# THE AFRO-AMERICAN

Readings

# THE AFRO-AMERICAN

## Readings

Edited by
**Ross K. Baker**
Rutgers University

VAN NOSTRAND
REINHOLD
COMPANY

New York
Cincinnati
Toronto
London
Melbourne

Van Nostrand Reinhold Company Regional Offices:
Cincinnati, New York, Chicago, Millbrae, Dallas

Van Nostrand Reinhold Company Foreign Offices:
London, Toronto, Melbourne

Published by Van Nostrand Reinhold Company
450 West 33rd Street, New York, N.Y. 10001

Published simultaneously in Canada by
D. Van Nostrand Company (Canada), Ltd.

10   9   8   7   6   5   4   3   2   1

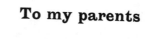
To my parents

# Preface

The long-overdue rush by scholars into the field of Afro-American studies has created a generation of "instant experts" who were either too young or too occupied elsewhere when men like Melville Herskovits, W. E. B. DuBois, E. Franklin Frazier and Rayford Logan were voices in the wilderness. Now that the civil rights struggle and the Black Power movement have confronted American scholarship with the fact of Black America's purloined past and contested future, the compensatory mechanisms of the learned professions are working overtime to rectify and revise.

Confronting the editor of an Afro-American reader are problems of emphasis, coherence, and relevance. The approach taken by this book of readings is to isolate one area and to focus on a single relationship while drawing materials from a number of disciplines and perspectives. The relationship is that one which has historically and contemporaneously prevailed between Black men in America and their ancestral homeland of Africa. To explore the relevance of this relationship to the cultural identity, self-concept, and social and political cohesion of the Black communities of North America is the aim of this reader. The selections that follow touch not only on the contemporary upsurge of interest in things African but also on the abiding, continuing, and ongoing relationships between a group of Americans and the region of their origin, and the effects and consequences of this relationship.

The assumption underlying this book is not to deny the Americanness of the Afro-American but, rather, to emphasize his Africanness in a country whose inhabitants are still preoccupied with their own ethnicity and national origins. Unlike the Polish-American or Irish-American, whose pride of origin, self, and group was never seriously impaired, the Afro-American's origins have been obscured, belittled, ridiculed, or ignored. We see today in Black communities across America a repudiation of the racist myths and shibboleths that have interposed themselves between Afro-Americans and Africa and a simultaneous effort to recapture a heritage. The consequences of this cultural and historical awakening generated from within the Black communities themselves have yet to have their full impact. It is hoped that this book will support the fullest manifestation of this great American cultural revolution.

The selections that follow represent a sampling of both primary and secondary source materials. By using such a format it is possible both to evaluate writings which were contemporaneous to a particular historical problem and also to profit by the increments in knowledge and historical perspective.

# Contents

# INTRODUCTION

The noted sociologist E. Franklin Frazier once wrote that in America the primary struggle of the Negro has been to acquire a culture. The problem, historically, has been what culture he has been struggling to acquire. This necessity for cultural choice that confronts Black Americans is a unique dilemma. The consequence of this choice will determine, in large measure, the place that this group of Americans will occupy vis-à-vis other groups of Americans. The choice is relevant not only for cultural identity itself but also for the political, economic, and social position the Black man occupies in this country. It is a choice which confronts no other ethnic or national group in America *as a group*. Culturally—and ethnically—linked traits, myths, symbols, and traditions were transmitted from generation to generation by Italian, Greek, and Irish immigrant groups, to name a few. The only choice facing the individual or family concerned whether or not such characteristics or beliefs were to be sustained. Group crises of identity were not particularly relevant in the broad societal context.

It is true that among Jews, for example, there is a continuing debate over assimilation, but the fact that assimilation can occur on an individual or primary-group basis without severe dislocation indicates the ease with which a group—even a group as culturally unique as the Jews—can lose its visibility and particularism without challenge by the dominant groups in society. If, on the other hand, an individual wishes to adhere to a highly visible and distinctive group such as a Williamsburg Hasidic community, or an Amish group in Pennsylvania, society will usually not compel his unwilling assimilation. Persecution per se, moreover, does not appear to either prevent or facilitate such assimilation. In the case of the American Indian, for example, despite systematic slaughter, removal, and concentration, no sustained attempt has been made to denigrate their traditions, rituals, or group-cohesion. As long as they caused no trouble and remained on the reservation, their cultural life was of no concern to the White man. Having been suppressed, isolated, and left in the benevolent care of the Bureau of Indian Affairs, they no longer posed a problem from the White man's perspective. In the case of the Black man, cultural suppression was both a precedent and concomitant of oppression. The master-slave relationship differed both in degree and kind from the colonist-indigene nexus. Efforts to enslave the Indian were never successful, not because his love of freedom was any greater than the Black man's, but rather because of his inability to endure the rigors of servitude.

The enslavement of non-indigenous Black men was, however, highly successful. The removal of the Black man from the seat of his heritage was the initial attack on cultural survival. The enslavement of Africans, from the perspective of White European Christians, could not be justified merely on the basis of commercial expediency and profit. Standing alone, that justification was simply too crass. If, however, this profitable venture could be rationalized in terms of religious salvation, paternalistic criteria, and rescue from a barbaric and sinful environment, the conscience of the slaver could be salved and commerce could proceed presumably unhindered by guilt or self-doubt. This rationalization, perhaps more than any other factor, accounted for the assault on African culture. It has become almost commonplace now to recognize the European cultural chauvinism which was supportive of the slave industry as a principal element in the obfuscation of Afro-American history and culture. What began as a justification, however, became internalized by the slavers and their clients and matured into a well developed attitudinal and perceptual syndrome. In addition to the more primitive and inelegant sentiments of the plantation owner and slave broker, a guilt-prone White America produced an illustrious and learned array of professors, clergymen, and ethnologists who were willing to pontificate on the natural inferiority and essential barbarity of the Black man and on the benevolence and enlightenment of the White man who saved him from heathenism and backwardness.

One such elaborate justification appeared in 1867. Reading it today one is struck by both its pseudo-scientific premises and also by its sanctimony and arrogance:

... what American will not rejoice at such a result [the presence of enslaved Blacks in America], if, when all the facts are known and tested by reason and conscience and the dictates of a true humanity, it is found that, however censurable the means employed may sometimes have been, the "slave trade," the original importation of African negroes by our ancestors, was right? The negro, as has been shown, from the necessities of his organism—the size and form of his brain—is, perforce, when isolated and by himself, a savage—an idle, non-advancing, and non-producing savage, and history, ancient and modern, in a word, all human experience, confirms this physiological and material fact.[1]

If the man himself is inferior, by extension, his culture is unworthy. The same observer noted that,

African travelers . . . have told fanciful tales about negro industry, thrift, and morality, while dreamers at home have indulged in even more absurd fancies still in regard to the future of Africa. . . . To talk of the civilization of the negro of Africa is like talking of the change of color of the negro, for it involves the same absurdities, the same impossibilities; and were not those who indulge in it utterly ignorant of the subject, one might say the same impieties, for the assumption that they can change the intellectual nature which God has given the negro, is as grossly impious as if they were to undertake his physical recreation.[2]

At the time the foregoing passages were written, slavery had been abolished. It then fell to those convinced of the inferiority of Blacks to find means to dispose of their troublesome presence. But even during the period before emancipation, the question of the status of freed or "manumitted" slaves had been a source of concern for both South and North. The establishment of the American Colonization Society in 1816 and its incorporation by Congress in 1820 were efforts to repatriate to Africa those Blacks who had been freed. Personal contact between free Blacks and slaves was regarded as potentially dangerous inasmuch as it was believed that such freedmen would encourage slave rebellion. The abortive uprising organized by Denmark Vesey in Charleston, S.C., in 1822 was adduced as evidence to support this contention. But as the rebellions of Gabriel, slave of Thomas H. Prosser, in 1800, Nat Turner in 1831, and numerous other plots and rebellions demonstrate, agitation by freedmen was neither a necessary nor a sufficient cause of uprisings. The desire for freedom and retribution among the slaves themselves was the more usual cause of rebellions. The fear of freedmen, regardless of how dubious its validity, provided the principal impetus for colonization efforts. The earliest and most enthusiastic support for colonization came from the slave states of Virginia and Maryland. The selection by Dwight Lowell Dumond in Chapter 3 explores the origins of the colonization movement.

Until the very moment of emancipation in 1863, efforts were being made to rid the United States of free Blacks and expatriate them either to Africa or to some other tropical area. The idea of colonization was staunchly opposed by the abolitionists who wanted not only to free the slaves but to integrate them into American life as free, productive citizens. The colonization forces however had strange allies. No less a man than Abraham Lincoln subscribed to this notion. In his statement to a deputation of free Black men in 1862, he made it very clear that the continued presence in the United States of emancipated Blacks would benefit neither them nor the White men whom they were suffered to live with. This interview (remarkable in light of the conventional popular adoration of the "Great Emancipator") is presented in its entirety in Chapter 3. Not until 1863, indeed, did the Civil War become, collaterally, a war of liberation. That Lincoln would have tolerated slavery to save the Union is abundantly clear. His private revulsion as an individual against slavery was submerged for the sake of political necessity while there was still some chance of maintaining the cohesion of the Union.

With the death of Lincoln and the termination of the Civil War, the policy of Lincoln's successor, Andrew Johnson, a Unionist from Tennessee, was to integrate the southern states into the Union by a *laissez faire* attitude in the conquered areas. What this resulted in was the rapid reacquisition of power by the same individuals who had supported slavery and rebellion. Repressive legislation to control the free Black population was initiated and enacted throughout the old Confederacy. The two years immediately following the war saw a repression of Blacks equal to, and in some cases, more intense than that which had existed during the era of legal slavery. Freed from the obligation to feed and clothe their human chattels, the former slave owners could concentrate on controlling and oppressing them without paternalistic constraints. Only with the onset of Congressional Reconstruction (or Radical Reconstruction, as it is usually characterized) was there any attempt to vest in the Black man a semblance of political power and social equality. Although it required the bayonets of Federal troops, Black militias, and the disenfranchisement of unreconstructed Confederates, the South found itself forced to accept a modicum of Black political participation, officeholding, and equality before the law. Even Radical Reconstruction, however, could not break the economic power which continued to reside in the hands of the secessionists whose ability to deny a livelihood to former slaves thwarted any fundamental change.

In less than a decade, the experiment in Reconstruction came to grief in the Hayes-Tilden election of 1876 when the hope of Black equality was bartered away for White southern support for the Republican candidate. With Federal troops withdrawn as part of the political covenant, the commitment of the United States to the Black struggle for equality evaporated. From Annapolis on the Chesapeake to El Paso on the Rio Grande; from Cincinnati on the Ohio to Biloxi on the Gulf, the curtain of oppression and subjugation was drawn on the hope of Black equality in the South. In the North, where most of the old radicals and abolitionists had passed from the scene, there was a retreat into complacency and smugness which would not be jarred for almost a century.

For the Black man, deprived of allies and legal protection, the choices which remained were emigration to the cities of the North where oppression was slightly less manifest, or continued residence in the South where compliance with organized, overt and institutionalized racism was the only means of survival. There was one other alternative, however, and that was physical removal from the society which had enslaved, formally emancipated, and then, in essence, re-enslaved the Black man. The logical place to which to remove was Africa.

When the disappointment, frustration, and feeling of helplessness became most acute, there was a resurgence of interest in Africa. After the failure of Reconstruction, Black men turned again to Africa as many had done before the Civil War when it appeared that Black slavery was forever established in America. The period following the Emancipation Proclamation had been one of hope, and of the prospect that some semblance of equality could be achieved. After 1876, however, the despair and disappointment of thwarted ambitions set in again. Liberia, the focus of Black immigration, had changed. Since outright slavery had been abolished, the various European and American colonization societies began to lose interest in Liberia. Liberia fell victim to the territorial ambitions of the colonial governments in the neighboring French and British protectorates. Between 1847 and 1910, Liberia lost 44 percent of her original territory to her colonial neighbors. There was a succession of financial scandals. In 1885 the British administration of Sierra Leone forced Liberia to cede considerable coastal area to that colony. In 1904 the maintenance of Liberian sovereignty became even more tenuous when the government was forced to invite British troops into the country to subdue marauding groups. When Liberia created a frontier police in 1908 and employed British officers to command it, France demanded equal numbers of her subjects on the force. The period of Liberia's most marked disintegration coincided with a major wave of interest in Liberia among Black Americans. The clash of Black American hopes and Liberian decline resulted in an even more pervasive feeling of hopelessness and bitterness. The rest of Africa had been divided by the European powers and the only republic where Black men could control their own destinies was no longer a going concern. In the selection by George Brown Tindall, "The Liberian Exodus," in Chapter 4, one can read of the frustration and disappointment of those who chose expatriation over oppression, but were forced to embrace the latter.

The travail of Liberia, the colonization of Africa, and the status of Black men in America created an identity crisis among Blacks and an intensified feeling of cultural superiority among Whites. Liberia was bankrupt, the rest of Africa was supine and exploited. Blacks in America were making only glacial progress toward educational, vocational, social, and economic attainment. Even among those Whites who regarded themselves as benevolent and understanding, a feeling emerged that perhaps what the racists had been telling them all along was correct. What had Black men accomplished anywhere? Where were the great cities, the universities, the scholars, and the artists? What was worthy, dignified, or magnificent about Black culture? The answer, had the White man sought to discover it, would have been highly displeasing to him.

The Africa that the White man saw was the victim of man's own avarice and ignorance. The great nations and cultures of West Africa had had their hearts cut out by slavery. What was left was prey to the scavengers of colonialism, and the grandeur of past empires was forgotten. In his own country, the White man could look upon his Black compatriot with scorn and disdain, simultaneously disregard the three hundred years of slavery and quasi-slavery, and marvel at the lack of Black advancement. How does one glorify the heritage of the man whom he has enslaved? To have accorded the Black men the same lofty origins, noble aspirations, and human desires would have been to deny the high-mindedness, democratic impulses, and benign attributes which the White man reserved for himself. It would have meant even more. It would have required him to pull down the Pantheon of secular saints who were worshipped in the republic. It would have required a revolution in thought to acknowledge the moral limitations of Washington the slaveholder, Jefferson the slaveholder, Madison, Monroe, and Jackson the slaveholders. How could men like these, shrouded as they were in myth and reverence, have done wrong? It was not they who had done wrong, for no wrong was done. They had merely participated in a somewhat morally ambiguous process which had rescued millions of souls from backwardness, disease and idolatry and brought them to a place on which God had clearly smiled. And after a brief dalliance with slavery which right-thinking men deplored all along, things were set right and the stigma of servitude was removed.

White America was in a quandary for it could not, for the sake of consistency, simultaneously recognize Afro-American culture and still portray America's national heroes without blemishes. This quandary was compounded after the collapse of Reconstruction when the sellout on Black equality could not be confronted squarely. There had to be a reason why the national government could no longer place its prestige and power on the line to foster Black integration into the mainstream of American cultural, economic, and political life. The only reasonable answer consistent with the patriotic perceptions of most Americans was that a period of tutelage of unspecified duration for the ex-slave was required in order to prepare him for full participation. His savage origins and arrested development under slavery necessitated a sort of collective apprenticeship: a process of protracted socialization and acculturation to the norms and beliefs of the dominant White culture, however defined. He had to be purged of his Africanness, the wretchedness of which caused him to succumb to the slaver for as one early twentieth century observer noted:

To our fair land of America he was brought as a captive—a happy captive one would think—and in a genial clime was given work, not too severe. . . . though for wholesome discipline cut with the whip a little sometimes when he moved too slowly.

And on his part, did he pine away and grow pale under his inhuman wrong? Ah, no! He laughed and grew fat, threw care to the winds, and slept undisturbed by thoughts of having to go into the boiling pot for somebody's breakfast in the morning. . . .

However horrid the crime of human slavery, however repulsive in all its forms and unprofitable in its operations, the fact remains that the negro was never so well off . . . as when he was the chattel of the chivalrous south. It was . . . a covert benediction, for until he found the blessings of bondage in North America his lot was truly a piteous one, a savage, and the master or the slave of savages.[3]

"The blessings of bondage in North America"—this curious clause is redolent of the plight of the Black man. He was harried and insecure in the best of times, victimized and slaughtered in the worst of times. Despite the efforts to expunge the Black man's past and the failure and reluctance to replace it with anything else, the Afro-American, usually in periods of the greatest turbulence and insecurity, turned to Africa.

At the turn of the century, the most powerful voice raised in favor of a return to Africa was Bishop Henry McNeal Turner of Georgia. This distinguished Black clergyman had served as a chaplain in the Federal Army during the Civil War and had served in the Reconstruction legislature in Georgia. For Turner, there was no hope for Black men in America. For Turner, however, time was out of joint. The partition of Africa by the European powers at the Berlin Conference in 1884 had decreed that although Africa was inhabited by Black men, it would be ruled by White men. Black emigrants from America could clearly not compete with the mighty powers of Europe for African territory. Booker T. Washington seized on this fact in 1899 to attack Turner. Washington labelled Turner's emigration schemes as escapism. Such escapism, in Washington's mind, was all the more abject due to the fact that Black men no longer owned Africa and that emigration would only exchange an American master for a European one.

From about 1900 until the First World War, Black American interest in Africa found its outlet in missionary activities. Money and missionaries from the largest urban churches to the smallest rural congregations were directed toward Africa. This effort was regarded suspiciously by the colonial governments who regarded American Black missions as centers for subverting colonial authority. A revolt led by an American-educated African, John Chilembwe, took place in Nyasaland (modern-day Malawi) in 1915. His association with American missionaries caused all such men to become suspect. But for the first two decades of the twentieth century, the Black American interest in Africa continued to be a religious one.

The First World War marked a period of relatively high expectations. Employment in war industries provided the opportunity for some economic betterment. For Blacks in the South, it provided the occasion to achieve a slightly better life in the cities of the North. The influx of Blacks in the crowded cities, however, occasioned clashes with the working-class Whites who resented their intrusion. Returning Black soldiers confronted the paradox of sacrifice abroad and subjugation at home and hope turned to frustration. The Ku Klux Klan was on the march across America, and again Black men turned to Africa as they had done after the collapse of Reconstruction. Especially among the least-favored and most desperate was the attraction of Africa most compelling.

The promise of deliverance came in the form of the Universal Negro Improvement Association and its leader, Marcus Garvey. This was Black Nationalism in its most intense form—not the separate development plan of Booker T. Washington which saw Black economic self-sufficiency as an avenue of acceptance, but a renunciation of White America. Garvey's U.N.I.A. was an effort to have Black Americans vote with their feet—to put miles between themselves and White America and to establish a better life in Africa. When Garvey was convicted for mail fraud and sent to prison, the hope of immediate repatriation for masses of Blacks evaporated. Like the plans of the 1870s and 1880s, the scandals surrounding emigration plans tended to discredit the idea for years. The program and fate of the U.N.I.A. are discussed in Chapter 4.

Throughout the thirties and forties, remnants of the Garvey movement attempted to keep the hope of emigration alive but the oft-burned Black communities of America were wary. With the coming of the Second World War hopes again rose. The patterns of migration from the rural South to the urban North, which had prevailed two decades earlier, were repeated and accentuated. The same paradox of twenty years earlier—men marching off to defend freedom in racially-segregated units—occurred again. There was also post-war frustration and tension but the immediate post-war years were not marked by the thought of return to Africa by Blacks on a mass scale.

There had been, however, a growing interest and curiosity about Africa, especially among Black American intellectuals. Beginning in the 1920s a familiarity and rough mutuality of interests prevailed between the growing Black intelligentsia in America and African intellectuals. Blaise Diagne of Senegal was well aware of the Garvey movement and was unalterably opposed to it. Others in Africa were likewise aware of the U.N.I.A. and embraced it. A U.N.I.A. chapter was established in Nigeria by two clergy-men, W. S. Euba and J. G. Campbell. Garveyism failed to stimulate much interest among the masses in Africa. Certain journalists in Nigeria espoused Garvey's Black Nationalism, however, and the concept was well-received among a small group of African intellectuals. The ordinary African was more than two decades away from the kind of militancy embodied in Gar-veyism. As Harold Cruse has pointed out, Garvey's plan came to grief as a result of opposition in Africa as much as it did by Garvey's own per-sonal shortcomings and the general mismanagement of the U.N.I.A. Cruse describes the friction between African and Afro-American intellectuals in Chapter 8.

Despite disagreement over emigration, nationalism, and cultural identity, there was significant contact in the pre-World War II era between Black literary figures in America and their Afro-Asian counterparts. Indeed, the establishment of the Pan-African Congress after World War I was the work of an Afro-American—W. E. B. DuBois—not an African. As Victor Fer-kiss has pointed out, it was not until the fifth Pan-African Congress in Manchester, England, in 1945 that Africans dominated the proceedings. Although such future luminaries as Kwame Nkrumah and Jomo Kenyatta were there, the guiding hand was clearly that of George Padmore, a U.S.-educated West Indian who had dedicated his life to Pan-Africanism.[4] Al-though the coming together of Black intellectuals from America and Africa was a crucial element in political and creative circles, it was restricted to a small group of intellectuals. Mass mutual concern between Black Ameri-cans and Africans was to come later.

The Supreme Court decision in the case of *Brown vs. The Board of Edu-cation of Topeka, Kansas* in April 1954, despite all of its shortcomings, verbal equivocations on enforcement, and false promises, did, however, arrest a trend toward increased pessimism and despair among large sections of the Black populace of America. On the heels of the successful bus boycott in Montgomery, Alabama, led by Dr. Martin Luther King, Jr., in the previous year, the decision appeared to mark a major breakthrough in civil rights. Although subsequent enforcement and compliance have been spasmodic, the decision, judged in the context of the times, was almost explosive in its impact.

The independence of the first Black African state—Ghana in 1957—coincided with a rising curve of Black expectations in America, brought about by the boycott and the court decision. The upsurge in the number of independent Black states brought more sub-Saharan students to America. Black diplomats became a common sight in Washington and New York and proceeded to run afoul of the Jim Crow laws in the South and border states. The "Route 40" cases became a national disgrace requiring propitiation at the highest level. African envoys who traveled the road from New York to Washington and were refused service in Delaware and Maryland were subsequently invited to lunch at the White House to soothe their feelings. This curious circumstance of a man rebuffed in a sleazy diner being feted at the White House pointed up a number of ironies, not the least of which was that the African in the United States was accorded a very special status not extended to American citizens who happened to be Black. The protection and prestige of the United States Government could be conferred on Black Africans but not necessarily Black Americans. Despite attempts by the Kennedy and Johnson administrations to push for legal equality through civil rights legislation, enforcement of judicial decisions, and executive orders, it required direct positive action on the part of American Blacks and White supporters through sit-ins, freedom marches, and demonstrations to provide and substantiate these actions. The price paid was lives, careers, and resources as generations of White southern reaction stiffened.

Until 1964 White northerners of liberal inclinations and sympathetic natures could look upon the civil right offensive and reactionary counteroffensives with approbation and disapproval, respectively. In the first of the "long, hot summers," however, the battles for equal treatment before the law, destruction of de facto segregation, and for an economic fair share were shifted to the northern cities. Long the repositories of a kind of superficial sympathy for the rights of Blacks in the South, the "northern liberal" became the embodiment and personification of marginal commitment and sanctimonious attitudes. As long as the front-line was in the South, many Blacks reasoned, self-styled White humanitarians were foursquare behind the drive for freedom, but when the locus of the struggle shifted to northern ghettos and when Black frustration with ghetto life manifested itself in riots which threatened their erstwhile friends, their sympathy and commitment dissolved. After years of heaping scorn and derision on the brutal South, the chickens were coming home to roost in the northerner's backyard.

If the Black man saw in the prosperous, well educated northern liberal an unwillingness to extend the battles of the South to his own home ground, he saw in the lower middle class, blue collar worker of recent immigrant stock something which he, the Black man, did not have and this was community power and group cohesion. From the Germans and the Irish in the 1840s through the Slavs in the 1880s to the Hungarians in the mid-1950s, all white ethnic groups had established themselves as forces to be reckoned with. Their power was amply demonstrated in their reluctance to accord the same mobility to Black men that they had achieved. Courted by politicians, sought after by labor unions, and driving hard into the solid middle class, the white ethnic groups had attained in a relatively short time what the Black man had failed to achieve in three hundred years.

Both White men and Black men asked themselves why and many came up with the same answer—slavery. For historians like Stanley Elkins and Frank Tannenbaum and social scientists like Daniel Patrick Moynihan, the slave system had corrupted and degraded the Black man to the point where his self-image, traditions, and family structure had been shattered. But slavery had ended over a century ago; surely the post-slavery generations had shaken off the burdens of servitude! Commentators on the Moynihan Report of March 1965 such as Herbert Gans acknowledged the role of slavery as the original cause of family instability among Black families documented in the Report. Moynihan's point was not to trace family instability back to slavery but to relate family disorganization to the imperfect socialization role of Black families. Elizabeth Herzog said that slavery was less the root of family disorganization than was the hundred years after slavery, and that White families that suffered severe continued deprivation were likely to suffer disorganization as intense as that of the Black family.[5]

For many Black writers, the Moynihan Report represented an effort to attribute pathological characteristics to the Black family and also to place an undue share of the blame for these putative problems on slavery which, manifestly, only the Blacks suffered from. To castigate slavery, furthermore, was to shift the burden of responsibility to an obsolete institution that operated principally in one section of the country and away from the role of American society as a whole. Some Black writers went even further and asserted that resistance to slavery rather than acceptance and docility characterized the Black man in bondage—that, indeed, there was a long and almost continuous historical record of plots and insurrections against servitude by slaves in America.

The focus of this controversy was the appearance in 1967 of an historical novel entitled, *The Confessions of Nat Turner,* by William Styron, a White Virginian. Styron prefaced his book by asserting that Nat Turner's rebellion in Southampton County, Virginia, in 1831 was the only important, sustained example of Black resistance to slavery. The battle was formally joined the following year (1968) with the publication of *William Styron's Nat Turner: Ten Black Writers Respond*. It represented an attack on the concept of the docile slave and, by extension, on the notion that slavery had so crushed and corrupted the slave that he entertained no thought of rebellion. It also implied that slavery alone could not be blamed for the plight of the Black man in modern America.

It is possible to view the argument of the Black writers as being fraught with contradictions—that one cannot attack the dehumanizing aspects of slavery while, at the same time, claiming that the self-image, feeling of efficacy and individual pride were not impaired. Such a perception, however, would miss the point which is that despite the deprivations and brutality of slavery, it was possible after emancipation to bend all efforts to make equality a fact as well as a law; that the experiment of Reconstruction pointed the way to such an effort but that its abandonment condemned Black men to another full century of pervasive hopelessness. Even if Black pride had been able to survive 250 years of slavery, it would have been difficult to sustain over an additional century of quasi-slavery. The disastrous effects of slavery and the succeeding twilight of equality are described in the articles by Thomas F. Pettigrew and Thomas E. Davis and in the speech of Edward A. Johnson in Chapter 6.

But putting controversy over the effects of slavery aside, one source of agreement was evident: that, at the very least, the period of slavery and its hundred-year aftermath had resulted in a serious erosion of the Afro-American's regard for his own culture. Every aspect of socialization from school textbooks to the principal sustaining myths of the society pointed to an America whose essence and contours were shaped by Whites. The most obscure White immigrant group was given its due as a contributor to American life and culture, but the impact of the Black African contribution was minimized or ignored. If individual pride were to be restored, it would be necessary to renew the esteem of the collectivity.

That the first breaches in the walls of segregation in America and the collapse of the colonial system in Africa should have roughly coincided is a fact of major importance. The assertion of self and community by Afro-Americans and the intense and contagious excitement of new Black republics being born began to instill in Black Americans a double source of pride. Americans of African descent could look for their heritage to a continent of free men while they, in America, fought to attain theirs. The new externalities of Black America—the "Afro" haircuts and *dashikis,* the desire to learn Swahili and Hausa—are only the outward manifestations of the quest for a culture. Beneath these outward symbols of cultural uniqueness appears to be a profound conviction that the establishment of pride in ancestral origins is linked to a feeling of community and that community-feeling is, in turn, linked to power. Common color and common oppression have been seen as insufficient aggregating factors. Perceptions of a broad range of uniting elements such as art, music, language, and a common ancestral locus may prove the most significant element in Afro-American cohesion and these, preeminently, are traceable to Africa. The heightened Black awareness of Africa in recent years is apparently not linked to a new wave of emigration to Africa. In a survey taken by Brink and Harris in 1964, indeed, only about five percent of those Black Americans responding indicated a desire to permanently remove to Africa. There are, to be sure, Black Americans who have moved to Africa or reside there on a more or less permanent basis. Anthony Astrachan of the *Washington Post* estimated in May 1969 that about 1,700 American Blacks are currently residing on the continent of Africa. One of the largest concentrations of recent immigrants is in Liberia. This group originally composed of about 175 members of the Hebrew Israelite movement has apparently dwindled since its establishment in Liberia in July 1967. A bill was introduced on the floor of the House of Representatives on March 13, 1969, by Congressman Robert N. C. Nix of Pennsylvania calling for U.S. financial and administrative support for the repatriation of American Blacks. The Congressman said that the idea did not originate with him but was suggested by a number of his constituents. There does exist a discernible group of Black Americans whose disillusionment with America is so great or whose love of Africa is so overpowering that emigration is pursued. The number of such advocates of emigration is, however, small. For the large majority of Afro-Americans believe that the struggle for equality must be waged in America.

For those Black Americans who have "made it" in America there is the established person's disinclination to change, but for those Afro-Americans who continue to live in poverty there is the equally strong conviction that as a race they have accumulated considerable economic, social, and political credit in America. They do not want to forfeit this credit. Quite the contrary, they mean to collect on it. The surest way to achieve the credit is through an increased feeling of group cohesion based on a shared perception of a common historical and cultural background.

Africa, then, represents not a potential future home for most Black Americans but a lodestone of identity and, by extension, power. Although definitions of Black Power are still imprecise, it is clear that community identity and cohesion are part of most definitions. A series of discussions of Black Power and its meaning are contained in Chapter 8. The various essays in that chapter will indicate the contention and dispute which surround the term "Black Power." There does, however, seem to be a base-line common to all and that is that Black Power is a power among powers, that it constitutes an effort to create a cohesive and efficacious community of Black Americans which possesses a corporate identity similar to that possessed by other ethnic or functional groups. The principal debate appears to be what its implications are and how much it can accomplish above and in coalition with other groups. Before these questions can be answered, however, the nucleus around which cohesion can occur must be solidified. At this time the most apparent focus of this cohesion is the broadening perception of a common African heritage. One point which this collection of essays seeks to make is the abiding nature of Afro-American interest in Africa, over time. Beginning with the excerpts from the journals of Ayuba Suleiman Diallo, who was enslaved in the eighteenth century, to Robert Campbell, who visited Africa in the mid-nineteenth century, through Garvey, who sought to be the Moses of his people in the twentieth century, and up to the recent interest in Africa, the homeland has never been out of the thoughts and dreams of Black Americans for very long.

It is necessary for Americans, especially White Americans, to appreciate what all this means. The manifestations of the awareness of Africa may, at times, seem puzzling. At a time in which Africans are striving to become Westernized, Black Americans are engaged in raising the saliency of their Africanness, both in terms of what Africa currently has to offer and in terms of the residuum of African culture which survived the slavery period and its aftermath. Paradoxes emerge such as the desire on the part of Black Americans to learn Swahili—a language spoken in an area of Africa from which only an estimated five percent of the ancestors of Black Americans derived. The cultural affinity among Black Americans for Africa is generalized and not directed at a single national state. It is difficult for a Black American to point to a single modern African state and say with certainty that it is his homeland. In a few cases, oral family traditions might allow this, but in most cases the regard for Africa is more diffuse and less focused on a single country.

Permanent relocation in Africa has never attracted the majority of Afro-Americans. Numerous surveys and studies have indicated that the attainment of equality, recognition, and success in the United States is the relevant objective for the preponderant number of Black Americans. Those Afro-Americans who have visited Africa have found, more often than not, that Africans regard them as Americans and not necessarily as fellow Africans. Given their lifelong exposure to the American value system, Black Americans often have trouble readily accepting such features of African life as the rurally-based and conservative tribal structures and the extended African family which decrees that many generations of a family live under one roof. Politically, socially, psychologically, and spiritually, the Afro-American differs markedly from the African. This syndrome, however, is only one aspect of the failure of latter-day emigration to catch on among Afro-Americans. More important, perhaps, is the fact that most Black Americans tend to subscribe to American norms and values. The impact of American education and American media have created aspirations among Black Americans which do not differ markedly from those of their White compatriots.

The point to bear in mind, however, is that the concern and involvement of Black Americans in their African heritage is not an end in itself. It is linked to the necessity to reconstruct a shattered and demoralized community and to forge a new and positive self-image on an individual basis and, by so doing, attain the kind of collective power and personal efficacy required to make equality a fact. The attainment of this equality is, pre-eminently, within the American context.

## NOTES

[1] J. H. Van Evrie, *White Supremacy and Negro Subordination; or Negroes A Subordinate Race* (New York: Van Evrie, Horton & Co., 1868), p. 169.

[2] Ibid., pp. 169–70.

[3] Hubert Howe Bancroft, *Retrospection* (New York: Bancroft Co., 1912), pp. 371–372.

[4] Victor C. Ferkiss, *Africa's Search for Identity* (New York: Meridian Books, 1967), p. 130.

[5] The Moynihan Report and the responses to it are contained in Lee Rainwater and William L. Yancey, eds., *The Moynihan Report and the Politics of Controversy* (Cambridge: M.I.T. Press, 1967).

# 1

## THE ABIDING TRADITION

The collection of essays which comprise the initial
section of this anthology deals with the early social
organization of Africa. The contributions by three noted
Africanists—W. E. B. DuBois, Basil Davidson, and
Melville Herskovits—treat that era of African history
which preceded and coincided with the first sustained
contact between Africans and Europeans. They provide
the reader with a broad overview of the contours of
tribal and imperial societies. The following essay, by
the Georgia Writers Project, discusses one aspect of
traditional African life which has survived in America
through centuries of slavery and oppression. It provides
a base-line for the consideration of the subsequent
relationships between Africa and America.

*The following selection, "The Peopling of Africa," is*
*from* The World and Africa, *one of fifteen books*
*written by W. E. B. DuBois, who died in 1961 in*
*Ghana at the age of 95. Born in Massachusetts, a*
*Harvard Ph.D., Professor of Greek at the University of*
*Pennsylvania, a founder of the NAACP, and Editor-in-*
*Chief of the* Encyclopedia Africana, *W. E. B. DuBois*
*was one of America's greatest men of letters. His*
*literate and eloquent description of the genesis and*
*variety of the humankind of Africa is crucial for the*
*consideration of the origins of Black Americans.*

# The Peopling of Africa

## W. E. B. DuBois

Seers say that for full two thousand million years this world out of fiery mist has whirled about the sun in molten metal and viscous crusted ball. That crust, congealing and separating the solids from the liquids, rose and fell in bulging ridges above the boiling sea. Five times the mass of land called Africa emerged and disappeared beneath the oceans. At last, at least a thousand million years ago, a mass of rigid rock lifted its crystal back above the waters and remained. Primeval Africa stretched from the ramparts of Ethiopia to where the copper, diamonds, and gold of South Africa eventually were found. More land rose, and perhaps three hundred million years ago Africa was connected with South America, India, and Australia. As the ocean basins dropped, the eastern half of Africa was slowly raised into a broad, flat arch.

The eastern side of this arch gave way, forming the Indian Ocean, and when the roof of the arch fell in there appeared the great Rift valley. This enormous crack, extending six thousand miles from the Zambesi to Ethiopia and Syria, is said to be the only thing that Martians can descry as they look earthward of a starry night. All the great East African lakes lie in the main rift, and doubtless the Red Sea and the Sea of Galilee are also part of this vast phenomenon. Later, about ten million years ago, a second rift occurred, and rifting and tilting kept on until perhaps a hundred thousand years before our era.

From W. E. B. DuBois, *The World and Africa* (New York: International Publishers Co., Inc., 1965), pp. 81–97.

Recurrent change came in geography and climate. Europe and Africa were united by land and separated. Lower Egypt was submerged, and the Mediterranean extended to Persia. Finally, what the geologists call the modern world emerged. In Egypt great rivers poured down the hills between the Red Sea, and the Nile found old and new valleys. The Sahara was crossed by a network of rivers, pouring into a vaster Lake Chad and uniting the Niger, the Congo, and the Nile.

Gondwanaland, the ancient united continent of Africa, South America, and Asia, was divided into three parts by the new changes which caused the rift valleys. The radioactivity of the inner earth made the crust break apart. We can see by the map how Africa broke from South America and Europe from North America. Changes in climate were caused by the sun, the earth's inner heat, and by two main glacial periods in Africa. The rainfall varied, bringing periods of flood between the glaciers.

The continent of Africa in its final modern form has been described as a question mark, as an inverted saucer, as the center of the world's continents. Including Madagascar, it is three times the size of Europe, four times the size of the United States; and the whole of Europe, India, China, and the United States could be held within its borders. In actual measurement it is nearly square: five thousand miles long by four thousand six hundred miles wide. But its northern half is by far the larger, with the southern half tapering off. In the middle, the equator cuts across Africa, and the whole continent lies mainly within the tropics.

Of the physical aspects of Africa, its relatively unbroken coastline has had the greatest effect upon its history. Although Africa is about three times larger than Europe in area, the coastline of Europe is four thousand miles longer than that of Africa. In other words, Africa has almost no peninsulas, deep bays, or natural harbors. Its low and narrow coast, almost level, rises rapidly to a central plateau with a depression in the center. Thus the great rivers fall suddenly to the ocean, and their navigation is impeded by rapids and falls.

Its five areas include the original Great Plateau with an average elevation of over thirty-five hundred feet, where mountains crowned with snow rise from thirteen to twenty thousand feet. Over these open spaces have always roamed herds of wild animals—elephants, rhinoceroses, and buffaloes.

The second area is the Great Depression, the basin of the Congo River draining nearly a million and a half square miles. Its average altitude is a thousand feet and it is the bed of a former inland sea. As Stanley described it: "Imagine the whole of France and the Iberian peninsula closely packed with trees varying from twenty to a hundred and eighty feet in height, whose crowns of foliage interlace and prevent any view of sky and sun, and each tree from a few inches to four feet in diameter." [1] In this area lies the Belgian Congo and French Equatorial Africa, Liberia and the British West African colonies.

The fourth area is the Sahara, extending from the Atlantic to the Red Sea. It covers three and a half million square miles and is divided into desert and fertile islands. In the past the Sahara was fertile and had a large population. Its surface today is often a hundred feet below sea level. In the east is Egypt and the Egyptian Sudan. North Africa lies on the Mediterranean with Algeria and Tunisia, Libya and Egypt. There are senses in which it is true that "Africa begins at the Pyrenees," and also that "Europe ends at the borders of the Sahara."

We may distinguish in Africa equatorial and tropical climates, and then over smaller areas climates peculiar to specific areas. The equatorial climate is divided into the climate of Central Africa and that of Guinea and East Africa. The first with constant heat, much rainfall, and humidity; the second with constant heat and smaller rainfall. In both these regions there is luxurious growth of plant life and dense forests. The East African climate is hot. There are savannahs and varied vegetation. Of the tropical climate, there is the Sudanese, with heat but less rain, and the desert type, with great heat but wide daily variation and little rain. Besides these, there is the climate peculiar to the Mediterranean, with hot summers and rain in winter; and to the Cape district, with more moderate summers and winters and less rainfall.

This is the climate of Africa today, but it has varied, and probably greatly, in the vast stretches of past time. The changes came with the distribution of land and water, the elevation and subsidence of land, the severance of the continent from Asia and South America, and the rise of the mountains in India and Europe that affect the air and sea currents. The rim of the great inland plateau which forms most of Africa falls to sea level near the coast and falls so steeply that the valleys of the rivers draining it do not spread into broad alluvial plains inviting settled populations. The history of tropical Africa would have been far different if it had possessed a Saint Lawrence, an Amazon, a Euphrates, a Ganges, a Yangtze, or a Nile south of the Sahara. The difference of land level within the continent brings strange contrasts.

Sixty million years ago vast reptiles and dinosaurs wandered over this continent. It became, as the years passed, a zoological garden with wild animals of all sorts. Finally there came domesticated cattle, sheep, and goats and a tremendous development of insects. As Sir Harry Johnston well remarks, "Africa is the chief stronghold of the real Devil—the reactionary forces of Nature hostile to the uprise of Humanity. Here Beelzebub, King of the Flies, marshals his vermiform and arthropod hosts—insects, ticks, and nematode worms—which more than in other continents (excepting Negroid Asia) convey to the skin, veins, intestines, and spinal marrow of men and other vertebrates the microorganisms which cause deadly, disfiguring, or debilitating diseases, or themselves create the morbid condition of the persecuted human being, beasts, bird, reptile, frog, or fish." [2]

Africa is a beautiful land; not merely comely and pleasant, but haunted with swamp and jungle; sternly beautiful in its loveliness of terror, its depth of gloom, and fullness of color; its heaven-tearing peaks, its silver of endless sand, the might, width, and breadth of its rivers, depth of its lakes and height of its hot, blue heaven. There are myriads of living things, the voice of storm, the kiss of pestilence and pain, old and ever new, new and incredibly ancient.

The anthropoid ape with the great brain who walked erect and used his hands as tools developed upon earth not less than half a million years ago. Traces of him have been found in Africa, Asia, and Europe and in the islands of the sea. Many types which developed have doubtless been lost, but one species has survived, driven hither and yon by cold and hunger, segregated from time by earthquake and glacier and united for defense against hunger and wild beasts.

Groups of this species must have inbred and developed subtypes over periods of tens of thousands of years. Of the subspecies thus developed, scientists have usually distinguished at least three, all of which were fertile in their cross-breeding with one another. In course of time they have given rise to many transitional groups and intermediary types, so that less than two-thirds of the living peoples of today can be decisively allotted to one or the other of the definite subspecies. These subspecies include the long-headed dark people with more or less crinkled hair whom we know as Negroids; the broad-headed yellow people with straight and wiry hair whom we call Mongoloids; and a type between these, possibly formed by their union, with bleached skins and intermediate hair, known as the Caucasoids.

No sooner had these variant types appeared in Central Africa, on the steppes of Asia, and in Europe than they merged again. The importance of these types was not so much their physical differences and likenesses as their cultural development. As Frobenius says: "With vast and growing weight there begins to emerge today out of the microscopic spectacles of blind eyes, a new conception among living men of the unity of human culture." Inquiring search has made clear "here Greek, there old Mexican spirituality; here European economic development, there pictures of the glacial age; here Negro sculpture, there shamanism; here philosophy, there machines; here fairy tale, there politics." [3]

Was Africa the cradle of the human race? Did it witness man's first evolution from the anthropoid ape to *Homo sapiens?* We do not know. Charles Darwin thought that "it is somewhat more probable that our early progenitors lived on the African continent than elsewhere." Sir G. E. Smith agrees with this and says that Africa "may have been the area of characterization, or, to use a more homely phrase, the cradle, both of the anthropoid apes and the human family." From Africa, Negroids may have entered Asia and Europe. On the other hand, the human race originating in Asia or even in Europe may have invaded Africa and become Negroid by long segregation in a tropical climate. But all this is conjecture. Of the origin of the Negro race or of other human races, we know nothing. But we do know that human beings inhabited Africa during the Pleistocene period, which may have been half a million years ago.

A memoir presented by a well-known Belgian scientist, Alfred Rutot, just before World War I, to the scientific section of the Académie de Belgique caused some stir. It was accompanied by a series of busts, ten in number, executed under careful supervision, by M. Louis Mascré. The busts were striking. The attempt to reproduce various prehistoric types, beginning with Pithecanthropus erectus, was characterized as "audacious," and, of course, much confirmation is necessary of the facts and theories adduced.

The chief interest of the paper was the reconstruction of the Negroids of Grimaldi, so-called from the finds at Mentone, France, helped out by similar remains found in the Landes and at Wellendorff in Lower Austria. How did specimens of Negroes so intelligent in appearance find themselves in the immediate presence of Caucasians, introducing amongst them the art of sculpture which presupposes an advanced stage of civilization? Science explains this phenomenon by the successive cataclysmic changes on our planet. For the quaternary period, Sicily formed part of the Italian mainland, the Strait of Gibraltar was nonexistent, and one passed from Africa to Europe on dry land. Thus it was that a race of more or less Ethiopic type filtered in amongst the people inhabiting our latitudes, to withdraw later toward their primitive habitat.

From the position of certain Negroid skeletons exhumed in France, some have concluded that this race carried and made use of the bow. This is uncertain; but it is well authenticated that these visitors brought to the white race the secret of sculpture, for their bones are almost invariably found in company with objects sculptured on steatite or stone, in high or low relief. Some of their sculptures are quite finished, like the Wellendorff Venus, cut in a limestone block. Of this Venus, Rutot's Negroid type of man is a replica out of mammoth ivory. The shell net of four rows adorning the head of this artistic ancestor is a faithful reproduction of the ornament encircling the cranium of the skeleton found in the Grotte des Enfants at Mentone. For the ancient Negroid woman, Mascré has gone to a figure in relief found in the excavations at Lausses (Dordogne). The marked horn held in the right hand is that of a bison, the bracelets and armlets are exact copies of the ornaments exhumed at Mentone.

These Negroid busts are most attractive and intelligent looking and have no exaggerated Negro features. The Cro-Magnon man of Dordogne is a Magdalenian, contemporary with the Negroid intrusion. The fine proportions of the skull indicate unmistakable intellectuality. The remains left by this race in the caves of Périgord reveal great skill in the art of sculpting and painting animals, whereas the Negroids of that time specialized in the representation of their own species. The daggers of that epoch, described in *Reliquiae Aquitaniae,* are engraved on reindeer horn, and the weapons underwent perhaps many practical improvements due to the effort, eventually successful, of the Magdalenians to drive out the Negroids, their artistic rivals.[4]

"There was once an 'uninterrupted belt' of Negro culture from Central Europe to South Africa. 'These people,' says Griffith Taylor, 'must have been quite abundant in Europe toward the close of the Paleolithic Age. Boule quotes their skeletons from Brittany, Switzerland, Liguria, Lombardy, Illyria, and Bulgaria. They are universal through Africa and through Melanesia, while the Botocudos and the Làgoa Santa skulls of East Brazil show where similar folk penetrated to the New World.' Massey says: 'The one sole race that can be traced among the aborigines all over the earth or below it is the dark race of a dwarf, Negrito type.' "[5]

It seems reasonable to suppose that Negroids originating in Africa or Asia appeared first as Negrillos. The Sahara at that time was probably covered with rivers and verdure and North Africa was in close touch with Mediterranean Europe. There came upon the Negrillos a wave of Negroids who were hunters and fishermen and used stone implements. The remains of an African stone age are scattered over a wide area with amazing abundance, and there is such a resemblance between implements found in Africa and those in Europe that we can apply, with few differences, the same names. The sequence in culture in Europe resembles the sequence in Africa although they may not have been contemporary.

The most primitive type of stone implement was found in Uganda and is known as the pebble tool. The same pebble industry extended to Tanganyika and the Transvaal. This gave way to the hand-ax culture, which extended over North Africa, the Sahara, Equatorial Africa, West and South Africa. Superb hand axes and other tools are the evidence. Then the middle Paleolithic flake-tool culture spread out over wide areas of Africa and is shown by perfect implements in South Africa and other places. The remains indicate a cave-dwelling people with a great variety of tools as well as beads and pottery.

During the Pleistocene period came a new Stone Age, with agriculture, domestic animals, pottery, and the grinding and polishing of stone tools. Evidence of this culture is found in Egypt and North Africa, the Sahara in West Africa, East and South Africa.

The Neolithic culture is of great significance. In Egypt it is found five thousand years before Christ. A thousand years later it changed from flint to copper. The Predynastic Egyptians who represented this culture were settled folk; they hunted and fished, and cultivated grain; made clothes and baskets, used copper, and were distinctly Negroid in physique. Probably they came from the south, from what is now Nubia. Later there came to Egypt other people of the type corresponding to the modern Beja, who lived in settled communities and used copper and gold. This brown Negroid people, like the modern Beja, Galla, and Somali, mixed increasingly with Asiatic blood, but their culture was African and extended by unbroken thread up the Nile and beyond the Somali peninsula.

The first wave of Negroes were hunters and fishermen and used stone implements. They gradually become sedentary and cultivated the soil and must have developed early artistic aptitudes and strong religious feeling. They built the stone monuments discovered in Negro Africa and the raised stones and carved rocks of Gambia. They did not mix with the Negrillos nor did they dispossess them, but recognized their ancestral land rights and seized unoccupied land. Thousands of years after this first wave of Negro immigrants there came another migration. The newcomers pushed north and west, dispossessed the Negrillos, and drove them toward the central forests and the deserts. They mixed more with the Negrillos, developed agriculture, the use of cattle and domestic fowl. They invented the working of iron and the making of pottery. Also, those who advanced farthest toward the north mixed with the Mediterranean race in varying degrees, so that sometimes the resulting population seemed white mixed with Negro blood and in other cases blacks mixed with white blood. The languages were mixed in various ways. Thus we had the various Libyan and Egyptian populations. All this migration and mixture took place long before the epoch of the first Egyptian dynasty.

There exists today a fairly complete sequence of closely interrelated types of human beings in Africa, leading from Australopithecus to such known primitive African types as Rhodesian Man and Florisbad Man. If these types are affiliated with, if not actually ancestral to, Boskop Man, the common presence of all three in the southern half of Africa is presumptive evidence that they all emerged on this continent from some common ancestral stock.

The name "Negro" originally embraced a clear conception of ethnology —the African with dark skin, so-called "woolly" hair, thick lips and nose; but it is one of the achievements of modern science to confine this type to a small district even in Africa. Gallas, Nubians, Hottentots, the Congo races, and the Bantus are not "genuine" Negroes from this view, and thus we find that the continent of Africa is peopled by races other than the "genuine" Negro.

Nothing then remains for the Negro in the "pure" sense of the word save, as Waitz says, "a tract of country extending over not more than ten or twelve degrees of latitude, which may be traced from the mouth of the Senegal River to Timbuktu." If we ask what justifies so narrow a limitation, "we find that the hideous Negro-type, which the fancy of observers once saw all over Africa, but which, as Livingstone says, is really to be seen only as a sign in front of tobacco-shops, has on closer inspection evaporated from almost all parts of Africa, to settle no one knows how in just this region. If we understand that an extreme case may have been taken for the genuine and pure form, even so we do not comprehend the ground of its geographical limitation and location. We are here in presence of a refinement of science which to an unprejudiced eye will hardly hold water." [6]

Palgrave says: "As to faces, the peculiarities of the Negro countenance are well known in caricature; but a truer pattern may be seen by those who wish to study it any day among the statues of the Egyptian rooms in the British Museum: the large gentle eye, the full but not overprotruding lips, the rounded contour, and the good-natured, easy, sensuous expression. This is the genuine African model; one not often to be met with in European or American thoroughfares, where the plastic African too readily acquires the careful look and even the irregularity of the features that surrounded him; but which is common enough in the villages and fields where he dwells after his own fashion among his own people; most common of all in the tranquil seclusion and congenial climate of Surinam plantation. There you may find, also, a type neither Asiatic nor European, but distinctly African; with much of independence and vigour in the male physiognomy and something that approaches, if it does not quite reach, beauty in the female. Rameses and his queen were cast in no other mould." [7]

What are the peoples who from vague prehistory emerged as the Africans of today? The answer has been bedeviled by the assumption that there was in Africa a "true" Negro and that this pure aboriginal race was mixed with a mythical "Hamitic race" which came apparently from neither Europe, Asia, nor Africa, but constituted itself as a "white element" in Negro Africa.

We may dismiss this "Hamitic" race as a quite unnecessary assumption and describe the present African somewhat as follows:

At a period as early as three thousand years before Christ the people of the North African coastal plains were practically identical with the early Egyptians and present two types: long-headed Negroid people and broad-headed Asiatics. Among the Berber types today are tall and medium long-headed people with broad faces, swarthy skin, and dark eyes. They have many Negroid characteristics, especially toward the south. Beside these there are short, broad-headed people.

These Berbers are the ones who correspond to the ancient Egyptians and who have close relationship to the Neolithic inhabitants of France. Among them today the Negro element is widely represented. It is in every part of Mauritania, where the reigning family itself is clearly of Negro descent. A large strain of Negro blood may also be found in Algeria.

In East Africa we have the Massai, Nandi, Suk, and others, tall, slender, and long-headed. In the case of the Massai the nose is thinner and the color tinged with reddish-brown. The Bari people are tall and the Lutoko very tall. Then there are the Nilotics in the Nile valley, extending south of Khartoum to Lake Kioga. Physically, as in the case of the Shilluk and Dinka, they are tall, very black, long-headed people, often with well-shaped features, thin lips, and high-bridged noses. The Nuba, tall, long-headed men, live in the hills of Kordofan. East of Kordofan are the Fung, with many tribes and with much Asiatic blood; and also broad-headed tribes like the Bongo and the Asande, a mixed people of reddish color with long heads.

On the other side of Africa, the lower and middle portion of the Senegal River forms a dividing line between West African types of Negroes and the Negroes of the Sudan. South of the river are the Jolofs and the Serers. With these are the Senegalese, including the Tukolor and Mandingo tribes. They are dolichocephalic with both broad and narrow noses. They are rather tall, some of them very tall, and their skin is very dark. The Mandingo, or Mandi, are among the most important groups of French Senegal and live between the Atlantic and Upper Niger. They are tall and slender with fine features, beards, and rather lighter skin than that of neighboring Negroes.

Among the most interesting of the West African people south of the Sudan are the Fulani, stretching from the Upper Niger to the Senegal River. They are Negroids, perhaps with Asiatic blood. They are straight-haired, straight-nosed, thin-lipped and long-headed, with slender physiques and reddish-brown color. The Songhay are tall and long-headed with well-formed noses and coppery-brown color. The people of Kanem and the Bagirmi cluster around Lake Chad. They are broad-nosed and dolichocephalic and resemble the Negroes on the Nile. In the east and South Africa are the Wachagga and the Fang and especially the Swahili, mixed people whose language dominates East Africa. They have all possible degrees of physical characteristics from Arabic to Negro. In South Africa there are the Bushmen, short, yellow, with closely-curled hair. Beside them live the Hottentots, probably Bushmen with Bantu admixture and later with white Dutch admixture which gave rise to the so-called "coloured" people.

The Negroes in the neighborhood of the Gulf of Guinea can be differentiated at present chiefly by their languages, which have been called Sudanic. Three great stocks prevail: the Twi, Ga, and Ewe. Belonging to these are the Asanti, moderately tall men, long-headed with some broad heads; the Dahomey, tall, long-headed, and black; the Yoruba, including the peoples of Benin and Ibo, dark brown or black, closely curled hair, moderate dolichocephaly, and broad-nosed. Their lips are thick and sometimes everted, and there is a considerable amount of prognathism. The Kru, hereditary sailors, are typically Negroid with fine physiques. The Haussa of the central Sudan are very black and long-headed but not prognathic and with thin noses.

Finally there are the Bantu, who are a congeries of peoples, belonging predominantly to Central and South Africa and occupying the southern two-thirds of black Africa. The Bantu are defined on purely linguistic criteria. The term "Bantu" primarily implies that the tribes included speak languages characterized by a division of nouns into classes distinguished by their prefixes (usually twelve to fifteen), absence of sex-gender in the grammar, and the existence of alliterative concord, the prefix of each class (noun-class) being repeated in some form or another in all words agreeing with any noun of that class in the sentence. It is the reappearance of the prefix in every word in agreement with the noun that gives the alliterative effect.

The southern Bantu outnumber all other groups of South Africa and are about four times as numerous as the Whites. They are divided into a large number of tribal units, each with its own distinctive name. In social organization and religious system they show broad resemblances to one another, but in details of history there are a number of important differences which permit of their being classified into four groups:

1. The Shona peoples of Southern Rhodesia and of Portuguese East Africa.
2. The Zulu-Xosa, chiefly in the coastal region south and east of the Drakensberg Mountains.
3. The Suto-Chwana occupy the greater portion of the high plateau north of the Orange River.

4. The Herero-Ovambo, in the northern half of Southwest Africa and in southern Angola.

In skin color the range is from the black of the Amaswazi to the yellowish-brown of some of the Bechuana. The prevalent color is a dark chocolate, with a reddish ground tint. The hair is uniformly short and woolly. The head is generally low and broad with a well-formed bridge and narrow nostrils. The face is moderately prognathous, the forehead prominent, cheekbones high, lips fleshy. The Negro facial type predominates in all groups, but side by side with it in the Zulu and the Thonga sections are relatively long, narrow faces, thin lips, and high noses.

The inhabitants of Natal and Zululand, divided originally into more than a hundred small separate tribes, are all now collectively known as "Zulus," a name derived from one of the tribes which, under the domination of Chaka, absorbed and conquered most of the others and so formed the Zulu nation which played so important a part in the political history of South Africa during the nineteenth century.

Tribes vary in size, some having from a few hundred to a couple of thousand members. Others are much larger, for example, the Bakwena, 11,000; the Batawana, 17,500; the Bamagwato, 60,000; the Ovandonga, 65,000; the Ovakwanyama, 55,000; the Amaswazi, again, number 110,000; while the Basuto, by far the largest of all and might be called a nation, number nearly half a million.

The area of the western Bantu includes the Cameroons (French), Rio Muni (Spanish), the Gaboon (French), French Equatoria, the Congo (Belgian), Angola (Portuguese), and Rhodesia, with the fraction of Portuguese East Africa north of Zambesi. This vast area is the true "Heart of Africa," the tropical rain forest of the Congo. Johnston enumerated over one hundred and fifty tribes in this area who speak Bantu or semi-Bantu tongues. The southern limit of the western Bantu is vague; the formation of the Lunda empire, the Yaggo raids, and the subsequent encroachments of the Bajokwe (Kioko) have played havoc with tribal organization. The Bateke occupy a vast region on the right bank of the Congo which is now largely peopled by the Fang, who in their various expeditions and conquests have left their mark on most tribes north of the Ogowe River. Finally, in the midst of Africa are the Negrillos or pygmies, small men with reddish-brown or dark skin and brachicephalic heads.[8]

These are but a few examples of the infinitely varied inhabitants of Africa. There is thus no one African race and no one Negro type. Africa has as great a physical and cultural variety as Europe or Asia.

This is the Africa of which Langston Hughes sings:

I've known rivers:
I've known rivers ancient as the world and older than the flow of human
    blood in human veins.
My soul has grown deep like the rivers.
I bathed in the Euphrates when dawns were young.
I built my hut near the Congo and it lulled me to sleep.
I looked upon the Nile and raised the Pyramids above it.[9]

## NOTES

[1] Henry M. Stanley, *In Darkest Africa* (New York: Charles Scribners' Sons, 1891),
Vol. II, p. 76.

[2] Harry H. Johnston, *The Negro in the New World* (London: Methuen & Co., 1910),
pp. 14, 15.

[3] Leo Frobenius, *Histoire de la Civilisation Africaine*, 6th ed., tr. from the German
by Back and Ermont (Paris: Gallimard, 1936), p. 56.

[4] Francis Hoggan, "Prehistoric Negroids and their Contribution to Civilization," *The
Crisis*, February 1920, p. 174.

[5] J. A. Rogers, *Sex and Race* (New York: published by the author, 1942–44), Vol. I,
p. 32.

[6] Friedrich Ratzel, *The History of Mankind*, tr. from the German by A. J. Butler
(London: Macmillan & Co., 1904), 2nd ed., Vol. II, p. 313.

[7] W. G. Palgrave, *Dutch Guiana* (London: Macmillan & Co., 1876). pp. 192–93.

[8] In this description of African peoples, I have relied principally on C. G. Selig-
mann's well-known studies.

[9] Langston Hughes, "The Negro Speaks of Rivers," *The Crisis*, June 1921, p. 71.

*Basil Davidson's contribution derives from his noted book,* The African Slave Trade (*originally entitled* Black Mother). *It follows the DuBois article by dealing with the social, political, and economic life of the many tribes and nations of Africa prior to their first important contact with the Europeans. It speaks of their strength and power and also of the weaknesses which caused them to succumb to the depredations of the slavers.*

# The African Slave Trade

## Basil Davidson

### BEFORE THE TRADE BEGAN

European ideas about Africa, before the years of discovery, varied remarkably with time and place. In southern Europe, face to face with North African power and commerce, there was beginning to be a good deal of solid information by the year 1500. Some knowledge of the scope and wealth of the lands beyond the Sahara was getting through to influential men. Yet even the well-informed ports of the Mediterranean could yield extraordinary fluctuations of judgment; and the facts they had to go on were encased, all too often, in a lavish covering of superstitious legend.

Much of this legend was learned from the Moors—Berbers and Arabs of the Moorish states of North Africa. Seldom could Christians penetrate the African interior, and only a handful of those who did have left any trace in the records. The earliest known European traveler's memoir from "inner Africa"—and it would stand alone for many years to come—dates from 1447, and was written by an Italian called Antonio Malfante in Tuat, an oasis of the northern Sahara. Tuat in those days was an important staging-post for trans-Saharan caravans which had come from the south with African slaves, whether as victims or as porters, since times beyond recall.

Malfante picked up the caravan gossip of Tuat, and already it was rich with strange misunderstandings. He explains to a friend in Genoa that to the south of Tuat and the Great Desert there are black peoples who have "innumerable great cities and territories." But these peoples of the south "are in carnal acts like the beasts: the father has knowledge of his daughter, the son of his sister. They breed greatly, for a woman bears up to five at a birth. Nor can it be doubted that they are eaters of human flesh." Already the image of Black Africa is beginning to be the image of Caliban.

Elsewhere in Europe, especially in northern Europe, where the trade with Africa was virtually unknown, opinions could be interestingly different. Northern Europe might understand Africa no more than Africa understood northern Europe: "Scotland," an Andalusian Arab writer had declared in 1154, "has neither dwellings, nor towns, nor villages." Yet even in remote Scotland a little was beginning to be known and thought of Africa by late medieval times; and the Scots, by the early years of the sixteenth century, had even welcomed a few visitors from Africa. Such rare "travelers" were evidently men and women taken out of Portuguese slaving ships by Scottish privateers. One or two of these visitors from the far south became famous in Edinburgh society, and not the least of these was that "black lady with the fulsome lips" of whom, in about 1460, the poet Dunbar wrote some memorable verses.

This black lady had her moment of fame. The occasion was a royal jousting at Edinburgh in 1508 or perhaps 1509—"the justing of the wild knycht for the black ladye." Fourteen men, it is recorded, carried her from Edinburgh Castle, where she was lodged, to the "barres and syne to the Abbey." The "wild knight" who was the challenger seems to have been a Frenchman; but it was the king himself, brawny James IV, who carried off the day and the prize. It was just as well for James that he acquitted himself well because the award for valor was as enviable as the penalty for cowardice was not. At least, according to Dunbar:

> Quhai for hir saik, with speir and scheld,
> Preiffis maist mychtele in the feld
>   Sall kiss, and withe her go to grippis;
> And fra thyne furth his luff sall weld
>   My ladye with the mekle lippis.

The gallant who stained his knightly name had less to hope for:

> And quhai in feld receawes schame,
> And tynis thair his knychtlie name,
>   Sall cum behind and kiss her hippis,
> And neivir to other comfort claime:
>   My ladye with the mekle lippis.

The times were broad, but at any rate they were not condescending.

And if European attitudes toward Africans in those early times displayed a wide range of contrast, they were generally uniform in one important respect. They supposed no natural inferiority in Africans, no inherent failure to develop and mature. That was to be the great myth of later years: the central myth of European expansion that first took shape on the deck of a slaving ship. Race contempt crept in when free men could justify their material interests by the scorn they had for slaves—for men, that is, to whom an unnatural inferiority had given every appearance of a natural inferiority. How otherwise would so intelligent a man as Thomas Jefferson have reached the conclusions that he did?

"Comparing them [Negroes in North America] by their faculties of memory, reason and imagination," Jefferson was writing after more than a century of intensive slaving had passed by, "it appears to me that in memory they are equal to the whites; in reason much inferior, as I think one could scarcely be found capable of tracing and comprehending the investigations of Euclid; and that in imagination they are dull, tasteless, and anomalous."

An American contemporary, as it happened, gave the answer to Jefferson. "Now I beg to know," wrote Imlay White in reply, "what can be more uncertain and false than estimating and comparing the intellect and talents of two descriptions of men: one enslaved, degraded and fettered in all their acts of volition . . . the other free, independent and with the advantage of appropriating the reason and science which have been the result of the study and labours of the philosophers and sensible men for centuries back?"

Was the charge of inferiority altogether a myth? To be treated as an inferior is often to become an inferior, and it is precisely because the judgments of Europe were applied, so persistently and repeatedly, to Africans who were slaves that the writing of African history for this period must involve an analysis of the European state of mind as well as of the African condition. If we keep that in view, we shall still not arrive at any final truth because history is not an exact science, susceptible of clear and completely objective categorization, but a more or less fallible means of explaining the present in terms of the past. It will be better or worse history according to the supply and use of fact. Propaganda, one may note, aims at just the opposite, explaining the past in terms of the present; a great deal of historical writing is propaganda. But Africa stands in dire need, not of propaganda, but of historical explanation.

And here one may take good heart, for in the matter of African history the supply of fact has immensely broadened and improved over recent years. Yet the task of coming to grips with this exciting and elusive theme will nonetheless remain a problem—and race contempt and its reactions define the reasons why—of coming to grips with oneself and with the limits of one's own development.

In the early years of discovery, men in Europe believed they had found partners and allies and equals in Africa. "Let them go and do business with the King of Timbuktu and Mali," Ramusio, secretary to the rulers in Venice, was urging the merchants of Italy in 1563, "and there is no doubt they will be well received there with their ships and their goods, and treated well, and granted the favours that they ask. . . ."

Four hundred years afterwards, other men in Europe were sure that Africans had never so much as known the rudiments of political organization, let alone the means of building powerful states and operating central governments; Africans, it would be commonly said, simply lacked the faculty for growing up. "Their inherent mental inferiority, almost more marked than their physical characters," Professor Keane was writing with assured Victorian complacency in 1896, "depends on physiological causes. . . ." Once an African grew beyond childhood, Richard Burton had decided a little earlier, "his mental development is arrested, and thenceforth he grows backwards instead of forwards."

If earlier Europeans had been closer to the truth, though having less information, they too were astray in their judgment. They avoided the crass absurdity of opinions such as those of Keane and Burton. They were right in thinking that their captains and caravels were discovering powerful states and potent commercial partners. But they were wrong in imagining that this Africa of lord and vassal and willing merchant was passing through the same political development as the states of Europe.

Looking back now, we can see that appearances were double-faced. On the one side, it was true that the "cultural gap" between the European discoverers and the Africans they found was narrow and was often felt to be nonexistent. On the other side, it was false that these appearances reflected a similar experience and potential of society in Africa and Europe. For the African states, evolving their governments and empires in lands remotely muffled from the heat and clash of European or Mediterranean competition, had reached a phase of relative stability. They could and would continue at much the same level of power and organization for a long time to come. But the states of Europe were anything but stable. On the contrary, they were about to trip the springs of all those piled-up tensions and turbulent contradictions that a restless and much-invaded past had compressed in their inheritance. Unlike the states of Africa, they were about to enter a time of fast and furious growth and change.

It was in these peculiar circumstances of great likeness and unlikeness that the African-European connection began. It was out of this equivocation that the confusion and misunderstanding of later years would grow.

## THE OLD STATES OF AFRICA

One outstanding fact about the old states of Africa, well understood in earlier times but afterwards forgotten, is that they were seldom or never conquered from outside the continent. They resisted invasion. They remained inviolate. Only here and there along the coast could European men-at-arms gain a foothold even when they tried to win more. The Moorish states of northern Africa had little luck with their overland invasions of the south, and were in the end frustrated and forced to withdraw.

Writers of the colonial period have sometimes explained this fact of successful African resistance by reference to the climate and the mosquito. Certainly, malaria and the sun were grim discouragers of foreign invasion. Yet the early records indicate another and more persuasive safeguard against conquest. They point to the striking-power of African armies. They show that it was the military factor, time and again, which proved decisive.

Even in the fifteenth century the Portuguese, then feeling their way around the long western coast, were vaguely aware of powers and principalities beyond the shoreward skyline whose alliance was desirable. "The King," wrote Barros, "began cautiously to send agents with messages to the important chiefs, and to involve himself as a close and powerful friend in their affairs and their wars." In the last quarter of the fifteenth century he sent "Pedro de Evora and Gonsalo Eannes to the Prince of Tekrur"—inland from the coast of Senegal—"and to the lord of Timbuktu." From further to the southward, the Portuguese also dispatched a mission up the Gambia River "to Mansa Mundi, one of the most powerful chiefs of the province of the Mandingo."

In 1481 they built their first fort on the Gold Coast, at a place they named Elmina, "the mine," believing that from here they could best tap the sources of African gold. Yet they built this fort by agreement with the chief of the people of the region, and not after conquest. At the close of a long plea by Diogo d'Azambuja, who commanded the Portuguese expedition, the chief in question consented to the building of a fort, but only on condition that "peace and truth must be kept." And one of the earliest actions that followed on the building of the castle at Elmina was not a military expedition to "the mines" of the interior, but a diplomatic mission of friendship and alliance. Messengers had come from Mamadu, lord of Mali. King John of Portugal ordered that these messengers should be accompanied back to their country by eight Portuguese emissaries, including two knights of the royal court, "with gifts of horses and mules and arms and other things prized in that country."

Elmina was no disappointment. It delivered the gold of Africa, and in large quantity through many years. But neither the Portuguese nor the Dutch nor any other European power ever secured access to the "land of gold" until the British fought their way into Ashanti in the nineteenth century. Forts were built, but they were never secure. Garrisons were placed in them and repeatedly replenished from Europe; time and again they were besieged and overwhelmed. Governors were installed; yet they were obliged to live in close agreement with African neighbors or else lose their power.

Opinion in Europe nonetheless grew common that European power held sway over the interior. "There is no small number of men in Europe," a Dutch factor on the Gold Coast wrote back to his employers in the year 1700, "who believe that the gold mines are in our power; that we . . . have no more to do but to work them by our slaves: though you perfectly know we have no manner of access to these treasures." By this time men in Europe were accustomed to seeing Africans only as men in chains, slaves without power, and they transferred their impressions to Africa and the states from which these slaves had come. The belief in African inferiority was already in full bloom.

Those who traveled in Africa knew better. "With nauseating presumption," complained Father Cavazzi of the states of the Congo in 1687, "these nations think themselves the foremost men in the world, and nothing will persuade them to the contrary. They imagine that Africa is not only the greatest part of the world, but also the happiest and most agreeable." The lords of Congo, he found, were even more arrogant. "Similar opinions are held by the king himself, but in a manner still more remarkable. For he is persuaded that there is no other monarch in the world who is his equal, or exceeds him in power or the abundance of wealth. . . ."

The reasons for this African self-confidence were not really obscure. They were the same reasons as those that had enabled Africans to resist invasion: the steady growth of Iron Age concentrations of power, the evolution of central government, the raising of armies, the swearing-in of vassals, or the elimination of rivals that had accompanied much of African social development for the previous thousand years. They were, in short, the reasons that had enabled African types of feudal rule to emerge and grow strong.

## SIMILARITIES

It would be an illusion to see the feudalism of Africa as being the same as the feudalism of Europe in these opening years of discovery. But the similarities were often strikingly close. They are worth dwelling on because nothing but powerful feudal organization can properly explain the military strength of many African states that were found by Europe in the fifteenth and sixteenth centuries, and respected by Europe (at any rate in the beginning) as allies and partners and equals.

To get at the true position, one must look at the nature of society as it had evolved in the maturity of Africa's Iron Age. A useful approach, especially in the light of what was to come, is from the standpoint of who was bond and who was free. In Western Europe during the Dark Ages, the formative period of feudalism, there had come a gradual transformation of slave into serf; and this change was accelerated in feudal times until "old slave" and "old freeman" were little by little merged together into "new vassal." In Africa, meanwhile, wherever strong states and empires shook and changed the old framework of tribal equality, there emerged the new phenomenon of mass subjugation of one people by another. This was not slavery as Europe understood the word—chattel slavery, the stripping from a man of all his rights and property—but serfdom, vassalship, "domestic slavery." Degrees of servility and obligation would immensely vary with time and place, as they would elsewhere; but this vassalship in Africa would become essentially the same as that of Europe.

An arresting parallel may be seen in land rights. "The Ashanti, under certain conditions not unlike those that existed in England at the time of the Norman conquest, seem to have evolved an almost exactly similar land code." This parallel of Rattray's can be greatly extended. Thus the titles and the rights of great lords, the obligations of the common people, the customs of trade and tribute, the swearing of fealty, the manners of war—all these and a hundred other manifestations have seemed to speak the same identical language of feudalism.

Not much more than a hundred years ago the little army of Amadou Hammadi, founder of the Fulani empire in the Macina grasslands of the Middle Niger, faced their much more powerful assailants in a battle for survival. They took the field in doubt and great anxiety. Amadou gave the command of his army to his henchman Usman and bestowed on him the title of Amirou Mangal, "great chief." Then tradition makes Amadou say to Usman: "Great chief, raise your eyes and look about you and tell me what signs you see." Amirou Mangal does as he is bidden and replies: "Verily, I see on every hand the signs of our victory. I see that God is with us." At this point there enters the herald of the "invincible" king of Segu. He rides up with his entourage in a grand flurry of horses and banners and demands that Amadou Hammadi should at once surrender, admit homage to the king of Segu, pay tribute, and be gone. "For otherwise the vultures shall tear your flesh."

Calm of heart, Amadou answers with a mocking smile and says to the herald: "A messenger can meet no evil. Be welcome here, bold herald, and you shall have refreshment." As for submitting to the king of Segu, "let him know that my submission is already to God and will be made to no man."

That is one example among many, and completely African. Yet King Henry V before the Battle of Agincourt said nothing different to the herald of King Louis of France, although he may have said it, thanks to Shakespeare, somewhat better:

> There's for thy labour, Mountjoy.
> Go, bid thy master well advise himself:
> If we may pass, we will; if we be hinder'd,
> We shall your tawny ground with your red blood
> Discolour: and so, Mountjoy, fare you well.

The medieval states of the Western Sudan repeatedly show how closely the condition of subjugated peoples—commonly referred to, alike by Arabs and Europeans, as "slaves"—resembled that of feudal vassals. In the Songhay Kingdom of the fifteenth century along the Middle Niger, "slaves" from the non-Muslim peoples of the forest verge were extensively used in agriculture. They were settled on the land and tied to it. In return for this livelihood they paid tribute to their masters both in crops and personal services. Their bondage was relative: time and custom gave them new liberties. Yet being generally restricted by feudal rule in the varieties of work they might undertake and the peoples among whom they might seek wives, these "slaves" tended to form occupational castes. They became blacksmiths, boat-builders, stablemen, makers of songs, bodyguards of their sovereign lord. Along with the "free peasants," whose social condition was really little different, these "vassal peasants" and "vassal artisans" formed the great bulk of the population.

Contrasts in status between the freemen who belonged to a conquering people and the "slave" who came of a conquered people would grow narrower as time went by and the system grew stronger; and in this too, there was a broad parallel with medieval Europe. Caste and even class divisions might emerge and sharpen among the mass of "commoners"; the dominant factor in society increasingly became the difference in power which separated prince and lords from the people, from all the people. This stratification occurred among the strong nations of the forest belt, behind the coast, just as it appeared among the Muslim peoples of the northern plains. It was narrowly limited by the nature of West Africa's feudal economy which remained largely one of subsistence and barter. It was greatly modified by the electoral principle of chiefdom and the checks and balances of customary rule. But the lord-and-vassal stratification nonetheless grew sharper among the groups who held power. There are many examples.

Early in the nineteenth century the old Hausa states of northern Nigeria were taken over by an invading army of Fulani. All the captains and leaders under Usman dan Fodio, the great Fulani leader, were then endowed with large landholdings seized from the defeated Hausa lords (except where these, as occasionally happened, had thrown in their lot with the new regime). The old Hausa royal title of *Sarki* was perpetuated, and the whole titular structure was bound directly to the newly created fiefs and regions of command. And this oligarchy came with time to exercise rights of life and death over the common people, and could call on them for labor in the fields or the building of houses or the maintenence of roads and river fords.

The case is especially instructive, since the origins of this Fulani invasion had lain in revolt against a gross social inequality. Explaining "the reasons for our holy war with the Hausa Sultans," a contemporary Fulani document, written some four years before Europe heard news of the Battle of Waterloo, says that in the beginning Usman dan Fodio "did not address himself to the kings. After a time his people grew and became famous, till they were known in Hausaland as *'The People.'* Men kept leaving their countries and coming to them. Of the ruling classes some repented"—for Usman preached a puritanical Islam, calling on the rich to abandon their wealth and calling on the poor to put their trust in God—"and came to him with all they possessed, leaving their [Hausa] Sultans. Then the Sultans became angry, till there ensued between them and their chiefs the war we remember."

Yet in freeing the people of the Hausa states from their old bondage, the Fulani reformers soon found themselves binding on a new one. However egalitarian Usman dan Fodio might be, his henchmen were ambitious men whose reforming zeal was tempered by a healthy territorial ambition. Besides, they were rulers of their time. They soon found they must either forfeit their new-found power and wealth or else revert to those very methods of bureaucratic government that they had set themselves to overthrow. And little by little, there being in any event no alternative but abdication, the new Fulani feudalism came to resemble the old Hausa system; except for a tightening of Islamic discipline, little was altered but the men at the top.

Usman himself resisted the trend toward feudal centralism. Many vivid stories tell of his shrewd prevarications when faced with the urgent pleas of his commanders. One day they came to him and said they must be allowed to sell land, as the Hausa lords had done before them, for otherwise they could not discipline the people. Usman had always laid it down that the land belonged to God and was not for anyone to sell. Now, faced with this new demand, he asked for a cupful of earth and sent it to the market place for sale; after a few days he inquired of his servants whether anyone had bid for it. They replied that none had made an offer. Whereupon Usman, calling his commanders together, declared that there could be no sense in giving them the right to sell land, since none desired to buy.

But the feudal bonds grew tighter. The early reforming vows were forgotten. The ruling emirs claimed more and more power. And in this increasingly stratified society, just as earlier in medieval Europe, the dividing line between bond and free among the common people became ever more hard to trace. The degree of freedom or unfreedom that distinguished the "free peasants" (*talakawa*) from the "serfs" (*cucenawa*) narrowed to the vanishing point: all were embraced as subjects, and perhaps the most that one can say about their difference in status was that some were more subjected than others.

Naturally, the process varied with circumstances. In nineteenth century Bornu, heir to the ancient state of Kanem in the region of Lake Chad, custom generally recognized three social groups beneath the noble families: the *kambe,* who were freemen drawn from the ranks of freed slaves and the children of freemen married to slaves; the *kalia,* who were slaves, whether foreigners or men and women captured in war; and the *zusanna,* the descendants of slaves, who were also the rank-and-file footsloggers of the army of Bornu. Yet the differences between the *kambe* and the *kalia* and the *zusanna* were undoubtedly less important, so far as the distribution of social power was concerned, than the differences between all these three on one hand and the nobles on the other. Here, once again, was a system recognizably feudal—a system, moreover, which had grown with Iron Age development from the earliest beginnings of the old pastoral empire of Kanem, forerunner of Bornu, during a period that was contemporary with the growth of European feudalism.

Such systems continued into modern times. One other example may be useful from another part of Africa, the kingdom of Ruanda, lying in a small country of tall mountains between the Congo and the East African lands of Uganda and Tanganyika. Ruanda possessed a close-knit social order that persists in large measure even today, so that anthropologists have been able to make direct reports about it.

This society is divided into three kinds of people. Foremost are the Watutsi—of late years much photographed for their splendid dancing—who may number about one-tenth of the population. They, says Maquet, "do no manual work and have leisure to cultivate eloquence, poetry, refined manners." Beneath them are the Bahutu, who "do not enjoy such gracious living," because "they have to produce for themselves and for the Watutsi." And beneath the Bahutu, in the third rank, are the Batwa—"so low in the social hierachy and . . . considered so irresponsible, that they have had a greater independence of action."

In Ruanda, accordingly, nobody is "free" in the modern sense of the word, for even the Watutsi are wedded to their laborers by a formal code of interwoven duties. Moreover, it is better for a Mututsi (that is to say, one Watutsi) to become the vassal of a strong man than to remain on his own. "We desire," Maquet's Watutsi informants told him, "to become the vassals of great chiefs, or even of the king, because we are then under the protection of somebody very important, we get more cows, and that allows us to have more 'clients' "—that is, more Bahutu workers who will labor in their turn so as to gain "protection."

Compare this "ladder of duty-and-obligation" with that of feudal Europe. Many European slaves were liberated—"manumitted" in the language of the times—but few were then able or desired to remain on their own. They found it better and safer to bind themselves to a master, and they chose the most powerful lord they could find. "The manumitter," Bloch has written of medieval France, "even if he agreed to give up a slave, wished to conserve a dependent. The manumitted himself, not daring to live without a protector, thus found the protection he desired." In Europe as in Africa, like causes produce like effects.

Next to Ruanda, in the neighboring Ugandan kingdom of Ankole, there was (and to some extent there still is) much the same system of rulers and ruled: Bahima nobles, in this case, and Bairu vassals. Such as were chattel slaves—genuine slaves without rights or claims—consisted, Oberg reports, "entirely of Bairu captured in raids made upon neighbouring kingdoms, [but] there is nothing to indicate that slaves were sold or exchanged, although chiefs gave each other slaves as presents . . . [and] from all accounts, slavery was restricted to the very wealthy, and slaves were restricted in numbers."

This was the broad type of centralized social organization in Africa that would prove, time and again in the coastal regions, too strong for challenge from outside. Along the seaboard of the Guinea Coast there emerged states and empires—Oyo, Benin, Denkyira, Akwamu, and many others—that European venturers would respect. And here, too, society had become increasingly divided into rulers and ruled, base and noble, bond and free, with weaker clans or even whole tribes reduced to this or that productive position in the social system of the stronger peoples.

Europeans of a somewhat later day often misunderstood the essentially vassal nature of this African subjection. Such slavery, argued the defenders of the slave trade, was no different from any other. This argument they used repeatedly in their eighteenth century battles against those who wished to abolish the trade. Do not prevent us from taking these poor savages away from Africa, the slavers urged, for otherwise you will condemn them to a fate much worse. Confirm us in our right to carry them off to America, and you will encourage "a great accession of happiness to Africa." The British Privy Council of Enquiry into the slave trade, which sat in 1788, was doubtfully impressed. One may note that other men would afterwards urge a continuance of the colonial system with much the same argument. Do not ask us to abandon our responsibilities for governing Africans, for you must otherwise confirm these peoples in a savage fate. . . . Support us in our powers of dominion, and you will ensure rich benefits for Africa. . . .

Yet the "slave" peoples of the coastal regions, like those of the Sudanese grasslands, were in truth serfs and vassals, often with valued individual rights. Their status was altogether different from the human cattle of the slave ships and the American plantations. Early European traders on the coast, though freely misusing the word "slave," repeatedly drew attention to this. "Those who come from the inward part of the country to traffick with us," Bosman reports of the Guinea Coast around the year 1700, "are chiefly slaves: one of which, on whom the master reposes the greatest trust, is appointed the chief of the caravan. But when he comes to us he is not treated as a slave, but as a very great merchant whom we take all possible care to oblige. . . . Indeed, I have observed that some of these slaves have more authority than their masters; for having long exercised command over their masters' dependents, by their own trading they are become possessors of some slaves themselves, and in process of time are grown so powerful, that their patrons are obliged to see with their eyes only. . . ."

One could multiply such observations, and for every part of Africa where the outside world had contact. Sometimes they were casual and inconclusive, mere traders' gossip of strange people and exotic countries. Now and then they were more than that. An early American Negro explorer of southern Nigeria, Martin Delany, spoke in sharper tones. "It is simply preposterous to talk about slavery, as that term is understood, either being legalised or existing in this part of Africa," he wrote. "It is nonsense. The system is a patriarchal one, there being no actual difference, socially, between slaves (called by their protector sons or daughters) and the children of the person with whom they live. Such persons intermarry and frequently become the heads of state. . . . And were this not the case, it either arises from some innovation among them or those exceptional cases of despotism to be found in every country. . . ." [1]

What was true of southern Nigeria was true of other "forest" peoples. In Ashanti, Rattray found "a slave might marry; own property; himself own a slave; swear an oath; be a competent witness; and ultimately become heir to his master. . . . Such briefly were the rights of an Ashanti slave. They seemed in many cases practically the ordinary privileges of an Ashanti free man. . . . An Ashanti slave, in nine cases out of ten, possibly became an adopted member of the family, and in time his descendants so merged and intermarried with the owner's kinsmen that only a few would know their origin. . . ." Captives, that is to say, became vassals; vassals became free men; free men became chiefs.

Set this highly mobile social order alongside the slave system of the United States, and the vital and enormous difference becomes immediately clear. There the slaves were entirely a class apart, labeled by their color, doomed to accept an absolute servitude; in Tannenbaum's words, "the mere fact of being a Negro was presumptive of a slave status." And slave status was forever. Manumission became increasingly difficult; often it became impossible. An early law of Maryland, dating from 1663, declared: "All Negroes or other slaves within the province, all Negroes to be hereafter imported, shall serve *durante vita";* but their children were to serve likewise. A few free Negroes there might be; yet they were tolerated with the utmost difficulty. A South Carolina law of 1740 provided that any free Negro should be sold at public auction if he had harbored a runaway slave or was charged "with any criminal matter." A Negro or mulatto in Mississippi could be sold as a slave unless he was able to prove himself a free man. As late as 1801 a Georgia law imposed a fine of two hundred dollars on any master who freed a slave without previous consent of the legislature. Seventeen years later the lawmakers of Georgia went even further. They imposed a fine of one thousand dollars on anyone who gave effect to a last will and testament freeing a slave or allowing him to work on his own account.

This is not to suggest that the life of an African vassal was one of un-alloyed bliss, but that the condition he suffered was in no way the same as plantation or mining slavery in the Americas. His condition often was comparable to that of the bulk of the men and women in Western Europe throughout medieval times. In this respect Africa and Europe, at the beginning of their connection, traded and met as equals. And it was this acceptance of equality, based on the strength and flexibility of feudal systems of state organization, that long continued to govern relations between Africa and Europe. Even in the matter of slaving their attitudes were much the same.

## SLAVES AND SLAVING

When the traders of Europe first began their traffic with the empire of Benin, not far from the coast of Nigeria, they found that captives could be purchased there without much difficulty.

"The trade one can conduct here," Pacheco was writing in about 1505, some thirty years after Portugal's earliest contact with Benin, "is the trade in slaves . . . and in elephants' tusks." But the traders also found that objection was taken at Benin to the enslavement of the natives of the country —of men and women, that is, who were within the protection of the Oba of Benin, a monarch whose power derived from God. By custom and by moral law, slaves ought to be men and women captured from neighboring peoples. They ought to be "outsiders," "unbelievers." This rule was often broken; but it was universally admitted.

Turning to the European records, one finds the leaders of Christianity busy endeavoring to apply precisely the same rule—and with about as much success. Slaves being a highly perishable commodity, the supply was always running short. Where possible, the European merchants who dealt in chattel slaves were accustomed to buy infidels or Jews; otherwise, they simply did as the Benin traders would do in somewhat later times. They bought "believers." They sold their "fellow-natives." Papal records show the Vatican repeatedly inveighing against this practice.

All the great city-states of medieval Italy appear to have dealt in Christian slaves. The Venetians and the Genoese were deep in the trade as early as the tenth and eleventh centuries. They continued in it, together with the Pisans and the Florentines and the merchants and mariners of ports as far apart as Lucca and Amalfi, until as late as the middle of the fifteenth century. Throughout the thirteenth century, European slaves were being carried in European ships to the Sultanate of Egypt despite all ecclesiastical rebukes and threats. "The excesses of the traders," Scelle records, "were such that Pope Clement V excommunicated the Venetians and authorised all Christian people to reduce them in turn to slavery."

Little more than half a century before the launching of the oversea slave trade from Africa, Pope Martin V published a bull of excommunication against the Genoese merchants of Caffa, Genoese city-state on the Black Sea, for their persistence in buying and selling Christians. This was as ineffectual as the earlier excommunication of the Venetians, and in 1441 the laws of Gazaria (as the Genoese called their little trading "empire" on the Black Sea coast) expressly provided for the sale and purchase of Christian as well as Muslim slaves.

Another aspect of this early equality between Europe and Africa, in respect to slaves and slaving, lies in the treatment of those who were captured. In Africa, as we have seen, slaves could almost at once begin climbing the ladder of liberation from their rightless condition. And it was not much different for the captives who were brought from Africa into fifteenth century Portugal and Spain. The many Negro slaves of Andalusia enjoyed a special code of law awarded by royal authority; and their principal judge, who was one of their own folk and represented them, was known as the "Negro count." With the passing of the years they mingled with their free neighbors and lost their ethnic identity.

Or consider the attitude of the fifteenth century Portuguese to the Negroes who were beginning to arrive in the earliest slaving ships. Zurara has described this in his famous chronicle of 1453. Finding these captives prepared to become Christians and "not hardened in the belief of the other Moors" —the Muslims of North Africa—the Portuguese "made no difference between them and their free servants, born in our own country. But those they took while still young, they caused to be instructed in the mechanical arts. But those whom they saw fitted for managing property, they set free and married to women who were natives of the land—making with them a division of their property, as if they had been bestowed on those who married them by the will of their own fathers. . . .

"Yes, and some widows of good family who bought some of these female slaves, either adopted them or left them a portion of their estate by will; so that in the future they married right well; treating them as entirely free. . . ." Portugal in the time of its greatness would thus anticipate Brazil.

As in Africa, so in Europe: the medieval slave, in one as in the other, was a captive who could soon win access to the system of mutual duty and obligation that bound noble and commoner together. And what went for the manners of society went for the morals of the merchants too—whether in Europe or Africa. European traders sold their fellow-countrymen to the oversea states of Egypt and North Africa. The lords of Africa would sell their own folk to the mariners who came from Europe.

It is important to establish this point. For it was the ground of departure on which the whole relationship between Europe and Africa was firmly set. Out of this common acceptance of bondage in a feudal situation there would flow, in postmedieval times, a common acceptance of the slave trade between the two continents. Thus the African notion that Europe altogether imposed the slave trade on Africa is without any foundation in history. This idea is as baseless as the comparable European notion that institutions of bondage were in some way peculiar to Africa.

Africa and Europe were jointly involved. Yet it is also true that Europe dominated the connection, shaped and promoted the slave trade, and continually turned it to European advantage and to African loss. And when one begins to examine why this was so, one sees how the similarities between European and African feudalism concealed differences that were more important—and were decisive.

## DIFFERENCES

Much has remained obscure about the early years of contact between Europe and Africa. One of the certainties, however, is that it was only from the north that discovery came. The little ships of that heroic enterprise came always from the ports of Western Europe, from Lisbon and Seville, Nantes and Boulogne and Plymouth, and never from the harbors of the Guinea Coast. Why was this? If leading peoples in Africa and Europe alike lived under systems of feudal rule, why was the initiative always European?

The answer has nothing to do with innate capacity, racial talent, intellectual or cultural potential, nor with any kind of natural superiority or inferiority. It lies in the profound difference in social content of these feudal systems—a difference that was the product of deep contrasts in environment and circumstance. These systems in Africa and Europe might often appear the same. At several points, as we have seen, they might actually be the same. Yet their formative backgrounds were altogether diverse. The similarities between them concealed an equivocation.

By the period of oversea discovery, Africa had reached a social equilibrium and evolved a society that was largely balanced in itself, any "overflow of discontent" being allowed to disperse across the endless lands. Yet Europe was anything but stable. Europe had already jumped from feudal equilibrium into the tumult of social progress through acquisitive advance. Spinning on its money-driven axis, heir to the peculiar pressures of its past, and impelled by a marvelous curiosity and will to know, Europe now moved across the threshold of a new age. Within eighteen years of the Portuguese arrival at Benin, Columbus had found land across the Atlantic. Within another seven years, Vasco da Gama had reached the golden East.

In this comparison of Africa and Europe in the fifteenth century, the equivocation between appearance and reality was the fruit of complex differences. The old system of society in Iron Age Europe had worked on the basis of a chattel slavery wherein men and women who were slaves had enjoyed no rights and held no property. This was the slavery of the Ancient World, of Greece and Rome and the empires of the Near East before them. It was a vital part of the social foundation of all those Iron Age concentrations of wealth and power that had given Europe its high civilizations of antiquity.

Then "tribal Europe" intervened. The nomad peoples of the north conquered Rome, assumed Roman civilization, were in turn absorbed in it, and yet destroyed the old and clear distinction between freeman and slave. And men in Europe, notably in Western Europe, became fused increasingly into a unified society, but a society in which the old divisions reappeared in another and more strictly hierarchical form. The feudal idea was enthroned.

Gradually, the chattel slaves of Roman Europe disappeared. The liberation, of course, was relative. Chattel slaves were transformed into tied laborers whose rights were few; even their old name, *servi,* being perpetuated in their new name, serfs. And as the slaves came up a little, so the freemen also went down, until the two classes came gradually to occupy positions that were not essentially different. However imperfectly, feudalism may thus be said to have enclosed Western Europe in a framework of social service, ideal of the medieval world. Only when the system broke down, as the cities grew and the barons and princes ruined each other in endless wars, was the way cleared for another unification—this time in terms of social equality, ideal of a later world.

The point here is that the system did break down. It broke down throughout medieval times, continuously if erratically, and gave way little by little, confusedly, obscurely, to the capitalism that would dominate the future of Europe. And it may well be—extending a parallel of Needham's—that the key component in this tortuous and onward-shifting machinery of social movement lay precisely in the industrial slavery of Roman Europe.[2] For it was this mass slavery—acid solvent of the old relations of "tribal equality" —which first "detribalized" large numbers of Europeans, concentrated wealth in the hands of a few men who were not necessarily kings and rulers, enabled these men to discover new ways of using and accumulating money, and created the mass of "masterless wights" who increasingly found a new life in towns and cities. And it was these cities and towns that were the makers of commerce, the gatherers of capital, the champions of individual liberty, the promoters of inquiry, the sources of new thought, and the powerful levers that switched the whole of Europe into new directions. It was here that the banker and merchant and entrepreneur were born and had their being and rose to power.

This explanation telescopes much history. Yet it may contain a good part of the reason why Africa and Europe, at the time of their early confrontation, were both living under systems that were recognizably feudal in character, and yet had reached sharply different stages of social growth.

There were towns in Black Africa before the coming of Europe, even large towns, but they were only another type of settlement for men who continued, for the most part, to live by the old rules of tribal loyalty and custom. Their inhabitants were seldom or never opposed to their feudal princes in the way that London was opposed to the barons, or the cities of the Holy Roman Empire to their kings and emperors. They were not the refuge of large numbers of men who sought to fashion a new society out of a new concept of freedom. They were powerless to impel Africa into new directions.

Exceptions to this there undoubtedly were, notably in the Western Sudan and along the East Coast, Djenné and Timbuktu, Malindi and Kilwa; but these exceptional cities were of marginal importance to the situation in continental Africa as a whole. The capitalist techniques they began to evolve—banking, lending, the use of currency—had little impact outside the relatively narrow limits of their mercantile connections across the Sahara and the Indian Ocean.

Why this contrast with Europe? There was, to begin with, the absence in Black Africa of any direct and steady influence from the high civilizations of the Mediterranean and the Middle East. Beyond its seas of sand and salt water, continental Africa was left to work out its own destiny. In fact, Africa worked out many destinies. Some African societies, their contact with the outside world muffled by immense forests and daunting plains, carried their ancient tribalism into very recent times. Even today, after half a century of incessant pressure for change, the loyalties and attitudes of ancient custom and morality often remain powerful and even decisive, and give life there a special accent and appearance.

Other African societies embarked on a process of social and economic change which brought them to forms of feudal unification. They passed from the Stone Age into a Metal Age (northern Nigeria, for example, began using iron for tools and weapons only a few centuries after northern Europe) and evolved new cultures, fashioned systems of centralized government, developed hierarchies of power, and extended their rule by imperial conquest. Islam, here and there, infused something of the same leveling and centralizing force that Christianity supplied in Europe.

Yet the "key component" was missing. There lay in the heritage of these feudal systems in Africa no great period of chattel slavery, no far-reaching process of "detribalization." That is why, I suggest, this Africa feudalism may reasonably be called "tribal feudalism," a system of centralized government that was almost always qualified by the precedents of "tribal equality." It was in some important ways nearer, not having arisen from a society which rested on slave labor, to the quasi-feudalism of pre-Roman Gaul or perhaps to the early feudalism of Anglo-Saxon England. When the Portuguese arrived in West Africa in times of European autocracy, they thought they found there the same stiff hierarchies of rule and precedence as those they knew at home. They hastened to interpret Africa in terms of fifteenth century Portugal. Vercingetorix and Boadicea, chiefs in Gaul and Britain long before, might have understood the situation better. The thegns and ealdormen of Alfred's England would certainly have done so.

Another explanation of why the kings and emperors of medieval Africa never developed the same autocracy and tyranny as their contemporaries in Europe may be found in the balance of weapon power. The European knight in steel from head to foot, riding a great horse, was immensely more powerful than the mass of freemen and serfs, at least until the coming of the longbow and later the gun. But the lords of medieval Africa were seldom much better armed or mounted than the plebes; even when they tried to behave as autocrats—and no doubt they often tried—their superiority in weapons could rarely allow them to succeed for long.

A third reason why African feudalism remained closely tied to its tribal past may lie in the far-ranging movement of African peoples. This was the ever-freshened impulse of migration that took them across the continent from northward to southward throughout the centuries of an Iron Age which began, for Africa, at about the same time as Europe knew the decline of Greece and the rise of the Roman Republic. There is scarcely a modern African people without a more or less vivid tradition that speaks of movement from another place. Younger sons of paramount chiefs would hive off with their followers, and become paramount themselves in a new land. Stronger peoples would conquer those who were weaker, marry their women, merge with them, weave yet another strand in the fabric of Negro life.

But this wandering of peoples clearly acted as a powerful preserver of the old system of tribal-feudal relationships, for it gave play to an elasticity and tolerance that could absorb and eliminate strains and stresses which must otherwise have forced a social crisis. Hence, to a large extent, the enduring stability of the general pattern of society in Iron Age Africa. Hence its appearance of immobility. For this continual making and weaving of new threads and strands strengthened rather than weakened the total fabric.

When Europeans first entered on their trading and political missions in Africa, here and there along the coast, it seemed for a time that their coming must provide the break and change whereby African society would move into a new form, mercantile and capitalist. The outcome was different. There were many shifts of power and many innovations; yet African society generally failed to undergo any radical and basic change of structure. What happened instead was a tremendous change in the African-European balance of power. And it was slaving that now occupied the center of the picture. It had stood there, indeed, from the very first. But then the cloud had been no bigger than a man's hand.

## NOTES

¹ I am indebted for this quotation to Dr. George Shepperson; it comes from the official report of the Niger Valley Exploring Party, published in New York, 1861, p. 40. Delany was a serious observer who traveled in West Africa between July, 1859, and August, 1860.

² J. Needham, "Science and Society in Ancient China," a paper prepared for the Conway Memorial Lecture Committee of the South Place Ethical Society.

*The late Melville Herskovits, one of the most outstanding*
*American scholars of Africa provides the following*
*excerpt from his book,* The Myth of the Negro Past.
*This work, published in 1941, was a scholarly attack on*
*the prevalent notion that Africa had contributed little*
*to American culture and that it was unworthy and*
*insignificant. It also deals with the compelling question of*
*"survivals" of African practices, organizations, beliefs,*
*and culture in the lives of contemporary Black Americans.*

# The Search for Tribal Origins

## Melville Herskovits

Fundamental to any discussion of the presence or absence of Africanisms in Negro custom in the New World is the establishment of a "base line"
from which change may be judged. Two elements enter into this; it is necessary to discover, as precisely as possible, the tribal origins of the slaves
brought to the New World, and on the basis of these facts to obtain as full
and accurate knowledge as we can of the cultures of these folk.

In this chapter, only the historical materials employed to determine tribal
provenience will be presented. Yet historical analysis, of itself, has not given
and cannot give the needed information. Only in coordination with the
ethnological phase of the dual attack implicit in the ethno-historical method
can documentation, otherwise meaningless, realize its greatest significance.
Historical scholars have for years considered the problem of the African
origins of the slaves, but without knowledge of the cultures of the regions
toward which the materials in the documents pointed, they were unable
to validate their hypotheses, even when, as was not always the case, they
had adequate acquaintance with the local geography of Africa and could
thus make effective use of the place names which recur in the contemporary
literature.

Here, indeed, the appropriate elements in our "mythology" played their
part well. Historians, with the principle that the slaves were derived from
most of the African continent and the convention of the "thousand-mile
march" of the slave coffles in mind, were understandably reluctant to draw
the conclusions their data indicated—that the greater number of Negroes

imported into New World countries came from a far more restricted area than had been thought the case. It is generally recognized that the ports from which slaves were shipped were preponderantly those along the western coast, and that south and east African points of shipment were rare. Yet coastal shipping points do not necessarily mean that the goods exported from them have not been gathered from a hinterland—in this case by distant native chieftains whose avarice was stimulated by the rewards held out to them by slavers.

Only when the scrutiny of the documents was complemented by acquaintance with the ethnography of Old and New World Negro communities, and the traits of the cultures of these groups were correlated with data from Africa to discover correspondences, did the question of African origins become susceptible of attack. A base line for the study of cultural change among New World Negroes—and, from the point of the focus of attention in this discussion, of the Negroes of the United States—has been established by means of this cross-disciplinary technique. We may thus turn to the results obtained from analyzing the historical documentation, leaving a consideration of survivals of tribal custom in New World Negro societies for a more appropriate later point.

*2*

The pattern for the prevailing conception of slaving operations was set by early writers, and this has been reinforced by the tendency to interpret African commercial relations in terms of European methods of trading, and a lack of knowledge of the density of population in West Africa. For it is not difficult to reason that, with a demand for slaves such as the American markets created, word of the commercial advantages in trading to the coast would spread to the hinterland, and captives would be brought to the factories of the European companies. It is said that slaves in some numbers were traded from tribe to tribe across the entire bulk of Central Africa, so that members of East African communities found themselves at Congo ports awaiting shipment to the New World! Yet this disregards not only the vast distances involved—some 3,000 miles—but also the dangers attendant upon such journeys in terms of the hostility between many of the tribes over the area and the absence of adequate lines of communication, to say nothing of the slight economic gain from such hazardous commerce even were the highest prices to be paid for such slaves.

The earlier writers gave astonishingly little justification, in their own works, for their statements on the extensiveness of the slave traffic. For example, though Bryan Edwards writes of the "immense distance to the sea-coast" traveled by slaves, yet of the cases he cites of Jamaican slaves he questioned about their African homes, only for "Adam, a Congo boy," is his assertion borne out, though even Adam is merely claimed to have come "from a vast distance inland." The four Negroes from the Gold Coast could not have lived far from the sea, the Ebo village Edwards speaks of was "about one day's journey from the sea-coast," while the fifth, a Chamba from Sierra Leone, also came from relatively near the coast.[1]

Mungo Park has given us our only firsthand account of the adventures of a slave coffle, but his description gives little support to those who emphasize the "thousand-mile" journeys made to the coast.[2] On April 19, 1797, Mr. Park departed from Kamalia, in the Bambara country, with slaves for the American market. The Gambia was reached on June 1, at a point some hundred miles from the sea where seagoing ships could come, and fifteen days later an American ship, bound for South Carolina, took slaves as cargo and Mr. Park as passenger. The distance traversed by the caravan was about 500 miles, or, for the 44 days in transit, an average of between 11 and 12 miles per day. The question may well be raised whether the translation of time into space, of the slow progress from sources of supply to the coastal factories, might not have been an important factor in giving the weight of logic to the conception of the slave trade as reaching far into the interior.

A source of information on the provenience of slaves which has remained almost entirely unexploited is the tradition about slaving in Africa itself. In Dahomey, for example, a kingdom on the Guinea coast which extended from its port, Whydah, some 150 miles into the interior, the annual "war" operated to supply the slave dealers. There are no traditions among these people that they acted as middlemen for traders farther inland; they were, in fact, avoided by the merchant folk, such as the Hausa, since the stranger in their kingdom was himself fair game. The peoples raided by the Dahomeans lived no farther from the coast than 200 miles, while most of their victims came from much nearer. Tribes to the east and west, rather than to the north, were the easiest prey, and hence the Nago (Yoruba) of Nigeria and the people of the present Togoland are found to figure most prominently in native lists of the annual campaigns.[3]

The coastal area of the Gold Coast was occupied by the Fanti tribes, who, because of their control of this strategic region, acted as middlemen for tribes to the north. Yet all evidence from recognizable survivals such as the many Ashanti-Akan-Fanti place names, names of deities, and day names in the New World are evidence that the sources of the slaves exported by the Fanti were in greatest proportion within the present boundaries of the Gold Coast colony. This is quite in accordance with the population resources of the coastal belt. The numerous villages, and the presence of cities of considerable size all through the area, suggest that the conception of an Africa depopulated by the slave trade, without the numbers necessary to support a drain that is to be figured in the millions, stands in need of drastic revision.

Senegal and the Guinea coast are two of the four principal areas mentioned in contemporary writings. The regions about the mouth of the Niger, named Bonny and Calabar in the documents, and the Congo are the other two, and it may be profitable to outline the situation with respect to the potentialities of the hinterland which was exploited for slaves there, and the nature of such historical facts as are available about the slave trade in these areas. The Niger Delta is a teeming hive, its low marshy plains densely inhabited by groups which, like those in the country lying behind it, are small and autonomous and thus, politically, in contrast to those larger entities, which we term kingdoms and empires, of the other parts of the slaving area. In this hinterland it was group against group, and kidnaping was probably more customary than anywhere else, though the oral tradition of the care taken by mothers to guard their children from unsupervised contact with strangers heard everywhere in West Africa and the use of folk tales to impress children with the danger of leaving the familial compound are eloquent of the fears engendered by the slavers in all the vast region.

Large numbers of slaves were shipped from the Niger Delta region, as indicated by the manifests of ships loaded at Calabar and Bonny, the principal ports. These were mainly Ibo slaves representing a people which today inhabits a large portion of this region. Their tendency to despondency, noted in many parts of the New World, and a tradition of suicide as a way out of difficulties has often been remarked, as, for example, in Haiti where the old saying *"Ibos pend' cor' a yo*—The Ibo hang themselves" [4] is still current. That this attitude toward life is still well recognized among the Ibo in Africa was corroborated in the field recently by Dr. J. S. Harris.[5] The same tendency was noticed among the "Calabar" Negroes—another generic name for Ibos among the slaves—in the United States, as is indicated by the remark of the biographer of Henry Laurens, that in South Carolina "the frequent suicides among Calabar slaves indicate the different degrees of sensitive and independent spirit among the various Negro tribes." [6]

To the east of the Cross River lie the Cameroons and Gaboon, which figured little in the slave trade. The worth of these Negroes was held to be slight, as the following quotation indicates:

The "kingdom of Gaboon," which straddled the equator, was the worst reputed of all. "From thence a good negro was scarcely ever brought. They are purchased so cheaply on the coast as to tempt many captains to freight with them; but they generally die either on the passage or soon after their arrival in the islands. The debility of their constitutions is astonishing." From this it would appear that most of the so-called Gaboons must have been in reality Pygmies caught in the inland equatorial forests, for Bosman, who traded among the Gaboons, merely inveighed against their garrulity, their indecision, their gullibility and their fondness for strong drink, while as to their physique he observed: "they are mostly large, robust well-shaped men." [7]

Raiding to the north or northeast of the Calabar area was rendered unlikely by the existence of better-organized political units, and consequently this locus of the trade fed on itself. This it could do, for with its dense peopling it could export the numbers it did without significant recourse to its neighboring territories, so that here again, where provenience is concerned, research must look to tribes well within a belt stretching, as a maximum, not more than two or three hundred miles from the coast as the area meriting closest attention.

For the Congo, relatively little information is available. We know from the data concerning two New World centers, Brazil and the Sea Islands off the Carolina Coast, that the peoples of Angola figured largely in the trade to these areas. Many traits of Congo religion and song have been recorded from Brazil [8] while linguistic survivals in the Gulla Islands, as studied by Dr. Turner,[9] likewise show a substantial proportion of words from this region. The works of Père Dieudonne Rinchon have dealt more carefully with the Congo slave trade than those of any other student of the history of slaving, and his testimony indicates that in the Congo, as elsewhere, the slavers were not compelled to range far from the coast to obtain their supply. The following passage, indeed, reinforces this hypothesis by the manner in which the case described in the last three sentences is singled out for special attention:

Les esclaves exportés sont principalement des Ambundus, des gens de Mbamba et de Mbata, et pour le reste des Nègres du Haut-Congo achetés par les Bamfumgunu et les Bateke du Pool. Quelques-uns de ces esclaves viennent de fort loin dans l'intérieur. Le capitaine négrier Degrandpré achète à Cabinda une Négresse qui lui paraît assez familière avec les Blancs, óu du moins qui ne témoigne à leur vue ni surprise, ni frayeur; frappé de cette sécurité peu ordinaire, le négrier lui en demande la cause. Elle répond qu'elle a vu précédement des Blancs dans une autre terre, où le soleil se lève dans l'eau, et non comme au Congo où il se cache dans la mer; et elle ajoute en montrant le levant *monizi monambu*, j'ai vu le bord de la mer; elle a été en chemin, *gonda cacata*, beaucoup de lune. Ce récit semble confirmer les dires de Dapper que parfois des esclaves du Mozambique sont vendus au Congo.[10]

A passage with such definite information is rare in the literature. It can most easily be utilized for our purpose if the excellent tribal maps of the Belgian Congo now available are consulted.[11] The Bamfumungu and the Bateke, living in the region of Stanley Pool on the upper Congo, are a bare 200 miles in the interior. The Bambata (the Mbata of the citation) are found about 100 miles from the coast; the Mbamba, given by Rinchon as living between 7° 5′ South and 14° East, are today included in the Portuguese colony of Angola, and hence not recorded on the Belgian maps. Aside from Rinchon's list, another clue to Congo origins is had in the name of a people mentioned often in Haiti, the Mayombe. This tribe lives directly behind Cabinda, which was the principal slaving port, and their most easterly extension is not more than 50 or 75 miles from the coast.

Material gained during field work further reinforces our hypothesis that the coastal area of West Africa furnished the greater proportion of the slaves. This information was recorded in the Hausa city of Kano, in northern Nigeria, where by the kindness of the Emir, it was possibly to query four old men who themselves, like their forebears for many generations, had been important slavers—"merchants," as they insisted on being called—trading with the Gold Coast. The route they traveled was some 1,800 miles long, and is still traversed today; and every point on it could be checked with standard maps. The distance involved was largely a matter of east-and-west travel rather than southwardly to the coast (Kano lies between 500 and 600 miles inland), since it was necessary, were they to remain in friendly Hausa and allied territory, to strike far to the west before moving southward —otherwise they would have encountered the hostile peoples of Dahomey and what is today western Nigeria. It is not necessary to repeat here information already available,[12] except to indicate briefly the operations of these men as they describe something of the numbers of slaves brought from this relatively deep point in the interior. That is, slaves were taken to the Gold Coast for trade with the Ashanti only as an incident to the major purpose; it was goods, not human beings, that were the object of their attention, and the slaves in the caravans were burden-bearers, and hence only for sale on the most advantageous terms. They were never, as far as these men knew, traded directly to the whites. The matter has been summarized in the following terms:

. . . though perhaps six or seven thousand slaves left Kano every year for the Gold Coast, two-thirds or three-fourths of that number returned north as carriers the capacity in which they had acted during the southward journey. And though we may suppose that more than five caravans departed from Kano each year when the slave trade was at its height, and that a smaller proportion of slaves than that named were returned as carriers of merchandise, even then the number who arrived at the coastal factories could constitute but a fraction of the enormous numbers of slaves whom the record tells us were shipped from Gold Coast ports.[13]

Let us permit the question of provenience, as it bears on the distance in the interior from which slaves were brought, to rest at this point. The present status of our knowledge permits us only to indicate that a reinvestigation of prevailing hypotheses in the matter of slaves brought to America deriving from vast distances inland is necessary. A qualification must, however, be made explicit and emphatic, for, as in other points at which research tends to contravene the accepted "mythology," an exception taken is interpreted as an assertion made. Hence it is necessary here to state unequivocally that in positing derivation from coastal tribes for the major portion of the slaves, it is not intended to convey that no slaves came from distant points inland or even from East Africa. Some undoubtedly traveled great distances—the case cited by Rinchon is to the point—since the demand, particularly in the later days of the slave trade, must have been so great that a certain number of captives were brought from the deep interior. The point at issue is not whether any slaves were derived from far inland, but whether enough of them could have been brought from these localities to the New World to place the stamp of their tribal customs on New World behavior; whether, that is, these extensions of the trade inland are significant for the study of African survivals in the United States and elsewhere in the New World. To answer this question we shall need to anticipate ethnographic materials to be given later; but it may here be stated that survivals of the known customs of such interior peoples are practically nonexistent in the Americas even where, and especially where, the most precisely localized African traits have been carried over. This means that, as we turn again to the documents, we may evaluate our findings without misgivings about whether or not points of shipment may be taken to be significant of points of tribal origin.

*3*

Before considering fresh data, let us examine some of the statements made on slave derivations. The late U. B. Phillips, outstanding as an historian of slavery, demonstrates handicaps under which the historian labors when he is not in a position to control the ethnography and geography of Africa as well as he does his documents. To illustrate this, an incident hitherto un-recorded may be set down. In discussing the problem of African tribal dis-tribution, Phillips, a few years ago, posed the following question: "Have you, in your field work in West Africa, ever encountered a people often mentioned in the literature, the Fantynes?" So varied has been the manner of writing tribal names that the meticulous technique of this historian did not permit him to deduce that the Fantynes of the documents and the great Fanti tribe of the present-day Gold Coast were identical, and that these people, who number considerably more than a million souls, were indeed the people meant in the slavers' reports. When the answer was given, the reaction of this scholar was primarily one of pleasure at having finally arrived at the solution to a problem that, as he stated at the time, had long troubled him.

Notwithstanding this, Phillips was essentially correct in his assumption on provenience, even though he felt compelled to endorse the patterned conception of the wide range of operations in Africa itself. For if this conception caused him to write:

The coffles came from distances ranging to a thousand miles or more, on rivers and paths whose shore ends the European traders could see but did not find inviting. . . . The swarm of their ships was particularly great in the Gulf of Guinea upon whose shores the vast fan-shaped hinterland poured its exiles among converging lines . . .[14]

he also reported many names of coastal tribes in giving the evaluations of the planters on various types of slaves they distinguished, and properly described the principal area of shipment in stating that:

The markets most frequented by the English and American separate traders lay on the great middle stretches of the coast—Sierra Leone, the Grain Coast (Liberia), the Ivory, Gold and Slave Coasts, the Oil Rivers as the Niger Delta was then called, Cameroon, Gaboon and Loango.[15]

Acting on a basic principle of his research—a principle that is of the soundest—that for purposes of the study of slavery the West Indies and the United States must be considered a unit, he details the categories of slaves recognized in Jamaica and elsewhere in the area. The names of these slave types are tribal or place names, all of which are to be found on present-day maps of Africa if one knows where to look and has sufficient detailed knowledge of the geography of Africa to facilitate equating the nomenclature of the period—Senegalese, Coromatees, Whydahs, Nagoes, Pawpaws, Eboes, Mocoes, Congoes, Angolas, Gambia (Mandingoes), Calabar—with that now used. Phillips indicated the types of Negroes advertised as fugitives from the Jamaica workhouse, in the following passage:

It would appear that the Congoes, Angolas and Eboes were especially prone to run away, or perhaps particularly easy to capture when fugitive, for among the 1046 native Africans advertised as runaways in the Jamaica workhouses in 1803 there were 284 Eboes and Mocoes, 185 Congos and 259 Angolas as compared with 101 Mandingoes, 60 Chambas (from Sierra Leone), 70 Coromantees, 57 Nagoes and Pawpaws, and 30 scattering, along with a total of 488 American-born negroes and mulattoes, and 187 unclassified.[16]

Other citations which indicate better knowledge than might be thought of the locale of slaving may also be quoted. Puckett—with proper qualification in regard to the "thousand-mile" hypothesis—under the heading "Sources of American Slaves" gives the following:

Roughly speaking, the six to twelve million Negro slaves brought to America came from that part of the West Coast of Africa between the Senegal and the Congo rivers. True enough these West Coast slave markets did in turn obtain some slaves from far in the interior of the continent, but the principal markets were about the mouths of the Senegal, Gambia, Niger and Congo, and the majority of the blacks were obtained from this West Coast region.[17]

The absence in this passage of any mention of the Gold Coast, "Slave" Coast (Dahomey and Togo), or western Nigeria is noteworthy, yet despite these omissions he reasons cogently regarding the population resources of this area, and the economic advantages of operation from it, though again he accepts explanations for the density in terms which, to say the least, are open to debate:

Here was the locality closest to America, the one with the densest population (more than half the total population of Africa was located in this western equatorial zone), with the inhabitants consisting largely of the more passive inland people driven to the coast by inland tribes expanding towards the sea. This mild and pacific disposition was enhanced by the tropical climate and excessive humidity of the coast.[18]

Reuter gives the conventional statement:

The Negroes brought to America were in the main of West African descent. For the most part they were bought or captured along the West Coast and the Guinea Negroes were by far the more numerous, constituting well over fifty per cent of the total importation. But the slaves secured along the Guinea Coast were by no means all of local origin. There were representatives of many different tribal stocks from many parts of the continent. The slave trails extended far into the interior of the continent and the slave coffles came by river and forest path sometimes for a thousand and more miles to the markets on the coast.[19]

Park likewise accepts the customary point of view:

The great markets for slaves in Africa were on the West Coast, but the old slave trails ran back from the coast far into the interior of the continent, and all peoples of Central Africa contributed to the stream of enforced emigration to the New World.[20]

Weatherford and Johnson, who discuss the problem of Negro origins on the basis of at least one contemporary source,[21] take a position somewhat more in accord with the facts. The conception of the "thousand-mile" trek to the coast here appears in somewhat reduced form—700 miles:

> The slaves brought to America came almost exclusively from the west coast. The English brought captives from the Senegal and Gambia rivers, from the Gold Coast, slave coast, and even as far south as Angola. The Dutch had forts on the Gold Coast, and in 1640 captured the Portuguese forts at Angola, where they gathered many slaves. The French had Fort Louis at the mouth of the Senegal river, and other forts scattered down the west coast. Anthony Benezet, who made a careful study of the slave trade, said that the slaves were regularly shipped from all points from the Senegal to Angola, a coast of nearly 4,000 miles. The heart of the trade was the slave coast and the Gold Coast, and behind this a territory extending into the interior for 700 miles or more. From this territory Senegalese Negroes, Mandingoes, Ibos, Efikes, Ibonis, Karamantis, Wydyas, Jolofs, Fulis, together with representatives of many of the interior Bantus were brought to America.[22]

It is not possible here to reproduce the detail in which Sir Harry H. Johnston indicates tribal origins, but the very richness of his suggestions, arising out of his acquaintance with the African scene itself, reinforces the point already made of the importance of a proper background in studying provenience.[23] Of interest here is his statement that, of the language of the Sea Island Negroes off the Carolina and Georgia coast, "the few words I have seen in print appear to be of Yoruban stock or from the Niger Delta." [24]

*4*

Recent data furnished by students of slaving and slavery give the historian far better information on all aspects of the trade than has hitherto been available. This is not to say that the resources, whether archival or of the earlier published works, have been exploited to the degree possible; for example, the works of French and Belgian students of the slave traffic, particularly as regards the trade out of the port of Nantes, seem to have been entirely ignored. Of these, one can cite the volumes of Rinchon, already mentioned in another connection, or of Gaston-Martin,[25] wherein many aspects of slavery, ordinarily subject to speculation, are treated with a wealth of fresh information. The importance of Rinchon's earlier work has already been indicated; his most recent volume presents, among other matters, the most precise data that have as yet been brought to light on the proportion of slaves shipped to the New World who lost their lives in the hazards of the "middle passage." In giving abstracts of the manifests of shipping out of Nantes, this author notes a startlingly low percentage of losses, as compared with previous estimates.[26] For he shows that, between 1748 and 1782, 541 slavers bought 146,799 slaves, and disposed of 127,133. The difference, 19,666, or 13 per cent, would indicate that the losses from all causes during shipment—and it by no means follows that these were deaths—were much smaller than has been thought.[27]

This failure to go to sources is especially difficult to understand in the case of the West Indies—a region that, as has long been recognized, took its slaves from the same localities of Africa as did the United States, and that, indeed, for many slaves served as an acclimatizing ground for Negroes resold to the mainland. The most precise information as to the sources of slaves in the Virgin Islands, between 1772 and 1775, is contained in a report of the inspector general of the Moravian Missions, C. G. A. Oldendorp.[28] A man who lived before the science of ethnology was known, or such a subject as applied anthropology was dreamed of, he produced a model report which goes far in enabling the student of today to understand why Africanisms have been forced so deeply underground in the life of these islands, when their inhabitants are compared to the Negroes in other parts of the Antilles. For in this rarely cited work, we find what a man could discover when he queried "salt-water" slaves—those born in Africa—and asked them their places of birth, the names of their tribes and the peoples bordering on the areas their own groups occupied, the names of their rulers, their gods, and various words from their vocabularies. The harvest for the student of New World Negro origins who uses this book is, as might be imagined, a rich one—so rich that only mere reference can here be made to its contents. So accurate is the reporting that almost every tribal name Oldendorp gives can be found on present-day maps of Africa—an accuracy that is doubly assured when we find that he correctly distinguishes such confusing tribal designations as Mandingo (Senegal) and Mondongo (Congo basin).[29] Hartsinck and Stedman, writing of Dutch Guiana,[30] or Moreau de St. Méry and Charlevoix and Père Labat,[31] reporting on the French West Indies, or Monk Lewis and Bryan Edwards for Jamaica,[32] have likewise been far too little employed. Of the many significant works written by those active in the slave trade, Bosman and Snelgrave[33] are almost exclusively encountered. Brantz Mayer's *Captain Canot*,[34] popularized through a recent reprint, is sometimes used, but without any apparent realization that the case is an abnormal one, since Canot was a slaver who operated during the last years of the trade, when all the accentuated viciousness of an outlawed traffic would be expected to appear.

The most precise information on the African sources of slaves brought to the United States is to be found in the documents published and analyzed by Miss Elizabeth Donnan.[35] Here, in convenient compass, has been assembled information of special significance to the students of the trade as it affected the United States; a sampling so extensive that it is doubtful whether data from other collections, English or otherwise—these volumes deal exclusively with British slaving operations—can do more than fill in details of the picture she outlines. Especially important are the abstracts of manifests of slaving vessels landing cargoes in ports of continental United States. Since only raw materials are given, it is necessary for one who uses this work to compute totals and analyze the data statistically, but once this is done, a remarkably clear idea is had of the degree to which the various parts of Africa were drawn upon for human materials. Such an analysis discloses that those portions of West Africa named in this chapter as the regions where the forerunners of survivals are to be sought are mentioned in greatest prominence.

These documents indicate the large difference in immediate sources of slaves brought to the northern colonies in the earlier days of the trade, on the one hand, and of those imported into the southern states. Phillips has remarked that the majority of the Negroes brought to the north were imported from the West Indies:

In the Northern colonies at large the slaves imported were more generally drawn from the West Indies than directly from Africa. The reasons were several. Small parcels, better suited to the retail demand, might be brought more profitably from the sugar islands whither New England, New York and Pennsylvania ships were frequently plying than from Guinea whence special voyages must be made. Familiarity with the English language and the rudiments of civilization at the outset were more essential to petty masters than to the owners of plantation gangs who had means of breaking in fresh Africans by deputy. But most important of all, a sojourn in the West Indies would lessen the shock of acclimatization, severe enough under the best circumstances. The number of negroes who died from it was probably not small, and of those who survived some were incapacitated and bedridden with each recurrence of winter.[36]

This statement is entirely borne out by Miss Donnan's figures, for of the 4,551 slaves received in New York and New Jersey ports between 1715 and 1765, only 930 were native Africans.[37] The small numbers of slaves in each cargo—the "retail" aspect of the trade to the North—is likewise shown in the few credited to each ship, more than ten per vessel being the exception, and the large majority of manifests listing but two or three. This "retail" nature of slaving operations to the North, furthermore, is a factor of some consequence in assessing differential rates of acculturation to European patterns as between northern and southern Negroes, since the opportunities for learning European ways were far greater for these northern Negroes than for slaves sent to the plantations of the South, or for those in the West Indies who lived even more remote from white contact.

From the point of view of the African provenience of northern Negroes, the manifests tell us little even where a shipment came direct, since the entry, "coast of Affrica," is the one most frequently set down; something which, indeed, contrasts interestingly with the specific names of the West Indian ports where the slaves were procured. What is important in the documents from the northern states are the letters of the slavers, who in reports to their owners mention the ports and the tribes which have been indicated as the source of New World slaves. Thus Captain Peleg Clarke, writing from "Cape Coast Roade" in the Gold Coast to John Fletcher under date of 6 July, 1776, says:

D'r Sir, In my former letters Pr Capt'ns Bold, Smith and others, I fully informed you in what manner I had disposed of my Cargo, and time agree'd on for payment was the middle of Augt. And Expected to be at Barbadoes in Novr and I Should purchase About 275 Slaves. I now add that Trade has been entirely Stop'd for this 6 Weeks pass'd, Owing to the Chief of the people a going back against the Asshantees to Warr, and are not yet returned, but there is no likelyhoods of comeing to battle as the Asshantees is returned back to their Country again, and it is not likely their will be any great matter of trade for this some time again, (as the Chiefest of our trade comes through the Asshantees).[38]

There is full documentation to prove the unity of sources for the New World Negroes in these accounts, particularly in instructions to the captains of slaving vessels as to ports of call to dispose of their cargoes, and in the reports of these men telling of the ports at which they were to call or actually had called. Thus Samuel Waldo, of Boston, on March 12, 1734, handed these instructions to Captain Samuel Rhodes, in command of Waldo's sloop Affrica:

You will be a Judge of what may be most for my Intrist, so I shall entirely confide that You'll act accordingly in the Purchase of Negros, Gold Dust or any other the produce of that Country with which You'll as soon as possible make your Return to me either by way of the West Indies or Virginia where You'll sell Your Slaves either for Gold Silver or good Bills of Exch'e. . . . If Your coming from off the Coast with Slaves will bring it towards Winter or late in the Fall before You can reach Virginia it will be best to go for the West Indies where by trying more or less the Islands You may probably do better than by selling att Virginia, . . .[39]

The abstracts of ships' manifests which account for slaves imported into the southern colonies give much exact information about the African regions where their cargoes were procured. As is to be anticipated from the comparison of direct trading between Africa and northern and southern ports, the proportion of slaves reimported from the West Indies drops sharply. A tabulation of the raw data found in the manifests recorded from Virginia between the years 1710 and 1769 gives the following results: [40]

| | |
|---|---:|
| Source of origin given as "Africa" | 20,564 |
| Gambia (including Senegal and Goree) | 3,652 |
| "Guinea" (from sources indicated as Gold Coast, Cabocorso Castle, Bande, Bance Island, and Windward Coast) | 6,777 |
| Calabar (Old Calabar, New Calabar and Bonny) | 9,224 |
| Angola | 3,860 |
| Madagascar | 1,011 |
| Slaves brought directly from Africa | 45,088 |
| Slaves imported from the West Indies | 7,046 |
| Slaves from other North American ports | 370 |
| | 52,504 |

It is to be observed that in addition to ships indicated as arriving from "Africa"—which gives no clue at all as to provenience except in so far as we wish to compare direct importation from that continent with the West Indian trade—the regions that figure most prominently are "Guinea," which means the west coast of Africa from the Ivory Coast to western Nigeria, Calabar, which represents the Niger Delta region, Angola, or the area about the lower Congo, and the Gambia.

The shipments from Madagascar are of some interest, if only because they indicate what small proportion of the slaves were drawn from ports other than those lying in the regions given as the principal centers of slaving operations. These 1,011 slaves out of 52,504 brought to Virginia—and, as will be seen shortly, the 473 listed as coming from Mozambique and East Africa out of 67,769 imported into South Carolina—merely underscore the points made as to provenience and indicate how relatively slight the exceptions were. More importantly, such figures show how little basis exists for the widespread idea that New World Negroes represent a sampling of the population of the entire African continent. Various other documents make this point—one of the most striking is the following decision handed down by the general court of Maryland:

Negro Mary v. The Vestry of William and Mary's Parish.
Oct. 1, 1796        3 Har. & M'Hen. 501

Petition for freedom. It was admitted the petitioner was descended from negro Mary, imported many years ago into this country from Madagascar, and the question was, whether she was entitled to her freedom.

It was contended that Madagascar was not a place from which slaves were brought, and that the act of 1715 related only to slaves brought in the usual course of the trade. On the other side, it was contended, that the petty provinces of Madagascar make war upon each other for slaves and plunder; and they carry on the slave trade with Europeans.

*Per. Cur.* Madagascar being a country where the slave trade is practiced, and this being a country where it is tolerated, it is incumbent on the petition to show her ancestor was free in her own country to entitle her to freedom.[41]

In view of all available figures, it is understandable how Negro Mary came to base her hope of freedom on the fact that she, of Malagasy descent, was to be exempted from bondage because her enslaved ancestress had been taken from a country outside "the usual course of the trade."

The slaves imported into South Carolina between 1733 and 1785 as listed by Miss Donnan, when tabulated, show them to have been derived from the following African sources: [42]

| | |
|---|---|
| Origin given as "Africa" | 4,146 |
| From the Gambia to Sierra Leone | 12,441 |
| Sierra Leone | 3,906 |
| Liberia and the Ivory Coast (Rice and Grain Coasts) | 3,851 |
| "Guinea Coast" (Gold Coast to Calabar) | 18,240 |
| Angola | 11,485 |
| Congo | 10,924 |
| Mozambique | 243 |
| East Africa | 230 |
| Imported from Africa | 65,466 |
| Imported from the West Indies | 2,303 |
| | 67,769 |

It would be of interest further to document the origins of the various groups of New World Negroes with comparable figures from the West Indies and South America, but far less data for these regions have been made available than for the United States. Such as do exist, however, support the assumption of essential unity stated in these pages. Rinchon's materials for the French West Indies name sources of origin of cargoes only in terms of "Senegal," "Guinea," "Angola," and "Mozambique," though figures even in such categories do offer supporting data in showing that only 17 out of the 1,313 cargoes listed for the years 1713 to 1792 came from East Africa. One interesting point is the small number of Senegalese shipments; which means that as far as the West Indian receivers in Haiti, Martinique, Cayenne, Trinidad, Cuba, Puerto Rico, and Suriname were concerned, the vast majority of the slaves they bought, from ships owned and operated out of the French port of Nantes, were from the region lying between the Gold Coast and Angola.[43] Mr. J. G. Cruickshank, archivist of British Guiana, has studied the materials to be found in the files of the *Essequibo and Demerary Gazette* for the years 1803–1807.[44] These materials consist mainly of advertisements of "new" Negroes, designated as to African type. When classified according to the regions given in the tables of figures calculated from Miss Donnan's work, they indicate the same points of origin: [45]

| | |
|---|---:|
| Windward Coast | 3,014 |
| Gold Coast | 3,593 |
| Evo (Calabar) | 820 |
| Angola | 1,051 |
| Others | 1,029 |

In 1789, Stephen Fuller, agent for Jamaica in London, published (by order of the House of Assembly of that colony) two reports for the Committee of the House which had been appointed to examine into the slave trade and the treatment of Negroes. Bryan Edwards, known for his *History of the British West Indies,* who gathered the materials, reproduced the accounts of five brokerage firms, giving records of the Negroes imported from Africa and sold by them. Four of these gave the sources of origin of their slaves in such fashion as to make tabulation possible. Combined in the following table, the four lists represent shipments for the years 1764–1774 for the first firm, 1782–1788 for the second, 1779–1788 for the third, and 1786–1788 for the last; the data themselves, when tabulated, support the position taken here: [46]

| | | |
|---|---:|---:|
| Gambia | | 673 |
| Windward Coast | | 2,669 |
| Gold Coast | | 14,312 |
|     Anamaboe | 8,488 | |
|     "Gold Coast" | 5,834 | |
| Togo and Dahomey | | 3,912 |
|     Pawpaw | 131 | |
|     Whydah | 3,781 | |
| Niger Delta | | 10,305 |
|     Benin | 1,039 | |
|     Bonny | 3,052 | |
|     Calabar and Old Calabar | 6,214 | |
| Gaboon | | 155 |
| Angola | | 1,984 |
| Total | | 34,010 |

With the principal areas of slaving established, and direct comparability in terms of the cultural background common to Negroes in all the New World proved by the documentary evidence, the final step in discovering the most significant tribal origins is greatly simplified. For we need merely turn to those works, written by men and women who surveyed the scene of slavery while it was at its height in the West Indies, and utilize the many tribal names contained therein—names which, when located in Africa, are found to lie within the regions indicated as those where the most intense slaving was carried on. The Ashanti and Fanti of the Gold Coast, the former most frequently termed Coromantees after a place name of their homeland, are mentioned most often by those who wrote of the British possessions, continental as well as insular. The Dahomean and allied peoples, at times called Whydahs, after the major seacoast town of Dahomey, or Pawpaws, from Popo, a town not far to the west, are especially prominent in the French writings. The French planters had little liking for the Gold Coast slaves, and these scarcely figure in Moreau de St. Mèry's listing of tribes represented in Haiti; in similar manner, the Dahomeans, who were the favorite slaves of the French, were not fancied by the English, as is to be seen when we contrast the 14,312 Gold Coast Negroes in our list of Jamaica imports with the 3,912 from Dahomey.

Another type of slave frequently mentioned is the Nago. This term is used for the Yoruba of western Nigeria, whose language is called by that name. Historical records for those parts of Latin America where present-day Negro customs have been studied, Cuba and Brazil, are not available. In the case of the latter, they were burned to wipe out every trace of slavery when the Negroes were emancipated in that country; and if they exist for Cuba, they have not been published. But such data as we have establish that the Nago slaves were favorites of the Spanish and Portuguese planters; from which it follows that it is logical to find Yoruban customs preponderant in the African survivals reported from these countries. For the rest of the slaving area, evidences of Africanisms are fragmentary. The Mandingo, Senegalese, and Hausa of the subdesert area to the north have left traces of their presence, principally in Brazil. The vast masses of Congo slaves that we know were imported have made their influence felt disproportionately little, though a few tribal names, a few tribal deities, some linguistic survivals, and more often the word "Congo" itself are encountered.

The mechanism that determined survival of customs and nomenclature of some African tribes in the New World, and not others, may probably be connected with the geographical spread of the slave trade itself. In the earliest days, before the trade became a major industry, Senegal was most important. Yet though in the aggregate many slaves were brought from this region, not enough from any one group came at this earlier period to make possible the establishment of their common customs in the new home. As the demand for slaves surpassed the human resources of this less densely populated region, the traders came more and more to seek their goods along the Guinea coast, and here most of the slaving was carried on during the last half of the eighteenth century. With the nineteenth century, the weight of the abolitionist movement began to make itself felt, and when the trade was outlawed, the captains of slave vessels had to cruise more widely than before. They found the Congo ports, under Portuguese control, most hospitable; and this is reflected in Miss Donnan's work, which on analysis makes it apparent that slaves were shipped from the Congo in increasing numbers toward the latter days of the traffic.[47]

The fact that the slave captains ranged more widely as time passed, perhaps because the difficulties of supplying their needs on the Guinea coast increased as the demands for slaves became greater, is likewise shown if a recapitulation be made of the ships sailing from Nantes, in terms of the African ports where they obtained their cargoes: [48]

| Year | Region of Origin of Cargo | | | |
| --- | --- | --- | --- | --- |
| | Senegal | Guinea | Angola | Mozambique |
| 1748 | — | 6 | 4 | — |
| 1749 | — | 24 | 9 | — |
| 1750 | 1 | 14 | 7 | — |
| 1751 | 1 | 11 | 5 | — |
| 1752 | 2 | 20 | 8 | — |
| 1753 | 3 | 17 | 8 | — |
| 1754 | 1 | 13 | 7 | — |
| 1755 | 1 | 5 | 5 | — |
| | * | * | * | |
| 1763 | — | 24 | 9 | — |
| 1764 | 2 | 20 | 8 | — |
| 1765 | — | 18 | 12 | — |
| 1766 | 3 | 11 | 11 | — |
| 1767 | — | 15 | 6 | — |
| 1768 | 1 | 13 | 4 | — |
| 1769 | — | 18 | 6 | — |
| 1770 | 2 | 10 | 8 | — |
| 1771 | 1 | 13 | 9 | — |
| 1772 | 2 | 8 | 6 | — |
| 1773 | 1 | 13 | 10 | — |

*Region of Origin of Cargo*

| Year | Senegal | Guinea | Angola | Mozambique |
|------|---------|--------|--------|------------|
| 1774 ......... | 2 | 6 | *10* | — |
| 1775 ......... | — | *11* | 6 | — |
| 1776 ......... | 1 | *12* | 5 | — |
| 1777 ......... | — | *11* | 2 | — |
| | * | * | * | |
| 1783 ......... | 8 | 11 | *18* | — |
| 1784 ......... | 3 | 8 | *9* | — |
| 1785 ......... | 11 | 11 | *14* | 2 |
| 1786 ......... | 6 | *19* | 15 | 3 |
| 1787 ......... | — | 15 | *17* | 1 |
| 1788 ......... | — | 16 | 16 | 2 |
| 1789 ......... | — | 19 | 22 | — |
| 1790 ......... | — | 18 | 22 | 2 |
| 1791 ......... | 1 | 9 | 27 | 2 |
| 1792 ......... | 2 | 8 | *18* | 3 |

Not until 1783, except for one year, does the Congo traffic exceed that from the Guinea coast; but after this time the French traders also, because of economic and political reasons that need not be gone into here, turned increasingly southward. And while not a single Mozambique cargo appears until 1785, after that year the demand seems to have been great enough to cause a few ships to be sent there annually. It must be observed, however, that the number is too slight to influence appreciably the demography of the New World Negro population.

Let us consider another facet of the problem. It is not difficult to see that the slaves who came late to the New World had to accommodate themselves to patterns of Negro behavior established earlier on the basis of the customs of the tribes represented during the middle period of slaving. In Haiti, Congo slaves are said to have been more complacent than those from other parts of Africa, and were held in contempt by those Negroes who refused to accept the slave status with equanimity. Tradition has it that when the blacks rose in revolt, these Congo slaves were killed in large numbers, since it was felt they could not be trusted. Mr. Cruickshank has advanced a cogent suggestion:

... from what I have learned from old Negroes ... it would appear that the three or four African Nations who were brought here in predominant numbers imposed their language, beliefs, etc., gradually on the others. In course of time there were not enough of the minority tribes on an estate to take part in customs, dances and the like, or even to carry on the language. There was nobody left to talk to! Children growing up heard another African language far oftener than their own; they were even laughed at when they said some of their mother's words—when they "cut country," as it was said—and so the language of the minority tribes, and much else—though probably never all—died out.[49]

Though African survivals in the United States are far fewer than in British Guiana, nonetheless, a similar process may well have operated. It might also be hazarded that, in the instance of early Senegalese arrivals, whatever was retained of aboriginal custom was overshadowed by the traditions of the more numerous Guinea coast Negroes; while as for late-comers such as the Congo Negroes, the slaves they found were numerous enough, and well enough established, to have translated their modes of behavior—always in so far as Africanisms are concerned, and without reference to the degree of acculturation to European habits—into community patterns.

The indisputable survivals in those parts of the New World where a considerable degree of African culture is found today in pure form are to be traced to a relatively restricted region of the area where slaving was carried on; this simplifies the problems we must face in drawing up our base line for the study of deviation from African tradition. The cultures of the tribes of the area must first be described as an aid to direct comprehension of the New World data, and this description must be compared with published accounts of the Negro's cultural heritage. We must then determine whether more generalized aspects of West African culture are to be discovered. For if such aspects are held in common both by the dominant tribes and by all the other folk of the entire area from which slaves were brought, we will be afforded further insight into those more subtle survivals which, because they represent the deepest seated aspects of African tradition, have persisted even where overt forms of African behavior and African custom have completely disappeared.

## NOTES

[1] *The History, Civil and Commercial of the British Colonies in the West Indies . . .* London, 1801 (3rd ed.), Vol. II, pp. 126 f.

[2] *Travels in the Interior Districts of Africa Performed Under the Direction and Patronage of the African Association in the Years 1795, 1796, and 1797*, London, 1799 (2nd ed.).

[3] Cf. M. J. and F. S. Herskovits, "A Footnote to the History of Negro Slaving," *Opportunity*, 11:178 f., 1933.

[4] M. L. E. Moreau de St. Méry, *Description . . . de la partie française de l'Isle Saint-Domingue*, Philadelphia, 1797–98, Vol. I, pp. 237 f.

[5] Personal communication.

[6] David D. Wallace, *The Life of Henry Laurens...*, New York, 1915, pp. 76 f.

[7] Phillips, *American Negro Slavery*, p. 43. Just how Phillips reached his conclusion regarding the pygmoid character of these Negroes cannot be said, but his comment bespeaks slight knowledge of the geography and ethnic types of the region.

[8] Cf. Ramos, *O Folk-Lore Negro do Brasil, passim.*

[9] Personal communication.

[10] *La Traite et l'Esclavage des Congolais par les Européens,* Wettern, Belgium, 1929, pp. 88 f. The reference to Grandpré, a slave trader whose experience covered more than thirty years along the African coast is contained in a volume by this dealer entitled, *Voyage à la Côte Occidentale d'Afrique fait dans les années 1786 et 1787,* Paris, 1801, Vol. I, pp. 223 f. For further discussion of the sources of Congo slaves by Rinchon see his *Le Trafic Négrier, d'après les livres de commerce du capitaine gantois Pierre-Ignace-Lévin Van Alstein,* Brussels, 1938, pp. 89 ff.

[11] J. Maes and O. Boon, "Les Peuplades du Congo Belge, Nom et Situation Géographique," *Monographies Idéologiques,* Publications de Bureau de Documentation Ethnographique, Musée du Congo Belge, Tervueren, Belgium, 1935, Vol. I, sér. 2.

[12] M. J. Herskovits, "The Significance of West Africa for Negro Research," *Journal of Negro History,* 21:15–30, 1936.

[13] *Ibid.,* pp. 21–22.

[14] *American Negro Slavery,* p. 31.

[15] *Ibid.,* pp. 30 f.

[16] *Ibid.,* p. 44; the data were gathered from the file of the *Royal Gazette* of Kingston, Jamaica, for 1803.

[17] *Folk Beliefs of the Southern Negro,* p. 3. The number of slaves imported is derived from the *Negro Year Book* for 1918–1919, p. 151. As so often in discussing Africa, Puckett took his statement of locale from Tillinghast, *The Negro from Africa to America,* in this case pp. 7 ff.

[18] *Ibid.,* pp. 3 f. The extraordinary statement concerning the docile coastal tribes— the warlike Ashanti and Dahomeans, for example!—is taken from Tillinghast's excogitations, to be found on page 10 of his work.

[19] *The American Race Problem,* p. 133.

[20] "The Conflict and Fusion of Cultures...," *Journal of Negro History,* p. 117.

[21] Anthony Benezet, *Some Historical Account of Guinea,* Philadelphia, 1771.

[22] *Race Relations,* p. 124. Where these authors obtained the spellings of tribal names they use cannot be said, but the errors are striking—Wydyas for Whydahs, Fulis for Fulas, etc.

[23] *The Negro in the New World,* pp. 82, 133, 275 f., 314.

[24] *Ibid.,* p. 470.

[25] *Nantes au XVIIIᵉ siècle; l'ère des Négriers (1714–1774), d'après des documents inédits,* Paris, 1931.

[26] E.g., Du Bois, *Black Folk, Then and Now,* p. 143.

[27] *Le Trafic Négrier...,* pp. 304 f., based on preceding tables.

[28] *Geschichte des Missionen der evangelischen Brüder auf den Inseln S. Thomas, S. Croix und S. Jan,* Barby, 1777, pp. 270 ff.

[29] Some of the relevant passages from Oldendorp are to be found in M. J. Herskovits, "On the Provenience of New World Negroes," *Social Forces,* 12:250 f., 1933.

[30] J. J. Hartsinck, *Beschryving van Guiana, of de Wilde Kust in Suid-America...*

Amsterdam, 1770; Capt. J. G. Stedman, *Narrative of a five years' expedition against the Revolted Negroes of Suriname,* London, 1776.

31 Moreau de St. Méry, *op. cit.;* F. X. Charlevoix, *Historie de l'Isle Espagnole ou de S. Domingue,* Paris, 1730–1731; Père J. B. Labat, *Nouveau Voyage aux Isles d'Amérique,* The Hague, 1724.

32 Lewis, *Journal of a West India Proprietor,* London, 1834; Edwards, *op. cit.*

33 Wm. Bosman, *A New and Accurate Description of the Coast of Guinea* ... (English trans.), London, 1721 (2nd ed.); Capt. Wm. Snelgrave, *A New Account of Some Parts of Guinea, and the Slave-Trade* ... , London, 1734.

34 *Captain Canot; or Twenty Years of an African Slaver,* New York, 1854.

35 "The Slave Trade in South Carolina Before the Revolution," *American Historical Review,* 33:809–828, 1928; *Documents Illustrative of the Slave Trade to America, Carnegie Institution Publication* No. 409, Vols. I–IV, 1930–1935.

36 *American Negro Slavery,* p. 113.

37 *Documents Illustrative of the Slave Trade to America,* Vol. III, pp. 462 ff.

38 *Ibid.,* p. 318.

39 *Ibid.,* pp. 43, 45.

40 M. J. Herskovits, "The Significance of West Africa for Negro Research," *loc. cit.;* computations from Donnan, *op. cit.,* Vol. IV, pp. 175 ff., *passim.*

41 J. D. Wheeler, *A Practical Treatise on the Law of Slavery* ... , New York, 1837; see also Jeffrey R. Brackett, *The Negro in Maryland* ... , Baltimore, 1889.

42 *Op. cit.,* Vol. IV, pp. 278 ff., *passim.* The points of origin in this table are equated as closely as possible with those in the preceding one; most notable is the fact that only 1,168 slaves were brought in ships sailing from "Benin," "Bonny," "New Calabar," and "Old Calabar."

43 *Le Trafic Négrier* ... , pp. 247 ff.

44 Personal communication.

45 These figures are to be found in M. J. Herskovits, "The Significance of West Africa for Negro Research," *loc. cit.,* p. 27.

46 Stephen Fuller, *Two Reports* ... *on the Slave-Trade,* London, 1798, pp. 20 ff.

47 Cf. also L. E. Bouet-Willaumez, *Commerce et Traite des Noirs aux Côtes Occidentales d'Afrique,* Paris, 1848; particularly Part II and maps.

48 Rinchon, *Le Trafic Négrier* ... , pp. 274 ff.; the author's sources are indicated on pp. 243 ff. of his book.

49 Herskovits, "The Significance of West Africa for Negro Research," *loc. cit.,* pp. 27 f.

*"St. Simons Island" is a section of a study undertaken
in 1940 by the Georgia Writers' Project, which was
a continuation of the federally financed writers' programs
sponsored by the W.P.A. during the recovery from the
Depression. It constitutes a specific example of the
research into African survivals in the New World which
Herskovits popularized in* The Myth of the Negro Past.
*It deals with the memories of Africa which were extant in
1940 among the inhabitants of a Georgia Sea Island.*

# St. Simons Island

## Georgia Writers' Project

St. Simons, one of the larger coastal islands, lies off the Georgia coast
not far from Brunswick on the mainland. For about fifteen years it has been
connected by causeway and bridge to the Coastal Highway. St. Simons has
always had a considerable Negro population, owing to the fact that from
early times many large plantations as well as smaller settlements flourished
on the island. This has given the Negroes considerable contact with white
people and of late years with the rather sophisticated type of tourist. Fearing
that the old customs would have been forgotten, we had little hope of good
field work here.

However, we had not worked half a day in the north end settlements of
the island before we were happily surprised. Around Harrington and Frederica there still live many old Negroes who remember the customs and
beliefs told them by their parents and grandparents. Most of them are
intelligent, reticent, and proud. Not easy of approach but with good manners, they responded to the request to help record the traditional beliefs
of their forefathers. Once they had realized the object of our conversation,
they talked freely and graciously, and several were outstanding for their
keen comprehension.

We went to see Catherine Wing,[1] who lives at the corner of the Harrington Road and the main Frederica Highway. Her comfortable frame house
was set in the midst of a flower garden and her washtubs were conveniently
placed under a grape arbor and spreading live oaks. On the side road stood

From Georgia Writers' Project, Works Projects Administration, *Drums and Shadows:
Survival Studies among Georgia Coastal Negroes* (Athens: University of Georgia
Press, 1940), pp. 173–185.

three stately pine trees from which hung silvery festoons of Spanish moss. Catherine was black, small, and lively at sixty-nine.

"Ise bawn in Meridian," she said, "but Ise lib mos muh life heah. Muh people belong tuh duh Atwoods uh Darien an tings heah on duh ilun is pretty much duh way dey wuz deah. Some tings is changed wut hadduh change, lak wen we hab a fewnul duh unduhtakuh come an git duh body an dey dohn lak yuh tuh hab no settin-up. In duh ole days we would sing an make prayuh all night an dey would come an measure duh body wid a string tuh make duh coffin tuh bury em in. Dey use tuh allus sen yuh home tuh bury [2] ef dey could git duh money but dey ain eben alluz do dat no mo. Dey nebuh use tuh bury no strainjuhs in duh buryin [3] groun but heah dat ain kep strick needuh."

We asked about the dances and festivals of her youth.

"We use tuh hab big times duh fus hahves,[4] an duh fus ting wut growed we take tuh duh chuch so as ebrybody could hab a piece ub it. We pray obuh it an shout. Wen we hab a dance, we use tuh shout in a ring. We ain hab wut yuh call a propuh dance tuhday.

"One uh duh dances wuz call duh Buzzud Lope.[5] It's a long time sence we done it, but I still membuh it. We ain hab much music in doze days but dey use a drum tuh call duh people tuhgedduh wen dey gonuh hab games aw meetin.[6] It sho bin a long time sence I tought bout dem days."

Catherine told us that Ryna Johnson, who lived about a mile down the Harrington Road, was one of the oldest people on the island. Leaving the main highway, we followed the narrow, less traversed side road. It was a heavily wooded section. We viewed the massive-trunked hoary oak trees through a misty curtain of hanging moss. The fences along the road were covered with honeysuckle and wild grape. Shortly before we arrived at our destination, the road divided to give way to a growth of towering oaks; then it joined again, resuming its winding trail through the quiet, shadowed countryside.

The little settlement now known as Harrington was formerly the property of the Demere family. A little less than a mile north of this settlement was Harrington Hall, home of Raymond Demere, who came to this country with Oglethorpe after serving ten years under Lord Harrington at Gibraltar.

To the left of the road was a small unpainted store operated by Ryna Johnson's daughter with whom she lived. Various advertisements on the front of the small building gave splashes of color to the green of trees and foliage.

Set back from the store was Ryna's house, surrounded by an expanse of short grass upon which a horse was grazing. The house was weathered with age, as were the vertical boards of the fence that enclosed the garden; here and there in the fence a new unpainted board, regardless of length, had replaced an old, and the top presented an irregular, jagged pattern. The cabin was the usual two-room affair but with a hall through the center and a lean-to in the back. The walls were papered with newspapers and, although there was a motley collection of objects and furniture, everything .was scrupulously clean.

Ryna [7] was blind from cataracts and had not been feeling very well; so she had just got up from bed. Although her body was bent and very feeble, her mind was still clear.

"Ise bout eighty-five yeahs ole, but I caahn tell zackly. I belong tuh duh Coupers wen I wuk on duh plantation. It bin sech a long time I mos stop studyin bout dem days. But I membuh we use tuh hab good times."

In answer to our inquiry regarding any Africans whom she had known during plantation days, Ryna told us, "Alexanduh, Jummy, an William, dey is all African. I membuh ole William well an he tell me lots bout times in Africa. Dey ain weah no cloze, he say, but a leedle clawt string roun em.

"William say dat dey ain hab much trouble gittin tings tuh eat in Africa cuz so much grow free. Dey cut duh tree an let duh suhrup drain out. Duh women tie duh leedle chillun an duh babies on tuh deah back tuh carry em roun.

"He say wen dey come in duh boats tuh ketch em, dey trail a red flag an dey ain use tuh see red an das duh way dey gut duh load. William he talk funny talk. He hab funny wud fuh tings. I use tuh know some ub em, cuz he teach em tuh me but it so long, missus, Ise fuhgit. But I membuh he say pot call 'sojo' and watuh 'deloe' and he call fyuh 'diffy.' He sho did dat, but das all I kin membuh. Ef uh study bout em, maybe I kin membuh some mo."

We wanted a description of William, the African.

"William a good size man, heaby set. He hab two leedle line mahk on he right cheek." [8]

Ryna mused: "Tings is sho change. Wen we is young, we use tuh hab big frolic an dance in a ring an shout tuh drum. Sometime we hab rattle made out uh dry goad and we rattle em an make good music." [9,10]

We wondered if she, too, remembered the Buzzard Lope and she assured us, "Yes'm, sho I knows it. Ebrybody knows it." [5]

Shortly afterward the conversation turned to conjure and the old woman told us, "I sho heah plenty bout da ting. Way back we hab plenty discussion bout root makuhs.[11,12] I membuh my huzbun Hillard Johnson speak bout a root makuh in Darien wut make duh pot bile widout fyah. My huzbun he frum Sapelo. He could tell yuh bout sech tings ef he wuz libin."

A short distance away lived Charles Hunter,[13] whose small board house was set well back from the road. The front yard enclosed by a wire fence was planted with a profusion of brightly colored flowers along the sandy walk leading to the house. Across the road to the left was a field which had been planted in corn.

Charles, a medium-sized, intelligent man, very black of skin and rather small-featured, talked to us about his people.

"Dey is long libin people," he began. "Muh fathuh lib until he a hundud an muh mothuh wuz ninety wen she die. Muh gran, she name Louise an come frum Bahama Ilun.[14] She lib tuh hundud an fifteen. Das duh way dey do an I guess I'll do duh same."

Did the people around Harrington believe in the old customs the way his mother and grandmother had believed in them?

"Yes'm, dey sticks tuh em but duh times is changin an yuh hab tuh change wid em. Duh unduhtakuh come now an mone lakly he bring yuh back tuh duh chuch an dey ain no watch an singin."

In the course of our talk he told us that the river baptisms were held by members of the local churches. "Yes'm, we still baptize in duh ribbuh," Charles said. "We hab one not long ago. We hab tuh wait till a Sunday wen a ebb tide come at a good time, cuz it duh ebb tide wut carry yuh sin away." [15]

Charles confirmed what the other residents had told us regarding conjure.

"Well, dey's some belieb in cunjuh and some wut dohn. Dey's lots wut say sickness ain natchul an somebody put sumpm down fuh yuh.[16] I ain belieb in it much muhsef but dey's curious tings happen. Now, wen I wuz a boy deah's a root makuh wut lib yuh name Alexanduh. He was African an he say he kin do any kine uh cunjuh wut kin be done and he kin cuo any kine uh disease.[12] He wuz a small man, slim an bery black. Alexanduh say he could fly.[17,18] He say all his fambly in Africa could fly. I ain seen em fly muhsef but he say he could do it all right. We's sked ub im wen we's boys an use tuh run wen we see im come."

During the interview Emma, Charles' wife, hovered nearby, seemingly very much interested in the proceedings. Finally we asked her to come and talk to us. Although she said that she was too young to remember much of the old times, she gave us some recollections regarding superstitions and African customs.

"Now muh gran Betty she wuz African an she plant benne seed. Once yuh staht plantin benne, yuh got tuh plant em ebry yeah aw yuh die. I tell yuh who kin tell yuh sumpm bout ole times an das Chahls Murray. He ain tell me how ole he is but I ketch he age jis duh same. Yuh go down tuh duh main road a lill way an duh road spring off tuh Chahls Murray house."

Emma also told us how to reach Ben Sullivan, one of the oldest men living on the island.

From Hunter's we turned left on a lane flanked by a thicket of low trees and bushes. After about two or three miles we came to a clearing where there was a scattering of houses and sheds.

A tall, spare man was plowing in a field to the left of the road. We hailed him and asked him if he could help us find Ben Sullivan. He left his mule and plow and came over to the car. He was tall, as straight as a soldier, with a lean agility that bespoke youthfulness. Over his long jaws and rather straight features his copper skin was smooth.

"Ise Ben Sullivan," [19] he said, and we were puzzled.

"But," we said, "the Ben Sullivan we are looking for is an old man."

"Ise duh only Ben Sullivan," he answered. "Ise eighty eight."

It seemed incredible that this active, intensely alive man could really be so old. We asked him who his people were and what he remembered about the old times.

"We belong tuh duh Coupers. Ise son tuh Belali. He wuz butluh tuh James Couper at Altama. I membuh we hab lots uh time tuh play wen we's chilluns." He smiled pleasantly at the memory.

This man, too, remembered native Africans he had known, for he told us, "I membuh lots uh Africans, but all ub em ain tame. But I knowd some ub em wut is tame an I knowd one tame Indian."

We asked again about old Alexander, the African root maker.

"Yes'm, I membuh him. He wuz a lill black man an he belong tuh duh Butlers but I ain know him well cuz we's diffunt people. Now ole man Okra an ole man Gibson an ole Israel, dey's African an dey belong tuh James Couper an das how I knows em. Dey tell us how dey lib in Africa. Dey laks tuh talk. It funny talk an it ain so easy tuh unnuhstan but yuh gits use tuh it. Dey say dey buil deah own camp deah an lib in it.

"Ole man Okra he say he wahn a place lak he hab in Africa so he buil im a hut. I membuh it well. It wuz bout twelve by foeteen feet an it hab dut flo and he buil duh side lak basket weave wid clay plastuh on it. It hab a flat roof wut he make frum bush an palmettuh an it hab one doe and no winduhs. But Massuh make im pull it down. He say he ain wahn no African hut on he place.

"Ole Israel he pray a lot wid a book he hab wut he hide, an he take a lill mat an he say he prayuhs on it. He pray wen duh sun go up and wen duh sun go down. Dey ain none but ole Israel wut pray on a mat. He hab he own mat. Now ole man Israel he hab shahp feechuh an a long pointed beahd, an he wuz bery tall. He alluz tie he head up in a wite clawt an seem he keep a lot uh clawt on han, fuh I membuh, yuh could see em hangin roun duh stable dryin."

Asked if he remembered any other Africans who tied their heads up, the old man told us, "I membuh a ole uhmun name Daphne. He didn tie he head up lak ole man Israel. He weah loose wite veil on he head. He wuz shahp-feechuh too an light uh complexion. He weah one ring in he eah fuh he eyes.[20] I hab refrence to it bein some kine uh pruhtection tuh he eyes. Wen he pray, he bow two aw tree times in duh middle uh duh prayuh."

We asked about the music they used to have and what they used for dancing in the old days.

"We ain dance den duh way dey dances now. We dance roun in a succle an den we dances fuh prayin.[21] I membuhs we use tuh hab drums fuh music and we beat duh drum fuh dances.[9]

"Now, ole man Dembo he use tuh beat duh drum tuh duh fewnul,[22] but Mr. Couper he stop dat. He say he dohn wahn drums beatin roun duh dead. But I watch em hab a fewnul. I gits behine duh bush an hide an watch an see wut dey does. Dey go in a long pruhcession tuh duh buryin groun an dey beat duh drums long duh way an dey submit duh body tuh duh groun. Den dey dance roun in a ring an dey motion wid duh hans.[23] Dey sing duh body tuh duh grabe an den dey let it down an den dey succle roun in duh dance.

"Dey ain hab no chuch in doze days an wen dey wannuh pray, dey git behine duh house aw hide someweah an make a great prayuh. Dey ain suppose tuh call on duh Lawd; dey hadduh call on duh massuh an ef dey ain do dat, dey git nine an tutty.

"Dey ain marry den duh way dey do now. Attuh slabery dey hadduh remarry. Dey hab big baptizin in duh ribbuh lak dey do tuhday and dey dip em on duh ebb tuh wash duh sins away an duh preachuh he make a great prayuh tuh duh ribbuh.[15]

"Ole man Okra he a great un fuh buil drum.[10] He take a calf skin an tan it an make duh side uh maple. Ise pretty sho it wuz maple. He stretch em obuh it good. It wuz bout eighteen inches wide an fifteen inches deep wen he finish it. He beat it wid a stick. Ole man Okra he sho kin chase a drum. Ole man Jesse he frum Africa, too, an he make he own drum."

When we asked Ben if he remembered any African words, he replied, "I know dat deah wuz a ole man, it bin so long I caahn relate his name, at duh plantation wut wehn roun wid ole man Okra an I membuh well he call all duh fish an ting uh duh ribbuh by duh name uh 'nyana' an den I heah pancake call 'flim.' Muh granmothuh Hettie, duh mothuh uh muh mothuh Bella, he come from Africa too an he huzbun come frum Africa. He name wuz Alex Boyd. Alex wuz bery small felluh but heaby an he hab dahk skin an shahp-feechuch. Yes, ma'am, he talk African but he stuttuh so he dohn talk much roun us chillun, cuz we make fun at im, an as I say befo, I wuz small lad den. Alex wuz knock-kneed an he tie he head up in a clawt."

Had his grandmother, Hettie, ever talked to him about Africa, we wanted to know.

Ben told us, "Many time. He tell some tings I membuh. He say he mus be bout tutteen aw foeteen wen dey bring im frum Africa. He say deah wuz great talk bout comin tuh dis country an some men tell em it would take only two aw tree days tuh git deah. Dey wuz all happy tuh come. Him an lot uh friens come tuhgedduh.

"Wen Hettie fus come, he say he feel worried cuz he couldn unnuhstan duh talk yuh an many udduh tings bein so diffunt frum he own country. He hab two sistuhs an tree brothuhs but dey couldn git a chance tuh come. He hab mo refrence tuh he mothuh dan tuh he fathuh. An he say dat in Africa he lib in a 'groun house.' It wuz a squeah house, an he say dat he didn lib close tuh a salt ribbuh but weah deah wuz a lot uh wile swamp. Wen he fus come tuh dis country, he didn unnuhstan bout fish. But he tell a lot bout monkey an parakeet. An, too, he say nuttn ebuh die way. Duh crops jis come back ebry yeah widout habin tuh be planted.

"Das all I membuh Hettie tellin bout Africa. Muh fathuh's fathuh come frum Africa too but wen muh fathuh Belali wuz a small young lad, muh granfathuh wehn tuh Dungeness on Cumberland Ilun tuh trade in slabes an nebuh wuz seen agen. It was muh fathuh Belali dat made rice cakes."

When asked about his father's mother, Ben continued, "Muh fathuh's mothuh lib at Altama. Huh name wuz Luna, but muh fathuh's fathuh wuz a unmarried man. Deah's many tings I do not membuh, it wuz sech a long time ago. I know dat wen deah wuz tuh be a buryin, dey alluz bury duh dead at night at duh plantation. Dey alluz come in frum duh tas befo dahk.

"In doze days deah wuz no way tuh git tuh Savannah cep by boat an wen Mr. Couper wannuh go, he use a boat bout fifty foot long an bout six foot wide. He take six strong oahsmen an dey would make it in ten aw twelve hours. I heahd tell ub a house buil by a man frum Africa, wid cawn stalks an mud an wid a straw filluh."

The flying story about old Alexander, the root maker, had interested us and we asked if Ben Sullivan had heard of it.

"I ain heahd specially bout him but Ise heahd plenty Africans talk bout flyin. Deah's plenty ub em wut could fly.[24, 25] I sho heahd em talk bout great doins an Ise heahd ole Israel say duh hoe could wuk by itsef ef yuh know wut tuh say tuh it.[26] It bin a long time sence Ise tought bout tings lak dat, but ef uh studies bout em, dey comes back tuh me."

On the way back from Harrington to St. Simons village we stopped at Nora Peterson's [27] small cabin to talk with her. Nora, the daughter of Tom Floyd, an African who came to this country on the *Wanderer* in 1858, is a nice looking, middle-aged woman, pleasant and up to date. She told us about her father.

"I wuz bery lill wen he died—not mone bout fo yeah ole, uh spec. I do know he come frum Africa. I membuhs dat an uh membuh muh Uncle Slaughtuh wuz his brothuh an he come frum Africa, too. I nebuh heahd him talk much bout it but maybe uh wuz too lill tuh membuh."

Although she had been so young at the time of her father's death, the woman still retained a vivid picture of him and she gave us the following description:

"He wuz shawt an dahk, an heaby buil. Yuh see, he wuzn but bout sixty yeah ole wen he died. Muh mothuh wuz Charity Lewis an uh got one brothuh, Caesar Prince, but he's younguh dan me an dohn membuh nothin."

From Nora's we went to the old tabby slave house of Floyd White [28] who was related to her. Floyd was of middle height, black, and of a powerful build. When we were uncertain and groping as to the right questions to ask, Floyd was clear and helpful.

"Ise nephew tuh Charity Lewis, so Nora is muh cousin, but Ise olduhn Nora an I membuh ole Tom Floyd well. I bout fifteen wen he die. He wuz shawt an tick set. I tinks he wuz Ibo. He used tuh whoop an holluh. He say dey do da way in Africa. He wuz doctuh too an he could cut yuh wid a knife an cop yuh. I wish he wuz yuh right now tuh cop me. I sho needs it an it make yuh feel lots bettuh.[12] I heah him talk plenty bout Africa but I caahn membuh so much ub it cuz uh wuz young boy den. He say he lib in a hut on a ribbuh an dey eat coconut an bread wut grow on a tree. Dey plant yam ebry seben yeah an dey dohn hadduh wuk it. Dey hab peanut an banana. He call it by anudduh name but I caahn membuh it. I seen plenty ub African people an dey all say dey plant duh crop an dey dohn hadduh wuk it. I heah lot ub em tell how dey git obuh yuh. Dey trap em on a boat wid a red flag."

Old Tom Floyd was not the only root doctor Floyd could remember. There were many others, he said, some still living and plying their trade.[12]

"I knows a root makuh now," he told us. "Uncle Quawt, he root makuh. Does yuh know him?"

We replied that we had known Quarterman for some time but that he had never told us he could work roots.

"Maybe he ain tell yuh but he kin wuk em all right.[12] He kin put a cunjuh on wid a goofa bag as good as anybody. Now, I tell yuh bout him. Deah's two felluhs in Brunswick wut does a lill killin an wen duh case is call, two buzzud light on duh cote house and wen duh men come up befo duh jedge, he let um go free. Now, Uncle Quawt, he had sumpm tuh do wid dat. Dey ain so many root makuhs lef."

Floyd, too, had heard of Alexander, the old African root maker.

"Yes'm, Ise heahd much bout im. He wuz still libin wen I wuz a boy. Ise heahd em tell plenty uh tales bout im. Dey say duh boat leab fuh Savannah an Alexanduh he yuh. He say good-bye frum yuh an tell em tuh go on widout im but he say he see em deah an wen duh boat git tuh Savannah, Alexanduh he in Savannah on duh dock tuh ketch duh line."

Pleasant memories associated with the social activities of the past caused Floyd to ponder abstractedly for a time. Finally he roused himself and told us, "We use tuh dance roun tuh a drum an a rattle goad. Dey could make good drum frum hawg an bass drum frum cow.[10] Doze days dey ain only beat duh drum fuh dancin; dey beat it on duh way tuh duh grabe yahd.[22] Dat wuz fuh duh det mahch wen dey use tuh carry duh body in a wagon. Dey hab lot uh singin den too an dey hab singin at duh baptizin. Den dey baptize em in duh ribbuh jis lak dey does now. Dey sing wid all duh candidates walkin in wite robes tuh duh ribbuh an duh preachuh he dip em on duh ebb tide an he pray duh ribbuh tuh take duh sin away.[15] Dey ain mine gittin wet in duh ribbuh.

"Heahd bout duh Ibo's Landing? Das duh place weah dey bring duh Ibos obuh in a slabe ship an wen dey git yuh, dey ain lak it an so dey all staht singin an dey mahch right down in duh ribbuh tuh mahch back tuh Africa, but dey ain able tuh git deah. Dey gits drown."

## NOTES

[1] *Catherine Wing, St. Simons Island.*

[2] *Burial at home*

a *Basden says of the Ibo:* "The desire of every Ibo man and woman is to die in their own town or, at least, to be buried within its precincts. For a long period it was very difficult to persuade a man to travel any distance from his native place, and if he were in need of medical assistance an Ibo would seldom agree to go from home in spite of assurances that he would be able to have better treatment elsewhere. In case of death occurring at a distance, if it can be done at all, the brethren will bring the body home for burial. It may be that this cannot be done for several days, according to distance and other circumstances."
*Among the Ibos of Nigeria, pp. 115–16.*

b *Bosman says of the Coast of Guinea:* "The Negroes are strangely fond of being buried in their own Country; so that if any Person dies out of it, they frequently bring his Corpse home to be buried, unless it be too far distant."
*Description of the Coast of Guinea, p. 232.*

c *Meek says of Nigeria:* "When a man dies at a distance from his home his body is always taken back, when possible, to his home, wrapped up in mats covered by a cloth and placed on a bier or cradle, which is carried on the shoulders of his relatives. The reason assigned for this is that the dead must not be severed from the company of other ancestors—they should be buried close to their living descendants on whom they are dependent for nourishment. Moreover, it is important that the ritual traditional to the kindred should be carried out accurately. This cannot be done by strangers."
*Law and Authority in a Nigerian Tribe, p. 309.*

d *Nassau says of the Bihe country:* "It is considered essential that a man should die in his own country, if not in his own town. On the way to Bailundu, shortly after leaving Bihe territory, I met some men running at great speed, carrying a sick man tied to a pole, in order that he might die in his own country."
*Fetichism in West Africa, p. 228.*

3 *Burial of relatives and strangers*
a *Pearce says of West Africa:* "There is a strong feeling of kinship in Africa and only relatives may be buried in the same piece of ground together." (Interview with John Pearce of Hinesville, Ga., an ex-missionary in West Africa.)

4 *Harvest festivals*
a *Ellis says of the Tshi-Speaking native:* "Yam, or Harvest Festivals:—These appear to be festivals held for the purpose of returning thanks to the gods for having protected the crop. There are apparently two; one held in September, when the yam crop is ripe, and another, called *Ojirrah,* in December, when it is planted. A minor festival, called *Affi-neh-dzea-fi,* which is held in April, appears, however, to be of the same nature. The September festival lasts a fortnight, and is commenced by a loud beating of drums. It is called by the Ashantis *Appatram,* and no new yam may be eaten by the people till the close of the festival."
*The Tshi-Speaking Peoples of the Gold Coast of West Africa, p. 229.*

b *Meek says of Nigeria:* "Public sacrifice to Ala may be offered periodically at the beginning of the agricultural season, before clearing new land, or after clearing old, before planting yams, or at the end of the yam harvest.
*Law and Authority in a Nigerian Tribe, p. 26.*

c *Rattray says of Ashanti:* "There appear to be at least three great festivals which are held by the Talense in connexion with the crops and harvest."
*The Tribes of the Ashanti Hinterland, II, 358–59.*

d *Talbot says of the Ibibio tribes:* "At the time of new yam planting, people came from far and near to beg protection and increase for their crops and herds. On such occasions the brow of the chief priest is bound with a fillet of white cloth, which may not be taken off till the time of sacrifice comes round again. He marks all the people with white chalk, as a sign that they have attended the festival and asked the blessing of the genius of the pool."
*Life in Southern Nigeria, p. 38.*

5 *Dances, buzzard lope, etc.*
a *Cuney-Hare says of the Bushman:* "They possess a variety of dances pertaining to social customs, each of which has its appropriate chant. One dance imitates the actions of different animals."
*Negro Musicians and Their Music, pp. 10–12.*

b *Melville and Frances Herskovits say of the Bush Negro of Dutch Guiana:* "Those who danced for the buzzard had no machetes, but went about in a circle, moving

with bodies bent forward from their waists and with arms thrown back in imitation of the bird from which their spirit took its name."
*Rebel Destiny, p. 330.*

c "Bush and town invoke the buzzard, *Opete,* so named in Ashanti, and sacred everywhere in West Africa. . . ."
*Rebel Destiny,* Preface, X.

d "The men were dancing to the great Kromanti spirits; the tiger-jaguar—and the buzzard, two of the three forms which the dreaded Kromanti *obia* can take. 'Obia! Huh! Huh!' one ejaculated, imitating the tiger, as his dancing became wilder and wilder."
*Rebel Destiny, p. 17.*

6 *Drum Messages*

a *Rattray says of Ashanti:* "A great deal is heard in Africa about the wonderful way in which news can be passed on over great distances in an incredibly short space of time. It has been reported that the news of the fall of Khartum was known among the natives of Sierra Leone the same day, and other equally wonderful instances are quoted to show that the native has some extraordinary rapid means of communicating important events. It must, however, be remembered that most of the instances that one hears quoted are incapable of verification, and would, moreover, probably be found to have been much exaggerated. Having said this much, however, it must be admitted that these natives have a means of intercommunication which often inspires wonder and curiosity on the part of Europeans. One of such means of communication is by drumming.

"This idea the European will readily grasp, and being familiar with various means of *signalling,* will suppose that some such a method might be adapted to drums; but among the Ashantis the drum is not used as a means of *signalling* in the sense that we would infer, that is by rapping out words by means of a prearranged code, but (to the native mind) is used to sound or speak the actual words."
*Ashanti Proverbs, pp. 133–34.*

b "I first became interested in this difficult subject many years ago. At that time it was generally known that the Ashanti, in common with certain other West Coast peoples, were able to convey messages over great distances and in an incredibly short space of time by means of drums, and it was thought that their system was based upon some such method as that with which Europeans are familiar in the Morse code."
*Ashanti, p. 242.*

7 *Ryna Johnson, Harrington, St. Simons Island.*

8 *Cicatrization*

a *Herskovits says of Dahomey:* "Another form which these positive injunctions take has to do with facial cuts, which vary from sib to sib. Thus the Adjalénû make no cuts at all. The Hwedánu who live in Whydah, make two cuts on each cheek. The Agblomenu, who are considered a group of autochthonous inhabitants of the plateau of Abomey, make three cuts on each side of the face, one on the temple called *àdjàkàsí* (tail of a rat), and two on the cheek, both in front of the ear. The Gedeví, another aboriginal group near Abomey, distinguish themselves by means of three cuts on each temple. At the present time all Dahomeans are supposed to have three cuts on the temple, though the Agblomenu have suppressed the two of these three and only cut the 'rat's tail.' "
*Dahomey,* I, *162.*

b "Twelve sets of cuts constitute a complete cicatrization."
*Dahomey, I, 292.*
c "The last design is placed between the breasts, and often takes the form of a series
of links or of straight lines radiating from a central point."
*Dahomey, I, 295.*
d *Livingstone says of South Africa:* "They mark themselves by a line of little raised
cicatrices, each of which is a quarter of an inch long; they extend from the tip of the
nose to the root of the hair on the forehead."
*Missionary Travels and Researches in South Africa, p. 576.*

⁹ *Drums*
a *Melville and Frances Herskovits say of the Paramaribo Negro:*
"Drums are the most important instruments in both Town and Bush, and the drummers, in these as in all Negro cultures, achieve a virtuosity of performance and an
intricacy of rhythm that come of long practice. It was impossible to obtain satisfactory recordings of drumming which would reveal the complexity of these rhythm-
patterns, chiefly because, lacking electrical recording apparatus, the inner rhythms
which in combination give a steady beat are lost, and only the points where the notes
of the several instruments coincide can be discerned.
"The drums have more than a musical significance in this culture. Tradition assigns
to them the threefold power of summoning the gods and the spirits of the ancestors
to appear, of articulating the messages of these supernatural beings when they arrive,
and of sending them back to their habitats at the end of each ceremony. Both in
Town and in the Bush, the dancers who are the worshippers,—one of the most important expressions of worship is dancing—face the drums and dance toward them,
in recognition of the voice of the god within the instruments."
*Suriname Folk-Lore, pp. 520–21.*
b *Milligan says of the West African:* "The fact is, however, that the only one of his
musical instruments which the African regards with profound respect is his dearly
beloved *tom-tom*—the drum to which he dances."
*The Fetish Folk of West Africa, p. 77.*

¹⁰ *Drums, manufacture of*
a *Du Puis says of Ansah:* "The large drums were carried on the heads of men, and
beaten in that posture; but the small ones were slung as kettle drums. These added
to calabashes and gourds filled with shot or small stones, concave bits of iron, and
striking sticks, will give an idea of the national taste in harmonic matters."
*Journal of a Residence in Ashantee, p. 43.*
b *Ellis says of the Gold Coast:* "Drums are made of the hollowed sections of trunks
of trees, with a goat's or sheep's skin stretched over one end. They are from one foot
to four feet high, and vary in diameter from about six to fourteen inches. Two or
three drums are usually used together, each drum producing a different note, and
they are played either with the fingers or with two sticks. The lookers-on generally
beat time by clapping the hands."
*The Tshi-Speaking Peoples of the Gold Coast of West Africa, p. 326.*
c *Herskovits says of Haiti:* "Drums, iron, and rattles are indispensable for a *vodun*
dance. The drums, of the characteristic hollow-log African type, tuned with pegs
inserted in the sides and reinforced with twine wound about the stretched heads of
cow-hide or goat-skin, are played in batteries of three, the largest being called *man-
man,* the middle the *seconde,* and the smallest the *bula.*"
*Life in a Haitian Valley, pp. 181–82.*

d *Herskovits says of Dahomey:* "Generally the drums are of the usual African type, made of a hollowed-out log with a more or less crudely carved foot, its head of animal skin being attached to pegs inserted into the body of the drum, just below its upper end. The drum-head is tightened by driving these pegs into the drum until the required note is sounded, since by this method the skin is stretched to produce the desired tone. Ordinarily the attachment of the head to the pegs is by means of strips of the skin itself; in some forms, however, a cord attachment is used. A small barrel drum, the only one of its kind observed, about eighteen inches high and twelve inches in diameter, and which does not have a foot, is used in the Sagbatá rites. The other more conventional drums range from two feet in size to a length of five feet and more."

*Dahomey,* II, *318.*

e *Moore says of the Mandingo:* "... with him came two or three Women, and the same Number of Mundingo Drums, which are about a Yard long, and a Foot, or twenty Inches diameter at the Top, but less at the Bottom, made out of a solid Piece of Wood, and covered, only at the widest End, with the Skin of a Kid. They beat upon them with only one Stick, and their left Hand, to which the Women will dance very briskly."

*Travels Into the Inland Parts of Africa, p. 64.*

f *Ward says of the Bakongo country:* "The natives were drumming on a goat-skin stretched tightly across the mouth of a hollowed-out log, and dancing round a fire lighted in their midst, one man singing a refrain, while others took up the chorus; and the mingled sound of the voices and the distant beating of other drums in neighboring villages helped to keep me awake."

*Five Years with the Congo Cannibals, p. 68.*

g *Beckwith says:* "The beating of the gombay drum is a familiar accompaniment of death."

*Black Roadways, p. 83.*

[11] *Diviners, Divining, Seed Casting, Etc.*

a *Delafosse says:* "Numerous fortune-tellers predict the future and reveal hidden things, by means of processes, many of which strangely resemble those which our own clairvoyants employ."

*Negroes of Africa, p. 237.*

b *Herskovits says of Dahomey:* "A third type, called *agŏkwíka,* employed two magically treated *agô* seeds tied to the ends of a cord long enough to go about the neck of the accused, and the seeds were buried lightly in the ground. Such was the spiritual power in these seeds, that if the accused was guilty of the crime, he could not remove them from the ground; if he succeeded in rising, he was declared innocent."

*Dahomey,* II, *18.*

c "In this myth, not only is the explanation found of how the prevalent system of divination came to man, but the principal outlines of the practices which characterize the Fá cult are to be discerned—that is, the sixteen palm-kernels employed in throwing the lots, the sixteen combinations in which they may fall, and which foretell the future. . . ."

*Dahomey,* II, *206.*

d "The details of this system by means of which the future is foretold may now be considered. In essence, Fá is based on the interpretation, by reference to appropriate myths, of the permutations and combinations obtained by the diviner when he manipulates the sixteen palm-kernels he employs for this purpose. Before him as he works

lies a rectangular wooden tray, on which powdered white clay or meal has been sprinkled. In one hand he holds his sixteen palm-kernels, and with great rapidity brings the hand which holds them into the palm of the other one, leaving either one or two seeds for an instant before they are once more picked up and the process is repeated. As soon as he has glimpsed the one or two kernels in his left hand, the right, with the palm-kernels, closes down upon it and the two clasp the seeds. The index and second fingers of the right hand are, however, left free and with these he describes marks in the white powder on the board in front of him. Moving his fingers away from him, he makes a double line for each single kernel, a single line if two seeds are left. The process is repeated eight times for a complete reading."
*Dahomey*, II, *209–10.*

e *Rattray says of the Ashanti:* "The soothsayer, oracle man, or diviner, as will be seen presently, takes a leading part in the everyday life of these people. He is consulted on almost every conceivable occasion. Hardly anything can be done until he has been asked. He is really a *medium,* a 'go-between' in the land of the living and the world of spirit ancestors. The root of the word used to describe this person is generally the same as that found in the word for shrine. The people consult him at some shrine, the spirit in which guides him and directs his answers."
*The Tribes of the Ashanti Hinterland*, I, *44.*

12 *Root doctors*

a *Cardinall says of the Gold Coast:* "With the belief that spiritual agents are the cause of misfortune and sickness, it follows that medical treatment consists generally in charms. There are certain men considered most proficient in the curative art. These are the *liri-tina* (Kassena), *tiindana* (Nankanni), *tinyam* (Builsa), (owner of medicine). Their medicines are drawn from the bush, and are usually bitter-tasting grasses, herbs, and barks. For poultices the same herbs are used mixed with shea-butter and charcoal and ashes. Usually they are covered with cow-dung. It is said that the stronger the smell the more easily will the evil spirit causing the sickness be driven away."
*The Natives of the Northern Territories of the Gold Coast, p. 46.*

b *Cruickshank says of the Gold Coast native:* "The natives of the Gold Coast have no despicable knowledge of the qualities of herbs. A collection of these was, at one time, sent home for analysis; and it was found generally that they possessed some qualities calculated to be of use in alleviating the diseases for which the natives applied them."
*Eighteen Years on the Gold Coast*, II, *147.*

c *Leyden says of the interior sections of West Africa, such as the Congo, the banks of the Senegal and the Gambia, etc.:* "The magicians appear to have been resorted to universally in cases of malady, which proved a hard trial on the faith even of the steadiest converts. When their children or near relations were seized with illness, they immediately began to cast a longing eye towards their old method of cure; and if they had not recourse to it, they even incurred reproach among their neighbors, as suffering their relation to die, rather than incur the expence of a magician."
*Historical Account of Discoveries and Travels in Africa*, I, *120.*

d *Meek says of Nigeria:* "The believer in witchcraft feels he has a right to protect himself by every means in his power, and chief among these is the employment of a witch-doctor . . . [who] is therefore considered just as essential in most negro communities as a medical practitioner is amongst ourselves, and, though some witch-

doctors may abuse their powers for selfish ends, as a class they are regarded as champions of morality."
*Law and Authority in a Nigerian Tribe, p. 345.*

e *Nassau, quoting Menzies' History of Religion, p. 73, says of the Benja, the Mpongwe, the Fang, and other West African tribes:* " 'There is generally a special person in a tribe who knows these things, and is able to work them. He has more power over spirits than other men have, and is able to make them do what he likes. He can heal sickness, he can foretell the future, he can change a thing into something else, or a man into a lower animal, or a tree, or anything; he can also assume such transformations himself at will. He uses means to bring about such results; he knows about herbs, he has also recourse to rubbing, to making images of affected parts in the body, and to various other arts. . . . It is the spirit dwelling in him which brings about the wonderful results; without the spirit he could not do anything.' "
*Fetichism in West Africa, pp. 86–87.*

f *Ward says of the Bakongo tribes:* "It is a general belief with the Bakongo that all sickness is the result of witchcraft exercised by some member of the community, and the services of the charm-doctor are employed to discover the individual who is *ndoki,* i.e., bedeviled, and guilty of devouring the spirit of the unfortunate invalid; and in the event of the sick person dying, the medicine-man is deputed by the relatives of the deceased to find out the witch who has 'eaten the heart.' "
*Five Years with the Congo Cannibals, p. 39.*

[13] *Charles Hunter, Harrington, St. Simons Island.*

[14] *A number of slaves accompanied their masters from the West Indies to this country. It was also the custom for slave ships to stop at the Bahamas en route to America with a cargo.*

[15] *Spirits, river*

a *Cardinall says of the Gold Coast:* "Spirits of rivers and water-holes are greatly respected. They are most powerful spirits, too. They can slay men and they can bring much good fortune. To them are brought many sacrifices of fowls and goats, etc. It is said that these spirits live below the river-bed."
*The Natives of the Northern Territories of the Gold Coast, p. 34.*

b *Melville and Frances Herskovits say of the Paramaribo Negro:* "A fourth group of *winti* are those which are associated with the river. This group, as all others, overlap the Snake gods, since the constrictor lives in the water as well as on land. However, there are other gods, among them the *kaima,* which are peculiar to the rivers alone. The river-gods are headed by the *Liba-Mama,* or *Watra-Mama,* respectively Mother of the River, or Mother of the Water, who, again, is not referred to by name. Among the Saramacca tribe of Bush-Negroes, the river-gods go under the generic name of Tone, and this name, like the name from the interior for the gods in general, is also sometimes employed in Paramaribo."
*Suriname Folk-Lore, pp. 64–65.*

c *Meek says of Nigeria:* "At Eha-Amufu (Nsukka Division) there is a river-cult, the priest of which is known as the Atama Ebe. Ebe is the spirit of the river and controls the fish, who are regarded as the spiritual counterparts of the inhabitants of Eha-Amufu. The big fish are the counterparts of the principal men of the village group, while the fry are the counterparts of persons of no consequence. When a villager dies a fish dies, and when a fish dies a villager dies. It is taboo, therefore, to catch fish in the river, and much annoyance has been caused by visits of foreign fishermen who disregard the local scruples. Ebe, the spirit of the river, being the guardian of the

fish, which are his children and messengers, is regarded as the giver of children to men, and is thus the object of public and private worship."
*Law and Authority in a Nigerian Tribe, p. 38.*

16 *Conjure, illness and death*

a *Ellis says of the Yoruba:* "They consequently attribute sickness and death, other than death resulting from injury or violence, to persons who have for bad purposes enlisted the services of evil spirits, that is to say, to wizards and witches."
*The Yoruba-Speaking Peoples of the Slave Coast of West Africa, p. 117.*

b *Meek says of the Jukun:* "Sudden deaths, especially of young people, are usually regarded as the work of sorcerers (*ba-shiko* or *ba-shibu*). If the deceased had been noted for his disrespect to his seniors his death would be ascribed to offended ancestors, and he would go to his grave with 'bloodshot eyes'; but otherwise it is thought that one who had died suddenly had met his death by the foul means of witchcraft and would take vengeance in his own time."
*A Sudanese Kingdom, pp. 223–24.*

c *Milligan says of a Mpongwe tribe:* "Sickness and death, they believe, may be caused by fetish medicine, which need not be administered to the victim, but is usually laid beside the path where he is about to pass."
*The Fetish Folk of West Africa, p. 39.*

d *Nassau says of West Africa:* " 'According to native ideas, all over Africa, such a thing as death from natural causes does not exist. Whatever ill befalls a man or a family, it is always the result of witchcraft, and in every case the witch-doctors are consulted to find out who has been guilty of it.' "
*Fetichism in West Africa, p. 117.*

e *Talbot says of the Ibibio tribes:* "When a man falls sick because his soul has gone forth and is being detained by an enemy, or when he believes that such an one is trying to entice it from out his body, he, in turn, goes to a Juju man known to have the power of seeing clearly."
*Life in Southern Nigeria, p. 121.*

f *Talbot says of the Yoruba:* "The Yoruba, like all other tribes here, considered that a large number of deaths was due to witchcraft or ill-will on the part of some enemy, and when many people died of famine or sickness, a general meeting was held and resort had to divination to find out the guilty persons, who were at once killed or offered in sacrifice to one of the Orisha."
*The Peoples of Southern Nigeria, III, 474–75.*

17 b *Meek says of Nigeria:* "Witches (*amozu*) and wizards (*ogboma*) have also animal counterparts, and so assume the forms of owls, lizards, vultures, and numerous species of night-birds. Consequently, if a night-bird comes and rests on a house, the owner loses no time in trying to drive it away or shoot it; and if he fails he will seize his *ofo* and call on his ancestors or any local deity to rid him of his enemy. A witch always assails at night. By magic means she attacks the throat, so that the victim is paralysed and cannot move or speak, and in the morning may be found lying senseless and naked outside his hut. . . . Witches can penetrate into a house through the smallest cracks in the wall, and can assume the form of the smallest insect. Flies and other creatures which bite are witches or the agents of witches, and if a person is severely bitten he may consult a diviner, who will order the patient to offer sacrifice to propitiate some witch, and induce the witch to remove the spell by transferring it to some one else. Witches can poison food or infect it with sorcery, and if any one eats a meal cooked by a witch he will become seriously ill or die.

Mothers, therefore, advise their children to avoid eating food outside their own homes."

*Law and Authority in a Nigerian Tribe, pp. 79–80.*

[18] c *Rattray says of Ashanti:* "Men and women possessed of this black magic are credited with volitant powers, being able to quit their bodies and travel great distances in the night. Besides sucking the blood of victims, they are supposed to be able to extract the sap and juices of crops."

*Ashanti Proverbs, p. 48.*

[19] *Ben Sullivan, St. Simons Island.*

[20] *Earrings*

a *Beckwith says of the Jamaica Negro:* "Parkes says that men who 'deal in spirits' wear a red flannel shirt, or a crosspiece of red under their ordinary clothes, and generally gold earrings. Not all men who wear earrings are Obeah Men; fishermen, for example, generally wear one earring. The gold is said to 'brighten their eyes to see ghosts,' but also a gold earring is put on to improve the natural sight."

*Black Roadways, p. 108.*

[21] *Dances, religious significance*

a *Rattray says of Ashanti:* "Dancing in Africa invariably has a religious significance."

*Religion and Art in Ashanti, p. 184.*

[22] *Drums, funeral*

a *Herskovits says of Dahomey:* "Outside the house the funerary zçli, a pottery drum, is played day and night. The drummers are the members of the *dókpwê* of the quarter where the dead man lived, or if he was a villager, of his village, and it is the head of this *dókpwê* who is the commanding *dókpwégâ* at the funeral."

*Dahomey, I, 355.*

b *Melville and Frances Herskovits say of the Bush Negro of Dutch Guiana:* "That night whenever we stirred in our sleep we strained for the sound of the drums, but the wind blew from the east, and though Gankwe, where the dead man lay in state, was but a ten-minute run down the rapids, we could hear nothing. In the morning, however, we heard them plainly, heard the invocations drummed by the grave diggers on their way to the burial ground deep in the bush on the opposite bank."

*Rebel Destiny, p. 3.*

c *Livingstone says of South Africa:* "Drums were beating over the body of a man who had died the preceding day, and some women were making a clamorous wail at the door of his hut, and addressing the deceased as if alive. The drums continued beating the whole night, with as much regularity as a steam-engine thumps, on board ship."

*Missionary Travels and Researches in South Africa, p. 467.*

[23] *Dances, funerals*

a *Moore says of a Mandingo funeral:* "They begin with Crying, and at Night they go to Singing and Dancing, and continue so doing till the Time they break up and depart."

*Travels Into the Inland Parts of Africa, p. 130.*

b *Rattray says of Ashanti:* "People from a far place who were related to the deceased and people from towns near by, also form their own companies. They dance the war-dances in the morning, and at 'the mouth' of evening, when the sun is slanting, they circle the grave. It is now that the corpse is taken to the grave."

*The Tribes of the Ashanti Hinterland, p. 194.*

24 c *Talbot says of Southern Nigeria:* "Witches often change into leopards and other animals."
*The Peoples of Southern Nigeria,* II, *219.*

25 b *Leonard says:* "In Brass the natives firmly believe that witches exist, and that certain persons by natural operations—or rather by co-operation with natural forces—possess the power of inflicting disease, injury, or death upon their neighbors. These individuals are divided into two classes—the harmful and the harmless. "The former are said to go out of their houses at night and to hold meetings with demons and their colleagues, to determine whose life is next to be destroyed. This is done by gradually sucking the blood of the victim through some supernatural and invisible means, the effect of which on the victim is imperceptible to others."
*The Lower Niger and Its Tribes,* p. 486.

26 *Hoe, magic*
a *Rattray repeats a Hausa folk tale:* "When he struck one blow on the ground with the hoe, then he climbed on the hoe and sat down, and the hoe started to hoe, and fairly flew until it had done as much as the hoers. It passed them, and reached the boundary of the furrow."
*Hausa Folk-Lore Customs, Proverbs, Etc.,* I, *74–76.*
b *Rattray tells an Ashanti folk tale:* "The Hoe turned over a huge tract (of land). Then they stopped work and went off, and the Porcupine took the hoe and hid it. And Kwaku, the Spider, saw (where he put it). He said, 'This hoe that I have seen, to-morrow very, very early I shall come and take it to do my work.' Truly, very, very, very early, the Spider went and got it; he took to his farm. Now, the Spider did not know how to make it stop, and he raised his song:
'Gyensaworowa, Kotoko, saworowa.
Gyensaworowa, Kotoko, saworowa,
Gyensaworowa.'
And the Hoe, when it commenced hoeing, continued hoeing. And it hoed until it came too far away. Now it reached the Sea-god's water. Thence it came to the Land of White-men-far, and the White men took it, and looked at it, and made

27 *Nora Peterson, St. Simons Island.*
28 *Floyd White, St. Simons Island.*

# 2

# THE UNWILLING MIGRATION

The essays in this section discuss the circumstances and conditions of the slave trade. Contained in this chapter are an account of the trade from the perspective of a commercial slaver and an evaluation of "the unwilling migration" by a modern writer. More significantly, however, there is also the narrative of one who was enslaved and subsequently repatriated. Presented, also, is an attempt to determine statistically the ethnic origins of those Africans taken as slaves. The rigors, horrors, and humiliation suffered by the slaves are coupled with empirical evidence of the devastating demographic effect of slavery on various societies of West Africa.

*In the following essay entitled "Blues," Janheinz Jahn*
*examines one area of African cultural survival in*
*the New World—music. The preeminent African nature*
*of jazz and blues has been established by numerous*
*studies. A recent book entitled* Early Jazz *by Gunther*
*Schuller has argued that not only the rhythms of jazz but*
*also the melodies and harmonies are of African origin.*
*"Blues" is an account of the Afro-American musical*
*heritage which the author relates to the broader question*
*of identity.*

# Blues: The Conflict of Cultures

## Janheinz Jahn

To keep from cryin' I opens my
mouth an' laughs.

LANGSTON HUGHES

## I. RESIDUAL AFRICAN ELEMENTS IN NORTH AMERICA

The peculiar development of African culture in North America began with the loss of the drums. The Protestant, and often Puritan, slave owners interfered much more radically with the personal life of their slaves than did their Catholic colleagues in the West Indies or in South America. The slaves were allowed no human dignity and their cultural past was ignored; or else it was considered a humane task to educate them into being 'better' human beings, and this process was initiated by teaching them to be ashamed of their African heritage. And to forbid the drums was to show a keen scent for the essential: for without the drums it was impossible to call the orishas, the ancestors were silent, and the proselytizers seemed to have a free hand. The Baptists and Methodists, whose practical maxims and revivals were sympathetic to African religiosity, quickly found masses of adherents.

Their nearness to God, their intimately personal relation to Him, and their ecstatic possession by the Holy Ghost won the highest praise for the converts in many Christian circles. People talked of the renewal of Christianity, of a 'fervour of faith akin to early Christianity',[1] and the like. And

From Janheinz Jahn, *Muntu, the New African Culture,* translated from German by Marjorie Greene (New York: Grove Press, 1961), pp. 217–236. © 1961 by Faber & Faber. Originally published by Eugene Diederichs Verlag Düsseldorf, West Germany.

certainly, the intensity of this religious feeling cannot be doubted, but the question whether it is really Christian might well provoke some theological dispute. According to Christian doctrine man designates by the word God that unworldly-supraworldly (transcendent) reality, by which he knows that the experienced world including his own being is governed and sustained.[2] But of what sort is the transcendence of the Christian God in the Negro churches of the United States, when the Pulitzer Prize winner Gwendolyn Brooks in one of her poems makes the preacher murmur at the end of his sermon:

> Picture Jehovah striding through the hall
> Of His importance, creatures running out
> From servant-corners to acclaim, to shout
> Appreciation of His merit's glare.
> But who walks with Him?—dares to take His arm,
> To slap Him on the shoulder, tweak His ear,
> Buy Him a Coca-Cola or a beer,
> Pooh-pooh his politics, call Him a fool?

Gwendolyn Brooks' preacher positively feels sorry for the Good Lord, because—to use our Haitian expression—he has to remain 'Bon Dieu' and is not allowed to become a loa like his son Jésus or the Holy Ghost. The revivalist ceremonies in the Negro churches, which no one describes better than the Afro-American poet James Baldwin in his novel *Go Tell it on the Mountain,* contain so many residual African elements, that the comparison with the Arada rite of Voodoo is inevitable. However, we are concerned here with the differences. In the first place the drums are missing. The percussion instruments are replaced by hand-clapping and foot-stamping. But no polymetry can be produced in this way and there are no specific formulas permitting the invocation of a number of loas. The singing is therefore directed to the *one* Christian divinity, to whom the sermon was also addressed, and the faithful, usually many of them at a time, are 'ridden' by a single divinity. The procedure which in the African orisha cult evokes ecstatic immobility, and in Haitian Voodoo different types of ecstatic movement, produces, in the Negro churches, 'mass ecstasy'.[4]

A faith like African art is an attitude. It is the relation between men on the one hand and one or more divine or deified beings on the other. In Christianity this relation is unequivocally determined by God alone: God created man, commanded him, forbade him; God enlightens, punishes and redeems him. The bond of man with God (*religio*) is expressed in man's obedience. In African religion this relation is reversed: *religio,* active worship, 'creates' God, as the expression 'She Orisha' [5] puts it: that is, the living person (muzima) in his active worship installs the divine being as such. Analogously to the designation of an image [6] we may speak of the *designation of divinity*. Necessarily, therefore, this divinity must be other than transcendent, for it is concretely present during the act of worship—or better, it is produced by the congregation during the act of worship. This occurs in the African cults, in Haitian Voodoo, in the Cuban santería, in the Jamaican pocomania, in the Brazilian macumba,[7] in the Winti cults of Guiana and in the Negro churches of the United States. But while the cults of the West Indies and South America have remained polytheistic, through the equation of the loas and orishas with saints (the equation is a pure act of designation), the Negro churches perform the designation of a single divinity.

With the designation of a Christian God Christian standards penetrate the cult, above all the sharp separation of good and evil; but the nature of worship, the *service* of God, remains to a great extent African. For God is not only served but invoked, called up and embodied by the faithful. As in art, so also in religion, the Kuntu is unchanging and remains the hallmark of African culture. Even the Christian images are treated in prayer in the African manner. Thus an old woman in Baldwin's novel *Go Tell it on the Mountain* prays: 'Lord, sprinkle the door-post of this house with the blood of the Lamb to keep all the wicked men away.' [8]

Musically, the change is expressed by the fact that with the loss of the drums, the polymetry which carries polytheism is lost, and all that remains is polyrhythm, which is constructed on the basis of a single metre. The hymns of Christian European origin used by the missions are Africanized, producing *jubilees,* 'original songs of praise, in which, as they are sung stanza after stanza, a more and more marked Africanization takes place, sometimes leading in the end to sporadic outbreaks of possession'.[9] Kuntu, the manner of singing, remains African, and where European melody and harmonics begin to penetrate, in the ballads, spirituals and blues, this becomes apparent through the fact that the African *way* of singing alters the melody in many ways unknown in Europe. First of all there is that melodic technique which Dauer calls 'heterophony of variants', impromptu variations by means of 'singing separately', for which in classical jazz 'the misleading title "improvization" has become widespread'.[10] Then there are changes of tone, of intonation, of pitch and timbre, variations, paraphrases and slurring of the text and many other African devices which Dauer expounds in detail.

Nor did the Afro-Americans have to wait to learn melody and harmony from European Americans. The very first slaves brought to America and passed on to their descendants their own tonality, harmony and a rich treasure of musical means of expression. 'If in this connection anything had surprised them in "white" music,' Dauer believes, 'it would have been at the most the fact of an amazingly large tonal and harmonic kinship.' [11] Yet the familiarization of the Afro-Americans with European church music (which was by no means always voluntary) produced 'a perceptible approach to the European melodic form and a new type of Afro-American harmony' [12] in the true spirituals, which differ considerably from the concert hall spirituals as they are presented by concertizing Negro choirs and soloists. For between 1860 and 1870 University choirs like the Fisk Jubilee Singers or the Hampton Student Singers began to collect spirituals in great numbers, to 'purify' them of 'ugly and unlovely' Africanisms and then to copy and record them in choral fashion. Through this 'purification' all the basic elements were destroyed.[13] The definiteness prevents designation, Nommo cannot take shape or be given shape; in the concert hall Kuntu freezes into a dead form. The true folk spirituals, on the other hand, are residual African folk art, and the part played in their origin by Christian influences is still considerably exaggerated.

The secular parallel to the jubilee and the spiritual is that music which is usually so completely misunderstood: the blues. 'A white song—black: that is, reduced to a simplified formula, blues.' [14] This is a widespread view. People also think that the *blue notes* and the modulation of tone exhaust the African part of the blues.[15] What is correct in all this is the fact that the blues did originate from the contact of African and European music. How the different contributions are divided, in what way these two very different styles affected one another, Dauer has described and determined. It is not the formula of the blues that is the true hallmark of blues but the sequence of voices, which is founded on the African antiphony. 'This consists in appeal and answer and explains the division of phrases in blues singing, as well as the function of the individual phrases. In the simplest case the phrase sequence runs A B and corresponds to the functions of an appeal and an answer. In the 12-beat blues, which have become classic, the sequence runs A A B, which corresponds to two appeals and one answer.' [16] Only in the blues the separate events of appeal by the first singer and answer by the chorus are 'consolidated into a single event, since they are all executed by a single voice.' [17] One song *in* the community becomes one song *before* the community, for the community is now only a listener. Instead of a chorus answering the singer, there are instruments accompanying the singing. In Africa the drums lead the singer's performance; one might say that the song accompanies the drums. In the blues this relation is reversed. First there is unaccompanied singing, then in the course of the development the instruments are added, but they are only accompaniment and the singing remains the most important part of the performance.

The texts of the blues follow the African narrative style almost entirely. They stem from the Afro-American ballads, which in turn continued the tradition of the African fable. 'In the fable', writes Senghor, 'the animal is seldom a totem; it is this or that one whom every one in the village knows well: the stupid or tyrannical or wise and good chief, the young man who makes reparation for injustice. Tales and fables are woven out of everyday occurrences. Yet it is not a question of anecdotes or of "material from life". The facts are images and have paradigmatic value.' [18] The boll weevil ballad, which comes from Texas, may serve as an example.[19] The weevil is the arch enemy of the cotton planter.

> Fahmah say to de weevil
> 'whut makes yore head so red',
> weevil say to de fahmah
> 'it's a wonder ah ain't dead,
> lookin' foh a home, lookin' for a home!'
>
> Nigger say to de weevil,
> 'ah'll throw yo in de hot san'!'
> Weevil say to de nigger
> 'ah'll stand it like a man,
> ah'll have a home, ah'll have a home!'
>
> Say de Capt'n to de Mistis
> 'what do you think ob dat?
> Dis Boll Weevil done make a nes'
> inside my Sunday hat;
> he will have a home, he'll have a home!'

The weevil, which bores into the bolls of cotton with its proboscis, is the plantation worker in his eternal search for a home. In the farmer's Sunday hat, his best piece of property, the weevil will have a home. Here again is the imperative future, which, in the form 'has made a nest', is set back into the perfect tense but means that the weevil *is to* make a nest there.[20] It is the same technique that Césaire uses. The ballad is a song that invokes liberation; in the most harmless fable it conceals the call to rebel.

The old ballad was later turned into a blues song, for the two types fade imperceptibly into one another. In the Boll Weevil Blues the weevil then becomes the living symbol of liberation.[21] The blues cannot therefore be reduced to the formula: 'a white song—black'; for both textual and musical structure stem from African traditions.

Nor are the blues 'sad', although the legend of 'melancholy' blues has been influential for a century and for a couple of decades there have in fact been melancholy blues. In accordance with the common view we do indeed find in the *Negro Caravan* of 1941 the statement: 'In contrast to the spirituals, which were originally intended for group singing, the blues are sung by a single person. They express his feelings and ideas about his experience, but they do this so fundamentally, in an idiom so recognizable to his audience, that this emotion is shared as theirs.' [22] But this is the exact contrary of the real situation.

For the blues singer does not in fact express *his* personal experiences and transfer them to his audience; on the contrary, it is the experiences of the community that he is expressing, making himself its spokesman.[23] Even when there is talk of loneliness, of the beloved who has run away, of the neglected wife, of nostalgia for the South, it is not the personal experience that is emphasized, but the typical experience of all those rejected by society in the Negro districts of the North. And even though indirectly, the note of rebellion is always heard too:

> I'd rather drink muddy water, sleep in a hollow log,
> dan to stay in dis town, treated like a dirty dog.[24]

The melancholy is a camouflage, the 'plaint' hides a *com*plaint.

If we read the text of the blues songs without prejudice and notice the double meaning, which all authors emphasize, we find them mocking, sarcastic, tragi-comic, tragic, dramatic and accusing, often crudely homorous— there is only one thing that they are only exceptionally, and then usually when they have been turned into a cabaret number, and that is—melancholy. Yet we read in the *Negro Caravan:* 'The mood is generally a sorrowful one; the word "blues" is part of the American vocabulary now as a synonym for melancholy, for unhappy moodiness.' [25] This widespread misinterpretation has various causes. The *blue notes* characteristic of the blues, which go back to the middle pitch of the West African tonal languages,[26] and have a modality between sharp and flat, sound sad to European ears. Besides, we are accustomed in Europe to interpret poetry and music psychologically as expressions of an individual soul. For African art, on the other hand, this means a confusion of means and meaning. Of the Afro-American *Work Songs,* which go back to the traditional form of communal work, and which are called *dokpwe* in Dahomey, *egbe* in Yoruba, *coumbite* in Haiti, *troca dia* in Brazil, and *gayap* in Trinidad, even Dauer writes: 'The basic law of the work song is to increase energy through music. Its effect consists in turning work into a kind of game or dance which in turn invokes an excitement that cannot be produced by pack mule work. This excitement increases energy and when reduced to a form that excludes all unnecessary movements itself becomes a driving force. The constant sequence of game and dance distracts the mind from the burdens of labour, the evenly rhythmic singing and playing becomes a (pretended) reality, work goes on automatically, and becomes subconscious.' [27] This interpretation of Dauer's correctly perceives the effects but not the causes. Song and dance do not have the purpose of lightening the work, but in song and dance Nommo is doing the real work, and conjuring up the latent forces of nature, while the work itself is only an addition.[28] The meaning of the work lies in the song and dance; they are not a purposive means for the end of lightening the work, even though their influence has that effect. The song is not an aid to the work, but the work an aid to the song.

The same is true of the blues. The blues are sung, not because one finds oneself in a particular mood, but because one wants to put oneself into a certain mood. The song is the Nommo which does not reflect but creates the mood. And this mood is melancholy only from the romantic point of view current since the time of the abolitionists. The picture of the poor slave full of yearning, singing his sad song, corresponded to the mood awakened by Harriet Beecher Stowe in *Uncle Tom's Cabin*. Much as we may admire the sentiments of the abolitionists, we must not overlook the fact that they saw the slaves as alienated, helpless beings who were longing for freedom but ought not to rebel: enslaved by white men, they should also be set free by them. So they were drawn as patiently suffering lambs, helpless, pitiable and sad. Help and support was to be given the slaves, but from agitators one kept one's distance and tried to pacify them. This attitude was apparent as late as the beginning of this century in the generous help that was given to the pacifist Booker T. Washington, while every possible obstacle was put in the way of W. E. B. DuBois, who made rigorous demands.

The abolitionists opposed their picture of the sad slave with his melancholy songs to the picture of the willing, confident, happy slave which the slave owners habitually drew. For the latter, the song of the disenfranchized sounded by no means melancholy; they considered it the expression of a carefree and happy mood. But both pictures are distorted. Frederick Douglass, the runaway slave, writes in his autobiography the telling sentences: 'The remark is not infrequently made, that slaves are the most contented and happy labourers in the world. They dance and sing, and make all manner of joyful noises—so they do; but it is a great mistake to suppose them happy because they sing. The songs of the slave represent the sorrows, rather than the joys, of his heart. Slaves sing to *make* themselves happy rather than to express their happiness through singing.' [29] The blues do not arise from a mood, but produce one. Like every art form in African culture song too is an attitude which effects something. The spiritual produces God, the secularized blues produce a mood. Even there residual-African Nommo is still effective.

## II. STATES OF CONFLICT

The blues lie at the boundary of African culture, where residual African elements pass over into American. They are always in danger of crossing the boundary but are held back by their musical traditions and mode of singing. Where, however, the song becomes a poem which is no longer sung, but written and printed, Africa is hardly even a memory. The poetry of the 'blues style' lives on both sides of the boundary. Often the 'I' no longer means a 'we,' and the exemplary expression on behalf of a community becomes the expression of individual feeling.[30]

Nevertheless the poetry stands closer to the African tradition than the prose. The Afro-American novelists have almost entirely adapted themselves to North American style. These writers often differ only in the colour of their skins from their European-American colleagues, and so the colour of their skin and the prejudice, contempt and oppression which accrue to them because of it form the theme of their books. The characters of their novels are split personalities who are struggling with their true selves and who furnish material for the widespread view that a split personality results from the conflict of two cultures.

It is not in the United States, however, where with a few exceptions only vestiges of African culture are still alive, and where even these are becoming more and more adapted to western forms—it is not there that two cultures come into conflict, but in Africa. In Africa men with European education do indeed stand between the civilizations.

> I'm tired
> I'm tired of hanging in the middle way
> —but where can I go? [31]

writes the Nigerian poetess Mabel Imoukhuede. And the Ghanaian Dei-Anang says:

> Here we stand—
> poised between two civilisations
> Backward? To days of drums

And festal dances in the shade
Of sun-kist palms.
Or forward?
Forward!
Toward?
The slums, where man is dumped upon man? . . .
The factory
To grind hard hours
In an inhuman mill
In one long ceaseless spell? [32]

This either-or is usually put before the African by the European with the demand that he make up his mind; and since there can be no turning back, he expects the answer that will make the African his pupil. This question corresponds to the schema which we mentioned at the beginning of our argument.[33] But the question is falsely put. Césaire said of it at the first world congress of Negro writers in Paris: 'They demand of us: "Choose . . . choose between loyalty, and with it backwardness, or progress and rupture." Our reply is that things are not so simple, that there is no alternative. That life (I say life and not abstract thought) does not know and does not accept this alternative. Or rather that if this alternative presents itself, it is life that will take care of its transcendence. We say that it is not only black societies that have to face this problem; that in every society there is always an equilibrium, always precarious, always in need of remaking, and in practice always remade by every generation between the new and the old. And that our black societies, our civilizations, our cultures will not escape from this rule. For our part and for that of our particular societies, we believe that in the African culture to come or in the para-African culture to come, there will be many new elements, modern elements, elements if you like borrowed from Europe. But we believe also that there will survive in that culture many traditional elements. We refuse to surrender to the temptation of the *tabula rasa*. I refuse to believe that the African culture of the future can oppose an end of total and brutal non-acceptance to the ancient culture of Africa. And to illustrate what I have just been saying permit me to use a parable. The anthropologists have described what one of them proposes to call cultural fatigue. The example that they cite deserves to be recalled, for that example rises to the level of a symbol. This is the story: it takes place in the Hawaian Islands. Some years after the discovery of the islands by Cook, the king died and was replaced by a young man, the prince Kamehameha II. Won over to European ideas, the young prince decided to abolish the ancestral religion. It was agreed between the new king and the high priest that a great festival would be organized and in the course of the ceremonies the taboo would be solemnly broken and the ancestral gods annulled. On the appointed day, at a sign from the king, the high priest hurled himself upon the divine images, trod them under foot, and broke them, while a great cry was heard: the taboo is broken. Several years later the Hawaians did indeed welcome the Christian missionaries with open arms. The sequel is known. It is the most complete case that we know of a cultural subversion preparing the way for enslavement. And then I ask if that renunciation by a people of its past, of its culture, is what they expect of us? I say simply: among us there will be no Kamehameha II!' [34]

Accordingly, African literature takes issue with the age, follows the traditional style even in European languages, and as we have shown in the chapters on Nommo and Kuntu in the cases of Tutuola and Laye, assimilates European elements to the African conception. In Peter Abrahams, Ferdinand Oyono, Mongo Beti and many others there may be passionate discussion of an African revival, of technology, progress and independence and of the place of tradition within the synthesis still to be produced—but the human being always remains sound. There is much talk to the effect that the African has been uprooted through the intrusion of western civilization—but the literature shows little indication of this. The African suffers, fights, rebels, seeks new paths, but he is not neurotic. There is a division of choice, an uncertainty of content, but existence is not split apart. Even where the traditional social order is shattered, where as in the slums of Johannesburg a new black proletariat has grown up, the individuals themselves have for the most part remained sound and well. Peter Abrahams, the great South African writer, in his novel *Mine Boy,* describes how an African woman named Leah fights for her existence against the inhuman oppression of apartheid. One night a stranger stands at her door seeking shelter. Abrahams characterizes the figures in brief dialogue: ' "Sister, do you know a place where a man can rest and maybe have a drink?" His voice is deep and husky. "It is late," the woman replied. "It is very late," the man said. "Make a light for me to see you," the woman said. "I have no matches." "What have you?" "Nothing." "And you want to rest and drink when it is so late?" The man inclined his head, but the woman could not see in the dark. "Have you money?" "No." "Huh. You're a queer one. What are you called? Are you new here?" "Xuma. I come from the North." "Well, Xuma from the North, stay here and I will be back with a light." ' [35] After the light has tested him Xuma from the North is given shelter in the house in which Leah is in charge of several people. ' "Then you can go to sleep," Leah said. Dladla and Ma Plank went out. Only the man who had been silent throughout remained. He looked at Leah and then at Xuma.

"What is it?" Leah asked him. "How do we know he's not from the police?" "I know," Leah replied and her whole face creased in a smile.' [36]

Psychological explanations are not necessary. Soul image and apparent image are identical, the meaning is revealed in the sign. Personalities recognize one another, and the boundaries are clearly marked. The conversation comes around to Leah's husband. ' "Yes," she repeated softly. "My man. He's in jail. He's been there for one year, and he must stay there for another two years. He killed a man. A big man with a big mouth who tried to kiss me. He is strong, my man, and he fights for his woman, and he kills for his woman. Not like Dladla who is all mouth and knife and nothing. He's a man, my man. You are a man yourself, Xuma, you are strong. But my man can break you like a stick! I don't lie, you can ask people . . . Here," said Leah, going into the little room, "this is where the teacher lives but she will not come till day after tomorrow so you can sleep here." She struck a match and lit the candle. "And listen to me Xuma from the North, don't you think because I do this I am soft or easy and you can cheat me, because if you do, I will cut you up so that your own mother will not want you . . ." Xuma laughed. "You are a strange woman. I don't understand you. The only thing I can understand is your kindness." "You're all right," she said softly. "But the city is a strange place. Good night." ' [37]

The people in Abrahams' novel are fighting against race madness and against oppression but they have no inferiority complex. They move from the country to the city, from village society to industrial society, as one exchanges a loin cloth for an overall. They remain the people they are, retain their values and their style, even if the struggle for existence forces on them new rules of play. They assert themselves in race society but do not accept it. There is no part of them which admits the rightness of their oppressors; if they defend themselves their consciences are clear. They are far from the dividedness of the coloured North Americans. Mofolo admired the white man's notions and rejected the African tradition. Recent African writers do not do this. Peter Abrahams describes the forces which are creating in Africa a modern, but an African society. The whites are for him not gods but fellow human beings, whose technology one accepts and whose arrogance one rejects. The cultural conflict that characterizes Africa today does not produce any split in consciousness. The slogan of the 'dividedness of the African' is wrong. The African writer who writes in a European language is not a divided person. He uses the freedom to choose one, another or any of a thousand hybrid forms, and by his decision brings past and future each time into harmony. Every decision is a weighing up, a compromise, a harmonization of contradictories.

Thus split consciousness and all the problems connected with it arise not in African writers but in the works of those Afro-Americans who know no conflict of cultures and to whom the freedom of choice is therefore denied. For centuries Afro-Americans have had no direct contact with African culture. In tradition, education and mother tongue they are Americans and do not want to be anything else. But the full citizenship of their homeland is denied them. Their colour, which alone is reminiscent of their African descent, becomes a stain which prevents their being entirely what they in fact are, namely Americans. They protest against the unjust prejudices of their lighter skinned fellow citizens, in order to become their equals —that is, in order to share their prejudices. Their situation is tragic. There is no alternative, no possibility of a choice, of a decision. Since only their skins prevent them from being Americans like other Americans, and since they are nevertheless Americans, they would like most of all to get rid of this burdensome skin of theirs. Therefore the hatred they feel against the resistance of their environment easily becomes hatred of their own skins, hatred of themselves. Added to this is the fact that their prejudiced neighbours are unwilling to see them as Americans, but see them as American Negroes, as people who are supposed to behave childishly, deferentially, and above all submissively—a type of behaviour which contradicts the democratic American attitude. Thus a role is forced on the Afro-American: he is supposed to be someone other than himself: a 'nigger' instead of an American—and he himself wants to be someone else, namely a light-skinned rather than a dark-skinned American. The role that he has to play revolts him and the role he wants to play he is not allowed to play, yet plays it all the more. So we find in Afro-American literature countless examples of split personalities. The Afro-American flees from the role forced on him into a thousand other roles, and changes his personality, the identity of his 'I', until the individual becomes invisible.

In his autobiography *Black Boy*,[38] Richard Wright shows how from childhood on an unnatural role is forced on the young Afro-American. In Ellison's novel *Invisible Man* there is a passage in which the narrator buys a pair of green sun-glasses and a big hat and so to his amazement falls into the role of another person, which he plays with effortless perfection.[39] When he is disguised the question of the identity of the person arises, and that means, it is placed in doubt. But the role one plays, so easily interchangeable, is what others see. The person behind the role, Ellison believes, is invisible. Everyone sees into the other person what he wants to see, but never the reality. The *designation of the person* has lost its sense and meaning: still a force, it becomes negative. It is as if 'wizards' were at work: instead of constituting personalities, unauthorized 'designators' have pushed man into the shadow-existence of a role and so dissolved his identity.

The same thing happens in the novel *Go Tell it on the Mountain* by James Baldwin. After a knifing a young man is brought wounded to his parents' house. But the father refuses to see that this son Roy, whom he loves, has brought the danger on himself, directs his reproaches against the brother John and slaps the mother when she defends her boy. Then the wounded Roy sits up and shouts at his father: ' "Don't you slap my mother. That's my mother. You slap her again, you black bastard, and I swear to God I'll kill you." In the moment that these words filled the room, John and his father were staring into each other's eyes. John thought for that moment that his father believed the words had come from him, his eyes were so wild and depthlessly malevolent.' [40]

Again the confusion of identity and also the hatred for one's own self. It is not enough that others strike one, one must strike oneself also. This dividedness cannot be ignored in any of these Afro-American writers. Alston Anderson writes about the two I's in his story 'Schooltime in North Carolina'. The pupil La Verne is lying in bed and thinking of his sweetheart, the coloured girl Del, but the image of the white founder of the school, Susanne Weber, becomes confused with her in his imagination: 'I'd try hard to see Del but I couldn't so I'd open my eyes and stare into the dark. When I closed them again I could see myself as Susanne Weber's husband but that wasn't the black me but the white me with wavy black hair and sideburns and a full dress suit.' [41]

Disunited with himself under the pressure of prejudice, the Afro-American is in a hopeless situation. Richard Wright gives one of the clearest pictures of this in his novel *Black Boy*. The young Richard has taken the liberty of asking his white overseers when he could learn something about the work. 'This is a white man's work around here,' is their answer, and from now on they persecute him with their hate. 'The climax came at noon one summer day. Pease called me to his workbench; to get to him I had to go between two narrow benches and stand with my back against a wall. "Richard, I want to ask you something," Pease began pleasantly, not looking up from his work. "Yes, Sir." Reynolds came over and stood blocking the narrow passage between the benches; he folded his arms and stared at me solemnly. I looked from one to the other, sensing trouble. Pease looked up and spoke slowly, so there would be no possibility of my not understanding. "Richard, Reynolds here tells me that you called me Pease," he said. I stiffened. A void opened up in me. I knew that this was the showdown. He meant that I had failed to call him Mr. Pease. I looked at Reynolds; he was gripping a steelbar in his hand. I opened my mouth to speak, to protest, to assure Pease that I never called him simply Pease, and that I never had any intention of doing so, when Reynolds grabbed me by the collar, ramming my head against the wall. "Now, be careful, nigger," snarled Reynolds, baring his teeth. "I heard you call 'im Pease. And if you say you didn't, you're calling me a liar, see?" He waved the steel bar threateningly. If I said: No, sir, Mr. Pease, I never called you Pease, I would by inference have been calling Reynolds a liar; and if I had said: Yes, sir, Mr. Pease, I called you Pease, I would have been pleading guilty to the worst insult that a Negro can offer to a southern white man. I stood trying to think of a neutral course that would resolve this quickly risen nightmare, but my tongue would not move.' [42]

The situation of the Afro-Americans in the United States is hopeless because for the most part they are distinguished from other Americans only by the colour of their skins, and often hardly by this, since 'the "Negro race" is', as Gunnar Myrdal writes in his important investigation sponsored by the Carnegie Foundation, *An American Dilemma,* 'defined in America by the white people. It is defined in terms of parentage. Everybody having a known trace of Negro blood in his veins—no matter how far back it was acquired—is classified as a Negro. Legislation in this respect tends to conform to social usage, although often it is not so exclusive. In some states one Negro grandparent defines a person as a Negro for legal purposes, in other states any Negro ancestor—no matter how far removed—is sufficient.' [43] Most of these 'Negroes' have entirely relinquished their African cultural heritage. There is no conflict of cultures and the 'race question' has to do with African culture only insofar as prejudices about it play a role in the debate. The problem itself belongs to western culture and can be resolved only within it. A book which has the aim of defining and describing African culture can dispense with its analysis. It offers a contribution to this problem only insofar as it shows that culture has nothing to do with 'race'. If African culture were tied to skin colour, the Afro-Americans would not be able to give up African culture and one would be able to see by the shade of each of them whether he belonged to African culture or not. When the Afro-American Richard Wright had visited Ghana, he wrote in the account of his journey, *Black Power,* 'I was black and they were black but it didn't help me.' [44] With as little understanding as any white-skinned American he stood before the Africans and their culture. It is therefore idle to make him, as so often happens, a star witness for African relations simply because of his colour.

Nothing shows more clearly than the North American 'Negro problem' that culture is not tied to chromosomes. Therefore one should not try to trace the character of African culture back either to physical or even psychological traits of the black race. Since history offers countless examples of the fact that on the one hand culture can be carried over and passed on, and that on the other hand it changes with the transformation of thought, the 'how', the Kuntu of a culture cannot be derived from the psychology of its bearers. When Senghor writes that the Negro is a sensual person, a being with open senses, that he is first of all sense, smells, rhythms, forms and colours, that he is sensation before vision as the white European is,[45] this attitude is indeed explicable as a consequence of African culture and the forming force of its style, but not as the physio-psychological cause of African culture, as Senghor suggests; for then the attitude would be a property, which could not be lost. For the analysis of African culture which Senghor presents, it is immaterial whether the attitude of the African is formed by the culture, or whether the culture arose from an attitude. Senghor would not really need to work with a false premise, for it changes nothing in his results. Since the attitude is directly derivable from the philosophy of the culture, there is no reason to reduce it to undemonstrable 'racial' characters. For the answer to the question why African philosophy and culture differ from other cultures, there are enough historical reasons which could be investigated, for one to do without physio-psychological arguments which are on the one hand vague and on the other dangerous.

## III. EUROPE, THE PARTNER

'It is a fact: the whites consider themselves superior to the blacks,' states Frantz Fanon. This proposition is indeed a generalization, yet unfortunately in most cases Fanon is right. This arrogant assumption is sometimes given a 'racial', sometimes a cultural, basis. The racial arrogance is easy to refute but hard to combat, since the majority of those who suffer from it are scarcely accessible to rational arguments. The cultural arrogance—which we must clearly distinguish from the self-consciousness which every culture needs and develops—is indeed hard to refute, so long as there is no universal standard for cultures and each, as we said at the outset, is superior to every other by its own standard; yet to objective argumentation this form of arrogance is less deaf. Only it is often unaware of itself and is frequently to be found in people who reject every form of arrogance. It is too easily hidden behind good will, unasked-for advice, or patronizing instruction.

In a world in which more than ever before everyone depends on everyone else, true partnership is a necessity of the hour and of reason. But it can come about only if every culture allows to every other its own unique nature and reciprocal influences and borrowings voluntarily follow. The attempt to force on others the acceptance of one's own views, forms of life and judgment, instead of simply offering it to them, lies so deep in the nature of western culture and of all its ideologies, that the hurtful presumption of such an attitude, especially towards Africans, is something of which the

European is often unaware. 'I am the Lord and thou shalt! . . .'—so speaks in effect, the military commander, the merchant, the farmer, the tourist, the big-game hunter, the dogma salesman. So they speak, whether they want to exploit Africa or to save her. They go along and teach and baptize in the name of the Father, in the name of civilization, in the name of democracy, in the name of communism.

And the one who is addressed, the African, is asked no questions. Freedom? Equal rights? 'Yes, but only when you have been baptized in the name of Christianity, in the name of civilization, in the name of economics, in the name of democracy, in the name of communism'—according to the particular faith in question. For all these Gods are the children of the one who says: 'I am the Lord . . . and thou shalt!'

Plans are elaborated, programmes made, books written as to what is to happen to Africa, how it should be opened up, in what direction it should be led. But the Africans are for the most part ignored. Nearly everyone who writes, speaks, arranges, recommends—disposes of them, because he thinks: 'I am . . . and thou shalt!'

'A true Copernican revolution must be imposed here,' writes Aimé Césaire, 'so much is rooted in Europe, and in all parties, in all spheres, from the extreme right to the extreme left, the habit of doing for us, the habit of arranging for us, the habit of thinking for us, in short the habit of contesting that right to initiative which is in essence the right to personality.' [47]

In their rejection of this constant guardianship neo-African writers have written many lines which scarcely sound flattering to European ears. Yet we find in neo-African poetry and literature less hatred and more co-operation than the state of things would lead us to expect. Neo-African intelligence, for all the self-consciousness with which it defends its own character, has not produced an opposing arrogance of 'racial' or cultural colour. The polytheistic basis of their culture permits them to be more patient towards foreign gods. And even where hatred is heard, it is in many cases love turned to its opposite. Thus the Barbadian writer George Lamming makes a labourer who hates the English as representative of all Europeans confess: '. . . if they'd just show one sign of friendship, just a little sign of appreciation for people like me an' you who from the time we born, in school an' after school, we wus hearin' about them, if they could understan' that an' be different, then all the hate you talk 'bout would disappear . . .' [48]

On the European side, if we leave aside those who are protecting vested interests, there is more ignorance than ill-will in the case. Europe has not yet played out all her sympathies. Guardianship can still be changed to partnership. But there does not seem to be much time left for this. Lamming makes his labourer say: '. . . because we'd be remembering that for genera-

tions an' generations we'd been offerin' them a love they never even try to
return. 'Tis why colonial wars will be de bloodiest . . .' [49]

Where the problems of neo-African culture are discussed, in the periodical *Présence-Africaine* in Paris, founded and edited by the Senegalese
Alioune Diop, in the world congresses of black writers and artists convoked
every second year by that periodical, in the poems, novels and essays of all
the poets who are at the same time active politically, and of all the politicians who are at the same time poets and whom we have presented in this
volume, the demands are moderate but firm. Over nearly all their publications and speeches stand as it were the verses of Césaire:

> . . . my heart, preserve me from all hatred,
> do not make of me that man of hate for whom I have but hate . . .
> you know that it is not through hate of other races
> that I make myself a digger . . .[49]

These are verses in which we hear self-control, but also concern lest the
partnership striven for fail through the hardness of folly of the other side,
and so force hatred to break out.

## NOTES

[1] Knesebeck, Paridam, *Spirituals,* München, 1955, p. 80.

[2] Cf. Simmel, Oskar, and Stählin, Rudolf, *Christliche Religion,* Frankfurt am Main,
1957, p. 111.

[3] Brooks, Gwendolyn, *A Street in Bronzeville,* New York and London, 1945, p. 13.

[4] Cf. Ch. 2, pp. 39 f.

[5] Cf. Ch. 3, p. 63 and Ch. 4, p. 115.

[6] Cf. Ch. 6, p. 157.

[7] Cf. Verger, Pierre, *Dieux d'Afrique,* Paris, 1954.

[8] Baldwin, James, *Go Tell it on the Mountain,* New York (1952), 1954, p. 59.

[9] Dauer, Alfons M., *Der Jazz, seine Ursprünge und seine Entwicklung,* Kassel, 1958,
p. 61.

[10] *ibid.,* p. 59.

[11] *ibid.,* p. 183.

[12] *ibid.,* p. 63.

[13] Cf. *ibid.,* p. 64.

[14] Berendt, Joachim Ernest, *Blues,* München, 1957, p. 11; *also see* Knesebeck, *op. cit.*

[15] Cf. *ibid.,* p. 12.

[16] Dauer, Alfons M., *Knaurs Jazz-Lexikon,* München, 1957, p. 53.

[17] Dauer, *Der Jazz, op. cit.,* p. 74.

[18] Senghor, Léopold Sédar, 'L'esprit de la civilisation ou les lois de la culture négro-
africaine', in *Présence Africaine* VIII-X, Paris, 1956.

[19] Original in Dauer, *Der Jazz,* pp. 146 f.

20 Cf. Ch. 5, pp. 136 f.

21 Dauer, *Der Jazz,* p. 60.

22 Brown, Sterling A., Davis, Arthur P., and Lee, Ulysses, *The Negro Caravan,* New York, 1941, p. 426.

23 Cf. Ch. 5, p. 149.

24 Brown-Davis-Lee, *op. cit.,* p. 429.

25 *ibid.,* p. 426.

26 Dauer, *Der Jazz,* p. 31.

27 *ibid.,* p. 53.

28 Cf. Ch. 5, pp. 124 ff.

29 Douglass quoted from Brown-Davis-Lee, p. 726.

30 Cf. Ch. 7, pp. 201 f.

31 Imoukhuede (Manuscript), German translation in Jahn, Janheinz, *Schwarzer Orpheus,* München (1954), 1955.

32 Dei-Anang, M. F., *Wayward Lines from Africa,* London and Redhill, 1946, pp. 23 f.

33 Cf. Ch. 1, pp. 11 f.

34 Césaire, Aimé, 'Culture et Colonisation', in *Présence Africaine* VIII-X, Paris, 1956, pp. 203 f.

35 Abrahams, Peter, *Mine Boy,* London (1946), 1954, pp. 11 f.

36 *ibid.,* p. 15.

37 *ibid.,* p. 17.

38 Cf. Wright, Richard, *Black Boy,* Cleveland (Ohio), 1945, pp. 59 f. and 160 ff.

39 Ellison, Ralph, *Invisible Man,* New York, 1947, p. 489.

40 Baldwin, *op. cit.,* p. 43.

41 Anderson, MS, also Anderson, Alston, *Lover Man,* London, 1959, p. 95, where the two selves are missing—at publisher's request?

42 Wright, *Black Boy, op. cit.,* pp. 164 ff.

43 Myrdal, Gunnar, *An American Dilemma,* New York-London, 1944.

44 Wright, Richard, *Black Power,* London, 1954, p. 123.

45 Senghor, *op. cit.,* p. 52.

46 Fanon, Frantz, *Peau Noire Masques Blancs,* Paris, 1952, p. 26.

47 Césaire, Aimé, *Lettre à Maurice Thorez,* Paris, 1956, pp. 12 f.

48 Lamming, George, *The Emigrants,* London, 1954, p. 186.

49 *loc. cit.*

*"The Middle Passage" taken from the 19th century memoir,* The Adventures of an African Slaver, *views the slave trade from the perspective of one who profited from commercialized bondage. The author justifies his role by placing the most favorable interpretation on the slave system. Read in conjunction with Pope-Hennessy's recent account, however, a more balanced picture emerges. Taken alone, it is the essence of justificatory autobiography.*

# The Middle Passage

## Theodore Canot

The 15th of March, 1827, was an epoch in my life. I remember it well, because it became the turning point of my destiny. A few weeks more of indolence might have forced me back to Europe or America, but the fortune of that day decided my residence and dealings in Africa.

At dawn of the 15th, a vessel was descried in the offing, and as she approached the coast, the initiated soon ascertained her to be a Spanish slaver. But what was the amazement of the river grandees when the captain landed and consigned his vessel to me!

*La Fortuna,* the property, chiefly, of my old friend the Regla grocer, was successor of the *Aerostatico,* which she exceeded in size as well as comfort. Her captain was charged to pay me my wages in full for the round voyage in the craft I had abandoned, and handed me besides a purse of thirty doubloons as a testimonial from his owners for my defence of their property on the dreadful night of our arrival. The *Fortuna* was dispatched to me for an "assorted cargo of slaves," while 200,000 cigars and 500 ounces of Mexican gold were on board for their purchase. My commission was fixed at ten per cent, and I was promised a command whenever I saw fit to abandon my residence on the African coast.

Having no factory, or barracoon of slaves, and being elevated to the dignity of a trader in so sudden a manner, I thought it best to summon all the factors of the river on board the schooner, with an offer to divide the cargo, provided they would pledge the production of the slaves within thirty days. Dispatch was all-important to the owners, and so anxious was

I to gratify them, that I consented to pay fifty dollars for every slave accepted.

After some discussion my offer was taken, and the cargo apportioned among the residents. They declined, however, receiving any share of the cigars in payment, insisting on liquidation in gold alone.

As this was my first enterprise, I felt at a loss to know how to convert my useless tobacco into merchantable doubloons. In this strait, I had recourse to the Englishman Joseph, who hitherto traded exclusively in produce; but being unable to withstand the temptation of gold, had consented to furnish a portion of my required negroes. As soon as I stated the difficulty to Don Edward, he proposed to send the Havanas to his Hebrew friend in Sierra Leone, where he did not doubt they would be readily exchanged for Manchester merchandise. That evening a canoe was dispatched to the English colony with the cigars; and on the tenth day after, the trusty Israelite appeared in the Rio Pongo, with a cutter laden to the deck with superior British fabrics. The rumor of five hundred doubloons disturbed his rest in Sierra Leone. So much gold could not linger in the hands of natives as long as Manchester and Birmingham were represented in the colony; and accordingly he coasted the edge of the surf, as rapidly as possible, to pay me a profit of four dollars a thousand for the cigars, and to take his chances at the exchange of my gold for the sable cargo. By this happy hit I was enabled to pay for the required balance of negroes, as well as to liquidate the schooner's expenses while in the river. I was amazingly rejoiced and proud at this happy result, because I learned from the captain that the invoice of cigars was a malicious trick, palmed off on the *Aerostatico's* owners by her captain in order to thwart or embarrass me, when he heard I was to be intrusted with the purchase of a cargo on the coast.

At the appointed day, *La Fortuna* sailed with 220 human beings packed in her hold. Three months afterwards, I received advices that she safely landed 217 in the bay of Matanzas, and that their sale yielded a clear profit on the voyage of forty-one thousand four hundred and thirty-eight dollars.*

An African factor of fair repute is ever careful to select his human cargo with consummate prudence, so as not only to supply his employers with athletic labourers, but to avoid any taint of disease that may affect the slaves in their transit to Cuba or the American main. Two days before embarkation, the head of every male and female is neatly shaved; and, if the cargo belongs to several owners, each man's *brand* is impressed on the body of his respective negro. This operation is performed with pieces of silver wire, or small irons fashioned into the merchant's initials, heated just hot enough to blister without burning the skin. When the entire cargo is the venture of but one proprietor, the branding is always dispensed with.

On the appointed day, the barracoon or slave-pen is made joyous by the abundant "feed" which signalises the negro's last hours in his native country. The feast over, they are taken alongside the vessel in canoes; and as they touch the deck, they are entirely stripped, so that women as well as men go out of Africa as they came into it—naked. This precaution, it will be understood, is indispensable; for perfect nudity, during the whole voyage, is the only means of securing cleanliness and health. In this state, they are immediately ordered below, the men to the hold and the women to the cabin, while boys and girls are, day and night, kept on deck, where their sole protection from the elements is a sail in fair weather, and a tarpaulin in foul.

At meal time they are distributed in messes of ten. Thirty years ago, when the Spanish slave trade was lawful, the captains were somewhat more ceremoniously religious than at present, and it was then a universal habit to make the gangs say grace before meat, and give thanks afterwards. In our days, however, they dispense with this ritual, and content themselves with a "Viva la Habana," or "hurrah for Havana," accompanied by a clapping of hands.

This over, a bucket of salt water is served to each mess, by way of "finger glasses" for the ablution of hands, after which a kidd—either of rice, farina, yams, or beans, according to the tribal habit of the negroes—is placed before the squad. In order to prevent greediness or inequality in the appropriation of nourishment, the process is performed by signals from a monitor, whose motions indicate when the darkies shall dip and when they shall swallow.

It is the duty of a guard to report immediately whenever a slave refuses to eat, in order that his abstinence may be traced to stubbornness or disease. Negroes have sometimes been found in slavers who attempted voluntary starvation; so that when the watch reports the patient to be shamming, his appetite is stimulated by the medical antidote of a cat. If the slave, however, is truly ill, he is forthwith ticketed for the sick-list by a bead or button around his neck, and dispatched to an infirmary in the forecastle.

These meals occur twice daily—at ten in the morning and four in the afternoon—and are terminated by another ablution. Thrice in each twenty-four hours they are served with half a pint of water. Pipes and tobacco are circulated economically among both sexes; but as each negro cannot be allowed the luxury of a separate bowl, boys are sent round with an adequate supply, allowing a few whiffs to each individual. On regular days—probably three times a week—their mouths are carefully rinsed with vinegar, while, nearly every morning, a dram is given as an antidote to scurvy.

Although it is found necessary to keep the sexes apart, they are allowed to converse freely during day while on deck. Corporal punishment is never inflicted save by order of an officer, and even then, not until the culprit understands exactly why it is done. Once a week, the ship's barber scrapes their chins without assistance from soap; and on the same day their nails are closely pared, to insure security from harm in those nightly battles that occur, when the slave contests with his neighbour every inch of plank to which he is glued. During afternoons of serene weather, men, women, girls, and boys are allowed to unite in African melodies, which they always enhance by an extemporaneous tom-tom on the bottom of a tub or tin kettle.

The greatest care, compatible with safety, is taken of a negro's health and cleanliness on the voyage. In every well-conducted slaver, the captain, officers, and crew, are alert and vigilant to preserve the cargo. It is their personal interest, as well as the interest of humanity, to do so. The boatswain is incessant in his patrol of purification, and disinfecting substances are plenteously distributed. The upper deck is washed and swabbed daily; the slave deck is scraped and holystoned; and, at nine o'clock each morning, the captain inspects every part of his craft; so that no vessel, except a man-of-war, can compare with a slaver in systematic order, purity, and neatness. I am not aware that the ship-fever, which sometimes decimates the emigrants from Europe, has ever prevailed in these African traders.

At sundown, the process of stowing the slaves for the night is begun. The second mate and boatswain descend into the hold, whip in hand, and range the slaves in their regular places; those on the right side of the vessel facing forward and lying in each other's lap, while those on the left are similarly stowed with their faces towards the stern. In this way each negro lies on his right side, which is considered preferable for the action of the heart. In allotting places, particular attention is paid to size, the taller being selected for the greatest breadth of the vessel, while the shorter and younger are lodged near the bows. When the cargo is large and the lower deck crammed, the supernumeraries are disposed of on deck, which is securely covered with boards to shield them from moisture. The strict discipline of nightly stowage is of the greatest importance in slavers, else every negro would accommodate himself as if he were a passenger.

In order to insure perfect silence and regularity during the night, a slave is chosen as constable from every ten, and furnished with a cat to enforce commands during his appointed watch. In remuneration for his services, which are admirably performed whenever the whip is required, he is adorned with an old shirt or tarry trowsers. Now and then, billets of wood are distributed among the sleepers, but this luxury is never granted until the good temper of the negroes is ascertained, for slaves have often been tempted to mutiny by the power of arming themselves with these pillows from the forest.

It is very probable that many of my readers will consider it barbarous to make slaves lie down naked upon a board, but let me inform them that native Africans are not familiar with the use of feather-beds, nor do any but the free and rich in their mother country indulge in the luxury even of a mat or raw-hide. Among the Mandingo chiefs—the most industrious and civilized of Africans—the beds, divans, and sofas, are heaps of mud, covered with untanned skins for cushions, while logs of wood serve for bolsters. I am of opinion, therefore, that emigrant slaves experience very slight inconvenience in lying down on deck.

But ventilation is carefully attended to. The hatches and bulkheads of every slaver are grated, and apertures are cut about the deck for ampler circulation of air. Wind-sails, too, are constantly pouring a steady draft into the hold, except during a chase, when every comfort is temporarily sacrificed for safety. During calms or in light and baffling winds, when the suffocating air of the tropics makes ventilation impossible, the gratings are always removed, and portions of the slaves allowed to repose at night on deck, while the crew is armed to watch the sleepers.

Handcuffs are rarely used on shipboard. It is the common custom to secure slaves in the barracoons, and while shipping, by chaining ten in a gang; but as these platoons would be extremely inconvenient at sea, the manacles are immediately taken off and replaced by leg-irons, which fasten them in pairs by the feet. Shackles are never used but for full-grown men, while women and boys are set at liberty as soon as they embark. It frequently happens that when the behaviour of male slaves warrants their freedom, they are released from all fastenings long before they arrive. Irons are altogether dispensed with on many Brazilian slavers, as negroes from Anjuda, Benin, and Angola, are mild, and unaddicted to revolt like those who dwell east of the Cape or north of the Gold Coast. Indeed, a knowing trader will never use chains but when compelled; for, the longer a slave is ironed, the more he deteriorates.

In old times, before treaties made the slave-trade piracy, the landing of human cargoes was as comfortably conducted as the disembarkation of flour. But now, the enterprise is effected with secrecy and hazard. A wild, uninhabited portion of the coast, where some little bay or sheltering nook exists, is commonly selected by the captain and his confederates. As soon as the vessel is driven close to the beach and anchored, her boats are packed with slaves, while the craft is quickly dismantled to avoid detection from sea or land. The busy skiffs are hurried to and fro incessantly till the cargo is entirely ashore, when the secured gang, led by the captain and escorted by armed sailors, is rapidly marched to the nearest plantation. There it is safe from the rapacity of local magistrates, who, if they have a chance, imitate their superiors by exacting "gratifications."

In the meantime, a courier has been dispatched to the owners in Havana, Matanzas, or Santiago de Cuba, who immediately post to the plantation with clothes for the slaves and gold for the crew. Preparations are quickly made through brokers for the sale of the blacks; while the vessel, if small, is disguised, to warrant her return under the coasting flag to a port of clearance. If the craft happens to be large, it is considered perilous to attempt a return with a cargo, or "in distress." Accordingly, she is either sunk or burnt where she lies.

When the genuine African reaches a plantation for the first time, he fancies himself in a paradise. He is amazed by the generosity with which he is fed with fruit and fresh provisions. His new clothes, red cap, and roasting blanket (a civilized superfluity he never dreamed of) strike him dumb with delight, and in his savage joy, he not only forgets country, relations, and friends, but skips about like a monkey, while he dons his garments wrongside out or hind-part before. The arrival of a carriage or cart creates no little confusion among the Ethiopian groups, who never imagined that beasts could be made to work. But the climax of wonder is reached when that paragon of oddities, a Cuban postilion, dressed in his sky-blue coat, silver-laced hat, white breeches, polished jack-boots, and ringing spurs, leaps from his prancing quadruped, and bids them welcome in their mother tongue. Every African rushes to "snap fingers" with his equestrian brother, who, according to orders, forthwith preaches an edifying sermon on the happiness of being a white man's slave, taking care to jingle his spurs and crack his whip at the end of every sentence, by way of amen.

Whenever a cargo is owned by several proprietors, each one takes his share at once to his plantation; but if it is the property of speculators, the blacks are sold to any one who requires them before removal from the original depot. The sale is conducted as rapidly as possible, to forestall the interference of British officials with the Captain-General.

Many of the Spanish governors in Cuba have respected treaties or at least have promised to enforce the laws. Squadrons of dragoons and troops of lancers have been paraded with convenient delay, and ordered to gallop to plantations designated by the representative of England. It generally happens, however, that when the hunters arrive the game is gone. Scandal declares that while brokers are selling the blacks at the depot, it is not unusual for their owner or his agent to be found knocking at the door of the Captain-General's secretary. It is even said that the Captain-General himself is sometimes present in the sanctuary, and after a familiar chat about the happy landing of "the contraband," as the traffic is amiably called, the requisite *rouleaux* are insinuated into the official desk under the intense smoke of a *cigarillo*. The metal is always considered the property of the Captain-General, but his scribe avails himself of a lingering farewell at the door, to hint an immediate and pressing need for "a very small darkey." Next day the diminutive African does not appear; but, as it is believed that Spanish officials prefer gold even to mortal flesh, his algebraic equivalent is unquestionably furnished in the shape of shining ounces.

The prompt dispatch I gave the schooner *Fortuna* started new ideas among the traders of the Rio Pongo, so that it was generally agreed my method of dividing the cargo among different factors was not only most advantageous for speed, but prevented monopoly and gave all an equal chance. At a "grand palaver" or assemblage of the traders on the river, it was resolved that this should be the course for trade for the future. All the factors except Ormond attended and assented; but we learned that the Mongo's people with difficulty prevented him from sending an armed party to break up our deliberations.

The knowledge of this hostile feeling soon spread throughout the settlement and adjacent towns, creating considerable excitement against Ormond. My plan and principles were approved by the natives as well as foreigners, so that warning was sent the Mongo, if any harm befell Joseph and Theodore, it would be promptly resented. Our native landlord Ali Ninpha, a Foulah by descent, told him boldly, in presence of his people, that the Africans were "tired of a mulatto Mongo"; and from that day his power dwindled away visibly, though a show of respect was kept up in consequence of his age and ancient importance.

During these troubles, the *Aerostatico* returned to my consignment, and in twenty-two days was dispatched with a choice cargo of Mandingos— a tribe which had become fashionable for house servants among the Havanese. But the luckless vessel was never heard of, and it is likely she went down in some of the gales that scourged the coast immediately after her departure.

## NOTES

* As the reader may scarcely credit so large a profit, I subjoin an account of the fitting of a slave vessel from Havana in 1827, and the liquidation of her voyage in Cuba:—

### 1.—Expenses Out

| | | |
|---|---|---|
| Cost of *La Fortuna,* a 90-ton schooner, .................. | $ 3,700 | 00 |
| Fitting out, sails, carpenter and cooper's bills .............. | 2,500 | 00 |
| Provisions for crew and slaves, .......................... | 1,115 | 00 |
| Wages advanced to 18 men before the mast, .............. | 900 | 00 |
| "          "      to captain, mates, boatswain, cook, and steward, ......................... | 440 | 00 |
| 200,000 cigars and 500 doubloons, cargo, ................ | 10,900 | 00 |
| Clearance and hush-money, ............................. | 200 | 00 |
| | $19,755 | 00 |
| Commission at 5 per cent, ............................. | 987 | 00 |
| Full cost of voyage out, ........................ | $20,742 | 00 |

### 2.—Expenses Home

| | | |
|---|---|---|
| Captain's head-money, at $8 a head, ..................... | 1,746 | 00 |
| Mates          "        $4      "     ................. | 873 | 00 |
| Second mate and boatswain's head-money, at $2 each a head, ........................................ | 873 | 00 |
| Captain's wages, ..................................... | 219 | 78 |
| First mate's wages, ................................... | 175 | 56 |
| Second mate and boatswain's wages, ..................... | 307 | 12 |
| Cook and steward's wages, ............................. | 264 | 00 |
| Eighteen sailors' wages, ............................... | 1,972 | 00 |
| | $27,172 | 46 |

### 3.—Expenses in Havana

| | | |
|---|---|---|
| Government officers, at $8 per head, ..................... | 1,736 | 00 |
| My commission on 217 slaves, expenses off, .............. | 5,565 | 00 |
| Consignees' commissions ............................... | 3,873 | 00 |
| 217 slave dresses, at $2 each, ......................... | 434 | 00 |
| Extra expenses of all kinds, say, ....................... | 1,200 | 00 |
| Total  expenses ............................. | $39,980 | 46 |

### 4.—Returns

| | | |
|---|---|---|
| Value of vessels at auction ........................... | $ 3,950 | 00 |
| Proceeds of 217 slavers, ........................... | 77,469 | 00 |
| | $81,419 | 00 |

### Resumé

| | | |
|---|---|---|
| Total  Returns, ........................ | $81,419 | 00 |
| "     Expenses ...................... | 39,980 | 46 |
| Net profit, .................... | $41,438 | 54 |

*"Westward Ho!" is a chapter from the book,* The Sins
of the Fathers, *by James Pope-Hennessy. It describes the
initial agonies of the slaves as they were taken from
the West African coast to the Americas. Pope-Hennessy's
vivid account is designed to leave little doubt in the
reader's mind that the "Middle Passage" was anything
but a Dantean horror. The brutality of the slaver should
be borne in mind, especially in light of later efforts
to justify the slave trade in terms of humanitarian or
spiritual goals.*

# Westward Ho!

## James Pope-Hennessy

I

We spent in our passage from St. Thomas to Barbados two months eleven
days . . . in which time there happened much sickness and mortality among
my poor men and negroes, that of the first we buried 14, and of the last 320 . . .
whereby the loss in all amounted to near 6560 pounds sterling. The distemper
which my men as well as the blacks mostly die of, was the white flux, which
was so violent and inveterate, that no medicine would in the least check it;
so that when any of our men were seized with it, we esteemed him a dead man,
as he generally proved.

Captain Thomas Phillips, from whose journal of the voyage of his slave
ship *Hannibal* in 1693 and 1694 this passage comes, had also one hundred
cases of smallpox amongst his slaves, only twelve of whom, however, actually died of it. A further twelve had drowned themselves off Whydah before
the voyage had begun, 'they having a more dreadful apprehension of Barbados than we can have of hell, tho' in reality they live much better there
than in their own country; but home is home etc.'

In taking a ship for the Atlantic crossing we can do much worse than
choose the *Hannibal,* a Guinea vessel of four hundred and fifty tons and
thirty-six guns, which had been bought for Phillips by his 'patron and benefactor', Sir Jeffrey Jeffreys, and had set sail from the Downs in October

From James Pope-Hennessy, *The Sins of the Fathers: A Study of the Atlantic Slave
Traders, 1441–1807* (New York: Alfred A. Knopf, 1968), pp. 97–116.

1693, in the reign of William and Mary. We could of course select any of a vast number of ships of different periods and different nationalities, since in our hindsighted case History itself is our travel agency. But Captain Phillips, a careful and not altogether unsympathetic man, will serve to get us off to Barbados, and instruct us on the way. His losses, both in slaves and seamen are, also, fairly typical of these lengthy and hazardous voyages on overcrowded ships; and in this connection it is necessary to remember that the conditions in which the sailors lived on board were almost as bad as those of the Negroes themselves. The crews' only relief came from drinking 'raw unwholesome rum' mixed with 'unpurged black sugar' with which, in the case of the *Hannibal,* they had secretly stocked up at São Tomé. Although Captain Phillips, who thought this drink caused illness, flogged men whom he found swilling it, and threw the punch into the sea, a good deal would seem to have remained on board, for the white flux did not set in until after the ship had sailed from the Gulf. For some reason which he could not understand, the white men and boys of his crew never contracted the smallpox, even though they were tending the Negroes who had caught it. The slaves themselves seemed to recover merely by drinking water and anointing their pustules with palm-oil: 'But what the smallpox spared, the flux swept off, to our great regret, after all our pains and care to give them their messes in due order and season, keeping their lodgings as clean and sweet as possible, and enduring so much misery and stench among a parcel of creatures nastier than swine; and after all our expectations to be defeated by their mortality.' Captain Phillips, who had several times fainted dead away in the 'trunk' or slave prison of the King of Whydah, did not relish his trade. 'No gold-finders can endure so much noisome slavery as they do who carry negroes; for those have some respite and satisfaction, but we endure twice the misery; and yet by their mortality our voyages are ruined, and we pine and fret ourselves to death, to think that we should undergo so much misery, and take so much pains to so little purpose.' Out of seven hundred Negroes embarked on the Guinea Coast, Phillips could deliver only three hundred and seventy-two alive in Barbados, where they sold for nineteen pounds a head.

Phillips' *cri de coeur* came at the very end of the voyage, and was provoked by its disappointing results. In other ways he was a thoughtful and even kindly man, who ran his ship well, let the Negroes out of their fetters once he was at sea, and saw to it that the slaves' chief food, a kind of porridge made of ground Indian corn, was flavoured with salt, malaguetta pepper and palm oil. Three days a week they were given boiled horse beans, at which, he relates, they would beat their breasts and cry out aloud with delight. When his officers urged him to follow the example of many slaving

captains and 'cut off the legs and arms of the most wilful' of the slaves
'to terrify the rest' he refused

to entertain the least thought of it, much less put in practice such barbarity
and cruelty to poor creatures, who, excepting their want of Christianity and
true religion (their misfortune more than fault) are as much the works of God's
hands, and no doubts as dear to him as ourselves; nor can I imagine why they
should be despised for their colour, being what they cannot help, and the effect
of the climate it has pleased God to appoint them. I can't think [he concludes]
there is any intrinsic value in one colour more than another, nor that white
is better than black, only we think so because we are so, and are prone to judge
favourably in our own case, as well as the blacks, who in odium of the colour,
say, the devil is white and so paint him.

Phillips organized his cargo with great care, appointing thirty or forty
Gold Coast Negroes as overseers of the Whydah ones, to keep the peace
and spy out any plotting. Each of these 'guardians' was given a cat-o'-nine-
tails as a badge of office 'which he is not a little proud of, and will exercise
with great authority'. The slaves were fed twice a day, at ten in the morning
and four in the afternoon; those sailors who were not distributing the victuals
manned the great guns and stood to arms to prevent any attempt at revolt.
Besides being filthy and long-drawn-out, the voyage of a loaded slave ship
was tense and nerve-searing for the handful of white men on board.

There is one aspect of Captain Phillips' account, which, though he does
not go into detail, is important and by its implications, unpleasant. The
Negro men, he tells us, were fed upon the main deck and forecastle, so as
to be 'under command of our arms from the quarterdeck'. The boys and
girls were fed upon the poop. But the African women 'eat upon the quarter
deck with us'. For the treatment of Negro women on slavers we must sup-
plement the *Hannibal*'s log from other equally reliable sources. Disagreeable,
indeed repellent, as this subject may seem, it is one of the greatest pertinence
to the history of the coloured populations of the West Indies, the Southern
States of America and other transatlantic slave plantations. For the humili-
ations which African women were forced to endure on the Middle Passage
cannot fail to have conditioned their attitude, and consequently that of their
descendants, to the white men who claimed to own them. We may begin
with the evidence of a Negro slave.

II

Ottobah Cugoano, the kidnapped Fantee who ended up as London servant to the miniaturist Cosway, and from whose book, published in 1787,

we have already quoted, had been taken as a boy to Cape Coast Castle, there sold, and transported to Grenada. He does not describe the voyage in much depth, just calling it 'the brutish, base but fashionable way of traffic'. He does, on the other hand, refer to a plot amongst the women and the boy slaves 'to burn and blow up the ship, and to perish all together in the flames; but we were betrayed by one of our own country-women, who slept with some of the head men of the ship, for it was common for the dirty filthy sailors to take the African women and lie upon their bodies; but the men were chained and penned up in holes'. John Newton, the famous slave-trader turned clergyman and Abolitionist, writes that while not necessarily universal in slave ships, the forced use of Negro girls by the officers and men on board ship was 'too commonly, and, I am afraid, too generally prevalent'. Newton himself tried to prevent such incidents on board his own ship: 'In the afternoon' (his Journal for a January day in 1753, when he was lying off Mana, records) 'while we were off the deck, William Cooney seduced a woman slave down into the room and lay with her brutelike in view of the whole quarter deck, for which I put him in irons. I hope this has been the first affair of the kind on board and I am determined to keep them quiet if possible. If anything happens to the woman I shall impute it to him, for she was big with child. Her number is 83.' But many slave-captains were not so scrupulous; Newton likens the white men's behaviour to that of a Cossack horde sacking a town. 'When the women and girls' (he writes) 'are taken on board a ship, naked, trembling, terrified, perhaps almost exhausted from cold, fatigue and hunger, they are often exposed to the wanton rudeness of white savages . . . In imagination the prey is divided on the spot, and only reserved till opportunity offers.' Although they could not speak English, these shivering creatures could not fail to understand the manners and the gestures of the seamen—the international language, the Esperanto, of lust.

'Perhaps' (Newton continues) 'some hard-hearted pleader may suggest that such treatment would indeed be cruel in Europe; but the African women are negroes, savages, who have no idea of the nicer sensations which obtain among civilized people. I dare contradict them in the strongest terms.' He explains that he 'had lived long and conversed much, amongst these supposed savages'; that he had been often alone in a town at night in a house filled with trade goods and with only a mat for a door, and had never suffered any harm. 'And with regard to the women, in Sherbro, where I was most acquainted, I have seen many instances of modesty, and even delicacy, which would not disgrace an English woman. Yet, such is the treatment which I have known permitted, if not encouraged, in many of our ships— they have been abandoned, without restraint, to the lawless will of the first-comer.' The sailors did not even trouble to ask a slave woman for her consent, and on most of the ships Newton had known 'the licence allowed, in this particular, was almost unlimited'. The surgeon, Alexander Falconbridge, who was a contemporary of John Newton, and published his *An Account of the Slave Trade* in 1788, writing of the slave-dances on deck in fine weather, when slaves 'who go about it reluctantly, or do not move with agility' were flogged with the cat-o'-nine-tails, and of the glass beads issued to the women to amuse them, likewise states that 'on board some ships, the common sailors are allowed to have intercourse' with the African women, although he believes it was only with those 'whose consent they can procure'. According to this witness some of these shot-gun romances ended in suicide, since African women had 'been known to take the inconstancy of their paramours so much to heart as to leap overboard and drown themselves. The officers are permitted to indulge their passions with them at pleasure, and sometimes are guilty of such brutal excesses as disgrace human nature'.

While both these authorities, and many others too, take care to be objective and to say that debauching the Negro women on board was not an undeniably universal practice, it would not be logical to suppose that there were many exceptions. To be a seaman on a slaver was, as we have seen, to live for months in conditions almost as dreadful as those of the slaves. The stench of death and disease was forever in your nostrils. In rough or wet weather the 'air-ports' on the slave decks were closed, and all fresh air shut out. Falconbridge, who had made many voyages as a slave ship surgeon, gives a solitary example of what, on such occasions, followed. 'Some wet and blowing weather' (he writes):

having occasioned the port-holes to be shut, and the grating to be covered, fluxes and fevers among the negroes ensued. While they were in this situation, my profession requiring it, I frequently went down among them, till at length their apartments became so extremely hot as to be only sufferable for a very short time. But the excessive heat was not the only thing that rendered their situation intolerable. The deck, that is the floor of their rooms, was so covered with the blood and mucous which had proceeded from them in consequence of the flux, that it resembled a slaughter-house. It is not in the power of the human imagination to picture to itself a situation more dreadful or disgusting. Numbers of the slaves having fainted, they were carried up on deck, where several of them died and the rest were, with great difficulty, restored. It had nearly proved fatal to me also.

And Falconbridge was serving on the better class of English slaver.

To work on ships which often were merely floating coffins—the ships taking slaves to Rio de Janeiro were in fact called *tumbeiros* from the Portuguese for tomb—was at once brutalizing and nauseous. Amongst other signal disadvantages of life aboard we may count a particularly bold breed of rat which infested the ships, destroying any clothing they found, biting men below deck, and defecating on the faces of those who slept. Seventeenth- and eighteenth-century ship conditions were bad enough, and the seamen of those days a rough lot. But the men who were persuaded, or who volunteered, to enlist on a slave ship were, in the words of the famous Liverpool slave-captain, Hugh Crow, who published his autobiography in 1830, 'the very dregs of the community'. Some had escaped from jails, others were criminals in fear of the law. Many were gentlemen's sons 'of desperate character and abandoned habits', who wished to escape creditors or to flee the country for some other reason. 'These wretched beings' writes Crow 'used to flock to Liverpool when the ships were fitting out, and after acquiring a few sea-phrases from some crimp [1] or other, they were shipped as ordinary seamen, though they had never been at sea in their lives. If, when at sea, they became saucy and insubordinate, the officers were compelled to treat them with severity; and, having never been in a warm climate before, if they took ill, they seldom recovered.' Under all these circumstances it is hard to suppose that any but a saintly captain would deny his sullen crew what diversion they could find with the slave women on a long and tedious Atlantic crossing; nor is it easy to see how even the strictest and most well-intentioned master could control the sexual activities of his men by day or night. The callous and wanton demoralization of these African women, at home so gay, so carefree, so courteous and so merrily clad, each with an allotted part to play in the busy life of her village community, surely formed one of the most criminal and, in its long-term results, one of the most durable by-products of the slave trade.

Amid so much accumulated horror, the ample records of which might make one permanently lose one's wavering faith in human nature, a single redeeming fact emerges—but it redeems neither captain nor crew. Writing of slavery in Jamaica as 'a situation that necessarily suppresses many of the best affections of the human heart', the historian Bryan Edwards remarked that if slavery 'calls forth any latent virtues, they are those of sympathy and compassion towards persons in the same conditions of life; and accordingly we find that the negroes in general are strongly attached to their countrymen, but above all to such of their companions as came in the same ship with them from Africa. This is a striking circumstance: the term *shipmate* is understood among them as signifying a relationship of the most endearing nature'. What is more poignant, what more revealing of the true character of Africans than such lifelong friendships forged in fetters and in blood? Yet, on arrival in the West Indian islands, or on the North American coast, even this solace was often denied the shipmates, for the processes of sale to the planters too frequently split up families, lovers or friends. Of all these processes perhaps the most barbarous was that known as 'sale by scramble'.

## III

When a ship laden with slaves dropped anchor off a West Indian port, excitement would prevail on board. The reaction of officers and men was very far removed from the fear and distaste with which they had made landfall in the Gambia or off the mangrove swamps of the Bight of Benin, just as the translucent green waters of the Caribbean Sea, the foam swirling gently over white coral reefs about which black-and-yellow-striped fish darted formed the antithesis to the dangerous thundering surf of the Gold Coast. The long and noisome voyage was over, the prospect of shore-time in European-run taverns and brothels was near, the second, and worst, lap of the Triangular Trade was completed once again. The lovely, melancholy islands of the Caribbean can never have been a more welcome or refreshing sight.

In their merciful ignorance, the slaves, too, rejoiced. Their irons were struck off, they were given fattening foods, and rubbed with oil until their black skins shone in the clear, cool dawn. Suddenly they felt a sense of freedom, curiosity and joy. But, as John Newton wrote:

This joy is short-lived indeed. The condition of the unhappy slaves is in a continual progress from bad to worse ... perhaps they would wish to spend the remainder of their days on ship-board, could they know beforehand the nature of the servitude which awaits them on shore; and that the dreadful hardships and sufferings they have already endured would, to the most of them, only terminate in excessive toil, hunger and the excruciating tortures of the cartwhip, inflicted at the caprice of an unfeeling overseer, proud of the power allowed him of punishing whom, and when, and how he pleases.

Today, the islands of the West Indies have become, for the undiscerning tourist, purely places of pleasure. In those days they were places of pain.

On shore, the arrival of a well-stocked Guineaman gave a thrill of anticipatory satisfaction to two mainly unattractive groups—firstly to the ships' agents and the slave-auctioneers, secondly to the owners of plantations and their vulturine overseers. Although, on the whole, the climate of most of the Caribbean islands is healthier and more balmy than that of West Africa, mortality amongst the Negro field-hands and other labourers was high.

I have earlier referred to a perennial controversy between certain planters as to whether it was best to give their slaves a moderate amount of work, feed them well and generally so treat them that they might live to an old age; or whether it were not more profitable to strain their strength to the utmost, use them harshly and feed them poorly, so as to wear them out 'before they became useless and unable to do service', purchasing new ones from the ships to replace those who had died. This controversy, the arguments on both sides of which had been calculated to a nicety, was, for instance, raging in the island of Antigua in the fifties of the eighteenth century. It had been concluded that to wear slaves out and buy a fresh stock was cheapest in the long run, and there were then a number of Antiguan estates on which slaves seldom survived more than nine years. Some planters, like the Codringtons who owned Betty's Hope plantation on Antigua, and the little islet of Barbuda as well, planned and operated 'slave nurseries' which were filled with little boys and girls bought off the boats.[2]

Even when the captain had successfully brought his ship to the West Indies his anxieties were not invariably over. Navigation down the islands was tricky; in 1791, for example, the deck and other portions of a small French Guineaman containing the bodies of some shaven slaves, was washed up on the beach at Antigua, and such was not a rare occurrence. At St. Christopher, in April 1737, there was a sensational mass suicide attempt by the slaves on board the *Prince of Orange,* out of Bristol, and commanded by a Captain Japhet Bird. 'At our arrival here' (a letter from on board, published in the *Boston Weekly News Letter,* relates):

I thought all our troubles of this voyage were over; but on the contrary I might say that dangers rest on the borders of security. On the 14th of March we found a great deal of discontent among the slaves, particularly the men, which continued till the 16th about five o'clock in the evening, when to our great amazement above an hundred men slaves jumped overboard . . . out of the whole we lost 33 of as good men slaves as we had on board, who would not endeavour to save themselves, but resolved to die and sunk directly down. Many more of them were taken up almost drowned, some of them died since, but not to the owner's loss, they being sold before any discovery was made of the injury the salt water had done them.

This particular panic was found to have been caused by a St. Christopher slave with a perverted sense of humour, who had trotted on board to tell the new arrivals that they were first to have their eyes put out and then be eaten. 'This misfortune' (the letter ends) 'has disconcerted the Captain's design of proceeding to Virginia'—where he hoped to sell slaves left on his hands in St. Christopher, then suffering from a shortage of sugar.

Once the slaves had been put ashore, selling began in earnest. The moribund or 'refuse' slaves were landed first, and sold off at a tavern *vendue* or public auction. In Grenada you could buy a slave who seemed to be dying of the flux for as little as one dollar; most of these refuse slaves, who were carried on shore, always died. Some captains would march the healthy slaves through the streets of the little tropical town at which they were landed, streets animated by that rather languid flurry peculiar to West Indian life, streets in which the 'seasoned' Negroes from previous ships would roll their sea-shell eyes at the procession of straggling bewildered newcomers. The fresh slaves would then be lined up in a yard for a minute physical examination by prospective purchasers. But a more popular mode of sale was often the 'scramble', the date and hour of which would be advertised beforehand.

The surgeon Falconbridge, who had attended many a scramble in his time, describes one at which he saw two hundred and fifty Africans sold on a Caribbean island which he does not name. In a scramble, all the Negroes, by an agreement between the captains and the purchasers, bore the same price. 'On a day appointed' (he writes) 'the negroes were landed, and placed altogether in a large yard belonging to the merchants to whom the ship is consigned. As soon as the hour agreed on arrived, the doors of the yard were suddenly thrown open, and in rushed a considerable number of purchasers, with all the ferocity of brutes.' The theory of the scramble was that any Negro, Negress or infant you could lay your hands on was yours to buy. 'Some instantly seized such of the negroes as they could conveniently lay hold of with their hands. Others, being prepared with several handkerchiefs tied together, encircled with these as many as they were able. While others, by means of a rope, effected the same purpose. It is scarcely possible to describe the confusion of which this mode of selling is productive.' Violent quarrels amongst the purchasers broke out. The Negroes themselves were so appalled by this bestial onslaught that several clambered up the walls of the yard and 'ran wild about the town'. These refugees were soon recaptured. On another voyage from Africa, Falconbridge witnessed a scramble on board ship. The Negroes were herded together on the main and quarter decks, which had been darkened by an awning of sailcloth so that the purchasers could not 'pick or choose'. 'The signal being given, the buyers rushed in, as usual, to seize their prey; when the negroes appeared extremely terrified, and near thirty of them jumped into the sea. But they were all soon retaken, chiefly by boats from other ships.' At one scramble at Port Maria, on the rocky north coast of Jamaica, Falconbridge says that the African women were especially alarmed, shrieking and clinging to each other 'through excess of terror at the savage manner in which their brutal purchasers rushed upon, and seized them'.

Such was the shattering prelude to life on the old plantation.

## IV

As a general rule, the captain's duty towards the slaves he had brought across the Atlantic ceased with the voyage. The owners' agents then took over and arranged sale by auction, scramble or private negotiation. Often, however, owing to the time of year—sugar was not ordinarily available before June, although it could at times be obtained in April and May—or to temporary poverty on one island, or to the poor quality of some of the slaves, the agent could not sell a whole shipload of Africans in the same island, or in a single mainland port such as Charleston. The captain had then to proceed from place to place, peddling his slaves piecemeal, sometimes for weeks or even months. In principle, however, once the captain had handed his human cargo over to the agents, he set about loading up with sugar when possible; if there was no sugar to be had, he returned home in ballast. Since, from fear of Negro revolts, Guineamen carried a larger crew than ordinary merchant ships, a number of the seamen would be paid off at, say, Barbados, and hang around there waiting for employment on some other ship. This employment was often hard to find. Bad captains were, indeed, known to have deliberately maltreated their men in West Indian ports, with the intention of forcing them to jump ship; others would sail for home without warning superfluous seamen who were carousing on shore. 'It was no uncommon thing' (according to one witness who attested before Parliament at the time of the Abolitionist agitation) 'for the captains to send on shore, a few hours before they sail, their lame, emaciated, and sick seamen, leaving them to perish.' The authors of *Black Cargoes* relate that these dying men were called 'wharfingers' in Kingston, Jamaica, where they would languish on the wharves. At more modest ports they were termed 'beach-horners'; and in the inscrutable, malevolent-looking island of Dominica, with its precipitous green mountains and lack of harbour, they were popularly described as 'scowbankers'—'scow' being the current word for large flat-bottomed boats or lighters.

Profits from the slave trade were large, but also chancy. In the autumn of 1774, for example, the snow *Africa,* a two-masted, square-rigged ship of one hundred tons burthen, which had been captured from the French during the Seven Years War, set sail from the port of Bristol for New Calabar.[3] The *Africa* had been bought and outfitted by a syndicate of eight Bristol merchants, and stocked up with the usual trade goods—brandy, rum, guns, laced hats and waistcoats, Indian and Manchester cottons, multi-coloured china beads, iron bars, copper rods and so on—to the total cost of £4,445 14s. 0d. A further £1,247 2s. 0d. had been spent on fitting the ship out, making a total of £5,692 16s. 0d. The syndicate appointed Captain George Merrick, who knew the Africa trade, to the command, and supplied him with the necessary certificates authorizing him to trade on the African coast and also in the Atlantic colonies. His written instructions ordered him to go to New Calabar, and there barter his cargo

for good healthy young negroes and ivory, and . . . not to buy any old slaves or children but good healthy young men and women, and buy all the ivory you can and when you are half-slaved don't stay too long if there is a possibility of getting off for the risk of sickness and mortality then become great . . . let no candle be made use of in drawing spirits or to go near the powder . . . We recommend you to treat the negroes with as much lenity as safety will admit and suffer none of your officers or people to abuse them under any pretence whatever, be sure you see their victuals well dressed and given them in due season . . . We recommend you to make fires frequently in the negroes' rooms as we think it healthy and you have iron kettles on board for that purpose. We recommend mutton broth in fluxes, so that you'll endeavour to purchase as many sheep and goats to bring off the coast for that purpose as you conveniently can.

In March of the following year, 1775, the syndicate, which called itself 'John Chilcott & Co.', write two letters. One was to Messrs. Akers and Houston, their agents on the island of St. Vincent, warning them that the *Africa* should be with them in the beginning of May, and asking them to take the cargo over from Captain Merrick and to sell the slaves for the usual promissory notes—'the sight of the bills we expect will not exceed twelve months, and if they are sold at St. Christophers we expect a part of somewhat shorter sight.' Their second letter was under cover to the first, and addressed to Captain Merrick, telling him to do whatever the agents required, to get rid of his Negroes quickly and to come back home 'unless a freight offers for Bristol worth staying a fortnight'. These merchants, some of those grave men we saw bending over a map at the opening of this book, ended this note: 'We recommend dispatch and frugality, Your friends and owners, John Chilcott.'

The crew of thirty-one—a ship of the *Africa*'s size engaged in normal trading would only have carried a complement of ten to fifteen men—were paid half their wages on arrival at St. Vincent; the slaves disposed of, Captain Merrick sailed his empty ship back to Bristol with a crew of seventeen, twelve of whom had set out thence on the voyage to New Calabar. The

Negroes had fetched a total of £5,128 12s. 6d. The total proceeds of the
voyage on the vessel amounted to £5,650 8s. 0d., which by deducting
miscellaneous operating charges left a net balance of £5,442 8s. 0d. This
meant that, for the owners of the *Africa,* not only was there no profit but a
very definite loss. The fact that the ship brought back no freight from the
Colonies and had, so to speak, achieved only two laps of the Triangular
Trade, would seem to have accounted for this dismal result.

The story of the skow *Africa* is interesting because it illuminates one of
the hazards of investment in the slave trade. The syndicate's instructions
on the treatment of Negroes were probably genuinely humane, although
they could be categorized under what one French writer on the subject has
neatly termed '*la sollicitude intéressée*'. The records of Captain Merrick's
murky doings in the Niger Delta, of the quantity of slaves he shipped, and
of how he fared on the Middle Passage seem, unfortunately, no longer to
exist. The saga of the *Africa* cannot, I think, be taken as typical, for is it
not otherwise unlikely that so many merchants of so many nations should
have plunged into the trade. More representative—to take ships' names at
random—is the case of the *Enterprize* from Liverpool, which left the Mersey
for Bonny in 1803, slaved quickly, and got rid of the whole cargo (save for
one Negro girl who was subject to fits) at Havana, returning to Liverpool
in 1804 with a net profit of nearly twenty-five thousand pounds. About 1800
the *Louisa,* also from Liverpool, returned from Jamaica with a profit of
nearly twenty thousand pounds. The owners of the *Fortune,* again a Liver-
pudlian vessel, which carried a cargo of Congolese slaves to the Bahamas
in 1805, made a profit of over thirteen thousand pounds, which the owners
judged insufficient. The *Fortune* scarcely lived up to its name, for the slaves
sold slowly, and during the long delay, the trading mate and one sailor
ran off, thirty-four of the seamen were impressed into, or volunteered for,
the Royal Navy at Nassau, the third mate and six seamen died on the voyage, and two of the other sailors were drowned.

V

'I hope the slaves in our islands are better treated now than they were
at the time that I was in the trade' (wrote the Reverend John Newton
retrospectively of the years 1736 to 1755, when he had been, off and on,
an eager young slaver). 'And even then, I know there were slaves who,
under the care of humane masters, were comparatively happy. But I saw
and heard enough to satisfy me that their condition, in general, was
wretched in the extreme.' The only islands which Newton had been able
to investigate personally had been Antigua and St. Kitts, but by the time

that he was writing his *Thoughts upon the African Slave Trade,* the legis-latures of some British West Indian colonies had passed certain ameliorative laws. In Jamaica, for example, the Consolidated Slave Law of 1784 abol-ished cruel and severe punishments, made regulations for slaves' working hours, their clothing, their spare time and the length of their meals. Female slaves who had borne six children were exempted from all labour. Scrambles on board ship were forbidden, and so was the separation of African families. This last prohibition (involving an interpreter) was awkward to enforce, but to the historian Bryan Edwards goes the credit for getting through the Jamaican House of Assembly a law by which 'the Guineamen' were com-pelled, under solemn oath, to do their utmost to see that this clause was respected. Nonetheless, Edwards strangely maintained that the West Indian planters were 'entirely innocent and ignorant of the manner in which the slave trade is conducted (having no other concern therein than becoming purchasers of what British acts of Parliament have made objects of sale)'; yet in fact the new slave regulations were primarily the planters' answer to rising criticism in Great Britain, and to the spread of the movement to abolish the slave trade, with all that movement's volcanic implications that the next step would be to abolish Negro slavery itself. A further strong influence in favour of improving slave conditions in the British West Indian possessions was the settlement there after the American Revolution of loyalists from the mainland states, who brought with them a type of slave altogether more advanced than those of the sugar islands. Young dis-charged officers settled there also, forming 'a better description' of planter, with a more civilized concept of duty towards their slaves.

Edwards, as we have seen, did strive to be historically impartial. He did not deny evidence of 'excessive whippings and barbarous mutilations' of slaves, and even glossed this with a condemnation: 'If they happened but seldom, they happened too often.' By and large, though, he took the Jamaican planter's traditional, roseate view of the state of West Indian Negro slaves. He describes those newly landed from the ships as 'presenting themselves, when the buyers are few, with cheerfulness and alacrity for selection, and appearing mortified and disappointed when refused'. He also comments on their 'loud and repeated bursts of laughter' at the discovery of a blemish on any of their fellows during the medical inspection which preceded sale. When the buyer had completed what Edwards calls 'his assortment' he clothed his new slaves in a coarse German cloth called oznaburgh, and gave them hats, handkerchiefs and knives. Since they could not know what work or conditions were in store for them, and since the squalors of the Middle Passage were now past, they may indeed have trudged off to their destinations in a genial, or at any rate an optimistic, mood.

On arrival at their future home, the new or 'unseasoned' Negroes were distributed amongst the huts and provision grounds of older, established and experienced slaves. On his own estates Edwards had at first forbidden this custom which he judged 'an insupportable hardship' for the slave hosts. These latter surprised him by begging that his decision be reversed—the young newcomers seemed to the old people to replace children who had died or had been left in Africa, and the girls (of whom there was always a shortage) were potential wives for their sons. An agreeable mutual relationship was quickly established, and the adoptive parents were venerated by the new arrivals as if they had in fact been their own progenitors. A further reason for this anxiety to adopt and guide was that the older Africans 'expected to revive and retrace in the conversation of their new visitors, the remembrance and ideas of past pleasures and scenes of their youth'. But the solace of adopting a young man or woman, boy or girl, fresh from Africa was frequently shortlived for, worn out by the Middle Passage, many of the 'new Negroes' died before their three-year seasoning period was over. On the Worthy Park plantation and its outlying properties in the parish of St John, Jamaica, for instance, in the year 1794 alone, thirty-one new Negroes died, chiefly from dysentery. There was also the heavy infant mortality usual amongst the slave population of the sugar colonies.

This infant mortality, together with the fact that the slave-women's birth-rate was often inexplicably low, increased the demand for 'new Negroes' off the ships. Professor Ulrich Phillips, who in 1914 published a study of the Worthy Park plantation, found that in the year 1792 there were three hundred and fifty-five slaves there. Of these one hundred and fifty constituted the main field gangs; thirty-four were artificers and jobbing foremen; forty were watchmen, gardeners and cattlemen; thirteen were in the hospital corps; twenty-four little boys and girls made up the 'grass gang'; thirty-nine were young children and thirty-three were invalids or superannuated. The domestic staff at Worthy Park was twenty-two slaves strong. That same spring the owner began buying Congoes and Coromantees from the slavers' agents—one hundred in 1792, and eighty-one more in the following year. It was amongst these new Negroes that the mortality rate was so high. Two of the thirty-one were thought to have committed suicide.

Robert Price, an absentee landlord of Penzance in Cornwall, was the owner of Worthy Park. He was presumably the sort of proprietor Edwards had in mind when, writing of 'the inheritance or accident' by which many of the white planters in the West Indies had acquired their land and their slaves, he points out that: 'Many persons there are, in Great Britain itself who . . . find themselves possessed of estates they have never seen, and invested with powers over their fellow creatures there, which, however extensively odious, they have never abused.'

Edwards was neither an enemy to the slave trade, nor to the state of slavery as such, although he rather ruefully admitted the innate injustice of perpetual servitude. Composing his monumental work in London, he looked back with nostalgia to 'the time of crop in the sugar islands' as 'the season of gladness and festivity'. During this harvest period the health of the Negroes and their inextinguishable vitality quite visibly improved, since all hands were allowed to chew as much luscious sugar-cane as they could manage. All of them—save those condemned to the Hades of the boiling-houses—grew temporarily strong and fat. The sick Negroes improved, and 'even the pigs and poultry' fattened on the cane-refuse. To Edwards, and to many other planting gentlemen of his kind, the blissful scenes on a well-run plantation at crop-time seemed 'to soften, in a great measure, the hardship of slavery, and induce a spectator to hope, when the miseries of life are represented as insupportable, that they are sometimes exaggerated through the medium of fancy'. But it was not the miseries of Negro slavery that were exaggerated through the medium of fancy; it was the depth and the duration of those limited outbursts of happiness in which the African slave managed, triumphantly, to indulge.

We have noticed that, on the steaming Gulf of Guinea, the comforting myth of the savagery and low mentality of Africans gained welcome sway over the minds of European slavers, and was spread by word of mouth and published books through Europe. Born of a callous and insolent ignorance, this myth crossed the Atlantic in the shark-ridden wake of the slave ships. There it took root and flourished in the sunlit, brooding islands of the West Indies, where the pale-green sugar-canes, acre upon acre, billowed and rippled in the breeze from the blue-green sea. It echoed through the high stuccoed drawing-rooms of the Bay Street mansions of the merchants and plantation owners in Charleston, South Carolina. In the bayous of Louisiana, in the Golden Isles of Georgia, in the cotton-fields beside the Mississippi River, in the thriving slave-markets of ominous New Orleans, in the trim offices of the Jewish slaving magnates of Newport, Rhode Island, it became an article of faith. So, in vast areas of the United States it appallingly remains today. But once established over the Atlantic, the myth not so much suffered a sea-change as it gained a new dimension. This appendix to the myth of Negro inferiority might be called the *Myth of the Merry and Contented Slave*—or, alternately, *Thanks for the Middle Passage*. Its components can best be envisaged as a series of vignettes in the mode of the lovely coloured engravings of slave festivals based on the pictures of the

eighteenth-century painter Agostino Brunyas. In this fictive slave existence
turbaned Negroes and Negresses sang as they worked the cane or cotton-
fields by day, spent the night drinking, dancing and making love, reared
happy families of sportive piccaninnies, and liked and respected the white
masters, their indolent whey-faced wives and their spoiled children. According to this theory, which swept back to Europe and was long believed there,
the slaves had, like Bryan Edwards' faithful old body, Clara, one further and
capital cause for gratitude—they had been saved from the funereal practices
of the Guinea Coast.

In an illogical, interlocking way these two myths, that of Negro stupidity
and that of slave happiness, supported one another mutually. Those planters
who, like the author of *Practical Rules for the Management of Negro Slaves*
(published in 1803), went so far as to admit that slavery 'is not so desirable
as freedom . . . because a slave is subject to an authority that may be exercised in a manner cruel, capricious or oppressive, from which the sufferer
has no means of relieving himself', asserted that even in the hands of a bad
master, a slave's 'lot is infinitely less deplorable than might be imagined;
for he does not sublime misery in the laboratory of the imagination. His
powers . . . are not felt if not applied to the organs of sense; and, let tyranny
cease but for a moment to act . . . the slave forgets his oppression, and discovers enjoyments more great than those of an epicure at a banquet . . .
Indulge to satiety his animal appetites, and a negro makes no account of
his degradation'.

This neat conviction that should a slave by some mischance fall from
his naturally happy state, he still could not suffer as a white man would
have suffered, was widespread. The shape of Negroes' skulls, their pigmenta-
tion, the way their hair grew, all were quoted to prove that they had a different and a much less delicate nervous system than Europeans. An exception
was sometimes made for the black mistresses of white men—either slave
girls or free Negresses. Here the superlative beauty of so many African
women was openly admitted. It was also on occasion praised. In 1765 an
elderly white Jamaican poetaster celebrated the imaginary arrival from
Africa of a negroid Venus—a classical Black Madonna, so to speak. We
may as well look at four of the verses of this curious eulogy, which was
entitled *The Sable Venus*. The country of origin of the sable Venus is indicated as being Portuguese Angola:

> Sweet is the beam of morning bright,
> Yet sweet the sober shade of night;
>     On rich Angola's shores,

While beauty clad in sable dye,
Enchanting fires the wond'ring eye,
   Farewell, ye Paphian bowers.

When thou, this large domain to view,
Jamaica's isle, they conquest new,
   First left thy native shore,
Bright was the morn, and soft the breeze,
With wanton joy the curling seas
   The beauteous burden bore.

Her skin excell'd the raven plume,
Her breath the fragrant orange bloom,
   Her eye the tropic beam:
Soft was her lip as silken down,
And mild her look as ev'ning sun
   That gilds the Cobre stream.[4]

Gay Goddess of the sable smile!
Propitious still, this grateful isle
   With thy protection bless!
Here fix, secure, thy constant throne;
Where all, adoring thee, do ONE,
   ONE deity confess.

Thus, in that period of calculated literary artifice, even the Middle Passage could be romanticized. Let us now dismiss myth and romanticism, and turn to scrutinize plantation realities.

## NOTES

[1] A crimp was a man who impressed or decoyed sailors.

[2] 'However, in my opinion, if I bought negroes, I would buy them at the age of 10 or 12 and send them to Barbuda; they would at that age come cheap, would live better and at little expense there, and I doubt not would do well' (letter to Sir William Codrington of Dodington Park, the absentee owner of Betty's Hope and of Barbuda, from his overseer who was also his nephew, June 1790; preserved among the Codrington Papers at Dodington).

[3] For details of the *Africa*'s voyage I am indebted to the interesting paper by my friend Professor Walter Minchinton, of Exeter University, published in *The Mariner's Mirror* for July, 1951.

[4] The Cobre, a river on the southern coast of Jamaica, on the western bank of which stands the old capital, Spanish Town.

*The remarkable narrative that follows is the account of*
*the capture, enslavement, manumission, and return*
*of Job, or Ayuba, Suleiman Ibrahima of Bondu (now*
*Western Mali). The son of a noble family, Ayuba was*
*captured in 1730 and transported to Maryland from*
*which he attempted to flee to Pennsylvania. He was*
*apprehended in Kent County, Delaware. He was*
*purchased from slavery by Thomas Bluett, who took*
*him to England where he became a court favorite.*
*He was subsequently repatriated to Africa. The account*
*of his adventures was recorded by Bluett.*

# The Capture and Travels
# of Ayuba Suleiman Ibrahima

## Philip D. Curtin

## INTRODUCTION

Having had occasion to inform myself of many considerable and curious circumstances of the life of Job, the African priest, in a more exact and
particular manner than the generality of his acquaintance in England could
do; I was desired by himself, a little before his departure, to draw up an
account of him agreeable to the information he had given me at different
times, and to the truth of the facts, which I had either been a witness to,
or personally concerned in upon his account. I have been solicited also by
several gentlemen, who were benefactors to Job, to publish what I knew
of him: and I am of opinion such an account is pretty generally wanted; at
least it cannot but be agreeable to those persons, who were pleased to do
kind offices to this stranger, merely from a principle of humanity, before
any particular account of him could be had. Therefore I have at length
resolved to communicate to the world such particulars of the life and character of this African gentleman, as I think will be most useful and enter-
taining; intending to advance nothing as fact, but what I either knew to be
such, or have had from Job's own mouth, whose veracity I have no reason
to doubt of.

Pursuant to this resolution, I shall not trouble my reader with any very

From Philip D. Curtin, *Africa Remembered: Narratives by West Africans from the
Era of the Slave Trade* (Madison: University of Wisconsin Press, © 1967 by the
Regents of the University of Wisconsin), pp. 34–59.

long and particular detail of the geography, history, or rarities of that country of Africa which Job belongs to; nor shall I meddle any farther with these matters, in the present account, than to relate such observations concerning them, as Job himself made to me in conversation; being either not generally known or so curious as to bear a repetition here, consistently with the design of these memoirs. However, I shall endeavour to make the whole as agreeable as the nature of the subject, and the limits of this pamphlet will allow; and therefore, without any farther preface, shall proceed to the thing proposed.

## SECTION I

Job's countrymen, like the Eastern people and some others, used to design themselves by the names of their ancestors, and in their appellations mention their progenitors several degrees backward; tho' they also have sirnames for distinguishing their particular families, much after the same manner as in England. Job's name, in his own country, is Hyuba, Boon Salumena, Boon Hibrahema; i.e., Job, the son of Solomon, the son of Abraham. The sirname of his family is Jallo [Diallo].[1]

Job, who is now about 31 or 32 years of age, was born at a town called Boonda [Bondu] [2] in the county of Galumbo (in our maps Catumbo) [3] in the kingdom of Futa [4] in Africa; which lies on both sides of the River Senegal, and on the south side reaches as far as the River Gambia. These two rivers, Job assured me, run pretty near parallel to one another, and never meet, contrary to the position they have in most of our maps.[5] The eastern boundary of the kingdom of Futa or Senega is the great lake, called in our maps Lacus Guarde. The extent of it, towards the north, is not so certain. The chief city or town of it is Tombut; over against which, on the other side of the river, is Boonda, the place of Job's nativity.[6]

About fifty years ago Hibrahim, the grandfather of Job, founded the town of Boonda, in the reign of Bubaker,[7] then King of Futa, and was, by his permission, sole Lord Proprietor and Governor of it, and at the same time High Priest, or *Alpha;* [8] so that he had a power to make what laws and regulations he thought proper for the increase and good government of his new city.[9] Among other institutions, one was, that no person who flies thither for protection shall be made a slave. This privilege is in force there to this day, and is extended to all in general, that can read and know God, as they express it; and it has contributed much to the peopling of the place, which is now very large and flourishing. Some time after the settlement of this town Hibrahim died; and, as the priesthood is hereditary there, Salumen his son, the father of Job, became High Priest.[10] About the same time Bubaker the King dying, his brother Gelazi [Geladio], who was next heir, succeeded him.[11] Gelazi had a son, named Sambo [Samba], whom he put under the care of Salumen, Job's father, to learn the Koran and Arabick language. Job was at this time also with his father, was companion to Sambo, and studied along with him. Sambo, upon the death of Gelazi, was made King of Futa,[12] and reigns there at present. When Job was fifteen years old, he assisted his father as *Emaum*,[13] or sub-priest. About this age he married the daughter of the Alpha of Tombut,[14] who was then only eleven years old. By her he had a son (when she was thirteen years old) called Abdolah; and after that two more sons, called Hibrahim and Sambo. About two years before his captivity he married a second wife, daughter of the Alpha of Tomga; [15] by whom he has a daughter named Fatima, after the daughter of their prophet Mahommed. Both these wives, with their children, were alive when he came from home.

## SECTION II

In February, 1730, Job's father hearing of an English ship at Gambia River, sent him, with two servants to attend him, to sell two Negroes, and to buy paper, and some other necessaries; but desired him not to venture over the river, because the country of the Mandingoes,[16] who are enemies to the people of Futa, lies on the other side. Job not agreeing with Captain Pike (who commanded the ship, lying then at Gambia,[17] in the service of Captain Henry Hunt, brother to Mr. William Hunt, merchant, in Little Tower-street, London) sent back the two servants to acquaint his father with it, and to let him know that he intended to go farther. Accordingly having agreed with another man, named Loumein Yoas,[18] who understood the Mandingoe language, to go with him as his interpreter, he crossed the River Gambia, and disposed of his Negroes for some cows. As he was returning home, he stopped for some refreshment at the house of an old acquaintance; and the weather being hot, he hung up his arms in the house, while he refreshed himself. Those arms were very valuable; consisting of a gold-hilted sword, a gold knife, which they wear by their side, and a rich quiver of arrows, which King Sambo had made him a present of. It happened that a company of the Mandingoes, who live upon plunder, passing by at that time, and observing him unarmed, rushed in, to the number of seven or eight at once, at a back door, and pinioned Job, before he could get to his arms, together with his interpreter, who is a slave in Maryland still.[19] They then shaved their heads and beards, which Job and his men resented as the highest indignity; tho' the Mandingoes meant no more by it, than to make them appear like Slaves taken in war. On the 27th of February, 1730, they carried them to Captain Pike at Gambia, who purchased them; and on the first of March they were put on board. Soon after Job found means to acquaint Captain Pike that he was the same person that came to trade with him a few days before, and after what manner he had been taken. Upon this Captain Pike gave him leave to redeem himself and his man; and Job sent to an acquaintance of his father's, near Gambia, who promised to send to Job's father, to inform him of what had happened, that he might take some course to have him set at liberty. But it being a fortnight's journey between that friend's house and his father's, and the ship sailing in about a week after,[20] Job was brought with the rest of the slaves to Annapolis in Maryland, and delivered to Mr. Vachell Denton, factor to Mr. Hunt, before mentioned. Job heard since, by vessels that came from Gambia, that his father sent down several slaves, a little after Captain Pike sailed, in order to procure his redemption; and that Sambo, King of Futa, had made war upon the Mandingoes, and cut off great numbers of them, upon account of the injury they had done to his schoolfellow.

Mr. Vachell Denton sold Job to one Mr. Tolsey in Kent Island in Maryland,[21] who put him to work in making tobacco; but he was soon convinced that Job had never been used to such labour. He every day showed more and more uneasiness under this exercise, and at last grew sick, being no way able to bear it; so that his master was obliged to find easier work for him, and therefore put him to tend the cattle. Job would often leave the cattle, and withdraw into the woods to pray; but a white boy frequently watched him, and whilst he was at his devotion would mock him, and throw dirt in his face. This very much disturbed Job, and added considerably to his other misfortunes; all which were increased by his ignorance of the English language, which prevented his complaining, or telling his case to any person about him. Grown in some measure desperate, by reason of his present hardships, he resolved to travel at a venture; thinking he might possibly be taken up by some master, who would use him better, or otherwise meet with some lucky accident, to divert or abate his grief. Accordingly, he travelled thro' the woods, till he came to the County of Kent,[22] upon Delaware Bay, now esteemed part of Pensilvania; altho' it is properly a part of Maryland, and belongs to my Lord Baltimore. There is a law in force, throughout the colonies of Virginia, Maryland, Pensilvania, etc. as far as Boston in New England, viz. that any Negroe, or white servant who is not known in the county, or has no pass, may be secured by any person, and kept in the common goal [sic], till the master of such servant shall fetch him.[23] Therefore Job being able to give no account of himself, was put in prison there.

This happened about the beginning of June, 1731, when I, who was attending the courts there,[24] and had heard of Job, went with several gentlemen to the goaler's [sic] house, being a tavern, and desired to see him. He was brought into the tavern to us, but could not speak one word of English. Upon our talking and making signs to him, he wrote a line or two before us, and when he read it, pronounced the words Allah and Mahommed; by which, and his refusing a glass of wine we offered him, we perceived he was a Mahometan, but could not imagine of what country he was, or how he got thither; for by his affable carriage, and the easy composure of his countenance, we could perceive he was no common slave.

When Job had been some time confined, an old Negroe man, who lived in that neighbourhood, and could speak the Jalloff [25] language, which Job also understood, went to him, and conversed with him. By this Negroe the keeper was informed to whom Job belonged, and what was the cause of his leaving his master. The keeper thereupon wrote to his master, who soon after fetched him home, and was much kinder to him than before; allowing him a place to pray in, and some other conveniencies, in order to make his slavery as easy as possible. Yet slavery and confinement was by no means agreeable to Job, who had never been used to it; he therefore wrote a letter in Arabick to his father, acquainting him with his misfortunes, hoping he might yet find means to redeem him. This letter he sent to Mr. Vachell Denton, desiring it might be sent to Africa by Captain Pike; but he being gone to England, Mr. Denton sent the letter inclosed to Mr. Hunt, in order to be sent to Africa by Captain Pike from England; but Captain Pike had sailed for Africa before the letter came to Mr. Hunt, who therefore kept it in his own hands, till he should have a proper opportunity of sending it. It happened that this letter was seen by James Oglethorpe, Esq.; [26] who, according to his usual goodness and generosity, took compassion on Job, and gave his bond to Mr. Hunt for the payment of a certain sum, upon the delivery of Job here in England. Mr. Hunt upon this sent to Mr. Denton, who purchased him again of his master for the same money which Mr. Denton had formerly received for him; his master being very willing to part with him, as finding him no ways fit for his business.

He lived some time with Mr. Denton at Annapolis, before any ship could stir out, upon account of the ice that lay in all the rivers of Maryland at that time. In this interval he became acquainted with the Reverend Mr. Henderson,[27] a gentleman of great learning, minister of Annapolis, and commissary to the Bishop of London, who gave Job the character of a person of great piety and learning; and indeed his good nature and affability gained him many friends besides in that place.

In March, 1733, he set sail in the *William,* Captain George Uriel Commander; in which ship I was also a passenger. The character which the Captain and I had of him at Annapolis, induced us to teach him as much of the English language as we could, he being then able to speak but few words of it, and those hardly intelligible. This we set about as soon as we were out at sea, and in about a fortnight's time taught him all his letters, and to spell almost any single syllable, when distinctly pronounced to him; but Job and myself falling sick, we were hindered from making any greater progress at that time. However, by the time that we arrived in England, which was the latter end of April, 1733, he had learned so much of our language, that he was able to understand most of what we said in common conversation; and we that were used to his manner of speaking, could make shift to understand him tolerably well.

During the voyage, he was very constant in his devotions; which he never omitted, on any pretence, notwithstanding we had exceeding bad weather all the time we were at sea. We often permitted him to kill our fresh stock, that he might eat of it himself; for he eats no flesh, unless he has killed the animal with his own hands, or knows that it has been killed by some Mussulman. He has no scruple about fish; but won't touch a bit of pork, it being expressly forbidden by their law. By his good nature and affability he gained the good will of all the sailors, who (not to mention other kind offices) all the way up the channel showed him the head lands and remarkable places; the names of which Job wrote down carefully, together with the accounts that were given him about them. His reason for so doing, he told me, was, that if he met with any Englishman in his country, he might by these marks be able to convince him that he had been in England.

On our arrival in England, we learned that Mr. Oglethorpe was gone to Georgia, and that Mr. Hunt had provided a lodging for Job at Limehouse. After I had visited my friends in the country, I went up on purpose to see Job. He was very sorrowful, and told me, that Mr. Hunt had been applied to by some persons to sell him, who pretended they would send him home; but he feared they would either sell him again as a slave, or if they sent him home would expect an unreasonable ransom for him. I took him to London with me, and waited on Mr. Hunt, to desire leave to carry him to Cheshunt in Hartfordshire; which Mr. Hunt complied with. He told me he had been applyed to, as Job had suggested, but did not intend to part with him without his own consent; but as Mr. Oglethorpe was out of England, if any of Job's friends would pay the money, he would accept of it, provided they would undertake to send him home safely to his own country. I also obtained his promise that he would not dispose of him till he heard farther from me.

Job, while he was at Cheshunt, had the honour to be sent for by most of the gentry of that place, who were mightily pleased with his company, and concerned for his misfortunes. They made him several handsome presents, and proposed that a subscription should be made for the payment

of the money to Mr. Hunt. The night before we set out for London from
Cheshunt, a footman belonging to Samuel Holden, Esq.; brought a letter
to Job, which was, I think, directed to Sir Byby Lake.[28] The letter was
delivered at the African House,[29] upon which the House was pleased to
order that Mr. Hunt should bring in a bill of the whole charges which he
had been at about Job, and be there paid; which was accordingly done,
and the sum amounted to fifty-nine pounds, six shillings, and eleven pence
half-penny. This sum being paid, Mr. Oglethorpe's bond was delivered up
to the Company. Job's fears were now over, with respect to his being sold
again as a slave; yet he could not be persuaded but that he must pay an
extravagant ransom, when he got home. I confess, I doubted much of the
success of a subscription, the sum being great, and Job's acquaintance in
England being so small; therefore, to ease Job's mind, I spoke to a gentleman about the affair, who has all along been Job's friend in a very remarkable manner. This gentleman was so far from discouraging the thing, that
he began the subscription himself with a handsome sum, and promised his
further assistance at a dead lift. Not to be tedious: several friends, both in
London and in the country, gave in their charitable contributions very
readily; yet the sum was so large, that the subscription was about twenty
pounds short of it; but that generous and worthy gentleman before mentioned, was pleased to make up the defect, and the whole sum was com-
pleated.

I went (being desired) to propose the matter to the African Company;
who, after having heard what I had to say, showed me the orders that the
House had made; which were, that Job should be accommodated at the
African House at the Company's expence, till one of the Company's ships
should go to Gambia, in which he should be sent back to his friends without
any ransom. The Company then asked me, if they could do any thing more
to make Job easy; and upon my desire, they ordered, that Mr. Oglethorpe's
bond should be cancelled, which was presently done, and that Job should
have his freedom in form, which he received handsomely engrossed, with
the Company's seal affixed; after which the full sum of the whole charges
(viz. fifty-nine pounds, six shillings, and eleven pence half-penny) was paid
in to their clerk, as was before proposed.

Job's mind being now perfectly easy, and being himself more known,
he went chearfully among his friends to several places, both in town and
country. One day being at Sir Hans Sloan's,[30] he expressed his great desire
to see the Royal Family. Sir Hans promised to get him introduced, when
he had clothes proper to go in. Job knew how kind a friend he had to apply
to upon occasion; and he was soon cloathed in a rich silk dress, made up
after his own country fashion, and introduced to their Majesties, and the

rest of the Royal Family. Her Majesty was pleased to present him with a rich gold watch; and the same day he had the honour to dine with his Grace the Duke of Mountague,[31] and some others of the nobility, who were pleased to make him a handsome present after dinner. His Grace, after that, was pleased to take Job often into the country with him, and show him the tools that are necessary for tilling the ground, both in gardens and fields, and made his servants show him how to use them; and afterwards his Grace furnished Job with all sorts of such instruments, and several other rich presents, which he ordered to be carefully done up in chests, and put on board for his use. 'Tis not possible for me to recollect the many favours he received from his Grace, and several other noblemen and gentlemen, who showed a singular generosity towards him; only, I may say in general, that the goods which were given him, and which he carried over with him, were worth upwards of 500 pounds; besides which, he was well furnished with money, in case any accident should oblige him to go on shore, or occasion particular charges at sea. About the latter end of July last [1734] he embarked on board one of the African Company's ships, bound for Gambia; where we hope he is safely arrived, to the great joy of his friends, and the honour of the English nation.

## SECTION III

I don't pretend here, as I hinted before, to trouble the reader or myself with a full and regular history of Job's country. Those who have the curiosity to inform themselves more particularly in the history of those parts of the world, may consult the voyages that are already published on that subject. I shall only take notice of some occasional remarks upon the customs of the country, as I had them in conversation from Job himself.

It is pretty commonly known that the Africans in general, especially those in the inland countries, are inured from their infancy to a hard and low life, being great strangers to the luxury and delicacy of most of the countries of Europe. They have the necessaries of life, 'tis true, and might have many of the conveniences of it too; but such is the simplicity of their manners, occasioned chiefly by their ignorance, and want of correspondence with the politer part of the world, that they seem contented enough with their plain necessaries, and don't much hanker after greater manners, tho' their country in many places is capable of great improvements.

In Job's country the slaves, and poorer sort of people, are employed in preparing the bread, corn, etc. And here they labour under a great many difficulties, having no proper instruments either for tilling the ground, or reaping the corn when it is ripe; insomuch that they used, in harvest-time, to pull it up, roots and all.[32] To reduce their corn to flour, they rub it between two stones with their hands, which must be very tedious. Nor is their fatigue in building and carriage less, for they perform the whole by mere dint of strength, and downright labour. The better sort of people, who apply themselves to study and reading, are obliged to read whole nights together by the light of the fire (having no candles or lamps, as we have) which must be very troublesome in that hot, sultry country. These, and several other difficulties which these people labour under, we hope will be removed by Job's return; his friends here having suited their presents very judiciously to the necessities of his countrymen; and there is scarce any tool or machine, that can be of real use to them, which Job has not had from some friend or other, and their several uses have been shown to him with a great deal of care.

Some of those people spend a great part of their time in hunting; particularly after the elephants, with whose teeth they drive a great trade. One of those hunters affirmed to Job, that he had seen an elephant surprise a lion (to which beast, it seems, the elephant bears a very great hatred) and carry him to a tree, which he split down, and putting the lion's head thro', let the tree close again on the lion's neck, and there left him to perish. Job did not say that he knew this fact to be true; but it seems to be the more probable, upon account of what he assured me he had been a witness to himself, viz. that an elephant having catched a lion, carried him directly to a great slough, and thrusting the lion's head under the mud, held him there till he was smothered.

One day Job finding a cow of his father's that had been killed and partly devoured, resolved, if possible, to surprise the devourer. Accordingly he placed himself in a tree, near the remains of the cow; and, in the close of the evening, he saw two lions making up to it with great caution, moving slow, and looking carefully about them. At last one came up, which Job shot with a poisoned arrow, and wounded so deadly, that he fell immediately upon the spot; the other coming up soon after, Job shot another arrow, and wounded him; upon which he roared out and fled, but the next morning was found dead about 300 yards from the place.

The poison they dip their arrows in is the juice of a certain tree: and is of such a nature that it infects the blood in a short time, and makes the creature quite stupid and senseless. Altho' it is so deadly a poison, it does not hinder their eating the flesh of the animal that is shot; for as soon as it is stupefied enough to drop down, they catch it, cut its throat, etc., as their law directs, and then eat it. If a man is wounded with one of these arrows, they have an herb, which, if immediately applyed, is a sure remedy, and extracts the poison.[33]

And here I would observe two things, as well from my own observations abroad, as from what I have just mentioned. First, that in all countries where these wild beasts are, at least where I have been, providence has so ordered it, that they will all fly at the sight of a man, and will never attack him, if they have any room to escape by flight. Secondly, that all poisons, of what nature soever, have their antidotes generally near them. One instance of which I shall mention, as being somewhat extraordinary.

The milk, or liquor that is squeezed from the cassavi,[34] or cassader roots (of which roots is made the bread of that name, used in Barbadoes, Jamaica, and all the Leward [sic], Caribbe Islands) is so deadly a poison, that one pint of it will soon kill any creature that drinks it. Yet I knew a cow, which drank a hearty draught of it, and immediately (as if sensible of the danger she was in) went and fed on a shrub, which grows common there, called the sensitive plant,[35] from the shrivelling up of its leaves upon the least touch; and altho' we expected every minute to see her fall down dead, it so expelled the poison, that she received not the least hurt by it.

The manner of their marriages and baptisms is something remarkable. When a man has a mind to marry his son (which they generally do much sooner than in England) and has found out a suitable match for him, he goes to the girl's father, proposes the matter to him, and agrees for the price that he is to pay for her; which the father of the woman always gives to her as a dowry. All things being concluded on, the two fathers and the young man go to the priest, and declare their agreement; which finishes the marriage. But now comes the great difficulty, viz. how the young man shall get his wife home; for the women, cousins, and relations, take on mightily, and guard the door of the house to prevent her being carried away; but at last the young man's presents and generosity to them, makes them abate their grief. He then provides a friend, well mounted, to carry her off; but as soon as she is up on horseback, the women renew their lamentations, and rush in to dismount her. However, the man is generally successful, and rides off with his prize to the house provided for her. After this they make a treat for their friends, but the woman never appears at it; and tho' the ladies here in England are generally more free after marriage than before, with the women in Job's country it is quite contrary; for they are so very bashful, that they will never permit their husbands to see them without a veil on for three years after they are married; insomuch, that altho' Job has a daughter by his last wife, yet he never saw her unveiled since marriage, having been married to her but about two years before he came from home. To prevent quarrels, and keep peace among their wives, the husbands divide their time equally betwixt them; and are so exact in this affair, that if one wife lies in, the husband lies alone in her apartment those nights, that are her turn, and not with the other wife. If a wife proves very bad, they put her away, and she keeps her dowry, and any one may marry her after her divorce; but they don't use to put them away upon slight occasions. If a woman puts away her husband, she must return him her dowry; and she is looked upon always after as a scandalous person, no man caring to have anything to do with her.[36]

All their male children are circumcised; but, besides, they have a kind of baptism for all children, of both sexes. When the child is seven days old, the people that are invited meet together at the father's house; the father names the child, and the priest writes the name of the child on a piece of smooth board. Then the father kills a cow or sheep, according to his ability; part of which is dressed for the company, and the rest distributed amongst the poor: after which the child is washed all over with fair water, and then the priest writes the child's name on paper, which is rolled up, and tied about the child's neck; where it remains, till it is wore or rubbed off.

The ceremony at their burials has nothing remarkable in it. They put the dead body in the earth, and cover it up as we do in England, saying some prayers over it, which Job told me were intended only for the benefit of the bystanders, and not of the dead person; for they are not of opinion that the dead can reap any advantage by their devotion at that time.

Their opinions and traditions, in matters of religion, are much the same with those of the generality of the Mahometans; [37] tho' the learned sort of them give a more plausible and refined turn to the gross and sensual doctrines of the Koran, than those in Turkey, and some other places. They have a strong aversion to the least appearance of idolatry, insomuch that they will not keep a picture of any kind whatsoever in their houses; and the popish worship, at the French factory in their neighbourhood, has much confirmed them in an opinion that all Christians are idolaters. But I shall not say any more here upon this head, since their religion, and the ceremonies relating to it, are pretty well known.

I might add several other particulars, concerning their dress, their houses, oeconomy, and the like; but these too being described at large in several books already published, I shall make an end of this section, and so pass on.

## SECTION IV

Job was about five feet ten inches high, strait limbed, and naturally of a good constitution; altho' the religious abstinence which he observed, and the fatigues he lately underwent, made him appear something lean and weakly. His countenance was exceeding pleasant, yet grave and composed; his hair long, black, and curled, being very different from that of the Negroes commonly brought from Africa.

His natural parts were remarkably good; and I believe most of the gentlemen that conversed with him frequently, will remember many instances of his ingenuity. On all occasions he discovered a solid judgment, a ready memory, and a clear head. And, notwithstanding the prejudices which it was natural for him to have in favour of his own religious principles, it was very observable with how much temper and impartiality he would reason in conversation upon any question of that kind, while at the same time he would frame such replies, as were calculated at once to support his own opinion, and to oblige or please his opponent. In his reasonings there appeared nothing trifling, nothing hypocritical or over-strained; but, on the contrary, strong sense, joined with an innocent simplicity, a strict regard to truth and a hearty desire to find it. Tho' it was a considerable disadvantage to him in company, that he was not sufficient master of our language; yet those who were used to his way, by making proper allowances, always found themselves agreeably entertained by him.

The acuteness of his genius appeared upon many occasions. He very readily conceived the mechanism and use of most of the ordinary instruments which were showed to him here; and particularly, upon seeing a plow, a grist mill, and a clock taken to pieces, he was able to put them together again himself, without any further direction.

His memory was extraordinary; for when he was fifteen years old he could say the whole Alcoran by heart, and while he was here in England he wrote three copies of it without the assistance of any other copy, and without so much as looking to one of those three when he wrote the others. He would often laugh at me when he heard me say I had forgot anything, and told me he hardly ever forgot anything in his life, and wondered that any other body should.

In his natural temper there appeared a happy mixture of the grave and the cheerful, a gentle mildness, guarded by a proper warmth, and a kind and compassionate disposition towards all that were in distress. In conversation he was commonly very pleasant; and would every now and then divert the company with some witty turn, or pretty story, but never to the prejudice of religion, or good manners. I could perceive, by several slight occurrences, that, notwithstanding his usual mildness he had courage enough, when there was occasion for it: and I remember a story which he told me of himself, that is some proof of it. As he was passing one day thro' the country of the Arabs,[38] on his way home, with four servants, and several Negroes which he had bought, he was attacked by fifteen of the Arabs, who are known to be common bandetti or robbers in those parts. Job, upon the first sight of this gang, prepared for a defence; and setting one of his servants to watch the Negroes, he, with the other three, stood on his guard. In the fight one of Job's men was killed, and Job himself was run thro' the leg with a spear.

However, having killed two of the Arabs, together with their captain and two horses, the rest fled, and Job brought off his Negroes safe.

Job's aversion to pictures of all sorts, was exceeding great; insomuch, that it was with great difficulty that he could be brought to sit for his own. We assured him that we never worshipped any picture, and that we wanted his for no other end but to keep us in mind of him. He at last consented to have it drawn; which was done by Mr. Hoare. When the face was finished, Mr. Hoare asked what dress would be most proper to draw him in; and, upon Job's desiring to be drawn in his own country dress, told him he could not draw it, unless he had seen it, or had it described to him by one who had: upon which Job answered, if you can't draw a dress you never saw, why do some of you painters presume to draw God, whom no one ever saw? I might mention several more of his smart repartees in company, which showed him to be a man of wit and humour, as well as good sense: but that I may not be tedious, what I have said shall suffice for this head.

As to his religion, 'tis known he was a Mahometan, but more moderate in his sentiments than most of that religion are. He did not believe a sensual paradise, nor many other ridiculous and vain traditions, which pass current among the generality of the Turks. He was very constant in his devotion to God; but said, he never prayed to Mahommed, nor did he think it lawful to address any but God himself in prayer. He was so fixed in the belief of one God, that it was not possible, at least during the time he was here, to give him any notion of the Trinity; so that having had a New Testament given him in his own language, when he had read it, he told me he had perused it with a great deal of care, but could not find one word in it of three Gods, as some people talk: I did not care to puzzle him, and therefore answered in general, that the English believed only in one God. He showed upon all occasions a singular veneration for the name of God, and never pronounced the word Allah without a peculiar accent, and a remarkable pause: and indeed his notions of God, Providence, and a future state, were in the main very just and reasonable.

His learning, considering the disadvantages of the place he came from, was far from being contemptible. The books in his country are all in manuscript, all upon religion; and are not, as I remember, more than thirty in number. They are all in Arabick; but the Alcoran, he says, was originally wrote by God himself, not in Arabick, and God sent it by the Angel Gabriel to Ababuker, some time before Mahommed was born; the Angel taught Ababuker to read it, and no one can read it but those who are instructed after a different manner from that in which the Arabick is commonly taught. However, I am apt to think that the difference depends only upon the pointing of the Arabick, which is of later date. Job was well acquainted with the historical part of our Bible, and spoke very respectfully of the good men mentioned in Scripture; particularly of Jesus Christ, who, he said, was a very great prophet, and would have done much more good in the world, if he had not been cut off so soon by the wicked Jews; which made it necessary for God to send Mahomet to confirm and improve his doctrine.

## AYUBA'S RETURN TO AFRICA

The next day [8 August 1734] about noon came up the *Dolphin* Snow, which saluted the fort with nine guns, and had the same number returned; after which came on shore the captain, four writers, one apprentice to the Company, and one black man, by name Job Ben Solomon, a Pholey [Pulo] of Bundo in Foota, who in the year 1731, as he was travelling in Jagra [Jarra], and driving his herds of cattle across the countries, was robbed and carried to Joar, where he was sold to Captain Pyke, commander of the ship *Arabella,* who was then trading there. By him he was carried to Maryland, and sold to a planter, with whom Job lived about a twelve month without being once beat by his master; at the end of which time he had the good fortune to have a letter of his own writing in the Arabic tongue conveyed to England. This letter coming to the hand of Mr. Oglethorpe, he sent the same to Oxford to be translated; which, when done, gave him so much satisfaction, and so good an opinion of the man, that he directly ordered him to be bought from his master, he soon after setting out for Georgia. Before he returned from thence, Job came to England; where being brought to the acquaintance of the learned Sir Hans Sloane, he was by him found a perfect master of the Arabic tongue, by translating several manuscripts and inscriptions upon medals: he was by him recommended to his Grace the Duke of Montague, who being pleased with the sweetness of humour, and mildness of temper, as well as genius and capacity of the man, introduced him to court, where he was graciously received by the Royal Family, and most of the nobility, from whom he received distinguishing marks of favour. After he had continued in England about fourteen months, he wanted much to return to his native country, which is Bundo (a place about a week's travel over land from the Royal African Company's factory at Joar, on the River Gambia) of which place his father was High-Priest, and to whom he sent letters from England. Upon his setting out from England he received a good many noble presents from her most Gracious Majesty Queen Caroline, his Highness the Duke of Cumberland,[39] his Grace the Duke of Montague, the Earl of Pembroke,[40] several ladies of quality, Mr. [Samuel] Holden, and the Royal African Company, who have ordered their agents to show him the greatest respect.

.  .  .  .  .  .  .  .  .  .  .  .  .  .

Job Ben Solomon having a mind to go up to Cower [Kau-Ur] [41] to talk with some of his countrymen, went along with me. In the evening we weighed anchor, saluting the fort with five guns, which returned the same number.

On the 26th [of August, 1734] we arrived at the Creek of Damasensa,[42] and having some old aquaintances at the town of Damasensa, Job and I went up in the yawl; in the way, going up a very narrow place for about half a mile, we saw several monkeys of a beautiful blue and red, which the natives tell me never set their feet on the ground, but live entirely amongst the trees, leaping from one to another at so great distances, as any one, were they not to see it, would think improbable.

In the evening, as my friend Job and I were sitting under a great tree at Damasensa, there came by us six or seven of the very people who robbed and made a slave of Job, about thirty miles from hence, about three years ago; Job, tho' a very even-tempered man at other times, could not contain himself when he saw them, but fell into a most terrible passion, and was for killing them with his broad sword and pistols, which he always took care to have about him. I had much ado to dissuade him from falling upon the six men; but at last, by representing to him the ill consequences that would infalliby attend such a rash action, and the impossibility of mine or his own escaping alive, if he should attempt it, I made him lay aside the thoughts of it, and persuaded him to sit down and pretend not to know them, but ask them questions about himself; which he accordingly did, and they answered nothing but the truth. At last he asked them how the king their master did; they told him he was dead, and by further enquiry we found, that amongst the goods for which he sold Job to Captain Pyke there was a pistol, which the king used commonly to wear slung about his neck with a string; and as they never carry arms without being loaded, one day this accidentally went off, and the ball's lodging in his throat, he died presently. At the closing of this story Job was so very much transported, that he immediately fell on his knees, and returned thanks to Mahomet for making this man die by the very goods for which he sold him into slavery; and then turning to me, he said, "Mr. Moore, you see now God Almightly was displeased at this man's making me a slave, and therefore made him die by the very pistol for which he sold me; yet I ought to forgive him, says he, because had I not been sold, I should neither have known any thing of the English tongue, nor have had any of the fine, useful and valuable things I now carry over, nor have known that in the world there is such a place as England, nor such noble, good and generous people as Queen Caroline, Prince William, the Duke of Montague, the Earl of Pembroke, Mr. Holden, Mr. Oglethorpe, and the Royal African Company."

On the 1st of September we arrived at Joar, the freshes being very strong against us. I immediately took an inventory of the company's effects, and gave receipts to Mr. Gill for the same. After which we unloaded the sloop, and then I sent her to Yanimarew [Niani-Maro] [43] for a load of corn for James Fort, where she stayed till the 25th, and then came back to Joar, during which time I made some trade with the merchants, though at a pretty high price.

On Job's first arrival here, he desired I would send a messenger up to his own country to acquaint his friends of his arrival. I spoke to one of the blacks which we usually employ upon those occasions, to procure me a messenger, who brought to me a Pholey, who knew the High Priest his father, and Job himself, and expressed great joy at seeing him in safety returned from slavery, he being the only man (except one) that was ever known to come back to this country, after having been once carried a slave out of it by white men. Job gave him the message himself, and desired his father should not come down to him, for it was too far for him to travel; and that it was fit for the young to go to the old, and not for the old to come to the young. He also sent some presents by him to his wives, and desired him to bring his little one, which was his best beloved, down to him. After the messenger was gone, Job went frequently along with me to Cower, and several other places about the country; he spoke always very handsome of the English, and what he said, took away a great deal of the horror of the Pholeys for the state of slavery amongst the English; for they before generally imagined, that all who were sold for slaves, were generally either eaten or murdered, since none ever returned. His description of the English gave them also a great notion of the power of England, and a veneration for those who traded amongst them. He sold some of the presents he brought with him from England for trading-goods, with which he bought a woman-slave and two horses, which were very useful to him there, and which he designed to carry with him to Bundo, whenever he should set out thither. He used to give his country people a good deal of writing-paper, which is a very useful commodity amongst them, and of which the Company had presented him with several reams. He used to pray frequently, and behaved himself with great mildness and affability to all, so that he was very popular and well-beloved. The messenger not being thought to return soon, Job desired to go down to James Fort to take care of his goods, I promising to send him word when the messenger came back, and also to send some other messengers, for fear the first should miscarry.

On the 26th [of September] I sent down the *Fame* sloop to James Fort, and Job going along with her, I gave the master orders to show him all the respect he could.

.    .    .    .    .    .    .    .    .    .    .    .    .    .

On the 29th [of January, 1734/35] came up from Damasensa in a canoa Job Ben Solomon, who, I forgot to say, came up in the *Fame* sloop along with me from James Fort on the 26th of December last, and going on shore with me at Elephants Island, and hearing that the people of Joar were run away,[44] it made him unwilling to proceed up hither, and therefore he desired Conner to put him and his things ashore at a place called India, about six miles above Damasensa, where he has continued ever since; but now hearing that there is no farther danger, he thought he might venture his body and goods along with mine and the Company's, and so came up.

On the 14th [of February] a messenger, whom I had sent to Job's country, returned hither with letters, and advice that Job's father died before he got up thither, but that he had lived to receive the letters sent by Job from England, which brought him the welcome news of his son's being redeemed out of slavery, and the figure he made in England. That one of Job's wives was married to another man; but that as soon as the husband heard of Job's arrival here, he thought it advisable to abscond: that since Job's absence from this country, there has been such a dreadful war, that there is not so much as one cow left in it, tho' when Job was there, it was a very noted country for numerous herds of large cattle. With this messenger came a good many of Job's old acquaintance, whom he was exceeding glad to see; but notwithstanding the joy he had to see his friends, he wept grievously for his father's death, and the misfortunes of his country. He forgave his wife, and the man that had taken her; for, says he, Mr. Moore, she could not help thinking I was dead, for I was gone to a land from whence no Pholey ever yet returned; therefore she is not to be blamed, nor the man neither. For three or four days he held a conversation with his friends without any interruption, unless to sleep or eat.

.    .    .    .    .    .    .    .    .    .    .    .    .    .    .

On the 8th [of April, 1735], having delivered up the company's effects to Mr. James Conner, and taken proper discharges for the same, I embarked on board the Company's sloop *James*, to which Mr. Hull accompanied me, and parted with me in a very friendly manner. Job likewise came down with me to the sloop, and parted with me with tears in his eyes, at the same time giving me letters for his Grace the Duke of Montague, the Royal African Company, Mr. Oglethorpe, and several other gentlemen in England, telling me to give his love and duty to them, and to acquaint them, that as he designs to learn to write the English tongue, he will, when he is master of it, send them longer epistles, and full accounts of what shall happen to him hereafter; desiring me, that as I had lived with him almost ever since he came here, I would let his Grace and the other gentlemen know what he had done, and that he was the next day going with Mr. Hull [45] up to Yani-marew, from whence he would accompany him to the gum forest, and make so good an understanding between the Company and his country people, that the English nation should reap the benefit of the gum trade; saying at last, that he would spend his days in endeavouring to do good for the English, by whom he had been redeemed from slavery, and from whom he had received such innumerable favours.

## NOTES

[1] The modern version of the Pular name would be Ayuba Suleiman Ibrahima Diallo and Ayuba's Arabic signature would be transliterated as Ayūb ibn Sulaymān Jāl. The *Yenodé,* or surname, of Diallo is in fact the name of one of the four major divisions of the Fulbe people. Ayuba's mother was Tanomata, the first wife of Suleiman (Nicholas, *Literary Anecdotes,* 6:90–91). His name as a slave was Simon, but he discarded this in favor of Job, the English equivalent of Ayuba.

[2] The phrase "a town called Boonda" might mean a town in Bondu, or might refer to the capital of the country, following a construction that was fairly common in the Western Sudan. For example, Abū Bakr al-Ṣiddīq (see Chap. 5) refers to Birnin Gazargamo, then the capital of Bornu, in an Arabic phrase translated as "the city of Bornu." In the same way, the phrase actually used by Ayuba in talking with Bluett may well have been something like "the city of Bondu," meaning its capital. It is more likely, however, that Bluett simply made a mistake. The capital at this period shifted from place to place with the movements of the ruler (Brigaud, *Histoire traditionelle du Sénégal,* p. 218; Rançon, "Le Boundou," pp. 433–63).

[3] Galumbo and Catumbo are variants of Galam, or, more correctly, Ngalam or Gadiaga.

[4] Fulbe kingdoms were often prefaced by Futa—as Futa Toro, Futa Jallon, and sometimes Futa Bondu. In this case, it appears to refer to Futa Toro and Bondu together. The *satigis* of Futa Toro may have claimed jurisdiction as far as the Gambia, but there is no evidence of their having more than a vague claim to suzerainty over the Ferlo wilderness or over Gadiaga, and this only at certain periods.

[5] In the eighteenth century the Niger River, which was known to Europeans only in its upper reaches and only through Arab reports, was believed to flow from east to west across the Western Sudan, dividing into two branches which emptied into the Atlantic as the Senegal and the Gambia. It was not until the nineteenth century that Europeans recognized the intricate system of waterways flowing into the Gulf of Guinea between the Bights of Benin and Biafra as the delta of the Niger.

[6] Bluett's reporting is confused by a little knowledge. Eighteenth-century Europeans knew Timbuktu as Tombut, mainly through the sixteenth-century account by Leo Africanus. Bluett was evidently trying to bring Ayuba's account into line with Leo Africanus. Thus, when Ayuba reported that the eastern boundary of Bondu was water —and it was, in fact, the Faleme River—Bluett translated this information to conform to seventeenth- and eighteenth-century maps of Africa, which showed Lacus Guarde about where Lake Débo now is, along the course of the Niger in Mali. In the same way, Ayuba reported the country of Bambuk across the Faleme from Bondu, but Bluett warped the information to make Bambuk appear as the city of Tombut.

7 The Denianke *satigi* of Futa Toro, Bubakar Sawa Lamu (*ca.* 1640–73).

8 *Alfa,* usually meaning simply a learned man, derived from the Arabic *al-fāqih,* a person learned in law.

9 The suggestion that Ayuba's town (or even the state of Bondu) was founded by authority of the *satigi* of Futa Toro runs counter to the dominant Sisibe tradition that Bondu was founded by Malik Si with the authority of the *tunka* of Tuabo. It is, however, far from impossible that population movements into the sparsely settled Bondu of the late seventeenth century could have been sponsored by several neighboring rulers who had claims to the territory. One variant tradition given in 1941 by Sada Abdul Si (a descendant of the Sisibe dynasty and canton chief of Koussan since 1917) reported that the Sisibe themselves came to Bondu under Tukulor authority, though not that of the Satigis (Bonnel de Mezières, "Les Diakanké," p. 23).

10 In present-day Bondu, the principal Islamic office in each village or town is that of Imam of the Mosque (Pular: *eliman*), who leads the Friday prayers. This office is frequently passed from father to son, just as the equivalent secular office of village head is also passed from father to son. The situation Ayuba describes, of having the two offices combined in a single person, is sometimes found today, though it is uncommon.

His information, however, provides a clue for the tentative identification of Ayuba's town. The largest concentration in present-day Bondu of people bearing the name Diallo is the town of Marsa, about fifteen miles southeast of Bakel. While village headship and the imamate of the mosque are not always held by the same individual, they often have been in the past; and both offices are hereditary in the Diallo family— the only instance in present-day Bondu where this is the case. Furthermore, the village still has an unusually strong Islamic religious tradition. While village traditions do not remember Ayuba by name (since they preserve only the names of the family head in each generation), the most prominent member of the family in recent times was Suleiman Diallo, village head and imam of the mosque in the 1850's. The customary practices of personal nomenclature suggest that one or more people named Suleiman Diallo had been prominent in the family during the more distant past. Possibly Ayuba's father, Suleiman, was one of them (personal communication from Mamadou Diallo, Imam of the Mosque, Marsa, and from other notables of Marsa).

This evidence at least creates a presumption that Ayuba came from Marsa, and the fact that the Diallo of present-day Bondu are mainly found in the region between Gabou and Kidira creates an even stronger presumption that he must at least have come from the northeastern part of Bondu. But people of Ayuba's social group, the Muslim clerics with mercantile interests, were easily mobile. He may have lived in a number of different places.

11 According to the local version of Islamic law, inheritance of the kingship was supposed to pass to the oldest member of the ruling family. In practice, this meant that it passed to the oldest living brother of the deceased monarch until no brothers remained, rather than passing directly to the sons of any of them. But pre-Islamic Futa Toro had been matrilineal. A male child inherited from his maternal uncle, not from his father. This had left a mark on Tukulor kinship patterns. As late as the twentieth century, a man's children were thought of as especially closely related to those of his sister. These cross-cousins were known as *dendirabe,* and marriage between *dendirabe* of the opposite sex was especially favored. The advantage in the case of inheritance is obvious. Property and heritable office could be passed to a man's descendants by both Islamic law and matrilineal succession (Henri Gaden, *Proverbes et maximes peuls et toucouleurs, traduits, expliqués, et annotés* [Paris, 1931], pp.

17–19). The Denianke of the late seventeenth and early eighteenth century played a similar game in seeking the office of *satigi* for their sons by arranging marriages that would reinforce the claim in Islamic law with a second, matrilineal claim (Labat, *Nouvelle Rélation*, 2:197–98).

The order of succession, however, was very confused in Futa Toro during the early eighteenth century. French reports make it clear that the intervention of Trarza and Morrocan forces made for brief reigns with many pretenders appearing, who might or might not be recognized in later tradition. King-lists therefore disagree with one another, and none of them takes account of repeated returns to power by a single ruler. It is clear, however, that Bubakar Tabakali was succeeded by his brother, as Ayuba's account says—but the brother in question was Sire Tabakali, not Geladio (see Table 1, above). Geladio Jegi came to the throne much later, being deposed in 1718 and dying shortly afterward (Delcourt, *Établissements français*, p. 155).

[12] According to one tradition, Samba Geladio Jegi was an adolescent when his father died (F. V. Equilbecq, *Contes indigènes de l'ouest africain français* [3 vols., Paris, 1913–16], 2:4). Since Ayuba would have been about seventeen in 1718, he and Samba Geladio Jegi were very nearly the same age, helping to confirm the identification of Ayuba's Samba with the traditional figure of Samba Geladio Jegi. But Samba was not universally recognized as king, though he fought for many years as a pretender to the satigiship and achieved some control of the country briefly in 1735. In 1737, he signed a treaty with the French official in charge of Fort Saint Joseph in Gadiaga, by which he was to secure French help against the reigning *satigi*, Konko Bubu Musa (for text of the treaty, see Delcourt, *Établissements français*, pp. 412–13). His literary fame, however, was far greater than his achievements. Ironically enough, Ayuba's report that Samba was a great king in Africa may well have led to the popularity of Sambo as a name for Afro-Americans (A. P. Middleton, "The Strange Story of Job Ben Solomon," *William and Mary Quarterly*, 5[3rd ser.]:342 [1948]). Within Africa, his long struggles against Konko Bubu Musa were turned into legend and then into epic poetry. In the end, he came to be the best remembered in the Western Sudan of all the Denianke dynasty. For various versions of the legend of Samba Geladio Jegi, see Siré Abbas Soh, in Delafosse and Gaden, "Fouta Sénégalais," pp. 31–32; Raffenel, *Nouveau voyage*, 2:320–44; Equilbecq, *Contes indigènes*, 2:3–42; L. J. B. Bérenger-Féraud, *Receuil des contes populaires de la Sénégambie* (Paris, 1885), pp. 39–49; Lanrezac, "Légendes soudanaises." *Revue économique française*, 5:607–19 (October 1907), pp. 615–19; Franz de Zeltner. *Contes du Sénégal et du Niger* (Paris, 1913), pp. 151–57.

[13] *Imam*, leader of prayer at the mosque.

[14] Unlikely to be Tombut, or Timbuktu, some 600 miles away. Should be understood as "an *alfa* from Bambuk."

[15] Damga, the southeasternmost part of the Tukulor kingdom bordering on Bondu and Gadiaga.

[16] Mandingo or Mandinka sometimes refers to all of the Mande-speaking peoples, and sometimes more narrowly to the Malinke. Malinke actually lived on both banks of the lower Gambia.

[17] Pike's ship was at Joar, near the present-day town Kau-Ur, about 110 miles upstream from the mouth of the Gambia and 200 miles from Bondu.

[18] He appears later in the correspondence of the Royal African Company as Lahmin Jay (Lamine Ndiaye). Ndiaye is a Wolof name, but the Ndiaye family, of Jollof origin, had already established themselves as the dominant family in Bakel. The concern Ayuba showed later in securing his return from slavery in America suggests that

Lamine was not a casual acquaintance in the Gambia, but one of the Ndiaye family of Bakel.

19 Ayuba and Lamine were captured in Jarra, the kingdom midway between Kiang and Niamina. Lamine was ransomed and returned to Africa in 1738.

20 Francis Moore, at James Island farther down the Gambia, gave this account in his journal of 11 April 1731: "Soon after came down the *Arabella,* Captain Pyke, a separate trader, from Joar, loaded with slaves; and having stay'd a day or two at James Fort, sail'd for Maryland, having among his compliment of slaves one man call'd Job Ben Solomen, of the Pholey [Fulbe] race, and son of the high-priest of Bundo in Foota, a place about ten days journey from Gillyfree [Jufureh, on the north bank of the Gambia opposite James Island]; who was travelling on the south side of this river, with a servant, and about twenty or thirty head of cattle, which induced the King of a country a little way inland, between Tancrowall [near present-day Janna-Kunda] and the Yamina [Niamina opposite Joar], not only to seize his cattle, but also his person and man, and sold them both to Captain Pyke, as he was trading at Joar. He would have been redeemed by the Pholeys, but was carried out of the river before they had notice of his being a slave" (Moore, *Travels,* p. 69).

21 The largest island in Chesapeake Bay, at its closest point about seven miles east of Annapolis. The eastern approaches to the Chesapeake Bay Bridge now cross the island.

22 Now Kent County, Delaware. In the eighteenth century, Kent, Sussex, and New Castle counties were in dispute between the rival proprietors of Pennsylvania and Maryland. They now form the separate State of Delaware, but at that time they were in the effective possession of Pennsylvania. Ayuba's escape therefore took him across the narrow channel separating Kent Island from the mainland of Queen Annes County, Maryland, then eastward across that county and across the colonial boundary into the Penns' jurisdiction, a distance of some thirty or forty miles in all.

23 This Pennsylvania legislation, passed in 1725–26, carried the penalty of ten lashes on the bare back for any slave found away from his master's house after nine at night, or more than ten miles from his master's property at any time, without written permission (E. R. Turner, *The Negro in Pennsylvania* [Washington, 1911], pp. 31–32).

24 Dover, Delaware, then, as now, the county seat of Kent County.

25 Wolof, a language related to Ayuba's native Pular.

26 James Edward Oglethorpe (1696–1785), M. P., 1722–54; founder of the colony of Georgia in 1732; director of the Royal African Company, 1730–32, and its deputy governor for a time in 1732. Oglethorpe was a philanthropist as well as a colonial promoter, and slavery was initially forbidden in Georgia; see A. A. Ettinger, *James Edward Oglethorpe, Imperial Idealist* (Oxford, 1936).

27 Jacob Henderson (d. 1751), born in Glenary, Ireland; ordained in the Church of England, 1710; served for a time as a missionary in Dover, Delaware, for the Society for the Propagation of the Gospel; resigned from S.P.G.; became the first clergyman in Annapolis, Maryland, and later (1715–23) Commissary to the Bishop of London for the Western Shore of Maryland; Commissary for the whole of Maryland in 1729–34 (Nelson W. Richtmyer, *Maryland's Established Church* [Baltimore, 1956], pp. 188–89). The connection between Henderson and Vachell Denton, the slave dealer, was evidently through the Church, since Denton was a vestryman at St. Anne's, Annapolis, where Henderson had once been rector (Ethan Allen, *Historical Notices of St. Ann's Parish, Ann Arundel County, Maryland* [Baltimore, 1857], p. 125).

[28] Sub-Governor of the Royal African Company.

[29] In the City of London, headquarters of the Royal African Company.

[30] Sir Hans Sloane (1660–1753), physician and botanist; conducted research in the West Indies; president of the Royal Society (1727–41); president of the Royal College of Physicians (1719–35); First Physician to King George II.

[31] John Montagu, second Duke of Montagu (d. 1749); courtier and one-time grantee of the West Indian islands of St. Vincent and St. Lucia; a noted Afrophile and patron of visiting Africans and Negro Americans.

[32] This is another instance of Ayuba's failure to make himself fully understood. The "corn" which the Bondunkobe pulled up roots and all was, of course, peanuts, which was already a common food crop and has since become the principal cash crop of the country.

[33] The poison is probably *Strophanthus hispidus,* widely cultivated in West Africa for the seeds, which form the base of the fluid extract into which arrows were dipped. Antidotes were usually kept secret, but several have been reported, including *Garcinia Iola,* or bitter kola, a forest plant which was nevertheless marketed in precolonial times in the savanna country as far north as Bondu (J. M. Dalziel, *The Useful Plants of West Tropical Africa* [London, 1948], pp. 91, 379–80; A. Chevalier, "Nos connaissances actuelles sur la géographie botanique et la flore économique du Sénégal et du Soudan," in Lasnet, Chevalier, Cligny, and Rambaud, *Une mission au Sénégal* [Paris, 1900]).

[34] Bitter cassava, *Manihot esculenta,* native to America but widely used in West Africa as a staple food. The poisonous hydrocyanic acid of the sap is removed by squeezing or soaking in water before cooking.

[35] Sensitive plant, *Mimosa pudica,* used as forage for cattle in certain parts of West Africa (Dalziel, *Useful Plants,* p. 217). I have seen no evidence that it neutralizes the hydrocyanic acid in uncooked cassava.

[36] For Fulbe marriage customs, see Monteil, *Les Khassonké,* pp. 170–214; Derrick J. Stenning, *Savannah Nomads* (London, 1959), pp. 111–16; and Marguerite Dupire. *Peuls nomades* (Paris, 1962), pp. 232–47.

[37] Bluett was misinformed. European travellers to Bondu in the later eighteenth century reported that a significant part of the population was still polytheist, and that the religion of the clerical class as well as popular Islam had important polytheistic elements at that time as it does today; see Park, *Travels,* 1:78, 89; and D. Houghton in *Proceedings of the Association for Promoting the Discovery of the Interior Parts of Africa* (2d ed., 2 vols., London, 1810), 1:247.

[38] This could refer to any of the Arabic-speaking region north of the Senegal in present-day Mauritania.

[39] William Augustus (1721–65), third son of George II and Queen Caroline.

[40] Henry Herbert (1693–1751), ninth Earl of Pembroke.

[41] Then one of the most important markets on the river, located in the state of Salum.

[42] In Jarra, the south-bank state in which Ayuba was captured.

[43] About twenty-five miles upstream from Joar and Kau-Ur.

[44] On account of a dynastic war in Salum during the latter part of 1734.

[45] Thomas Hull, nephew of Richard Hull who was then governor at James Fort.

*The problem of determining the origins of Afro-
Americans is a compelling one which challenges not only
scholars but Black Americans as well. Indeed, the
more precise location of one's ancestral home is intimately
linked to the question of identity. The following article
by Curtin and Vansina is an attempt, by the use of
historical records, to determine with greater precision
the areas from which Black Americans derive.*

# Sources of the Nineteenth-Century
## Atlantic Slave Trade

### Philip D. Curtin and Jan Vansina

The Atlantic slave trade was the most important link between Africa
and other continents for at least two full centuries from 1650 to 1850, yet
relatively little is known about the sources of the trade, its commercial organization within Africa, or the overall consequence for African societies. Estimates of the number of slaves exported each year or decade are mainly
educated guesses. For certain periods it is relatively easy to determine the
number of slaves carried by the ships of one or other of the European maritime powers, but many different nations participated in the trade. Statistical
information is widely scattered in a dozen different archives, and historical
demographers have not yet attempted a systematic exploration of these diffuse sources of information. The national origins of slaves have also been
studied at the receiving end, within the national context of a single American
country. While this kind of investigation is important for the history of Mexico or Brazil, no country in America received a true sample of all slaves
entering the trade. The sources of the trade were, indeed, subject to change
from time to time, and the distribution of the slaves in America shifted
constantly in response to all kinds of political and economic changes in
Europe and in the Americas themselves.

The British attempt to suppress the slave trade of the early nineteenth
century, however, produced data about the European slave trade as a whole.
When the British attempted to capture slavers at sea, they also captured the
slaves in transit. From 1808 to 1842, the great majority of these recaptives,

From *The Journal of African History,* V, No. 2 (1964), 185–208. Reprinted by permission of the authors and the Cambridge University Press.

or "liberated Africans," as they were usually called at the time, were landed and settled in Sierra Leone. To the degree that the Royal Navy captured a random sample of slaves entering the trade, the national origins of the population of Sierra Leone in the 1840s will reflect the range of national origins for the Atlantic slave trade as a whole.

Fortunately there are some excellent qualitative data about origins of the Sierra Leone population, and some quantitative data as well. These are contained in two separate surveys of the later 1840s. By far the most detailed was the work of Sigismund Wilhelm Koelle, who spent five years (December 1847 to February 1853) in Sierra Leone as a linguist employed by the Church Missionary Society. One aspect of his research, mainly carried out in 1849, was the collection of sample vocabularies of African languages spoken by the liberated Africans and other visitors to the colony. In all, he collected some 160 languages, occasionally with a number of dialectical variants. These were ultimately published in the great *Polyglotta Africana*. The value of the work is more than linguistic. Since he tried to make his survey as exhaustive as possible, his list of languages represents very nearly all of those spoken by the liberated Africans in Sierra Leone. Koelle also kept very careful notes about his informants, giving the name, the country of origin, the date of departure from that country, and the number of each informant's fellow countrymen present in the colony.

The second survey was the Sierra Leone census of 1848, which included data on "tribal origins" for Freetown and vicinity. The census's "tribal" categories were not the same as those of Koelle, but the enumeration fills the most important gap in Koelle's quantitative data. Koelle's informants could report the numbers of their fellow countrymen accurately enough when they were very few, but they could not supply quantitative data about the very large groups, like the Yoruba or Ibo. Thus, while Koelle gives a list of groups present in Sierra Leone, and reasonably accurate statistics about the size of the smaller groups, the census figures give the broader picture of regional origins. The two together thus present a reasonably full and complementary picture.

While the two surveys together reveal the broad patterns of the nineteenth-century slave trade, they have certain limitations. First of all, the Sierra Leone population of 1848–9 was not completely representative of the liberated Africans as a whole. About three-quarters of all slaves recaptured by British ships between 1808 and 1840 were landed in Sierra Leone. Thereafter, about half were taken to the West Indies instead. Furthermore, the surveys conducted at the end of three decades necessarily contain an age bias and an emigration bias. That is, they will certainly under-represent the older people among those captured early in the century. They will also under-represent groups from the hinterland of Sierra Leone or other coastal regions to which it was relatively easy to return.

The distances these liberated Africans could travel are sometimes surprising. Koelle's Wolof informant makes it clear that virtually all of the Wolof in Sierra Leone returned to Senegal. Some of the Yoruba recaptives returned by sea to Badagri and Lagos during the 1840s, and more were to follow. Discrepancies between the number of liberated Africans landed in the colony and the total colonial population are probably accounted for by emigration of this kind. By 1841, 70,000 recaptives had been landed, while the total population of Sierra Leone was only 37,000.

A second weakness in the data comes from the fact that the Navy patrolled some parts of the coast more frequently than others. It concentrated on West Africa, from the Gambia to the Cameroons. The sample of recaptives from this region is therefore the most nearly representative of Africans entering the trade. Even for this region, however, the operations of the cruisers would not have produced a perfectly random sample. Freetown was the most important British base in tropical Africa between 1808 and 1827. During this period, cruisers patrolled most frequently along the "Windward Coast" on either side of Sierra Leone. Then, from 1827 to 1832, the British established a base at Fernando Po, and even after this base was withdrawn they used Fernando Po informally and patrolled more frequently in the Bights of Benin and Biafra. The sample may therefore be expected to represent the western section of the coast more accurately from 1810 to the mid-1820s, and the eastern section from the mid-1820s onward.

The sample may also be biased by the legal niceties of the blockade. French and American ships could not be captured legally by British cruisers, though they were occasionally captured by the naval patrols of their own nationality. Illegal French slavers probably operated more frequently off the coasts of Senegal. Groups from the Senegambian interior may therefore be under-represented. Not enough is known about the geographical range of illegal, American-flag slavers to predict the possible influence of their operations.

The influence of changing blockade tactics is also difficult to assess. The number of ships on station varied from time to time, and so did the number of slaves recaptured. It was less than 500 in 1820 and more than 8,500 in 1837. Blockade tactics also varied according to coastal conditions of wind and current. Along the coast between Cape Palmas and the Cameroons the prevailing wind and current are both westerly. Ships inbound from the Americas therefore tended to follow the coastline. Once the cargo was loaded, however, they dropped south of the equator to find the southeast trades and avoid the contrary currents off the coast. The usual naval procedure until after 1839 was to wait well off shore in the hope of catching a loaded slaver making off for the south, as they all had to do if they were to reach the Americas. This tactic was forced on the Navy by the fact that the courts would not condemn slavers unless slaves were actually found on board. In 1835, however, a new treaty with Spain made it legal to capture ships equipped for the slave trade (and, for the first time, to capture Spanish ships south of the equator). The same provisions were extended to Portuguese ships by an Act of Parliament in 1839. From then onward, a close blockade was possible. Ships inbound down the coast were searched for the equipment of the slave trade, and the blockade was supplemented from time to time by raids against the shore installations of the slave traders. Of the two modes of operation, off-shore cruising was more likely to yield a random sample of slavers in the trade. The sample from the Bights of Benin and Biafra is probably more nearly representative than that of the Windward Coast hinterland. The sample from any part of the coast before 1839 will also be more accurate than that of the 1840s. By then, it was possible to make a strategic decision to clean out the slave trade from one section of coast at a time.

But these considerations apply only to West Africa. South of the equator the anti-slavery operations were quite different, and the numerical data shown in maps 4 and 5 are not directly comparable with those of maps 1, 2, and 3. The sample from southern areas is smaller (relative to their total slave trade) than the West African samples. The legal position of the Navy was not assured against Spanish slavers south of the equator until 1835, against Portuguese until 1839, nor against Brazilians until 1845. Naval patrols on the Congo and Angola coast, or northward from Cape Town to the Mozambique Channel, began only in the 1840s. Most of the earlier Brazilian slave trade was therefore absent from the Sierra Leone data, and slavers bound for North America and the Caribbean were not likely to be captured until they had reached American waters. Koelle's list of Central African peoples entering the slave trade is nevertheless the most comprehensive we have for any period before the 1840s.

With all these qualifications, the data still throw some light on the sources of slaves entering the trade. In Central Africa, for example, the evidence confirms what was already suspected on other grounds. Thus most of the slaves shipped from the west coast came from the immediate hinterland of Luanda—from such groups as the Ambundu—or else from the hinterland of the slave-trade ports north of the Congo mouth—from such groups as the Vili, Yombe, Boma, Nsundi and Kongo. The numbers finding their way into the trade decreased with increasing distance from the coast. The inland sources were also predictably those living along the principal trade routes into the interior. One route ran from the Congo-mouth harbors to Stanley Pool, and thence up the Congo, with a branch to the upper Ogowe and the Teke and Tsayi country. A second ran from Luanda to Cassange and Lundaland, and a third ran from Benguela to the Ovimbundu country.

The most striking pattern of the east-coast trade is the absence of slaves from the Swahili coast and its hinterland. The trade apparently divided in the vicinity of Cape Delgado, the northern segment flowing to Zanzibar, the Red Sea and the Persian Gulf, while a southern, Portuguese segment flowed both to the islands of the Indian Ocean and to the Americas. The Mozambique slaves, however, came mainly from the immediate hinterland of Inhambane, Quilimane, Mozambique, and Tete, with an extension along the Yao-operated trade route from Lake Nyasa to the coast. This route, incidentally, explains why Koelle's Medo informant was able to speak Yao.

The pattern of the West African slave trade was more complex, and it was more clearly associated with recent political events. Its most striking feature is the apparent absence of the trade from the Ivory Coast and its hinterland.

In the 1680s this region had been considered the most profitable area in the whole slave trade of the Royal Africa Company. The causes of its neglect in the nineteenth century were mainly geographical. The long unbroken coastline was dangerous for shipping in the best of circumstances. Cargoes had to be landed across a steeply shelving beach with a heavy surf. In earlier centuries it was reckoned to be useless in time of war. Privateers and commerce raiders could all too easily sweep down a coast so nearly free of any chance for concealment. The same conditions made it dangerous for illicit slavers, and they apparently left it alone in favor of better conditions to the east or west.

The Windward Coast from the Gambia to Cape Palmas was far better suited to illegal slave trading. Hiding places were plentiful in the river mouths or in the maze of creeks and channels of Guiné. The Gambia itself, however, was now effectively closed to slavers by the British post at Bathurst, just as the Senegal was closed by the French post at Saint-Louis. Slaves were still taken in the Senegambia, but they were no longer brought down the rivers. Instead, they were carried overland to various points on the open coast. This may account for the fact that few slaves of the sample originated at any great distance from the coast, whereas in the eighteenth century a long-distance inland trade brought slaves from the Bambara country near the upper Niger, first overland and then down the Senegal or Gambia by boat.

The real heart of the nineteenth-century slave trade lay behind the stretch of coast from Popo on the west to Douala on the east. From the later seventeenth century, the western section of this coast—the "Slave Coast," roughly the shores of the present Togo and Dahomey Republics—had been a center for the slave trade, drawing in prisoners of war and other people from the ill-organized segmentary societies of northern Togo and Dahomey. This westward extension of the Nigerian "middle belt" was still well represented in Koelle's sample, but the early nineteenth century also saw the collapse of Oyo as a political entity and the rise of the Fulani domination in northern Nigeria. The fall of the one and the rise of the other account for most of the pattern shown in maps 2 and 3. The only major exception was the Ibo area of eastern Nigeria, which had been a long-term supplier of slaves.

Koelle's informants also confirm our knowledge of the West African slave-trade routes in this period. The Yoruba slaves were brought directly to the coast and sold, either at the older slave-trading port of Whydah, or at newly developed Badagri and Lagos. The captives of the Fulani, however, arrived at the coast by a variety of routes. The Niger and the Benue provided a water route for carrying canoe-loads of slaves to the ports of the Niger delta, such as Brass or Bonny. There were also well-used overland routes. One led from the Niger in the vicinity of Rabba, through Yorubaland to the slave posts on the Bight of Benin. Another led directly south from the lower Benue, overland to Bonny. A third left either the upper or middle Benue for the slave markets of Old Calabar on the Cross river.

When the Fulani led long-distance raids to the south of their own territory, they did not necessarily take the slaves back to the north with them. The captives of the great Fulani raids southward from Adamawa in the 1820s, for example, were mainly sold to other peoples in the vicinity, and thus passed from hand to hand until they were finally sold to the Europeans in Old Calabar. Other captives, however, were taken back into the heart of the Fulani empire before being sold down whichever route was convenient at the time. Thus the Wute informant (appendix I, no. 147) made a journey of well over a thousand miles before being sold to the Slave Coast via Yorubaland, even though his home country was less than five hundred miles from Douala.

As in East Africa, there was a division between the Muslim and the Christian slave trade. Some West African slaves were shipped north to the Maghrib or Egypt, while others went south to the European dealers on the coast. The Sierra Leone sample throws some light on this division, if only through its *lacunae*. The Fulani *jihad* in Massina, for example, must have produced a body of war prisoners from the Niger valley just above the great northern bend of the river. Some merchants from this region were represented in Sierra Leone, but no slaves appear. Apparently these prisoners were either retained for local use or sold to North Africa. In the same way, prisoners taken in the fighting associated with the stabilization of Bornu under Muhammad al-Kanami (d. 1835) apparently were sold to the north, rather than to the Europeans. Kanuri prisoners captured by the Fulani during the Holy War of 1804–30, however, were sent to the coast in at least some proportion. Although only thirty Kanuri remained in 1849, Koelle's informant (appendix I, no. 67a) reported that there had formerly been about 200 in Sierra Leone. The large number of Hausa is a further reflection of the Fulani *jihad* in northern Nigeria. Even the Habe of Gobir, to the north of the Fulani empire, appear to have sold at least a part of their prisoners to the coast. Three Hausa and Fulani informants (numbers 133a, 133b and 134d) had been slaves of the Gobirawa before they were sold to the foreign slave trade.

Weak as these data are from a strictly statistical point of view, they nevertheless fill a gap in our knowledge of the African slave trade of the nineteenth century. They also suggest the possibility that further research into the slave-trade records of the seventeenth and eighteenth centuries may make it possible to accumulate similar data for those periods. If so, a glimpse of the shifting patterns of the trade within Africa over the decades and the centuries would surely help to solve the major problem of assessing the impact of the Atlantic slave trade on African societies.

# 3

# THE FIRST RETURN:
# THE COLONIZATION MOVEMENT,
# 1817–1865

The colonization movement which sought to repatriate freed slaves to Liberia was initiated not by Blacks, but by White slaveowners fearful of the effect of freedmen on their slaves. It was by no means universally popular among Blacks, either free or slave. The opposition to it is discussed in the essay by Dumond. The operation of the colonization movement in one state is considered by Sydnor. The contemporaneous account by Robert Campbell represents a Black man's alternative to Liberia, and the visit of a White U.S. Naval officer to the fledgling Liberia colony is evocative of a somewhat condescending attitude toward African accomplishments. The essays are prefaced by the request by colonization adherents for Congressional recognition. The final contribution describes the attitudes of Lincoln toward colonization on the eve of Emancipation.

*The Memorial to the U.S. Congress by the American
Colonization Society represents the effort, on the part of
those White Americans desirous of repatriating freed
slaves to Africa, to obtain Congressional recognition for
their efforts. Fear of servile rebellion instigated by
freedmen served as the principal impetus for the
foundation and operation of this group whose charter
members were principally Virginians and Marylanders.
The desire to restore Blacks to their homelands must
be counted as a collateral goal. The efforts of the
American Colonization Society culminated in the
establishment of the Liberia colony and the repatriation,
between 1822 and 1862, of twelve thousand freed slaves.*

# American Colonization Society: A Memorial
## to the United States Congress

### Annals of Congress

*To the Senate and House of Representatives of the United States:*
The President and Board of Managers of the American Colonization
Society respectfully represent that, being about to commence the execution
of the object to which their views have been long directed, they deem it
proper and necessary to address themselves to the legislative council of their
country. They trust that this object will be considered, in itself, of great
national importance, will be found inseparably connected with another,
vitally affecting the honor and interest of this nation, and leading, in its
consequences, to the most desirable results.

Believing that examination and reflection will show that such are its con-
nexions and tendency, they are encouraged to present themselves, and their
cause, where they know that a public measure, having these advantages,
cannot fail to receive all the countenance and aid it may require.

The last census shows the number of free people of color of the United
States, and their rapid increase. Supposing them to increase in the same

From *Annals of Congress,* 16th Congress, 1st Session (February 3, 1820), pp. 1047–51.
Reprinted in Albert P. Blaustein and Robert L. Zangrando, eds., *Civil Rights and the
American Negro,* pp. 69–74, by permission of Washington Square Press, a division
of Simon & Schuster, Inc. Copyright © 1968 by Washington Square Press, Inc.

ratio, it will appear how large a proportion of our population will, in the course of even a few years, consist of persons of that description.

No argument is necessary to show that this is very far indeed from constituting an increase of our physical strength; nor can there be a population, in any country, neutral as to its effects upon society. The least observation shows that this description of persons are not, and cannot be, either useful or happy among us; and many considerations, which need not be mentioned, prove, beyond dispute, that it is best, for all the parties interested, that there should be a separation; that those who are now free, and those who may become so hereafter, should be provided with the means of attaining to a state of respectability and happiness, which, it is certain, they have never yet reached, and, therefore, can never be likely to reach, in this country.

The last two reports of the Society, to which your memorialists beg leave to refer, show the success of their mission to Africa, and the result of their inquiries upon that continent. From those it is manifest that a situation can be readily obtained, favorable to commerce and agriculture, in a healthy and fertile country, and that the natives are well disposed to give every encouragement to the establishment of such a settlement among them. Thus, it appears, that an object of great national concern, already expressly desired by some of the States, and truly desirable to all, receiving, also, the approbation of those upon whom it is more immediately to operate, is brought within our reach.

But this subject derives, perhaps, its chief interest from its connexion with a measure which has, already, to the honor of our country, occupied the deliberations of the Congress of the United States.

Your memorialists refer, with pleasure, to the act, passed at the last session of Congress, supplementary to the act formerly passed for the suppression of the slave trade. The means afforded, by the provisions of that act, for the accomplishment of its object, are certainly great; but the total extirpation of this disgraceful trade cannot, perhaps, be expected from any measures which rely alone upon the employment of a maritime force, however considerable.

The profits attending it are so extraordinary, that the cupidity of the unprincipled will still be tempted to continue it, as long as there is any chance of escaping the vigilance of the cruisers engaged against them. From the best information your memorialists have been able to obtain, of the nature, causes, and course of this trade, and of the present situation of the coast of Africa, and the habits and dispositions of the natives, they are well assured that the suppression of the African slave trade, and the civilization of the natives, are measures of indispensable connexion. . . .

Since the establishment of the English settlement at Sierra Leone, the slave trade has been rapidly ceasing upon that part of the coast.

Not only the kingdoms in its immediate neighborhood, but those upon the Sherbro and Bagroo rivers, and others with whom the people of that settlement have opened a communication, have been prevailed upon to abandon it, and are turning their attention to the ordinary and innocent pursuits of civilized nations.

That the same consequences will result from similar settlements cannot be doubted. When the natives there see that the European commodities, for which they have been accustomed to exchange their fellow-beings, until vast and fertile regions have become almost depopulated, can be more easily and safely obtained by other pursuits, can it be believed that they will hesitate to profit by the experience? Nor will the advantages of civilization be alone exhibited. That religion, whose mandate is "peace on earth and good will towards men," will "do its errand"; will deliver them from the bondage of their miserable superstitions, and display the same triumphs which it is achieving in every land.

No nation has it so much in its power to furnish proper settlers for such establishments as this; no nation has so deep an interest in thus disposing of them. By the law passed at the last session, and before referred to, the captives who may be taken by our cruisers, from the slave ships are to be taken to Africa, and delivered to the custody of agents appointed by the President. There will then be a settlement of captured negroes upon the coast, in consequence of the measures already adopted. And it is evidently most important, if not necessary, to such a settlement, that the civilized people of color of this country, whose industry, enterprise, and knowledge of agriculture and the arts, would render them most useful assistants, should be connected with such an establishment.

When, therefore, the object of the Colonization Society is viewed in connexion with that entire suppression of the slave trade which your memorialists trust it is resolved shall be effected, its importance becomes obvious in the extreme. The beneficial consequences resulting from success in such a measure, it is impossible to calculate. To the general cause of humanity it will afford the most rich and noble contribution, and for the nation that regards that cause, that employs its power in its behalf, it cannot fail to procure a proportionate reward. It is by such a course that a nation insures to itself the protection and favor of the Governor of the World. Nor are there wanting views and considerations, rising from our peculiar political institutions, which would justify the sure expectation of the most signal blessings to ourselves from the accomplishment of such an object. If one of these consequences shall be the gradual and almost imperceptible removal of a national evil, which all unite in lamenting, and for which, with the most intense, but, hitherto, hopeless anxiety, the patriots and statesmen of our country have labored to discover a remedy, who can doubt, that, of all the blessings we may be permitted to bequeath to our descendants, this will receive the richest tribute of their thanks and veneration?

Your memorialists cannot believe that such an evil, universally acknowledged and deprecated, has been irremovably fixed upon us. Some way will always be opened by Providence by which a people desirous of acting justly and benevolently may be led to the attainment of a meritorious object. And they believe that, of all the plans that the most sagacious and discerning of our patriots have suggested, for effecting what they have so greatly desired, the colonization of Africa, in the manner proposed, presents the fairest prospects of success. But if it be admitted to be ever so doubtful, whether this happy result shall be the reward of our exertions, yet, if great and certain benefits immediately attend them, why may not others, still greater, follow them?

In a work evidently progressive, who shall assign limits to the good that zeal and perseverance shall be permitted to accomplish? Your memorialists beg leave to state that, having expended considerable funds in prosecuting their inquiries and making preparations, they are now about to send out a colony, and complete the purchase, already stipulated for with the native kings and chiefs of Sherbro, of a suitable territory for their establishment. The number they are now enabled to transport and provide for, is but a small proportion of the people of color who have expressed their desire to go; and without a larger and more sudden increase of their funds than can be expected from the voluntary contributions of individuals, their progress must be slow and uncertain. They have always flattered themselves with the hope that when it was seen they had surmounted the difficulties of preparation, and shown that means applied to the execution of their design would lead directly and evidently to its accomplishment, they would be able to obtain for it the national countenance and assistance. To this point they have arrived; and they, therefore, respectfully request that this interesting subject may receive the consideration of your honorable body, and that the Executive Department may be authorized, in such way as may meet your approbation, to extend to this object such pecuniary and other aid as it may be thought to require and deserve.

Your memorialists further request, that the subscribers to the American Colonization Society may be incorporated, by act of Congress, to enable them to act with more efficiency in carrying on the great and important objects of the Society, and to enable them, with more economy, to manage the benevolent contributions intrusted to their care.

Signed by John Mason, W. Jones, E. B. Caldwell, and F. S. Key, committee.

WASHINGTON
*February 1, 1820*

*"Colonization" is a chapter from Professor Dwight
Lowell Dumond's* Antislavery: The Crusade For
Freedom in America. *In this selection, the author takes
to task the motives and operations of the supporters of
colonization. By so doing, he questions the humanitarian
motives of such prominent Americans as Clay, Jefferson,
and Monroe, who were staunch advocates of colonization.*

# Colonization

## Dwight Lowell Dumond

"Under the Federal Government which is now established, we have
reason to believe that all slaves in the United States, will in time be emancipated, in a manner most consistent with their own happiness, and the true
interest of their proprietors. Whether this will be effected by transporting
them back to Africa; or by colonizing them in some part of our own territory, and extending to them our alliance and protection until they shall
have acquired strength sufficient for their own defense; or by incorporation
with the whites; or in some other way, remains to be determined. All these
methods are attended with difficulties. The first would be cruel; the second
dangerous; and the latter disagreeable and unnatural. Deep-rooted prejudices entertained by the whites; ten thousand recollections, by the blacks,
of the injuries they have sustained; new provocations; the real distinction
which nature has made; besides many other circumstances which would
tend to divide them into parties, and produce convulsions, are objections
against retaining and incorporating the blacks with the citizens of the several
states. But justice and humanity demand that these difficulties should be
surmounted." [1] So wrote Jedediah Morse in his *American Geography* in
1789.

Morse saw clearly the evil of slavery, but his approach to the problem of
emancipation was that of Madison and Washington and Jefferson and Patrick Henry. Those men were perfectly willing to spread carnage over the
face of the earth to establish their own claim to freedom, but lacked the
courage to live by their assertions of the natural rights of men. Twenty years
later emancipation had run its course; Virginia had become the breeding
ground of slaves for the emerging cotton kingdom, and slavery was so

From Dwight Lowell Dumond, *Antislavery: The Crusade for Freedom in America*
(New York: W. W. Norton, 1966), pp. 126–132. © 1961, The University of Michigan.

deeply rooted in the Black Belt as to be indestructible. The Southern position was made crystal clear in the debates over prohibiting the foreign slave trade. It was to be perpetual slavery or civil war. Three powerful pillars supported the superstructure: slaves constituted the labor force; slaves gave the white people tremendous political power; and slaves were the living proof of racial superiority.

In no respect was this determination to strengthen and perpetuate the institution more clearly demonstrated than in the movement to colonize the free Negroes. Morse was correct when he said to transport the Negroes to Africa would be cruel; it was all of that—as cruel as death. Everyone who studies the documents on this subject should start with Benjamin Franklin. In the "Address to the Public from the Pennsylvania Society for Promoting the Abolition of Slavery, and the Relief of Free Negroes Unlawfully Held in Bondage," Franklin said:

"The unhappy man, who has long been treated as a brute animal, too frequently sinks beneath the common standard of the human species. The galling chains that bind his body do also fetter his intellectual faculties, and impair the social affections of his heart. Accustomed to move like a mere machine, by the will of a master, reflection is suspended; he has not the power of choice; and reason and conscience have but little influence over his conduct, because he is chiefly governed by the passion of fear. He is poor and friendless; perhaps worn out by extreme labor, age, and disease.

"Attention to emancipated blacks, it is therefore to be hoped, will become a branch of our national policy; but, as far as we contribute to promote this emancipation, so far that attention is evidently a serious duty incumbent on us, and which we mean to discharge to the best of our judgment and abilities.

"To instruct, to advise, to qualify those who have been restored to freedom, for the exercise and enjoyment of civil liberty; to promote in them habits of industry; to furnish them with employments suited to their age, sex, talents, and other circumstances; and to procure their children an education calculated for their future situation in life,—these are the great outlines of our annexed plan, which we have adopted, and which we conceive will essentially promote the public good, and the happiness of these our hitherto too much neglected fellow creatures." [2]

This statement of Franklin was in the finest tradition of Woolman and Benezet and of the Quakers generally. It was the program of the several state societies affiliated in the American Convention. It constituted an important part, in some respects the most important part, of the work of antislavery societies down to the Civil War. Franklin said this program should be a part of national policy. This was precisely what was being argued in the House of Representatives in February 1790, when petitions from the several societies were introduced. It will be recalled that the House undertook to discuss the limits of congressional power in regard to slavery in great detail and finally adopted a self-denying resolution leaving treatment of slaves within the purview of state governments.

The mere existence, North or South, of free Negroes was a constant torment to slaveholders. Their presence in a slave community increased the individual slaveholder's problems. Marriages between slaves and free Negroes, though not recognized by law or by the churches, created all sorts of difficulties, particularly absences and running away. The mere presence of Negroes who were free increased the slaves' desire for freedom. They constituted a potential source of conspiracy and insurrection. They were proof of the Negroes' ability to progress, a denial of his animal status. The slave states simply refused to countenance any program of assistance to these people. They tried to discourage manumissions. They tried to force free Negroes to move out. They finally tried to get them back into slavery. The objective always was to strengthen slavery, not to aid the Negro.

Against this background of antislavery efforts to educate and train free Negroes for individual competence and intelligent citizenship on the one hand, and proslavery efforts to prevent emancipation, stands the organization of the American Colonization Society in 1817. President Thomas Jefferson and Governor James Monroe of Virginia tried to inaugurate colonization in 1800 and failed. The scheme lay dormant until 1816 when Henry Clay revived it.

Virginia wanted to get rid of her free Negroes. The legislature requested the governor, December 23, 1816, to make representations to the President of the United States for a territory in Africa or elsewhere outside this country to which they might go or be sent. The resolution did not clearly indicate whether this was to be voluntary or compulsory. It is of little consequence, since direct action by Congress was never obtained. Some days later a private meeting of some prominent men in Washington, D.C., was held to discuss the matter, and out of this meeting came the American Society for Colonizing the Free People of Color of the United States, commonly called the American Colonization Society. Its constitution declared its purpose "to promote and execute a plan for colonizing (with their consent) the free people of color, residing in our country, in Africa, or such other place as Congress shall deem most expedient. And the Society shall act to effect this object in Cooperation with the general government, and such of the states as may adopt regulations upon the subject." [3]

The organization was nourished and kept alive, not by pride in its achievements, but by blind devotion to the doctrine of racial inferiority. The arguments of its sponsors were always subtle, always specious, and always bad in their effects upon race prejudice. President Monroe was so completely captivated by them as to say that the manumission of slaves in Virginia at the time of the Revolution (these are the words of John Quincy Adams, Secretary of State) "had introduced a class of very dangerous people, the free blacks, who lived by pilfering, and corrupted the slaves, and produced such pernicious consequences that the Legislature were obliged to prohibit further emancipation by law. The important object now was to remove these free blacks, and provide a place to which the emancipated slaves might go; the legal obstacles to emancipation might then be withdrawn, and the black population in time be drawn off entirely from Virginia." [4] Adams refused, as secretary of state, to have anything to do with putting the United States into the business of supporting colonies, Negro or otherwise, and he was too shrewd an observer of domestic affairs to credit the founders of the society with the charity and sagacity of long-range emancipation objectives. Among those supporting the organization, he said, were "some exceedingly humane, weak-minded men, who have really no other than the professed objects in view, and who honestly believe them both useful and attainable; some, speculators in official profits and honors, which a colonial establishment would of course produce; some, speculators in political popularity, who think to please the abolitionists by their zeal for emancipation, and the slaveholders by the flattering hope of ridding them of the free colored people at the public expense; lastly, some cunning slave-holders, who see that the plan may be carried far enough to produce the effect of raising the market price of the slaves." [5]

Most of the support for colonization, through the years, actually came from the politicians and from people who, like politicians, were in positions where it was profitable to maintain an appearance of antislavery feeling without supporting the cause. Antislavery people would have no part of it.

It was just as cruel, just as inhuman, just as much an invasion of man's natural rights as the rape of Africa had been in the first place. It was rooting people out of their homeland, tearing them away from their families and friends, transporting them across the sea to a strange, new environment. It was robbing them of whatever property they had accumulated, depriving them of an opportunity for an education and economic advancement, snatching away from them the opportunity to live a free life in the country their unrewarded labor had helped so largely to build.

The very idea of sending the free Negroes out of the country was, on the face of it, an endorsement of biological inequality and racial inferiority. It was either an attempt to remove from society an element in the population believed to be incapable of progress, or an attempt to avoid the expense and effort of compensating, by special devotion to the task, for the years of soul-destroying oppression. Antislavery people denied the rationalization and scorned the evasion.

Free Negroes could not be persuaded to go to Africa or anywhere else of their own free will. They had been born in the United States. This was their home, and however underprivileged they might be, there was nothing at the other end of the migration pulling them. Africa was a continent, strange and far away. Nobody knew what conditions existed there, what the climate was like, what opportunities there were for making a living. Actually, the Negroes showed no interest whatever in migrating. Some few went, largely slaves who were offered freedom if they would go, but there never were enough volunteers to justify the effort.

Antislavery people quickly realized three developments. Slaveholders, to the degree they were supporting the organization, were interested only in removing an element from the population thought to be dangerous and known to create by its presence alone a restlessness among the slaves. Their purpose was to strengthen slavery and make it more secure. Antislavery men realized, also, that the cost of removing the free Negroes was beyond the limits of private resources and that no appreciable number of slaves would ever be emancipated and sent out of the country. Finally, they knew the free Negroes were needed here for leadership of their people when emancipation came.

There were three powerful reasons why slave-holders would never go along with the program of colonization. Even granting they could have been persuaded to forego the ease, and luxury, and wealth derived from slave ownership, they could never have sent their labor supply out of the country. They would not have agreed, and never did, to any expenditure of public funds for colonization, because it would have opened the way to a full-scale program of emancipation. They would have demanded compensation for their slaves, something antislavery people would never have supported.

The combination of antislavery opposition to colonization and proslavery opposition to government participation prevented Congress from taking any action. Congress, however, amended the act prohibiting the foreign slave trade (March 3, 1819), thus disposing of the old problem of what to do with Negro captives of intercepted slave traders. Whether the provision for their sale as slaves in the Act of 1807 had served as an incentive to violations, as antislavery people had claimed, or not, there had been violations, and there was as much reason to oppose sale in 1819 as there had been at an earlier time. The revised law authorized naval patrol of African and American waters; equal division of all prize money between the United States government and the officers and crew of the ship making a seizure;

payment of twenty-five dollars to the officers and crew for safe delivery of each Negro rescued to United States officials; return of such Negroes to Africa; appointment of a resident agent there to receive them; prosecution of any person holding Negroes unlawfully imported; payment of fifty dollars to the informer for each such Negro so determined by a jury; and expenditure up to $100,000 for enforcement of the Act.[6] President Monroe interpreted the act broadly and appointed a member of the Colonization Society as agent of the government in Africa, thus giving to the society semi-official recognition. This did not provide financial assistance, but it did provide prestige at home and abroad.

The society encountered much the same difficulties establishing a permanent settlement in Africa that the London Company had experienced in Virginia. A much higher percentage of Negroes taken to Africa died during the period of acclimatization than of slaves brought to America. The first settlement, on Sherbo Island (1820), was a total failure, and it was not until 1822 that the region later known as Liberia was secured. Another decade passed before the colony reached the point of assured permanence. In 1830 there were 2,000,000 slaves in the United States, and 319,000 free Negroes. The Colonization Society sent out only 2,228 before 1831, fewer than four thousand in twenty years. In 1832 the society had 228 auxiliary societies throughout the country, but its income was only $43,000, and the number of emigrants sent to Liberia was only 796. Ohio had thirty-seven auxiliary societies by 1832, but sent out only fifty-five emigrants by 1860. Kentucky, a slave state, had thirty-two auxiliary societies, but sent out less than six hundred emigrants by 1860; and from the entire country only twelve thousand went by the end of the Civil War. In short, few, if any, national organizations ever failed so miserably. It had no money to send emigrants, and Negroes refused to go. It never made provision for the care of emigrants after they reached Africa. Its importance lies in its effect upon the progress of emancipation, upon the status of the free Negro, and upon the growth of race prejudice.

The American Convention reported in 1818 that it had not "been able to discern, in the constitution and proceedings of the American Colonization Society, or in the avowed sentiments of its members, anything friendly to the abolition of slavery in the United States." [7] Three years later (1821) it said "a colony, either in Africa, or in our own country, would be incompatible with the principles of our government, and with the temporal and spiritual interests of the blacks." [8] Instead of colonization, it urged, as preliminary steps in a general plan of emancipation, that all migration, transportation, and sale of slaves be prohibited; that they be attached to the soil, paid wages, and allowed to work some land as renters; that the children be given an education; and that all arbitrary punishments cease, and a system of humane laws for control be enacted.[9]

The Colonization Society received strong support from humanitarians for a few years. The interval between the close of the War of 1812 and the late 1820's embraced the early years of the Colonization Society and the late years of the American Convention. The antislavery people won their first real victories in these years. They had suffered only defeats since the Ordinance of 1787, until the act for the control of the foreign slave trade was amended in 1819 and the Missouri Compromise line was established in 1820. The era of benevolent enterprises and moral reform began. It was not to end until slavery was abolished; in fact, that reform was long overdue and quickly took precedence in absorbing the interests and efforts of humanitarians. It was perfectly natural, therefore, that colonization should have appeared to a great many people to be the simple, quick, and complete solution of the racial problem.

The colonizationists presented their program to the country as a benevolent enterprise, designed to accomplish four primary objectives; to remove the free Negro population from an atmosphere of prejudice and oppression to one of wholesome freedom, equality, and opportunity; to pave the way for thousands of slaveholders voluntarily to free their slaves, which state laws presently forbade; to provide in Africa the nucleus of an intelligent, Christian civilization for redemption of the continent; and to remove from society an element which was, in the free states, idle and vicious, and in the slave states a corrupting influence upon the slaves. Said Henry Clay: "Can there be anything, to a reflecting freeman, more humiliating, more dark and cheerless, than to see himself, and to trace in imagination his posterity, through all succeeding time, degraded and debased, aliens to the Society of which they are members, and cut off from all its higher blessings." [10]

In this statement of Clay's we have the key to the history of the organization, in fact to the entire history of race relations: *acceptance of the immutability of Negro inferiority*. The first annual report of the society devoted nearly one half its space to a letter from Robert G. Harper, United States senator, Federalist candidate for the vice-presidency in 1816, and a founder of the organization. Said Harper: "These persons are condemned to a state of hopeless inferiority and degradation, by their colour; which is an indelible mark of their origin and former condition, and establishes an impossible barrier between them and the whites. This barrier is closed forever . . . you may manumit the slave, but you cannot make him a white man. He still remains a negro or a mulatto. The mark and the recollection of his origin and former state still adhere to him; the feelings produced by that condition, in his own mind and in the minds of the whites, still exist; he is associated by his colour, and by these recollections and feelings, with the class of slaves; and a barrier is thus raised between him and the whites, *that is* between him and the free class, which he can never hope to transcend." [11] The publications and the speeches of the colonizationists contain enough repulsive stimulants to race prejudice, many of them so vicious as to be almost unprintable, to fill an encyclopedia.[12] This was the first reason for the importance of the society. Men talked of the inherent incapacity and depravity of Negroes until they came to believe it themselves and inflexibly opposed emancipation. They converted thousands to the same belief, thus creating an unreasoned proscription of Negroes and antislavery leaders in hundreds of communities and precipitating a major contest over civil rights. The task of attaining equal protection of the laws for Negroes became more difficult, and emancipation of the slaves was long delayed.

The second reason for the importance of the colonization movement was that it provided anchorage for men who sought escape from the responsibility or penalty of taking a forthright stand for or against slavery. Thomas Jefferson, James Madison, John Marshall, John Randolph, John Taylor of Caroline, Bushrod Washington, and Henry Clay are typical of prominent men who favored colonization and either gave active support to the organization or allowed their names to be used. These men were but mildly opposed to slavery if at all. They were slaveholders; and they were politicians. Marshall voted against the abolition of slavery in Virginia. Bushrod Washington, first president of the Colonization Society, sold his fifty slaves to the commercial traders when they became restless. Charles Carroll, second president, owned 1,000 slaves and never freed any. James Madison, third president, left 100 slaves to his heirs. Henry Clay, fourth president, was always firm in his defense of slavery. Thomas Jefferson appears to have favored compulsory emigration, and always subscribed to the doctrine of racial inferiority. John Randolph and Henry Clay both emphasized the fact that colonization of the free Negroes would strengthen slavery. It is a moot question whether the men to whom the American Colonization Society was "bread and butter" sought out persons prominent in political and religious life to lend dignity and prestige to the activities of the society, or whether these persons attached themselves to the society for security reasons.

Equally important is the fact that neither the parent society, nor the auxiliary societies, nor any of the great variety of persons speaking before and for the societies ever gave more than casual lip service to the improvement of the status of Negroes in society. They did not recognize that the deficiencies of the Negro resulted from the debasing effects of slavery, from the black laws of the free states, and from all kinds of prejudice and denials.

They did a great deal of talking about the wretched status of the Negro, but they did nothing to secure the repeal of oppressive legislation, nor to accelerate emancipation, nor to educate or train free Negroes, nor to protect them against violence and abuse. Negroes were not underprivileged people in the eyes of colonizationists; they were undesirable people. Colonizationists sought relief, not for the Negro, but for society from the Negro's presence. Their objective was not to assist the Negro but to put him away from sight. Neither did the colonizationists move against slavery. They did nothing to prevent kidnapping, or to repeal the laws by which free Negroes could be reduced again to slavery; or to repeal the laws of the slave states circumscribing the activities of the slaves and forbidding their education. The parent society itself formally disclaimed any intention of doing these things, saying: "The moral, intellectual, and political improvement of people of color within the United States, are objects foreign to the powers of this Society." [13]

The third reason for the importance of the colonization movement was the violent reaction of the lower South, under the leadership, as it had been since 1787, of South Carolina and Georgia. Colonization, debated by Congress and financed by the federal government, would open the way to emancipation of the slaves. Colonization, also, to whatever degree it succeeded either with or without government assistance, would deprive the slave states of political power; they would lose votes in Congress and in the Electoral College. They would also lose their labor supply, but that seems to have been of secondary importance to them at this time. The first great debate directly involving the question of slavery in the states had occurred over the foreign slave trade. The second, as we shall see, was over the question of using the public lands to finance colonization. The subject was brought up during the debates in 1820 and emerged as a major issue in 1825.

The legislature of Ohio passed resolutions (January 17, 1824), recommending gradual emancipation. The plan called for all children of slaves to be given freedom at age twenty-one, providing they agreed to colonization. The resolution said: "It is expedient that such a system should be predicated upon the principle that the evil of slavery is a national one, and that the people and the States of this Union ought mutually to participate in the duties and burthens of removing it." These resolutions were sent to the other state governments and to Congress.[14] Vermont, Massachusetts, Connecticut, Pennsylvania, New Jersey, Delaware, Indiana, and Illinois approved the plan. The states of the Black Belt—South Carolina, Georgia, Alabama, Mississippi, and Louisiana—disapproved most emphatically.

One year later (February 18, 1825) Rufus King of New York, whose unceasing war upon slavery dated back to the Ordinance of 1787, offered a resolution in the United States Senate to pledge all future proceeds of the public land sales "to aid the emancipation of such slaves, within any of the United States, and to aid the removal of such slaves, and the removal of such free persons of color, in any of the said States, as by the laws of the States, respectively, may be allowed to be emancipated, or removed to any territory or country without the limits of the United States of America." [15] Jefferson had favored this method of financing emancipation, either under a broad definition of federal power or by constitutional grant of power through amendment.[16] Madison also favored it, by amendment, if necessary.[17] John Marshall, a vice-president of the American Colonization Society and chief justice of the United States, frankly said Congress had the power and should use it.

Finally, the American Colonization Society petitioned Congress, January 29, 1827, for assistance. The petition embraced a short history of the movement, described the colony in Africa, and carefully defined its objectives in the narrow terms of removing from this country only the free Negroes willing to go. It said the Colonization Society lacked the authority and power to govern a distant colony, and lacked sufficient funds to finance the undertaking. It requested assistance, without being specific, relying upon the wisdom of Congress to act effectively and expressing confidence in its constitutional power to act "to provide for the common defense, and promote the general welfare." [18] In this connection, it is a singular fact, worthy of careful attention, that the two men who had written the Virginia and Kentucky Resolutions, Jefferson and Madison, and John Marshall, chief justice of the United States, slaveholders all, and all opposed to emancipation without deportation, and Rufus King whose public career extended back into the Congress of the Confederation—all of these venerable statesmen—should have believed the powers of Congress adequate to take direct action in expending federal funds to encourage and accelerate emancipation. It is important because Robert Y. Hayne who had not been born when Franklin, Jefferson, Madison, and King were founding the nation, and John C. Calhoun and George Troup, who were babies at the time, presently undertook to lecture them and the country on the nature and constitutional powers of the government.

It all began with the Ohio resolutions of January 1824. The Senate of South Carolina termed them "a very strange and ill-advised communication." It protested against any interference with "that part of her property which forms the colored population of the state," and refused to permit that property "to be meddled with, or tampered with, or in any manner ordered, regulated, or controlled by any other power, foreign and domestic, than this legislature." [19] Other states in the Black Belt supported this position.[20]

While state after state was passing resolutions for or against the Ohio proposal, Rufus King offered his resolution in the Senate (February 18, 1825). King had avoided all debate on his resolution by having it read, printed, and laid on the table. This prevented debate, and Robert Y. Hayne of South Carolina took the unusual course of laying on the table a counterresolution which said that Congress possessed no power to appropriate public lands to aid in the emancipation and removal from the country of slaves, and that such action "would be a departure from the conditions and spirit of the compact between the several States; and that such measures would be dangerous to the safety of the States holding slaves, and be calculated to disturb the peace and harmony of the Union." [21] Once more, then, here was the threat of war—delivered with a little more finesse than the threats of Jackson and Early but of the same character.

Governor Troup of Georgia, who never seemed to tire of setting up straw men and of tearing them down and who spent many waking hours snarling at the government of the United States, warned the legislature of his state: "Soon, very soon, therefore, the United States Government, discarding the mask, will openly lend itself to a combination of fanatics for the destruction of every thing valuable in the Southern country; one movement of the Congress unresisted by you, and all is lost. Temporize no longer—make known your resolution that this subject shall not be touched by them, but at their peril ... If this matter be an evil, it is our own—if it be a sin, we can implore the forgiveness of it—to remove it we ask not even their sympathy or assistance; it may be our physical weakness—it is our moral strength ... I entreat you, therefore, most earnestly, now that it is not too late, to step forth, and having exhausted the argument, to stand by your arms." [22]

The memorial of the Colonization Society to Congress was promptly challenged by Hayne (Feb. 7, 1827), who said "he denied the Constitutional power of the Government so to act; and if they had the power, he should still deny the policy, justice and humanity of such proceeding." [23] He argued against the government's embarking upon a colonial policy, and that was his strongest argument against the proposal. He insisted that the government would become a purchaser of slaves to be sent to Africa, that resolutions and speeches in state legislatures would soon force down the price of slaves, and that general emancipation would inevitably follow, all of which was logical and probably correct. Then he followed the usual pattern of defense: "The only safety of the Southern States is to be found in the want of power on the part of the Federal Government to touch the subject at all. Thank God, the Constitution gives them no power to engage in the work of colonization, or to interfere with our institutions, either for good or for evil. This is the very 'Ark of the Covenant' in which alone we will find safety." [24]

# NOTES

1 Jedediah Morse, *The American Geography; or, A View of the Present Situation of the United States of America* (Elizabeth Town, 1789), p. 67. Morse's Geography was an important antislavery publication because of its wide circulation over a long period. Only a few paragraphs were devoted to slavery but they were sharply critical and incisive. For example: "The Africans are said to be inferior in point of sense, understanding, sentiment and feeling to white people. Hence the one infers a right to enslave the other. The African labours night and day to collect a small pittance to purchase the freedom of his child. The white man begets his likeness, and with much indifference and indignity of soul, sees his offspring in bondage and misery, and makes not one effort to redeem his own blood. Choice food for satire! Wide field for burlesque! Noble game for wit! Sad cause for pity to bleed, and for humanity to weep!" *Ibid.,* p. 66.

2 Albert Henry Smyth (ed.), *The Writings of Benjamin Franklin* (10 vols, New York, 1905–7), X, pp. 66–69. Franklin's plan, adopted by the Pennsylvania Society, *ibid.,* pp. 127–29, was to establish a committee of twenty-four persons which should resolve itself into a Committee of Inspection, a Committee of Guardians, a Committee of Education, and a Committee of Employment.

3 *The First Annual Report of the American Society for Colonizing the Free People of Color, of the United States; and the Proceedings of the Society at Their Annual Meeting in the City of Washington, on the First Day of January, 1818* (Washington, City, 1818), p. 3.

4 Charles Francis Adams (ed.), *Memoirs of John Quincy Adams, Comprising Portions of His Diary from 1795 to 1848* (12 vols, Philadelphia, 1874–77), IV, p. 293.

5 *Ibid.,* p. 292.

6 *Annals of Congress,* 15 Cong., 2 Sess., II, pp. 544–46.

7 *Minutes of a Special Meeting of the Fifteenth American Convention for Promoting the Abolition of Slavery, and Improving the Condition of the African Race, Assembled at Philadelphia, on the Tenth Day of December 1818, and Continued by Adjournment until the Fifteenth Day of the Same Month, Inclusive* (Philadelphia, 1818), p. 49.

8 *Minutes of the Seventeenth Session of the American Convention for Promoting the Abolition of Slavery, and Improving the Condition of the African Race, Convened at Philadelphia, on the Third Day of October, 1821* (Philadelphia, 1821), p. 57. Said the Convention "We think it worthy of consideration, how far any measure should be recommended that may tend to draw from our country the most industrious, moral, and respectable of its colored population, and thus deprive others, less improved, of the benefit of their example and advice. . . . Deeply injured as they have been by the whites, the coloured people certainly claim from us some degree of retributive justice."

9 *Ibid.,* pp. 50–55.

10 *The First Annual Report of the American Society for Colonizing the Free People of Color, of the United States,* p. 18.

11 *Ibid.,* pp. 30–31.

12 *The African Repository and Colonial Journal* (68 vols., Washington, 1825–1889), IV, p. 118.

13 *The African Repository and Colonial Journal,* VII, p. 29.

[14] Herman V. Ames (ed.), *State Documents on Federal Relations: the States and the United States* (Philadelphia, 1904), V, pp. 11–12.

[15] *Register of Debates in Congress,* 18 Cong., 2 Sess., I, p. 623.

[16] Jefferson to Jared Sparks, February 4, 1824, in A. A. Liscomb and A. L. Berg (eds.), *The Writings of Thomas Jefferson* (20 vols., Washington, 1903), XVI, pp. 8–14.

[17] James Madison to Thomas R. Dun, February 23, 1833 in Gaillard Hunt (ed.), *The Writings of James Madison* (9 vols., New York, 1900–1910), IX, pp. 498–502.

[18] *House Documents,* 19 Cong., 2 Sess., Doc. No. 64.

[19] Herman V. Ames (ed.), *State Documents on Federal Relations: The States and the United States,* No. 5, p. 15.

[20] Georgia, December 7, 1824; Mississippi, February 1, 1825; Louisiana, February 16, 1826, and Alabama January 1, 1827.

[21] *Register of Debates in Congress,* 18 Cong., 2 Sess., pp. 696–97.

[22] Herman V. Ames (ed), *State Documents on Federal Relations: The States and the United States,* No. 5, p. 17.

[23] *Register of Debates in Congress,* 19 Cong., 2 Sess., p. 289.

[24] *Ibid.,* p. 329.

❦⟨◯⟩❧

*Originally published in 1933, this section of Charles S.
Sydnor's book,* Slavery in Mississippi, *details the
experience of one of the state colonization societies
affiliated with the American Colonization Society. It
discusses the emigration of freed slaves from southwestern
Mississippi, who settled in the area of Greenville, in
Liberia. The Mississippi Society, which was founded in
1831 and ceased to function about 1840, was responsible
for sending over five hundred ex-slaves to Liberia.
The author, unlike Professor Dumond, is favorably
disposed toward the colonization movement.*

# The Mississippi Colonization Society

## Charles S. Sydnor

In 1830, the year before the founding of the Mississippi Colonization
Society, there were 519 free negroes and mulattoes in Mississippi. It seems
hardly reasonable that this small number should have caused any serious
concern to the white people of the State, particularly as there were many
more in several other slave States.[1] On the other hand, a large proportion
of this class lived in the southwestern counties of Mississippi where the
slaves greatly outnumbered the white population.[2] Slaveholders feared that
the mere existence of free negroes among slaves might make the latter dissatisfied, and there was always a possibility that some of the free negroes
might actively endeavor to create discontent. This anxiety was accentuated
in 1830 and 1831 as rumors reached Mississippi of slave insurrections in
Virginia and North Carolina.[3] The middle States were also suspected of
trying to unload their slaves on the markets of the lower slave States as a
step toward abolishing slavery.[4] Finally, the rapid growth of the slave population of Mississippi was considered alarming. For these reasons a strong
and apparently unanimous desire arose to abolish the free negro class, with
certain exceptions, and in 1831 a law was passed which required all adult
free negroes to leave Mississippi.[5] It is significant that almost the whole
of this agitation came from the southwestern corner of the State; the newspapers that were most vigorous in the crusade were in Wilkinson and Adams
Counties; from the latter county came the petition which induced the legis-

From Charles S. Sydnor, *Slavery in Mississippi* (Baton Rouge: Louisiana State University Press, 1966), pp. 203–238. © American Historical Association, 1959.

lature to require that free negroes be removed from the State; [6] and this law of 1831 was framed by a committee drawn almost entirely from representatives of southwestern counties.[7]

In addition to making laws to force free negroes to leave Mississippi, there was a slight interest in schemes to persuade them to leave voluntarily. In 1824, seven years before the Mississippi Colonization Society was created, Mississippi free negroes were informed that they could find good homes in Haiti. For twenty issues the *Woodville Republican* prominently displayed a large advertisement of the advantages to be gained by removing to that island.[8] There were also several news items telling of the rise and decline of the Haiti movement.[9]

Had there been no free negro class in Mississippi, the Mississippi Colonization Society would probably not have been created. The purpose of this organization, as officially and publicly expressed, was to remove free negroes from the State. Embedded in its constitution were the words: "The object to which the Mississippi Society shall be exclusively devoted, shall be to aid the Parental Institution at Washington, in the colonization of free people of color of the United States on the coast of Africa. . . ." [10] In the early speeches and writings of the Mississippi colonizers there was never a plea for colonizing slaves. Speaking before part of the society, Daniel Williams, of Wilkinson County, affirmed that its members proposed "to transport back to Africa the land of their fathers, such free persons of colour as may choose to emigrate—and with any other views that party or prejudice may blend with this object, they totally disclaim all connection." [11] While there was more freedom of expression in private correspondence, we find Dr. John Ker, a leader in the movement in Mississippi, writing to Major Isaac Thomas of Louisiana, "You and I, and I think all men of sound judgement and sober reflection, will agree, that as to the *slaves,* neither the Society nor our Government can in the remotest degree meddle with them." [12] Clearly, it was the official opinion of the organization, and the private opinion of some of its leaders, that the removal of free negroes was the only concern of the society. With such an objective, the society could appeal to those planters who thought that free negroes had a harmful influence upon slaves and to humane persons who believed free negroes would be happier and more prosperous, if removed to regions where slavery did not exist.

Even with its purpose restricted to the transportation of free negroes alone, the colonization movement had some enemies. One of these declared that while he had no objection to the removal of free negroes, he was by no means sure that the methods and ultimate aims of the American Colonization Society were above reproach. He particularly objected to a pro-

posed bill by which congress would appropriate money for returning free
negroes to Africa, fearing that, if the competency of the national government to legislate in this field were once established, there might be a repetition of the fable of the camel that was allowed to put his nose in the tent.
Congress might soon attempt to control the entire question of slavery.[13]

As early as 1827, citizens of Mississippi began to read of the work of the
American Colonization Society, and, naturally, the thought presented itself
that this organization might be useful in solving Mississippi's free negro
problem. The newspaper controversy just mentioned was in 1827, and in
this same year, so far as we knew, occurred the first attempt to advance
the work of the American Colonization Society in Mississippi. An inquiry
was addressed to Rev. William Winans, a prominent Methodist minister
of the State, asking whether it would be wise to have an agent work in
Mississippi. Winans answered in the affirmative, but he warned the society
that great care must be exercised in selecting this individual. In saying this,
he probably had in mind the hostile attitude of some in the community.[14]
In September, 1827, there appeared in the *Woodville Republican* a letter
describing the good state of affairs in Liberia,[15] and less than a month later
this paper gave two columns to an article on the same subject.[16] In December of the following year there was a lengthy discussion of the aims of the
American Colonization Society.[17]

As early as July 4, 1826, Mississippians began to contribute to the colonization movement and by 1829 nearly $1,000 had been collected, largely
through the zeal of Winans, from over seventy persons, churches, and
Masonic lodges.[18] Each of two Mississippians agreed, in 1829, to give $100
a year for ten years.[19] All this was contributed before a colonization society
was founded in the State.

An attempt was made near Natchez, in the fall of 1828, to form a Mississippi Colonization Society, but it failed because the impression was gained
by the slaves that its object was their immediate emancipation. It was, therefore, necessary to suspend activities for a time.[20]

The Mississippi Colonization Society was organized in June, 1831. Probably because of the false start in 1828, its birth seems not to have been
preceded by any publicity through the press or in open meetings. Some of
its leaders were also interested in the organization of the Louisiana society
and, therefore, the procedures in these States were possibly similar. We
know from a letter of Dr. Ker, who was vitally concerned in the creation
of both societies, that the plan in Louisiana was to organize quietly and
thereby avoid conflict with any oppositon before the movement was well
started. A constitution was prepared and the signatures of prominent per-

sons were privately secured, with the result that the society, as it were, began life full grown. Ker also considered publishing a compilation of some of the articles that had appeared in the official publications of the American Colonization Society. He thought this might be valuable, if it were discreetly edited, for "the regular publications of the society, excellent as they are, contain some things which are calculated to jar upon the Southern prejudices." [21]

On the first day of June, 1831, there was a meeting in Natchez in which a constitution was adopted and a full set of officers elected. The text of the constitution was as follows:

### CONSTITUTION

Of the Mississippi Colonization Society, adopted at a meeting of the citizens of the State, held at Natchez, on the 1st day of June, 1831.

Art. 1st. This society shall be called the Colonization Society of the State of Mississippi, and shall be auxiliary to the American Colonization Society.

2nd. The object to which it shall be exclusively devoted, shall be to aid the Parent Institution at Washington, in the colonization of free people of color of the United States, on the coast of Africa, and to do this not only by the contribution of money, but by the exertion of its influence to promote the formation of other Societies.

3rd. An annual subscription of one dollar or more, shall constitute an individual member of the Society, and the payment at any time of twenty dollars, a member for life.

4th. The officers of this Society shall be a President, nine Vice Presidents, and twenty-three Managers: Secretary and Treasurer to be elected annual by the Society.

5th. The Presidents, Secretary and Treasurer shall be (ex-officio) Members of the Board of Managers.

6th. The Board of Managers shall meet on their own adjournment or by order of the President, to transact the business of the Society.

7th. The Treasurer shall keep the accounts of the Society, as well as take charge of its funds, and hold them subject to an order of the Board of Managers.

8th. The Secretary shall keep the records of the Society, and of the Board of Managers, and shall conduct under the direction of the Board of Managers, the correspondence of the Society with the Parent Society, and other Societies.

9th. The annual meeting of the Society shall be held on the first Wednesday of March in each year, at which meeting the officers of the Society shall be elected, who shall hold their offices for one year thereafter, and until others are elected in their places.

10th. Fifteen members at all meetings of the Society, and seven members at all meetings of the Board of Managers, shall constitute a quorum to proceed to business.[22]

Few organizations have existed in Mississippi that could claim a group of officers equal in character and influence to those of the Mississippi Colonization Society. There has been preserved a list of those chosen at the creation of the society in 1831, as well as another list of those elected in December, 1838. At both times, the president was Dr. Stephen Duncan, of Natchez, physician, successful planter, president of the Bank of Mississippi and one of the wealthiest men in the State.[23] Among the other officers was Gerard C. Brandon, Governor of Mississippi, and Cowles Mead, formerly Secretary and Acting-Governor of Mississippi Territory, who remained a leader in public affairs after the State was created. His home was near Clinton, in Hinds County.[24] James Railey owned a large plantation,[25] and David Hunt, another officer, was a man of considerable wealth.[26] Near Rodney lived Thomas Freeland, an affluent planter, who was a delegate to the Baltimore convention that nominated General Winfield Scott for president.[27] The Rev. William Winans has already been mentioned. This prominent Methodist preacher spent most of his life at Mount Pleasant, sixteen miles southeast of Woodville. Isaac R. Nicholson, a lawyer of Natchez, attained the speakership of the House of Representatives of Mississippi, and was later a member of the supreme court of the State.[28]

Two of the officers were Presbyterian ministers, Zebulon Butler, for many years pastor at Port Gibson,[29] and J. Chamberlain, for a long time president of Oakland College, located thirty-five miles north of Natchez.[30] Surveyor-General Levin Wailes, of Washington, Mississippi, and Natchez, was in the list of officers,[31] as was Edward McGehee of Wilkinson County. The latter was a wealthy planter, pioneer railroad builder, and philanthropist, who refused the secretaryship of the treasury offered him by President Taylor. He was one of the largest slaveholders of the State, owning possibly a thousand negroes.[32] The Rev. B. M. Drake, a prominent Methodist minister, was for a time president of Elizabeth Female Academy, located in Washington, Mississippi.[33] Three of the officers, Joseph, Robert T., and Dr. William Dunbar, bore a name that had been famous in southwestern Mississippi since William Dunbar attained prominence during the Spanish régime. John Henderson, a venerated and respected citizen of Natchez, controlled large plantations and numerous slaves in Louisiana as well as in Mississippi.[34] Dr. John Ker likewise had plantations on both sides of the great river, to which he gave most of his attention, though he was by profession a physician.[35]

The remaining officials of the Mississippi Colonization Society, as recorded in the lists of those elected in 1831 and in 1838, were: the Rev. D. C. Page, Alexander C. Henderson, James G. Carson, William Harris, J. Beaumont, the Rev. S. G. Winchester, William St. John Elliott, William C. Conner, the Rev. Benjamin Chase, William Bisland, Edward Turner, John L. Irwin, Joseph Johnson, the Rev. George Potts, William L. Chew, Joseph Sessions, the Rev. John C. Burruss, William B. Melvin, R. M. Gaines, John H. Magruder, William Lattimore, Dr. A. P. Merrill, John Perkins, Dr. Rush Nutt, Felix Huston, B. R. Grayson, Alvarez Fisk, and H. W. Huntington. There is not space to comment on each of these men, but the student of the history of Mississippi will recognize the names of many who were prominent.[36]

Several citizens of Mississippi were officers of the American Colonization Society. Among these were, Dr. Stephen Duncan, the Rev. William Winans, Dr. John Ker, James Railey, the Hon. Robert J. Walker, Edward McGehee, and the Rev. Robert Paine, who were vice-presidents, and Francis Griffin, who was a life director.[37]

It is evident that the officers of the Mississippi Colonization Society were prominent in educational and religious life as well as in business and politics. Several of them were known far beyond the boundaries of their own State. They were not malcontents, failures, or sentimentalists. Practically all were permanent residents of Mississippi, and many of them were owners of large plantations and of numerous slaves. Further, a majority of them were residents of the counties in southern Mississippi that border the Mississippi River, that is, the counties of Warren, Claiborne, Jefferson, Adams, and Wilkinson.

The heyday of the Mississippi Colonization Society was from its founding to about 1839 or 1840. We will first consider its activities during this period.

Three weeks after the creation of the society there was a meeting of the board of managers in the Methodist Church at Natchez. An address to the public was prepared in which the objectives of the organizations were stated. These were: to arouse interest in colonization, to persuade free negroes to return to Africa, and to raise money for this end. It was estimated, in an optimistic moment, that twenty dollars was sufficient to send a negro to Africa. Included in the address was a description of the Liberian colony as well an account of the work of the American Colonization Society. After meeting a few of the criticisms that were being directed against the movement, a plea was made for the creation of local auxiliary societies.[38] At least four of these were formed: the Woodville and Wilkinson County, the Port Gibson and Claiborne County, the Vicksburg and Warren County, and the Clinton and Hinds County Societies.[39]

The Woodville and Wilkinson County Society functioned in 1831 and at least through the following year. Its activities were largely a microcosm of those of the Mississippi society. In addition to holding meetings, it collected funds, discussed through the press the evil conditions of free negroes and the advantages to them and to Mississippi of their removal to Africa, and defended the American Colonization Society and the colony in Liberia.[40]

In 1832 the Mississippi Colonization Society published its first annual report, which shows, so far as its published statements were concerned, that it was still interested exclusively in removing free negroes. This account also indicates that its work was in the formative period, for no negroes had been removed. The following is a part of this report:

> The Society is increasing in numbers, ... some subscriptions have been obtained, and ... this has had a happy effect; the free people of color in this neighborhood have become awakened to the subject, and the advantages held out to them by a removal from their degraded political position here, to the land of their ancestors, where they can enjoy the rights and privileges of freemen, have created a great desire on their part to be better informed on the subject. They have called a meeting among themselves, appointed two of their own color to visit Liberia, to examine the country, and, make a report of the state and condition of the colony.
>
> A fund nearly sufficient to defray the expenses of their agents, in going and returning, has been raised among them. It is expected that they will set out immediately under the care and direction of the Society, and will return as soon as the trip can be performed to make their report.
>
> Your Board of Managers have been informed that a vessel will be fitted out by the parent society, and will sail from New Orleans in the month of May next, for the purpose of conveying emigrants to Liberia: a number will come from some of the western States, and it is contemplated to take as many from this State as may be ready to go. And the Board are happy to say, that they have understood several are now making preparations, and intend to avail themselves of the first opportunity to leave the State for Africa.[41]

Though the removal of free negroes continued to be the only publicly avowed purpose of the Mississippi Colonization Society, its actual work soon veered toward the colonization of slaves. The justification for this enlargement of aims is well stated in a letter written by Dr. John Ker less than two months after the formation of the Mississippi society. After discussing the humaneness and expediency of returning free negroes, he added:

> All experience I think goes to show at least the great probability, that the spirit of emigration will spread, and that for a long time the *demand* for means will only *increase* with its *supply*. Laws will probably be made in the slave holding states to prevent emancipation, except on condition of immediate emigration to Liberia. Those who have been withheld from emancipation by the conviction that it would be prejudicial to society to do so, will no doubt gratify their wishes, when this objection shall no longer exist. But will this be cause

of complaint or regret to others? Will it not on the contrary benefit other slave holders, rather by removing some examples of loose and injuriously indulgent discipline, the effect of mistaken feelings of Humanity? Will it not have the effect also, of enhancing the value of those who may be left? Will not the hands of slavery be strengthened as to those who shall remain, except from the only ground of hope to the slave, the voluntary act of his master? Will it not have the effect of lessening the evils of slavery, both with regard to the bond and their masters, by creating such a state of things as will enable the latter to relax the former unavailable rigor of discipline? It is manifest to every slave holder that many evils arise from the existence of the free colored people amongst the slaves: and it would be unnecessary to expatiate upon this point.[42]

Here are certain reasons for favoring colonization that did not appear in the formal reports of the society, for in these the suggestion that emancipated slaves might be returned to Liberia is nowhere to be found. In suggesting that the society transport emancipated slaves, it seems that Ker's idea was somewhat as follows: the majority of the people of Mississippi did not object to the manumission of a slave, if the negro were immediately removed to Africa. But, most of the people did fear the word *emancipation,* particularly when it was used in connection with the federal government or even a national society. Since the colonization society was asking the central government to aid in returning negroes, it was best not to mention slaves in this connection. In the mind of the public the fear would arise that the government, after returning the slaves of owners who willingly emancipated them, might attempt to go further and remove the slaves of unwilling owners.

In the vigorous period of the life of the Mississippi Colonization Society, that is from 1831 to 1840, a considerable amount of money was collected. R. R. Gurley, the efficient secretary of the parent society, estimated that between January, 1834, and January, 1838, the societies of "Mississippi and Louisiana spent probably not less than fifteen or twenty thousand dollars in founding the settlement at the mouth of the Sinou river." [43] Later he stated that this figure was probably much too small. The president of the Mississippi society, Dr. Duncan, promised to give $300 a year for five years, an amount which he subsequently augmented.[44] Eleven years later, in 1842, we find that Dr. Duncan had given $2,500, probably in addition to the first $1,500, and in the following year he promised to give another $1,500.[45]

The largest contribution in Mississippi for colonization during the early years of the movement was for colonizing the slaves of Judge James Green. In 1836 it was stated that $7,000 had already been spent by Green's executors for this purpose and that it had been determined to devote an additional $25,000 to completing the task. In the same year, Gurley wrote: "Without my personal application to a single individual, and with my detention hardly for a day," $2,000 was raised in Mississippi.[46]

James G. Birney collected $1,400 as a result of two meetings held the same Sunday in Natchez and was thereby moved to comment on the good spirit in all benevolent things in the older parts of Mississippi.[47] Another agent, H. B. Bascom, collected over $1,300 on a visit to Mississippi in 1831.[48] In the spring of 1832 friends of the movement about Natchez subscribed over $6,000.[49]

David Hunt, who lived near Rodney, contributed $500 and occasionally $1,000 a year from about 1850 to 1860 and in addition made two donations of $5,000 and one of $25,000.[50]

These and many small contributions [51] show that close to $100,000 was contributed to the colonization movement from Mississippi. Indeed, in 1833 the Mississippi society became the creditor of the parent society by lending it $3,000 from its surplus with the understanding that the latter should expend that amount in colonizing Mississippi negroes when requested to do so by the Mississippi society.[52] Two years later the Mississippi society met with little success in an endeavor to hold the American society to this agreement.[53] In 1836 the secretary of the latter society stated in his report that he considered Mississippi and Louisiana the best fields in the Union for securing both emigrants and money.[54]

Few points were more frequently reiterated in the letters from the parent society to the Mississippi society than the necessity of employing an agent to work in the State, possibly devoting part of his time to Louisiana.[55] Several citizens of these two States were suggested as agents, among them the Rev. William Winans, but there is no record of their having formally become agents of the society. However, Winans was appointed by the Methodist conference to solicit funds in Mississippi and Alabama for the colonization society. He was probably more valuable to the society than any of its paid agents in the Southwest.[56] Gurley himself visited Mississippi at least twice in the interests of the cause, once in 1836 and again in 1839.[57] Cresson, a representative who worked mainly in the North, must have been in the State at least once, and the Rev. J. B. Pinney was in Mississippi in 1845.[58] James G. Birney, the lawyer of Huntsville, Alabama, who changed from slaveholder to abolitionist, represented the society in Mississippi in 1833. Shortly after this visit several of his articles were reprinted in the Mississippi press.[59] Another minister, H. B. Bascom, who was in Mississippi in the summer of 1831, was an energetic agent who was especially active in forming local societies.[60] He was followed within a few months by Robert S. Finley who returned a number of times to the State where he made speeches, secured contributions, and superintended the embarkation of emigrants. Finley seems to have been better liked than any of the out-of-the-state agents who worked in Mississippi and when the Mississippi society separated for a time from the mother society, Finley was employed as agent of the Mississippi society.[61]

The success of the Mississippi Colonization Society in the middle of the 'thirties encouraged its leaders to independent action. The society was flourishing and was, indeed, a creditor of the American society. The flush of success and something of State rights feeling led to a decision to form a separate African colony for Mississippi emigrants. It is also probable that the leaders of the movement in Mississippi felt that it would be wiser, since there was some local animosity toward the American Colonization Society, to steer a fairly independent course. Accordingly, in 1836, land was secured 130 miles south of Monrovia. "Mississippi in Africa" was to be the name of the colony and "Greenville" was to be its capital, being so named in honor of Judge James Green of whom more will be told later. As has been stated, the Mississippi society employed R. S. Finley as its separate agent.[62] The executive committee of the Mississippi society estimated that $20,000 a year for five years would place their colony on a basis of permanent and progressive prosperity.[63]

As Maryland already had a separate African colony, and as Louisiana was moving with Mississippi in its secession from the parent society, the officers of the latter sought to block this step. Acting with considerable artfulness they first sought to dampen the self-reliance of the Mississippi society by intimating that the land purchased was unsatisfactory and that a native of great power was hostile to the enterprise.[64] Also, Gurley came to Mississippi in June, 1839, to attempt to bring the Mississippi society back to the fold.[65]

In the meantime, a revision of the constitution of the American Colonization Society made his task more difficult. Under the new constitution the Mississippi society, along with the others of the South, suffered because the voting strength of each State was now made proportional to its contributions in money, no account being taken of the large value of emancipated slaves.[66] In spite of this handicap, Gurley succeeded in a prolonged conference with the Mississippi society in patching up a truce between the two organizations. Though there were attached to the agreement some provisos —designed to keep "Mississippi in Africa" a separate unit in Liberia—by the end of 1840 the Mississippi society was on good terms with the American society.[67]

It might also be remarked that by 1840 the Mississippi society was nearly defunct. By this time the initial steps had been taken to secure the colonization of most of the negroes who were transplanted from Mississippi to Africa, although the negotiations necessary to effect the freedom of many of them extended considerably past 1840. The apparent activities after 1840 were but the reapings of earlier sowings. The force of the movement was spent about ten years after its birth.

Two causes of the decline of the Mississippi society have been mentioned, the revision of the constitution of the American society and the partial failure of the ambitious "Mississippi in Africa" plan. A third cause of waning interest in Mississippi was an article in the *Repository* written by Gurley. In it were statements that were strongly disapproved by Dr. Duncan, a most valuable and liberal member of the Mississippi society and for many years its president. Though the writer explained his position and in a measure apologized, Dr. Duncan's active interest seems to have ceased.[68] The patched-up friendship of 1839 between the two societies was completely destroyed when the Rev. William McLain displaced Gurley as secretary of the parent society. Soon after this event, Ker, the last influential and active friend of colonization in the State, became hostile to the management of the American Colonization Society. The subject is best explained in a letter from Ker to McLain. A Mr. T. M. Whiteside, who sought the position of agent of the society in Mississippi, was referred by McLain to Ker, who thereupon wrote to McLain: "I had no knowledge of Whiteside whatever & . . . I am somewhat surprised at *such* a reference to me and from *yourself*. In the first place I am only a single individual without any authority. . . . Our society has been essentially defunct for some years. It has for many years existed only in an Ex. Committee of which I was a member." Ker declared that the individual zeal of the members of this committee had been nearly extinguished because of the disregard of their rights and claims by the Executive Committee of the American Colonization Society and by its secretary, McLain.

Ker further stated that he had a personal ground for complaint against McLain. After the article in the *Repository* that was so much disliked by Duncan, Ker made two attempts to effect a reconciliation. McLain did not even reply to these letters. As a result, Duncan struck from his will a bequest to the society, and his feelings on the subject were so strong that Ker could not even discuss the matter with him.

A final indictment that Ker brought against McLain was that of failure to coöperate in the emigration of a large shipment of Mississippi negroes with the unfortunate result that many of them died of cholera. Their exposure was in part due to McLain's hurried and cowardly flight from New Orleans when he found that cholera was there.[69]

There is small wonder, in view of all these things, that the Mississippi society should have lost interest in the cause. Local conditions also tended to diminish its influence. One was the increase in cotton production and a consequent decline of interest in anything that would remove the sinews of this business. Another factor was the growth of the abolitionist movement and the confusion, in the popular mind, of this cause with that of colonization.[70] By 1842 public opinion in Mississippi was so stirred that a law was passed declaring that no slave could be set free by will, even if this was conditioned on his leaving the State forever.[71] This law, strictly enforced, would of course have greatly hampered the work of the colonization society. Indeed, as will be pointed out later, it was enacted for this very purpose.

After the death of the Mississippi Colonization Society, about the year 1840, a few of the leaders strove to complete tasks that had been begun. Occasional efforts were made to take new steps, but without success. For example, R. S. Finley, who worked in Mississippi over a month in the spring of 1847, was not able to collect enough money to meet his frugal expense account of fifty dollars. His failure is the more evident when we realize that he worked in the section of the State that had earlier been most interested in colonization, namely, at Natchez, Vicksburg, and Oakland College.[72] This fiasco is a fair index to the change of sentiment that had taken place in a very few years. Occasional newspaper references to colonization can be found after 1844, but in general they were brief and frequently hostile. For example, in 1852, a criticism of the idea of emancipating slaves for the purpose of returning them to Africa appeared in one of the State newspapers. A short time after, the same paper had in its columns a copy of a letter of Governor Collier of Alabama relative to the American Colonization Society. He favored returning free negroes to Africa but not slaves.[73]

Through its entire history there was a close connection between the colonization movement and the religious bodies in Mississippi. About one fifth of the officers of the Mississippi society were ministers. Furthermore, the only two meetings that have been noticed were held in the Presbyterian and Methodist churches of Natchez,[74] and these same churches were thrown open for colonization addresses by James G. Birney.[75] The Wilkinson County Colonization Society seems to have been always welcome in the local Methodist church.[76] Finally, resolutions endorsing the movement were passed by these two denominations. In 1833, the Presbytery of Mississippi expressed "unabated confidence" in the colonization society and the following year pledged itself to contribute $100 a year for ten years.[77] Fourteen years later this confidence seems to have continued unshaken, for R. S. Finley was allowed to address a meeting of this Presbytery in the interests of the movement.[78] Likewise, the Mississippi Annual Conference of 1835 of the Methodist Episcopal Church, though denouncing the abolitionists, declared its esteem for the American Colonization Society, which it considered truly friendly to the whole African race and not harmful to the white.[79] This body continued to approve the movement in 1845.[80] The missionary society of Oakland College planned to send a young white man as a missionary to "Mississippi in Africa," [81] and the Presbyterian Synod of Mississippi coöperated with that of Alabama in purchasing a negro man and his family for $2,500 to be sent as missionaries. The slave, Harrison Ellis, was an intelligent blacksmith who had studied Latin and Greek and had made some progress in Hebrew.[82]

Having discussed various phases of the genesis, life, and decline of the colonization movement in Mississippi, there remains the question of what it actually accomplished in settling Mississippi negroes in Africa.

A few Mississippi slaves emigrated to Africa before June 1, 1831, when the Mississippi society was formally organized. The most noted of these was a Natchez slave known as Prince who was discovered to have been a man of rank in Africa. His freedom was given to him so that he could return there. Before sailing he was able to raise sufficient money to purchase his slave wife, and in the spring of 1829 the aged couple departed from the United States in the "Harriet." A year and a half later his eight children and grandchildren, all recently freed from slavery, sailed from Norfolk in the "Carolinian." [83]

In August, 1831, eighteen slaves, set free by Mr. Elizabeth Greenfield who lived near Natchez, embarked for Liberia.[84]

As the avowed purpose of the Mississippi society was to remove free negroes from the State, especial interest attaches itself to the next emigrants, Gloster Simpson and Archy Moore. Doubtless they were the men referred to in the first annual report of the Mississippi Colonization Society, which stated that some free negroes were interested in emigrating and that two of their number expected to go to Liberia and bring back a report of conditions there. The journey of these explorers, for so they might be called, was well described in 1835 by Simpson himself.

For a long time I had desired to find a place of refuge, where I might enjoy liberty and such advantages as I could not here in the South—not that I was treated unkindly in Mississippi. I have many dear friends there. But it is not possible for colored people to enjoy among white men all the privileges and advantages of liberty. I heard a great deal about Liberia, and read a good deal. Good people told me a heap about it, and I wanted to see it. So did some of my friends. One said to another, "Will you go and see it for us." But all were too busy. They sent to me to know if I would go. I said yes. So did Archy Moore. We started. First we came to New Orleans, but the vessel we expected to go in had sailed. Then we had to go to an eastern port. We started for Washington City. Met with many discouragements. In Fredericktown a lady said to me, "Where are you going?" To Africa. "Where?" to *Africa.* "What—you such a fool as to go to Africa? Don't you know that the niggers will kill you and eat you there?" [A laugh] So other persons tried to dishearten and dissuade us from going, till we found Mr. Gurley in Washington. He received us in a friendly manner—encouraged us to go on, and provided for us a passage from Norfolk. Our voyage was much pleasanter than I expected. I found many Christian friends among the emigrants in the ship. We arrived at Monrovia the last day of June.[85]

Thus the two colored emigrants reached Africa, in 1832, and returned the same year. Nearly three years later they went to Africa again, this time leading a company of seventy-one emigrants, who sailed on the brig "Rover" from New Orleans on March 4, 1835.[86] Simpson and Moore had been prevented from returning earlier because their families were in bondage. Although Robert Cochrane,[87] the owner of Simpson's wife and five children, had formally given them to Simpson, they were not able to migrate before 1834 because they had been hired out. Not only did Cochrane relinquish his title to these slaves, valued at $4,000, but he also bequeathed $100 to each of Simpson's five children. Simpson himself owned a farm of 150 acres and was of sufficient prominence to have been invited to deliver a farewell message at the close of the sermon in Bethel church, the church of the white people of his community.

Archy Moore was less fortunate, in that he was compelled to purchase his son for $1,000 and his daughter for $750. However, interested white persons contributed $1,100 for this purpose.[88]

Another emigrant was David Moore, brother of Archy. David had been set free about nine years before for meritorious services. Not only was he successful in managing his own farm of 280 acres, but in addition he received $450 a year for managing an adjoining plantation. He was accompanied to Africa by his wife, for whom he had paid $500, by a female slave purchased at the same price, and by his six children and three grandchildren, for whom he had paid $3,500. He took with him a cotton-gin, about $1,000 worth of agricultural and mechanical tools, provisions and trade goods to an equal value, and about $3,000 in specie. He was probably the wealthiest emigrant to go from Mississippi to Africa.

Also, there was the free negro, Preston Spottswood, who had been employed as second barkeeper in a hotel in Port Gibson. His wife and three children remained in the United States, for he proposed to examine Liberia himself before taking them there.

One other emigrant free negro family was that of Richard Saunders, mechanic and cotton-gin wright. After the death of his owner in 1827, the executor of the estate allowed him to hire his own time for $250 a year and to keep whatever he earned over that amount. At the end of four years he was able to purchase himself for $1,000 in addition to having paid his annual hire. A few days before leaving Mississippi he purchased his wife and son for $1,125, and he also took to Africa a good set of tools for his trade.[89]

These were the chief free negroes on the "Rover." With them sailed a number of negroes who had been freed by their owners for the direct purpose of sending them to Africa. Among these were eleven who had belonged to a Mrs. Bullock of Claiborne County. She had also contributed $700 for their outfit.[90]

Twenty-six slaves were from the estate of Judge James Green, who had been a prominent citizen of Adams County. As executors and trustees he had named his two sisters, Eliza C. Wood and Matilda S. Railey, and his brother-in-law, James Railey. After distinctly excluding all other heirs-at-law, particularly Cowles Mead and any of his descendants, he devised his personal and real property to the three executors, subject to certain exceptions which will be mentioned presently.

One negro man, Granger, was specifically set free, and the executors were enjoined to make ample provision for him, the sum of $3,000 being suggested as proper. To each of the three executors were devised a number of slaves, who were mentioned by name: to Eliza C. Wood, forty-seven; to Matilda S. Railey, seventeen; and to James Railey, nine. Toward the close of the codicil to the will is the following matter, which is particularly relevant to colonization.

... My desire and will is that my following named negro slaves, to-wit, Henry Rust and children Hampton and Nael and Misha if Rusts wife at the time together with any children she may have by him Henry Hubbard and his child Lawson Sam Delany and his wife Suckey and child Sally, Adam his wife Charlotte and their children Dave Bunch and his brother George Jack Armstrong and his Silla Old George and his wife Peg be liberated by my said Executors and trustees acting for the time being at such times as they shall think proper if in their opinion said negroes or any of them from their continued good conduct be entitled to their freedom according to my wishes.

And in the event of any or all of said negroes and their children being emancipated as aforesaid and removing to Liberia to reside my desire in that event is that my executors and trustees give each of them so removing a liberal provision and I suggest a sum not less than two hundred Dollars nor more than five hundred Dollars to each one over twelve years of age and also an outfit to each; and a liberal sum and outfit to each under twelve years of age; to be paid out of my estate by my said acting Executors and trustees. And in the event said negroes or any of them being emancipated and not going to Liberia then the provision out of my estate for any who do not go to be regulated and given by my Executors and trustees as aforesaid according to their best judgments.

I also will and Desire that my negro Charlotte Butler wife of my negro man Granger liberated in my will be set apart and allotted to said negro man Granger by my said Executors and trustees. And after all my bequests devises and dispositions of my Property and directions to my said Executors and trustees contained in my last will & testament in this codicil thereto or expressed in any writing or verbally to my said Executors and Trustees (who are to determine the same) shall have been carried into effect executed and complied with most fully and liberally in every respect according to my intentions and wishes which are fully understood by my said Executors and trustees I give and bequeath all the rest and residue of my Estate of any Description to my said acting Executors & Trustees as provided in my will to be appropriated to the purpose and aid of emancipating negroes in the state of Mississippi and in the event of that not being practicable then towards the establishing or aiding in the endowing of an academy or school or other charitable objects as my said Executors and trustees for the time being shall deem best and think proper leaving it to their discretion, they being fully apprized of my wishes upon this subject.[91]

Judge Green died shortly after he made this will on May 15, 1832, for it was admitted to record at the June term of court in the same year.[92] A few months later at least part of the estate was advertised for sale: "The Forest Plantation," about eight miles below Vidalia, Louisiana, comprising 1,080 acres; "The Point Plantation" of 280 acres, which was seven miles below the first tract of land; and "Boling Green" in Claiborne County, Mississippi, comprising 1,500 acres.[93]

The executors thus entered at once upon their duties. It should be remembered that they were themselves slaveholders and were also among the legal heirs of the testator. Even though the negroes would otherwise have become their own property, they faithfully executed the will of Judge Green. They contributed from the estate $1,000 toward chartering the "Rover," $1,600 in outfitting the twenty-six slaves of Judge Green who sailed on this vessel, and shipped $4,400 in specie to the Governor of Liberia with a memorandum showing how the money should be divided among these slaves.[94] It is probable that a number of other slaves were sent subsequently from this estate.[95] A year later the executors advanced $2,500 toward defraying the expenses of the schooner "Swift," and the officers of the colonization society expected them to devote an additional $25,000 to the cause.[96]

The free negroes, the slaves of Mrs. Bullock and the slaves of Judge Green's estate, who composed most if not all of the passenger list of the

"Rover," were in New Orleans several weeks before they sailed, and Mrs. Wood and Mr. Railey were there part of the time to superintend the embarkation of the twenty-six in whom they were interested. During the delay at New Orleans there were two interesting meetings, one on January seventeenth and the other on February twenty-third. The latter was a farewell meeting and was addressed by Simpson and Moore, the two free negroes who had already been to Africa; by Finley, agent of the American Colonization Society; by Zebulon Butler; and by others. The earlier meeting was the occasion of the formation of all the emigrants into a Temperance Society. The program was impressive; there were numerous testimonies of good character; the pledge was taken by all the emigrants; and all was properly set off by the story of one negro, a brother of one of the emigrants, who pleaded with tears to be allowed to go, but was rejected because he was a drunkard.[97]

It is probable that the next emigrants from Mississippi to Africa sailed on the "Swift" in April, 1836. William Foster, who died near Natchez in 1834, had provided in his will that four families, twenty-one negroes in all, should be separated from his slaves and sent to Liberia, the rest remaining in bondage. In the same vessel were an additional twenty-one slaves who had formerly been the property of a Mr. Randolph, who lived near Columbus, Mississippi. The question of how to finance the transportation of the Randolph negroes had been the subject of some communication between the Mississippi and the American societies in the previous year. The former sought to recover for this purpose a considerable sum earlier loaned to the American Colonization Society. The latter practically repudiated the debt and at least confessed its inability to return the money at that time. However, its secretary promised to write to the Kentucky and Tennessee societies and to urge them to coöperate in supplying means and equipment for the expedition. If necessary, the American society would supply any deficit in funds, but its secretary devoutly hoped that the shortage would not be great. Mr. R. S. Finley was suggested as the best person available to manage the embarkation of the negroes at New Orleans and it is probable that he undertook the task.[98]

In March, 1836, James Leech of Wilkinson County, died, having provided in his will that his servant Delila and her four children should be set free and sent either to Indiana or to Liberia, whichever they chose. One lot in Woodville was willed separately to Delila, and the rest of the property was to be sold and divided equally between her and three of her children, Jack, Harriet, and Nancy. Certain relatives of Leech claimed that the law prohibiting emancipations within the State except with special permission of the legislature [99] was in conflict with this will for the executors were directed

—notice the order of the words—"to set the slaves free and remove them to Liberia." The courts, however, held that the sense of the will was to send the slaves away from the State and then free them, a procedure that was not contrary to law. Thus the will was upheld and it is possible, though not certain, that Delila and her children were sent to Liberia either in 1838 or 1839.[100]

Thirty-seven colored emigrants from Mississippi sailed on the "Mail" from New Orleans in May, 1838. Among these was Robert Leiper, an aged free negro of Natchez. Though his children would not go with him, he was accompanied by his daughter-in-law and her two children. It is probable that the other thirty-three negroes were from the estate of Judge Green. These were the first negroes to go to the new town of Greenville, Liberia, so named in honor of Judge Green. The Mississippi emigrants who had sailed on the "Rover" three years before and who had settled near Monrovia were invited to move to this new town in "Mississippi in Africa" and some, including Gloster Simpson, did so.[101]

The largest number of slaves to go to Liberia from any one Mississippi estate were those of Captain Isaac Ross, a native and resident of Jefferson County. He died in January, 1836. The part of his will and the codicils attached that relate to colonization have been summarized as follows:

1. To his grand-daughter Adelaide Wade, he gave his cook, a woman named Grace, and all her children living at the time of his demise, unless the said Grace should elect, of her own free will, to go to Africa, in which case she and her children were to be transported there with his other slaves as hereinafter provided for. And then the said Adelaide, in lieu thereof, was to have an additional $2,000 besides her other bequests.

2. His aforesaid grand-daughter shall take charge of and maintain comfortably, during their natural lives, testator's negro man Hannibal, and his three sisters, and he gave to Hannibal $100, annually, for life, and to each of his sisters $50, annually. But should they elect to go to Africa, they shall be permitted to go with and on the same footing with the other slaves; and should he so elect he shall be paid when he embarks $500, in silver, in lieu of the aforesaid legacy.

3. Enoch, wife and children were to be conveyed free of expense, in twelve months, to the free State they might prefer, there to be manumitted and receive $500, in coin, or to Africa if they chose, on the same footing with the others, and receive $500.

4. Excepting Tom, William, Joe, Aleck and Henrietta, and Jeffers, (who are to be sold as hereinafter provided,) all the slaves aged twenty-one and upward, within ten days after the growing crop shall be gathered, shall be called together by the executors and the provisions of the will be fully explained. Those electing to go shall be sent to Africa under the authority of the American

Colonization Society. And the remainder of his estate, real, personal and mixed, (excepting always the negroes whose names are mentioned above,) be offered for sale at public auction, one-half the purchase money to be paid in cash and the balance in twelve months. The proceeds of the sale, and any money on hand or due, after deducting enough for the aforesaid legacies, to be paid over to the A. C. S., provided it will consent to appropriate it as follows, to-wit: 1st. To pay the expense of transporting to Africa of such of my slaves as may elect to go. 2d. To expend the remainder for their support and maintenance while there.

5. Should the slaves refuse to go there, they (except those that have been specially named) are to be sold, and the proceeds paid over to the A. C. S., to be invested at 6 per cent., the interest to be employed for 100 years, in maintaining an institution of learning in Liberia, in Africa. If there shall be no government in Liberia, the said fund to be transferred to the State of Mississippi for a similar institution.

6. Daniel Vertner, James P. Parker, Dr. Elias Ogden, Isaac Ross Wade, and John B. Coleman were appointed executors without bond.[102]

This was the substance of the will of Isaac Ross, an officer in the American Revolutionary army and an eminent citizen of his State, who possessed at the time of his death about 160 or 170 slaves. However, their colonization was not to take place before the death of his daughter, Mrs. Margaret A. Reed, widow of United States Senator Thomas Buck Reed.

Captain Ross combined unusual business acumen with kindness and benevolence. One who knew him wrote:

The slaves who are the subjects of his bounty were kept disconnected from those on other plantations, and constitute one great family of *one hundred and seventy persons,* who have been treated more like children than slaves. They are represented to have no superiors among their cast in good morals, industry, and intelligence. To render them happy appears to have been a principal object of their owner. He was an excellent planter; yet for many years, instead of endeavoring to increase his estate, he developed and applied its great resources to increase the comforts of his people. Some conception of its extent may be formed from the statement that the crop on it for the present year will pay all the debts, and that it may hereafter accumulate at the rate of *twenty thousand* dollars per annum. [103]

"Prospect Hill," located nine miles from Port Gibson, was the center of the Ross estate. The value of the property, over and above that of the negroes, was estimated at $150,000 at the time of the owner's death. With an estate of such value, producing a net income of $20,000 a year, there should have been ample funds to carry out the desires of Captain Ross. Unfortunately, some years elapsed before the negroes set sail. During this period the value of the estate shrank almost to the vanishing point; the number of slaves largely increased.

The initial difficulty was that the executors with the single exception of Isaac Ross Wade, a grandson, failed to qualify; while he, with some of the other excluded heirs, laid plans to break the will although he took no legal action to that end. This was highly provoking to Mrs. Reed and Isaac Ross, junior, both of whom were in sympathy with the desires of their father. Indeed, they each made wills providing for the emancipation of at least part of their own slaves. Isaac Ross, junior, died in 1836. Slaves from his estate may have been among the seventy-seven Mississippi emigrants on the "Renown," which sailed in June, 1843, and was wrecked on the Cape Verde Islands where a supply of horses, jacks, and provisions was sought. No lives were lost, however, and with the assistance of the American consul another vessel was secured and the voyage to Liberia was completed.[104]

After witnessing the difficulties that were met in administering the will of her father, Captain Ross, Mrs. Reed, who died in 1838, willed her slaves, including those she inherited from her father, in fee simple to Zebulon Butler and Stephen Duncan. Both of these men, the former a Presbyterian minister of Port Gibson and the latter a wealthy resident of Natchez, favored colonization and understood the desire of Mrs. Reed. Though the slaves were given them outright by Mrs. Reed, they knew that she wanted them sent to Liberia. After a legal fight this was done, though it was "said that Dr. Duncan actually obtained his portion of the slaves by having them run away from the plantation and secreted on the banks of the Mississippi until a steamboat was hailed to take them on to Louisiana, whence he sent them to Liberia." [105]

The Reed negroes sent to Africa by Butler and Duncan composed all but twenty of the ninety-two Mississippi emigrants on the brig "Lime Rock," which sailed from New Orleans on March 10, 1844. The cost of returning the entire ninety-two, including provisions for the first six months in Africa, amounted to at least $5,394.80. The "Lime Rock" was two months on its journey, anchoring at Monrovia on May sixth. Two of the emigrants died at sea; nineteen settled at Monrovia; and the others, presumably the Reed negroes, went down to Sinoe and settled in the Mississippi colony in and about Greenville.[106] Other slaves from the estate of Mrs. Reed had sailed with an earlier expedition, either on the "Mail," in 1838, or the "Renown," in 1843, and had also settled at Greenville.[107]

We will not attempt to follow the intricate and extended litigation concerning the will of Captain Isaac Ross, senior. It is sufficient to state that in its December, 1840, term the State supreme court decided against the heirs. In referring to the law which prohibited the emancipation of slaves in

Mississippi, except with the approval of the legislature in each instance,[108] the court concluded that though this "might seem to prohibit emancipation out of as well as within the State by a citizen, yet such a construction would be manifestly contrary to the spirit of the law. . . . The evil contemplated by the legislature was the increase of free negroes by emancipation. The removal of slaves belonging to citizens of the State, and their emancipation in parts beyond her territorial limits was no injury to her." [109]

Though it would seem, after this decision, that the will of Captain Ross could now be administered, there remained much trouble ahead. Wade and the other defeated heirs carried the fight into the legislative halls of the State. They even spread the rumor that, if the legislature did not block the emancipation of the Ross slaves, there were 500 armed men who had sworn to use force to keep the negroes from being colonized. In addition to bringing this pressure to bear on the legislature, the heirs also declared that Isaac Ross was not in sound mind when he made his will, but was under the influence of "the terrors of death and judgement, inspired by 'priests and fanatics.' " The measure that the heirs sought to force through the legislature would make illegal any bequests of slaves for purposes of emancipation, and would be retroactive over the will of Isaac Ross. It was chiefly due to Dr. John Ker, who was a member of the upper house, that the close lobby maintained by Wade was not entirely successful. Though a bill was finally passed, in 1842, that forbade any manumission of slaves by will, the law was not retroactive. In case a will was already probated, one year was allowed in which the slaves could be removed from the state.[110]

The last clause of this law made necessary the removal of the Ross emigrants from the State within twelve months. This could not be accomplished because of the further maneuvers of Wade, the administrator and manager of the estate. Ker had by this time accepted the position of agent and attorney of the American Colonization Society in this case. A bill was filed within the year in the name of the society to compel the executor to carry out the provisions of the will. As a result of this further litigation the supreme court held that the one-year clause of the act of 1842 would not apply here because "the acts of the executor constituted such a fraud, that neither he nor anyone claiming by virtue of his acts acquired any rights." [111]

Thus ended all legal obstacles to the return of the slaves. Great demands had been made on the time and patience of Dr. Ker and other friends of colonization. The expense of the litigation had been so great that the estate of Captain Ross was now found insufficient to meet the cost of transporting the negroes to Africa. The estate was further impoverished by the fees due Wade for his twelve-year executorship.[112] As the estate could not furnish sufficient money to send the negroes to Africa, other sources had to be discovered. Some funds were secured by contributions from the officers of the Mississippi society.[113] The American Colonization Society was also approached and presumably gave aid. A pamphlet of thirty-six pages was published by the New York Colonization Society, in 1848, giving a good account of the history of the Ross slaves and making a plea for at least $8,000, the amount necessary to consummate the will of Captain Isaac Ross.[114]

The way was finally cleared of all financial and legal obstacles and in January, 1848, thirty-four of the Ross slaves and an additional one from the estate of Mrs. Reed sailed on the "Nehemiah Rich." [115] A year later one hundred and forty-one Ross slaves and one Reed slave sailed on the "Laura" from New Orleans.[116] The total number of Ross emigrants was variously estimated at from 235 to 300. This wide lack of agreement may be accounted for in part by the natural increase of the slaves during the twelve years between the death of their benefactor and the time of their emigration and in part by the question of what slaves to count in making up to the total. In addition to the slaves under the executorship of Wade, there were the slaves bequeathed by Isaac Ross, senior, to Mrs. Reed and liberated by her; the slaves earlier owned by Mrs. Reed; and the slaves liberated by Isaac Ross, junior.

An unfortunate occurrence marred the departure of the "Laura." The Ross emigrants were sent on a river steamboat to New Orleans by Ker, who expected them to be met by McLain, secretary of the American Colonization Society. Cholera suddenly developed in New Orleans and McLain immediately departed without providing for the safety of the slaves. For a time Ker feared that they would be returned to him, which would probably have resulted in their permanent enslavement under the law of 1842. He believed that, if a ship had been ready, it would have been less dangerous to send the slaves on than to retain them anywhere in Mississippi or Louisiana. But McLain left without doing anything. Thus, the slaves were exposed to the disease and, as a result, many deaths occurred on the voyage to Liberia. Those of the Ross slaves who had sailed about a year earlier seem to have suffered no casualties.[117]

After the sailing of the "Laura" there was no large group of emigrants to leave Mississippi for Africa at any one time. Among the twenty-one negroes on the "Clintonia Wright," which sailed from New Orleans in April, 1849, two were from Mississippi. These were Isaac and Cally Morris, both old and probably free negroes.[118] Henry Boatner, who gave his occupation as musician, emigrated in January, 1852. He had been emancipated by J. B. Byrne, of Centerville who had also contributed $50 toward the passage of this thirty-seven-year-old slave.[119] In May of the same year Edward and Susan Bolles of Lafayette County sailed on the brig "Ralph

Cross" from Baltimore. Though both had been born slaves, they had purchased their freedom. On the same boat were Peter Adams and his son, Wesley, who had been set free by Mrs. Land of Centerville.[120] G. J. Vick of Vicksburg freed eight of his slaves and they sailed on the "Zebra" from New Orleans in December, 1852.[121] A family of five slaves emancipated by Mrs. Nancy Jennings of Kemper County sailed from Baltimore in 1853.[122] On the "Elvira Owens" from Savannah in May, 1856, sailed fourteen negroes liberated by Mrs. Elizabeth Holderness of Columbus.[123] James West, who had been freed by C. C. West of Woodville, sailed in December of the same year.[124] The last emigrants from Mississippi to Liberia before the Civil War were fifteen free negroes from Pontotoc who sailed in May, 1860. All bore the surname Manns, and all but two had been born free.[125]

The total number of negroes to go to Liberia from Mississippi was about 571, which was approximately one twentieth of all the emigrants sent from the United States by the American Colonization Society and its auxiliaries.[126] It is probable that at least 500 of these were slaves freed by their owners with the object of colonizing them.

Some Mississippi slave-owners failed in their attempts to free their slaves and send them to Liberia. In December, 1827, Silas Hamilton of Adams County requested the American Colonization Society to provide passage early in June for his twenty-three negroes. This was four years before the Mississippi society was formed. Hamilton hoped to supply agricultural implements and carpenters' tools but was unable to finance the transportation of his slaves. His letter to the society shows how strongly he felt slavery to be a moral and religious evil. In language that would have warmed the heart of the most ardent abolitionist he welcomed the creation of the American Colonization Society, which afforded the means whereby, "I may be enabled to wipe from my character the foulest stain with which it was ever tarnished and pluck from my bleeding conscience the most pungent sting." [127] But Hamilton was not to see his wish fulfilled so early. Three years later he was still writing to the society in regard to his slaves. No evidence of their return has been found.

Drury W. Brazeale, resident of Claiborne County, died in 1834, after providing by will for freeing four families of negroes, supplying them with a suitable outfit, and sending them to Africa. In 1836, the American Colonization Society planned to transport them at an early date,[128] but, in 1839, the superior court of chancery of Mississippi enjoined the executors from carrying this part of the will into effect. It is, therefore, most improbable that the slaves of Brazeale were sent to Liberia.[129]

N. H. Hooe, of King George County, Virginia, provided in his will for the emancipation and colonization of over a hundred of his slaves in Mississippi as well as some in other States. He desired his estate to furnish means for transporting them and to give each one twenty-five dollars when he reached Africa. Gurley was made the executor of this will. The difficulty was that Hooe both made his will and died in the year 1844, two years after the passage of the law of Mississippi that prohibited such a bequest. When the will was brought before the courts of Mississippi, its defense was, of course, undertaken by the colonizationists, but the supreme court declared the will invalid so far as the emancipation of slaves domiciled in Mississippi was concerned.[130]

Another unsuccessful attempt to colonize Mississippi slaves appeared in the will of Robert Lusk, who gave all his slaves "to John H. B. Latrobe, Rev. Wm. McLean, and W. W. Seaton, in trust for the American Colonization Society," and also $3,500, presumably to be expended in removing the slaves to Liberia. These men were leaders in the colonization movement. The court declared the will of Robert Lusk invalid. Part of the decision in this case was in marked contrast to an opinion of the same body handed down just sixteen years before. In 1840, the court stated, in substance, that it was not against the policy of the State of Mississippi for an owner to send his slaves out of the State for the purpose of manumussion.[131] In 1856, in referring to the American Colonization Society, the same court stated that "its operation was calculated strongly to promote emancipation, and it may, therefore, be regarded as founded on a principle not consistent with the growth and permanency of the institution of slavery." [132] It is evident that the court had changed its mind in regard to the policy of the State toward emancipating slaves.

Among the futile attempts to remove negroes from Mississippi to Africa was one that involved free negroes. In 1854, the board of police of Pike County was authorized by a special act of the State legislature to hire out annually at public auction all free negroes in the county with the surname *Lundy*. The money derived from the hiring of these negroes should be loaned at 8 per cent until the total reached $6,000. At that time, a contract should be made with some person or persons to transport the Lundy negroes to Liberia and provide comfortable lodging and board for twelve months.[133] No record has been found of whether the plan was put into operation, but it is almost certain that none of these free negroes were transported. The Lundy negroes were mulattoes with an evident scandal connected with their origin, and this may account for the desire to remove them from the State. They were a peaceful lot who were well behaved during the Civil War and took no part in the disturbances of reconstruction.[134]

These instances of unsuccessful attempts to colonize slaves cannot serve as an accurate measure of the desire of Mississippi planters to send their negroes to Africa. There were doubtless others who would have colonized their slaves, but who were deterred by the knowledge that it was impossible to accomplish this by will after the passage of the law of 1842. For instance, Edward McGehee, of Wilkinson County, an officer of the Mississippi Colonization Society and one of the largest slaveholders of the State, seriously considered planting a colony of his slaves on the coast of Liberia.[135]

As has already been stated, the land at the mouth of the Sinoe River, located about 130 miles southeast of Monrovia, was purchased by the Mississippi and Louisiana Colonization Societies. At the town of Greenville, laid out on this tract, Mississippi emigrants began to settle in 1838.[136] Just as Greenville was named in honor of the former master of the first large group of emigrants, so also other small neighboring settlements were given the names of other Mississippi and Louisiana benefactors of the colonists.

Several years before the founding of Greenville, Liberia, the land was viewed by two free negro men, Moore and Simpson, who have already been presented. Their description of the country is interesting both because of what they said and of the occasion on which they spoke; they were on the verge of conducting a number of their friends to that region. After some preliminary remarks, Moore stated to the assembled emigrants chiefly from the Green estate:

As to the natural productions of the country, they exceed anything I ever saw in all my travels elsewhere. Besides such fruit as we have here, they have a great variety, that grows only there. They have fine grapes. I ate delicious English grapes there. The palm tree I had often heard of, and it is mentioned in the Bible. I saw it growing. It is a singular tree. I saw some two or three feet over. They grow very high, without a single branch or limb. Right on the top is a cabbage, or what looks so much like a cabbage you couldn't tell the difference a little way off. The leaves they use for covering their houses, from the trunk they get a juice, that makes wine, and an oil, that is used for butter and lard. I ate of it, and found it very good. The fibre they used instead of flax and hemp. [Of this fibre he exhibited a specimen—also a piece of the cam wood, a valuable dye wood, of a beautiful red color.] This wood is worth sixty dollars a ton, is abundant and easily obtained. It is as good as gold and silver to trade with.

As to the style of living among the Colonists, it was quite superior to what I expected to see. Many houses, where I visited, look like those of respectable white families, and had I not seen the occupants, would have supposed them inhabited by white people. One Sabbath we were invited by Mr. Devany to dine with him. We went home with him. He introduced us into his sitting room. It was well furnished with carpet, chairs, two elegant sofas, two handsome mirrors, etc. In a little while the folding doors, separating the parlor from the dining room, were thrown open, and we were invited to take seats at the table there, richly set and well supplied with every good thing to eat. Now, some may think because I have lived in the country in Mississippi, I have never seen good style. But I have lived in the first families of the country. I lived many years with Governor Claiborne of your State. Twenty years ago, I know, the furniture in the best houses in the western country, was not better than what I saw in common use in Liberia. I go willingly. I have got a living here in slavery; and now that I am free, if I can't, with health, get a living there, then let me suffer. There is no winter there. I believe I can live easier and better there than I can here.[137]

There was something affecting in this description of Africa by one who had just visited it, and who was encouraging a number of his fellows as they set forth for the land of their ancestors. The occasion was well likened, by an interested spectator, to the report of the spies whom the Israelites had sent into the land of Canaan. And so they returned, and Greenville was founded. Several interesting letters came back from this town, one of which will serve as a fair sample. This communication was addressed to Dr. John Ker.

Greenville Sinoe, October 12th, '49.

Respected Sir—As an opportunity occurs by the Liberia "Packett" I embrace it by writing you these few lines to inform you that I'm still spared & alive, hope they may fine you and your family enjoying good health.

Jeff is well and haughty, and is on his farm trying by the assistance of the Almighty to make a living, and his children are also well, and expresses their thankfulness to you, for your kind & affectionate influence & contrivance of his being in Africa with them, where they have labored long under fearful apprehensions of ever meeting him in this life. Of the last of our people [*i.e.*] the Ross Set that came out here twenty-five have died from the effects of the *Cholera* taken in New Orleans on their way out here.

You will please write me by the first opportunity how all the remaining Ross people are. Old man Hannibald is well & family and wishes to know from, if you have done anything for his daughter Cecelia.

Now, my dear sir, knowing you were always kindly & friendly disposed towards me, even when Capt. Ross were alive, and I now am old & helpless, can't work, let me intrude upon you, not withstanding past events. Simply by begging you to send me a little Soap, Rappa Snuff & any old clothes that you may judge to be of service to the old man in Africa, and a razor. A number of the last emigrants that is our people died on their passage out here, among whom were as follows: James Cole, Grace Julia [in N. Orleans].

This settlement [Greenville, Sinoe] is rapidly improving & increasing in population, &c., and have been upon the continual increase ever since I have been here, and I believe the Spirit & necessity of Education have been awakened considerable.

Now, dear Sir, I hope & trust by the very first opportunity to hear from you and let me hear from all of our people there. Having [no] more of interest to communicate I conclude, praying that the Lord may continue to add his blessings toward you.

Yours very Respectfully,<br>
*Hector Belton.*

P.S.—Old man Scipio & Sampson is dead.[138]

There has also been preserved an account of the Mississippi settlement as it appeared about 1852, a few years after its founding.

The Sinou, a small but placid river, was selected about eighteen years ago by colonists from Mississippi and Louisiana, with a few from South Carolina, who, after acclimating at Monrovia, founded the town of Greenville on the right bank, just above the river's mouth.

From the sea this settlement presents an attractive appearance . . . Greenville faces the sea, and the river flows behind it. It is regularly laid out, and Mississippi Avenue with a row of dwellings on one side and open to the sea on the other, is a delightful promenade. The houses I considered by far the neatest I had seen—two of them were quite handsome two-story ones; and the gardens were in better condition than those of Monrovia. There are about sixty houses and between three and four hundred inhabitants in the settlement. The churches are the least reputable features of the place; but although unprepossessing in their exterior, their congregations were creditable in costume and deportment. My visit was at the time of the annual Baptist association, and the members of that persuasion thronging the settlement gave it quite a lively appearance.

There are a number of mechanics in Greenville, particularly carpenters, and in the outskirts of the town I saw a steam saw-mill, to which lumber was rafted from the river by an artificial canal. . . .

Above Greenville were founded the settlements of Rossville and Readville [Reedville was the proper spelling]; but the country around them, although slightly rolling, is subject to inundation. Other nearby towns were Lexington and Louisiana.[139]

It may not be amiss to include a brief statement of present-day conditions (1930) in Greenville, Liberia, even though this indicates that many of the early hopes have not been fulfilled.

Greenville is the capital and principal port of Sinoe County, Liberia, and is generally known simply by the name of Sinoe. At present it has a population of about six Europeans, perhaps one hundred civilized Liberians and about two thousand natives. There is practically no business or trade carried on except in connection with small cargoes of miscellaneous supplies landed for local consumption and the shipping of a hundred tons or so of piassava. There are no railroads in Liberia and no roads in Sinoe County except native trails which are impassable to any wheeled vehicles.

Economically Greenville is suffering from the same great depression which prevails throughout Liberia and in general it may be said that the inhabitants are living only from day to day on home raised garden produce and poultry.[140]

In concluding the history of the Mississippi Colonization Society, a few additional remarks may be proper. The high position of the leaders of the movement has been indicated. If one will but read the correspondence of the few who were especially active in the work, the conviction will be created that they were unselfishly devoted to the cause, and this was in the face of a popular mistrust which developed in the later 1830's and increased until all interest in colonization was lost.

The colonization movement in Mississippi was mainly confined to the southwestern part of the state. It was here that most of the free negroes lived and that most of the criticism against them arose. And it will be remembered that the removal of this class was the primary purpose of the society. It was also in these same counties that most of the money was raised to finance the work, and from this section came most of the emancipated slaves who emigrated to Africa. The leaders of the movement lived in this part of Mississippi which, significantly, was also a Whig stronghold. The Mississippi Colonization Society might accurately be called the Southwestern Mississippi Colonization Society.

Certain of the tangible accomplishments of the society can be easily listed. About 571 negroes were provided with the necessary equipment and sent to begin their new life on the coast of Africa. The large majority of the emigrants were ex-slaves. It is also certain that a considerable sum of money was contributed; and though the total can never be given, it is probable that a hundred thousand dollars would be a conservative estimate.[141] When the value of the negroes who were emancipated is added to this, the worth of Mississippi's gift to colonization looms large. To complete the record, we should remember the gifts and emancipations offered in good faith which could not be accepted by the society because of legal prohibitions.

One of the main objectives of the Mississippi Colonization Society was to rid the State, particularly its southwestern corner, of free negroes. In this regard the society failed signally. While the free negroes did not keep pace with the great increase in Mississippi's population in the score of years after 1830, this was chiefly due to adverse legislation which caused many of them to move to other States.[142] Colonization may have had an indirect influence on the size of this class by permitting the removal to Africa of slaves who might otherwise have been emancipated within the State by their masters.

One other result of a material nature was the creation and settlement of Greenville on the coast of Liberia, a town that remains to this day as a monument to the Mississippi Colonization Society. The Liberians of this locality doubtless had some share in developing the State of Liberia, in combating the slave-trade, and in civilizing the neighboring parts of Africa.[143] However, such good work as was done seems to have almost ceased. Present-day reports of conditions in Liberia, including Greenville and its vicinity, indicate that the high hopes of the Mississippi Colonization Society have not been fulfilled. Liberians who are descendants of Mississippi emigrants, if we may judge this by their names, are among those whose conduct has recently brought condemnation upon their country.[144] Whatever may be the cause of present conditions, Greenville was settled by a well-chosen group of emigrants who were superior to the average negroes in Mississippi. They were well equipped for their venture, and were sent on their journey by earnest, intelligent, and unselfish citizens of Mississippi.

## NOTES

[1] *Compendium of the Census of 1850,* pp. 45, 63, 83.

[2] *Ibid.,* p. 260.

[3] Franklin L. Riley, "A Contribution to the History of the Colonization Movement in Mississippi," in *P. M. H. S.,* IX, 355. "Free Negroes, and their Influence and Danger among Slaves," is the title of one chapter in W. B. Trotter, *A History and Defense of African Slavery.*

[4] Mitchell *v.* Wells, 37 Miss. 235.

[5] *Hutchinson's Code,* p. 533.

[6] Syndor, "Free Negro in Miss.," in *American Historical Review,* XXXII, 785.

[7] *Jour. Gen. Assem. of Miss.,* 1831, House Jour., pp. 3, 8, and Sen. Jour., pp. 3, 7.

[8] *Woodville Republican,* Sept. 21, 1824, through Feb. 9, 1825.

[9] *Ibid.,* Oct. 5, 1824, and occasional notices until the middle of 1825.

[10] *Ibid.,* Aug. 6, 1831.

[11] *Ibid.,* July 16, 1831.

[12] Riley, "Colonization Movement," in *P. M. H. S.,* IX, 349.

[13] *Woodville Republican,* July 14, Aug. 4, 11, and 18, 1827.

[14] E. L. Fox, *The American Colonization Society, 1817–1840,* p. 81, in *Johns Hopkins University Studies in Historical and Political Science,* XXXVII. *P. M. H. S.,* II, 171, 174.

[15] *Woodville Republican,* Sept. 22, 1827.

[16] *Ibid.,* Oct. 6, 1827.

[17] *Ibid.,* Dec. 16, 1828.

[18] *African Repository,* II, 324; III, 127, 233, 384; IV, 256.

[19] *Ibid.,* V, 182.

[20] *Ibid.*

21 "Colonization Movement," in *P. M. H. S.,* IX, 344–348.

22 *Woodville Republican,* Aug. 6, 1831. A "Form of a Constitution for an Auxiliary Society" was from time to time printed on the paper jackets of the *African Repository.* This "Form" evidently served as a basis for the drafting of the constitution of the Mississippi society.

In 1838 the constitution was amended in several particulars. Among other changes the number of vice-presidents was increased to twelve, and the number of managers was decreased to this same size.—"Colonization Movement," in *P. M. H. S.,* IX, 406–408.

23 Claiborne, *Mississppi,* p. 409; J. D. Shields, *Life and Times of Seargent Smith Prentiss,* p. 13; Dunbar Rowland, *Mississippi,* I, 666.

24 Rowland, *Mississippi,* II, 213–214.

25 *American Colonization Society,* p. 198.

26 Rowland, *Mississippi,* I, 908.

27 *Memoirs of Mississippi,* I, 769.

28 Rowland, *Mississippi,* II, 341.

29 *Memoirs of Mississippi,* I, 475.

30 Rowland, *Mississippi,* II, 349.

31 *P. M. H. S.,* V, 261.

32 Rowland, *Mississippi,* II, 186–187.

33 *P. M. H. S.,* II, 172.

34 Rowland, *Mississippi,* I, 858.

35 "Colonization Movement," in *P. M. H. S.,* IX, 337–341.

36 The officers for 1831 were listed in the *Woodville Republican,* Aug. 6, 1831, and the list for 1838 appeared in the Natchez *Weekly Courier and Journal,* Dec. 28, 1838. The latter item was cited in Riley, "Colonization Movement," in *P.M.H.S.,* IX, 406–407.

Of the ten persons who made gifts in excess of $5,000 to Oakland College, half were officers of the Mississippi Colonization Society. John Ker gave that college $20,000 and David Hunt's munificence was so great that his name has been incorporated into that of the institution.—Edward Mayes, *History of Education in Mississippi,* pp. 66, 71.

37 These persons appear among the lists of officers of the American Colonization Society that were printed in the following pamphlets: *Report of the Naval Committee to the House of Representatives, August, 1850, in Favor of the Establishment of a Line of Mail Steamships to the Western Coast of Africa. . . . Twenty-eighth Annual Report of the American Colonization Society.* C. K. Marshall, *The Exodus: Its Effect upon the People of the South.*

38 *Woodville Republican,* Aug. 6, 1831.

39 *African Repository,* VII, 207.

40 *Woodville Republican,* July 9 and 16, Dec. 17, 1831; June 30, 1832.

41 *Ibid.,* Mar. 31, 1832.

42 "Colonization Movement," in *P. M. H. S.,* IX, 350–351. *American Colonization Society,* p. 158.

43 R. R. Gurley, *Mission to England,* p. 261.

44 "Colonization Movement," in *P. M. H. S.,* IX, 347.

45 *Ibid.,* pp. 377, 380.

46 *American Colonization Society,* pp. 171, 198.

47 William Birney, *James G. Birney and His Times,* pp. 122–123.

48 *African Repository*, VII, 206.

49 *Ibid.*, VIII, 61, 81, 93, 122.

50 *Ibid.*, XXIX, 219; XXXII, 19–20; XXXIII, 151; XXXIV, 64, 82; XXXVI, 95; XXXVII, 160.

51 Several free negroes, presumably not emigrants, contributed small sums to the cause.—*Ibid.*, XVIII, 47; XXX, 287.

52 *Ibid.*, IX, 57.

53 "Colonization Movement," in *P. M. H. S.*, IX, 365.

54 *African Repository*, XII, 336.

55 "Colonization Movement," in *P. M. H. S.*, IX, passim.

56 *Ibid.*, p. 369. *African Repository*, V, 182; VI, 80.

57 "Colonization Movement," in *P. M. H. S.*, IX, 408. American Colonization Society, p. 198.

58 *Ibid.*, p. 188. *African Repository*, XXI, 160.

59 *James G. Birney*, pp. 122–128. *Woodville Republican*, June 15, July 27, Aug. 17, 1833.

60 *African Repository*, VII, 138–139, 206–207.

61 *Ibid.*, VII, 345; VIII, 315; XI, 64, 250–252; XIII, 63–64. *American Colonization Society*, p. 101. "Colonization Movement," in *P. M. H. S.*, IX, 366, 369.

62 *African Repository*, XIII, 63–64.

63 *South-Western Journal, a Magazine of Science, Literature and Miscellany*, vol. I, no. ii (Dec. 30, 1837). Published semimonthly by the Jefferson College and Washington Lyceum.

64 *African Repository*, XII, 36; XIII, 192. *Mission to England*, p. 240.

65 *African Repository*, XV, 200–201.

66 *American Colonization Society*, pp. 119–122.

67 *African Repository*, XV, 200–201; XVII, 43, 158; XVIII, 59–60. "Colonization Movement," in *P. M. H. S.*, IX, 408–411.

68 "Colonization Movement," in *P. M. H. S.*, IX, 383–384.

69 *Ibid.*, pp. 358–361.

70 Robert J. Walker stated in the United States senate that "among the unfortunate consequences which had been produced in Mississippi, owing to the movements of the Abolitionists was the unpopularity of the Colonization Society, which previously, on the contrary had been extremely popular. There were many individuals in the state who had been beneficient contributors to it but who now were opposed to it." Speech of Jan. 27, 1837. *Congressional Debates*, vol. XII, part I, p. 535.

71 *Hutchinson's Code*, p. 539.

72 "Colonization Movement," in *P. M. H. S.*, IX, 396–399.

73 Natchez *Mississippi Free Trader*, Jan. 10 and 28, 1852.

74 "Colonization Movement," in *P. M. H. S.*, IX, 406–411.

75 *James G. Birney*, p. 122.

76 *Woodville Republican*, July 9, Aug. 6, 1831; June 30, 1832.

77 *American Colonization Society*, p. 94. *African Repository*, X, 29.

78 "Colonization Movement," in *P. M. H. S.*, IX, 397.

79 *Woodville Republican*, Dec. 5, 1835.

80 *American Colonization Society*, p. 165.

81 *African Repository*, XVI, 216.

82 *Ibid.*, XXII, 356; XXIII, 46–48.

83 *Ibid.*, III, 364–367; IV, 77–81, 243–250; V, 94, 281; VI, 60, 187.

[84] *Ibid.*, VII, 217. *American Colonization Society*, pp. 212–215.

Mrs. Greenfield, formerly Mrs. Roach, was the donor of the land and buildings at Washington, Miss., for that pioneer institution for the education of women, Elizabeth Female Academy.—*Education in Mississippi*, p. 38.

[85] *Emigrants from New Orleans*, p. 3.

[86] The supplies that emigrants needed were, in the opinion of Robert S. Finley as follows: "Bacon, beef, flour, corn meal, leaf tobacco, salt, nails, hinges, pots, skillets and all kinds of hardware, house earthen ware, pound beans, coarse cottons, and callicoes, hemp, linen, etc. etc."—*Woodville Republican*, Nov. 6, 1831.

[87] Cochrane donated the 250 acres of land on which Oakland College was built.— *Education in Mississippi*, p. 66.

[88] *African Repository*, XI, 153.

[89] *Ibid.*, XI, 154.

[90] *Ibid.*, XI, 250–251.

[91] From a certified copy of Last Will and Testament, and the codicil thereto, of James Green, deceased. Record of Wills Book 2, pages 8 to 12 inclusive, Chancery Court, Adams County, Mississippi.

[92] Letter from W. H. Hale, chancery clerk, Adams County, Miss.

[93] *Woodville Republican*, Nov. 24, 1832.

The legislature of Louisiana passed an act authorizing the executors of the estate of Judge Green to move the administration of the part of the property that was in Louisiana to Adams County, Mississippi.—*Laws of Louisiana*, 1836, p. 148.

[94] *African Repository*, XI, 251–252.

[95] Claiborne, *Mississippi*, p. 388. *American Colonization Society*, p. 198.

[96] *African Repository*, XII, 236.

[97] *Ibid.*, XI, 123–127, 251–252. *Emigrants from New Orleans*, pp. 1–2.

[98] *African Repository*, XI, 336. *American Colonization Society*, pp. 199, 212–215. "Colonization Movement," in *P. M. H. S.*, IX, 365–367.

[99] *Hutchinson's Code*, p. 523.

[100] Leech *v.* Cooley, 14 Miss. 93.

[101] *African Repository*, XIV, 93–94; XV, 71–88.

[102] Claiborne, *Mississippi*, pp. 389–390, thus condenses the part of the will dealing with colonization.

[103] *A Brief History of The Ross Slaves*, pp. 11–12.

Jefferson Davis, though opposed to colonization, was probably referring to the Ross emigrants when he stated that he knew and highly esteemed the slaves who had been sent to Africa by one master.—Rowland, *Jefferson Davis, Constitutionalist*, IV, 522–523.

[104] *African Repository*, XV, 71–88; XIX, 81–82.

[105] *A Brief History of The Ross Slaves*, p. 31.

[106] *Twenty-eighth Annual Report of the American Colonization Society* (1845).

[107] *African Repository*, XX, 284–286.

[108] *Hutchinson's Code*, p. 523.

[109] It is worthy of note that Seargent S. Prentiss was a counsel in this case, serving those who were endeavoring to fulfill the will of Isaac Ross.—*Seargent S. Prentiss*, p. 313.

[110] *Hutchinson's Code*, p. 539.

[111] "Prospect Hill," where Wade and his family lived, was burned in 1845. There is evidence to show that the negroes, who had become restive under the long delay,

did this with the hope of destroying Wade whom they considered the chief obstacle to their being freed.—Anna Mims Wright, *A Record of the Descendants of Isaac Ross and Jean Brown*, pp. 72–74.

[112] *Ibid.*, pp. 69–74. *A Brief History of the Ross Slaves*, p. 35.

[113] "Colonization Movement," in *P. M. H. S.*, IX, 377, 380.

[114] *A Brief History of The Ross Slaves*.

[115] *African Repository*, XXIV, 59–61, 77, 210–211.

[116] *Ibid.*, XXV, 118–121.

[117] The following sources supplied the material for the discussion of the colonization of the Ross Slaves: Riley, "Colonization Movement," in *P. M. H. S.*, IX, 331–414; Claiborne, *Mississippi*, pp. 388–391; *American Colonization Society*, pp. 202–204; Ross *et al. v.* Vertner *et al.*, 6 Miss. 305; Wade *v.* American Colonization Society, 12 Miss. 670; Wade *v.* American Colonization Society, 15 Miss. 663; *African Repository*, XV, XIX, XX, XXIV, XXV; *A Brief History of The Ross Slaves*.

[118] *African Repository*, XXV, 218.

[119] *Ibid.*, XXVII, 122; XXVIII, 128.

[120] *Ibid.*, XXVII, 183.

[121] *Ibid.*, XXIX, 70.

[122] *Ibid.*, XXIX, 220.

[123] *Ibid.*, XXXII, 253–254.

[124] *Ibid.*, XXXIII, 25.

[125] *Ibid.*, XXXVI, 143.

[126] A tabulation of emigrants to the end of the year 1859 is given according to States in the *African Repository*, XXXVI, 115. In *ibid.*, XXXIII, 152–155 is a table which shows the number of emigrants each year from each State to the end of 1857. To the totals given in these tables I have added the fifteen free negroes who departed from Pontotoc in 1860, too late to be included in either table. I have also added Prince and his wife and the eighteen slaves freed by Mrs. Greenfield, who sailed in 1829 and 1831 respectively. Though there is ample evidence that these twenty emigrated to Africa, they were either omitted from the tables mentioned above or listed under some other State which was probably due to their having departed from Mississippi before the State colonization society was organized.

[127] *American Colonization Society*, p. 193.

[128] *African Repository*, XI, 36; XII, 235

[129] Clarke *v.* McCreary, 20 Miss. 347.

[130] Mahorner *v.* Hooe *et al.*, 17 Miss. 247. "Colonization Movement," in *P. M. H. S.*, IX, 398. *American Colonization Society*, p. 206.

[131] Ross *et al. v.* Vertner *et al.*, 6 Miss. 305.

[132] Lusk *v.* Lewis *et al.*, 32 Miss. 297.

[133] *Laws of Miss.*, 1854, pp. 358–359.

[134] All Pike County Records were destroyed by fire in 1882. The above information was gained from old residents of the county.

[135] Rowland, *Mississippi*, II, 187.

[136] *Mission to England*, p. 240.

An early map of Liberia showing the location of Greenville and the neighboring villages of Rossville and Reedville can be found in *African Repository*, XXVII, 193.

[137] *Emigrants from New Orleans*, p. 4.

Devany, whom Moore met in Liberia, was doubtless Francis Devany, formerly of

Philadelphia, who was in 1830 high sheriff of the colony of Liberia.—*African Reposi-*
*tory,* III, 250; VI, pp. 97 ff.

138 "Colonization Movement," in *P. M. H. S.,* IX, 401–402. In this place are two
other letters from Mississippi negroes who had emigrated to Africa.

139 *Report of Commander W. F. Lynch to the Secretary of the Navy,* Sept. 5, 1853
(House Document). In addition to the report just cited, there is a description of
Greenville in *Sketches of Liberia* by J. W. Lugenbeel, at one time Colonial Physician
and United States Agent in Liberia.

140 From a letter dated July 19, 1930, to the writer from C. H. Hall, Jr., American
Chargé d'Affaires ad interim, Monrovia, Liberia.

141 In addition to the gifts that have been mentioned before, there was also a bequest
of $45,000 left to the Society by David Hunt of Adams County.—*American Coloniza-*
*tion Society,* p. 63.

142 "Free Negro in Miss," in *American Historical Review,* XXXII, 769–788.

143 *American Colonization Society,* chapt. V.

144 *Report of the International Commission of Inquiry into the Existence of Slavery*
*and Forced Labor in the Republic of Liberia,* pp. 22–23. In 1860 Jefferson Davis
avowed his opposition to sending confiscated cargoes of Africans to Liberia on the
ground that Liberian colonists excluded uncivilized Africans from participation in
churches and schools, and practically enslaved them.—Rowland, *Jefferson Davis,*
*Constitutionalist,* IV, 521.

Davis seems to have known in 1860 what the rest of the world did not learn until
1931.—*Slavery and Forced Labor in Liberia.*

*Although colonization efforts in the United States tended to focus on Liberia, other areas of Africa were also considered as areas of settlement. One of the initiators of a plan to purchase land for freed slaves at Abeokuta (in present-day western Nigeria) was Robert Campbell of Philadelphia. A Black man, Campbell was one of the Commissioners of the Niger Exploring Party, Chairman of the Scientific Department of the Institute for Colored Youth in Philadelphia, and a member of the International Statistical Congress of London. His journey to seek settlement lands took place in 1859 and 1860. The concluding section of his journal is presented here as it was published in 1861.*

# A Pilgrimage to My Motherland

## Robert Campbell

The native authorities, every where from Lagos to Ilorin, are willing to receive civilized people among them as settlers. It is hardly fair to say merely that they are willing; they hail the event with joy. They know and appreciate the blessings which must accrue to them by such accessions. They would, however, be opposed to independent colonies, the establishment of which among them, not only on this account, would be highly inexpedient.

The sea-coast, from the prevalence of mangrove-swamps, is unhealthy, but it is a fact that many persons, even Europeans and Americans, enjoy good health there, and many of the deaths are more to be attributed to alcoholic indulgence than to the character of the location. Abbeokuta, and all other interior towns we visited, are healthy, but even in these an occasional attack of bilious fever must be expected for a year or two, or until the process of acclimature is completed. Emigrants should remember that in new countries it is always necessary to exercise great watchfulness and discretion.

The expense of a voyage to Lagos directly from America, should not exceed $100 for first-class, and $60 for second-class: via Liverpool, besides the expense of the voyage thither, it would cost $200 for first-class, and

From Robert Campbell, *A Pilgrimage to My Motherland: An Account of a Journey Among the Egbas and Yorubas of Central Africa, in 1859–60* (New York: Thomas Hamilton, 1861), pp. 134–145.

$150 for second-class: $25 should include all expense of landing at Lagos, and of the journey to Abbeokuta.

The best protection on which a settler should rely in Africa, is that which all men are disposed to afford a good and honest man. The proper kind of emigrants want no protection among the natives of the Egba and Yoruba countries. We have had, however, from Lord Malmesbury, late Foreign Secretary in the British Cabinet, a letter to the Consul at Lagos, by which the protection of that functionary, as far as he can afford it, is secured for settlers.

Although land for agricultural purposes may be obtained, as much as can be used, "without money and without price," yet town-lots will cost from $2 to $50 and even $100. Some fine fellows may get a very suitable lot for a trifle, or even for nothing; much depends upon the person.

The commercial and agricultural prospects are excellent, but there is much room for enterprise and energy. There is a decided demand for intelligent colored Americans, but it must be observed that one who is only prepared to roll barrels would have to compete with the natives under great disadvantages. Agriculturists, mechanics, and capitalists, with suitable religious and secular teachers, are most required.

Emigrants should never leave the States so as to arrive at Lagos in the months of June, July or August: the bar is then bad, and there is great risk to person and property in landing at such season. For safety I might include the last of May and first of September. During all the rest of the year there is no danger. The difficulties of the bar are not, however, insuperable; small vessels can always easily sail over it into the fine bay within, where they can load or unload with little trouble and without risk. It is not so easy to go out again, however, for then it would be necessary to "beat" against the wind, but a small steamboat could at once take them out in tow with perfect safety. I was informed that slavers used always to enter the bay: they could, of course, afford to wait for a favorable wind with which to get out.

Emigrants going to Abbeokuta, according to the second article of our treaty, will be permitted the privilege of self-government, but this can only be municipal, and affecting too only themselves. There is no doubt, however, that in time it will assume all the functions of a national government, for the people are fast progressing in civilization, and the existing laws, which from their nature apply only to heathens, would be found inadequate for them. Even now, as soon as any one of the people assumes the garb or other characteristics of civilization, they cease to exercise jurisdiction over him. He is thenceforward deemed an "oyibo," or white man.* The rulers, of course, will not be unaffected by those influences which can bring about such changes in their people, and thus they too will find it expedient to modify the laws to meet the emergency. But emigrants must ever remember that the existing rulers must be respected, for they only are the *bona fide* rulers of the place. The effort should be to lift them up to the proper standard, and not to supersede or crush them. If such a disposition is manifested, then harmony and peace will prevail; I am afraid not, otherwise.

Of course the succession of seasons in northern and southern latitudes below the 24th parallel, does not exist. There are two wet and two dry seasons. The first wet begins about the last of April, and continues until the close of June. The second begins in the last of September, and ceases with the end of October. The period between June and September is not entirely without rain. Both the wet seasons are inaugurated by sharp thunder and lightning, and an occasional shower. The harmattan winds prevail about Christmas time. They are very dry and cold: I have seen at 8 A.M., the thermometer at 54° Fahr., during the prevalence of these winds. The mornings and evenings, however warm the noon might be, are always comfortable. The general range of the temperature is between 74° and 90° Fahr. I have experienced warmer days in New-York and Philadelphia.

With due prudence there is nothing to fear from the African fever, which is simply the bilious fever, arising from marsh miasmata common to other tropical countries, as well as to the southern sections of the United States. I have, myself, experienced the disease, not only in Africa, but in the West-Indies and Central America, and know that in all these places it is identical. Emigrants to the Western States of America suffer severely from typhoid fever, which often renders them powerless for months together; but with the African fever, which is periodical, there is always an intermission of from one to three days between the paroxysms, when the patient is comparatively well. Persons of intemperate habits, however, are generally very seriously affected. I suffered five attacks during my sojourn in Africa. The first, at Lagos, continuing about eight days, was induced by severe physical exertion in the sun. The four other attacks were in the interior. By a prompt application of suitable remedies, neither of them lasted longer than four or five days, and were not severe. The treatment I found most efficacious was, immediately on the appearance of the symptoms, to take two or three anti-bilious pills, composed each of two and a half grains comp. ext. Colocynth, and one fourth grain Podophyllin, (ext. May-apple root.) For the present of a box of these pills I am indebted to Messrs. Bullock & Crenshaw, druggists, Sixth, above Arch street. This treatment always had the effect of greatly prostrating me, but the next day I was better, although weak. I then took three times daily about one grain sulphate of quinine, as much as will lie on a five-cent piece. This quantity in my own case was always sufficient, but it must be observed that the same dose will not answer for every constitution. It should be taken in a little acidulated water, or wine and water. Mr. Edward S. Morris, 916 Arch street, has a preparation which from experience I found better than the pure quinine. The practice of physicking while in health to keep well is very unwise: try to keep off disease by living carefully, and when in spite of this it comes, then physic, but carefully. Many suffer more from medicines than from disease. Quinine should not be taken during the recurrence of the fever. Hard labor or unnecessary walking in the sun must be avoided, but with an umbrella one might go out for an hour or two with impunity in the warmest weather.

Cotton from Abbeokuta has been an article of export to the British market for about eight years. In the first year only 235 pounds could be procured, but from that time, through the efforts of Thomas Clegg, Esq., of Manchester, and several gentlemen connected with the Church Missionary Society, London, the export has more than doubled every year, until, in 1859 the quantity reached about 6000 bales or 720,000 pounds. The plant abounds throughout the entire country, the natives cultivating it for the manufacture of cloths for their own consumption. Its exportation is, therefore, capable of indefinite extension. In the seed it is purchased from the natives at something less than two cents per pound. It is then ginned and pressed by the traders, and shipped to Liverpool, where it realizes better prices than New-Orleans cotton. The gins now in use by the natives affect injuriously the fibre, so as to depreciate it at least two cents per pound. Properly cleaned, it would bring far more than New-Orleans cotton, and even as it is, the value is about four cents more than the East-India product. The plant in Africa being perennial, the expense and trouble of replanting every year, as in this country, is avoided. There are flowers and ripe cotton on the plants at all seasons of the year, although there is a time when the yield is greatest. Free laborers for its cultivation can be employed each for about one half the interest of the cost of a slave at the South per annum, and land at present can be procured for nothing. These are advantages not to be despised.

The domestic animals comprise horses, which are plentiful and cheap; mules and asses at Ilorin; fine cattle, furnishing excellent milk, which can be purchased at about two cents per quart; sheep, not the woolly variety; goats, pigs, dogs, cats, turkeys, ducks, chickens, Guinea-hens, (also wild ones in abundance,) pigeons, etc. Of agricultural products there are cotton, palm-oil, and other oils; Indian-corn, which is now being exported; sweet potatoes, yams, cassava, rice; Guinea-corn, a good substitute for wheat; beans, several varieties; arrow-root, ginger, sugar-cane, ground-nuts; onions, as good as can be obtained any where; luscious pine-apples, delectable papaws, unrivalled oranges and bananas, not to mention the locust and other fine varieties of fruit.

Of minerals there is an abundance of the best building granite. I have seen no limestone, but Lagos furnishes, as already observed, an unlimited supply from oyster-shells. Plenty of rich iron-ore, from which the natives extract their own iron.

Of timber there is plenty of the African oak or teak—*roko,* as the natives call it—which is the material commonly used for building. Of course there are other fine varieties of timber. Water is easily procured every where. In the dry season some find it convenient to procure it from wells only a few feet deep, say from three to twelve feet. The Ogun furnishes good water-power; there are also fine brooks which could be so used, but not all the year. The sugar-cane I have seen every where.

There is certainly no more industrious people any where, and I challenge all the world besides to produce a people more so, or capable of as much endurance. Those who believe, among other foolish things, that the Negro is accustomed lazily to spend his time basking in the sunshine, like black-snakes or alligators, should go and see the people they malign. There are, doubtless, among them, as among every other race, not excepting the Anglo-American, indolent people, but this says nothing more against the one than the other. Labor is cheap, but is rising in value from the increased demand for it.

The following is a copy of the treaty we concluded with the native authorities of Abbeokuta:

## TREATY

This Treaty made between his Majesty Okukenu, Alake; Somoye, Ibashorun; Sokenu, Ogubonna, and Atambala, on the first part; and Martin Robison Delany and Robert Campbell, of the Niger Valley Exploring Party, Commissioners from the African race of the United States and the Canadas in America, on the second part, covenants:

### ARTICLE FIRST

That the King and Chiefs on their part agree to grant and assign unto the said Commissioners, on behalf of the African race in America, the right and privilege of settling in common with the Egba people, on any part of the territory belonging to Abbeokuta not otherwise occupied.

### ARTICLE SECOND

That all matters requiring legal investigation among the settlers be left to themselves to be disposed of according to their own customs.

### ARTICLE THIRD

That the Commissioners on their part also agree that the settlers shall bring with them, as an equivalent for the privileges above accorded, intelligence, education, a knowledge of the arts and sciences, agriculture, and other mechanical and industrial occupations, which they shall put into immediate operation by improving the lands and in other useful vocations.

### ARTICLE FOURTH

That the laws of the Egba people shall be strictly respected by the settlers; and in all matters in which both parties are concerned, an equal number of commissioners, mutually agreed upon, shall be appointed, who shall have power to settle such matters.

As a pledge of our faith and the sincerity of our hearts, we, each of us, hereunto affix our hands and seals, this twenty-seventh day of December, Anno Domini one thousand eight hundred and fifty-nine.

his<br>
OKUKENU × ALAKE<br>
mark.

his<br>
SOMOYE × IBASHORUN,<br>
mark.

M. R. DELANY,<br>
ROBERT CAMPBELL.

Witness:

    SAMUEL CROWTHER, JR.

Attest:

    SAMUEL CROWTHER, SR.

---

We landed at Liverpool, Dr. Delany and myself, on the 12th May, 1860, in good health, although we had been to—Africa!

## NOTES

\* This term, which literally signifies stripped off, was applied to white men, from the belief that their skin was stripped off. It is now applied indiscriminately to civilized men. To distinguish, however, between black civilized and white civilized men, the terms *dudu* for the former, and *fufu* for the latter, are respectively affixed.

*As the lieutenant commanding the U.S. Brig* Perry *in 1850 and 1851, Andrew H. Foote visited the Cape Palmas area of Liberia. This region had been settled with ex-slaves through the efforts of the Maryland Colonization Society. The rather patronizing account of Foote casts a favorable and optimistic light on the Liberia experiment. His narrative, however, was contemporaneous with the heyday of colonization before the Civil War. Later accounts will describe the decline of the colony after Emancipation when interest in colonization waned in the United States.*

# Africa and the American Flag

### Andrew H. Foote

Notwithstanding the heterogeneous population of Liberia, a commendable degree of order, quiet, and comparative prosperity prevails. With such men as President Roberts, Chief-Justice Benedict, Major-General Lewis, Vice-President Williams, and many other prominent persons in office and in the walks of civil life, the government and society present an aspect altogether more favorable than a visitor, judging them from the race when in contact with a white population, is prepared to find. The country is theirs —they are lords of the soil; and in intercourse with them, it is soon observed that they are free from that oppressive sense of inferiority which distinguish the colored people of this country. A visit to Monrovia is always agreeable to the African cruiser.

Monrovia, the capital, is situated immediately in the rear of the bold promontory of Cape Mesurado, which rises to the altitude of 250 feet. The highest part of the town is eighty feet above the level of the sea. The place is laid out with as much regularity as the location will admit. Broadway is the main or principal street, running nearly at right angles with the sea. Besides this, there are twelve or fifteen more. The town contains not far from two thousand inhabitants. Many of the houses are substantially built of brick or of stone, and several of them are handsomely furnished. The humidity of the climate has greatly impaired the wooden buildings. The State-House, public stores, and the new academy are solid, substantial build-

From Andrew H. Foote, *Africa and the American Flag* (New York: D. Appleton & Co., 1854), pp. 192–212.

ings, appropriate to their uses. There are five churches, and these are well attended. The schools will compare favorably with the former district schools in this country, which is not saying much in their favor.

The soil in the vicinity of the rocky peninsula of Mesurado is generally sandy and comparatively unproductive, except where there are alluvial deposits along the margin of the streams or creeks. The lands on the banks of the rivers—of the St. Paul's, for instance, four or five miles north of Monrovia—are very rich, of loamy clay soil, equalling in fertility the high lands of Brazil, or any other part of the world. Here more care is devoted to the culture of sugar, and increasing attention is given to agriculture. These lands readily sell at from forty to fifty dollars per acre. A fork of this river flows in a southeasterly direction, and unites with the Mesurado River at its mouth. This fork is called Stockton's Creek, in honor of Commodore Stockton. The largest rivers of Liberia are navigable only about twelve or fifteen miles before coming to the Rapids.

As the country becomes settled, and the character of its diseases better understood, the acclimating fever is less dreaded. In fact, it now rarely proves fatal. This having been passed through, the colored emigrants enjoy far better health than they did in most parts of the United States. The statistics, as President Roberts stated, show some three per cent. smaller number of deaths than in the New England States and Canada among the same class of population. The thermometer seldom rises higher than 85°, nor falls lower than 70°.

The productions of the soil are varied and abundant,—capable of sustaining an immense population. The want of agricultural industry, rather than the incapacity of the country to yield richly the fruits of the earth, has been the difficulty with the Liberians. With well-directed labor, of one-half the amount required among the farmers of the United States, a large surplus of the earth's productions, over the demands of home consumption, might be gathered. The country certainly possesses elements of great prosperity.

"A bill for the improvement of rivers and harbors" should be forthwith passed by the Liberian legislature. A country exporting articles annually amounting to the sum of eight hundred thousand dollars, and this on the increase, might make an appropriation to render landing safe from the ducking in the surf to which one is now exposed. Sharks, in great abundance, are playing about the bars of the rivers, eagerly watching the boats and canoes for their prey. Dr. Prout, a Liberian senator, and several others, have been capsized in boats and fallen victims to these sea-tigers.

A full and very interesting description of the geography, climate, productions and diseases of Africa has been published by Dr. J. W. Lugenbeel, late colonial physician, and the last white man who was United States agent in Africa.

In devising measures for the benefit of Liberia, one thing was pre-eminently to be kept in view, which was, that the people be prevented from sinking back to become mere Africans. It is believed that this danger was wholly past under the energetic administration of Buchanan, to whom too much praise cannot be awarded. He infused life and spirit into the nation, and brought out such men as Roberts and others, in whose hands we believe the republic is safe. A large majority of the emigrants having been slaves, and dependent on the will and dictation of others, many of them are thereby rendered in a measure incapable of that self-reliance which secures early success in an enterprise of this kind.

Slaves do not work like freemen. The question, then, arises—Is this the case because they are slaves, or because they are negroes? Those who have been emancipated in the British territories have hitherto cast no favorable light on this inquiry. They do not now work as they did when compelled to work, although they are free. Neither do the Sicilians, Neapolitans, or Portuguese work as men work elsewhere. There are no men freer than the slavers, who steal children and sell them, in order that they themselves may live in vicious idleness. It is the freeman's intelligence and his higher motives of action, which produce his virtues.

The slave-trade being extirpated within the boundaries of Liberia, and the natives brought under new influences, the necessity produced for new kinds of labor has become favorable to the improvement of the African. There is now the will and ability of the native population to work in the fields. The low rate of remuneration which they require, favors the employ-ment of capital, but keeps wages for common labor very low. It is of no use to urge upon colonists to employ their own people in preference to natives, when the former want eighty cents a day and the latter only twenty-five. These things must take their natural course. The increase of capital must be waited for ere wages can rise. But it all tells strongly in favor of settlers securing grants of land, and becomes a great inducement for colored men emigrating to Liberia who have some little capital of their own.

It is in Liberia alone that the colored man can find freedom and the incentives to higher motives of action, which are conducive to virtue. There these sources of good are found in abundance for his race. In this country he can gain the intelligence of the free population, but is excluded from the vivifying motives of the freeman. In Liberia he has both. Means are needed to sustain this condition of things. The first of these is religion, which to a great degree, pervades the community there: it is true that some of the lower forms of a vivid conception of spiritual things characterize the people; but far preferable is this, to the tendency of the age elsewhere—towards attempting to bring within the scope of human reason the higher mysteries of faith. The second is the school, which keeps both intelligence and aspiration alive, and nurtures both. Roberts is aware of this, and keeps it before the people. They will transfer, therefore, what the United States alone exemplifies, and what is vitally important to free governments, namely, a system of free public education in the common schools; such a system is that of the *graded schools* in many parts of our country, far surpassing most of the select schools, where a thorough education may be freely obtained by all the children of the community.

Liberia contains a population exceeding one hundred and fifty thousand inhabitants; not more than one-twentieth of this number are American colonists. Its growth has been gradual and healthy. The government, from its successful administration by blacks alone, for more than six years, appears to be firmly established. The country is now in a condition to receive as many emigrants as the United States can send. To the colored man who regards the highest interest of his children; to young men of activity and enterprise, Liberia affords the strongest attractions.

We would not join in any attempt to crush the aspirations of any class of men in this country. But it is an actual fact, whatever may be thought of it, that here the colored man has never risen to that position, which every one should occupy among his fellows. For suppose the wishes of the philanthropist towards him to be fully accomplished,—secure him his political rights; unfetter him in body and intellect; cultivate him in taste even; then while nominally free, he is still in bondage; for freedom must also be the prerogative of the white, as well as of the black man; and the white man must likewise be left free to form his most intimate social relations; and he is not, and never has been disposed, in this country, to unite himself with a caste, marked by so broad a distinction as exists between the two races. The testimony on these two points of those who have had abundant advantages for observation, has been uniform and conclusive. For the colored man himself then, for his children, Liberia is an open city of refuge. He there may become a freeman not only in name, but a freeman in deed and in truth.

Liberia has strong claims upon Christian aid and sympathy. Its present and prospective commercial advantages to our country, will far counterbalance the amount appropriated by private benevolence in planting and aiding the colony and the republic. Its independence ought to be acknowledged by the United States. This, according to the opinion of President Roberts, would not imply the necessity of diplomatic correspondence, while the moral and political effects, would be beneficial to both parties. England, by early acknowledging the independence of Liberia, and cultivating a good understanding with its government and people, has greatly subserved her own commercial interest, while responding to the call of British philanthropy.

.      .      .      .      .      .      .      .      .      .      .      .

The Maryland Colonization Society resolved to establish a colony at Cape Palmas. Dr. James Hall, their agent, secured the consent of the chiefs to cede the required territory, without employing the wretched medium of rum. These kings, to their credit, have retained sensible names of their own, redolent of good taste and patriotism, being Parmah, Weah Boleo, and Baphro. As has ever been done by all wise people on that coast, a fort was expeditiously erected, overlooking in a peremptory way the native villages and the anchorage; since it is not, for a time at least, safe to trust in such affairs to the conscience of the natives.

Cape Palmas is well suited for such an establishment; the climate is as good as any in tropical Africa. The Cape itself is a small elevation or insulated hill, sloping down towards the continent, into the general expanse of wooded plain or forest; this, to the north and east of the Cape, stretches out into a wide fertile flat, the waters of which drain towards the long line of sea-beach, receiving the heavy surf of the equatorial Atlantic. The surf throws a long bulwark of sand along the mouths of the fresh-water streams, and checks them in a lagoon of ten miles in length, by about a quarter of a mile in breadth. This water is fresh or brackish, according as either element gains the mastery, and serves the natives as a precious and fruitful fish-pond.

Of this region, a tract extending about twenty miles along the sea-shore, and as much inland, was, by purchase, brought under the jurisdiction of the Maryland Society. Provision was made for retaining the resident natives on the lands they cultivated. Here, in the month of February, 1834, the Maryland Colonization Society attached itself to Africa, by landing fifty-three emigrants from that State.

Their temporary dwellings were soon put up; and their fortifications erected near to populous towns crowded with natives supplied with fire-arms and ready to use them. Vessels continued to arrive, bringing more settlers to their shores. In 1836, an additional tract of country, east of the Cape, was procured; extending the colonial territories along the broad, rapid stream of the Cavally, to the distance of thirty miles from its mouth. In succeeding years new settlers arrived to occupy the lands so acquired; yet all these acquisitive proceedings gave rise to scarcely any noticeable opposition. A little blustering occurred on the part of one chief, who attempted to monopolize the selling of rice to the colonists when in want; but a kind and resolute firmness removed the difficulty. Scarcely, in fact, does an instance occur in history, of an administration so uniformly successful in the operations for which it was established; and, whatever the future may offer to equal it, nothing certainly in the past has a higher claim for sympathy, than these efforts of Maryland for the benefit of her colored population.

With the same wisdom which had characterized the previous measures of the society, in 1837 Mr. Russwurm, a colored man, was appointed governor of the colony. He fulfilled the expectations formed of him. Thus one step was judiciously taken, to disengage the colored men of Africa from dependence on foreign management.

Considering, however, that Cape Palmas has been colonized from a slave state alone, and that the government has been retained in the hands of the state society, it is scarcely to be expected that the same vigor and activity should be found in its internal operations, or the same amount of influence exercised over the surrounding natives, as has been manifested in Liberia. Notwithstanding this, the beneficial influence of this colony also, on the surrounding natives, has been considerable. Six kings, of their own accord, applied to Governor Russwurm, and ceded their territories, that they might be incorporated with the colony. Every treaty contained an absolute prohibition of the slave-trade.

Cape Palmas colony, then, may be considered as now extending from the confines of her elder sister at the river Jarraway, as far to the eastward as Cape Lahou. The inland boundary may be anywhere, as the future shall settle it. The cultivated or cleared land extends parallel to the coast, over distances varying from twenty-five to fifty miles. Here comes on the dark verdure of forest, undulating over the rising lands which lead to the mountains, or whatever they may be, which feed the rivers. These streams act as lines of communication. But here also the old Portuguese influence has aimed at a monopoly of trade. Some explorations have disclosed the fact that there are powerful tribes in these lands, who, in spite of an obstacle of this kind, will soon be brought within the commercial influence of the colony.

This line of coast has at many points been a frequent haunt of slavers, and the atrocities due to native superstition have been shocking, and rendered more villainous by European trade. Commodore Perry, in 1843, as will be seen in the notice of squadrons, did justice on some of their villages, convicted of murder and robbery of an American vessel. The officers delivered several of the natives from torture under the accusations of sorcery. To control such fierce materials into quietness, or melt them to Christian brotherhood, will require much grace from Providence, and much kind and patient dealing from men.

In carrying out the the objects of the colony, an effort was made by the Maryland Colonization Society, which seemed in its nature singularly promising. This consisted in establishing a joint-stock trading company, or line of packets for carrying out emigrants and returning with produce. It was expected that the colored people of the state would, to some considerable extent, invest capital in shares. With these expectations the "Liberia Packet" was launched in 1846, and made many voyages. It was found necessary to increase the size of vessels thus employed. But these operations were checked by the wreck of the "Ralph Cross." It was also found that comparatively little interest in this undertaking was awakened among the colored population, or that they had not the means for investment in it, as only about one-eighth of the whole amount of stock was held by them. It is, however, an incident of value in the history of Africa, that through facilities thus afforded, many emigrants revisited this country for short periods, and thus established a return line of intercourse, inquiry, or business, which binds Africa more strongly to this land.

A movement for the elevation of the colony into an independent state, has been made by the people at Cape Palmas, and a commission has visited this country to make arrangements for the purpose. That there be full political independence granted to this people, is requisite, as an element of the great achievement now going on. This contemplates something far higher than creating merely a refuge for black men, or sticking on a patch of colored America on the coast of Africa like an ill-assorted graft, for which the old stock is none the better. Liberia is the restoration of the African in his highest intellectual condition to that country in which his condition had become the most degraded. The question is to be settled whether that condition can be retained, or so improved that he may keep pace with the rest of the world.

It is a necessary element in this proceeding that he be self-governing. It is to the establishment of this point that all men look to decide the dispute, whether negro races are to remain forever degraded or not. Time and patience, however, and much kind watchfulness, may be required before this experiment be deemed conclusive. Let many failures be anticipated ere a certain result is secured. Let no higher claims be made on the negro than on other races. Would a colony of Frenchmen, Spaniards, Portuguese, Sicilians, if left to themselves, offer a fairer prospect of success than Liberia now offers? Few persons would have confidence in the stability of republican institutions among these races, if so placed.

Let then the black man be judged fairly, and not presumed to have become all at once and by miracle, of a higher order than old historic nations, through many generations of whom the political organization of the world has been slowly developing itself. There will be among them men who are covetous, or men who are tyrannical, or men who would sacrifice the public interests or any others to their own: men who would now go into the slave-trade if they could, or rob hen-roosts, or intrigue for office, or pick pockets, rather than trouble their heads or their hands with more honorable occupations. It should be remembered by visitors that such things will be found in Liberia; not because men are black, but because men are men.

It should not be forgotten that the experiment in respect to this race is essentially a new one. The nonsense about Hannibal, and Terence, and Cyprian, and Augustine, being negro Africans, should have been out of the heads of people long ago. A woolly-headed, flat-nosed African, in ancient times, would have created as great a sensation at the head of an army, or in the chair of a professor, as it would now in the United States or in England. These men were Asiatics or Europeans, rather than Africans: the Great Desert being properly the northern boundary of the African race. The African has never reached in fact, until the settlement of Liberia, a higher rank than a king of Dahomey, or the inventor of the last fashionable grisgris to prevent the devil from stealing sugar-plums. No philosopher among them has caught sight of the mysteries of nature; no poet has illustrated heaven, or earth, or the life of man; no statesman has done any thing to lighten or brighten the links of human policy. In fact, if all that negroes of all generations have ever done, were to be obliterated from recollections forever, the world would lose no great truth, no profitable art, no exemplary form of life. The loss of all that is African would offer no memorable deduction from any thing but the earth's black catalogue of crimes. Africa is guilty of the slavery under which she suffered; for her people made it, as well as suffered it.

The great experiment, therefore, is as to the effect of instruction given to such a race from a higher one. It has had its success, and promises more. But many patient endeavors must still be used. The heroism of the missionary is still needed. Such men as Mills, Ashmun, Wilson, and Bishop Payne, will be required to give energy to this work in various forms. But there will be henceforth, it is to be hoped, less demand for the exposure of American life. There should be found in the colored people of the United States, with whom the climate agrees, the source of supply for African missions, till, in a few years, Liberia itself send them forth, with words of life to their brethren throughout the length and breadth of the continent.

Like all sinful men, the African needs faith. But you must dig deeper in him, before you find any thing to plant it on. The grain of mustard-seed meets a very hard soil there, and the thorns are deep. It is a conquest to get him to believe that there is any virtue in man. They have never had a Socrates, to talk wisdom to them; nor a Cyrus, who was not a slave-merchant; nor a Pythagoras, to teach that kindness was a virtue. Hence the difficulty which the Christian missionary has had with them, has been to satisfy their minds as to the miraculous phenomenon of there being a good man. It has been always found that there was many a consultation among their sages as to the peculiar trade or purpose the missionary might have in view, in coming as he came; and very generally the more good they saw, the more evil they suspected. The first thing which, in most instances, opened their eyes, has been in his inculcating peace; for they saw no fees coming to him for it, and of course no looking out for plunder.

The civilized world, as well as the savage, need the example of the missionary. The true courage of faith is a blessing to mankind. Besides his devotion to the highest interests of men, the world also owes much to the educated and enlightened missionary, who has not only greatly contributed to the cause of science and literature, but has often been the means of developing the commercial resources of the countries where he has been stationed. Women, with their own peculiar heroism, which consists in fearless tenderness and patience, have also shared in this work of faith. Mrs. Judson is seen wandering through a Burman village teaching the people, with a sick child in her arms, while her husband lies in prison. And Mrs. Wilson, highly cultivated and refined, sacrificing her property, and surrendering a position in the best society of the country, is found teaching negro children in the dull and fetid atmosphere of African schools. This is true heroism, such as the gospel alone can inspire.

Christianity has, with watchful kindness, been seeking to penetrate Africa from various points of the coast. Abyssinia has long professed the Christian faith, although in a corrupt form. Its church, and that of Egypt, must soon fall under the influence of the line of communication through the Red Sea. English missionaries are at Zanzibar, and have brought to light, by their explorations in the interior, the group of mountains which raise their snowy heads south of the equator in that neighborhood. Missionaries from the same country are also to be found at Sierra Leone and in the Bight of Benin. From the extremity of the continent they have, in conjunction with those of five other nations, been penetrating all the interior of the southern angle.

The United States have also missionaries at four or five points. There are those of the Liberian republic, Cape Palmas, and the Mendi mission. In these places different denominations work kindly and earnestly together. The first obvious sign of their presence is peace. Nowhere in the world was this more needed, or more welcome, than in the regions north and east of

Liberia, where men, for many years, had had to fight for their own persons, that they might remain their own, and not be sold. Every thing, as might be expected, had fallen into utter confusion. Tribes of historic character were in fragments; towns depopulated, cultivation suspended, and the small knots of families which kept together, were perishing. "The women and children," says Mr. Thompson, "were often obliged to go out in search of berries and fruits to keep themselves from starving." To this country, which lies along the sources of the Sierra Leone and the Gallinas rivers on the northern confines of Liberia, the captives on board the *Amistad* had gone in 1842. But such was the confusion in that quarter, that it was not until 1851, that the missionary found it practicable to commence his efforts for peace. They told Mr. Thompson "that no one but a white man could have brought it about;" and that "they had long been praying to God to send a white man to stop the war."

The Gaboon mission, since its disturbance by the French in 1844, has been re-established, and has experienced courteous treatment at the hands of the French authorities. This mission occupies the important position at which the great southern nation and language come in contact with the more energetic men of the equatorial region, and at which great light is likely to be thrown on their relations. The French also have a mission at the Gaboon.

The mission to the Zulus, in the healthy region at the southern end of the Mozambique Channel, was at one time divided between the two branches of that tribe; but in consequence of wars, was afterwards united and established in the colony of Natal. The commercial crisis in the United States in 1837, led to the proposal that this mission should be abandoned. But its influence had been so beneficial, that the Cape colonists and their government proposed to take measures to support it. Circumstances, however, enabled the American Board to decline this proposal, and they continue their operations. An effort is being made by this mission to unite all similarly engaged, in a common and uniform mode of treating the language of the south.

The Portuguese have missions, both on the east and west side of the continent.

Commander Forbes, R. N., says: "In all the countries which have given up the traffic in their fellow-men, the preaching of the Gospel and the spread of education have most materially assisted the effects of the coercive measures of our squadron."

*On August 14, 1862, President Abraham Lincoln
received a group of prominent Black citizens of
Washington at the White House. In the course of the
discussion, Lincoln suggested that it would be best for
both Whites and Blacks if all free Blacks were to emigrate
from the United States. Although he praised the
prospects of Liberia, Lincoln suggested that the
Caribbean or Latin America might be a more desirable
locale due to their proximity to the United States.
Lincoln, at this time, was under pressure from certain
northern financial interests to colonize sections of the
Isthmus of Panama and Haiti with free Blacks who could
be used as laborers in the enterprises owned by these
businessmen. Colonization efforts took place in both
locations but soon collapsed amidst protest by Latin
American governments and scandal in the United States.
The greatest losers were the colonists.*

# Address on Colonization
# to a Deputation of Negroes [1]

## Abraham Lincoln

August 14, 1862

This afternoon the President of the United States gave audience to a
Committee of colored men at the White House. They were introduced by
the Rev. J. Mitchell, Commissioner of Emigration. E. M. Thomas, the
Chairman, remarked that they were there by invitation to hear what the
Executive had to say to them. Having all been seated, the President, after
a few preliminary observations, informed them that a sum of money had
been appropriated by Congress, and placed at his disposition for the purpose
of aiding the colonization in some country of the people, or a portion of
them, of African descent, thereby making it his duty, as it had for a long
time been his inclination, to favor that cause; and why, he asked, should
the people of your race be colonized, and where? Why should they leave
this country? This is, perhaps, the first question for proper consideration.
You and we are different races. We have between us a broader difference

From *The Collected Works of Abraham Lincoln* (Roy Basler, ed.) (New Brunswick,
N.J.: Rutgers University Press, 1953), pp. 370–375.

than exists between almost any other two races. Whether it is right or wrong I need not discuss, but this physical difference is a great disadvantage to us both, as I think your race suffer very greatly, many of them by living among us, while ours suffer from your presence. In a word we suffer on each side. If this is admitted, it affords a reason at least why we should be separated. You here are freemen I suppose.

A VOICE: Yes, sir.

The President—Perhaps you have long been free, or all your lives. Your race are suffering, in my judgment, the greatest wrong inflicted on any people. But even when you cease to be slaves, you are yet far removed from being placed on an equality with the white race. You are cut off from many of the advantages which the other race enjoy. The aspiration of men is to enjoy equality with the best when free, but on this broad continent, not a single man of your race is made the equal of a single man of ours. Go where you are treated the best, and the ban is still upon you.

I do not propose to discuss this, but to present it as a fact with which we have to deal. I cannot alter it if I would. It is a fact, about which we all think and feel alike, I and you. We look to our condition, owing to the existence of the two races on this continent. I need not recount to you the effects upon white men, growing out of the institution of Slavery. I believe in its general evil effects on the white race. See our present condition—the country engaged in war!—our white men cutting one another's throats, none knowing how far it will extend; and then consider what we know to be the truth. But for your race among us there could not be war, although many men engaged on either side do not care for you one way or the other. Nevertheless, I repeat, without the institution of Slavery and the colored race as a basis, the war could not have an existence.

It is better for us both, therefore, to be separated. I know that there are free men among you, who even if they could better their condition are not as much inclined to go out of the country as those, who being slaves could obtain their freedom on this condition. I suppose one of the principal difficulties in the way of colonization is that the free colored man cannot see that his comfort would be advanced by it. You may believe you can live in Washington or elsewhere in the United States the remainder of your life [as easily], perhaps more so than you can in any foreign country, and hence you may come to the conclusion that you have nothing to do with the idea of going to a foreign country. This is (I speak in no unkind sense) an extremely selfish view of the case.

But you ought to do something to help those who are not so fortunate as yourselves. There is an unwillingness on the part of our people, harsh as it may be, for you free colored people to remain with us. Now, if you could give a start to white people, you would open a wide door for many to be made free. If we deal with those who are not free at the beginning, and whose intellects are clouded by Slavery, we have very poor materials to start with. If intelligent colored men, such as are before me, would move in this matter, much might be accomplished. It is exceedingly important that we have men at the beginning capable of thinking as white men, and not those who have been systematically oppressed.

There is much to encourage you. For the sake of your race you should sacrifice something of your present comfort for the purpose of being as grand in that respect as the white people. It is a cheering thought throughout life that something can be done to ameliorate the condition of those who have been subject to the hard usage of the world. It is difficult to make a man miserable while he feels he is worthy of himself, and claims kindred to the great God who made him. In the American Revolutionary war sacrifices were made by men engaged in it; but they were cheered by the future. Gen. Washington himself endured greater physical hardships than if he had remained a British subject. Yet he was a happy man, because he was engaged in benefiting his race—something for the children of his neighbors, having none of his own.

The colony of Liberia has been in existence a long time. In a certain sense it is a success. The old President of Liberia, Roberts, has just been with me—the first time I ever saw him. He says they have within the bounds of that colony between 300,000 and 400,000 people, or more than in some of our old States, such as Rhode Island or Delaware, or in some of our newer States, and less than in some of our larger ones. They are not all American colonists, or their descendants. Something less than 12,000 have been sent thither from this country. Many of the original settlers have died, yet, like people elsewhere, their offspring outnumber those deceased.

The question is if the colored people are persuaded to go anywhere, why not there? One reason for an unwillingness to do so is that some of you would rather remain within reach of the country of your nativity. I do not know how much attachment you may have toward our race. It does not strike me that you have the greatest reason to love them. But still you are attached to them at all events.

The place I am thinking about having for a colony is in Central America. It is nearer to us than Liberia—not much more than one-fourth as far as Liberia, and within seven days' run by steamers. Unlike Liberia it is on a great line of travel—it is a highway. The country is a very excellent one for any people, and with great natural resources and advantages, and especially because of the similarity of climate with your native land—thus being suited to your physical condition.

The particular place I have in view is to be a great highway from the Atlantic or Caribbean Sea to the Pacific Ocean, and this particular place has all the advantages for a colony. On both sides there are harbors among the finest in the world. Again, there is evidence of very rich coal mines. A certain amount of coal is valuable in any country, and there may be more than enough for the wants of the country. Why I attach so much importance to coal is, it will afford an opportunity to the inhabitants for immediate employment till they get ready to settle permanently in their homes.

If you take colonists where there is no good landing, there is a bad show; and so where there is nothing to cultivate, and of which to make a farm. But if something is started so that you can get your daily bread as soon as you reach there, it is a great advantage. Coal land is the best thing I know of with which to commence an enterprise.

To return, you have been talked to upon this subject, and told that a speculation is intended by gentlemen, who have an interest in the country, including the coal mines. We have been mistaken all our lives if we do not know whites as well as blacks look to their self-interest. Unless among those deficient of intellect everybody you trade with makes something. You meet with these things here as elsewhere.

If such persons have what will be an advantage to them, the question is whether it cannot be made of advantage to you. You are intelligent, and know that success does not as much depend on external help as on self-reliance. Much, therefore, depends upon yourselves. As to the coal mines, I think I see the means available for your self-reliance.

I shall, if I get a sufficient number of you engaged, have provisions made that you shall not be wronged. If you will engage in the enterprise I will spend some of the money intrusted to me. I am not sure you will succeed. The Government may lose the money, but we cannot succeed unless we try; but we think, with care, we can succeed.

The political affairs in Central America are not in quite as satisfactory condition as I wish. There are contending factions in that quarter; but it is true all the factions are agreed alike on the subject of colonization, and want it, and are more generous than we are here. To your colored race they have no objection. Besides, I would endeavor to have you made equals, and have the best assurance that you should be the equals of the best.

The practical thing I want to ascertain is whether I can get a number of able-bodied men, with their wives and children, who are willing to go, when I present evidence of encouragement and protection. Could I get a hundred tolerably intelligent men, with their wives and children, to "cut their own fodder," so to speak? Can I have fifty? If I could find twenty-five able-bodied men, with a mixture of women and children, good things in the family relation, I think I could make a successful commencement.

I want you to let me know whether this can be done or not. This is the practical part of my wish to see you. These are subjects of very great importance, worthy of a month's study, [instead] of a speech delivered in an hour. I ask you then to consider seriously not pertaining to yourselves merely, nor for your race, and ours, for the present time, but as one of the things, if successfully managed, for the good of mankind—not confined to the present generation, but as

> From age to age descends the lay,
>     To millions yet to be,
> Till far its echoes roll away,
>     Into eternity.

The above is merely given as the substance of the President's remarks.

The Chairman of the delegation briefly replied that "they would hold a consultation and in a short time give an answer." The President said: "Take your full time—no hurry at all."

The delegation then withdrew.

## NOTES

[1] New York *Tribune,* August 15, 1862. An act "releasing certain persons held to labor in the District of Columbia" and providing $100,000 for colonization, became law on April 16, 1862, and an act approved on July 16, freed slaves in the hands of the army and granted $500,000 for colonization. Since October, 1861, the Chiriqui Project for colonization had been under cabinet consideration (see Lincoln to Smith October 23 and 24, 1861, *supra*). The appointment of Reverend James Mitchell of Indiana as agent of emigration is not listed in the *Official Register,* but contemporary records indicate that he operated in the Department of Interior as early as May 28, 1862, when he sent Lincoln his long letter on colonization printed by the Government Printing Office. His activity in July and August brought the matter of colonization to a head with the arrangement for an interview between Lincoln and the committee of Negroes headed by Edward M. Thomas on August 14. Thomas was president of the Anglo-African Institute for the Encouragement of Industry and Art. The committee's reception of Lincoln's views is indicated by a letter from Thomas written on August 16:

"We would respectfully suggest that it is necessary that we should confer with leading colored men in Phila New York and Boston upon the movement of emigration to the point recommended in your address.

"We were entirely hostile to the movement until all the advantages were so ably brought to our view by you and we believe that our friends and co-laborers for our race in those cities will when the subject is explained by us to them join heartily in sustaining such a movement. . . ." (DLC-RTL).

Subsequent developments, however, indicated that Negroes in the District of Columbia received the colonization proposal with hostility. A Negro meeting held at Union Bethel Church was reported in the Baltimore *Sun* on August 23 as protesting against the plan: "Such dissatisfaction had been manifested in regard to the course of the committee who lately waited on the president . . . that they did not attend. It was hinted that they had exceeded their instructions."

Plans were fully matured in August, however, to send Senator Samuel C. Pomeroy with "500 able-bodied negroes as the first colony" to be settled on a site on the Isthmus of Chiriqui to be selected by Pomeroy (New York *Tribune,* September 15, 1862). A letter of authority from Lincoln to Pomeroy was prepared for Lincoln's signature, probably by the State Department, under date of September 10, 1862, but remains unsigned in duplicate copies in the Lincoln Papers. The project was abandoned when first Honduras and later Nicaragua and Costa Rica protested the scheme and hinted that force might be used to prevent the settlement.

# 4

# THE DECLINE OF COLONIZATION

The two essays in this section discuss the fortunes of the
Colonization movement after the Civil War and
Reconstruction. With the hope of any real motion in
the direction of equality thwarted with the demise
of Reconstruction, the Black population of the southern
states were forced to reappraise their American
nationality in the face of repressive measures by a
vindictive southern population. Most either remained in
the South or fled to the North. Others considered
Africa as an alternative. The circumstances and results
of this second wave of colonization are considered here.

*In Georgia, where the post-Reconstruction period was especially harsh on the Black population, the urge to emigrate was overpowering. Despite the calamitous attempts of their South Carolina brethren to resettle in Liberia, the Georgia Blacks were smitten by the prospect that somewhere on the face of the earth they could find relief from oppression. The feedback from the South Carolina failure served to reduce the number of potential colonists but substantial interest did exist. Clarence A. Bacote's article describes the conditions prevalent in Georgia after Reconstruction which help to explain the continued Black interest in emigration despite previous failures.*

# Negro Proscription, Protests, and Proposed Solutions in Georgia, 1880–1908

## Clarence A. Bacote

Following reconstruction in Georgia, the Negro was not only the victim of political disfranchisement and educational discrimination, but also suffered humiliation in the form of "Jim Crow" laws, lynching, and the convict-lease system. These forms of racial proscription brought forth numerous protests from Negroes but to no avail; hence, convinced of the futility of striving for first-class citizenship in such an environment, some Negro leaders proposed three avenues of escape, namely: (1) back to Africa, (2) exodus to the North, and (3) colonization in the frontier West. By these means, they hoped, Negroes might be able to acquire those rights and privileges guaranteed by the United States Constitution.

"It is paradoxical," says Woodward, "that the barriers of racial discrimination mounted in direct ratio to the tide of political democracy among the whites." [1] Antagonism between the poor whites and Negroes dated back to the ante bellum period and continued after the Civil War, but it was intensified as the two groups became competitors in the labor market. Knowing that they were despised by both the upper-class whites and the freedmen, the poor whites struggled to maintain a floor below which no whites would fall and which at the same time would serve as a ceiling to the rise of Negroes. [2]

From *Journal of Southern History*, XXV, No. 4 (November, 1959), pp. 471–498. Copyright 1959 by the Southern Historical Association. Reprinted by permission of the Managing Editor.

Meanwhile, the upper-class whites, who did not wish to see the Southern social and economic structure fractured by a coalition of the poor whites and Negroes, aided and abetted this racial friction by stressing to the poor whites the importance of maintaining white supremacy. Thus white supremacy was the principal theme, and the average white voter was blind to the fact that "Negro domination" was a fantastically false appeal of politicians who had finally succeeded in enslaving the white voter through propaganda. To strengthen the allegiance of the poor whites to the existing social and economic arrangements, the ruling class proceeded in a limited way to establish schools and factories for them. The result was a widening of the educational and economic gap between the poor whites and Negroes.[3]

In 1870, as a result of a bill introduced in the Georgia Legislature by two Negro members, James Porter of Chatham County in the house and George Wallace in the senate,[4] an act was passed which stated that "all common carriers of passengers for hire in the State of Georgia shall furnish like and equal accommodations for all persons, without distinction of race, color, or previous condition."[5] But by 1890, the growing antagonism between the poor whites and Negroes was reflected on the state level when the Alliancemen gained control of the Georgia Legislature by electing 160 of the 219 members.[6] While the Alliancemen advocated a liberal platform,[7] at the same time they enacted several laws which were definitely designed to emphasize the inferior status of the Negro; the most vicious of these was the "Jim Crow" law.

When Representative S. W. Johnson of Appling County introduced a bill in the Georgia House on July 20, 1891, requiring the railroads to furnish separate coaches for whites and Negroes with equal accommodations for both races, Representative Lectured Crawford, a Negro from McIntosh County, told the House that

The railroads would not give equal accommodations if this act were to become law, and as long as I buy a first class ticket I have a right to such accommodations, whether I am considered below the other race or not. . . . The railroads sell us first class tickets and then put us into cars where white men come in and smoke, use all kinds of indecent language, drink whiskey out of water cups, and they call this first class passage.[8]

While this bill was under discussion in the House, the Georgia Colored Alliancemen were holding their state meeting in Atlanta. A committee to memorialize the legislature was appointed, with J. W. Carter as chairman, to ask for better laws, not race legislation, but "such laws as will better the condition of the colored race, and promote their happiness and advance the cause of education."[9] On July 23, the members of this committee visited the legislature and took seats in the gallery. Representative J. M. Holzendorf, Negro member from Camden County, obtained permission from the house to allow a representative from the Negro Alliance to address them for ten minutes. Just before their spokesman, J. W. Carter, began to speak, the Alliance members were invited to take seats on the floor of the house. In his plea against the bill, Carter said in part:

The white people . . . have sold themselves to the Negroes. . . . You ask them to vote for you, and when you ask the Negro to vote for you, you are due him a return of the compliment. We Negroes are voting for you now. Some of these days we expect you to vote for us.

After complimenting the Alliance legislature on its successful campaign, Carter turned to the social relationship of the races.

We don't want social equality. All the Negro wants is protection. You white people attend to your business and let us alone. . . . The politicians and the lawyers say you must keep us Negroes down. But that is not right. . . . If you have a sow that has a lot of pigs, some white ones and some black ones, you don't kill the black ones, do you? No sir. You think just as much of the black pigs as you do the white ones. . . . If this old state of ours should be threatened, these Negroes—your mothers in black—would be the first to offer themselves in her defense.[10]

It was unusual for a Negro visitor to be extended an invitation to address the legislature from the floor, but the speech was well received. Many of the members congratulated Carter for his keen logic. However, despite Crawford's protest and Carter's appeal for justice, the "Jim Crow" bill was passed by both houses and was signed by Governor Northen on October 21, 1891. The law required the railroads to provide equal accommodations in separate cars for whites and Negroes but this did not apply to sleeping cars. In addition, the law authorized streetcar conductors to separate the races as far as possible.[11]

This "Jim Crow" law drew nationwide attention. The Chicago *Appeal* declared that

A state cursed with such a legislative body almost deserves commiseration. . . . The state of "Wisdom, Justice, and Moderation" is thus set back in this enlightened age by the recent wretched legislation which was a Farmer's Alliance body.[12]

Negroes themselves were disappointed in this group, whose platform seemed to incorporate ideas of justice and fair play. In a lengthy editorial, the Savannah *Tribune* observed:

The past twelve months have been more prolific of legislation in the Southern States directly antagonistic to the Negro than any similar period since the days of Reconstruction.

. . . in the states dominated by the Farmer's Alliance, and in those legislatures where their influence has been strongest and most commanding, has this tendency to reactionary legislation been most active and pronounced. . . . These exhibitions of prejudice . . . are simply an expression of hostility to the Negro injected by the white farmers of the South into the great currents of passing political opinion. They represent the feeling of the agricultural class always more strongly wedded to old ideas and less susceptible to the newer teachings of an enlarged and and progressive humanity. They have their origin in an order dominated from its incipiency by a feeling of enmity to the Negro.[13]

Negroes pleaded with Governor Northern to force the railroads to provide equal accommodations for both races, and the Negro Press Association of Georgia drew up resolutions advocating such accommodations.[14] These pleas were ignored; consequently, Negroes were herded into crowded coaches without ice water, towels, or soap, and men and women were forced to use the same lavatory facilities.[15]

Since the railroads refused to provide better facilities for Negroes, the latter were advised to stop patronizing railroad excursions and save their money. In most instances these excursions were frequented by the worst element of Negroes, which did the race much harm.[16] The Reverend J. W. Carter, pastor of the Boulevard A. M. E. Zion Church in Atlanta, said "the colored people keep plenty of money ahead in the railroad treasury from the excursion business to take care of and repair all the Jim Crow cars, where the Negroes and dogs ride together. . . . Enough money is spent in one season by Negro excursions to buy one-fourth of the Indian territory." When Negroes returned home from such excursions, continued the Reverend Mr. Carter, they usually found themselves with insufficient money to pay their rent, to buy food, and to provide for their children.[17]

"Jim Crow" trains were followed by "Jim Crow" streetcars in various cites in Georgia. For years Negroes were privileged to occupy any seat in the streetcars, but beginning with Atlanta in the early part of the 1890's, all Georgia cities gradually enacted ordinances providing for "Jim Crow" seating arrangements on public transportation. This action by the Atlanta City Council prompted Negroes to initiate a movement to boycott the streetcars. "The time has come," declared a group of Negro women in Atlanta, "when such actions are necessary to secure our rights. What's the use of giving any man or corporation our patronage when it is not appreciated." [18] To Negroes, the "Jim Crow" policy was absurd. "It is no more contaminating . . . for colored persons to ride in the same car with white persons than for them to cook for them and do other domestic duties." [19]

Savannah did not establish "Jim Crow" streetcars until 1906, although efforts had been made earlier without success. When such a proposal was made in 1902, President Baldwin, of the Savannah Electric Railway, told a reported for the Savannah *Morning News* that

It is really not a question of the separation of the races, but of the cleanly from the uncleanly. Now I do not mind sitting by a decent clean Negro on a street car, and I believe there are few people who do. Uncleanly persons of either race are objectionable, however, so that it may be seen that it is really not a question of segregation of races.

Whenever the effort to separate the races has been made it has resulted unsatisfactorily. . . . People recognize its inconveniences and difficulties, and they are soon ready to revert to the old system of getting a seat wherever you can.

It is difficult to make the people take the places set apart for them by law. A policeman would have a ride on every car to enforce a measure for the separation of the races. They had to do it in Jacksonville. The white people are worse, too, than the Negroes. A Negro will sit where he is told, as a rule, but a white man will kick. Let a white passenger find all seats in the section reserved for his race taken and he will move down to the Negro section, if there are vacancies there. He will probably think the law all right, but that it wasn't intended for him.[20]

These views of the official and the better element of Savannah prevented passage of the "Jim Crow" ordinance by the city council at that time. Shortly after this, a second "Jim Crow" bill was introduced in the council but was defeated, and the councilman who sponsored the measure failed to win re-election.[21] However, by 1906 the minds of white people had been inflamed against the Negro by the race-baiting tactics of Hoke Smith in the gubernatorial race of that year. Furthermore, many poor whites were moving into the city from the rural areas, bringing with them their deep-seated prejudices against the Negro.[22] Thus the time seemed propitious for a "Jim Crow" streetcar law, and such a measure was proposed a third time in the city council. At first the ordinance was withdrawn, but a resolution was passed suggesting that the city police be authorized to enforce the state segregation law. This was adopted immediately, and the streetcar company complied.[23]

Negroes were incensed and immediately laid plans to boycott the streetcars. Hackmen and street wagons were pressed into service to carry Negroes at a reduced rate. The pastor of the Second Baptist Church, the Reverend J. J. Durham, advised his members to stay off the cars. A group of enterprising Negroes organized the United Transport Company which planned to invest in vehicles to meet the emergency. Negroes were advised to walk because walking was healthy. If they lived a long distance from their destination, they were advised to start earlier, "thereby increasing your health and your wealth." [24] Those who defied the request were castigated as traitors to the race—especially the preachers. "For a few paltry dollars they will sell their manhood rights and endeavor to ruin those who are weak enough to follow them." [25] Despite this defection among the Negroes, the boycott was not a complete failure, for President Baldwin of the Savannah Electric Railway told the city council that the "Jim Crow" law had cost his company fifty thousand dollars in revenue.[26]

Lynching, which added to the social degradation of the Negro, was another weapon used by the Southern whites to keep the Negro in his place. Between 1888 and 1903 there were 241 Negroes lynched in Georgia, which made the state second only to Mississippi with 294 for the same period.[27] Despite the pleas of Negroes to the federal government, urging that legislation be enacted for their protection against this barbarous practice, nothing was done. The Republican party was as lukewarm in this respect as the Democrats.[28] Although there was an anti-lynching law passed during the administration of President Benjamin Harrison, it was inspired by the protests of the Italian government against the lynching of eleven Italians in New Orleans and was designed to protect foreign nationals rather than the Negro. In his last message to Congress, on December 6, 1892, Harrison made the first presidential recommendation to Congress to adopt measures for curbing this evil practice. Since only three months remained in his term, no action was taken. It remained for the only Negro congressman at the time, George White, of North Carolina, to introduce on January 20, 1900, "the first bill to make lynching of American citizens a federal crime," but it died in the Judiciary Committee.[29]

Lynchings were so prevalent in Georgia that Negroes became convinced that few of the victims were actually guilty. In fact, it was proposed that Negroes should set aside Memorial Day, May 30, for the purpose of paying respect to the innocent victims of mob violence, and ministers were urged to enlist the support of their congregations for such a movement.[30] Although rape was the most publicized reason given for lynchings, actually only about one-fourth of them were attributed to that crime. But because Negroes were occasionally guilty of rape, the prejudices of the whites toward them were intensified. On the other hand, while countless Negro women were forced to submit to the lust of white men, Southern "justice" made no provision for this. As the Savannah *Tribune* observed, "The very men who are abridging our rights are the ones who are ruining our daughters." [31]

In the gubernatorial race of 1892, Governor Northen, with the majority of Negro voters supporting him, was re-elected over his Populist opponent, W. L. Peek, and this despite the fact that the bosses of the state Republican organization endorsed the Populist candidate.[32] Most Negroes, like Bishop McNeal Turner of the African Methodist Episcopal Church, felt that Northen deserved the Negro vote because of the courage of his convictions. Furthermore, many Negroes were suspicious of the Populist party, feeling that its members represented the uneducated classes in the state and were responsible for the proscriptive legislation passed by the Alliance legislature of 1890–1891.[33] The governor became very popular among Negroes by recommending in his inaugural address that a more stringent law to prevent lynching should be passed. By his proposal a sheriff who was negligent in protecting a prisoner in his custody would be subject to a fine and imprisonment and suspension or dismissal from office.[34]

This position induced the Negro Press Association of Georgia at its meeting in Atlanta on June 20, 1893, to adopt a resolution endorsing the governor's stand as well as the support given him by the better element of whites. The meeting also expressed its appreciation to the Atlanta *Constitution,* Augusta *Chronicle,* and other papers for the interest they manifested in the general welfare of the Negro.[35] When the legislature passed a law incorporating many of the recommendations of Governor Northen, Bishop Turner issued a call for Negro mass meetings to be held Emancipation Day, January 1, 1894, to give thanks for the new law against lynching. From now on, said Bishop Turner, Georgia would serve as a model for the other states; no state in the Union was blessed with such an honorable body of men to represent them in government. "Prosperity shall enthrone her future." [36]

These were noble words from the acknowledged spiritual leader of the Negroes in Georgia. The lawless element of the white population, however, did not heed them, for lynchings continued unabated. In his message to the legislature on October 23, 1895, Governor W. Y. Atkinson deplored the lynchings and asked the assembly to enact a law which would empower him to remove from office a law officer who permitted a mob to take a man from his custody. In addition, he proposed that the administrator of the victim should have the right to recover from the county the full value of his life. His message was courageous:

What excuse can be given for this conduct when our race has control of the Legislature and the courts, furnishing both the judges and the jurors? No white man should insist upon the infliction of punishment in a case where he is unwilling to entrust the trial to the most intelligent and upright of his race.[37]

The mounting number of lynchings brought forth impassioned protest from Negro leaders. Bishop Turner was so provoked by the callousness of the Republican party toward lynchings in the South that he announced his intention to support William Jennings Bryan for president in 1900 as opposed to Willam McKinley. He claimed that he was neither a Democrat nor a Republican but a Prohibitionist who would vote for Bryan

... five times before I would vote for William McKinley ... because we have tried McKinley for four years and he is of no benefit to the black man, except in giving some of them just a few offices, but the great bulk of my race receive no more recognition at his hands than a man who has been dead twenty years.
... I am willing as a negro to try some other white man. ... Grover Cleveland turned out to be one of the ablest and best presidents that ever graced the nation. ... Ohio has given us three presidents, and if any of them was ever any account, so far as the negro is concerned, I have yet to learn about it.

Turner declared that the vital questions concerned discrimination, proscription, disfranchisement, and lynchings, the last having increased almost fourfold since McKinley had been president. Bryan, he thought, would take the necessary measures to curb them.[38]

However, with the disfranchisement movement burgeoning at the turn of the century, many white supremacists attributed lynchings to politics. Mrs. Rebecca Felton, the widow of the leader of the Independent movement in Georgia during the 1880's, declared that "when you take the Negro into your embrace on election day to control his vote ... so long will lynching prevail." She proudly proclaimed that the white women of the South had to be protected from Negroes, even if it was necessary to lynch one thousand weekly.[39] In explaining a lynching that occurred in Newnan, Governor Candler said that the trouble could be laid to one factor, politics.[40] Ex-governor Northen, who was elected in 1890 and 1892 with the aid of Negro votes, told the Congregational Club at Tremont Temple in Boston on May 23, 1899, that the politics learned by Negroes during Reconstruction were responsible for all the ills that beset the South. Furthermore, he accused the Negro of being ungrateful in that he voted against his best friends in most elections. As long as these conditions prevailed, concluded Northen, lynchings and outrages would continue in Georgia.[41]

Probably the worst lynching outrage occurred when two Negroes convicted of murdering four members of the Hodges family were burned at the stake in Statesboro, Georgia, on August 16, 1904, a crime so heinous that even the Charleston (S.C.) *News and Courier* exclaimed that "The eyes of the country and the civilized world are fixed on Georgia. What will she do?" [42] Referring to this incident in a speech at Spartanburg, South Carolina, Senator John Sharp Williams of Mississippi declared that the Statesboro lynching cost the Democrats the support of a quarter of a million votes throughout the country in the national election of 1904. "The very affair itself," said Williams, "is a confession on the white man's part of his incapacity for self-government under his own laws. . . . I feel it my duty to say to a southern audience that things like the Statesboro affair must stop." [43] This statement, coming from one "who was a little more polished than other demagogues," [44] was a serious indictment against those who advocated Negro disfranchisement but favored preserving the white vote, even though the whites were not educated, because of their "inherited" qualities.

To say that all white citizens in Georgia approved of the open defiance of law and order would be misleading. There was a small minority that voiced its protest, but to an ever diminishing audience. One of these individuals was Superior Court Judge Richard B. Russell of Winder, father of United States Senator Richard B. Russell, Jr. As a judge he proved himself one who desired to see justice prevail regardless of the parties involved. This attitude was demonstrated in 1904 when he ordered the grand jury of Franklin County to bring the lynchers of one John Ware, a Negro, to trial. He denounced lynching as a relic of barbarism, and declared that when mob rule replaced authority "you have created something that is subversive of every principle of good government." [45]

Further degradation of the Negro in Georgia was caused by the peonage-like convict-lease system established by the state to secure cheap labor. This practice was in keeping with the economy program adopted by the Bourbon Democrats, since it relieved the state of supporting the penitentiary and, in theory, was to provide revenue. To provide an abundant supply of convict labor, the criminal code was revised to make petty offenders subject to very little sympathy from the courts. The legislature was generous in granting to vested interests, planters, and politicians, long-term leases extending from ten to thirty years, from which concessions they reaped immense profits.[46]

When the "Prison Reform Bill" was presented to the Georgia House in 1876, Representative James Blue, Negro member from Glynn County, made an impassioned plea for justice to the Negroes. He opened his speech by declaring that he was vitally interested in this question since his people composed three-fourths of the convicts, and that therefore he opposed the practice of farming them out in squads. Citing numerous cases of inhuman treatment, he begged the legislature to make the necessary reforms so that when the prisoners had served their sentences, they "would not go back into the world cripples and invalids in health or outlaws in morals," but come out as reformed men ready to take their places in society once more. The speech was so well received that it had much effect in securing the passage of the reform bill in the house by an overwhelming vote. Later the governor, on April 14, 1876, proclaimed "an act to regulate the leasing of convicts by the Governor, authorizing him to make contracts in relation thereto and for other purposes." [47]

Despite the passage of the bill, abuses continued to be practiced in the convict camps, and a serious debate ensued in the legislature on this issue in 1881. Representative T. W. Milner, a white man, feeling that present safeguards were inadequate, introduced a bill "to provide for the better inspection and control of the convicts of the state." He cited the case of a young white convict in Dougherty County "with a Negro guard on one side, and a Negro guard on the other side, and a Negro guard behind . . . whipping him," and asked that the system be abolished,[48] although his motives seemed to have been based on different grounds than those which were to be expressed by the Negro legislators.

Two of the five Negro members of the house spoke against the convict-lease system. One was Representative Ishmael Lonnon of Dougherty County, who said:

I am not opposed to leases but to the system. It ought to be abolished, not for awhile, but it ought to be such forever in the indistinguishable ruin of death. Convicts are so terrified that they are afraid to tell how badly they are treated.[49]

The other Negro member to speak against the system was Representative John McIntosh of Liberty County, an 1877 graduate of Atlanta University. He stated that, as a representative of one-half the population of Georgia, he was seeking justice for his people, and referring directly to the convict-lease system, asserted: "I am not afraid of men but when I have seen convicts in charge of guards, these guards looked so ferocious that I felt a horror of them." While he favored the abolishment of the system, he doubted that it would come about and so wished some action would be taken to alleviate the situation created by it. Making a humble plea to the white legislators for justice, he declared:

Men talk seriously about regulating railroads, and yet smile when we ask them to talk about the system of punishing criminals. . . . The colored people of the South will be as true to you in freedom as they were in slavery. . . . They were true to you then at home and often on the field of battle, and they will be true to you yet if you will protect them. . . . The colored people come to you and in the name of pity ask you to do something to improve the system.[50]

But powerful groups in the state, headed by corporations, influential planters, and politicians, opposed any change. The Atlanta *Constitution,* which was the spokesman for the Bourbon oligarchy, declared that the system was satisfactory, that the issue was raised by scheming politicians to mislead the Negroes.[51] The real fact was, however, that Negroes found themselves the chief victims of this infamous system. The very circumstance that the better element of white people shirked jury duty made the lot of the Negro more precarious, and lacking the power of the ballot, he was subject to the whims of judges and other court officials elected by white voters.[52]

Some state superior court judges used this system to enhance their political fortunes. In order to curry favor with the Democratic bosses of the state, who by and large were the corporations, the planters, and prominent politicians, these judges in meting out punishment to Negroes would sentence them to long terms on the chain gang, which benefited the lessees. The Democratic bosses in turn would show their appreciation by supporting the judges for Congress.[53] Judge John W. Maddox of Rome was alleged to have defeated Congressman Everett from the seventh congressional district in 1892 largely by this method. A Negro, Sam Jackson of Rome, was fined one thousand dollars or a term on the chain gang for gambling, while John M. Vandiver, a white man who later became postmaster of Rome, was fined ten dollars for the same offense.[54] Judge Charles L. Bartlett of Macon was notorious for sending Negroes to the chain gang for trivial offenses. He sentenced one Negro to fifteen years on the chain gang for stealing some milk, and a twelve-year-old Negro boy to twelve years of hard labor on the chain gang for taking a horse to ride a few miles and back.[55]

Such miscarriages of justice resulted in the fact that Negroes constituted about nine-tenths of the prisoners in the convict camps. Since the income from crime rather than the rehabilitation of the criminal was the primary objective, the future of the Negro prisoner was beyond redemption. In 1895, a prison inspector reported to Governor Atkinson that he had visited thirty-four chain gangs in twenty-three counties and found 795 convicts, of whom 19 were Negro women and only 27 white men. No provision was made for separating the sexes either at work or in sleeping quarters, which increased sexual immorality.[56] From 1879 to 1899 the number of Negro convicts in Georgia increased from 1,109 to 1,953 while for the same period the number of whites increased from 121 to 248.[57]

Although it was obvious that the Negro was the victim of various forms of proscription, some Negro leaders were the first to profess that the Negro was not altogether blameless. The Reverend L. B. Maxwell,[58] Atlanta University and Hartford Theological Seminary graduate and pastor of the First Congregational Church (Negro) of Savannah, in a sermon delivered to his congregation in July 1896, declared that

More than a quarter of a century has passed since the black man first entered the political arena and yet it is true that he holds today a place of influence very little advanced of what he did in the beginning. . . . The common reasons given have been race prejudice and bad leadership, but tonight I beg to take exception to the wholesale acceptance of these reasons. . . . The greatest obstacle has been neither race prejudice nor bad leaders, but something which . . . is far more harmful, it is that curse of narrow, selfish, concentrated individualism which hinders race concentration, race combination and race cooperation.[59]

All of the various proscriptions stimulated Negroes to think seriously of fundamental solutions to the race problem in America. The most crude and reactionary elements of the community appeared to be taking over, and the traditional Southern liberals, always few in number, seemed almost non-existent at the time. When the latter did insist on speaking out in behalf of the Negro, they found themselves subject to threats and abuse from members of their own race. A typical example was that involving the editor of the Hawkinsville (Ga.) *Dispatch,* who received a letter from one of the white citizens of the county dated July 13, 1891, and threatening him or any other white person who might defend any Negro in his rights. The citizen wrote:

Mr. Editor if the foling article appears in your Paper Five Dolers will appear in the (PO) addressed to you. But if it don't appear 25 of your subscribers will sure to stop and we will stop all the rest We can Your White Brothers.

Notice, We hereby forewarn any and all Persons from taking up for the nigroes in any shape form or fashion We the undersign will declare any white man that Takes Sides With any nigroes against a white person no matter how lodown he or She is just so they are White We are White men organized For the Perpose of protecting the White Race and we are going to carry out or Plans at the Pearl of our Lives Dark Nights and cool heads Will our work quitly Mr. Editor if this fail to appear in the next issue of Your Paper Will Consider you in favor of civil wrights and We Will deal you properly Many Sitersons.[60]

In view of this growing tension, several suggestions for the improvement of race relations were offered by Negroes. One was for the white press to cease publishing anti-Negro articles. It was pointed out that Southern papers made deliberate efforts to portray Negroes in the most unfavorable light, such as referring to them as "big burly brutes," and branding them as the "aggressors" whenever there was a misunderstanding with the whites.[61]

Some Negroes, however, believed it impossible to reason with the Southern whites, that the Negro had extended the olive branch for twenty-five years and the net result was Southern hate and barbarism. Therefore, rather than remain in an environment offering little hope for the future, the Negro should seek greener pastures if he was to realize the privileges that went along with first-class citizenship.[62]

The first of such plans of escape was the "Back-to-Africa" movement. Foremost advocate of this idea in Georgia, if not in the United States, was Bishop Henry McNeal Turner, of the African Methodist Episcopal Church. The Bishop not only was well acquainted with the Negro and his ills in all parts of the United States, but had actually lived and traveled in Africa. He was convinced that the Negro in America had no future above that of an inferior being. If he had any doubts before 1883, said the Bishop, the United States Supreme Court, when it killed the Civil Rights Act of 1875, completely removed these doubts. He emphasized that this decision was written by a Republican justice and every member of the Court was a Northerner except one, Associate Justice John Marshall Harlan, of Kentucky, who ironically enough, cast the only dissenting vote.[63] Turner was so disappointed in the Republican party that he deserted its banner for that of the Prohibitionists and even supported the Democratic candidates for the presidency in 1900 and 1908. He and others made vigorous attempts to secure appropriations from Congress in support of voluntary colonization of American Negroes in Africa where they could enjoy first-class citizenship. "The Negro . . . is an outlawed inhabitant of the country," said Turner, "for a people divested of their civil rights can hope for nothing but degradation and contempt." [64]

In 1892 the popularity of the "Back-to-Africa" movement reached its crest among a few of the more credulous Negroes in Georgia. This enthusiasm was partly caused by the "Jim Crow" law that recently had been passed by the state legislature, as well as by the election of Grover Cleveland for his second term as president. On the Sunday following this election a few Negro ministers predicted a dark future for their race. At Big Bethel Church, one of the largest in Atlanta, a minister advised his listeners "to leave Georgia and go to their own country, Africa, where they would have equal rights and help govern and have street cars of their own." At the annual Republican picnic in Blackshear, I. J. White, a Negro, exclaimed "We would rather be eaten by wild Negroes than to be lynched by white men in the South." Some Negroes of Polk County sent a memorial to the Georgia House of Representatives requesting permission to go to Africa or some free country.[65] As late as 1903, a group of Negro women sent a petition to the Georgia House requesting the legislature to appropriate two thousand dollars in order that they might take themselves and their families to Africa. Amid much mirth, the petition was referred to the Committee of Emigration.[66]

These efforts bore no fruit, and few Negroes actually went to Africa. By and large, Negro leaders and the Negro press were opposed to the idea. For example, Representative Lectured Crawford, Negro member of the legislature, declared that the only solution was through education which would reveal to the Negro the folly of such a project.[67] Frederick Douglass, the titular leader of the Negro race at the time, in a speech in Atlanta on May 23, 1892, said "the glory of Africa is in her palm trees and not her men," and that the Negro's home was America.[68] Others thought that it was "dangerous to fly to evils that we know not of." Some suggested that Bishop Turner might demonstrate his sincerity by going to Africa himself instead of remaining in America. It was even hinted that any movement that had as its goal the sending of Negroes to Africa would mean having to take half of the white race, since it was difficult to distinguish almost a third of the Negroes from Caucasians. The Negro Press Association of Georgia advised Negroes to "remain where they are: go to work industriously with renewed vigor," and "cultivate a friendly feeling with their white neighbors." [69]

The crowning blow to the movement, however, was the testimony of Negroes who actually had been to Africa and reported their experiences on their return home. Such was the case of Green B. Parks, who left Atlanta on May 24, 1891, for Monrovia and returned to Atlanta in September of the same year. He told Negroes that Monrovia was a very undesirable place in which to live and denounced the African movement and those who sponsored it. "The only hunting in Liberia," he said, "is to hunt a way to leave." [70]

Testimony of a more realistic nature was that given by C. H. J. Taylor, a Negro lawyer of Atlanta and prominent Democratic politician who served as United States minister to Liberia during Cleveland's first administration and as recorder of deeds in Washington, D. C., in his second term.[71] While expressing deep admiration for Bishop Turner as a leader of the Negro race, Taylor questioned his glowing accounts of the great possibilities that awaited the Negro in Liberia. Taylor understood, however, that Turner would naturally be inclined to urge African emigration, since the Bishop was Liberian consul in this country, and it was his duty to promote the development of Liberia. He declared that the conditions in Liberia were so degrading that a law should be passed making it a felony for anyone to encourage the Negro to leave the United States for that country. To convey the idea that by going to Liberia Negroes could become officeholders, statesmen, and financiers was absurd. A Negro policeman in Atlanta, he said, would be envied by a cabinet officer in Liberia. Describing the government while he was a resident of Liberia, he stated:

They have a president . . . cabinet officers in name only . . . a secretary of the treasury, but not a dollar in the treasury . . . a secretary of war with no guns . . . a postmaster general with no postal system. . . . In 1886 the total vote cast for president in the whole republic by all parties was 2,325; of this number of voters, and only Liberians are allowed to vote, 1,333 were officeholders. There were 817 men in the republic's military regiment, 787 of whom were military officers and 30 privates.[72]

While the "Back-to-Africa" movement failed to gain many converts, some Negroes suggested that the salvation of the race lay in a mass exodus to the North. Had not the North been responsible for their emancipation? Did not many Northern orators frequently emphasize human and civil equality? Did not Northern teachers come South after the Civil War to preach social equality to Negroes and urge that they should be protected in their civil and political rights? Thus it was only natural that many Negroes became obsessed with the idea that only by going North could they realize those privileges that were associated with first-class citizenship.

Much to their disappointment, many Negroes who left the South for the North in the 1880's and 1890's to escape Southern proscription found conditions anything but ideal. Although they were not "Jim Crowed" to the extent that they were in the South, they found it extremely difficult to obtain work, since many of the trade unions excluded them from membership. What advantage was there in being able to ride on non-segregated trains, attend non-segregated schools, and enjoy non-segregated amusements if they did not have the money to avail themselves of these opportunities?[73]

Even in New England few jobs were open to Negroes and great pains were taken to prevent Negroes from competing with whites. E. J. Bruce, a Negro of Savannah who went to Providence, Rhode Island, in the 1870's and secured a job with the largest contracting firm in the state, declared that while Negro civil rights were observed more in the North, the economic opportunities were far more limited than in the South. He cited numerous cases in which Negro mechanics were denied work because the whites threatened to strike if they were hired.[74] The Washington (D.C.) Bee, a Negro paper, stated that Negroes in the North, even the educated ones, could work only as waiters, caterers, porters, or barbers; and as far as political activity was concerned, they might have their ego inflated by being appointed as doorkeepers at the Republican national conventions.[75] W. R. Davis, a Negro who left the South to live in New York, declared that while Negroes in 1885 had most of the jobs as waiters in hotels and restaurants, by 1895 only a few remained. Even the Negro bootblack was replaced by the Italian. So many opportunities for work had been denied the Negro man that the responsibility for supporting the family fell upon the women, who were forced to take in washing to keep the family from becoming a burden on the community. The situation was becoming so desperate, Davis said, that the Negro was "almost denied the right to breathe." [76]

As a substitute for the "Back-to-Africa" and "Exodus-to-the-North" projects as means of solving the race problem, another distinguished Georgia Negro, Bishop Lucius H. Holsey of the Colored Methodist Episcopal Church, proposed that the federal government set aside out of the public domain a separate state where Negroes might enjoy first-class citizenship. He declared that "two distinct peoples can never live together in the South in peace, when one is Anglo-Saxon and the other Negro, unless the Negro, as a race or *en masse,* lives in the submerged realm of serfdom and slavery." [77] To justify his stand, he pointed out the refusal of the South to provide adequate educational facilities for the Negro, and the antagonism expressed toward the educated Negro; the denial of political privileges; the "Jim Crow" policy; the lack of protection for Negroes in rural areas; and the prevalence of mob violence.

Under these conditions, said Bishop Holsey, it was not practical to continue to allow the South to settle this problem, since it was national in scope, involving national honor and national law. Therefore, in order that the Negro might enjoy all the privileges that were guaranteed by the United States Constitution, he requested the federal government to establish a Negro state in part of the Indian Territory, New Mexico, or in some other part of the public domain in the West. In this territory white persons would be ineligible for citizenship, except through marriage, and only those white persons who had some official connection with the government would be permitted to reside therein. By having responsibilities of government thrust upon his shoulders, the Negro would become inspired and more willing to help the Anglo-Saxon race to develop a greater civilization in this country.[78]

While the leaders of these movements to provide an escape for the Negroes had good intentions, they failed to convince the Negro masses that their conditions would be improved by leaving the South. A number of Negroes followed "Pop" Singleton to Kansas in 1879 and to several Northern communities, but there was no significant migration northward until World War I. It appears that the Negro masses were resigned to staying in the South, hoping eventually that the tide would turn in their favor. Such a development, they believed, was dependent upon two factors: (1) the ability of the Negro to improve his social, economic, and educational status in order to win the respect of his white neighbors, and (2) the willingness of the whites to cease vilifying the Negro in the white press and at the same time to extend the Negro his constitutional rights.

Not only were Negroes critical of the white press but also of the Northern Negro press for meddling with affairs pertaining to the Negroes in the South. Many of these Northern Negro journals criticized the Southern Negro press for not taking a more militant stand against Southerners who were responsible for repressive measures aimed at the Negroes. This was especially true of the New York *Age,* whose editor, T. Thomas Fortune, became a nationally known figure through his condemnation of the South in his paper. The editor of the Savannah *Tribune* advised Fortune that if he desired to "be so base and outspoken" toward the South, then he should come down to the "seat of battle" and give vent to his feelings.[79]

White people were admonished that the South could not possibly advance unless the Negroes were given the same opportunities as the whites, that it was necessary to encourage Negroes to participate in politics in order that they might have an interest in the community and the community an interest in them. Furthermore, Negroes urged that it was the duty of the parents and teachers of both races to teach their children to respect each other, since the South, unlike the North, had only two races, "both of whom are true American citizens who love themselves, their country and its flag and their neighbors." As the Negro had proven himself to be a faithful worker for over two hundred and fifty years, the whites were advised not to import foreigners as laborers in the South, for such a policy might result in a tragedy similar to the Haymarket riot in Chicago. "Let the Southern Negro and Southern white man ever remain and stick together for they understand each other as no one else understands them." [80]

This sentiment was concurred in by many white people who believed that the Southern whites were the true friends of the Negro. Negroes of Atlanta were reminded of this when an unusual cold spell struck the city in the winter of 1895 and caused considerable hardship for thousands of people. To meet this emergency, the white people formed a relief committee which raised five thousand dollars to care for the victims, and of this amount, forty-five hundred dollars went to the relief of Negroes. The Atlanta *Journal* claimed that while many Negroes owned property and were gainfully employed, they contributed only three dollars and fifty cents to the effort to alleviate the misery among their own people. "If the Negroes will think over this and many similar events," observed the *Journal,* "they will discover who their true friends are and will pay less attention to lying Negro preachers and politicians who preach doctrines of hate and revenge." [81]

Furthermore, the unfortunate experiences of Negroes who had gone North and West to escape Southern proscription convinced the Negro masses that the future of the Negro lay in the South where, even though he received lower wages, he was not denied work on account of his color.

Because of the perpetuation of the old slave idea that work was only for "niggers and poor whites," Negroes were able to engage in labor activities which were closed to them in the North. Numerous cases were cited in which Negroes worked alongside of whites without incident, where Southern Negro contractors frequently hired whites and Negroes on jobs.[82] Southern white people were urged to "take away mob violence, court injustices . . . and let us have in full the constitutional rights of this country, and the South, if anywhere, . . . is the best for us. We are more united and progressive there than in any other section of the land." [83]

The Reverend Charles T. Walker, pastor of the Tabernacle Baptist Church in Augusta, and next to Bishop Turner probably the most widely known Negro churchman in the state, declared that it was a mistake for the Negro to leave the South, since prejudice was national and not sectional. He admitted that the North did not disfranchise the Negro nor "Jim Crow" him to the same extent as did the South; but, on the other hand, he noted that the North did not guarantee the same economic security. He advised the Negro to remain in the South, buy land, engage in business, and educate his children, for it was only a matter of time until the best people of the South would come to his aid and defend him in all of his rights.[84]

The Negro editor of the LaGrange (Georgia) *Enterprise,* W. S. Cannon, believed that it was far better to develop friendly relations with the white people of the South, and promised the support of his paper to any movement that would create a spirit of good will between the races, which in the long run would advance the interests of both groups.[85] The point was constantly stressed by many Negroes that the South was the natural home of the Negro and it was his duty to make himself indispensable to the community. "If we cannot vote for president, we can vote five dollar bills in a bank to our credit all day and the cashier will count them. . . . If we cannot govern, we can produce that which the ruling class must have." By doing this, Negro leaders said, the road to political equality, which was the dream of the Negro, would be paved.[86] Furthermore, Negroes were reminded that in certain places in the North Negroes were forced to leave the community in which they lived just because they wanted to earn an honest living. Such was the case in Dent, Ohio. In cities like Boston and Chicago there were signs reading, "No Negro help wanted." In Indiana, upon learning that Negroes were planning to come to the state to work, white men met them at the state line with guns and forced them back. As the Atlanta *Independent* aptly put it: "In the south we make them get a move on them because they won't work, but in the north, they make you move because you want to work." [87]

The economic plight of the Negro in New York by 1908 had become so acute that the Committee for Improving the Industrial Conditions of the Negro in New York, composed of both races and headed by William Jay Schiefflin, addressed a communication to the Negro editors and ministers of the South asking their aid in stemming any further migration of their people to the North. This communication pointed out that due to discrimination against Negroes in the labor field, inferior housing facilities, unfavorable climate, and the increasing crime rate among Negroes as a result of these factors, living conditions in the North were almost intolerable. In their opinion, the solution to the race problem in the South had to be worked out through the cooperation of the better elements of both races, which in the final analysis would prove beneficial to the material and moral growth of the South.[88]

Thus the Negro masses were resigned to staying in the South, hoping eventually that sentiment and conditions would move in their favor. Probably the general attitude of the Negro in Georgia at this time was best expressed by the Reverend C. L. Bonner, pastor of the St. Paul Colored Methodist Episcopal Church of Savannah. At the annual Emancipation Day exercises held in that city on January 1, 1902, the Reverend Mr. Bonner said:

There are men who are more profound in thought, loftier in ideas ... than I am ... who think and express their thoughts differently to me. ... There is my own Bishop Holsey's doctrine of segregation, Bishop Turner's emigration, ex-Senator Butler's expatriation, John Temple Graves' colonization, T. Thomas Fortune's ... amalgamation, Ben Tillman's extermination. My doctrine is, if you let me coin a word, *"stayhereation"* and when I say that, I mean stay here as a separate and distinct race, and the God that has brought us thus far can carry us on.[89]

And "stayhereation" it was, as the vast majority of Negroes, either by preference or by circumstances over which they had no control, remained in the South despite segregation, political disfranchisement, mob violence, and other forms of race proscription. As the twentieth century wore on, the Negro would find an increasingly hostile environment. Despite his efforts to improve his economic status, his struggle to educate himself, and his attempts to promote his social betterment, his hopes of attaining first-class citizenship were to be engulfed by the wave of white supremacy which grew in volume and intensity after the turn of the century.

## NOTES

[1] C. Vann Woodward, *Origins of the New South* (Baton Rouge, 1951), pp. 211–212.

[2] Gunnar Myrdal, *An American Dilemma: The Negro Problem and Modern Democracy* (2 vols.; New York, 1944), I, 582.

[3] W. J. Cash, *The Mind of the South* (New York, 1957), pp. 178–183.

[4] *Journal of the House of Representatives of the State of Georgia, at the Annual Session of the General Assembly Convened at Atlanta, January 10, 1870* (Atlanta, 1870), Part I, p. 309; *Journal of the Senate of the State of Georgia, at the Annual Session of the General Assembly, Atlanta, January 10, 1870* (Atlanta, 1870), Part II, p. 261, Part III, p. 508.

[5] *Acts and Resolutions of the General Assembly of the State of Georgia, 1870* (Atlanta, 1871), p. 390.

[6] Rebecca Latimer Felton, *My Memoirs of Georgia Politics* (Atlanta, 1911), p. 646.

[7] The platform proposed (1) increasing the powers of the railway commission to prevent discrimination, (2) abolishing the convict-lease system, (3) tax revision, (4) public school improvements, and (5) primary and election reforms. Alex M. Arnett, *The Populist Movement in Georgia* (New York, 1922), pp. 105–106.

[8] *Journal of the House of Representatives of the State of Georgia at the Adjourned Session of the General Assembly, at Atlanta, Wednesday, July 8, 1891* (Atlanta, 1891), p. 176; *Constitution* (Atlanta), July 21, 1891.

[9] *Ibid.*, July 23, 1891.

[10] *Ibid.*, July 24, 1891.

[11] *Acts and Resolutions of the General Assembly of the State of Georgia, 1890–1891* (Atlanta, 1891), I, 157–158. In order to preserve white supremacy at its lowest level, the Alliance legislature passed an act forbidding white and colored prisoners being chained together while at work. *Ibid.*, pp. 211–212.

[12] Quoted in *Tribune* (Savannah), November 28, 1891.

[13] *Ibid.*, October 17, 1891.

[14] *Ibid.*, November 15, December 31, 1892.

[15] *Independent* (Atlanta), September 5, 1908.

[16] "A Plea Against Excursions," *Voice of the Negro* (Atlanta), II (August, 1905), 530–531.

[17] *Independent* (Atlanta), January 19, 1907.

[18] *Tribune* (Savannah), November 5, 1892, August 29, 1906. Albert Thornton, president of the Union Street Railway Company of Atlanta, admitted that "the Negro is the best patron of the streetcar. If he has a nickel and is going anywhere he will ride; while the white man will walk. . . ." *Constitution* (Atlanta), March 1, 1891.

[19] *Tribune* (Savannah), May 22, 1893.

[20] *Morning News* (Savannah), quoted in *Tribune* (Savannah), July 12, 1902.

[21] *Tribune* (Savannah), September 1, 1906.

[22] *Ibid.*

[23] *Ibid.*, September 15, 1906.

[24] *Ibid.*, September 22, 29, October 6, 1906, and March 9, 1907.

[25] *Ibid.*, June 8, 1907.

[26] *Ibid.*, March 9, 1907.

[27] Ellis P. Oberholtzer, *A History of the United States Since the Civil War* (5 vols.; New York, 1917–1937), V, 716.

[28] Rayford W. Logan, *The Negro in American Life and Thought: The Nadir, 1877–1901* (New York, 1954), p. 76.

[29] *Ibid.*, pp. 77, 91.

[30] W. E. B. Du Bois, *Some Notes on Negro Crime, Particularly in Georgia* ("Atlanta University Publications," No. 9 [1904]), p. 60; *Tribune* (Savannah), May 7, 1892.

[31] *Ibid.*, May 21, 1892.

[32] *Journal* (Atlanta), September 27, 1892. Northen, who ran on the Alliance platform in 1890, was the Democratic candidate for re-election in 1892.

[33] *Ibid.*, September 30, 1892; *Bulletin of Atlanta University*, November, 1892, 4.

[34] *Journal* (Atlanta), October 27, 1892.

[35] *Tribune* (Savannah), July 1, 1893.

[36] *Journal* (Atlanta), December 23, 1893.

[37] *Message of the Governor of Georgia to the General Assembly, October 25, 1895* (Atlanta, 1895), pp. 19–20.

[38] *Journal* (Atlanta), September 6, 1900. For other protests, see *Tribune* (Savannah), January 7, May 25, 1899.

[39] *Journal* (Atlanta), November 15, 1898.

[40] *Ibid.*, April 24, 1899. As a rejoinder, the *Tribune* (Savannah), August 5, 1899, stated: "Our governor may be true after all . . . when he says that the placing of the ballot in the hands of the Negro is the cause of so much lynching. The lynching record in this state . . . shows they are trying to get rid of the Negro voters."

[41] *Journal* (Atlanta), May 23, 1899.

[42] *Ibid.*, August 17, 19, 1904.

[43] *Ibid.*, December 3, 1904.

[44] Logan, *op. cit.*, p. 90.

[45] *Journal* (Atlanta), September 28, 1904.

[46] Woodward, *op. cit.*, pp. 212–213. One of the big lessees was Joseph E. Brown who owned the Dade coal mines. He, along with the other lessees like General John B. Gordon, paid the state twenty dollars annually for each convict, or less than seven cents a day. Arnett, *op. cit.*, pp. 27–28.

[47] Quoted in *Telegraph and Messenger* (Macon), March 4, 1876; *ibid.*, April 22, 1876.

[48] *Constitution* (Atlanta), August 10, 1881.

[49] *Ibid.* Lonnon was dark-complexioned and had a soft tenor voice. He was about five feet three inches tall and weighed about one hundred and sixty pounds. He operated a blacksmith shop in Albany. Although he lacked formal education, he could read and write. Interview with George A. Towns, professor emeritus of Atlanta University, June 2, 1951.

[50] *Constitution* (Atlanta), August 10, 1881. Other Negro leaders registered bitter complaints against this iniquitous system, but to no avail. At Negro conventions resolutions were adopted condemning the practice as well as demanding that Negroes be included on jury lists. *Ibid.*, April 1, September 19, 1888; Du Bois, *Some Notes on Negro Crime*, p. 66.

[51] *Constitution* (Atlanta), September 7, 1881.

[52] Du Bois, *op. cit.*, p. 65.

[53] Felton, *op. cit.*, pp. 655, 658–659.

[54] Rebecca Latimer Felton, *Country Life in Georgia in the Days of My Youth* (Atlanta, 1919), p. 196.

[55] Felton, *Memoirs of Georgia Politics*, pp. 658–659.

56 *Journal* (Atlanta), November 12, 1895. In the Maddox camp in northeast Georgia about twelve children were born of Negro mothers and white fathers (*Tribune* [Savannah], April 28, 1894).

57 *Second Annual Report of the Prison Commission of Georgia from October 1, 1898 to October 1, 1899* (Atlanta, 1899), pp. 5–6. In this number were included three white women and sixty-eight Negro women convicts.

58 The Reverend Mr. Maxwell finished Atlanta University in the class of 1886, and at the commencement exercises he spoke on "A Man Is a Man for That." After he had finished, Senator Colquitt of Georgia walked over and shook his hand and congratulated him on his excellent speech. For a number of years he was the international Sunday School lecturer for Negroes of the Congregational Church. He died in 1902. *Tribune* (Savannah), March 22, 1902.

59 *Ibid.*, August 1, 1896.

60 Quoted *ibid.*, September 12, 1891.

61 *Ibid.*, December 10, 1898.

62 *Ibid.*, February 11, 1893.

63 *Journal* (Atlanta), August 12, 1893. Turner further stated that this decision was even more revolting than the Dred Scott decision since Chief Justice Taney "only voiced the condition of things as they existed in the days of slavery, while Justice Bradley issued a decree on behalf of the supreme court that nullified the plain acts of congress and the expressed provisions of the constitution of the United States."

64 *Constitution* (Atlanta), July 13, 1891; *Journal* (Atlanta), August 12, 1893.

65 *Ibid.*, November 22, 1892, November 30, 1894; *Tribune* (Savannah), May 26, 1894.

66 *Journal* (Atlanta), June 25, 1903.

67 *Constitution* (Atlanta), November 22, 1890.

68 *Ibid.*, May 24, 1892.

69 *Tribune* (Savannah), July 18, 1891, September 3, 30, November 12, 1892.

70 *Constitution* (Atlanta), September 15, 1891.

71 *Tribune* (Savannah), June 3, 1899. At the time of his death in 1899, Taylor was editor of the Atlanta *Appeal* and dean of Morris Brown College. He was born in Alabama in 1856 but spent most of his boyhood in Savannah. He attended the University of Michigan, where he earned the bachelor's and master's degrees. In 1882 he was an assistant prosecuting attorney in Kanas City, Missouri, receiving his appointment from a Democratic mayor and council. After practicing six years there, he was sent to Liberia by President Cleveland. *Constitution* (Atlanta), December 21, 1887.

72 *Journal* (Atlanta), January 29, 1898.

73 Thomas J. Bell, "Does the Colored Man Have a Chance in the North," *Bulletin of Atlanta University*, January, 1894, 2. Bell was a member of the Atlanta University class of 1891 and served as YMCA secretary in New York, Denver, and Brockton, Massachusetts. "Who's Who Among Atlanta University Graduates and Former Students," *Phylon*, III (Second Quarter, 1942), 166.

74 *Tribune*, (Savannah), May 2, 1903.

75 Quoted *ibid.*, January 24, 1903.

76 "Give the Negro Work," *Press* (New York), quoted in *Journal* (Atlanta), April 10, 1895. For a description of the hardships experienced by Negroes who went to Kansas in 1879, see Logan, *op cit.*, pp. 133–134.

77 Lucius H. Holsey, "Race Segregation," in *The Possibilities of the Negro in Symposium*, ed. Willis B. Parks (Atlanta, 1904), pp. 102, 109.

78 *Ibid.,* pp. 104–119.

79 *Tribune* (Savannah), December 2, 1893.

80 *Ibid.,* June 5, 1897, February 4, 1893.

81 *Journal* (Atlanta), March 2, 1895.

82 Bell, *op. cit.,* 3.

83 *Tribune* (Savannah), May 2, 1903. Even Bishop Turner admitted that while Northern whites might be more friendly politically toward the Negro, the South afforded him better economic opportunities. He stated that employment was opened to Negroes in almost every field except that of operating railroad locomotives. *Constitution* (Atlanta), July 14, 1890.

84 *Presbyterian Herald* (New York City), quoted in *Tribune* (Savannah), December 29, 1900.

85 Quoted in *Journal* (Atlanta), January 9, 1901.

86 *Independent* (Atlanta), March 26, 1904, April 8, 1905.

87 *Ibid.,* April 8, 1905.

88 *Tribune* (Savannah), May 9, 1908.

89 *Ibid.,* January 18, 1902 (italics mine).

*"The Liberian Exodus" is a chapter from George Brown Tindall's* South Carolina Negroes, 1877–1900, *which treats the upsurge of interest in emigration to Liberia after the collapse of Reconstruction. With considerable support from political leaders in the North, White South Carolinians encouraged colonization among that state's Black population. The decline of Liberia and the shady nature of its promotion combined with the desperation of the Blacks to create a debacle and to discredit emigration for the next fifty years.*

# The Liberian Exodus

## George Brown Tindall

The Negro penchant for migration which became notorious after the Civil War was the outgrowth of unsettled conditions and the novelty of freedom, but was kept alive by the poverty that Negroes experienced as the mudsills of a depressed agriculture. Without worldly goods, Negroes could easily pull up stakes and move off in search of better conditions and better employers. The mobility of the Negro sharecropper has been a constant factor in the South since the Civil War. In addition to the mobility brought about by the search for improved economic conditions, railway excursions became an important part of Negro social life. The Negroes, said a white observer, "are literally crazy about travelling. The railroad officials are continually importuned by them to run extra trains, excursion trains, and so on, on all sorts of occasions: holidays, picnics, Sunday-school celebrations, church dedications, funerals of their prominent men, circuses, public executions. . . . They attract whole counties of negroes, and it is delightful to witness their childish wonder and enjoyment and behavior on the cars." [1]

So common had these practices become that by the end of Reconstruction it was axiomatic among whites that delight in travel was a racial characteristic of the Negroes. "The Negro rarely possesses any home attachments," said one. "He is continually on the wing . . . ; and as he can with facility ingratiate himself among strangers of his own color, he would not be disconcerted were he as quickly transported from one State to another as Aladdin's wife or as Noureddin in the Thousand and One Nights." [2]

From George Brown Tindall, *South Carolina Negroes, 1877–1900* (Columbia: University of South Carolina Press, 1952), pp. 153–168. © 1952 University of South Carolina Press.

The violent political campaign of 1876 and its aftermath brought widespread uncertainty among the Negroes of the state and interest in the possibility of emigration. The great interest in emigration was not confined to South Carolina but was a Southwide phenomenon that had as its causes not only the political weakness of the Negroes and the general restriction of civil rights but also their economic subordination and the general difficulty of getting ahead in agriculture, their chief source of livelihood. It culminated in 1879 in the wholesale removal of great numbers of Negroes from the lower Mississippi Valley to the West, particularly Kansas.[3] In South Carolina, on the other hand, interest was at first centered almost altogether on Liberia, both because of its greater accessibility from the east coast and because of the work already undertaken by the American Colonization Society in transporting small numbers of Negroes to Africa.[4]

Congressman Richard H. Cain, Negro minister and newspaper publisher of Charleston, noted in January, 1877, a "deep and growing interest taken by the Colored people . . . in the subject of Emigration," and wrote to the secretary of the Colonization Society for information on arrangements for passage to Liberia. "The Colored people of the South," he said, "are tired of the constant struggle for life and liberty with such results as the 'Missippi [sic] Plan' and prefer going where no such obstacles are in their way of enjoying their Liberty." [5] During the first four months of 1877, while the rival Chamberlain and Hampton governments were struggling for ascendancy, Cain reported interest in the possibility of emigration to be spreading daily.[6] In his *Missionary Record* he reported "communications from various persons and from all sections of the country on the subject of emigration to Africa. Thousands of colored people in South Carolina would leave if the means of transportation were furnished them." [7] Movements to organize for removal to Liberia were reported in the counties of Abbeville, Laurens, Oconee, Pickens, Newberry, Lexington, Marlboro, Georgetown, Colleton, Barnwell, Aiken, Edgefield, Beaufort, and Charleston.[8]

Negroes were particularly eager to leave Edgefield County, center of the "Straightout" white supremacy Democrats. H. N. Bouey, Republican probate judge, retired by the election of 1876, said that if a ship could be started for Liberia from Charleston or Beaufort in January it would not be able to carry the fifth man who was ready to go. "Of course, this upheaval is caused by their political and general mistreatment in this County—But I advise them to take it all quietly and christianly, for I believe God is in the move." [9] Bouey himself was ready to return to school teaching, "and in Liberia at that," and expressed sincere hope that some way would be made available to carry "the best men and women of this county" who wished to go in January after their crops had been gathered.[10]

Bouey was to be an important figure in the organization of the effort to carry out a mass exodus. In the spring of 1877 he was selected as a juror in the United States District Court in Charleston, and there met George Curtis, another juror, native of British Guiana and resident of Beaufort, who was also full of the spirit of emigration. The two men sought out the Reverend B. F. Porter, pastor of Morris Brown A. M. E. Church, who was very enthusiastic about the idea. By chance, Professor J. C. Hazeley, a native African, was in Charleston at the same time to deliver lectures on the advantages of emigration. On the fourth of July a celebration was held at the Morris Brown Church at which a number of addresses were delivered on behalf of emigration.[11] On July 26 a mass meeting was called to celebrate the thirtieth anniversary of the Liberian Declaration of Independence. A parade culminated at the Mall where four thousand Negroes gathered to hear George Curtis read the Liberian Declaration of Independence and the Reverend B. F. Porter deliver a twenty minute address in favor of the exodus. A proposition made by Porter for the formation of a stock company with thirty thousand shares of stock at $10 a share "met with much evident favor," [12] and the Liberian Exodus Joint Stock Steamship Company with B. F. Porter as president and H. N. Bouey as secretary was soon thereafter organized.[13]

Obvious enthusiasm for the project all over the state caused immediate white reaction against the prospect of losing cheap colored labor. A rumor went about that J. C. Hazeley was being paid $200 a month by the American Colonization Society to get the Negroes to leave and that Senators Blaine, Conkling, and Morton were getting up subscriptions of $2,000,000 in the North to send Negroes to Liberia in order to ruin the whites in the South.[14] Prominent white lawyers and businessmen in Charleston were accused of trying to bribe Hazeley to lecture against the emigration scheme.[15] In Edgefield the whites charged the leaders of the emigration movement "with seeking revenge against them on account of their political ascension in this state and county," and sought to dissuade colored laborers by paying them only in drafts on merchants, which would be good only in Edgefield, and would therefore keep them from leaving.[16] In addition, John Mardenborough, a Negro attorney of Edgefield, wrote to William Coppinger, "Sir, you cannot imagine the deplorable condition of the colored people here," and reported white planters to be spreading a rumor that the emigration scheme was really an effort to entice the Negroes away to Cuba, where they would be sold in slavery.[17]

But white opposition and efforts at obstruction served only to fan the flames. R. H. Cain kept in his *Missionary Record* a standing editorial headed "Ho for Africa! One million men wanted for Africa." [18] Martin R.

Delany, recently appointed trial justice in Charleston, was quickly brought into the movement. He had travelled extensively in Africa before the Civil War and had been in the fifties active on behalf of a scheme to colonize the Niger Valley with Negroes from the United States.[19] B. F. Porter appeared in Columbia in August to speak on behalf of the colonization scheme, and in the northern tier of counties June Mobley, a colored citizen of Union County, travelled about making speeches in favor of Liberian emigration to all who would listen. He argued that it would be impossible for whites and blacks to live together in South Carolina as citizens. The black man would always "take his place in the kitchen," to use the speaker's words. He saw no way in which Negroes could prosper, for in order to prosper they must become landowners. That would be extremely difficult, he argued, because of the repeal of the lien law. Mobley, however, warned against precipitate action, and asked for contributions so that he could make a trip to Africa and bring back a report on conditions.[20]

Rumors of the fertility of the Liberian soil and the salubrity of the Liberian climate reached fantastic proportions. One laborer told a reporter he understood potatoes grew to such proportions in Liberia that one would more than supply a large family for a whole day, that it was necessary when one wanted sugar or syrup only to bore a gimlet hole in a tree, that certain trees produced bacon, and that fires were almost unknown, the heat of the sun being enough for cooking purposes.[21] Jasper Smith of Union, having heard that Congress had appropriated $100,000 for emigration, sent a petition for aid signed by a number of his neighbors, to be presented to the Congress.[22]

The Negro churches were at first opposed to the movement for fear of losing some of their best members, but as time went by they fell in line with the general hue and cry, applying their zeal to "their appointed work" of carrying the religion of Christ into the jungles of Africa. In addition, colored ministers advanced the argument that the discontented should be encouraged to emigrate because their presence would be a general detriment to the communities in which they lived if they were unable to get away.[23]

The responsive chord that emigration propaganda struck among Negroes all over the state is indicated by the volume of mail that was received from various points in the state by William Coppinger, Secretary of the American Colonization Society. Although Coppinger's group was not organically connected with the company formed in Charleston during 1877, it was to him that many, including the officers of the Charleston group, turned for information. William G. White of Claflin University wrote to get information because, he said, "Many are desirous of emigrating. . . ." [24] William Martin of Columbia reported that he had received more than fifty requests for information from different parts of the state.[25] I. H. Rivers reported from Blackville that Negroes in his neighborhood were making up clubs to aid the emigration movement and that his club wanted five hundred copies of the latest issue of the *African Repository*.[26] Samuel J. Lee wrote from Aiken that he had had numerous inquiries about conditions in Liberia and wanted reliable information.[27] James G. G. A. Talley of Mount Jory, Union County, planned to make up a company in his neighborhood, and E. J. Furby of Society Hill estimated that two hundred families from Marlboro County would go, one hundred having already signed to go if they could get help.[28] From a farm near Guthriesville in York County, George Black wrote that he had heard much talk among the colored people of his neighborhood about Liberia and had heard June Mobley say "the colonization society out nort have send sum of our people to liberia." He wrote for "sum of papers that would give me a better understanding about going to liberia as I am won among the menny that am in favor of going." He had a wife and three children and was willing to sacrifice everything he had "to give them there liberty which I consider very sacraid." [29]

George W. West, leader of a group that had collected in Charleston, wrote that if they could not get away, "the poor people Will Die with grief from the treatments they have to incout [*sic*] with. We have to keep our mouths shut for Everything they say to us We are no more then dogs here in S. C. and i am going to Lookout a place for them on the St. Paul's River and try through the Lords help to get them out." [30] Nelson Davies of York-ville, however, reported in February, 1878, that a party he had collected to emigrate had been dissuaded by people who had been to Liberia and returned, having become dissatisfied.[31] There was a large group of these in York County, apparently some of those who had been sent by the Colonization Society during the Reconstruction period.

In Chester the Negroes of the county were reported during August, 1877, to be "afflicted with the Liberia fever. . . . Their feelings have been so wrought upon . . . that there is no doubt that a large number of them, if not a majority, would take their departure with little or no preparation. . . . At some places in the county the desire to shake off the dust of their feet against this Democratic State is so great, that they are talking of selling out their crops and their personal effects, save what they would need in their new home." [32] But the reporter who made this observation concluded that the emigration excitement would end in talk, for the very simple reason that those who wanted to go were destitute of the means to go. The white press attempted to dissuade those who wanted to emigrate by warning that the entire scheme was fraudulent. The Columbia *Daily Register* headed its account of a meeting addressed by B. F. Porter, "The Liberian Fraud," [33] and warned the Negroes that the "whole scheme is gotten up by a few sharpers of your own race and a lot of white rascals, who would delude you by first robbing you of your little hard earnings and then leave you to die in the jungles of the native wilds of your ancestors. . . ." [34] From Ellenton it was reported that the Negroes took no stock whatever in the "Liberian humbug," although numbers of them were migrating from Barnwell to Beaufort, "a sort of negro paradise." [35] The Orangeburg *Taxpayer* expressed fear "that many an honest darkey has been deluded into this trap by designing and dishonest men." [36] In January, 1878, when parties of Negroes began to arrive in Charleston, having heard that a ship was available to take them to Liberia, they found none available, and the officers of the exodus association offered to get them jobs in the nearby phosphate works. The *News and Courier* bemoaned the fact that whipping had been abolished as a punishment in South Carolina, but suggested that "if the deluded colored people, from Georgia and South Carolina, were to vigorously apply forty lashes save one, to the fat backs of the sharpers who have swindled them, public opinion would not condemn the deed very severely!" [37]

Meanwhile, however, the exodus association had acquired a fund of $6,000 from the sale of stock and its president, B. F. Porter, under pressure from the emigrants who had arrived prematurely in Charleston, left in January to select a ship.[38] On March 18 the bark *Azor* arrived in the port of Charleston, "gaily decorated with flags which fluttered in the brisk breeze." It was of clipper build, of 411 and 97-100ths tons burden, with "a rakish look, indicative of fast sailing." Having come from Boston in fourteen days, the captain estimated that he could make Monrovia in twenty-five. The vessel had 19 berths for cabin passengers, and 140 berths for steerage passengers.[39]

On the twenty-first of March the bark was consecrated at a special religious service at White Point Garden, in the presence of five thousand Negroes. The ladies of St. Joseph's Union presented to Martin R. Delany the flag of Liberia and several addresses were made, all breathing missionary zeal. B. F. Porter remarked that the consecration of a ship was a little unusual, "but the colored race was one that eminently believed in God, and was learning to believe in the evangelization of the millions of their people who now sat in darkness." The Reverend Henry M. Turner told the crowd that the vessel "was not only to bear a load of humanity, but to take back the culture, education, and religion acquired here. The work inaugurated then would never stop until the blaze of Gospel truth should glitter over the whole broad African continent." [40]

During the following month arrangements were made for the departure of the vessel, and exactly one month after the consecration the *Azor* sailed out of Charleston with 206 emigrants aboard, 175 having been left ashore when it was discovered that the emigrants, in their enthusiasm, had over-loaded the ship. The association purchased a plantation on the Wando River for them to occupy until it returned.[41] Two churches were organized among the emigrants, the African Methodist Episcopal Church under the Reverend S. Flegler, and the Shiloh Baptist Church, with a clerk and seven deacons.[42] The *News and Courier,* still doubtful of the wisdom of the emigration, said the friends of the race wished the emigrants, "most sincerely, complete success in their undertaking, and bid them with one voice, Godspeed!" [43]

A. B. Williams, then a young reporter for the *News and Courier* accompanied the emigrants on their voyage to Monrovia and wrote a comprehensive account of the trip. On the way over he found that various motives had animated them. Some were going because they thought they would have a better chance to "rise in the world" with easily procured land and social equality with their neighbors, while others were tired of renting or working out and wanted to be their own masters. An emigrant from Georgia said that farm laborers had no security for their earnings and therefore no reason to work. Others "ground the 'Outrage Mill' " freely, and complained of "Ku-Klux," "Night Hawks," and "political persecutions." "By constant repetition of and additions to these tales of horror they get to put implicit confidence in them, and such groundless fears have probably really something to do with this movement. It seems though that in the main various and widely differing opinions and views brought the emigrants to Charleston. Once there, they were soon rallied under the general watchwords of 'Political persecution and 'Social equality.' " [44]

The management of the association was guilty of several serious blunders which caused a frightful mortality from fever; 23 of the 206 emigrants died before reaching Africa.[45] The water supply was insufficient and gave out shortly before the arrival at Sierra Leone. The flour was coarse and black, the meal poor, being stigmatized as "kiln-dried stuff, only fit for hogs to eat," the rice was broken and dirty, and the meat was only enough to last when carefully doled out; although all of it except five barrels belonged to the "six months' stores," intended for the support of the emigrants after their arrival in Liberia, all of it was used on the voyage.[46]

In addition, despite the law requiring the presence of a doctor on board, there was no doctor on the vessel. Arrangements had been made by B. F. Porter for Dr. J. W. Watts of Washington to accompany the *Azor,* but when he failed to arrive George Curtis volunteered to be the physician and was so presented to the Custom-House officials. Although he had never practiced, he claimed to have a knowledge of medicine, and since his wife was a regular nurse it was thought that the passengers could get along.[47] Williams observed that Curtis knew about as much of medicine "as a street car mule." During the voyage he prowled about the decks with a small book called *The Mariner's Medical Guide* in one hand and compounds extracted from the medicine chest in the other. "It is horrible," said Williams, "to think of a blundering ignoramus like this man having charge of the health of some three hundred people, a large majority of whom were women and children. It is only Heaven's mercy that there are not even more deaths to record." [48]

The vessel arrived at Sierra Leone on May 19, where additional debts were incurred by the captain for supplies, pilotage, and, when the vessel became becalmed, for towage. The passengers were finally delivered in Monrovia on June 3.[49] After a forty-two days' journey, with the replenishing of supplies at Sierra Leone, there were still barely three weeks' supplies for the emigrants, including the ship's stores, which were turnd over to them by the captain. Mitchell Williams, an emigrant who died on the voyage, had receipts for $558.20 for provisions, a share in a grist mill, dry goods, a due bill, and stock. His widow found in Monrovia that she had only the stock, dry goods, about fifteen dollars' worth of provisions, and the papers. There was no sign of any grist mill.[50]

The additional expenses incurred at Sierra Leone proved to be the burden that broke the back of the Liberian Exodus Joint Stock Steamship Company. Late in May, 1878, bills for $1,680 reached the company, $1,050 of which was for towage charged by the British steamer, *Senegal*.[51] Appeals for help were sent out to the American Colonization Society, and offers were made to transport its emigrants on the *Azor* more cheaply than Yates and Porterfield, the company with which the society had been dealing.[52] Captain Holmes, who had been trying to buy the *Azor* at the time it was purchased by Porter for the Company, was hired on the understanding that he was familiar with the coast of Africa and would open a profitable trade to the profit of the company and himself. Holmes, however, returned to Charleston without any freight, "but breathing death and slaughter to all concerned." He then obtained a full freight for London, worth $3,000 or more, but the income was all squandered on expenses. From London he wrote that he would sail to Africa for a home freight, but was next heard from late in 1878 off the Charleston bar, without freight or revenue. He was naturally suspected of engineering a swindle in order to get possession of the vessel.[53]

In January, 1879, the Company announced another trip to Liberia, with the object of clearing the vessel of the heavy debt against her. This time the voyage was not for the stockholders of the company, but a regular fare of $40 for steerage passengers and $65 for cabin passengers was charged.

The officers of the company admitted that they had bought the vessel when they had but $6,000 on hand, because emigrants were already pouring into Charleston, and that more than three hundred had been left in the city who were unable to make the trip, but they promised that "No such blunders will be permitted to occur again." [54] The departure date was set at February 20, but the ship never left.

Meanwhile, a libel against the *Azor* had been filed in the United States Admiralty Court in Charleston by Captain W. E. Holmes and Mate Sidney E. Horne for back wages and money loaned to the company, by the firm of Fuller and Chase for the cost of the anchor, and by Anna M. Gaillard, wife of a former state senator from Charleston who had gone on the first trip of the *Azor,* for $1,021 advanced for the purpose of fitting out the bark.[55] Late in March the company announced a mass meeting at Gibbs Farm near Charleston to raise not less than $5,000, "which must be raised at once or our property will go into the hands of Northern sharpers. . . ." [56] It was apparently unsuccessful, however, for Major Edward Willis, a white legal representative of the company, wrote to John H. B. Latrobe of the American Colonization Society in October that the company would require a loan to save the *Azor*.[57]

In November the vessel was sold at auction by order of the court, and was purchased for $2,950 by Edward Willis, representative of the company, acting for F. S. Rodgers, a wealthy white merchant.[58] This transaction was undertaken on the understanding that the Liberian Exodus Joint Stock Steamship Company would repurchase the vessel from Rodgers. At the time of Rodgers' purchase the company furnished $450 of the purchase price and made a contract authorizing it to repurchase the vessel for the remainder of the price Rodgers had paid plus $175, or a total of $2,675, provided the amount was in Rodgers' hands by November 11, 1880.[59] Rodgers, however, sold the vessel to parties in Boston five months before the expiration of the contract, and when the company presented him the $2,675 on the due date, the vessel had long since been out of his hands. "The transaction has surprised everybody," wrote Martin R. Delany, "as this merchant is very wealthy, was commended as being very reliable, and generally reputed to be a gentleman of unswerving integrity." [60] A suit which was entered by the company to recover $7,325 on the contract from Rodgers dragged on through the courts until 1884. A circuit court ruled in 1883 that the company was not a legal corporation because it was incorporated under a law that gave no authority to incorporate navigation companies, but this decision was reversed in 1884 by the state Supreme Court, which ruled that the defendant had contracted with the Liberian Exodus Company, and therefore had no right to question its legal existence later; the Court also ruled that the charter could be taken away from the company only by suit commenced by the attorney general of the state. It then remanded the case to the lower court.[61] There is, however, no evidence that the company was ever able to recover, since Rodgers had ample resources and the company did not have enough to continue the litigation.

Liberia was not made more attractive by the reports which were spread far and wide of mismanagement and fatalities on the first *Azor* voyage nor by the subsequent reports of emigrants who returned to the United States. In May, 1879, Spencer Reeves of Milledgeville, Georgia, an *Azor* emigrant, returned to his home, complaining that Liberia had been misrepresented to him. He had lost his wife and youngest child.[62] But the *Monrovia,* on which Reeves had returned to New York, was reported to be preparing a return voyage to Liberia with about eighty Negroes, many of them from the northern counties of South Carolina.[63] In December, 1879, the *Monrovia* brought back to New York eighteen more *Azor* emigrants who reported that not one in the *Azor* party would remain if he had the means to return. Most of them, because of their poverty and the dissipation of their supplies during the voyage, were said to have been thrown on the charity of the Liberians.[64]

Success in Liberia was achieved, but the reports of successful emigrants did not arrive until years after the assumption of general failure had been widely accepted. One emigrant wrote in 1880: "Almost every week I see some of the *Azor* people living at Poor Bar, and they report themselves as doing well. Those at Bonneville are greatly elated at their success. I don't think that there is one of them that could be induced to return to America on any account—things remaining in that country as they are now." The same correspondent reported 173 of the *Azor* emigrants, to his own knowledge, to be still in Liberia, and others perhaps in the interior, contrary to stories that the majority had died or returned to America.[65]

Saul Hill, a native of York, reported four years later that he had established a successful coffee farm of seven hundred acres, the entire crop of which he sold to a Philadelphia firm, and was planning to send for his father. His success, however, was attributed by the Columbia *Daily Register* to the fact that he had been in good financial circumstances when he left. "A number of other colored men went to Liberia at the same time, but some of them returned in a year or so afterward as poor as church mice and thoroughly disgusted with the new country." [66]

In 1890 it was reported that Charleston had furnished to Liberia some of its most prominent citizens. C. L. Parsons, Chief Justice of the Liberian Supreme Court, was a native of Charleston. Clement Irons, another native of Charleston, had built the first steamship constructed in Liberia. It had been launched on the St. Paul's River in December, 1888.[67] In 1891 the

Reverend David Frazier, an emigrant from South Carolina, was elected to the Liberian Senate. He had opened a coffee farm with twenty thousand trees and was hoping to have thirty thousand the following year.[68]

But despite the success of these individuals, the Liberian Exodus Joint Stock Steamship Company must be put down as a failure. The causes of failure are numerous, but they cannot all be attributed to the officers of the company. The difficulties experienced on the voyage from want of supplies were the natural error of inexperienced persons. Porter claimed that the depletion of the water supply had resulted from extravagant waste.[69] The additional heavy expenses incurred at Sierra Leone were entirely unforeseen, but the company could be blamed for operating on such a close margin that unforeseen expenses could not be handled. The officers of the company sought to explain this away as having resulted from the enthusiasm of the emigrants who had gathered in Charleston in great numbers early in 1878 and had practically forced the company to purchase the *Azor* before it had sufficient funds on hand.[70] The plan of B. F. Porter to organize a regular trade between Charleston and Monrovia was not altogether impractical, but was undone by either the swindling, or the incompetency, of the white captain of the vessel. The final loss of the *Azor* was due to a man who took advantage of the financial stringency of the company to make a contract which he later violated, perhaps on the assumption that the company could not raise the money to reclaim the ship.

The whole project was destroyed by the accumulation of unforeseen debts, the remorseless pressure of creditors, the pitiless propaganda by the white press that "Curtis & Co. are humbugs," [71] and, finally, by lengthy and devious litigation. Although the idea of emigration to Africa was an unrealistic solution for the problems of Southern Negroes, there was sufficient interest in South Carolina to have made the Liberian Exodus Company a minor success had it not been destroyed by the concatenation of unfortunate circumstances.

## NOTES

[1] A South Carolinian, *Atlantic Monthly*, XXXIX (February, 1877), 682.

[2] *Ibid.*, p. 677.

[3] Woodson, *A Century of Negro Migration* (Washington, 1918), pp. 134–43; Vernon Lane Wharton, *The Negro in Mississippi, 1865–1890* (Chapel Hill, 1947), pp. 106–17.

[4] Simkins and Woody, *South Carolina During Reconstruction*, 234; *African Repository*, LIII (January, 1877), 26–27.

[5] Richard Harvey Cain to William Coppinger, January 25, 1877, American Colonization Society Papers, Vol. 196, Library of Congress.

[6] R. H. Cain to W. Coppinger, February 12, 1877, *ibid.*

7 *African Repository,* LIII (April, 1877), 39, quoting Charleston *Missionary Record.*

8 *Ibid.*

9 Harrison N. Bouey to W. Coppinger, May 23, 1877, American Colonization Society Papers, Vol. 197.

10 H. N. Bouey to W. Coppinger, May 31, 1877, *ibid.*

11 J. C. Hazeley to W. Coppinger, July 4, 10, 14, 1877, *ibid.,* Vol. 198; Charleston *News and Courier,* April 16, 1878.

12 Charleston *News and Courier,* July 27, 1877.

13 H. N. Bouey to W. Coppinger, November 27, 1877, American Colonization Society Papers, Vol. 199.

14 J. C. Hazeley to W. Coppinger, July 10, 1877, *ibid.,* Vol. 198.

15 J. C. Hazeley to W. Coppinger, July 14, 1877, *ibid.*

16 H. N. Bouey to W. Coppinger, July 10, 1877, *ibid.*

17 John Mardenborough to W. Coppinger, June 6, 1877, *ibid.,* Vol. 197.

18 Charleston *News and Courier,* April 16 1878.

19 Frank A. Rollin, *Life and Public Services of Martin R. Delany* (Boston, 1883), pp. 84–85, 96; Charleston *News and Courier,* April 16, 1878.

20 Columbia *Daily Register,* August 21, 1877; Yorkville *Enquirer,* September 27, October 1, 1877.

21 Charleston *News and Courier,* August 21, 1877.

22 Jasper Smith to W. Coppinger, January 3, 1878, American Colonization Society Papers, Vol. 200.

23 Charleston *News and Courier,* April 16, 1878.

24 William G. White to W. Coppinger, March 14, 1877, American Colonization Society Papers, Vol. 196.

25 William Martin to W. Coppinger, May 3, 1877, *ibid.,* Vol. 197.

26 I. H. Rivers to W. Coppinger, August 8, 1877, *ibid.,* Vol. 198.

27 Samuel J. Lee to W. Coppinger, September 19, 1877, *ibid.*

28 James G. G. A. Talley to W. Coppinger, October 1, 1877, *ibid.,* Vol. 199.

29 George Black to W. Coppinger, October 16, 1877, *ibid.*

30 George West to W. Coppinger, November 19, 1878, American Colonization Society Papers, Vol. 203.

31 Nelson Davies to W. Coppinger, February 5, 12, *ibid.,* Vol. 200.

32 Yorkville *Enquirer,* August 30, 1877.

33 Columbia *Daily Register,* August 21, 1877.

34 *Ibid.,* August 19, 1877.

35 Charleston *News and Courier,* January 22, 1878.

36 Charleston *News and Courier,* March 26, 1878, quoting Orangeburg *Taxpayer.*

37 Charleston *News and Courier,* January 3, 1878.

38 *Ibid.; For Africa! Special Voyage to Monrovia, Liberia,* broadside dated January 16, 1879, in American Colonization Society Papers, Vol. 204.

39 Charleston *News and Courier,* March 19, 1878.

40 *Ibid.,* March 22, 1878; *see also African Repository,* LIV (July, 1878), 77–78.

41 Charleston *News and Courier,* April 23, 1878.

42 *African Repository,* LIV (July, 1878), 78.

43 Charleston *News and Courier,* April 18, 1878.

44 Williams, *The Liberian Exodus* (Charleston, 1878), p. 11.

45 Charleston *News and Courier,* June 17, 1878.

46 Williams, *The Liberian Exodus,* p. 2.

[47] Report of interview with B. F. Porter in Baltimore, July 9, 1878, in dispatch to New York *Herald,* n.d. See unidentified clipping in volume titled *Azor* in Edward Willis Pamphlets, South Carolina Historical Society.

[48] Williams, *The Liberian Exodus,* p. 6. The ebullient and irresponsible George Curtis was a constant source of difficulty to the movement. When the Liberian Exodus Company was barely under way he had had illusions of getting the Charleston Chamber of Commerce to join with the Liberian government in raising a loan of $2,000,000 with which to establish a line of steamers between the two countries "on a grand scale." Later, an appeal through the *News and Courier* for help for the emigrants had to be disavowed by Martin R. Delany, who wrote, "Mr. Curtis of his own volition has not attended, except casually, the meetings of the board of directors for several months, and consequently could know but little of what was going on. His article and call for help was gratuitous, entirely unauthorized, and no such aid . . . is needed." Meanwhile it was disclosed he had deserted his wife, two of his own children, and three of hers by a previous marriage when he moved to Charleston. His only defense was, that "If every *liaison* is to be deemed a marriage, then we have a sufficient number of Utahs without going to the particular Territory of that name." It was later reported by a returning emigrant that he had deserted in Liberia the wife who had migrated there with him and had "a sweetheart" in Liberia. Charleston *News and Courier,* August 6, 17, 1877; *ibid.,* April 5, 6, 17, 1878; *ibid.,* May 13, 1879; George Curtis to William Coppinger, July 27, 1877, American Colonization Society Papers, Vol. 198.

[49] Charleston *News and Courier,* June 17, 24, 1878.

[50] Williams, *The Liberian Exodus,* p. 33.

[51] Martin R. Delany to Eli K. Price, July 12, 1878, American Colonization Society Papers, Vol. 202.

[52] *Ibid.,* H. N. Bouey to W. Coppinger, January 16, 1879, *ibid.,* Vol. 204.

[53] Unidentified clipping from a Negro newspaper, *Azor,* Edward Willis Pamphlets, South Carolina Historical Society.

[54] *For Africa! Voyage to Monrovia, Liberia,* in *Azor,* Edward Willis Pamphlets.

[55] Charleston *News and Courier,* February 1, March 12, July 7, 1879; Edward Willis to John H. B. Latrobe, October 2, 1879, American Colonization Society Papers, Vol. 207.

[56] *Save Our Ship the Azor!,* broadside dated March 31, 1879, in *Azor,* Edward Willis Pamphlets.

[57] E. Willis to J. H. B. Latrobe, October 2, 1879, American Colonization Society Papers, Vol. 207.

[58] Charleston *News and Courier,* November 9, 1879.

[59] *Liberian Exodus Joint-Stock Steamship Company v. Rodgers,* 21 S. C. Reports, p. 27.

[60] M. R. Delany to W. Coppinger, December 18, 1880, American Colonization Society Papers, Vol. 211.

[61] *Liberian Exodus Joint-Stock Steamship Company v. Rodgers,* 21 S. C. Reports, p. 27.

[62] Charleston *News and Courier,* May 9, 13, 1879.

[63] *Ibid.,* May 9, 1879.

[64] Yorkville *Enquirer,* December 11, 1879, quoting New York *Herald.* A comical aspect of the difficulties experienced in Liberia was presented when the Charleston *News and Courier* reported that the Unitd States minister in Liberia had sent the

State Department an account of the secession of a number of native tribes in the interior in which he attributed the secession fever to the *Azor* emigrants who had brought to Liberia the heresy of state rights. Charleston *News and Courier,* August 18, 1879. It later appeared that the trouble was engineered by British imperialists looking toward a seizure of Liberia. *Ibid.,* August 26, 1879.

65 D. B. Warner to W. Coppinger, January 5, 1880, letter published in Philadelphia *Christian Recorder* and quoted in Charleston *News and Courier,* March 13, 1880.

66 Columbia *Daily Register,* December 17, 1884.

67 *African Repository,* LXVI (January, 1890), 28–29.

68 Columbia *Daily Register,* July 24, 1891, quoting Winnsboro *News.*

69 Report of interview with B. F. Porter in Baltimore, July 9, 1878, in a dispatch to New York *Herald,* n.d. See unidentified clipping in *Azor,* Edward Willis Pamphlets.

70 *For Africa! Voyage to Monrovia, Liberia,* in *Azor,* Edward Willis Pamphlets.

71 Charleston *News and Courier,* June 19, 1878.

# CHAPTER

# 5

# BACK TO AFRICA: WORLD WAR I AND THE RESURGENCE OF EMIGRATION

Between the last decade of the 19th century and the end of of World War I, Black interest in African emigration flagged. Not until the end of that conflict when thwarted Black hopes coincided with the rise of White extremism, especially from the Ku Klux Klan, was the ground prepared for another wave of interest in emigration to Africa. The genesis and focal point of the renewed interest was a Jamaican, Marcus Garvey, whose Universal Negro Improvement Association represented the first organized colonization movement founded and directed by a Black man. Like some prior efforts, however, the U.N.I.A. came to grief amidst scandal and recrimination. Condemned by such eminent leaders as W. E. B. Du Bois, the U.N.I.A. induced cleavages in the Black community of America which still exist today.

*The following selection from* The Philosophy and
Opinions of Marcus Garvey *is an appeal to the racial
pride of the Black American and the promise of Africa
which was so characteristic of Garvey's movement. In
a country shaken by race riots and jarred by militant
White racism, the impact of Garvey's words on the
Black listener was considerable.*

# The Future As I See It

## Marcus Garvey

It comes to the individual, the race, the nation, once in a life time to
decide upon the course to be pursued as a career. The hour has now struck
for the individual Negro as well as the entire race to decide the course that
will be pursued in the interest of our own liberty.

We who make up the Universal Negro Improvement Association have
decided that we shall go forward, upward and onward toward the great goal
of human liberty. We have determined among ourselves that all barriers
placed in the way of our progress must be removed, must be cleared away
for we desire to see the light of a brighter day.

### THE NEGRO IS READY

The Universal Negro Improvement Association for five years has been
proclaiming to the world the readiness of the Negro to carve out a pathway
for himself in the course of life. Men of other races and nations have become
alarmed at this attitude of the Negro in his desire to do things for himself
and by himself. This alarm has become so universal that organizations have
been brought into being here, there and everywhere for the purpose of
deterring and obstructing this forward move of our race. Propaganda has
been waged here, there and everywhere for the purpose of misinterpreting
the intention of this organization; some have said that this organization
seeks to create discord and discontent among the races; some say we are
organized for the purpose of hating other people. Every sensible, sane and
honest-minded person knows that the Universal Negro Improvement Association has no such intention. We are organized for the absolute purpose
of bettering our condition, industrially, commercially, socially, religiously
and politically. We are organized not to hate other men, but to lift ourselves,

From *The Philosophy and Opinions of Marcus Garvey* (A. J. Garvey, ed.) (New
York: Humanities Press Inc., 1968), pp. 73–78.

and to demand respect of all humanity. We have a program that we believe to be righteous; we believe it to be just, and we have made up our minds to lay down ourselves on the altar of sacrifice for the realization of this great hope of ours, based upon the foundation of righteousness. We declare to the world that Africa must be free, that the entire Negro race must be emancipated from industrial bondage, peonage and serfdom; we make no compromise, we make no apology in this our declaration. We do not desire to create offense on the part of other races, but we are determined that we shall be heard, that we shall be given the rights to which we are entitled. . . .

## "CROCODILES" AS FRIENDS

Men of the Negro race, let me say to you that a greater future is in store for us; we have no cause to lose hope, to become faint-hearted. We must realize that upon ourselves depend our destiny, our future; we must carve out that future, that destiny, and we who make up the Universal Negro Improvement Association have pledged ourselves that nothing in the world shall stand in our way, nothing in the world shall discourage us, but opposition shall make us work harder, shall bring us closer together so that as one man the millions of us will march on toward that goal that we have set for ourselves. The new Negro shall not be deceived. The new Negro refuses to take advice from anyone who has not felt with him, and suffered with him. We have suffered for three hundred years, therefore we feel that the time has come when only those who have suffered with us can interpret our feelings and our spirit. It takes the slave to interpret the feelings of the slave; it takes the unfortunate man to interpret the spirit of his unfortunate brother; and so it takes the suffering Negro to interpret the spirit of his comrade. It is strange that so many people are interested in the Negro now, willing to advise him how to act, and what organizations he should join, yet nobody was interested in the Negro to the extent of not making him a slave for two hundred and fifty years, reducing him to industrial peonage and serfdom after he was freed; it is strange that the same people can be so interested in the Negro now, as to tell him what organization he should follow and what leader he should support.

Whilst we are bordering on a future of brighter things, we are also at our danger period, when we must either accept the right philosophy, or go down by following deceptive propaganda which has hemmed us in for many centuries.

## DECEIVING THE PEOPLE

There is many a leader of our race who tells us that everything is well, and that all things will work out themselves and that a better day is coming.

Yes, all of us know that a better day is coming; we all know that one day we will go home to Paradise; but whilst we are hoping by our Christian virtues to have an entry into Paradise we also realize that we are living on earth, and that the things that are practised in Paradise are not practiced here. You have to treat this world as the world treats you; we are living in a temporal, material age, an age of activity, an age of racial, national selfishness. What else can you expect but to give back to the world what the world gives you, and we are calling upon the four hundred million Negroes of the world to take a decided stand, a determined stand, that we shall occupy a firm position; that position shall be an emancipated race and a free nation of our own. We are determined that we shall have a free country; we are determined that we shall have a flag; we are determined that we shall have a government, second to none in the world.

## AN EYE FOR AN EYE

Men may spurn the idea, they may scoff at it; the metropolitan press of this country may deride us; yes, white men may laugh at the idea of Negroes talking about government; but let me tell you there is going to be a government, and let me say to you also that whatsoever you give, in like measure it shall be returned to you. The world is sinful, and therefore man believes in the doctrine of an eye for an eye, a tooth for a tooth. Everybody believes that revenge is God's, but at the same time we are men, and revenge sometimes springs up, even in the most Christian heart.

Why should man write down a history that will react against him? Why should man perpetrate deeds of wickedness upon his brother which will return to him in like measure? Yes, the Germans maltreated the French in the Franco-Prussian war of 1870, but the French got even with the Germans in 1918. It is history, and history will repeat itself. Beat the Negro, brutalize the Negro, kill the Negro, burn the Negro, imprison the Negro, scoff at the Negro, deride the Negro, it may come back to you one of these fine days, because the supreme destiny of man is in the hands of God. God is no respecter of persons, whether that person be white, yellow or black. Today the one race is up, tomorrow it has fallen; today the Negro seems to be the footstool of the other races and nations of the world; tomorrow the Negro may occupy the highest rung of the great human ladder.

But, when we come to consider the history of man, was not the Negro a power, was he not great once? Yes, honest students of history can recall the day when Egypt, Ethiopia and Timbuctoo towered in their civilizations, towered above Europe, towered above Asia. When Europe was inhabited by a race of cannibals, a race of savages, naked men, heathens and pagans, Africa was peopled with a race of cultured black men, who were masters in art, science and literature; men who were cultured and refined; men who, it was said, were like the gods. Even the great poets of old sang in beautiful sonnets of the delight it afforded the gods to be in companionship with the Ethiopians. Why, then, should we lose hope? Black men, you were once great; you shall be great again. Lose not courage, lose not faith, go forward. The thing to do is to get organized; keep separated and you will be exploited, you will be robbed, you will be killed. Get organized, and you will compel the world to respect you. If the world fails to give you consideration because you are black men, because you are Negroes, four hundred millions of you shall, through organization, shake the pillars of the universe and bring down creation, even as Samson brought down the temple upon his head and upon the heads of the Philistines.

## AN INSPIRING VISION

So Negroes, I say, through the Universal Negro Improvement Association, that there is much to live for. I have a vision of the future, and I see before me a picture of a redeemed Africa, with her dotted cities, with her beautiful civilization, with her millions of happy children, going to and fro. Why should I lose hope, why should I give up and take a back place in this age of progress? Remember that you are men, that God created you Lords of this creation. Lift up yourselves, men, take yourselves out of the mire and hitch your hopes to the stars; yes, rise as high as the very stars themselves. Let no man pull you down, let no man destroy your ambition, because man is but your companion, your equal; man is your brother; he is not your lord; he is not your sovereign master.

We of the Universal Negro Improvement Association feel happy; we are cheerful. Let them connive to destroy us; let them organize to destroy us; we shall fight the more. Ask me personally the cause of my success, and I say opposition; oppose me, and I fight the more, and if you want to find out the sterling worth of the Negro, oppose him, and under the leadership of the Universal Negro Improvement Association he shall fight his way to victory, and in the days to come, and I believe not far distant, Africa shall reflect a splendid demonstration of the worth of the Negro, of the determination of the Negro, to set himself free and to establish a government of his own.

*The following selection by C. Eric Lincoln is not without
its elements of criticism for Garveyism. It makes
abundantly clear, however, the astounding impact this
movement had among Black Americans. It will become
apparent, while reading this essay, that many of the
appeals for Black pride and dignity made by Garvey
are strikingly similar to current campaigns for pride
in heritage and self.*

# Black Nationalism: The Minor Leagues

## C. Eric Lincoln

### POLITICAL NATIONALISM: THE GARVEY MOVEMENT

The name of Marcus Garvey is one of the best known in recent Negro
history, yet it is one that the Negro leadership would like very much to
forget. Few Negroes have elicited such consummate scorn from their fellows
as did this belligerent little man, caricatured by a contemporary as:

A Jamaican of unmixed stock, squat, stocky, fat and sleek, with protruding
jaws, and heavy jowls, small bright pig-like eyes and rather bulldog-like face.
Boastful, egotistic, tyrannical, intolerant, cunning, shifty, smooth and suave,
avaricious . . . gifted at self-advertisement, without shame in self-laudation . . .
wthout regard for veracity, a lover of pomp and tawdry finery and garish
display.[1]

Yet, for all the castigations of his many critics, Garvey enjoyed the
admiration of hundreds of thousands of lower-class Negroes, who followed
him with enthusiasm and money, and who received from him a new estimate
of their worth and their future. His movement fired the imaginations of a
people desperate for a new hope and a new purpose, however unrealistic.
"Its spirit of race chauvinism had the sympathy of the overwhelming majority of the Negro people, including those who opposed its objectives. For this
was the potent spirit of race consciousness and race pride that informed the
'New Negro' " of the 1920s [2]—a period of cultural renaissance and racial
militancy among the Negro intelligentsia.

The Garvey movement must inevitably be seen against the background
of the post-World War I era, a crucial and difficult time for Negroes in the

From C. Eric Lincoln, *The Black Muslims in America* (Boston: Beacon Press, 1961),
pp. 56–66.

United States. They had helped to win a war for democracy overseas, only to return to the customary bigotry at home. They had risked death fighting beside the white man in the trenches of France, only to die in America at the white man's hand. In the first year after the war, seventy Negroes were lynched, many of them still in uniform. Fourteen Negroes were burned publicly by white citizens; eleven of these martyrs were burned alive.[3] During the "Red Summer" of 1919, there were no fewer than twenty-five race riots across the country. A riot in the nation's capital lasted three days; in Chicago, thirty-eight people were killed and 537 injured during thirteen days of mob rule.[4]

Along with the actual physical violence, there was intimidation everywhere. The Ku Klux Klan had been revived; and New York, Illinois, Indiana, Michigan and several New England states had been added to its traditional roster of Southern states.[5] There was an increasing competition between Negroes and whites for housing and jobs. Despair and militancy were the alternate moods of the Negro veterans who had fought "to make the world safe for democracy." They were disillusioned about the share of democracy America had reserved for them, but they were determined to bid for their rights—loud and clear.

In the summer of 1914, Marcus Garvey had returned home to Jamaica from a visit to London, his mind seething with plans for a new Universal Negro Improvement Association. Ironically, his sense of mission had been triggered by a reading of *Up From Slavery*, the autobiography of Booker T. Washington, who had been despised by many Negroes for his life-pattern of compromise and accommodation.

I read *Up From Slavery* ... and then my doom ... of being a race leader dawned upon me. ... I asked: "Where is the black man's Government? Where is his King and his kingdom? Where is his President, his country, and his ambassador, his army, his navy, his men of big affairs?" I could not find them, and then I declared, "I will help to make them." [6]

And he did. Putting aside Washington's reminiscences of restraint and gratitude for white favors, he originated a movement devoted to extreme black nationalism and self-improvement. As a result, he came to share with Washington the bitter contempt of Negro intellectuals—though for the opposite reason.

The manifesto of the UNIA called attention to "the universal disunity existing among the people of the Negro or African race." It challenged "all people of Negro or African parentage" to subscribe to the UNIA program, which read in part:

To establish a Universal Confraternity among the race; to promote the spirit of race pride and love; to reclaim the fallen of the race ... to strengthen the imperialism [self-determination] of independent African States ... to establish Universities, Colleges and Secondary Schools for the further education and culture of the boys and girls of the race to conduct a world-wide commercial and industrial intercourse.[7]

The motto of the Association was: "One God! One Aim! One Destiny!"—a motto which has recently been adopted by the rabid Ras Tafarian cult, which also emanates from Jamaica.

In 1916, Marcus Garvey "came screaming out of the British West Indies onto the American Stage." [8] He landed in New York, where at first little attention was paid to his street-corner speeches. Undaunted, he set out to tour thirty-eight states in order to study conditions of Negro life in America. When he returned to New York a year later, he had formulated certain opinions which were later to shape the largest mass movement in the history of the American Negro. Important among these conclusions was the amazing discovery that the "so-called Negro leaders ... had no program, but were mere opportunists who were living off their so-called leadership while the poor people were groping in the dark." [9] He seems to have concluded that too much of the leadership was concentrated in the hands of mulattoes and that these "part-white Negroes" could not be trusted.[10] He was exceedingly disturbed that Negro leadership depended so heavily upon white philanthropy—an impossible paradox. He was most contemptuous because this dependent leadership seemed willing "to turn back the clock of progress" at the whim of the white benefactors.

The New York division of the UNIA soon became the headquarters of a world-wide organization. By midsummer of 1919, Garvey claimed to have two million members in thirty branches.[11] His newspaper, *The Negro World,* was printed in French and Spanish, as well as in English, at its peak, it claimed a circulation of more than 200,000, "reaching the mass of Negroes throughout the world." The paper devoted itself mainly to a recapitulation and reinterpretation of the Negro's contribution to history. It recalled "the stirring heroism of such leaders of American slave rebellions as Denmark Vesey, Gabriel Prosser, and Nat Turner. The struggles of Zulu and Hottentot warriors against European rule, the histories of Moorish and Ethiopian empires, and the intrepid exploits of Toussaint L'Ouverture ... were not neglected in the effort to make Negroes conscious and proud of their racial heritage." [12] Readers were encouraged to speak out on racial matters, and Garvey himself "delighted in references to the greatness of colored civilizations at a time when white men were only barbarians and savages." [13]

At the First International Convention of the UNIA, held in New York in August 1920, no fewer than twenty-five countries were represented. A mammoth parade—led by the African Legion, the Black Cross Nurses and other organizations of the UNIA—wound through Harlem and on to Madison Square Garden, where Garvey set the tone of the month-long convention with an opening address to 25,000 Negroes:

We are the descendants of a suffering people; we are the descendants of a people determined to suffer no longer. . . . We shall now organize the 400,000,-000 Negroes of the world into a vast organization to plant the banner of freedom on the great continent of Africa. . . . If Europe is for the Europeans, then Africa shall be for the black peoples of the world. We say it; we mean it. . . .[14]

Later, the UNIA delegates drafted a "Declaration of the Rights of the Negro Peoples of the World," which was adopted on August 13, 1920. The declaration spelled out the Negro's rights in terms of political and judicial equality, racial self-determination and an independent Africa under a Negro government. It alleged that the League of Nations (which had just been organized in Switzerland) "seeks to deprive Negroes of their liberty." The League, it said, is "null and void as far as the Negro is concerned."

The convention also approved a flag for the movement: "red for the blood of the race, nobly shed in the past and dedicated to the future; black to symbolize pride in the color of its skin; and green for the promise of a new and better life in Africa." [15] An order of nobility was created; honorary orders were established; salaries were voted for the leadership; and Garvey was elected Provisional President of the African Republic. Gabriel Johnson, mayor of Monrovia, capital of the free African Republic of Liberia, was named secretary of state in the Provisional Cabinet at a salary of $12,000 a year. So impressed was Johnson that, on his return home, he announced that his office in Garvey's Provisional Government gave him diplomatic precedence over the President of Liberia.

When the convention ended, the Garvey movement had attained world significance. " 'Up, you mighty race,' Garvey thundered, 'you can accomplish what you will,' and the Negro people responded with an enthusiastic determination born of centuries of frustration and despair." [16] They poured a million dollars into the UNIA's Black Star Steamship Line—organized to link the black peoples of the world in commerce and trade, and to transport America's black millions back to their African "home." They gloried in the cooperative possession of grocery stores, laundries, restaurants and hotels. They took an unconcealed pride in staffing the Universal Black Cross Nurses, the Universal African Motor Corps, the Black Eagle Flying Corps and other UNIA auxiliaries with "Black men and women." An unarmed but smartly uniformed Universal African Legion paraded spectacularly through the streets of Harlem, and the admiring Negroes massed along the route whispered knowingly about the liberation of Africa by force of arms. Uncritical Negroes everywhere, and especially the despairing millions in the crowded slums of black America, acclaimed Garvey as the true leader of a new race.

Garvey's political ambitions were never made wholly explicit. The Ku Klux Klan and the fanatical Anglo-Saxon Clubs of that era assumed that he intended to lead all the Negroes in America to Africa; for this reason, they gave him their open support. But Garvey declared, "We do not want all the Negroes [to settle] in Africa. Some are no good here, and naturally will be no good there." [17] His real intentions seem to have been not unlike those of modern Zionism. He wanted to build a state, somewhere in Africa, to which Negroes would come from all over the world, bringing with them a wealth of technical and professional skills. Within a few years, he hoped, the new state would gain such prestige and power that it would be recognized as a symbol of accomplishment and protection for Negroes all over the world. For Garvey was convinced, as is Elijah Muhammad, that the Negro can hope for neither peace nor dignity while he lives in a white society. Like Muhammad, he saw only one solution: the establishment of a separate nation "so strong as to strike fear" into the hearts of the oppressor white race.[18]

But, unlike the Zionists, Garvey did not rest his ambitions here. The eventual liberation of all Africa was never far from his thinking. Presumably his black state, when it became sufficiently peaceful, would begin a revolution that would free all Africa, for he spoke mysteriously of the hour of "Africa's Redemption": "It is in the wind. It is coming. One day, like a storm, it will be here." He told a white audience that "you will find ten years from now, or 100 years from now, Garvey was not an idle buffoon but was representing the new vision of the Negro. . . ." In what was perhaps a prophetic warning, he declared: "We say to the white man who now dominates Africa that it is to his interest to clear out of Africa now, because we are coming . . . 400,000,000 strong." And again, "We shall not ask England or France or Italy or Belgium, 'Why are you here?' We shall only command them, 'Get out of here.' " [19]

Garvey's beachhead on the African continent was to be Liberia, the little country founded on the west coast by American slaves in 1847. The Liberian government had promised to "afford the association every facility legally possible in effectuating in Liberia its industrial, agricultural, and business projects." Specified settlements were laid out by the Liberian government and set aside for colonization, but Liberia's Acting President Edwin

Barclay felt it necessary to warn Garvey that "the British and French have enquired. . . . But it is not always advisable nor politic to openly expose our secret intentions. . . . We don't tell them what we think; we only tell them what we like them to hear—what, in fact, they like to hear." [20]

Garvey's movement was essentially political and social; he did not rest his doctrines and program upon any religious premise. Yet he did not neglect the wellspring of religious fervor—and discontent—in the Negro community. Then as now, many Negroes resented the white man's presumption in depicting God and Jesus as Caucasians, in filling the Christian churches and Bibles with pictures of a white God, a white Savior and an all-white heavenly host. Garvey seized on this resentment and carried it to a logical extreme. Since whatever is white cannot be beneficial to the black man, he pointed out, a white God cannot be the God of the Negro people. This was the God of the white man. The Negro's God must be black.

To promulgate a black religion, Garvey named as Chaplain General of the UNIA a former Episcopal rector, the Reverend George Alexander McGuire. In the Episcopalian fold, Bishop McGuire had long been a nettlesome critic, first agitating in vain for independent status for the Negro congregations, then organizing an Independent Episcopalian Church. This group followed him into the Garveyite movement and became the nucleus of a new, UNIA-sponsored African Orthodox Church. In his new position, McGuire was ordained a bishop by Archbishop Vilatte of the Syrian Orthodox Church,[21] thus bringing to the African Orthodox Church direct apostolic succession from one of the oldest bodies in Christendom.

Under Garvey's aegis, Bishop McGuire set out to re-order the religious thinking of the vast membership of the UNIA. He established a cathedral and a seminary (named Endich, after an alleged Ethiopian mentioned in the New Testament) for the training of a new order of black priests. The liturgy, based on the Episcopalian ritual, was colorful and impressive. And the new church set high moral demands, seeking "to be true to the principles of Christianity without the shameful hypocrisy of the white churches." [22] But the church was distinguished primarily by its appeal to race consciousness. "Forget the white gods," the bishop demanded. "Erase the white gods from your hearts." By 1924, after four years of his ministry, the Black Madonna and Child had become a standard picture in the homes of the faithful, and the worship of a Black Christ was openly advocated.

In August 1924, at the fourth annual convention of the UNIA, Bishop McGuire issued a public appeal to Negroes "to name the day when all members of the race would tear down and burn any pictures of the white Madonna and the white Christ found in their homes." [23] The Negro clergy was loud in protest, and the Negro press derided the idea of a "black Jesus."

But the African Orthodox Church had long since spread its missions through several states and into Canada, Cuba and Haiti. On both fronts, religious and political, Garvey's black nationalism was riding high.

From the start, however, Garvey had not been without his troubles. His movement had been kept under constant surveillance by New York State Assistant District Attorney Edwin P. Kilroe, whose interest bordered on harassment. The federal government was hardly sympathetic to Garvey's international ambitions; and abroad, the various colonial governments viewed him with outright alarm. His newspaper—in its English, French and Spanish editions—had been quickly suppressed throughout the colonial world. In America the newspaper was among several Negro organs cited by the U. S. Department of Justice in a 1919 report on alleged radicalism and sedition among American Negroes. The following year the Lusk Committee, investigating sedition in New York State, cited the *Negro World* as one of the most radical elements of the New Negro press. Both the committee and the Department of Justice portrayed Garvey as a dangerous agitator, inimical to the interests of his own people and of the country as a whole; but neither group was able to substantiate its charges.

Meanwhile, the governments of Great Britain and France became increasingly alarmed over the implications of the Garvey movement and spared no effort to keep it out of Africa—even to the extent of bringing indirect pressure to bear on the Republic of Liberia, which had agreed to provide for the settlement of about a hundred thousand Garvey followers in that country. The UNIA had been enthusiastically welcomed there, and the mayor of Monrovia had accepted a post as secretary of state in Garvey's provisional government. Garvey sent several missions to Liberia, one as late as June 1924, to prepare for the settlement of his followers, who were scheduled to begin arriving in October, 1924.

In the summer of 1924, the pressure from the British and French (who governed the territories surrounding Liberia) took effect. The Liberian government, under President Charles D. B. King, sent a diplomatic note to the United States announcing that it was "irrevocably opposed both in principle and fact to the incendiary policy of the Universal Negro Improvement Association, headed by Marcus Garvey." The lands promised to Garvey were leased instead to the Firestone Rubber Corporation, and when the new Garvey mission arrived, the members were arrested for immediate deportation. Thereupon, the Liberian president was lionized by the British for his "courage and statesmanship." The British press hailed him for putting "his foot down very firmly on such misguided movements for the people of his own race, as that sponsored . . . by Marcus Garvey and other agitators." The French government made him a Chevalier of the French Legion of Honor.[24]

At home, Garvey was encountering increasing resistance within the Negro community. The emerging black bourgeoisie and the Negro intellectuals would have no part of him.[25] Their attempt to mold the public image of Negroes as an intelligent, sophisticated people was undermined by his constant harangues and the spectacle of thousands of his followers parading in flamboyant uniforms through the streets of New York City. At first they simply ignored his movement; but as its notoriety increased, it drew the fire of most of the well-known Negro leaders, including A. Philip Randolph, Chandler Owen and W. E. B. DuBois. DuBois criticized the UNIA as "bombastic and impractical," although he later admitted that competition from Garvey had greatly hampered the development of his own Pan-African Congresses.[26] The NAACP also criticized Garvey's movement, as did the National Urban League.

Nor did Garvey spare his critics. He characterized such leaders as DuBois, James Weldon Johnson and Eugene Kinkle Jones as "weak-kneed and cringing . . . sycophant to the white man." He warned that "the 'Uncle Tom' Negroes must give way to the 'New Negro,' who is seeking his place in the sun." [27]

Thus Garvey's troubles closed down upon him. His own lack of business acumen had kept him embroiled in legal wrangles over the Black Star Line and other commercial ventures of the UNIA.[28] Now the apprehensions of the ruling powers on three continents were joined with those of America's conservative Negro leadership in a demand that the dangerous little Jamaican be cut down to size. The *Messenger* magazine, edited by Chandler Owen and A. Philip Randolph, led the Negro intellectuals in a direct attack. "Garvey must go!" became the rallying cry of many individuals who could agree on no other single issue.

Early in 1922, at the urging of the Negro press, Garvey had been indicted for using the mails to defraud in the promotion of stock in the UNIA's Black Star Steamship Line. But the government's case was weak, and the federal authorities made no move to prosecute. In January 1923, however, the calm was shattered by the murder of James W. H. Eason, an early Garvey admirer who had split with the movement the previous year and was now rumored to have offered himself as a key prosecution witness in the mail-fraud case. There was no evidence linking Garvey or the UNIA to the crime, which remains unsolved, but the hostility of the responsible Negro leadership was whetted. Less than a week after the murder, a "Committee of Eight"—all prominent American Negroes, most of them active in the NAACP—sent an open letter to the U. S. Attorney General. The letter condemned Garveyism as a philosophy seeking "to arouse ill-feeling between the races" and urged that he "use his full influence completely to disband and extirpate the vicious movement, that he vigorously and speedily push the government's case against Marcus Garvey for using the mails to defraud." [29]

Garvey responded with a bitter denunciation of the "good old darkies" who had treacherously sought to curry favor with the white man at the expense of their "fellow Negroes whose only crime has been that of making an effort to improve the condition of the race." [30] But in May the government brought the case to trial and won a conviction. Garvey was fined and sentenced to imprisonment for the maximum term of five years. He remained at liberty for seventeen months while his lawyers vainly appealed the decision, but in February 1925 he was taken to the federal penitentiary at Atlanta, Georgia. In December 1927 his sentence was commuted by President Coolidge; but Garvey had never become an American citizen, and since he had been convicted of a felony, the law required that he be immediately deported. From abroad he labored hard to keep his movement in the United States alive, but it quickly faded, and his death in London in 1940 was scarcely mentioned in the American press.

Garveyism is not dead. William L. Sherrill, once Garvey's representative to the League of Nations, still maintains UNIA headquarters in Detroit and serves as president of the straggling movement. The African Orthodox Church also survives, but its membership has dwindled to less than seven thousand. Various nationalistic cults in America, Africa and Jamaica still celebrate "Garvey Day" each August 1 with appropriate speeches and ceremony. And Garvey's own stature continues to grow as more and more observers concede that, for all his faults, he had a profound awakening effect on the American Negro community. Yet Garveyism lives on not really as a movement but as a symbol—a symbol of the militant Negro nationalism which so many black Americans see as their only alternative to eternal frustration and despair.

## PREPARING THE WAY FOR ALLAH

By the late 1920s, then, Noble Drew Ali was dead and Marcus Garvey deported. Their movements, shorn of their charismatic leadership, were in rapid decline. But there was no change in the experience that gave rise to both movements—the experience of being black among a white majority. This condition was, if anything, more intolerable than ever, for the Negro masses had been vividly reminded of their human dignity and their proud racial heritage. The failure of the Moorish and Garveyite movements left in the Negro lower class a constrained silence, a vacuum of extremist protest against racial indignities that were soon to be aggravated by the tensions of the Depression. Either America had to come quickly to its senses and live up to its democratic ideals, or a new black nationalist movement would move in to fill that vacuum.

It was just at this time, in the summer of 1930, that Wallace D. Fard appeared in Detroit. Many of those who first came under his spell had been followers of Garvey or Noble Drew. Fard was not alone, of course, in seeking to win over the masses already conditioned to black nationalism, especially those who had flocked to the black, green and crimson banner of the UNIA. Other black nationalist groups were also active, among them the National Movement for the Establishment of a Forty-Ninth State, the National Union of People of African Descent, the Peace Movement of Ethiopia and the United African Nationalist Movement. But none of these groups had a leader with Fard's charisma or his ability to seize on the Moorish and Garveyite passions and transform them into a new force, in which religious and political energies were fused. Fard's movement was destined to become the vanguard of black nationalism and, by solving the problem of succession on which earlier movements had foundered, to give that ancient ambition a fresh permanence and power.

## NOTES

[1] Dr. George W. Bagnall in a discourse entitled, "The Madness of Marcus Garvey," quoted in Edmund Cronon, *Black Moses* (Madison: University of Wisconsin Press, 1948), p. 107. Cronon's book is probably the best recent study of the Garvey Movement.

[2] J. Saunders Redding, *They Came in Chains* (Philadelphia: J. B. Lippincott Co., 1950), p. 261.

[3] John Hope Franklin, *From Slavery to Freedom* (New York: Alfred A. Knopf, 1956), p. 472.

[4] *Ibid.,* pp. 473–474.

[5] *Ibid.,* p. 471.

[6] Cronon, *Black Moses,* p. 16.

[7] *Ibid.,* p. 17.

[8] Redding, *They Came in Chains,* p. 259.

[9] Cronon, *Black Moses,* p. 41.

[10] Garvey's understanding of the American caste system was probably faulty. In his native Jamaica, the mulattoes formed a more or less distinct class between the whites and the unmixed blacks. In America, a Negro is commonly identified as anyone having any Negro ancestry whatever; and all Negroes of whatever color are relegated to a common caste.

[11] Cronon, *op. cit.,* p. 44.

[12] *Ibid.,* p. 47.

[13] *Ibid.*

14 Quoted in *ibid.*, p. 65.

15 *Ibid.*, p. 67.

16 *Ibid.*, p. 70.

17 *Ibid.*, p. 185.

18 *Ibid.*, p. 187.

19 *Ibid.*, p. 184.

20 *Ibid.*, pp. 124–125.

21 Elmer T. Clark, *The Small Sects in America*, p. 172.

22 Cronon, *op. cit.*, p. 178.

23 *Ibid.*, p. 179.

24 *Ibid.*, pp. 129–132.

25 See E. Franklin Frazier, *Black Bourgeoisie* (Glencoe, Ill.: The Free Press, 1957), p. 123. These Negroes "who were acquiring middle-class status," Frazier says, "did not only regard his program as fantastic, but they did not want to associate with his illiterate poor black followers, especially since West Indians were prominent in the movement." See also, J. Saunders Redding, *op. cit.*, pp. 260–261.

26 See John Hope Franklin, *op. cit.*, p. 482.

27 Frazier, *Black Bourgeoisie*, p. 260.

28 Cronon, *op. cit.*, pp. 113 ff.

29 *Ibid.*, p. 111.

30 *Ibid.*

# 6

# THE BLACK SELF-IMAGE
# IN MODERN TIMES:
# PRECONDITIONS FOR PRIDE

The inclusion of these four essays may, at first glance,
seem to diverge from the format of this anthology.
But in order to understand the present phenomenon of
the "Black Pride" movement and the glorification of
things African by Black Americans, one must be
confronted with what came before. The devastating
effects of poverty, racism, and oppression left their mark
on the Black man and his perceptions of his culture
and ancestry.

*The study by Thomas E. Davis on racial attitudes of
Black students appeared in the* Journal of Negro
Education *in April 1937. The degree to which oppression
manifested itself in the attitudes and perceptions of
these grade-school and college students gives some
indication of the decrease in group pride and personal
regard of these young Americans.*

# Some Racial Attitudes of Negro College
# and Grade School Students

## Thomas E. Davis

The purpose of this investigation is to reveal some of the specific attitudes possessed by Negro children, of the pre-adolescent, adolescent, and
post-adolescent periods of development, which are distinctly unfavorable to
their own racial group. The origins of the attitudes can be traced to many
sources; personal experiences in family discussions, in play groups, in reading newspapers and other printed matter, in contacts with other racial
groups, and in the schools. These attitudes often become so fixed as to form
definite stereotypes which in turn become an unconscious part of these
individuals' thoughts and actions towards other members of their group.
The removal of these attitudes is an as-yet-unaccomplished task of Negro
education. This task must have more definite results in order that one of the
most important phases of Negro life, independence through a sound and
strong business structure, may keep pace with the other phases of Negro life.

One of the pioneers in measuring racial attitudes of students was Emory
S. Bogardus.[1] Some others doing work along the same line are Reinhardt,[2]
Young,[3] Rice,[4] Thurstone,[5] and Lasker.[6] These studies were confined to
the inter-racial attitudes of these students. The most recent effort to study
the attitudes of Negroes towards themselves has been that of Baumgardner.[7]
His scientific approach to the subject has resulted in a scale which has not
as yet been generally applied to selected groups of Negroes. Another pioneer
in the field of measuring intra-racial attitudes of Negroes is W. A. Robinson,
Principal of the Laboratory School at Atlanta University. He has devised
two tests, the first of which is an informal questionnaire of the positive and
negative answer procedure for answering, to be used for college students,

From *The Journal of Negro Education,* Vol. VI, No. 2 (April, 1937), pp. 157–165.

and the second of which is of the multiple choice type with a ranking of the attitudes and is to be used in testing grade school students.

## GENERAL PROCEDURE

The present investigation is based on the results of these two tests and cannot be represented as being absolutely scientific since these tests are still in the process of standardization by Mr. Robinson.[8] The results are important only in indicating the general trends to be found in some specific attitudes of students which might be comparable to the attitudes of a larger general group of Negroes in the communities from which they have come and in which they now live. The author claims neither a scientifically achieved validity nor absolute reliability for the results since they represent phases of behavior which are themselves invalid and unreliable. Only when these attitudes are found to be consistent with the general trends of thought and activity of Negroes, as reflected in their socio-economic relations, can they be said to be worthy of consideration.

The test used for the college students is a mimeographed form called an Attitudes Test. The students were directed to place a plus sign before the statements if, after having read them over once, they agreed with them more than they disagreed. If they disagreed more than they agreed with the statements they were directed to place a minus sign before the statements. Partial agreement was to be indicated by a plus sign in a circle placed before such statements as fell in that category. This indication was considered, in tabulating the tests, as agreement and was devised by the author of the test to catch those students who wanted to excuse themselves for thinking as they did.

The Attitudes Test consists of 57 statements (reproduced in Table I) grouped as follows; 1–18, general traits of Negroes; 19–28, Negro Business; 29–37, Negro Professions; 38–41, Negro Ministry; 42–52, Negro Industry; 53–57, Negro Militancy (so-called by the author of the test to indicate the amount of hopefulness Negroes have that will operate to make them think effort is worth while). This is a no-time-limit test. All statements which had fifty per cent or more plus answers, including plus in a circle answers, were considered as being generally believed by the group and possibly by the majority of Negroes. The students were also asked to give their age, sex, training, and home states, but not their names.

The test for the grade school students is called a What-I-Think Test (Table II). It is designed for use with children in grades 3, 4, 5, and 6. The children are shown how to answer the items in the test by being directed to answer a practice item at the beginning of the test. This is also a no-time-limit test, and has ten items which deal with various characteristics of Negro behavior.

In neither test is there any statement in the directions which would indicate that they deal with racial attitudes. This in itself helps to prevent any conditioning of the students which might cause them to develop scruples against revealing their personal attitudes.

The college students were selected without regard to year classification, the tests being given to as many classes as it was possible to secure permission from the teachers. In this way the test was given to 107 students who comprised about a fourth of the entire student body at Fisk. These students were divided by their sex into 34 per cent male and 66 per cent female. Half of the students were from the South, 15 per cent from border states and 35 per cent from the North. They were about evenly divided in the age groupings of under twenty years and twenty years and over. All of these percentages agree closely with those for the entire student body, which indicates a representative sample group.

The grade school students were all from Ashcraft School in the Nashville city school system. Tests were administered to 125 third- and sixth-grade students. The average age of the 28 third-grade boys was 10.3 years, which represents one and three-tenths years of retardation for the group. The 27 third-grade girls were only nine-tenths of a year retarded with an average age of 9.9 years. The 37 sixth-grade boys had an average age of 12.8 years and a retardation of eight-tenths of a year, and the 33 sixth-grade girls had an average age of 11.5 years and were five-tenths of a year advanced in their age-grade relationship. The advantage of three years of age and school experience makes differences in the attitudes of students as the detailed results (Table II) will indicate. There is also a noticeable difference in the attitudes of the retarded classes. There is a definite range from the third-grade boys, who have the greatest amount of retardation, up to the sixth-grade girls who are advanced in relation to their age-grade relationship. The attitudes of the third-grade students are more varied than is true of the sixth-grade students but they are consistent enough to serve as a basis for comparison. There is also a noticeable difference in the attitudes of the boys and girls which is due partly to the different interests of the two groups as well as on the different experiences of the two sexes.

## RESULTS AND CONCLUSIONS

### The Attitudes Test (College Students)

Table I gives the percentage of positive answers of Fisk Students to the Robinson Attitudes Test grouped according to sex and test item. These

**TABLE I**  PERCENTAGE OF POSITIVE ANSWERS OF FISK STUDENTS TO THE ROBINSON ATTITUDES TEST GROUPED ACCORDING TO SEX AND TEST ITEM

| ITEMS | MALE | FEMALE |
|---|---|---|
| 1. An ignorant white man has more sense than an educated Negro | 00.0 | 00.0 |
| 2. Negroes like red more than other people | 13.9 | 18.3 |
| 3. Negroes like to show off more than other people | 27.8 | 7.0 |
| 4. Negroes never go crazy from worry like other people because when they get worried they go to sleep | 22.2 | 22.5 |
| 5. Any close observer can see that Negroes are more afraid of cold weather than white people are | 27.8 | 25.4 |
| 6. Negroes are the only people in the world who shout and get noisy in church | 22.2 | 4.2 |
| 7. Unlike other people if the average Negro remains quiet for a few minutes he goes to sleep | 13.9 | 14.1 |
| 8. Another way in which Negroes are different from other people is that they can hardly have a big gathering without a fight | 22.2 | 19.7 |
| 9. Negro children are so bad mannered on street cars and in public places that separation of the races could almost be justified on that basis alone | 16.7 | 18.3 |
| 10. When the facts are faced white people can hardly be blamed for not wanting Negroes to use their swimming pools | 41.7 | 61.6 |
| 11. A white park keeper, when asked for a few privileges for a Negro group, replied that Negroes are never satisfied with going far enough but they always go too far and spoil things. He was right. | 47.2 | 52.1 |
| 12. "Jimcrowing" on the street cars seems almost justified by the way Negro workmen come on the cars dirty and smelly and insist on sitting down by people | 47.2 | 60.6 |
| 13. People who try to get Negroes to attend meetings have discovered that they are different from other people in that the only way to get them to meet is to serve food | 30.6 | 35.2 |
| 14. Negroes are worse than other people about being late. If a meeting of Negroes is expected to begin at 8:00 o'clock, it is necessary to call it for 7:30. | 80.6 | 78.9 |
| 15. Much of the poverty of the South can be directly traced to the inborn laziness and unproductiveness of the large proportion of the Negro population | 16.7 | 29.6 |
| 16. The greatest problem which Negro teachers have to face is that Negro parents are not as interested in their children as other people are in theirs | 55.6 | 53.5 |
| 17. It is extremely difficult for American Negroes to overcome the handicap of their savage African ancestry | 19.4 | 18.3 |
| 18. When Negroes remember that they are descended from savage Africans they cannot be blamed for a tinge of embarrassment at that fact | 11.1 | 15.5 |
| 19. The trouble with Negro business is that Negroes have never learned to organize and work together | 94.4 | 93.0 |
| 20. Whatever the future may bring forth, the story of Negro business in the past has been smartness taking advantage of ignorance | 55.6 | 59.2 |

| ITEMS | MALE | FEMALE |
|---|---|---|
| 21. The average Negro had rather trade in a white store than in a Negro store even when the prices are the same | 69.4 | 73.2 |
| 22. Negroes with more sense than race pride will take out insurance with white companies | 83.3 | 70.4 |
| 23. The average Negro who goes around selling things is a sharpster who will cheat you if he can | 16.7 | 26.8 |
| 24. It is characteristic of Negro business that one Negro business will not cooperate with another | 77.8 | 84.5 |
| 25. The average Negro business man is too lazy to keep his business place clean and decent | 33.3 | 47.9 |
| 26. Whatever we may say about it we know that Negro bank failures are the direct result of business inefficiency and dishonesty | 33.3 | 57.7 |
| 27. No banks are entirely safe, probably, but any person honest with himself knows that Negro banks are not as safe as white banks | 55.6 | 57.7 |
| 28. One can feel much safer about a checking account in a Negro bank than about a savings account | 69.4 | 66.2 |
| 29. If a member of my family were dangerously ill and I had the choice of either a white or a Negro doctor, no one could blame me for calling the white doctor | 41.7 | 29.6 |
| 30. No matter how much race pride a Negro has he could not be expected to risk the treatment of his eyes to a Negro doctor who claims to have specialized on the eyes | 22.2 | 32.4 |
| 31. The average Negro doctor will refuse to serve a patient if he is not sure of getting his money | 13.9 | 29.6 |
| 32. One bad thing about Negro doctors and lawyers is the loose way in which they discuss the affairs of their patients and clients | 44.4 | 69.0 |
| 33. The main reason that Negroes prefer white lawyers is that Negro lawyers just cannot do for them what white lawyers can | 66.6 | 52.1 |
| 34. The average Negro lawyer charges too much for his services as compared with white lawyers serving Negro clients | 22.2 | 21.1 |
| 35. There are beginning now to be some few decent drug stores, but the average Negro drug store is a disgrace | 30.6 | 35.2 |
| 36. Negro teachers do not have enough patience with Negro children | 22.2 | 14.1 |
| 37. The average Negro teacher is interested only in her pay check | 27.8 | 36.6 |
| 38. White ministers try to appeal to the reason of their congregations, but Negro ministers appeal to the emotions of their congregations | 75.0 | 78.9 |
| 39. One main difference between white preachers and Negro preachers is that the Negro preachers are always begging for money | 58.3 | 49.3 |
| 40. The average Negro minister unlike the average white minister spends more of his time begging money than he does trying to save his congregation | 41.7 | 45.1 |
| 41. The average Negro congregations are better satisfied with an ignorant, noisy preacher than with an educated man in the pulpit | 63.9 | 59.2 |
| 42. The average Negro workman would rather work under a white foreman than under a Negro foreman | 66.6 | 78.9 |
| 43. Employers with very responsible work to be done can hardly be blamed for employing white workers instead of Negro workers | 25.0 | 32.4 |

**TABLE I**—*Continued*

| ITEMS | MALE | FEMALE |
|---|---|---|
| 44. A man who had invested a thousand or more dollars in a car would be foolish to risk it with a colored mechanic | 8.3 | 9.9 |
| 45. Any one who has had dealings with a Negro contractor will advise you to get a white contractor if you want a decent job | 16.7 | 29.6 |
| 46. The business of being an air mail pilot requires both courage and skill and the government cannot be blamed for refusing to allow Negroes to enter the air service | 8.3 | 7.0 |
| 47. The big trouble with Negro workmen is that you have to hire too many people to watch them so as to keep them busy | 11.1 | 32.4 |
| 48. The only time a Negro mechanic can be depended upon to do a first rate job is when a white man is standing over him | 2.8 | 14.1 |
| 49. The quickest way to ruin a good car is to turn it over to a Negro mechanic | 5.6 | 4.2 |
| 50. The average Negro mechanic takes a Ford car down and somehow gets it together again and then thinks he is a mechanic | 27.8 | 23.9 |
| 51. The average Negro barber shop is usually so dirty that one feels that almost any kind of disease can be contracted there | 41.7 | 45.1 |
| 52. When you get a Negro to do something for you, he expects you to be satisfied with poor work just because he is colored | 47.2 | 38.0 |
| 53. Negro lawyers can never hope to succeed in a state like Alabama or Mississippi | 41.7 | 52.1 |
| 54. There is no chance of a "Jimcrow" law ever being repealed in any state where it has ever been passed | 22.2 | 35.2 |
| 55. Negroes might just as well give up expecting to get into the manufacturing end of production | 8.3 | 16.9 |
| 56. With political conditions as they are in the South there is no hope for higher salaries for Negro teachers | 36.1 | 40.8 |
| 57. There is positively no chance for a Negro ever to be elected to the legislature of a state like Georgia | 33.3 | 50.7 |

percentages are based on the total of 107 students taking the test. The range of percentages is from zero up to 94.4. The sections dealing with Negro business and Negro ministry had the highest percentages of agreement while the section dealing with Negro industry had the lowest percentages of agreement.

The sectional differences indicate that generally the students from the North have higher percentages of agreement with the statements than those from the border states and the South. In the matter of statements definitely involving comparison with the white race the percentages show no great variances except in the matter of swimming pools (statement 10). Here the percentages agreeing were higher among the Northern students because they probably meet with such problems more often than do students in the South. Northern students also had a higher percentage of agreement with statements 26 and 27 dealing with the greater safety of white banks over Negro banks. The most outstanding belief of students from the South was that Negroes have a natural preference for white stores. Students from the border states had high percentages of agreement with statements which indicated that Negro preachers spent most of their time begging money, and that white doctors are superior to Negro doctors.

Age differentials are mainly confined to the statements that "Negroes are embarrassed over their African ancestry," in which three times as many students under 20 years of age agreed as students 20 years and over; "Negroes contribute the noise and shouting in churches," in which about four times more students under 20 years agreed than students 20 years and over; and "Negro children are bad mannered in public places and conveyances," in which over twice as many students under 20 agreed that they should be therefore segregated as was true for the students 20 years and over.

Of interest are some of the marked differentials in agreement with certain statements by the male and the female students. Statement 32 has the highest difference between the sexes in their percentage of agreement. While the belief is high among both sexes that "doctors and lawyers reveal the affairs of their patients and clients," there is a much higher percentage of agreement among the women students than among the men. The men having more confidence in the members of these two professions since they predominate in them. The same reason is probably true in the much higher percentages of agreement of the women over the men with statements 26, 47, 48, 57, 25, and 23. A higher percentage of males than females agreed with statement number 3—"Negroes like to show off more than other people." The same is true in the percentage of agreement with statement 6 regarding the "noise and shouting Negroes do in churches." Other statements having this same trend are numbers 29 and 36.

There were 17 statements, about 30 per cent of all of the statements, with which a half or more of either or both sexes agreed. The highest percentage of agreement with any statement was with statement 19, expressing the idea that "Negroes have never learned to work together" as being the trouble with Negro business. The next highest was statement 14 concerning the general lateness of Negroes to meetings as compared with "other people." The third highest was statement 24 dealing with the non-cooperation of Negro businesses. The fourth highest was statement 22 which indicated that sensible Negroes would deal with white rather than Negro insurance companies.

### What-I-Think Test (Grade Students)

Following are given the What-I-Think Test, and Table II indicating per cent of replies to each question:

Read each statement and then read the answers that come after the statement and mark an X by the number of the answer that you think is the best answer.

Example:

A little boy got sick at school one day. What do you think the teacher did?

1. She gave him an apple.
2. She was angry with the little fellow.
3. She called up the little boy's mother and let the little boy go home.
4. She made the little boy stay at school.

Number 3 is the best answer so we place X by the 3. Read all of the statements and mark the best answer in each in the same way that it is marked for this statement.

I. Johnnie was a little colored boy whose mother was very poor. One day she asked Johnnie to stay at home and work in the garden. What do you think Johnnie did?

1. He was too lazy to work in the garden.
2. He went to sleep under a tree like all little colored boys.
3. He was a smart boy and worked hard for his poor mother.
4. He went fishing because he was too lazy to work.

II. One day a man's car broke down. The only place near was a service station run by a colored man. He called the colored man to fix his car. What do you think the colored man did to his car?

1. He found the trouble and fixed the car.
2. He ruined the man's car.
3. He got a white man to help him find the trouble because he couldn't find it.
4. He half fixed the man's car and charged him for the job.

III. A colored man named Henry had been janitor of a jewelry store for 20 years. One night the jeweller thought he had put all of the diamonds in the safe but he had dropped one. As Henry was sweeping the floor early next morning he found the diamond on the floor. What do you think the colored man did with the diamond?

1. He was honest and gave the diamond back to the jeweller.
2. He was dishonest and stole the diamond.
3. He was afraid to keep it so he gave it away.
4. He hid it until it was safe to sell it.

IV. Mary's father bought some coal from a colored coal man. He put some of the coal in his furnace. What do you think happened?

1. The colored man's coal made the furnace smoke.
2. The coal burned as well as the coal from a white coal man.
3. The colored man's coal would not burn.
4. The coal was too cheap.

V. Bettie was a little colored girl. Her mother sent her to buy a loaf of bread. There was a white store on one side of the street and a colored store on another side. Where did Bettie go for her bread?

1. She went to the white store.

2. She did not care which store she went to.

3. She went to the white store because she liked the way it looked.

4. She went to the colored store because she wanted to buy from a colored store.

VI.  If you went to a flying field to take a ride in an airplane and there was a colored man driving the plane that day, what would you do?

1. Go on and take a ride with the colored man.

2. Be afraid to go up with the colored man.

3. Wait until some day when there was a white man driving the airplane.

4. Go to another field where they had white drivers for the airplanes.

VII.  A colored soldier in the war saw his friend fall wounded but still alive. The place where the friend fell was a dangerous place to go because the enemy's guns were shooting in that direction. What do you think the colored soldier did about his friend?

1. He was afraid to go and save his friend and left him to die.

2. He risked his life to save his friend.

3. He tried to get someone else to go for the man because he was afraid.

4. He was afraid like all colored people.

VIII.  A little colored boy had a story in his book at school about some English soldiers trying to capture an African village but the African chief and his men drove the soldiers away and killed some of them. How do you think he felt as he read the story?

1. He felt like laughing at the Africans.

2. He felt very proud that the Africans were so brave.

3. He felt ashamed of the way the Africans treated the English soldiers.

4. He felt angry because the Africans fought the English.

IX.  Aladdin was the son of a poor tailor. He lived in Pekin, the capital city of China. He was always idle and lazy and liked to play better than to work. What kind of a boy do you think he was?

1. French

2. Negro

3. Indian

4. Chinese

X.  What do you think about colored children as compared to other children?

1. Colored children are worse than any other children.

2. Colored children do not act like other children.

3. Colored children are as good as any other children.

4. Colored children will not behave as other children.

Table II presents the percentage of replies to each question by grade and sex.

The most significant result from this test was the high percentage of 6th grade girls who selected what may be termed the "good qualities" in Negro behavior. All of these girls believed that Negroes were honest (III),

**TABLE II** PERCENTAGE OF STUDENTS CHECKING ANSWERS TO STATEMENTS IN THE ROBINSON WHAT-I-THINK TEST GROUPED ACCORDING TO GRADE AND SEX

| ANSWERS' NUMBER | | THIRD GRADE | | SIXTH GRADE | | BOTH GRADES |
|---|---|---|---|---|---|---|
| | | BOYS | GIRLS | BOYS | GIRLS | AND SEXES |
| I | 1 | 17.9 | 18.5 | 18.9 | 6.1 | 15.2 |
| | 2 | 7.1 | 7.4 | 8.1 | | 5.6 |
| | 3 | 50.0 | 40.8 | 67.6 | 90.9 | 64.0 |
| | 4 | 25.0 | 33.3 | 5.4 | 3.0 | 15.2 |
| II | 1 | 30.8 | 26.9 | 70.3 | 69.7 | 52.4 |
| | 2 | 19.2 | 23.1 | 2.7 | 3.0 | 10.7 |
| | 3 | 19.2 | 26.9 | 10.8 | 21.2 | 18.9 |
| | 4 | 30.8 | 23.1 | 16.2 | 6.1 | 18.0 |
| III | 1 | 39.3 | 25.9 | 81.1 | 100.0 | 64.8 |
| | 2 | 10.7 | 22.3 | 10.8 | | 10.4 |
| | 3 | 25.0 | 33.3 | 2.7 | | 13.6 |
| | 4 | 25.0 | 18.5 | 5.4 | | 11.2 |
| IV | 1 | 11.1 | 19.2 | 8.1 | 9.1 | 11.4 |
| | 2 | 44.5 | 38.5 | 81.1 | 81.8 | 64.2 |
| | 3 | 33.3 | 26.9 | 10.8 | 3.0 | 17.1 |
| | 4 | 11.1 | 15.4 | | 6.1 | 7.3 |
| V | 1 | 3.7 | 7.4 | 5.4 | | 4.1 |
| | 2 | 11.1 | 14.8 | 18.9 | 12.1 | 14.5 |
| | 3 | 33.3 | 18.5 | 18.9 | 3.0 | 17.7 |
| | 4 | 51.9 | 59.3 | 56.8 | 84.9 | 63.7 |
| VI | 1 | 30.4 | 38.4 | 78.4 | 87.9 | 63.0 |
| | 2 | 8.7 | 23.1 | 13.5 | 6.1 | 12.6 |
| | 3 | 34.8 | 23.1 | 8.1 | 3.0 | 15.1 |
| | 4 | 26.1 | 15.4 | | 3.0 | 9.3 |
| VII | 1 | 4.0 | 15.4 | | 3.0 | 5.0 |
| | 2 | 32.0 | 46.2 | 78.4 | 90.9 | 65.3 |
| | 3 | 28.0 | 19.2 | 13.5 | | 14.0 |
| | 4 | 36.0 | 19.2 | 8.1 | 6.1 | 15.7 |
| VIII | 1 | 20.8 | 7.7 | 8.1 | | 8.3 |
| | 2 | 8.3 | 23.1 | 51.4 | 51.5 | 36.7 |
| | 3 | 41.7 | 38.4 | 21.6 | 33.3 | 32.5 |
| | 4 | 29.2 | 30.8 | 18.9 | 15.2 | 22.5 |
| IX | 1 | 13.6 | 20.0 | | | 6.3 |
| | 2 | 18.2 | 20.0 | 29.7 | 33.3 | 26.8 |
| | 3 | 40.9 | 15.0 | 8.1 | 12.1 | 16.9 |
| | 4 | 27.3 | 45.0 | 62.2 | 54.6 | 50.0 |
| X | 1 | 5.3 | 12.0 | 5.4 | 3.0 | 6.2 |
| | 2 | 10.5 | 16.0 | 16.2 | 12.1 | 14.0 |
| | 3 | 47.4 | 52.0 | 59.5 | 78.8 | 61.4 |
| | 4 | 36.8 | 20.0 | 18.9 | 6.1 | 18.4 |
| Total | | 28 | 27 | 37 | 33 | 125 |

while 90 per cent or more believed that Negroes were industrious (I) and fearless and loyal (VII). The third grade girls had the highest percentage of adverse beliefs concerning Negro behavior in the first four statements but yielded this position to the third grade boys for the remainder of the statements. These third grade boys agreed with a larger number of the items than did the third grade girls. Next in order were the sixth grade boys and the sixth grade girls who by their smaller range of agreement indicated more agreement or disagreement with the statements. This probably indicates the beginning of maturity in their thinking and ideation about the behavior characteristics of Negroes.

The widest range of agreement was confined to those statements dealing with Negro business and industry. The greatest amount of doubt being expressed concerning the mechanical ability of Negroes (II) and the preference of stores according to the racial identity of their owners (V).

## Conclusions

The results of the two tests clearly indicate the adverse attitudes all of the students had about Negro business. The suggestion that the attitudes of this small sample are comparable to those of a large majority of the Negro population does have some bases for fact. One basis is that attitudes are generally universal among a group and tend to remain constant when no undue pressure is exerted to change them. Another basis is the consistency of beliefs of this sample of 232 students who represent a wide range of ages, geographical locations, educational experiences, and socio-economic status. If these attitudes are as general as this investigation might indicate, then there is much work to be done by those who would redirect and reorganize Negro education. The existence of these attitudes among both the youth and the adults of the Negro race is a serious indictment of Negro education. Schools and colleges are attempting major programs of vocational and occupational guidance based upon aptitudes without the inclusion of a consideration of intra-racial attitudes. There is no logic in training Negroes for businesses if they continue to believe in the ultimate failure of most Negro enterprises, or if they must operate in locales where the population has no confidence in Negro business. If the psychologically important factor of self-confidence is to operate, it must of necessity be rid of the added burden of adverse attitudes about the general field of business. The failure of business, the ministry, and other specialized fields to attract more educated Negroes who could insure higher percentages of success is due in part to the general attitudes held by Negroes towards them. Changing attitudes would also mean removing one of the most important obstacles to the progress of Negro business. Herein lies a challenge to those who would improve the economic status of the Negro.

## NOTES

[1] E. S. Bogardus, "Social Distance and its Origins," *Journal of Applied Sociology,* **9**:216–226 (1925).

[2] J. M. Reinhardt, "Students and Race Feeling," *Survey,* **61**:239–240 (1928).

[3] Donald Young, "Some Effects of a Course in American Race Problems on the Race Prejudices of 450 Undergraduates at the University of Pennsylvania," *Journal of Abnormal and Social Psychology,* **22**:235–242 (1927).

[4] S. A. Rice, " 'Stereotypes': A Source of Error in Judging Human Character," *Journal of Personnel Research,* **5**:267–276 (1926–27).

[5] L. L. Thurstone, "An Experimental Study of Nationality Preferences," *Journal of General Psychology,* **1**:405–425 (1928).

[6] Bruno Lasker, *Race Attitudes in Children,* New York: Henry Holt and Co. (1929).

[7] H. W. Baumgardner, "Measuring Negro Self Respect," JOURNAL OF NEGRO EDUCATION, **4**:490–9, O 1935.

[8] Permission for use of these tests was given the author by Mr. Robinson who is preparing a comprehensive report of the results from administering them to a large number of college and grade school students.

*Thomas F. Pettigrew's* Profile of the Negro American,
*written in 1964, relates the lack of a positive self-image
and favorable disposition toward one's color to the
poverty and oppression suffered by Black Americans.
He analyzes the effects of these long-standing forces on
the personality and family structure in much the same
way that Moynihan did a decade later. He also assesses
the favorable impact of Black liberation in Africa on the
Afro-American and how it may serve to re-instill pride.*

# The Role and Its Burdens

## Thomas F. Pettigrew

A small Negro boy came regularly to his play therapy sessions. Each week he entered the playroom, sat at the table, propped back his chair, placed his feet upon the table, and then folded his arms majestically over his chest. Week after week, the child came to the playroom, repeated the performance, and sat with an impassive expression on his face until the session ended. Finally, he asked the therapist if she knew what he had been playing. Eagerly, she confessed that she had no idea. "I've been playing white man!" he announced.

This incident aptly illustrates the translation of societal racism into personal terms, the effect of racial discrimination upon the individual Negro. But discrimination does not affect all Negroes in the same way. There are, of course, as many Negro American personalities as there are Negro Americans. As Gordon W. Allport and others emphasize, each individual has his own unique personality, shaped by his special endowments and experiences. But the ubiquity of racial prejudice in the United States guarantees that virtually every Negro American faces at some level the impersonal effects of discrimination, the frightening feeling of being a black man in what often appears to him to be a white man's world.

## PLAYING THE ROLE OF "NEGRO"

Like all human interactions, discriminatory encounters between whites and Negroes require that both parties "play the game." As the small Negro boy astutely recognized, the white must act out the role of the "superior";

From Thomas F. Pettigrew, *A Profile of the Negro American* (Princeton, N.J.: D. Van Nostrand Co., 1964), pp. 3–26.

by direct action or subtle cue, he must convey the expectation that he will be treated with deference. For his part, the Negro must, if racist norms are to be obeyed, act out the role of the "inferior"; he must play the social role of "Negro." And if he should refuse to play the game, he would be judged by the white supremacist as "not knowing his place," and harsh sanctions could follow.

The terror such a subordinate role can have for a white person, inexperienced in its subtleties, is revealed by John Griffin in his *Black Like Me*. Artificially darkening his skin and traveling in the South as a "Negro," Griffin discovered viscerally what it is like to play the lowly role. He describes the "hate stare" intensely bigoted whites cast upon Negroes:

It came from a middle-aged, heavy-set, well-dressed white man. He sat a few yards away, fixing his eyes on me. Nothing can describe the withering horror of this. You feel lost, sick at heart before such unmasked hatred . . .

Griffin concludes:

The Negro is treated not even as a second-class citizen, but as a tenth-class one. His day-to-day living is a reminder of his inferior status. He does not become calloused to those things—the polite rebuffs when he seeks better employment; hearing himself referred to as nigger, coon, jigaboo; having to bypass available rest-room facilities or eating facilities to find one specified for him. Each new reminder strikes at the raw spot, deepens the wound.

The socially-stigmatized role of "Negro" is the critical feature of having dark skin in the United States. "It is part of the price the Negro pays for his position in this society," comments James Baldwin, "that, as Richard Wright points out, he is almost always acting." At the personality level, such enforced role adoption further divides the individual Negro both from other human beings and from himself. Of course, all social roles, necessary as they are, hinder to some extent forthright, uninhibited social interaction. An employer and employee, for example, may never begin to understand each other as complete human beings unless they break through the formality and constraints of their role relationship, unless they "let their hair down." Likewise, whites and Negroes can never communicate as equals unless they break through the role barriers. As long as racial roles are maintained, both parties find it difficult to perceive the humanity behind the façade. Many whites who are by no means racists confuse the role of "Negro" with the people who must play this role. "Negroes are just like that," goes the phrase, "they are born that way." Conversely, many Negroes confuse the role of "white man" with whites. "Whites are just like that, they are born thinking they should be boss."

Intimately associated with this impairment of human relatedness is an impairment of the individual's acceptance and understanding of himself. Both whites and Negroes can confuse their own roles as being an essential part of themselves. Whites can easily flatter themselves into the conviction that they are in fact "superior"; after all, does not the deferential behavior of the role-playing Negro confirm this "superiority"? And Negroes in turn often accept much of the racists' mythology; for does not the imperious behavior of the role-playing white confirm this "inferiority"?

These are not mere speculations of existentialist philosophy. A large body of psychological research convincingly demonstrates the power of role-playing to change deeply-held attitudes, values, and even conceptions of self.[1] Moreover, these remarkable changes have been rendered by temporary role adoptions of an exceedingly trivial nature when compared to the life-long role of "Negro."[2] Imagine, then, the depth of the effects of having to play a role which has such vast personal and social significance that it influences virtually all aspects of daily living. Indeed, the resulting confusion of self-identity and lowering of self-esteem are two of the most serious "marks of oppression" upon Negro American personality.

## SELF-IDENTITY AND SELF-ESTEEM

The quest for self-identity is the search for answers to the all-important questions: Who am I? What am I like as a person? And how do I fit into the world? These are not easy questions for anyone to answer in our complex, swiftly-changing society. Yet they offer even greater difficulties for Negro Americans.

We learn who we are and what we are like largely by carefully observing how other people react to us. But this process is highly structured for the Negro by the role he is expected to play. When he attempts to gain an image of himself on the basis of his typical contacts with white America and the general culture, he often receives a rude jolt. While he is totally American in every conceivable meaning of the term, he finds that most Americans are white and that somehow the mere color of his skin puts him into a unique and socially-defined inferior category. And when the Negro looks around him—except in the spheres of athletics and entertainment—he discovers very few Americans with his skin color who hold important positions in his society. Save for the mass media expressly tailored for Negro audiences, he sees only white models in advertisements and only whites as heroes of stories. When he does see Negroes in the general mass media, they are likely to be cast in low-status roles and appear as "amusingly ignorant."[3] Little wonder, then, that the question, who am I?, raises special difficulties for him.

Identity problems are unusually acute during certain periods in a person's life. These periods, these identity-crises, often occur in the preschool years, later in adolescence, and again in young adulthood. All three of these periods impose additional stress on Negroes. Negro parents confess to great anxiety and ambivalence over telling their preschool children what it means to be a Negro in American society. Should youngsters be shielded from the truth as long as possible? Or should they be prepared early for blows that are sure to come?

The importance of identity problems for young Negro children has been demonstrated by a series of ingenious investigations. Following the classical work of Kenneth and Mamie Clark,[4] these researches have utilized a wide assortment of techniques in a variety of segregated Southern and integrated Northern nursery and school settings and have consistently arrived at the same critical conclusions. Racial recognition in both white and Negro children appears by the third year and rapidly sharpens each year thereafter. Of special significance is the tendency found in all of these studies for Negro children to prefer white skin. They are usually slower than white children to make racial distinctions, they frequently prefer white dolls and white friends, and they often identify themselves as white or show a tense reluctance to acknowledge that they are Negro. Moreover, young children of both races soon learn to assign, realistically, poorer houses and less desirable roles to Negro dolls. This early "mark of oppression" is illustrated by the behavior of a small Negro boy who participated in one of these studies conducted in Lynchburg, Virginia. Asked if he were white or colored, he hung his head and hesitated. Then he murmured softly, "I guess I'se kinda colored."

Some of this direct manifestation of "self-hate" disappears in later years, though similar studies of older Negro children find residual symptoms. One investigation of children aged eight to thirteen years in an interracial summer camp found that Negroes tended at first to be oversensitive to unfavorable behavior of their Negro peers and to avoid choosing other Negroes as friends. A successful experience in an egalitarian, interracial setting, however, can alleviate these inclinations. In this study, a two-week experience in interracial camping is shown to have significantly modified these expressions of self-hate in the young Negro campers.

In the teens, sex becomes an acute issue. This is a period of great strain for most American adolescents, but for the Negro child in the North who has close friendships with white children, it frequently means a sudden parting of paths. After puberty, the Negro child is no longer invited to his white friends' parties, for at this time the deep racist fears of miscegenation harbored by many white parents enter on the scene. For the majority of Negro youth of this age who have no white friends, the early teens introduce their own version of identity-crisis. From his teachers, his peer group, his contacts with the white world beyond his immediate neighborhood, the Negro teenager encounters new shocks. The full awareness of his social devaluation in the larger society in addition to the sharp strains felt by all teenagers in a complex society can assume the dimensions of a severe emotional stress-situation.

If the ambitious Negro has successfully weathered these earlier crises, he must face yet another series of identity-shocks in young adulthood. Employment discrimination may keep him from the job for which he trained, and housing segregation may restrict him from securing the type of housing he wants for his family. Who am I? What am I like as a person? And how do I fit into the world? The old questions from childhood continue to require answers when he is refused a job for which he is qualified and a house for which he has the purchase price.

This confused identity in adulthood even reveals itself among the most militant and articulate Negroes. A careful statistical analysis of Richard Wright's autobiography, *Black Boy,* strongly suggests this famous Negro writer lacked a basic identification with other Negroes. Four-fifths of his descriptions of Negroes are unfavorable and do not at all coincide with his recurrent self-descriptions. "My life at home," wrote Wright, "has cut me off, not only from white people but from Negroes as well."

These identity problems are inextricably linked with problems of self-esteem. For years, Negro Americans have had little else by which to judge themselves than the second-class status assigned them in America. And along with this inferior treatment, their ears have been filled with the din of white racists egotistically insisting that Caucasians are innately superior to Negroes. Consequently, many Negroes, consciously or unconsciously, accept in part these assertions of their inferiority. In addition, they accept the American emphases on "status" and "success." But when they employ these standards for judging their own worth, their lowly positions and their relative lack of success lead to further self-disparagement. Competition with successful whites is especially threatening. Laboratory experimentation demonstrates that even when Negroes receive objective evidence of equal mental ability in an interracial situation they typically feel inadequate and respond compliantly.

The sweeping changes of recent years, however, have begun to alter this situation. The old wounds of confused identity and damaged self-esteem have not sufficiently healed, but recent events are potent medicines. Supreme Court decisions, in particular, brought new hope. A 1963 *Newsweek* national poll found that two-thirds of all Negroes credited the Supreme Court for their biggest breakthroughs. "It started the ball rolling," voiced one respondent. And another added, "The Supreme Court gave us heart to fight." Moreover, the Negro's own protests and assertion of civil rights, his increasing educational and economic opportunities, the findings of social science, and the emergence of proud new African nations all have salved the old wounds.

It is difficult for white Americans to grasp the full personal significance of these events for Negro Americans. But imagine how a Negro feels today. All of his life he has been bombarded with white-supremacy ideas and restrictions. Moreover, he has shared much of the naïve conception of Africa as the dark continent of wild and naked savages. Now he is greeted with evidence from all sides that the white supremacists are wrong. On television, he sees segregationists desperately defying his national government in their losing battle to maintain Jim Crow, he sees his President conferring with black chiefs of state with full pomp and circumstance, and he sees his nation's representatives wooing the all-important black delegates to the United Nations. He sees all this, and his wounds begin to heal. The special role of "Negro" remains, but is undergoing drastic change. James Baldwin puts the matter forcefully:

... the American Negro can no longer, nor will he ever again, be controlled by white America's image of him. This fact has everything to do with the rise of Africa in world affairs. At the time that I was growing up, Negroes in this country were taught to be ashamed of Africa. . . . One was always being mercilessly scrubbed and polished, as though in the hope that a stain could thus be washed away. . . . The women were forever straightening and curling their hair, and using bleaching creams. . . . But none of this is so for those who are young now. . . . by the time they were able to react to the world, Africa was on the stage of history. This could not but have an extraordinary effect on their own morale, for it meant that they were not merely the descendants of slaves in a white, Protestant, and puritan country: they were also related to kings and princes in an ancestral homeland, far away. And this has proved to be a great antidote to the poison of self-hatred.

The recent rise of Africa is especially important in the changing self-images of very dark Negro Americans. A survey of working-class Negroes in Boston related skin color to attitudes and knowledge of Africa. Figure 1 presents the results. Note that dark Negroes most often agreed that African independence enhanced the self-conceptions of Negro Americans and disagreed that Africans are of no help in the American civil rights struggle. Furthermore, the better-educated dark Negroes were best informed about Africa. Though they identified Negro-American leaders less accurately than other Negroes, darker respondents with at least a high school education more often knew who Haile Selassie I and Kwame Nkrumah were.

## THE HOSTILE ENVIRONMENT

Another widespread reaction to racism is a generalized perception of the world as a hostile, threatening place. Horace Cayton considers this a critical feature of the "oppression phobia" experienced by many Negro Americans: an expectancy of violent mistreatment combined with a feeling of utter helplessness. Negroes questioned in *Newsweek*'s national poll groped for words to describe this phobia: "the feeling of being choked," said one; "feels like being punished for something you didn't do," said another. Such feelings are also experienced by other minority groups. Many Jews, for instance, have reported a preoccupation with anti-Semitism and a vague sense of impending doom, of haunting anxiety, hovering over them.

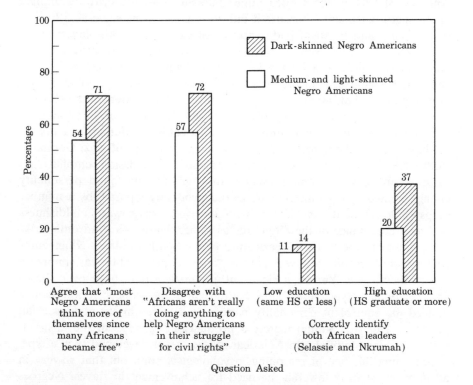

**Figure 1.** Skin Color and Orientation Toward Africa
(Data from T. F. Pettigrew, "Skin Color and Negro American Personality," unpublished paper.)

Psychological studies of young Negro children reveal that this phobia has early roots. One such investigation utilized the Thematic Apperception Test (TAT), a set of imagination-provoking pictures on the basis of which respondents compose brief stories. It found that a sample of nine-to-fourteen-year-old Negro boys viewed the environment as a far more hostile, dangerous entity than comparable white boys.[5] These Negro youths typically told stories in which the hero—presumably themselves—is hated, reprimanded, restricted, or injured. By contrast, the white youths generally fashioned heroes who, unencumbered by environmental barriers, were greatly admired and respected.

Reality testing is involved here, of course, for the world *is* more often a treacherous, threatening place for Negroes. Consider the social scars of discrimination throughout Negro American history that make this true. Slavery cast the longest shadow. Compared with the institution in Latin America, slavery in the United States had an unusually crushing impact upon Negro personality, because it did not recognize the slave as a human being. Spain and Portugal had centuries of experience with slavery prior to the founding of the New World, hence Iberian law had evolved a special place for the slave as a human being with definite, if limited, rights. By contrast, England had no previous involvement with the "peculiar institution," and so its law, adopted by the American colonies, treated the slave as mere property—no different legally from a house, a barn, or an animal.

Recently, one historian ventured a parallel between Southern slavery on the large, cotton plantations and the concentration camps of Nazi Germany. Both were closed systems, with little chance of manumission, emphasis on survival, and a single, omnipresent authority.[6] The profound personality change created by Nazi internment, as independently reported by a number of psychologists and psychiatrists who survived, was toward childishness and total acceptance of the SS guards as father-figures—a syndrome strikingly similar to the "Sambo" caricature of the Southern slave. Nineteenth-century racists readily believed that the "Sambo" personality was simply an inborn racial type. Yet no African anthropological data have ever shown any personality type resembling Sambo; and the concentration camps molded the equivalent personality pattern in a wide variety of Caucasian prisoners. Nor was Sambo merely a product of "slavery" in the abstract, for the less devastating Latin American system never developed such a type.

Extending this line of reasoning, psychologists point out that slavery in all its forms sharply lowered the need for achievement in slaves. Negroes in bondage, stripped of their African heritage, were placed in a completely dependent role. All of their rewards came, not from individual initiative and enterprise, but from absolute obedience—a situation that severely depresses the need for achievement among all peoples. Most important of all, slavery vitiated family life. Since many slaveowners neither fostered Christian marriage among their slave couples nor hesitated to separate them on the auction block, the slave household often developed a fatherless, matrifocal (mother-centered) pattern.

Strong traces of these effects of slavery, augmented by racial discrimination, have persisted since Emancipation because of bitter poverty and the uprooted life of migrants far from home. Poverty is not limited to Negroes, of course, but it takes on a special meaning when due in part to the color of one's skin. Though a substantial number of Negroes have improved their status economically, a much greater percentage of Negroes than whites comprise the nation's most destitute citizens. For these Negroes, poverty means living in the degraded slums of our largest cities in close proximity to the worst centers of the nation's vice and crime. Poverty means less education, less opportunity, and less participation in the general culture. And it means less ability to throw off the effects of past oppression. A Negro drug addict and ex-felon expresses the matter bluntly:

. . . a young kid growing up in Harlem, the only people he sees who have money are the pimps, the prostitutes, the people in the sporting world. So then maybe he go home and maybe his mother ain't working and he asks her for money and she ain't got none and maybe sometimes there ain't no food. Then he grows up and gets a job and all his money goes for rent and food and clothes. . . . You ain't got nothing. Then you see the sporting people and they seem always to have it, right in their pockets. A man got to be pretty strong to resist that temptation.

Furthermore, Negro Americans are often lonely, recent arrivals to huge metropolitan areas, strangers detached from their home moorings. Between 1950 and 1960, over one-and-a-half million Negroes left the South and came to cities in the North and West; others came to Southern cities from the farms. These migrants are frequently ill prepared for the demands of urban life, with only an inferior Southern rural education and few if any job skills. Consequently, they must fit onto the lowest rungs of the occupational ladder and hope for economic survival in an age when automation is dramatically reducing the number of jobs for unskilled workers. Small wonder such individuals come to view the world as a hostile place.

## FAMILY DISORGANIZATION AND PERSONALITY

Both poverty and migration also act to maintain the old slave pattern of a mother-centered family. Not only does desperate poverty disturb healthy family life through dilapidated housing, crowded living conditions, restricted recreational facilities, and direct contact with the most corrupting elements of urban disorganization, but it makes the ideal American pattern of household economics practically impossible. Employment discrimination has traditionally made it more difficult for the poorly-educated Negro male to secure steady employment than the poorly-educated Negro female. In many areas of the nation, North as well as South, this is still true, with Negro females always able to obtain jobs as domestics if nothing else is available. When the unskilled Negro male does manage to secure a job, he generally assumes an occupation that pays barely enough to support himself—much less a family. Such conditions obviously limit the ability of lower-class Negroes to follow the typical American pattern—that is, a stable unit with the husband providing a steady income for his family.

The Negro wife in this situation can easily become disgusted with her financially-dependent husband, and her rejection of him further alienates the male from family life. Embittered by their experiences with men, many Negro mothers often act to perpetuate the mother-centered pattern by taking a greater interest in their daughters than their sons. For example, more Negro females graduate from college than Negro males, the reverse of the pattern found among white Americans.

Family stability also suffers from the effects of migration, with its tensions over relocation and its release of the migrant from the sanctions of his home community. When all of these factors are considered, the prevalence of divorce, separation, and illegitimacy among poor Negroes should not come as a surprise. For when American society isolates the lower-class Negro from contact with the general norms and prevents him from sharing in the rewards which follow from abiding by these norms, it guarantees the emergence of a ghetto subculture with different standards of conduct, motivation, and family life.

Census data for 1960 illustrate the depth of this family disorganization among Negroes: over a third (34.3 per cent) of all non-white mothers with children under six years of age hold jobs as compared with less than a fifth (19.5 per cent) of white mothers with children under six; [7] only three-fourths (74.9 per cent) of all non-white families have both the husband and the wife present in the household as compared with nine-tenths (89.2 per cent) of white families; [8] and only two-thirds (66.3 per cent) of non-whites under eighteen years of age live with both of their parents as compared with nine-tenths (90.2 per cent) of such whites. These data do not cancel out the effects of social class differences between the two groups; rough comparisons between the lower classes of each race, however, still reveal a greater prevalence of father-absence among Negroes. The scar of slavery upon Negro family life, perpetuated through poverty and migration, is still evident.

Recent psychological research vividly demonstrates the personality effects upon children of having been raised in a disorganized home without a father. One such study reveals that eight-and-nine-year-old children whose fathers are absent seek immediate gratification far more than children whose fathers are present in the home. For example, when offered their choice of receiving a tiny candy bar immediately or a large bar a week later, fatherless children typically take the small bar while other children prefer to wait for the larger bar. This hunger for immediate gratification among fatherless children seems to have serious implications. Regardless of race, children manifesting this trait also tend to be less accurate in judging time, less "socially responsible," less oriented toward achievement, and more prone toward delinquency. Indeed, two psychologists maintain that the inability to delay gratification is a critical factor in immature, criminal, and neurotic behavior.[9]

Sex-role adoption is a second personality area which distinguishes children from intact homes from those in homes without fathers. One study found that five-to-fourteen-year-old Negro youths without fathers experienced unusual difficulty in differentiating between male and female roles. Thus, boys and girls without fathers described themselves in very similar ways, while boys from whole families described themselves in considerably more masculine terms than girls from whole families. Another investigation of high school students reported far sharper differences between the sexes in their values among white than among Negro children. This occurred primarily because the Negro girls revealed interests generally associated with males; compared with the white girls, they valued theoretical and political concerns more and religious and esthetic concerns less. Significantly, these Negro children more often came from families without fathers than did the white children.

Studies of white American boys whose fathers left them during World War II and of Norwegian boys whose sailor-fathers ship out for years at a time report related phenomena. These father-deprived boys are markedly more immature, submissive, dependent, and effeminate than other boys both in their overt behavior and fantasies. Eight-and-nine-year-old, father-absent Norwegian boys, for instance, when playing with self-representative dolls, put them in a crib rather than a bed. As they grow older, this passive behavior may continue, but, more typically, it is vigorously overcompensated for by exaggerated masculinity. Juvenile gangs, white and Negro, classically act out this pseudo-masculinity with leather jackets, harsh language, and physical "toughness."

The reasons for these characteristics of father-absent children seem clear. Negro girls in such families model themselves after their mothers and prepare to assume male as well as female responsibilities. And various investigations have demonstrated the crucial importance of the father in the socialization of boys. Mothers raising their children in homes without fathers are frequently overprotective, sometimes even smothering, in their compensatory attempts to be a combined father and mother. Burton and Whiting persuasively contend that the boys whose fathers are not present have initially identified with their mothers and must later, in America's relatively patrifocal society, develop a conflicting, secondary identification with males. In other words, they must painfully achieve a masculine self-image late in their childhood after having established an original self-image on the basis of the only parental model they have had—their mother.

Several studies point to the applicability of this sex-identity problem to lower-class Negro males. Two objective test assessments of widely different groups—Alabama jail prisoners and Wisconsin working-class veterans with tuberculosis—found that Negro males scored higher than white males on a measure of femininity. This measure is a part of the Minnesota Multiphasic Inventory (MMPI), a well-known psychological instrument that requires the respondent to judge the applicability to himself of over five hundred simple statements. Thus, Negroes in these samples generally agreed more often with such "feminine" choices as "I would like to be a singer" and "I think that I feel more intensely than most people do."

Psychiatrists have noted the prevalence of pseudo-masculine defenses among neurotic Negro male patients. And an investigation employing the personality-probing Thematic Apperception Test (TAT) with a representative national sample revealed Negro males to be unusually high in their need for social power and dominance. This need is apparently a compensatory reaction to their lowly role, for it, too, grows partly out of the broken home situation. The same study demonstrated that a strongly-felt need for power is a typical personality trait among men, Negro and white, raised by only one parent as opposed to men from intact homes. Finally, a survey of working-class Negroes in Boston matched 21 adult males whose fathers had been absent during their early childhoods, with 21 men who possessed similar social characteristics (age, income, education, region of birth, etc.), but whose fathers had been present during their early childhoods. Figure 2 illustrates the differences between these matched groups. The most critical distinction involves marriage; the first group of men was more likely to be either single or divorced—another manifestation of their disturbed sexual identification. They also felt more victimized, less in control of the environment, and more distrustful of others (Figure 2).

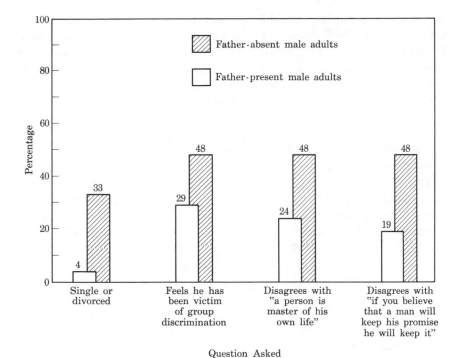

**Figure 2.** Father Absence and Adult Negro Personality
(Data from T. F. Pettigrew, "Father Absence and Negro Adult Personality: A
research note," unpublished paper.)

These findings reflect not only the effects of family disorganization but
also the effeminate aspects of the "Negro" role many of these men must play
in adult life. Servility is often required, and most low-paying service occupations typically open to unskilled Negro males—for example, cook, waiter,
orderly, dishwasher—generally carry a connotation in American culture of
being "women's work." Thus, the sex-identity problems created by the
fatherless home are perpetuated in adulthood.

Personality development of children in families without fathers may also
be related to three recurrent problems among Negro Americans: juvenile
delinquency, crimes against persons, and schizophrenia. More research is
necessary to link definitely these symptoms of social disorganization to
impaired family structure, but present data are most suggestive. In predict-
ing juvenile crime, Eleanor and Sheldon Glueck find that more delinquent
boys, when compared with non-delinquents, come from broken homes.
Other researchers, focusing upon the "good" boy in high delinquency neigh-

borhoods, note that such non-delinquents typically come from exceptionally stable, intact families. These boys think of themselves as "good" and score favorably on a personality measure of socialization. Family disorganization upsets this normal socializing influence of the home and creates the potential for juvenile delinquency. Community institutions such as the school and the church, which sometimes can help deter delinquent acts, simply do not possess the same meaning for unsocialized children from impaired families as they do for other children. In fact, one investigator finds that Negro delinquents tend to come from homes even more unstable than those of comparable white delinquents.

The findings connecting personal crime and schizophrenia with family structure are more tenuous. One ingenious study of a variety of non-literate societies throughout the world reveals that those with high rates of crime against persons are characterized by: mother-child households with inadequate opportunity to identify with the father; mother-child sleeping arrangements which foster a strong dependent relationship between the child and his mother; an abrupt and anxiety-producing preparation for independence; and a general distrustfulness of others (as in Figure 2). Perhaps personal crime is merely one aspect of the masculine façade which mother-raised boys tend to present as they enter "the man's world." Concerned about their sexual identity, they assert their masculinity through person-directed violence. In any event, this suggestive lead deserves further attention in research among Negro Americans. Likewise, a matrifocal situation, particularly a family composed of a strong mother and a present but weak father, seems to be positively related to schizophrenia. Since this pattern is common even among intact lower-class Negro families and this particular psychosis is especially prevalent among lower-class Negroes, future research along these lines is also indicated.

These considerations have led social scientists to emphasize the stability and structure of the home as crucial factors in counteracting the effects of racism upon Negro personality. A warm, supportive home can effectively compensate for many of the restrictions the Negro child faces outside of the ghetto; consequently, the type of home life a Negro enjoys as a child may be far more crucial for governing the influence of segregation upon his personality than the form the segregation takes—legal or informal, Southern or Northern. One psychologist maintains that full awareness of his social devaluation and role as a "Negro" does not usually impinge upon the individual until early adolescence. Just how the Negro bears up under this severe emotional stress is largely a function of the degree of ego-strength that has developed in his earlier, family-centered years. The ego-strong Negro, nurtured in a stable and complete family, may come out of this stressful encounter harboring some self-hatred, but he generally manages to dissociate his basic personality from his socially-defined role of "Negro." He maintains his self-respect as a unique and worthwhile human being apart from the position of inferior being that the racists insist he assume. As one elderly Negro candidly expressed it, "Being a Negro is no disgrace, but it sure is an inconvenience."

By contrast, the "psychologically vulnerable" Negro, crippled by weak ego development from earlier family disorganization, is more likely to fall prey to mental illness, drug addiction, or crime, depending on his particular life history. He has few personality resources to withstand the gale winds of discrimination that strike him full force in adolescence. Thus, segregation has its most fundamental influence on Negro personality in the manner in which it affects Negro family functioning.

Case studies bear out these contentions. In their psychoanalytic investigation of 25 Negroes, *The Mark of Oppression,* Kardiner and Ovesey studied "O. D.," a twenty-nine-year-old, lower-class male. Although he was a trained automobile mechanic, O. D. had been forced by the usual pattern of employment discrimination to take a series of poorly-paid service jobs with their typically effeminate features—dishwasher, short order cook, and hospital orderly. His mother had been warm yet strict, but he had never known a stable father-figure during his poor, and sometimes hungry, childhood. As an adult, O.D. had substituted an aggressive, educated wife for his mother and had become very dependent upon her. Also consistent with the father-deprived personality pattern were his serious difficulties in adopting a masculine role; he suffered from problems of sexual impotency and an almost complete inability to express anger. The case of O. D. offers an example of a lower-class Negro who, made "psychologically vulnerable" by an impaired family background, expressed his serious personality difficulties in sexual disturbance.

The case studies of New Orleans Negroes conducted by Rohrer and his associates provide further examples. This research consisted of a re-examination of individuals who, as children nearly two decades earlier, had served as subjects for a pioneer study of Negro personality, published as *Children of Bondage.* Again the devastating personality scars rendered by the absence of fathers in matrifocal family life were apparent in many of the lower-class Negroes. Girls raised in such households tended as adults to establish similar households for themselves and to live either with or very close to their mothers. Boys from this background evidenced the familiar pattern of conflict over sexual identity. Many of them as youths had joined gangs of older boys and acted out this conflict within the gang in the form of compulsive masculine behavior. "The gang member," conclude the investigators, "re-

jects this femininity in every form, and he sees it in women and in effeminate men, in laws and morals and religion, in schools and occupational
striving." This blanket rejection by gang members of the values and institutions of society is obviously not likely to lead to an ambitious struggle
out of the lower class. In fact, such alienation often leads directly into a
life of crime, drug addiction, and deep despair.

## "THE SELF-FULFILLING PROPHECY"

If, like these gang members, you believe the world to be a hostile place,
you will probably act in such a manner as to cause the world to become
in fact hostile toward you. In this sense, a person's own beliefs about a
social situation can contribute to shaping the situation. Such beliefs, then,
are "self-fulfilling prophecies."

This phenomenon of social interaction is often crucially important in the
exacerbation of the Negro's "marks of oppression." The compliant Negro's
behavior may serve both to "prove" the racists' contentions and to heighten
and make more serious the personality scars inflicted by being classified
and treated as an "inferior." A vicious circle can thus be established: the
deeper the scars from discrimination, the more in keeping with the discrimination is the Negro's behavior, the greater the reinforcement of the
discriminatory pattern, and thus the deeper the scars.

This vicious circle can be broken only by "outside" influences. Economic
and political forces can restructure the discriminatory situation; new experiences, formal education, and the mass media can change the participants
directly. These influences weaken the discriminatory pattern and begin a
benign circle of allowing the scars of oppression to heal. And once these
scars begin to heal, once the Negro gains a new image of himself and the
situation, he can initiate change himself and further accelerate the self-
correcting benign circle.

## THE ROLE AND ITS BURDENS

"Suffering which falls to our lot in the course of nature, or by chance,
or fate," commented Schopenhauer, "does not seem so painful as suffering
which is inflicted on us by the arbitrary will of another." This sage observation has special force for Negro Americans. And the evidence reviewed in
this chapter suggests that much of their "painful suffering" has been medi-
ated through two social processes: the inferior role of "Negro" and severe
family disorganization.

Being a Negro in America is less of a racial identity than a necessity to
adopt a subordinate social role. The effects of playing this "Negro" role
are profound and lasting. Evaluating himself by the way others react to him,
the Negro may grow into the servile role; in time, the person and the role

become indistinguishable. The personality consequences of this situation can be devastating—confusion of self-identity, lowered self-esteem, perception of the world as a hostile place, and serious sex-role conflicts.

By no means all Negro Americans succumb to these problems. Those reared in stable, accepting families generally develop the psychological resources to withstand the most debilitating aspects of the "Negro" role. But racial discrimination, from the time of slavery to the present, creates a type of family disorganization which causes many Negroes to be especially vulnerable to the role's full effects. The absence of the father in a sizable minority of Negro homes is particularly critical for personality development. Socialization without the agency of the father may be an important contributor to three persistent problems—juvenile delinquency, crime against persons, and schizophrenia. These, then, are the bitter fruits of racial prejudice and discrimination.

## NOTES

[1] Psychotherapists have long utilized this process in "psycho drama" and other clinical techniques. Recently, social psychologists have subjected the process to intensive laboratory investigation in their study of attitude-change.

[2] The studies cited in Footnote 1 either required a single public presentation orally of a position counter to that held by the subject or a written essay counter to the subject's opinion. Yet all of them demonstrated significant shifts in opinion.

[3] Mass media stereotypes of minority group members are currently becoming more favorable.

[4] The Clarks' work was prominently cited in the famous Footnote 11 of the United States Supreme Court 1954 public school desegregation ruling.

[5] A similar perception of the world as a hostile and threatening place has been noted among Arabs who were establishing themselves in cities and who were at the time being treated as an inferior minority group by the French.

[6] One important psychological difference did exist, however, between the two situations. After the first generation of slaves in America, Negroes were born into slavery and had never experienced any other condition of life. Jews, by contrast, had known the life of free men prior to their internment by the Nazis.

[7] During 1950, 35 per cent of all non-white mothers under forty-five years of age held jobs compared with 19 per cent of similarly-aged white mothers.

[8] The vast majority of incomplete Negro households is lacking the husband. Frazier estimated in 1950 that the male parent was missing in roughly 20 per cent of Negro households. In addition to divorce and separation, part of this phenomenon is due to a higher Negro male death rate. The percentage of widows among Negro women fifty-four years old or less is roughly twice that of white women.

[9] Contributing to this situation is the fact that where fathers are not present children more often have the additional stigma of being illegitimate. Although illegitimacy is more naturally accepted in lower-class Negro culture, careful research reveals better school and personal "adjustment" among legitimate Negro children.

*The essay by Abram Kardiner and Lionel Ovesey from
their noted book,* The Mark of Oppression, *explores
the aspects of a problem raised by Pettigrew and
Herskovits in their essays and treated extensively in the*
Moynihan Report. *That problem is the origin of the
matriarchal family group of American Blacks and
whether it constitutes a survival of West African practice
(as Herskovits suggests) or is a product of the
systematic degradation of the Black male and the sexual
utility and relative occupational success of the Black
female. Kardiner and Ovesey tend to come out on
the side of Pettigrew and, like Moynihan, relate the
so-called "uterine family" to a dysfunctional pattern
of socialization in Black families.*

# The Social Environment of the Negro [1]

## Abram Kardiner and Lionel Ovesey

### I. THE HISTORICAL BACKGROUND OF SLAVERY

For our purposes, the African background of the Negro is of importance only with regard to the extent that his aboriginal culture survived in
his new habitat. There is a good deal of difference of opinion on this subject.
Two authorities, Herskovits,[2] and Frazier,[3] differ widely in their interpretation. There is little doubt that vestigial remains of aboriginal African culture
have survived into the present. Herskovits believes that African survivals
can be discovered in almost every phase of current Negro life. This is undoubtedly a great exaggeration. The Negroes came from widely scattered
areas of the West Coast of Africa. There may even have been, and probably
was, some similarity in the institutions of the various aboriginal tribes. However, there is every reason to believe that the conditions of slavery were such
that no aboriginal culture could survive the impact. This is the position of
Frazier, and also our own. If there were survivals, they would have to be
in areas that lie outside the main problems of human adaptation. We can
assume that art forms, musical idioms, and the like can long survive in the
new environment. Even religion can do so—but only for a while.

This issue of origins and survivals is of some consequence because there

From Abram Kardiner and Lionel Ovesey, *The Mark of Oppression* (Cleveland:
World Publishing Co., 1968), pp. 39–47.

are anthropologists who insist that many features of Negro life in America are what they are because they represent survivals of African culture. This is claimed to be especially true of the uterine family (a mother-child unit in the absence of the father), which is supposed to be common in West Africa. We propose to show that the present state of the Negro family structure is a function of the social adaptation of the Negro in America and not an aboriginal survival.

The basic issue in this question is whether ways of living have an adaptive function or whether they exist irrespective of such function. We can point to many features of our own institutional structure that are functionally useless, yet, nevertheless, persist. This would seem to upset the assumption that all institutions have an adaptive function. Some of these institutions in our culture, which have outlived their usefulness, are either given new explanations, or no explanations at all are given, for no one knows what the original function was. In other words, it is the way it is because it has always been that way. Such an answer merely begs the question because of ignorance. In the case of the uterine family, such as it is, we are on much safer ground. We find it limited in the Negro to the lower classes. This means, in effect, that the pull, when possible, is toward the middle classes with their orthodox American family structure. The so-called uterine family is not institutionalized, but the accidental end product of transient socio-economic conditions. The father deserts because his masculine prerogatives are undermined by the inability to find consistent and gainful employment.

The most conspicuous feature of the Negro in America is *that his aboriginal culture was smashed,* be it by design or accident. The importance of this basic fact for the Negro in America cannot be overestimated. It means, in effect, that the old types of social organization and all their derivatives could not continue, but a new type of emergent adjustment derived from the new conditions would have to be established. This kind of situation has arisen many times in human history. The incentives for such emergent changes in adaptation are usually the inadequacy of the environment in which the group finds itself. The movement of the Comanche Indians from the plateau to the plains was caused by such exhaustion of the adaptive possibilities in the old environment. This led to the attempt to make a fresh start in a new one. This is an example of a voluntary change of environment to improve the living conditions of the group.

The Negro did not come to America under such circumstances. It was not necessity that brought him here, but a forced transportation against his will. Also, for the greater part, his communication with other slaves was limited by the conditions of slavery. In other words, when we say that Negro culture was destroyed, we are implying three things: (1) that the old types of organization were rendered useless; (2) that the minimal conditions for maintaining a culture, or for developing a new one, were lacking; and (3) that his adoption of American culture was, by the same token, limited. Hence, the term *acculturation* cannot be applied to the Negro, at least not during slavery.

This raises an important question, What are the minimal conditions for the continuation of a culture? They are as follows:

(1) Its constituents must be able to survive in sufficient numbers to be able to propagate.

(2) The institutions must have a functional relevance to the problems that confront the group. For example, the old Tanala [4] culture was smashed by the exhaustion of dry rice and the necessity for seeking valleys for wet rice cultivation. Here the family organization could not continue because it was unsuited to the new environment. The resultant family breakdown had far-reaching consequences.

(3) The relations between the various statuses in the society—age, sex, and social role—must be able to continue in such a way that mutual aggression and antagonism do not disrupt essential cooperation.

(4) Minimal instinctual satisfaction must be permitted each constituent to preserve a workable balance between frustration and gratification. Otherwise, the comfort and the effectiveness of the constituents are destroyed.

(5) Each constituent must be permitted minimal access to participation in the whole culture. A caste system destroys this to a large measure.

(6) Emotional reciprocal interaction between each other must be permitted the various constituents. This is also destroyed by a caste system.

In the light of these criteria, we can compare the Negro under slavery with the Ghetto Jew. The latter did not have his culture destroyed, but rather the whole culture was transplanted to a new environment—the Ghetto. Full participation in his own culture inside the Ghetto was permitted the Jew, but only limited participation in the master culture outside of it. Family organization, religion, tradition could continue unchanged. The ideals of the group were drawn from traditional sources, and the ideals of accomplishment were drawn from the intrinsic culture. The master culture in which the Ghetto was located was treated with disdain, and its ideals were rejected. The subservient position the group had to the master culture was, to a good measure, canceled out by the exaggerated value of the intrinsic culture. The extrinsic culture was "foreign." It was this contrast that kept the culture of the Jews alive for two thousand years.

The case of the Negro was completely different from that of the Jew.

There was not only limited participation in the extrinsic culture, but this could only take place by identification with the master's status. In other words, participation was vicarious—through the agency of another person. Moreover, slavery destroyed the intrinsic culture by depriving the old institutions of functional relevance and by destroying the functional interaction of various statuses. All of the latter were leveled to one status, that of a vested interest belonging to someone else. Minimal instinctual gratification had to be permitted to preserve the utility of the slave, but much of his comfort and effectiveness were destroyed. Reciprocal action between members of the intrinsic group (slave) was extremely limited, and with the extrinsic group (master) was completely absent. There was also another disrupting feature: one of the statuses—the female—had more participation with the extrinsic group through her value as a sexual object and as a mother surrogate. This was immediately better for the female, but it sowed seeds for a serious disruptive influence in the intrinsic group.

## II. THE PSYCHOLOGY OF SLAVERY

We can best begin our discussion on the psychology of slavery by describing several types of human relationships: (1) to a machine; (2) to a domesticated animal; (3) to a slave; and (4) to an equal.

The relationship to a machine is governed entirely by *utility*. The machine is created by man to serve a specific utilitarian end, and if it is effective, a high degree of dependency can be attached to it. It then becomes an extension of some organ of man—of a foot, hand, eye, ear. An automobile is an extension of the foot, used for transportation; a lathe is an extension of the hand; a telescope an extension of the eye, a radio an extension of the ear, etc. A simple tool like a hammer needs no attention other than to use it when necessary; when not needed, the tool has no existence and has only a potential utility. In the case of more complex tools, like an automobile, the properties of the apparatus must be maintained in good condition to keep the potential utility in constant readiness. This means that the conditions for functioning must be preserved: it must be oiled, parts must be replaced, etc. The greater the care bestowed to preserve this potential utility, the greater the effective utility will be. However, regardless of the amount of care devoted to the machine, it cannot be said to have *needs* to which the owner must respond. A machine has no needs; it has only conditions under which it will function.

The relationship of man to a domesticated animal, such as a horse, is quite like that to a machine, but with one exception: an animal has *needs* and not merely conditions—like oiling—for effectiveness. Food, for example, is a condition for effectiveness, as well as a need. But sexual appetite in a horse is a *need* without qualification. This need can interfere with the utility value of the animal. Hence, what man does to the animal is to castrate it, thus obviating any interference from that source to its utility. There is thus no opportunity for the animal to influence his master except where the utility of the animal is concerned.

The relation of a man to a slave is quite the same as to a horse, and yet there are important differences. It is the same, insofar as the prime objective is to exploit the utility value of the slave, and to perpetuate the conditions which favor his maximum utility. All other conditions for cultural existence are ignored or prevented by force. It would have been uneconomical to castrate the male Negroes, because in permitting propagation, his utility was greatly enhanced, notwithstanding the time lost by the females to bear the infants and pay a minimal amount of attention to them. In order to carry out the program of maximum utility of the slave, it was necessary to suppress all cultural practices which were injurious to utility and permit only those over which no control could be exercised.

Thus, physiological needs, including sexual activity, would have to be satisfied. Entertainment of the kind the slaves could create among themselves, while at work or after, could be permitted. But a family organization, either of the kind to which they were accustomed in their native habitat, or like that of the whites, could not be permitted. Thus, the only permissible kind of family organization would be one that would not interfere with utility. This set of conditions prescribes in a large measure what kind of family organization was possible. Neither paternity nor permanent marriage could be recognized, for this would interfere with the free mobility of the slave for sale purposes.

The chief conclusion that emerges from these considerations is that *reciprocity of feeling* between master and slave was destroyed. There was no possibility for emotional interchange. If a slave was sick, he would be treated like a sick horse, to restore his utility. The rage or protest of the slave could be *ignored* or treated with violence. The only really effective form of protest was *flight*.

Communication between slaves could not be completely destroyed, but its effectiveness could be impaired by the limited opportunities for concerted action. However, organized revolts and flight could and did take place, but never on a scale that permanently benefited the status of the slave. The forces arrayed against him were too great.

The relation between equals is characterized by complete emotional reciprocity. There is no barrier between identification of equals capable of mutual influence. For example, the anger of one party will influence the overt behavior and emotional tone of the other party. The latter is free to register his protest. Reconciliation is possible between equals, but not necessarily submission. If there is submission, it is of a voluntary and not of a coercive kind. In large groups of equals, the reciprocal influence is maintained by certain *conventions*. For example, property rights are largely a convention among equals; their force is maintained by mutual support of the conventions, and the invocation of commonly ordained agencies of enforcement, should one of the parties violate the convention. This is effected through police and courts of law. Reciprocity is also extended among equals to all forms of positive affects, such as love, sexual union among the sexes, marriage, friendship, and the like. Reciprocity of feeling also involves the convention of access to conviction. One can argue with a friend or a fellow citizen in the attempt to get his consent to common action. He is not forced or commanded.

If *culture* is the name for the collective methods or patterns of social adaptation, then it follows that whatever culture or cultures the Negroes had to start with could not survive under these new conditions, except in the form of fragmentary remnants. As regards the *new* culture in which the slave found himself, this was forced upon him. But, even here, he could only adopt those features of the culture in which he was permitted limited participation. He was thus obliged to learn the new language and adopt a new religion, which was not evolved out of his old cultural conditions, but was foisted on him as a new credo, with no bearing—except in one detail to be discussed below—on his current problem of adaptation.

One cannot, therefore, speak of a new Negro culture that would spring up emergently from the new stipulations for living. The conditions of slavery were such that they not only destroyed the possibility of reciprocal interaction between master and slave, but, in a large measure, free emotional interaction between slaves was seriously impaired. No *culture* can arise under these limitations.

The fate of the Negro family under slavery is a case in point. Marriage was not recognized; paternity was not recognized. Offspring became the property of whoever owned the *mother*. The child-mother relationship had to be respected, at least until the utility potential of the child was realized, i.e. until the child was able to work, and, therefore, had a sale value. The biological father had no social significance, whether he was white or colored. There were, however, exceptions to this. White fathers occasionally did recognize and care for offspring from Negro mistresses. On the whole, marriage between Negroes was a loose arrangement without mutual obligations. However, slaveowners did recognize the fact that the cohesion of the slave group was greater where the family was allowed to remain intact, and that flight was commonest where the families were broken up.

This takes us to a feature of slavery, which altered the relations between white and Negro, and that is the relation of the white male to the Negro female. This could not be confined to the domain of pure utility, as it was with the male. The Negro female did have the opportunity for more emotional interaction with white masters by virtue of her sexual attractiveness. This can never be confined within the limits of *utility*. A white master (or his son) could become attached emotionally to his Negro mistress. He could care for his Negro offspring and could discriminate in their favor, or free them.

A second function of the Negro female, commonly underestimated, is the role of the Negro nursemaid. Here the attachment of the growing child to the Negro mammy could have become very strong indeed, and even predispose the white male to a predilection for the Negro woman as a sexual object. There is little question that the Negro female was attractive to the white male for mating purposes. The universality of laws prohibiting marriage of whites and Negroes is an eloquent testimonial to this fact. These two features, the sexual usefulness of the female and her role as a mammy, could only have the effect of increasing the white man's fear of the Negro male, her rightful mate and legitimate possessor. This could not help but lead to the fantastic exaggeration in the white man's mind of the Negro male's sexual prowess. And this, in turn, would necessitate more repressive measures against the Negro male—all caused by the white man's guilt and anxiety. The necessity to "protect" the white female against this fancied prowess of the male Negro thus became a fixed constellation in the ethos of the South.

It is easy to see from this discussion what the destruction of a *culture* means. The most rudimentary type of family organization was not permitted to survive, to say nothing of the extensions of the family. The mother-child family with the father either unknown, absent, or, if present, incapable of wielding influence, was the only type of family that could survive in the new environment. This is known as the *uterine family,* and it is this type of family that is supposed to be common in the native African habitat of the Negro. Hence, it is regarded by some as a cultural *survival*. This is not the case. No matter what the type of family organization was in Africa—it was an institutionalized type. Under the conditions of slavery, the uterine family was not institutionalized, but incidental to a host of conditions that held priority of claim.

The effects of the uterine family could, however, be enduring. There would be created a definite type of emotional relationship of mother-child, father-child, and of the siblings toward each other. These constellations, of course, would be of quite a different order than those created by the patriarchal family organization of Western culture. Let us track down the effects of the emotional patterns that prevailed in the Negro family.

The mother-child relationship must have been affected because the care the mother could give the child was limited. White children had priority, if the mother was a nursemaid or a mammy; if, in addition, she worked in the fields, she then could devote little or no time to her own children. The effects of this on the development of affectivity, or emotional potential, are well known. They are inevitably diminished.[5]

However, in comparison with the mother, the father image suffered a great deal more. It must not be forgotten that the white man's culture was *male-oriented*. In contrast, the anonymity or continuous absence of the father made the mother the central and focal point of the Negro family. The father could not be idealized as protector and provider, for he was neither. The mother could be idealized to a certain extent, and this is what actually happened. Thus, greater and more protracted proximity to the mother, together with her protective role, rendered her the central point of orientation in the family. In the lower classes this orientation still persists, and has been reinforced by conditions which perpetuated the higher status and prestige of the Negro female after emancipation.

Nor can it be overlooked that under conditions of slavery, it was the *white master,* who, despite his role as exploiter and persecutor, was also protector. And it was in this role that the white owner became an idealized, though hated figure. This idealization enhanced the adaptation of the Negro to the slave status. It strongly reinforced his unconscious perception of the white man's power. The identification of the Negro with his master was facilitated by the difference in status between house slaves and field slaves, the former being more desirable. The competition and mutual hatred of field and house slaves did not help the Negroes as a group.

The psychological effects of the slave status on the individual were probably very complex; but a few features of this adaptation can be inferred with certainty:

(1) Degradation of self-esteem.
(2) Destruction of cultural forms and forced adoption of foreign culture traits.
(3) Destruction of the family unit, with particular disparagement of the male.
(4) Relative enhancement of the female status, thus making her the central figure in the culture, by virtue of her value to the white man for sexual ends and as mammy to the white children.

(5) The destruction of social cohesion among Negroes by the inability to have their own culture.

(6) The idealization of the white master; but with this ideal was incorporated an object which was at once revered and hated. These became incompatible constituents of the Negro personality.

Can anything be said about the slave status that was favorable from the adaptational point of view? Only one thing. There was an absence of strong pressure on the individual to achieve status, a feature that was very conspicuous in the white man's culture. When status is frozen, one cannot successfully direct one's aspirations toward goals that are beyond the possibility of attainment. Some inner peace can be achieved by ceasing to struggle for it. The adaptation of the slave was essentially by a process of passivity. Such adaptation can be at least partially effective, provided that all instinctual needs are satisfied—particularly hunger and sex.

Another compensatory feature of slavery was the vicarious participation in the culture through identification with the master. The slave could get some prestige by belonging to a wealthy or influential household. This, together with the gradations of status between field and domestic slaves, laid the base for status differentiation between Negroes. Gradations of color became a fixed method of determining status which persists to this day. In conclusion, it need hardly be said that the disadvantages of the slave state so far outweighed the advantages, that any comparison is ludicrous.

## NOTES

[1] The authors do not intend this chapter to be a summary of the vast literature dealing with the subject, and certainly not a substitute for it. The works of Frazier and Myrdal are still standard in this field. We have included the statement that follows rather as a text for discussion than as an exhaustive account of the Negro's social environment.

[2] Herskovits, Melville, *The Myth of the Negro Past,* Harper, 1942.

[3] Frazier, E. Franklin, *The Negro in the United States,* The Macmillan Company, 1949.

[4] Ralph Linton in Kardiner, A., *The Individual and His Society,* Columbia University Press, 1939.

[5] *See* Kardiner, *op. cit.*

*The final contribution in this section is a remarkable*
*speech made by Edward A. Johnson in 1932 at the*
*annual meeting of the Association for the Study of Negro*
*Life and History. It is remarkable in the sense that it is*
*both militant and despairing. Johnson rhetorically asks*
*the Black Americans why they did not resist enslavement*
*but seems to infer that the time for effective resistance*
*is past. He looks, instead, for the salvation of the Black*
*races to Africa where the blight of slavery, in his*
*analysis, did not erode pride and self-esteem.*

# Is Not the African Negro Undergoing
# a More Desirable Development
# Than the American Negro?

## Edward A. Johnson

Development here may be considered improvement along different
lines, as usually relates to the progress of a group of people educationally,
economically and spiritually. In the first place, the African Negro has a
better spiritual background than the American Negro: that is, dating back
from the advent of the American Negro into America when he lost his
African contact. While the Negroes' two hundred and fifty years in America
has served to give them training in education and industry, and helped them
to accumulate considerable property, yet this hiatus in his African and
American existence has served to develop a certain inferiority complex that
differentiates the American Negro from the African. The African seems to
feel himself equal to any other man on earth, and brooks no superior. He
shows this in his actions and in his talk while the American Negro has had
instilled into him a subserviency that has almost made of him a defeatist
who by his acts and talk does not consider himself the equal of other men.

The American Negro, however, is an equal among his fellows and
brooks no superior among them. He accepts much from the white man that
he will not accept from one of his own race. Bad treatment from a white
man may be constantly imposed and soon forgotten while the same treatment from a colored man would be instantly resented and long remembered.

An address delivered at the Annual Meeting of the Association for the Study of Negro
Life and History in Atlanta, Georgia, November 16, 1932. From *Journal of Negro
History*, Vol. XVIII (1933), pp. 71–77.

Statistics show that the Negroes of Atlanta and other Negro centers of population commit 80% of the murders; and 70% of these murders are killings of Negroes by Negroes. The American Negro, along economic lines, has developed a hostility to his compatriots of color to the extent that he reluctantly gives him his patronage in business or in the trades and professions. The Negro doctor, the Negro dentist, and the Negro undertaker have conquered this prejudice to a great extent in communities where there are either no such white professional and business men, or where the whites refuse to serve them. The Negro in religion has long ago tabooed the white minister. He will not allow him the privilege of caring for his spiritual affairs. The white lawyer may give him a deed to his land on earth, but the white minister cannot give him the deed to the promised land above. He will trust the white man to draw his will, to dispose of his earthly possessions. But a white minister cannot give him a ticket to his heavenly abode or advice as to the disposition of his soul.

The American Negro has developed a number of undesirable traits during his existence in this country that seem not to be characteristic of his African brother, and it would appear that he has very much to unlearn that he has too well learned in America, if he is to be lifted to the level with his African brother. In the first place, it is very probable that physically the American Negroes, both among women and men, are not equal to the African. This may be due to natural causes resulting from a change from a nomadic and free and easy life in the tropics, to a North Temperate Zone where the hazards against health are more pronounced and have developed many diseases and ailments characteristic of this zone. The native African, however, who comes in contact with the white traders and adventurers along the coast region of Africa are showing signs of contracting many of the diseases characteristic of the people who live in the North Temperate Zones. They have not only taken on many of the diseases of the white man, but many of his vices. This is noticeable to travelers along the coast region and stands out in contrast to the condition of things in the hinterland where the white man has not penetrated to any great extent, and the African remains in his accustomed habits and ways.

The American Negro has been subjected to a long list of treatments and conditions during his American existence such as relegating him to the back alleys and streets along the railroads and river banks, and giving him for a long time no schools at all, and, since schools were established, segregating him in a system with inferior provisions for maintenance and development.

As he has been discriminated against in educational matters so he has been thwarted in his development in the industrial sphere. It is said that he is the "last to be hired and the first to be fired." His wage scale is also generally less than that of other fellows. In the effort to earn a living, then, the Negro is under considerable handicaps.

Usually, too, the colored community in America is neglected by political officials of the city or village, and the disposition is to allow their sanitation and ordinary civic affairs to go neglected. This may be due to the fact that the Negro is not a political factor in the election of many of these municipal functionaries, who, therefore, do not recognize them as voters. The voter, if he is white, obtains recognition while the non-voter, who may be of Negro descent, is not thus considered. In many instances the Negroes do not vote where they have the opportunity and might thus exercise some influence in their own political development. This fault is in their own "dear stars." The ballot was intended as a defense against such things, and the man, white or black, who is so inept as to not use it, has himself to blame.

The American Negro's development has been limited within certain lines. He stands like some caged bird in an acre of space enclosed. He may move around inside of the enclosure and fly from tree to tree and from post to post, and he can feel free to a certain extent in doing so; but when he gets out of the cage or enclosure, public sentiment requires that he be taught that he has a place, and must go back or must be put back and there remain. This decree of public sentiment may be called the unwritten law in reference to the American Negro. No such unwritten law applies in Africa in the sense that we refer to. And it is not strange that the American Negro in two hundred and fifty years of such restriction, should to some extent, develop an inferiority complex and become a defeatist.

There were at the close of the Civil War when the Negroes emerged from slavery into freedom many laws restricting his freedom in citizenship. For instance, the colored man could not bear arms in self defense, one of the special privileges of the United States Constitution. He could not give testimony in the courts where a white person's interest was involved. He could not sit on juries, and he could not hold land. These provisions, however, being part of the Black Code of Reconstruction, were finally expunged from the statutes and, so far as the law now reads, a Negro is on an equality with all other citizens of the republic. But this is not all. While the Black Codes were not allowed to exist because of the passage of new laws in their stead, yet, there has developed an unwritten law or custom which dominates and controls in every community. For instance, although a policeman in Mooneville he cannot go into the parks; and, on the other hand, although permitted to go into the parks in Sunville, he cannot be a policeman. In other words, custom runs a zigzag course. His privileges as a citizen are controlled by customs in the community in which he lives. Some are very drastic and

others are less so. The harshness of the custom is the barometer of the
religion of the white people of the section. The Negro is the victim of whatever custom or imposition or favor that the dominant sentiment of the
community in which he lives dictates. And to a great extent the American
Negro has modified or increased the harshness of this custom by either submitting to it or refusing to conform thereto. Usually the custom prefers an
Uncle Tom Negro, and if the mass of the colored people of the community
accept a position of Uncle Tom, they get Uncle Tom treatment. If they
resist, other consequences may follow.

The American brand of Negro is somewhat of a putty man, which is
indigenous perhaps to the American soil. He "stays put." If he is given
the vote, he votes to some extent. If it is taken away from him, he does not
vote and makes little to do about it. If he has no school or the school fund
is misappropriated as it has been in many cases, then he contents himself
without the school. He seems to enjoy following Paul's advice "to be content
in whatever lot he is placed." It is even alleged that, in the District of Columbia, the Capital of the Nation, where the laws are made and the president
resides, the school fund is divided unequally—the Negro with twenty-six
per cent of the population getting only nineteen per cent of the school fund.
We could give figures to cover many other places and communities with the
same disproportion in the division of the school fund. It is said even that
we got only three hundred and forty thousand dollars out of six million
and a half dollars appropriated by the National government for schools,
when as a matter of fact we, with one tenth of the population, ought to
receive one tenth of the six million and a half so appropriated.

From the foregoing we may observe to some extent what kind of development the American Negro has undergone during his existence in this country, and it is seriously to be considered whether or not such a scheme of
development as the American Negro has received should be imposed upon
his brethren in Africa. The training of a people consists in giving them something else besides schools and churches. The idea of giving the Negro a full
dose of religion minus Christianity seems to predominate among certain
of the white church organizations that are fostering mission schools in
Africa. The idea seems to be to save the soul after death rather than preserve both soul and body before death. Millions for soul saving, but only
a few pennies for man saving, in spite of the fact that forty years ago the
question arose in the Presbyterian board for examining foreign missionaries
as to whether or not there was probation for the African soul after death.

We might remark here that there never was a time when the American
Negro could not get a larger donation for a church than for anything else
and the African seems to be fed out of the same altruistic spoon smelted

especially for his benefit—all out of a misconceived idea of many white religionists as to what is good for any others than themselves. If the African is being trained *a la Americana,* as seems to be true in many instances, and as also seems to be devoutedly wished by many, then in two hundred and fifty years from now we expect him to arrive at the same stage of development of the American Negro, that is, reducing his illiteracy ninety-eight per cent after the Civil War to twenty-five per cent at present and bringing up his accumulations from practically nothing then to about two billions now, but in spite of this still remaining as an untouchable pariah in the make up of the American ethical placements.

The African owing to his background and freedom from many of the American Negroes' subserviency handicaps may not become molded into the same sort of individual as his American brother in the course of time by undergoing the same treatment. Let us hope that the ability of the African to employ mass action may gain him more in the future than the American Negro has gotten from his regimen of diet tossed over to him by pseudo-religious-political sentiment seemingly agreed upon as best fitted for his non-absorbable existence in the American plan of citizenship, and which has practically kneaded most of the American Negro's mass action out of his aspirations.

The American Negro's failure to develop mass action has caused him to lose much that he otherwise might have. He has developed, however, an overwhelming propensity for mass action in social, lodge and church affairs. He can easily grope all night at hard work for a social function, or march all day in a parade, but it seems difficult for him to cooperate for his educational, economic and political welfare. The same effort is being made to prevent mass action among the Africans as was made to prevent it among American Negroes. Africa is divided up among the different nations of Europe, and the control of the natives is, therefore, in the hands of these nations that hold sovereignity over them, but the Africans are learning that their best interest lies in hanging together, to prevent, as Benjamin Franklin would say, "their hanging separately."

Harking back to Jamestown when the twenty Negro slaves landed there in 1619 some one wonders why they did not hang together and resist enslavement. It had been sought to enslave the poor whites of this colony, but they took themselves to the hills and mountains. It was also sought to enslave the Indians and make them do the work and thus avoid the period known as the "starving time," but the Indians said something to John Smith and the "F.F.V.'s" of Virginia that sounded something like "Oh yeah?" They did not work, but grabbed a tomahawk. It was left to the twenty Negroes and their descendants to do the work and save the colony. Whitfield wrote from Bethesda colony in South Carolina, "For the Lord's sake, send us more Negroes, for one Negro has produced more in a year than 150 whites." With the African slaves, then, came the bread winners, and their numbers increased until by new arrivals and multiplication of those who had already come, the number reached approximately four million at the end of the Civil War. The whites fed them on religion and told them about the paved streets and golden slippers of the new Jerusalem and how it all might be theirs if they would obey Paul's advice, saying, "Servants, be obedient unto your masters." The Jamestown slaves and their descendants looked into the good book provided for them by their masters and taking the master's interpretation of the word said it must be so because the Bible says so. With their eyes on the great expanse of the ocean lying between them and their African homeland and with shackles and the lash waiting their disobedience to the rule of their new environment they philosophically, perhaps mistakenly, adopted the white man's idea of scriptural interpretation instead of interpreting the word to suit themselves. The African is not being developed along these lines, and this bespeaks for him a more substantial progress in manhood rights in the future than his American brother has attained during the past.

# CHAPTER

# 7

# INDEPENDENT AFRICA
# AND EMERGING BLACK AMERICA

The encounter between Americans of African descent
and Africa and its people is often an emotional
experience with widely varying results. Some Afro-
Americans come away from the experience with a
profound realization of the differences which separate
them, as Americans, from Africa and Africans. Other
Black Americans embrace Africa as their homeland
and identify themselves with its fate. Between
disillusionment and cultural conversion, however, there
is a vast area. The experiences of the Crossroads
Africa volunteers, described by Harold Isaacs, shows
how one group responded. But Africa, embraced or
rejected, is of momentous consequence to a people in
search of identity. The point is forcefully made in the
essay by Charles E. Silberman.

*Charles E. Silberman, an editor for* Fortune *Magazine,*
*contributes the following chapter from his 1964 book,*
Crisis in Black and White. *In this selection, he considers*
*the history of Africa, the distortion of the Black past,*
*and the necessity for the Afro-American to restore and*
*recapture it.*

# Lost and Found: Africa and the Negro Past

## Charles E. Silberman

*1*

Most discussions of Malcolm X and the Black Muslims have seen
them as a threat to the white community. Certainly the danger of violence,
inspired by Malcolm or led by him, can't be discounted, particularly if the
white reaction to Negro advances itself takes the form of violence, as it has
in Mississippi and Alabama, and to a lesser and more sporadic degree, in
Philadelphia and Chicago and other Northern cities. While the number of
Muslim members is small and static, there are many "fellow travelers" who
may be attracted by Malcolm's movement, and there is every reason to
believe that Negro anger and impatience will increase rather than diminish
in the next several years.

But the Muslims represent a much greater threat to the leaders of the
Negro community and to that community's dominant institutions, for their
existence bears testimony to these leaders' failure, thus far, to capture the
imagination and allegiance of their constituents. Even more, the Muslims'
success in transforming the lives of its members dramatizes the failure to
date of the traditional institutions—the Negro church, the civil rights groups,
the white settlement houses—to make any real headway with the psychological, social, and economic problems of the Negro poor.

The growth of black nationalism, moreover, exposes the real differences
of opinion, and the very real conflicts of interest, that exist around the question of integration. A good many Negro businessmen and politicians, for
example, might be hurt by integration; their livelihood and their status derive from the existence of segregation. Hence their advocacy of integration
tends to diminish as its existence draws nearer. The problem is posed for

From Charles E. Silberman, *Crisis in Black and White* (New York: Random House,
1964), pp. 162–188.

politicians in quite concrete terms when, for example, there is discussion
about the best location for a new public housing project: should it be built
within the existing Negro community, in which case it will almost certainly
be segregated; or should it be built on available land somewhere else in the
city, which might lead to depopulation of the politicians' district?

The more important problem is a good deal subtler: what do Negroes
really mean by "integration"? As C. Eric Lincoln asks the question, do
Negroes want "true integration," or do they want what he terms "a conspicuous, superficial integration which relieves them of the self-hatred and
insecurity that come from second-class citizenship, but which also relieves
them of the responsibility that full participation would mean." Too many
Negroes, Professor Lincoln fears, prefer the latter; when the Atlanta Negro
community won the right to attend the Atlanta Symphony concerts and to
eat in a few leading downtown restaurants, for example, a good many
upper-class Negroes concluded that the battle at long last had been won.
What else, they wondered, was there left to do?

Atlanta, needless to say, is still a highly segregated city. So are New York
—and Washington and Detroit and Los Angeles, for that matter. But what
are the hallmarks of "true" integration? Does it imply the disappearance
of the Negro community and the all-Negro churches, fraternal orders, and
other institutions; does it require the redistribution of the Negro population
more or less evenly throughout the white community? Or is integration compatible with the perpetuation of a distinctly Negro community? Is perpetuation desirable, or simply inevitable? What attributes of the Negro community
are worth preserving? Is there a specifically Negro culture that is worth
preserving, or are so-called Negro culture traits simply an outgrowth of
Jim Crow? Should kudos be granted to Negroes who move into previously
all-white neighborhoods—or alternatively, should any onus be attached to
people who prefer to remain in all-Negro enclaves? Is an all-Negro neighborhood necessarily a ghetto? Is an all-Negro school necessarily inferior?

The answers are by no means obvious; they require nothing less than a
redefinition of what it means to be a Negro in the United States and a new
appraisal of the ways in which Negroes can best relate to whites. The redefinition is long overdue; perhaps because achievement of integration has
always seemed so far away, Negroes have given surprisingly little thought
to what they actually mean by the term—to what kind of relationship they
really want with whites or, for that matter, with other Negroes. The ideology
of the civil rights movement, as we have seen, developed at the beginning
of the century, when liberal thought was dominated by the notion of "the
melting pot." In fact, Israel Zangwill's influential play, *The Melting Pot,* in

which the term originated, opened on Broadway the year before the NAACP was founded.

But the crucial thing about the melting pot was that it did not happen: American politics and American social life are still dominated by the existence of sharply-defined ethnic groups.[1] To be sure, these groups have been transformed by several generations of life in America; the immigrants of three or four or five generations ago would be unable to recognize the Italian-Americans, the Irish-Americans, the Jewish-Americans of the 1960s; the latter groups, in turn, would disavow kinship with their ancestors. And yet the ethnic groups are not just a political anachronism; they are a reality. The WASPs (White Anglo-Saxon Protestants), the Irish-Americans, the Italian-Americans, the Jewish-Americans do differ from each other in essential ways. They vote differently, raise their children differently, have different ideas about sex, education, religion, death, etc.[2] And so if Negroes are to assimilate, if they are to integrate with the white American, the question has to be asked: with *which* white American? With the WASP? Or with the Irishman? The Italian? The Slovak? The Jew? For in truth there is no "white American"; there are only white Americans.

More to the point, the experience of the European ethnic groups suggests that integration need not mean assimilation, that integrating the Negro into the main stream of American life does not depend—indeed, cannot depend —on "making color irrelevant by making it disappear as a fact of consciousness." Consciousness of color is not likely to disappear unless color itself disappears, or unless men lose their eyesight. For color is not merely a political fact, as James Baldwin argues; on the contrary, it is a social and personal reality, just as being Protestant or Catholic or Jewish is a reality, just as being Italian or Irish or German is a reality. One of the contributions the Muslims have made is their insistence that solution of "the Negro problem" cannot depend on the Negro's disappearance.

This is not to say that the attempts of Professor Handlin or Professor Hauser to equate the Negro migration with the European migrations are correct. It is infinitely harder for white Americans to accept the fact of color than it was for their fathers or grandfathers to accept the fact of ethnic difference. And it is vastly harder for Negro-Americans to come to grips with their Negro-ness than, say, for Jewish-Americans to come to grips with their Jewishness, or Italian-Americans to come to grips with their Italian-ness. (Neither group, in fact, has completely resolved the complex conflicts that still exist between being an Italian or a Jew and being an American.) Negroes are both more than an ethnic group and less: though their color makes them far more identifiable than any ethnic group, they lack the common history and cultural traditions which the other groups share. The

Negro's central problem is to discover his identity, or to create an identity for himself. What history suggests is that when the Negro solves his problem of identity, he will have gone a long way towards finding the means of relating himself to every other American group.

2

Solution of the problem of Negro identity seems much closer than appeared likely only a few years ago. The biggest factor in this change has been the rise of the African states, which is making it possible for American Negroes to admit their relationship to Africa—which in fact is encouraging them to reconstruct their history and restore the cultural ties to Africa destroyed by slavery. It is hard to exaggerate the importance of Africa for the problem of Negro identity in the United States. Today, Africa is contributing enormously to Negro self-pride; yesterday, Africa contributed even more to Negro self-hate.

To understand why, it is necessary to recall the image of Africa that prevailed just a few years ago—the image which, indeed, still dominates most white thinking. Africa, in this view, is the Dark Continent, "a continent without history," a place of savagery and ignorance whose people had contributed nothing at all to human progress. "All the continents begin with an 'A' except one," begins a chapter of V. M. Hillyer's *A Child's Geography of the World,* a favorite when I was a child, and still a popular children's book. "Asia is the largest continent. Africa is the next largest. But Africa was an 'In-the-Way' continent," the chapter continues. "It was in the way of those who wanted to get to Asia. Everyone wanted to get *around* Africa. No one wanted to get *to* it. Sailors have been shipwrecked on its shores, but few lived to tell the tale of jungles, of wild animals, and wild black men. Africa was called the Dark Continent because no one knew much about it or wanted to know about it . . . On one edge—along the Mediterranean Sea —white men lived, but south of that edge was a great desert that men feared to cross, and south of that wild black men and wild animals. . . ."

Public school textbooks were even more deprecating. In the texts used when today's adult Negro population attended school, the inevitable pictures of "the five races of man" almost always showed the African man at his most primitive. In contrast to "the Emersonian white man in his study, the Japanese aristocrat, the Malay nobleman, and the Indian chief—all obviously selected to depict the highest social rank in each case," Professor Harold R. Isaacs has written, the "African" appeared as "a prehistoric figure of a man, naked, stepping out of primeval ooze, carrying an antedeluvian club and shield." [3] One text, Isaacs reports, classified the states of man as "savage" ("all black or red"), "barbarous" ("chiefly brown"), "half-civilized" ("almost wholly yellow"), and "civilized" ("almost all belong to the white race.") Movies were even more devastating: Hollywood almost invariably showed Africa as a land populated by half-naked cannibals.

Against this debasing picture of "the African," the Negro child had no defense; he had no way of knowing that the picture happened to be false. On the contrary, this "evidence of the black man's inferiority," as Isaacs puts it, "was borne in upon him with all the weight and authority of the all-knowing, all-powerful, all-surrounding white world," thereby confirming the sense of his own worthlessness that white attitudes and actions had already established. This confirmation played an important, frequently a crucial, role in the development of Negro children's conception of themselves. In the interviews with a hundred seven leading Negroes that formed the basis of *The New World of Negro Americans,* Isaacs found "that in nearly every instance" the early discovery of the African background had been "a prime element" in shaping the individual's knowledge of and attitude toward himself and his world—so much so that most of the subjects could recall the details of the pictures and the names of the texts with agonizing clarity forty, fifty, and even sixty years later!

In general, therefore, Africa served to alienate the Negro not just from America but from the whole human race. In self-defense, he tried to dissociate himself from Africa. As the Negro historian Carter G. Woodson, a pioneer in the study of Negro history in Africa and in the United States, put it in 1937, Negroes "accept as a compliment the theory of a complete break with Africa, for above all things, they do not care to be known as resembling in any way 'these terrible Africans.'" Negroes not aware of the academic debate over just how many African cultural traits had survived did, however, emphasize their Indian or white ancestry, if they had any. And they proceeded to use "African" as an epithet and an insult. If a Negro had dark skin and kinky hair, lighter-skinned Negroes would wither him with a "You look like a black African." Indeed, to call someone a "black African" became an even greater insult than to call him a "nigger."

The key word was "black." For a Negro to dissociate himself from Africa meant, after all, to dissociate himself from the African's color, hair, features —from the Negroidness that stared at him from the pictures in the public-school textbooks and that assaulted his senses from the movie screen. But in the last analysis, dissociation was impossible, the perverse fact of color remained. And so the Negro's rejection of Africa was, at bottom, a rejection of himself.

African independence is profoundly altering American Negroes' relation to Africa and to themselves. Few Negroes can fail to feel a flush of pride as jet-black African ambassadors, presidents, and prime ministers are received at the White House or take their places in the United Nations. Negroes who had shuddered inwardly at the mention of Africa are developing an interest in African art and poetry; men who had fled from blackness are pondering the meanings and debating the attributes of *Negritude;* adolescents and young adults whose idols had been some entertainer or athlete now worship the memory of Lumumba or make a hero of Nkrumah. And ordinary Negro women who a short time ago were buying hair-straighteners and skin-bleaches now wear the new "African look" in hair styles.

Negroes of all social classes and all educational levels, moreover, are developing an interest in African history. They are discovering, as a result, that their past—or at least that part of their past which belongs to Africa—is a lot easier to accept than they had thought. For Africa does have a history which enables black men to hold their heads aloft. We do not know nearly enough about that history, to be sure, but we know considerably more than most people (or most scholars, for that matter) realize. And what we do know makes it clear that Arnold Toynbee erred grievously when he wrote that of all the races of mankind, "The Black races alone have not contributed positively to any civilization." [4]

The contribution of the black race may have started at the very beginning; there is some evidence to suggest that Elijah Muhammad's claim that the black is "original man" may not be as wide of the mark as it sounds. A number of distinguished archaeologists, anthropologists, paleontologists, and other "prehistorians," now believe that human life first developed in Africa. As the eminent Oxford anthropologist L. S. B. Leakey, puts it, "Africa's first contribution to human progress was the evolution of man himself." Professor Leakey's view is based on fossils and skeletons he has discovered in Africa. The evidence, needless to say, is circumstantial, but it is persuasive nonetheless. The distinction between man and other primates is that man makes and uses tools. The earlies toolmaker so far known is a creature called Zinganthropus, discovered by Professor Leakey in northern Tanganyika. Zinganthropus lived nearly two million years ago, and was more apelike than human; thousands of generations of evolution were needed before he came to resemble what we call *Homo sapiens,* whose brain is more important than his brawn and whose hands are more useful than his teeth. As the historians Roland Oliver and J. D. Fage have put it, "there is little doubt that throughout all but the last small fraction of this long development of the human form, Africa remained at the center of the inhabited world." [5] All the so-called "pebble tools" that have been discovered so far have been found in Africa or close by, and far more "hand axes" (the next tool to be developed) have been found in Africa than anywhere else.

However vague the evidence may be concerning the origin of man in Africa, it is clear that black men played a far greater role in the civilizations of antiquity than most historians have acknowledged. What we call "civilization" began at about the same time, some seven thousand years ago, in Mesopotamia and in Egypt. Whether the Mesopotamians were black is open to question, though there is some evidence indicating that they were. But there is no doubt that black men played a significant role in Egyptian civilization from the very beginning. The Egyptians were, in all probability, a mixed breed; in their own paintings, they depicted themselves as black, reddish-brown, or yellow; white-skinned figures usually represented foreigners or slaves. Examination of skeletons and other remains, moreover, indicate that a substantial proportion of the Egyptian population—perhaps a third or more—was clearly Negroid. And Herodotus described the fifth-century B.C. Egyptians as "black and curly-haired."

There was contact, extending over millenia, moreover, between the Egyptians and the Ethiopians, who considered themselves the spiritual fathers of Egyptian civilization.[6] Diodorous Siculus, the Greek historian of the first century B.C., wrote that "The Ethiopians conceived themselves to be of greater antiquity than any other nation; and it is probably that, born under the sun's path, its warmth may have ripened them earlier than other men. They supposed themselves to be the inventors of worship, of festivals, of solemn assemblies, of sacrifices, and every religious practice." There was a good deal in Greek legend to support the Ethiopian claim. The *Iliad* speaks of the Gods feasting among the "blameless Ethiopians," and Homer elsewhere praises Memnon, king of Ethiopia, and Eurybates:

> Of visage solemn, sad, but sable hue,
> Short, wooly curls, o'erfleeced his bending head . . .
> Eurybates, in whose large soul alone,
> Ulysses viewed an image of his own. . . .

The Old Testament, whose historical reliability is being validated more and more by the findings of archaeology, provides perhaps the best evidence of the role black men played in the development of ancient civilization. Chapter X of Genesis, for example, catalogues the principal races and nations known at the time, describing them all as branches of one great family owing common ancestry to Noah. (This chapter is thus the first assertion of the unity of the human race, a concept which follows logically from the Hebrew belief in the Unity of God.) "These are the groupings of Noah's descendants," says the author of Genesis, "according to their origins, by their nations; and from these the nations branched out on the earth after the Flood." The Israelites themselves claimed direct descent from Shem, the first Semite and Noah's oldest son. The Medes, the Greeks, the Scythians, and the Cimmerians, among others—"the maritime nations"—were descended from Japheth, Noah's youngest son. Noah's middle son, of course, was Ham. His name in Hebrew—*Cham*—means black; it also means Egypt.[7]

The Biblical language itself thus shows clearly that the ancients viewed Egypt as a black society. Lest there be any doubt of the role of black men in that period, the author of Genesis continues by listing the sons of Ham. The oldest was *Cush,* the Biblical name for Ethiopia and, down to the present, the vernacular Hebrew term for a black African. (Genesis reports that in addition to a number of other children, Cush "begot Nimrod, who was the first man of power on earth. He was a mighty hunter by the grace of the Lord," not to mention his having been the founder of Babylonia. The Israelites clearly believed that the Babylonians and Assyrians were of African origin—a belief shared by some contemporary historians.) The other children of Ham included *Mizraim,* the most common Biblical name for Egypt; *Put,* or Libya; and *Canaan,* a name derived from a root meaning "to be low"; and referring originally to the low-lying coast of Phoenicia and the lowlands of the Philistines, later to all of western Palestine.

It was Ham's son Canaan, incidentally, and not Ham himself, upon whom Noah laid his famous curse, "a servant of servants shall he be to his brethren." For centuries, the so-called "curse of Ham" (Genesis, IX, 25–27) has been cited to prove Biblical justification for Negro slavery and inferiority. Rarely has a greater hoax been perpetrated, for Noah's curse is completely unambiguous: "And he said: Cursed be Canaan; A servant of servants shall he be unto his brethren. And he said: Blessed be the Lord, the God of Shem; and let Canaan be their servant. God enlarge Japheth . . . And let Canaan be their servant." In short, the curse was laid not on Ham and his descendants, *i.e.,* on the black race, but on Canaan—the traditional enemy of the ancient Israelites.[8]

What happened to end the large, perhaps central, role which Africa played in world progress for some five or six thousand years or more?[9] In Professor Leakey's opinion, Africa lost this role for two reasons: the expansion of the desert "cut off Africa from the rest of the world" (except for the Nile); and the African climate reduced human incentive by providing an abundance of food, and reduced capacity because of an abundance of disease. The truth undoubtedly is a good deal more complex. For one thing, the Sahara was nothing like the obstacle to communication that so many historians assume; on the contrary, the trans-Saharan trade connecting

North Africa with the western Sudan, and through the Sudan, with the Gold Coast, continued on a large scale down to the nineteenth century, and indeed is still carried on. For another, the expansion of the desert does not explain the decline of Egypt—once the pinnacle of civilization and of wealth, now one of the poorest and most backward of lands. Indeed, few things in history are as dimly understood as the causes for either the rise or the fall of the great civilizations.

Be that as it may, the fact remains that although Africa lost its leadership, it did not sink into savagery or barbarism. On the contrary, Negro cultures and cultures led by mixed groups of Negroes, Berbers, and whites flourished in West and Central Africa and on the eastern coast until the sixteenth century, and in lesser degree down to the establishment of European hegemony in the nineteenth century.[10] These societies were known to the Europeans of their day; knowledge of them disappeared in modern times in part because black Africa has no written history, and our literate age tends to assume that an absence of written record means an absence of anything worth recording. But knowledge of African culture and history disappeared also because, as Du Bois put it, "the world which raped it had to pretend that it had not harmed a man but a thing."

In good measure, however, the history of black Africa was obscured by the interpenetration of Moslem and Negro cultures during the Moslem ascendance that ran from the seventh to the sixteenth centuries. It is now clear that much of what had been considered the history of Arab or Moslem or Moorish societies was the history of Negro and Negroid people as well.[11] The term "Arab" or "Moor" was applied to anyone professing the faith of Islam; the large proportion of Negroid blood among the Berbers and other peoples of North Africa is evident to anyone who has traveled in the area. Thus, Elijah Muhammad's identification of Negroes with Islam and the Arabic world, while grossly exaggerated, reveals a truth that has been generally ignored and unknown.

From its beginnings, in fact, Mohammedanism contained substantial Negroid elements. One of the greatest figures in the development of Islam, for example, was Bilal-i-Habesh, or Bilal of Ethiopia, a liberated slave who became Mohammed's closest friend, and to whom Mohammed yielded precedence in Paradise. Mohammed adopted another Negro, Zayd bin Hareth, as his son; Zayd became one of the Prophet's greatest generals. The Moorish army which invaded and conquered Spain included a great many Negroes and dark-skinned Berbers as well as "white" Arabs; if Shakespeare's *Othello* is any indication, the Europeans considered the Moors to be Negroes. Thus, Othello's color is described as "sooty," and Iago refers unflatteringly to "the thick lips." [12]

The main impact of Islam on the Negro peoples began in the eleventh century, when a Puritanical sect of Berber warriors, the Almavorids, crossed the Sahara, conquered the ancient empire of Ghana,[13] and converted to Islam the rulers (but not much of the population) of the whole fertile belt that stretches across Africa from the Western Sudan to the hills of Ethiopia. At the time of the Almavorid conquest, Ghana was noted for its wealth throughout the Arab world; the Arab geographer El Bikri reported in 1067 that the king of Ghana had a nugget of gold so large that he could tether his horse to it. After the conquest, however, Ghana went into a decline.

The next great empire to emerge in the Sudan was Mali. Its history goes back to the seventh century, but Mali became important in the thirteenth century when a Moslem convert, Sundiata, came to power, and reached its apex in the fourteenth century under Mansa (Emperor) Musa, who ruled from 1307 to 1332. Mansa Musa put Mali on the map [14] through his pilgrimage to Mecca in 1324, which was carried out with incredible pomp and style; the enormous store of gold he took on the journey was a source of awe throughout the Moslem world and much of Europe as well. On his return, he brought with him an Arab poet and architect who built mosques in Timbuctu and other cities. Twenty years after Musa's death, Ibn Battuta, the John Gunther of the fourteenth century, spent nearly two months in Mali. Its inhabitants, he reported, "are Moslems, punctilious in observing the hours of prayer, studying books of law, and memorizing the Koran." The women were "of surpassing beauty." All in all, Ibn Battuta, who visited virtually every state from Africa's west coast straight across to China, was impressed with what he saw in Mali:

The Negroes possess some admirable qualities. They are seldom unjust, and have a greater abhorrence of injustice than any other people. Their sultan shows no mercy to anyone who is guilty of the least act of it. There is complete security in their country. Neither traveler nor inhabitant in it has anything to fear from robbers or men of violence. They do not confiscate the property of any white man who dies in their country, even if it be uncounted wealth. On the contrary, they give it into the charge of some trustworthy person among the whites, until the rightful heir takes possession of it. . . .

In short, Mali was a state whose organization and civilization compared favorably with those of the Moslem kingdoms or indeed the Christian kingdoms of the same epoch.

One hundred and sixty years later, this part of the Sudan was still the site of a flourishing civilization, though the Mali empire had been replaced by a former vassal, the kingdom of Songhay, whose capital was seven hundred miles to the east. Timbuctu had become a city of perhaps 100,000 inhabitants; its University of Sankore was famous throughout the Moslem world for the study of law and surgery. Leo Africanus, a member of the Papal Court of Leo X, the Medici Pope, visited Mali in about 1510 and was considerably impressed.[15] "The people of this region," he reported "excel all other Negroes in wit, civility, and industry, and were the first that embraced the law of Mohammad." In Timbuctu itself, he reported, there were "great stores of doctors, judges, priests, and other learned men that are bountifully maintained at the king's costs and charges. And hither are brought diverse manuscripts or written books out of Barbary, which are sold for more money than any other merchandise." (Timbuctu's intellectual and cultural life was carried on in Arabic, since the African languages had never been committed to writing.) But Leo's visit came near the end of Sudanese glory. At the end of the sixteenth century, the Songhay empire was destroyed by an invasion from the North—this time by Moors who, possessing gunpowder, had no trouble subduing the black population. From the time the capital of Gao fell in 1591, the Sudan went into a decline from which it never recovered. Once the central government was destroyed, the Songhay empire dissolved into tribal kingdoms. The Sudan became a battleground, fought over by Tuareg nomads infiltrating from the desert and pastoralists coming from the west.

The history of the forested southern half of West Africa—what the Europeans called Guinea—is more obscure than that of the Sudan, since it was not visited by the Arab authors who wrote about the Sudan between the eighth and fifteenth centuries. By the thirteenth century, however, the Negroes of Guinea had begun to develop states rather similar in pattern to those of the Sudan, and when the European slave traders came, they dealt with highly organized, and militarily powerful states. The societies of the Guinea area, though agricultural, were also urban in character; settlements ranged from small villages to substantial towns. Most of these towns were barred to Europeans until the nineteenth century, when the Europeans finally succeeded in penetrating beyond the coastal strip. The town of Benin, in what is now Nigeria, was an exception; Benin was one of the "ports of trade" to which the European slave traders were restricted. Sixteenth- and seventeenth-century European traders, whose descriptions survive, quite clearly regarded Benin as a great city, quite comparable with the major European cities of the time. In 1602, for example, a Dutch trader reported that:

> The town seemeth to be very great; when you enter into it you go into a great broad street, not paved, which seems to be seven or eight times broader than Warmoes street in Amsterdam ... At the gate where I entered on horseback, I saw a very high bulwark, very thick of earth, with a very deep broad

ditch ... Without this gate there is a great suburb. When you are in the great street aforesaid, you see many great streets on the sides thereof, which also go right forth ... The King's Court is very great, within it having many great foursquare plains, which round about them have galleries, wherein there is always watch kept. I was so far within the Court that I passed over four such great plains, and wherever I looked, still I saw gates upon gates to go into other places ... It seems that the King has many soldiers; he has also many gentlemen, who when they come to court ride upon horses. ...

Today, Benin is best known for its magnificent bronze art, which exerted a powerful influence on Picasso and other contemporary painters. The rulers of such states as Benin and Dahomey maintained their Authority over large areas, and as noted, were able to keep the Europeans out until the late-nineteenth century. In the middle of the nineteenth century, when Dahomey was still under African control, the English trader and writer, John Duncan, was impressed by the country's law and order. "During my stay at Abomey," he wrote, "I was never asked by any individual for an article of even the most trifling value, nor ever lost anything, except what was stolen by my people from the coast. The Dahoman laws are certainly severe, but they have the desired effect."

3

Looking at the broad sweep of African history, it seems clear that Negroes need not feel ashamed of their race on account of its past. There are, to be sure, enormous gaps in our knowledge of African history, and a great many mysteries as well. Why did the culture of the Western Sudan atrophy after the sixteenth century? (The region did not come under European control until the nineteenth century.) And why did black Africa never develop a written language?

The point at issue, however, is not whether black African civilization was the equal of European or Arabic civilizations, whatever "equal" may mean; we understand too little of the reasons for either the rise or the fall of any of the great civilizations of the past. If progress requires the stimulation that comes from contact with other cultures, as many historians and anthropologists believe, then black Africa commands particular respect: it has been more isolated from contact with other cultures than any other society save the Indians of North and South America. And how do we measure one culture against another? Were the pagan (or the Moslem) blacks, for example, the moral inferiors of the whites who came from Catholic Spain and Portugal or Protestant England and Holland to trade in human flesh? And if black Africans failed to develop a written language, what are we to make of African art; how do we rate a culture in which esthetic expression is an experience in which the entire population participates? (In Africa, as Lerone Bennett, Jr., has observed, art "was not for art's sake, but for life's sake.")

Whether African societies were "better" or "worse," "more civilized" or "less civilized" than the societies developed by white men, in short, is not really germane. What is crucial is simply the fact that Negroes can hold their heads aloft in the knowledge that men of black skin have contributed to human progress, that they have created and maintained societies and civilizations of a high order. Having been denied a place in history for so long, it is essential that Negroes be allowed to claim their rightful place in the story of mankind. It is equally important that white men understand that Negroes do in fact have that place.

If Negroes are to claim the past that is rightfully theirs, however, they will have to assume the risks that go with it. Acquisition of a past is necessary, but it is also perilous—for it means an end to innocence. Just as the Negro past shows beauty and grandeur, so does it show meanness, cruelty, injustice. The Europeans, after all, did not invent the slave trade; they exploited and expanded a commerce that Africans had been carrying on from time immemorial, and diverted it into new channels. (Slaves had always been one of the staples of the trans-Saharan trade.) Indeed, the European slave traders themselves almost never enslaved an African, for they were not permitted to enter the interior. They were, instead, restricted to the coastal trading settlements by the African kings and emperors who wanted to keep the monopoly of the slave trade in their own hands. It was Africans who waged war periodically in order to enslave other Africans, and it was Africans who chained the slaves together and marched them hundreds of miles to the sea, to be sold to the Europeans for guns or cloth.

The attempt to establish kinship with contemporary Africa raises even deeper problems. It is only when he visits Africa that the American Negro realizes how much of an American he really is and how wide is the cultural gap between him and the African Negro; it is only when he visits Africa that the American Negro realizes how deep are the wounds that Africa has inflicted on him. Richard Wright's experiences provide a case in point. When friends first suggested that he go to Africa, Wright wrote:

I heard them, but my mind and feelings were racing along another and hidden track. Africa! Being of African descent, would I be able to feel and know something about Africa on the basis of a common "racial" heritage? ... Or had three hundred years imposed a psychological distance between me and the "racial stock" from which I had sprung? ... Am I African? Had some of my ancestors sold their relatives to white men? What would my feelings be when

I looked into the black face of an African, feeling that maybe his great-great-great-grandfather had sold my great-great-great-grandfather into slavery? Was there something in Africa that my feelings could latch onto to make all of this dark past clear and meaningful? Would the Africans regard me as a lost brother who had returned? . . . According to popular notions of race, there ought to be something of "me" down there in Africa. Some vestige, some heritage, some vague but definite ancestral reality that would serve as a key to unlock the hearts and feelings of the Africans whom I'd meet. . . .

The key did not work; Wright's meeting with Africa was disastrous, for his mind and tastes were too American. He was horrified to find that belief in magic was not limited to the uneducated; he was shaken by what he saw of African culture; and he found that Africans regarded him as a stranger to be evaded or fooled. "I found the African an oblique, hard-to-know man who seems to take a kind of childish pride in trying to create a sense of bewilderment in the minds of strangers," Wright reported. "I found the African almost invariably underestimated the person with whom he was dealing; he always placed too much confidence in an evasive reply, thinking that if he denied something, then that something ceased to exist. It was child-like." More important, perhaps, he found a universal distrust; "This fear, this suspicion of nothing in particular came to be the most predictable hall-mark of the African mentality that I met in all of the Gold Coast, from the Prime Minister down to the humblest 'mammy' selling *kenke* on the street corners." [16]

Wright traveled to Africa in 1954, when African independence was just beginning, but his experience seems to be repeated by many Negroes who "return" for any length of time. They discover an enormous cultural gap, far beyond anything they have been prepared for: they are troubled by telephones and plumbing that do not work, by appointments that are not kept and promises that are not fulfilled, if indeed they are even remembered the next day—in short, by hundreds of factors, large and small, that remind him that Africa is not really "home." "It's ridiculous," one American Negro in Africa told Harold Isaacs, "but I had never before realized how much of my life had nothing to do with the race problem at all. I mean just the way you do everything you do, what you mean when you say something, and how you understand what the other fellow means."

Nor are the difficulties of communicating the only things that serve to alienate the American Negro in Africa; he is upset also by the corruption and brutality of much of African political life. (Nkrumah has been jailing political opponents since he first came to power, under a law that permits him to hold men for four years—recently extended to eight—without trial or charges.) Nor does it take much sensitivity to see that the new black ruling classes frequently are as contemptuous of their subjects, and as condescending toward them, as was the most arrogant white colonial. Thus it is not surprising that American Negroes who visit frequently find it more upsetting than rewarding. Almost every American Negro he met in Africa in 1960, Isaacs reports, had "discovered that he was much more alien in Africa. Whether he liked it or not, he found that he was American, and that in Africa he became an American in exile."

It is in the United States, in short, and only in the United States, that American Negroes will be able to resolve their problems of identification. To be sure, Negroes must recapture their African past, because denying them a place in history has been one of the means whites have used to keep them down; and they must find some basis on which to relate to Africa, because denying that relationship has been central to Negro self-hatred. But building a bridge to Africa past and Africa present is simply a means of erasing the old stigma of race; it is not a base on which Negroes can erect a new identity. For American Negroes have been formed by the United States, not by Africa; Africa gave them their color, but America gave them their personality and their culture. The central fact in Negro history is slavery, and Negroes must come to grips with it, must learn to accept it not as a source of shame (the shame is the white man's) but as an experience that explains a large part of their present predicament. Only if they understand *why* they are what they are, can Negroes change *what* they are. Identity is not something that can be found; it must be created.

It is clear, however, that pride in race must play a part in the new identity. The Negro is not struggling to become free, Ralph Ellison argues, simply in order to disappear. For one thing, he cannot disappear; to argue, as does a liberal intellectual like Norman Podhoretz, that "the Negro problem can be solved in this country in no other way" than through assimilation and miscegenation is to argue that no solution is possible for several centuries. Equally important, Negroes are beginning to think that maybe they do not *want* to disappear, that perhaps there are specifically Negro values and cultural traits that should be kept.

This new pride in race must be carefully nurtured, for it is not yet deeply entrenched. The process is bound to lead—has already led—to a considerable degree of racial self-consciousness, indeed, to out-and-out race chauvinism. Whites who encounter it tend to react with surprise or indignation: how can Negroes, who have been (and who still are) the victims of racial persecution, now turn around and talk about mystical notions like Negritude, "soul," and the like? The answer is simple: the reaction to centuries of being ashamed and humiliated by the color black is not likely to be a calm and dispassionate analysis of racial characteristics. Only by swinging in the opposite direction can the pendulum find the center. But Negro self-consciousness is not entirely irrational; to some degree it involves what the French existentialist philosopher and playwright Jean-Paul Sartre calls "anti-racist racism." Before differences can be abolished, they must be respected; given past history, neither Negroes nor whites will learn to respect blackness unless the virtues of being black are emphasized and over-emphasized. Once racial differences are respected, however, people can proceed to ignore them, or to transcend them. Thus, Solly Saunders, the hero of John Oliver Killen's novel, *And Then We Heard the Thunder,* is transformed by reading a copy of Richard Wright's *Twelve Million Black Voices* which his race-conscious sweetheart had sent him.

The photography by Edwin Russkam together with Wright's overpowering word images awoke inside of Solly emotions long asleep and almost forgotten. Sometimes he would be reading a passage, or sometimes a face would stare at him from the pages, and he would hear the voices, and he would feel a trembling in his stomach and a fulness in his own face, and he would feel his own blackness deeply, and be proud to be a black man.

This pride in self dissolves Solly's hatred of the white.

One day he was reading the book, and it suddenly came to him, and he said to himself, if I'm proud of me, I don't need to hate Mr. Charlie's people. I don't want to. I don't need to. If I love me, I can also love the whole damn human race. Black, brown, yellow, white. . . .[17]

The danger, of course, is that the pendulum does not always come back to center; anti-racist racism does not necessarily lead to a belief in the common humanity of man. The bitterness of Killens' novel shows that clearly enough; Killens' hero may have been able to overcome his suspicion and hatred of every white man, but Killens himself was not. More to the point, the two mass movements that have been most successful in developing self-pride among Negroes—the Garveyites and the Black Muslims—did so in large measure by preaching undying hatred of everything white. The problem is not peculiarly Negro; on the contrary, one of the central questions of our time is whether any group, be it a religion, a nationality, or a race, can instil a commitment among its members without at the same time derogating other groups. It is fortunate, perhaps, that the search for Negro identity is coming to a head at a time when the great religions of the West are seriously grappling with this problem—when they are discovering, in fact, that faith without prejudice *is* possible.[18]

As they struggle to create an identity for themselves, Negroes inevitably find the present particularly painful to live through. They are caught in the tensions of two worlds. For a great many Negroes, as we have seen, segregation had become a crutch on which they leaned very heavily; the concept of Negro inferiority relieved them of the need to compete in a sternly competitive society, and absolved them of responsibility for their behavior or their fate. For other Negroes, segregation provided a convenient scapegoat to excuse their personal failures.

But now the crutch is being broken and the scapegoat cast aside; the old identity is being destroyed before the new one has been completed. The winds blowing from Africa (and from within the United States as well) are forcing Negro Americans into new and uncharted territory—into a terrain that terrifies as much as it invites. Clearly the conditions of life have changed, the opportunities have broadened enormously. Yet just as clearly, the white world is still mined against the Negro. Or is it? One is never really sure; part of the price of being a Negro in America is a degree of paranoia. The obstacles are no less frightening for being imagined—and many are real enough, for the United States has a long, long way to go before discrimination disappears. Hence the Negro must keep his guard up while adjusting to the new world that is opening. All this, moreover, while he is still searching for his identity, while he is still struggling to assimilate and understand the varied messages with which his mind and heart have been assaulted, to put the pieces together in a way that makes sense.

The result is a terrible strain as old customs and habits and patterns of thought are eroded and the familiar and the unfamiliar merge in a kaleidoscope of changing impressions. "The tensions among Negroes," says Harold Isaacs, "become less and less the tensions of submission and endurance, and more and more the tensions of change and self-assertion. But both kinds of tension continue to co-exist in almost every Negro individual . . . they jostle each other in a constant and bruising inward turmoil as each person seeks to discover the new terms of life—the older person fighting both to hold on to and to throw off the older habits of mind and outlook; the younger person trying to find the new ground to stand on amid all the tangled fears and angers and despairs and exhilarations." No Negro can remain as he was; the poverty-stricken Negro in the Mississippi Delta and his cousin in the Chicago slum, the lawyer or doctor holding his head up high in an integrated suburb of New York, and the president of a Negro college in the South, who still must bow and scrape to keep his school alive —all are being forced to see themselves and to see others in new and unsettling ways.

# NOTES

[1] For a discerning analysis of the role of ethnic groups in American life, *see* Nathan Glazer and Daniel P. Moynihan, *Beyond the Melting Pot,* Cambridge, Mass.: MIT Press and Harvard University Press, 1963.

[2] In an article describing the rapidly growing phenomenon of the public dance for single men and women—as many as 150 such affairs are held on a single weekend in New York—*The New York Times* reported that separate dances for persons of Irish, German, Polish, Greek, Italian, and Hungarian extraction are advertised in neighborhood papers and in the foreign-language press.

[3] Anyone concerned with the impact of Africa on Negro consciousness is indebted to Professor Isaacs for *The New World of Negro Americans* (New York: John Day, 1963).

[4] Toynbee's error may be due less to outright prejudice than to a century-old tradition that has simply excluded Africa from serious historical or archaeological study. Thus, the 600-page Somervell abridgement of Toynbee's *Study of History* contains no more than three indexed references to Africa. The tradition continues: a recently published 1,300-page study called *The World of The Past* contains no section on any part of Africa save Egypt.

[5] R. Oliver and J. D. Fage, *A Short History of Africa,* Baltimore: Penguin Books, 1962.

[6] In antiquity, "Ethiopia" referred to the Egyptian Sudan, as well as to the land on *both* sides of the Red Sea.

[7] For direct references to Egypt as "the land of Ham" (in Hebrew, *eretz Cham*), see Psalms CV, verses 23 and 27, and CVI, verse 22, which describe the Israelites' slavery in Egypt and the Exodus.

[8] The erroneous belief that Ham was cursed stems in part from the ambiguity of the verses immediately preceding the curse, in part from mistranslation. They are usually translated: "Ham, the father of Canaan, saw his father's nakedness and told his two brothers outside. And Noah awoke from his wine and *knew what his youngest son* had done unto him." [Emphasis added] The first verse does suggest that the sin (of looking at Noah's nakedness) was committed by Ham—but the text curiously identifies Ham as "the father of Canaan." The fact that it was Canaan and not Ham who was guilty seems clear from study of the next few verses. For one thing, the curse is clearly directed at Canaan, not at Ham. For another, the line preceding the curse is invariably translated incorrectly. It should read "and Noah knew what his *grandson* had done unto him." The Hebrew word *beno hakatan* may either be translated "his youngest son" or "his grandson" (the latter meaning is similar to the French *petit fils*). But "grandson" is the correct—indeed, the only possible—translation in this instance, for Ham was *not* Noah's youngest son. Japheth was the youngest; Ham was the middle son. (*See* Genesis VI, 1; VII, 13; IX, 18; X, 1.)

[9] Archaeologists have unearthed a primitive abacus in the Congo that is approximately 8,000 years old—probably the world's oldest.

[10] I am indebted to Professor Morroe Berger of Princeton University for his help in interpreting African history, especially its Moslem elements.

[11] *Cf.,* Morroe Berger, *op. cit.;* Oliver and Fage, *op. cit.;* Basil Davidson, *The Lost Cities of Africa,* Boston: Atlantic Monthly Press, 1959; J. D. Fage, *An Introduction*

*to the History of West Africa,* Cambridge, England: Cambridge University Press, 1962; W. E. B. Du Bois, *Black Folk, Then and Now,* New York: Henry Holt & Co., 1939, and *The World and Africa,* New York: The Viking Press, 1947; Henri Labouret, *Africa Before the White Man,* New York: Walker & Co., 1962; Lerone Bennett, Jr., *Before the Mayflower,* Chicago: Johnson Publishing Co., 1962.

[12] Shakespeare's play suggests how deep European prejudice against Negroes had already become—witness the horror and fury with which Desdemona's father receives the news of her marriage to Othello. (He is sure she must have been drugged by some magic potion.) But the play also demonstrates that however much Europeans may have frowned on miscegenation, their image of the Negro was as far from the "Sambo" stereotype as can be imagined: Othello—a former slave—is described as "the noble Moor" and as the greatest general of his day. (He convinces the Duke of Venice that he did not use any magic to win Desdemona's love by explaining that she fell in love with him while overhearing him tell the story of his military exploits.)

[13] Ancient Ghana was located considerably north and west of present-day Ghana. The state, which included most of present-day Senegal and part of Mali, was founded in about the fourth century A.D. by North African Berbers.

[14] Quite literally so: the first map of West Africa ever drawn in Europe, in 1375, showed Mali and its "Land of the Negroes."

[15] Leo Africanus was an Arab Moslem who was captured in Spain. Impressed by his learning, his captors presented him to Pope Leo who freed him, converted him to Christianity, and made him a member of his court.

[16] *Black Power, A Record of Reactions in a Land of Pathos,* New York: Harper & Row, Publishers, Inc., 1954.

[17] John Oliver Killens, *And Then We Heard the Thunder,* New York: Alfred A. Knopf, Inc., 1963.

[18] *See,* for example, Bernhard E. Olson's pioneering examination of Protestant religious school curricula in *Faith and Prejudice,* New Haven: Yale University Press, 1963.

*Crossroads Africa, a precursor of the Peace Corps and
the first voluntary program aimed at channeling the
talents and enthusiasm of young Americans toward the
solution of problems of development, was evaluated by
Professor Harold Isaacs of the Massachusetts Institute
of Technology in 1960–1961. The section of his study
called* Emergent Americans, *which deals with the
reactions of Black American volunteeers and African
reactions to them, is contained in the following pages.*

# Race

## Harold Isaacs

On the subject of race, which so dominated African thinking about
America, our Crossroaders learned a good deal. What they learned was life-
changing for a few, critical for some, important for all.

For the white Crossroaders it was most commonly the experience of
being exposed to Negroes as friends and peers, often for the first time in
their lives; of having the problems and emotions of race relations and race
attitudes brought more closely and more intimately into their lives than
ever before. They not only discovered, as though it were new, the impact
of this matter on the American society, on Negroes, and on themselves, but
in the African setting they also learned about the great new impact of this
matter in world affairs.

For Negro Crossroaders the learning experience was even more complicated. They were meeting and living with white peers on a sustained and
intimate basis, and for some of them also this was a quite new experience.
They were able both to teach and to learn something about the meaning
of the race problem in the society and in their own lives. At the same time
vis-à-vis Africans, they had the peculiar and difficult task of "explaining"
what it meant to be a Negro in America while also, each one within himself,
somehow facing up to the need to re-examine and redefine their identities
as individuals and as Negro Americans. This was a complex, painful, and
mostly inconclusive experience.

On this matter I can report here in detail only on the 44 Crossroaders
with whom I discussed these matters at length before, during and/or after

the summer. This group included 33 whites and 11 Negroes, 8 of the whites and 2 of the Negroes from the South, and 25 whites and 9 Negroes from other parts of the country.

## NORTHERN WHITES

As far as the white Crossroaders were concerned, it followed from the conditions of both self-selection and selection that they had—or earnestly tried to have—the "right" attitudes on the race problem whether they came from North or South. This meant that they were usually what is called "liberal"; i.e., they decried prejudice and were against racial discrimination.

If they were from the North, they generally held these views and attitudes without having had many (or any) occasions to act upon them in any way. They might have had a sprinkle of Negroes as classmates in high school or (even more rarely) in college, or known one or two Negroes as teammates or fellow participants in school activities. They shared public eating and transport facilities with Negroes as a matter of normal course. But only quite rarely would friendship, acquaintance, or, indeed, any contact with any Negroes extend beyond the school hours of the day into the home or social hours. "It was," remarked one new Ivy League graduate, "just like five o'clock anti-Semitism." There were only one or two limited exceptions to this pattern in the entire group, one or two high school friendships (including a few awkward and usually one-sided visits to homes), and in one case a summer spent with some Negro fellow volunteers at a settlement house. As a rule, there was neither occasion nor opportunity for any Negro-white relationships on an equal basis to occur either in the home, neighborhood, or social circles in which all these young people moved. The home neighborhoods were usually far apart. In white homes a Negro appeared most commonly only as servant, sometimes "a wonderful person" or "just like one of the family," but still no peer; and even such contacts have been decreasingly common, since most of our Crossroaders grew up when servants had largely disappeared from American middle class life. Their parents, as a rule, either automatically accepted the prevailing prejudice patterns of their communities or else passively deplored them up to some point. Only in a few cases were they actively or more militantly "liberal." These boys and girls grew up with some awareness of the established system of discrimination, denials, and exclusions affecting Negroes (and other minority groups), but in most cases, if they were members of the majority group, it did not intrude in any direct way upon their lives. It never became a close or emotionally sensitive issue. One read about it in the newspapers or heard about it, but most of the time there had been no need to think about it at all. Until the sit-in movement started by Negro students in the South in the spring of 1960, very few of these young men and women had ever felt called upon to make this a matter of their own personal concern and action. A few Crossroaders were even caught up sharply by the discovery that they had unthinkingly joined fraternities and sororities that still practiced racial and ethnic discrimination. Some took up an active role in picketing and demonstrating in support of the sit-ins during the spring, but this was still only a small number.

In sum, with only a few exceptions, our Crossroaders from northern states either "never knew any Negroes" or had had only the most fleeting contacts with any; and, although they held more or less "liberal" views about race problems, they had had only the scantiest kind of involvement in the fight for civil rights in the country, and this was still largely the case right up until the day they presented themselves to join their Crossroads group for orientation in June just before leaving for Africa.

## SOUTHERN WHITES

Our southern white Crossroaders had no greater contact with Negroes than their northern counterparts, perhaps even less. ("My parents moved to a community with no Negroes"; "I never knew any Negroes until we moved when I was twelve"; "I had no contact with Negroes at all until I grew up"; "When I was little I played with our maid's daughters.") What was different for these Southerners was not the amount of contact, but the saliency of the whole matter of race relations in their homes and in their social environment generally, especially in these years of steadily rising pressure and tension within the established system. In the North the patterns of prejudice or non-prejudice in most Crossroaders' homes might vary, but would ordinarily remain of a passive order; i.e., it would not be a matter of daily or vivid concern or become a cause for action or conflict within the family or with society. Our southern Crossroader parents, by contrast, divide sharply into at least two groups, both with strong feelings and community involvements. On the one hand there are the "liberals" who felt the need to find some way of humanizing their own and their children's thinking and behavior in relation to Negroes. On the other hand there are the parents who generally conformed more or less strongly to the stereotyped racialist patterns of the community. There was sometimes a division between parents (e.g., "My father thought Negroes were inferior, but my mother never allowed me to use the word 'nigger.' "), but either way, it was a highly sensitive matter, setting up strong emotional currents within the family and governing much of its relation to the world outside. The years in which these boys and girls were moving through high school into college, moreover, were the years following the Supreme Court decision of 1954, full of drawn issues, open conflicts, and violence: Little Rock, Clinton, the Lucy case in Alabama, the lynch murder of Mack Parker in Mississippi, and the Tallahassee rapes. No one remained untouched by these events and pressures. Everyone felt pushed, forced, driven on the issue. The young men and women of whom we write here, and their parents, had to react; the problem would no longer leave them alone. "My parents always taught me to respect the equality of people," said one girl, "but living up to it here was so hard!"

Several of these students had found some new ground to stand on through church youth groups making their slow way toward changed ideas and practices. Three of them had attended church student conferences conducted on an integrated basis in Ohio, where for a weekend they sat at tables and in conference rooms and shared dormitory rooms with Negroes and joined together also at social evenings. Only one of them had become, last spring, an active participant in the sit-in movement. I believe it is fair to say that all but one or two of these young white Southerners stood at varying distances but still quite far from the new Negro view that change had to come *now;* that Negroes were still unknown to them as individual people; that their expressed opinions on race matters continued to be deeply undercut by a host of unexpressed uncertainties, hesitations, and ambivalences, and that these were uppermost in their minds as they came to New York last June to join Crossroads.

## EXPOSURES

The first big thing that happened to all of them, wherever they came from, was the simple business of being exposed to Negroes as individuals. This began right there in New York during the orientation sessions held at the Union Theological Seminary. The groups formed up, and each group had one or more Negro members. They shared rooms in the dormitories, ate together, socialized together—including dancing—and of course attended the meetings, at which many of the speakers were distinguished Negroes in various fields. For a remarkable number of these Crossroaders— and not only the Southerners—this was the beginning of a radically new experience. They passed for the first time, many of them, the barriers that normally prevent whites in our society from meeting and knowing Negroes in the normal and ordinary ways in which one meets and knows all sorts of people. One young man, Midwest-born and New England-educated, said:

That week in New York was my largest dip into Negro society, my largest single contact with Negro intellectuals. The speakers at the orientation opened up to me the vast and competent Negro leadership I had not been exposed to before—I got my greatest lessons on this whole question in that first week.

Some were faced, really for the first time, with the need to overcome habits and trepidations acquired in a lifetime of emotion-laden conditioning. Two examples:

I had never really known Negroes before living in this atmosphere, there in the subways, in the restaurants, all the Negroes. You really notice it, and in church too that Sunday, it was startling, it was so different.... To me there was a kind of barrier at first, then we got to know them as part of the group, and throughout the summer we did everything together. Color in the American Negroes and the tribal marks on the Africans made no difference after a while. You just stopped noticing it.

Again:

I was put in a situation I had never been in on a social basis. I went into the project with the big idea of brotherhood in my mind. The actual situation I first met in New York was nerve-racking for me. I was always aware of sitting and eating with Negroes. But finally this disappeared and I just stopped thinking about it. It just became a matter of person to person. But it was hard at first. I couldn't realize how submerged I was. I thought I could handle anything like this, until I was actually put into it. It took time. Now I have come back, and see all these people here [in the South] again and it is so difficult. But when I went to Atlanta for a Crossroads conference, right away it was just like Africa again. What can I do about this? There is not much opportunity in this setting to carry on that kind of relationship. I have tried to tell some of my friends here what this experience is like. I have wondered whether to stay here in the South to try to do good here, but I want to be a free individual without hurting my family. I'm not sure I can do that here, even if I have the stamina or determination to try it.

This process of mutual discovery continued throughout the summer, and for some Crossroaders, especially among whites from the South, it was the summer's main business. Said one:

I had never been in contact with educated American Negroes before and I made a real effort to come to terms with the two in our group. It was a real education for me, all new to me, like discovering a new society.

Another felt a great sense of liberation:

The outstanding thing [of the summer] was to be able to move freely with American Negroes in our group without the sword of segregation over our heads. Strange that you had come to Africa to do that. This summer was the freest I have ever been in terms of race, gave me the first opportunity I've ever had to become friends with a Negro, and I held this very high, because I have never had such a chance before.

A girl from the South said, "It came to me sharply how the barb of inequality hits a person."

A boy from the Midwest said, "I had never understood what it was to be a Negro in America. I suppose I still don't, but I understand it more now."

## IN AFRICA

In Africa the learning experience about race became a triangular affair. While they were coming to some new terms with each other, Negro Americans and white Americans both had to meet Africans' demands and queries on this matter. They found all Africans interested in it wherever they went, and they had to answer more questions on this subject than on anything else. Some of this interest was relatively mild, some of it suspicious, some of it hostile. These differences were often a matter of politics. Africans still more favorably disposed toward the United States were usually less aggressive about the race problem. Africans politically antagonistic toward the United States used the race issue as a weapon, attacking as hard as they could at an obvious point of American weakness. But whether it was milder than expected or dismayingly strong, feeling on the race issue plainly held a major place in the African view of America.

Even in places like Guinea and Senegal, where Crossroaders were able to learn at first hand what the Communist-inspired assault on the race issue was like, they also learned that African ideas on the subject did not come merely from exposure to Communist propaganda. The facts about the American situation spoke loudly enough for themselves, and African black men had ample reason within themselves to react to what they heard. Long before Communists ever became an important element in the education of any Africans, British and French colonial authorities had seen to it these American facts of life—often carefully selected and highlighted—were made known to their black colonial charges. Even in crypto-Communist Guinea the young Guineans who worked with Crossroads had gotten their ideas and information about American racism not primarily from their more recent Communist sources (though these were not meager) but a long time before, from their French teachers, who in school, in the press, and on the radio had for so long taught them everything they knew about the world outside. The facts of American racism were extremely useful to the colonialists in inoculating young Africans against being infected by American democratic ideas and suggesting that, compared to American democracy, the colonial regimes were perhaps not so bad. The young Guineans who met our Crossroaders watched them narrowly in the first days to see if any of the Americans would hold back from any of the unremitting handshaking that goes on among these late children of French culture; they had been told that Americans never *touched* Negroes, not even to shake hands. They were soon satisfied on this score, but only our individual Crossroaders, not the American people, got the credit:

We came to be regarded as exceptions, not as representative of the majority of the American population, which they still thought of as racist.

As they made their way through repeated discussion of these matters with sharply questioning Guineans, members of the group went through a certain evolution:

On race, we all tried to be defensive, to say it wasn't so bad. Then we quit trying to justify the situation in the United States and became more frank, with the Guineans and with ourselves.

One Crossroader in this group belonged to another American minority group and since he was burdened neither by the guilt of the whites nor the defensiveness of the Negroes, he was able to add another dimension to the experience for all of them:

The whites in the group were saying: "Yes, but we've made progress." At the end of the summer they were pretty well rid of their efforts at rationalization. What I tried to do was point out that we should be talking about discrimination in general. It annoys me to hear Negroes talking so violently about discrimination when they themselves have all sorts of it. And when I asked the Africans about intermarriage, I found they were against it too. They felt that Africans should remain pure in the same way that the white racists do. Yet they were critical of America on this very score. One African I talked to thought mulattos were inferior to him. So obviously Africans have their own system of discrimination. All of us, Mexicans, Negroes, Jews, Africans, show some kind of discrimination—and we have to oppose all of it.

The dialogue, starting from the large and the impersonal, moved readily to the particular and the personal, as in this account:

Things like dating would come up in the form of being asked whether I would date a Negro, whether my parents would mind, whether I would marry a Negro. I said I would date a Negro, that my parents would not mind, that I might marry a Negro, but would be reluctant to do so because of the many problems. It was strange, being in a land of black people, but I got used to it. I got more of a conception of what race is and what it isn't. I had never dated a Negro at home. I went out with an African in Dakar and felt strange about it. In the beginning some of our girls would not dance with Africans. I was interested in my own reactions to this experience. It was something new. It was not different, yet it *was* different. I realized how much race was in our own minds, that we always are conscious of color, and that we do notice what race people are. I wanted to feel that race did not mean anything to me. I was brought up to be overly conscious of persons being Negro because they are a special group. You never get used to it because they are special, you have to be so careful, anything you might say or think might be construed as prejudice. When I was a child, Negroes were just apart, the people who lived "over there." I had no feelings about them, they were not involved in my life at all but in high school a Negro girl was my best friend. I think during the summer I lost most of this race consciousness. All the girls in the group eventually came around to dancing more freely with the Africans. They were sensitive at first. But then you just sort of forget about it.

## BACK HOME

It is not easy to try to judge the longer-range impact of these encounters on each individual. As one Crossroader put it during the summer: "Now we all feel strongly about it because we are here in this situation. But what will it be like a month from now when we are home?"

Not one month, but six months later when I talked of this again to most of these young men and women, they located themselves at various points along a path of change. One girl who had felt while she was in Africa that ". . . you can, you *really* can forget the whole business of race and color, you can do it in finding love and friendship with another person," now said, in some painful confusion:

I really don't know. You can't fight racial feeling as one person. I don't agree with the feelings people have, and I hope they will change. I think things will resolve themselves, but it will take generations. Our generation is still too instilled with prejudice. I know we can't afford it, so who knows what will happen? I don't know.

Many spoke, like this young man, with a strong sense of commitment:

I never was concerned before with the problem as I am now. I never gave it thought before. Now I do. I take a strong stand. I am concerned about it. I think about it and care about it, and about the effect of this thing in the rest of the world.

He had come back to New England, and I could not discover that his new feeling had as yet been translated into any new behavior. But some southern Crossroaders who carried this same feeling back to their homes and their campuses found it almost immediately put to test, in some instances in a critical and deeply personal way. One girl came back to a fiancé whom she saw now with new eyes and heard with new ears, discovering with shock and dismay that he shared the conventional racist views of the community. The issue had simply not forced itself upon them before and she had not noticed it. But she noticed it now, because when she spoke of her experiences and her new outlook, these two young people who had believed themselves in love found themselves sharply divided; and when she joined a lunch counter sit-in demonstration, she found that it meant not only breaking southern "tradition" but also breaking her engagement.

Another young woman who returned to a southern environment found herself in a major crisis within her family:

I have had to make a big decision. We had never even discussed this kind of thing before. I had never known a Negro personally as a friend until this summer. I had worked with them, but never on an equal basis. We never really had occasion to talk about this. It all came to a big blow-up. . . . It was the first time I had ever talked to my father that way, and I'm twenty-three now. I just had to decide that they had their view and I had mine. They are different. I must lead my own life. None of this is so far away from me any more. Now it is all so real.

I think this was the essence of what a great many white Crossroaders learned about the race problem across the summer—that it is real.

## THE NEGRO EXPERIENCE

The experience of Negro Crossroaders on this matter of race was much more complicated. Partly it was like that of their white comrades, a new association on a new basis of intimacy with members of the opposite group, yielding up some new knowledge and new insight. I think this was a meaningful experience for some of these individuals, though only for a few could it have that great impact of newness that so many of the whites felt. Negroes generally have not been able to afford to be as unaware and ignorant of whites as whites have been of Negroes. Almost all those I interviewed had had some working contact with whites, whether at school or in job situations, and each had in varying degree his or her share of defensive sophistication about the varieties of white behavior. Still, most of them got to know some white Crossroaders better than they had ever known any whites before, and they could feel that some of the whites had got to know some of them. As one of them remarked: "I think the whites found out from us that there are all kinds of Negroes, and we could find out—if we didn't know it already—that there are all kinds of whites." They learned something also about some of their own prejudices. "I even found myself liking some of the Ivy League types," said one girl. "I had never met people like this before." Nor, for that matter, had she ever met Negroes like some of the highly intellectual, high-achieving individuals who were with Crossroads, whether as students or as staff. On both counts she greatly improved and sharpened her perceptions.

Relating to the white Crossroaders was a fresh experience for many, but it was much more in relation to the Africans that these Negro Americans found themselves on new and much more uncertain ground. To begin with, there was a thrill in seeing new nations of black men asserting themselves and their individuality, a thrill in seeing black men free of white domination, occupying the seats of power, making history, commanding respect. It was possible for some to feel a certain satisfaction as they watched their white American comrades take the full weight of the African reaction to American racism. This was what they had been hearing about. This was evidence that the world *was* changing, that the whites of the world now, at last, had to listen with respect to non-whites and begin yielding up some of their self-deceptions and hypocrisies. This was no small sensation, to feel the great wind blowing at your back, thrusting you forward, instead, as always hitherto, blowing in your face, holding you back. But this, too, some soon discovered, was a mixed sensation. One individual, for example, found out what it was like to enjoy discrimination in reverse: he was served out of turn in front of a line of waiting Europeans. "I must say I enjoyed it," he said, "but then I started feeling guilty about enjoying it. It was just the same as discrimination against us, and it was bad." This young man was angry at himself for not being able to take greater relish in this new experience. He *wanted* to relish it. He had a long, long score to settle. But he also understood the nature of that score; it was not going to be settled by a simple reversal of roles because *he* knew too well what it was like to be on the receiving end. There was a mordant kind of irony in his inability to be as complacent about this as he was tempted to be. He had hated white men for their contempt and their baseness and had always thought how good it would be to be in their place, and yet, when the moment offered itself, he found, to his own great irritation, that he could not get down to that level, or at least that he could not remain there long.

Another virtue, the need to respect the truth, intruded on some of these encounters. The realities of American racism are harsh enough. When Africans went way beyond them, as they often did, Negro Crossroaders found themselves patiently trying to correct, to explain, to set them straight. Such was the case, for example, when Africans seemed to think that segregation and separation were total in all American life, that there was *no* association and *no* contact at all between Negroes and whites, that Negro children under segregation did not go to *any* school, and even that the United States was a country, like South Africa, with a majority black population ruled by a white minority.

This process of correction was more than a matter of merely getting the facts straight. For one thing, it involved the Negro's self-respect. Most of these distortions suggested that Negroes were putting up with conditions worse than they actually were. But here a different and subtler element entered the dialogue; for in trying to explain the facts of life to Africans, these young Negroes often found that they were explaining these facts also to themselves, that they were getting a new sense of their own values as products of the American culture. This occurred at different levels, some simple ("I was appalled by the lack of any concept of health standards"), some more complicated ("When I looked at the African women, I realized that as an American woman I am free and independent"). One Negro Crossroader had to try to convince his hosts that he was quite free to speak as critically as he wished of the social and political regime in America, that he would not be penalized, imprisoned, or "hanged" for speaking his mind, as they said they feared he might be. He had to try to explain how different American democracy was from the African non-democracy in which they lived and in which they were, indeed, in some peril if they ever spoke out in any such critical vein. Here is the way another Negro Crossroader who had a similar experience in yet another African country described the matter:

I think the most important thing for me in the summer was this business of trying to explain the situation in the United States. I had never been put on the defensive this way before. What *is* democracy, I had to ask myself, and what *did* you do about it? I found this very difficult. I had been warned of things like this, but you never know what it is like until you actually experience it. I had to re-think through the ideals of America and then to think about what I saw happening around me. As I listened to the Africans talk, I still thought I was going to have a better chance in our democratic system even if it was slower. . . .

When the African attack opened up, as it sometimes did, into a generalized assault on the American society as a whole, some of these young Negroes, whatever their own angers or feelings of alienation, found themselves coming to its defense.

I found myself defending America, its policies, the racial situation, the situation of American whites and Negroes in a way that I could not imagine myself doing.

Wrapped up in this experience was the discovery, or the confirmation, of the fact that will it or not, like it or not, these individuals were integrally and inescapably part of the American society and American culture, committed to its struggles and its goals, and could not be otherwise. In the small group of individuals who shared some glimpses of this experience with me there was only one limited exception to this, one girl who at the end of her summer's African experience felt ready to spend the rest of her life in Africa rather than in America. She felt this way because her struggle for her integrity as a person had revolved not around the issue of Negro versus white but the issue of darker Negro versus lighter Negro, and among Africans she had found for the first time in her life not rejection but acceptance— and precisely because of her color. At least for the moment, this sensation blotted out all others. Even so, as she spoke of plans that might take her back to Africa for good, she spoke also of first getting an advanced degree that would help her counteract the low status of women in African society, and she clearly had no thoughts of surrendering her culture, her citizenship, her essentially American identity. It was clear that whatever travails her plans might bring if they were realized, her prospective African husband was due to learn what it means to have an American, and not an African, for a wife.

In the encounter between these young Negro Americans and Africans are matters that lie deeper than perhaps we are called upon to go in these pages. They share parts of a common ancestry around which there are thick clusters of tangled notions and emotions, lost history, an inheritance of mutual rejection and self-rejection. They have seen each other dimly across great distances of time-space and culture-space, and where they meet, pools of prejudice and ignorance lie between them that are in some ways even deeper than those that lie between white and non-white. This has had many forms in the past and takes many different forms in the changing present, and it gets linked to all our current history. Both groups, the African and the American, are emerging into a world in which white supremacy, as a set of ideas and a system of power, is coming to a great wrenching end and a massive rearrangement of human affairs is taking place. In their part of this experience Negro Americans and Africans are having to find new and more mutually acceptable images of themselves, each other, and their relationship. Africans are able to move into the new epoch first by establishing their own new nation-states, no longer such a difficult task in this time of disintegrating empires. Negroes in this country have the more complicated task of taking their part in the American struggle to achieve an open, plural, free society. Between the two, from the purely personal to the massively impersonal, a whole new history is to be made, and our young Negro Crossroaders, in this summer of 1960, brushed up against some of its beginnings.

# BLACK AFRICA, BLACK AWARENESS, AND BLACK POWER

The objective of this final section of the anthology is to
assess the current state of relations between Black
Americans and Africa across a broad range of
phenomena—from cultural indicators to perceptions of
political power to the future of Afro-American
nationalism and the prospects for future Afro-American
emigration to Africa. It also subsumes a dialogue on
the nature and configuration of Black Power and how
this poorly understood concept is related to the Black
American's assessment of his Africanness and what
operational consequences flow therefrom.

*"Black Power: Its Needs and Substance," is the second chapter of the 1967 book,* Black Power, *by Stokely Carmichael and Charles V. Hamilton. They posit a very clear relationship between the realization of a common African ancestry, a feeling of community among American Black men, and the acquisition of political and economic power in the context of American political-bloc organization. They repudiate the necessity for alliances with White power groups until such time as a powerful and autonomous Black Power group, directed and shaped by Black men, can establish itself. Only then, will coalition with White men of good-will be feasible.*

# Black Power: Its Needs and Substance

## Stokely Carmichael and Charles V. Hamilton

"To carve out a place for itself in the politico-social order," V. O. Key, Jr. wrote in *Politics, Parties and Pressure Groups,* "a new group may have to fight for reorientation of many of the values of the old order" (p. 57). This is especially true when that group is composed of black people in the American society—a society that has for centuries deliberately and systematically excluded them from political participation. Black people in the United States must raise hard questions, questions which challenge the very nature of the society itself: its long-standing values, beliefs and institutions.

To do this, we must first redefine ourselves. Our basic need is to reclaim our history and our identity from what must be called cultural terrorism, from the depredation of self-justifying white guilt. We shall have to struggle for the right to create our own terms through which to define ourselves and our relationship to the society, and to have these terms recognized. This is the first necessity of a free people, and the first right that any oppressor must suspend.

In *Politics Among Nations,* Hans Morgenthau defined political power as "the psychological control over the minds of men" (p. 29). This control includes the attempt by the oppressor to have *his* definitions, *his* historical descriptions, *accepted* by the oppressed. This was true in Africa no less

From Stokely Carmichael and Charles V. Hamilton, *Black Power* (New York: Random House, 1967), pp. 34–56.

than in the United States. To black Africans, the word "Uhuru" means "freedom," but they had to fight the white colonizers for the right to use the term. The recorded history of this country's dealings with red and black men offers other examples. In the wars between the white settlers and the "Indians," a battle won by the Cavalry was described as a "victory." The "Indians' " triumphs, however, were "massacres." (The American colonists were not unaware of the need to define their acts in their own terms. They labeled their fight against England a "revolution"; the English attempted to demean it by calling it "insubordination" or "riotous.")

The historical period following Reconstruction in the South after the Civil War has been called by many historians the period of Redemption, implying that the bigoted southern slave societies were "redeemed" from the hands of "reckless and irresponsible" black rulers. Professor John Hope Franklin's *Reconstruction* or Dr. W. E. B. Dubois' *Black Reconstruction* should be sufficient to dispel inaccurate historical notions, but the larger society persists in its own self-serving accounts. Thus black people came to be depicted as "lazy," "apathetic," "dumb," "shiftless," "good-timers." Just as red men had to be recorded as "savages" to justify the white man's theft of their land, so black men had to be vilified in order to justify their continued oppression. Those who have the right to define are the masters of the situation. Lewis Carroll understood this:

"When I use a word," Humpty Dumpty said in a rather scornful tone, "it means just what I choose it to mean—neither more nor less."

"The question is," said Alice, "whether you *can* make words mean so many different things."

"The question is," said Humpty Dumpty, "which is to be master—that's all." [1]

Today, the American educational system continues to reinforce the entrenched values of the society through the use of words. Few people in this country question that this is "the land of the free and the home of the brave." They have had these words drummed into them from childhood. Few people question that this is the "Great Society" or that this country is fighting "Communist aggression" around the world. We mouth these things over and over, and they become truisms not to be questioned. In a similar way, black people have been saddled with epithets.

"Integration" is another current example of a word which has been defined according to the way white Americans see it. To many of them, it means black men wanting to marry white daughters; it means "race mixing" —implying bed or dance partners. To black people, it has meant a way to improve their lives—economically and politically. But the predominant white definition has stuck in the minds of too many people.

Black people must redefine themselves, and only *they* can do that. Throughout this country, vast segments of the black communities are beginning to recognize the need to assert their own definitions, to reclaim their history, their culture; to create their own sense of community and togetherness. There is a growing resentment of the word "Negro," for example, because this term is the invention of our oppressor; it is *his* image of us that he describes. Many blacks are now calling themselves African-Americans, Afro-Americans or black people because that is *our* image of ourselves. When we begin to define our own image, the stereotypes—that is, lies— that our oppressor has developed will begin in the white community and end there. The black community will have a positive image of itself that *it* has created. This means we will no longer call ourselves lazy, apathetic, dumb, good-timers, shiftless, etc. Those are words used by white America to define us. If we accept these adjectives, as some of us have in the past, then we see ourselves only in a negative way, precisely the way white America wants us to see ourselves. Our incentive is broken and our will to fight is surrendered. From now on we shall view ourselves as African-Americans and as black people who are in fact energetic, determined, intelligent, beautiful and peace-loving.

There is a terminology and ethos peculiar to the black community of which black people are beginning to be no longer ashamed. Black communities are the only large segments of this society where people refer to each other as brother—soul-brother, soul-sister. Some people may look upon this as *ersatz,* as make-believe, but it is not that. It is real. It is a growing sense of community. It is a growing realization that black Americans have a common bond not only among themselves, but with their African brothers. In *Black Man's Burden,* John O. Killens described his trip to ten African countries as follows:

Everywhere I went people called me brother.... "Welcome, American brother." It was a good feeling for me, to be in Africa. To walk in a land for the first time in your entire life knowing within yourself that your color would not be held against you. No black man ever knows this in America [p. 160].

More and more black Americans are developing this feeling. They are becoming aware that they have a history which pre-dates their forced introduction to this country. African-American history means a long history beginning on the continent of Africa, a history not taught in the standard textbooks of this country. It is absolutely essential that black people know this history, that they know their roots, that they develop an awareness of their cultural heritage. Too long have they been kept in submission by being told that they had no culture, no manifest heritage, before they landed on the slave auction blocks in this country. If black people are to know themselves as a vibrant, valiant people, they must know their roots. And they will soon learn that the Hollywood image of man-eating cannibals waiting for, and waiting on, the Great White Hunter is a lie.

With redefinition will come a clearer notion of the role black Americans can play in this world. This role will emerge clearly out of the unique, common experiences of Afro-Asians. Killens concludes:

I believe furthermore that the American Negro can be the bridge between the West and Africa-Asia. We black Americans can serve as a bridge to mutual understanding. The one thing we black Americans have in common with the other colored peoples of the world is that we have all felt the cruel and ruthless heel of white supremacy. We have all been "niggerized" on one level or another. And all of us are determined to "deniggerize" the earth. To rid the world of "niggers" is the Black Man's Burden, human reconstruction is the grand objective [p. 176].

Only when black people fully develop this sense of community, of themselves, can they begin to deal effectively with the problems of racism in *this* country. This is what we mean by a new consciousness; this is the vital first step.

The next step is what we shall call the process of political modernization —a process which must take place if the society is to be rid of racism. "Political modernization" includes many things, but we mean by it three major concepts: (1) questioning old values and institutions of the society; (2) searching for new and different forms of political structure to solve political and economic problems; and (3) broadening the base of political participation to include more people in the decision-making process. These notions (we shall take up each in turn) are central to our thinking throughout this book and to contemporary American history as a whole. As David Apter wrote in *The Politics of Modernization,* ". . . the struggle to modernize is what has given meaning to our generation. It tests our cherished institutions and our beliefs. . . . So compelling a force has it become that we are forced to ask new questions of our own institutions. Each country, whether modernized or modernizing, stands in both judgment and fear of the results. Our own society is no exception" (p. 2).

The values of this society support a racist system; we find it incongruous to ask black people to adopt and support most of these values. We also reject the assumption that the basic institutions of this society must be preserved. The goal of black people must *not* be to assimilate into middle-class America, for that class—as a whole—is without a viable conscience as regards humanity. The values of the middle class permit the perpetuation of the ravages of the black community. The values of that class are based on material aggrandizement, not the expansion of humanity. The values of that class ultimately support cloistered little closed societies tucked away neatly in tree-lined suburbia. The values of that class do *not* lead to the creation of an open society. That class *mouths* its preference for a free, competitive society, while at the same time forcefully and even viciously denying to black people as a group the opportunity to compete.

We are not unmindful of other descriptions of the social utility of the middle class. Banfield and Wilson, in *City Politics*, concluded:

> The departure of the middle class from the central city is important in other ways. . . . The middle class supplies a social and political leavening in the life of a city. Middle-class people demand good schools and integrity in government. They support churches, lodges, parent-teacher associations, scout troops, better-housing committees, art galleries, and operas. It is the middle class, in short, that asserts a conception of the public interest. Now its activity is increasingly concentrated in the suburbs [p. 14].

But this same middle class manifests a sense of superior group position in regard to race. This class wants "good government" *for themselves;* it wants good schools *for its children.* At the same time, many of its members sneak into the black community by day, exploit it, and take the money home to their middle-class communities at night to support their operas and art galleries and comfortable homes. When not actually robbing, they will fight off the handful of more affluent black people who seek to move in; when they approve or even seek token integration, it applies only to black people like themselves—as "white" as possible. *This class is the backbone of institutional racism in this country.*

Thus we reject the goal of assimilation into middle-class America because the values of that class are in themselves anti-humanist and because that class as a social force perpetuates racism. We must face the fact that, in the past, what we have called the movement has not really questioned the middle-class values and institutions of this country. If anything, it has accepted those values and institutions without fully realizing their racist nature. Reorientation means an emphasis on the dignity of man, not on the sanctity of property. It means the creation of a society where human misery and poverty are repugnant to that society, not an indication of laziness or lack of initiative. The creation of new values means the establishment of a society based, as Killens expresses it in *Black Man's Burden,* on "free people," not "free enterprise" (p. 167). To do this means to modernize—*indeed, to civilize*—this country.

Supporting the old values are old political and economic structures; these must also be "modernized." We should at this point distinguish between "structures" and "system." By system, we have in mind the entire American complex of basic institutions, values, beliefs, etc. By structures, we mean the specific institutions (political parties, interest groups, bureaucratic administrations) which exist to conduct the business of that system. Obviously, the first is broader than the second. Also, the second assumes the legitimacy of the first. Our view is that, given the illegitimacy of the system, we cannot then proceed to transform that system with existing structures.

The two major political parties in this country have become non-viable entities for the legitimate representation of the real needs of masses—especially blacks—in this country. Walter Lippmann raised the same point in his syndicated column of December 8, 1966. He pointed out that the party system in the United States developed before our society became as technologically complex as it is now. He says that the ways in which men live and define themselves are changing radically. Old ideological issues, once the subject of passionate controversy, Lippmann argues, are of little interest today. He asks whether the great urban complexes—which are rapidly becoming the centers of black population in the U.S.—can be run with the same systems and ideas that derive from a time when America was a country of small villages and farms. While not addressing himself directly to the question of race, Lippmann raises a major question about our political institutions; and the crisis of race in America may be its major symptom.

Black people have seen the city planning commissions, the urban renewal commissions, the boards of education and the police departments fail to speak to their needs in a meaningful way. We must devise new structures, new institutions to replace those forms or to make them responsive. There is nothing sacred or inevitable about old institutions; the focus must be on people, not forms.

Existing structures and established ways of doing things have a way of perpetuating themselves and for this reason, the modernizing process will be difficult. Therefore, timidity in calling into question the boards of education or the police departments will not do. They must be challenged forcefully and clearly. If this means the creation of parallel community institutions, then that must be the solution. If this means that black parents must gain control over the operation of the schools in the black community, then that must be the solution. The search for new forms means the search for institutions that will, for once, make decisions in the interest of black people. It means, for example, a building inspection department that neither winks at violations of building codes by absentee slumlords nor imposes meaningless fines which permit them to continue their exploitation of the black community.

Essential to the modernization of structures is a broadened base of political participation. More and more people must become politically sensitive and active (we have already seen this happening in some areas of the South). People must no longer be tied, by small incentives or handouts, to a corrupting and corruptible white machine. Black people will choose their own leaders and hold those leaders responsible to *them*. A broadened base means an end to the condition described by James Wilson in *Negro Politics,* whereby "Negroes tended to be the objects rather than the subjects of civic action. Things are often done for, or about, or to, or because of Negroes, but they are less frequently done *by* Negroes" (p. 133). Broadening the base of political participation, then, has as much to do with the quality of black participation as with the quantity. We are fully aware that the black vote, especially in the North, has been pulled out of white pockets and "delivered" whenever it was in the interest of white politicians to do so. That vote must no longer be controllable by those who have neither the interests nor the demonstrated concern of black people in mind.

As the base broadens, as more and more black people become activated, they will perceive more clearly the special disadvantages heaped upon them as a group. They will perceive that the larger society is growing more affluent while the black society is retrogressing, as daily life and mounting statistics clearly show (see Chapters I and VIII). V. O. Key describes what often happens next, in *Politics, Parties and Pressure Groups:* "A factor of great significance in the setting off of political movements is an abrupt change for the worse in the status of one group relative to that of other groups in society. . . . A rapid change for the worse . . . in the relative status of any group . . . is likely to precipitate political action" (p. 24). Black people will become increasingly active as they notice that their retrogressive status exists in large measure because of values and institutions arraigned against them. They will begin to stress and strain and call the entire system into question. Political modernization will be in motion. We believe that it is now in motion. One form of that motion is Black Power.

The adoption of the concept of Black Power is one of the most legitimate and healthy developments in American politics and race relations in our time. The concept of Black Power speaks to all the needs mentioned in this chapter. It is a call for black people in this country to unite, to recognize their heritage, to build a sense of community. It is a call for black people to begin to define their own goals, to lead their own organizations and to support those organizations. It is a call to reject the racist institutions and values of this society.

The concept of Black Power rests on a fundamental premise: *Before a group can enter the open society, it must first close ranks.* By this we mean that group solidarity is necessary before a group can operate effectively from a bargaining position of strength in a pluralistic society. Traditionally, each new ethnic group in this society has found the route to social and political viability through the organization of its own institutions with which to represent its needs within the larger society. Studies in voting behavior specifically, and political behavior generally, have made it clear that politically the American pot has not melted. Italians vote for Rubino over O'Brien; Irish for Murphy over Goldberg, etc. This phenomenon may seem distasteful to some, but it has been and remains today a central fact of the American political system. There are other examples of ways in which groups in the society have remembered their roots and used this effectively in the political arena. Theodore Sorensen describes the politics of foreign aid during the Kennedy Administration in his book *Kennedy:*

No powerful constituencies or interest groups backed foreign aid. The Marshall Plan at least had appealed to Americans who traced their roots to the Western European nations aided. But there were few voters who identified with India, Colombia or Tanganyika [p. 351].

The extent to which black Americans can and do "trace their roots" to Africa, to that extent will they be able to be more effective on the political scene.

A white reporter set forth this point in other terms when he made the following observation about white Mississippi's manipulation of the antipoverty program:

The war on poverty has been predicated on the notion that there is such a thing as a community which can be defined geographically and mobilized for a collective effort to help the poor. This theory has no relationship to reality in the deep South. In every Mississippi county there are two communities. Despite all the pious platitudes of the moderates on both sides, these two communities habitually see their interests in terms of conflict rather than cooperation. Only when the Negro community can muster enough political, economic and professional strength to compete on somewhat equal terms, will Negroes believe in the possibility of true cooperation and whites accept its necessity. En route to integration, the Negro community needs to develop a greater independence—a chance to run its own affairs and not cave in whenever "the man" barks—or so it seems to me, and to most of the knowledgeable people with whom I talked in Mississippi. To OEO, this judgment may sound like black nationalism. . . .[2]

The point is obvious: black people must lead and run their own organizations. Only black people can convey the revolutionary idea—and it is a revolutionary idea—that black people are able to do things themselves. Only they can help create in the community an aroused and continuing black consciousness that will provide the basis for political strength. In the past, white allies have often furthered white supremacy without the whites involved realizing it, or even wanting to do so. Black people must come together and do things for themselves. They must achieve self-identity and self-determination in order to have their daily needs met.

Black Power means, for example, that in Lowndes County, Alabama, a black sheriff can end police brutality. A black tax assessor and tax collector and county board of revenue can lay, collect, and channel tax monies for the building of better roads and schools serving black people. In such areas as Lowndes, where black people have a majority, they will attempt to use power to exercise control. This is what they seek: control. When black people lack a majority, Black Power means proper representation and sharing of control. It means the creation of power bases, of strength, from which black people can press to change local or nation-wide patterns of oppression—instead of from weakness.

It does not mean *merely* putting black faces into office. Black visibility is not Black Power. Most of the black politicians around the country today are not examples of Black Power. The power must be that of a community, and emanate from there. The black politicians must start from there. The black politicians must stop being representatives of "downtown" machines, whatever the cost might be in terms of lost patronage and holiday handouts.

Black Power recognizes—it must recognize—the ethnic basis of American politics as well as the power-oriented nature of American politics. Black Power therefore calls for black people to consolidate behind their own, so that they can bargain from a position of strength. But while we endorse the *procedure* of group solidarity and identity for the purpose of attaining certain goals in the body politic, this does not mean that black people should strive for the same kind of rewards (i.e., end results) obtained by the white society. The ultimate values and goals are not domination or exploitation of other groups, but rather an effective share in the total power of the society.

Nevertheless, some observers have labeled those who advocate Black Power as racists; they have said that the call for self-identification and self-determination is "racism in reverse" or "black supremacy." This is a deliberate and absurd lie. There is no analogy—by any stretch of definition or imagination—between the advocates of Black Power and white racists. Racism is not merely exclusion on the basis of race but exclusion for the purpose of subjugating or maintaining subjugation. The goal of the racists is to keep black people on the bottom, arbitrarily and dictatorially, as they have done in this country for over three hundred years. The goal of black self-determination and black self-identity—Black Power—is full participation in the decision-making processes affecting the lives of black people, and recognition of the virtues in themselves as black people. The black people of this country have not lynched whites, bombed their churches, murdered their children and manipulated laws and institutions to maintain oppression. White racists have. Congressional laws, one after the other, have not been necessary to stop black people from oppressing others and denying others the full enjoyment of their rights. White racists have made such laws necessary. The goal of Black Power is positive and functional to a free and viable society. No white racist can make this claim.

A great deal of public attention and press space was devoted to the hysterical accusation of "black racism" when the call for Black Power was first sounded. A national committee of influential black churchmen affiliated with the National Council of Churches, despite their obvious respectability and responsibility, had to resort to a paid advertisement to articulate their position, while anyone yapping "black racism" made front-page news. In their statement, published in *The New York Times* of July 31, 1966, the churchmen said:

We, an informal group of Negro churchmen in America, are deeply disturbed about the crisis brought upon our country by historic distortions of important human realities in the controversy about "black power." What we see shining through the variety of rhetoric is not anything new but the same old problem of power and race which has faced our beloved country since 1619.

. . . The conscience of black men is corrupted because having no power to implement the demands of conscience, the concern for justice in the absence of justice becomes a chaotic self-surrender. Powerlessness breeds a race of beggars. We are faced with a situation where powerless conscience meets conscienceless power, threatening the very foundations of our Nation.

We deplore the overt violence of riots, but we feel it is more important to focus on the real sources of these eruptions. These sources may be abetted inside the Ghetto, but their basic cause lies in the silent and covert violence which white middle class America inflicts upon the victims of the inner city.

. . . In short, the failure of American leaders to use American power to create equal opportunity *in life* as well as *law,* this is the real problem and not the anguished cry for black power.

. . . Without the capacity to participate with power, i.e., to have some organized political and economic strength to really influence people with whom one interacts, integration is not meaningful.

. . . America has asked its Negro citizens to fight for opportunity as *individuals,* whereas at certain points in our history what we have needed most has been opportunity for the *whole group,* not just for selected and approved Negroes.

...We must not apologize for the existence of this form of group power, for we have been oppressed as a group and not as individuals. We will not find our way out of that oppression until both we and America accept the need for Negro Americans, as well as for Jews, Italians, Poles, and white Anglo-Saxon Protestants, among others, to have and to wield group power.

It is a commentary on the fundamentally racist nature of this society that the concept of group strength for black people must be articulated—not to mention defended. No other group would submit to being led by others. Italians do not run the Anti-Defamation League of B'nai B'rith. Irish do not chair Christopher Columbus Societies. Yet when black people call for black-run and all-black organizations, they are immediately classed in a category with the Ku Klux Klan. This is interesting and ironic, but by no means surprising: the society does not expect black people to be able to take care of their business, and there are many who prefer it precisely that way.

In the end, we cannot and shall not offer any guarantees that Black Power, if achieved, would be non-racist. No one can predict human behavior. Social change always has unanticipated consequences. If black racism is what the larger society fears, we cannot help them. We can only state what we hope will be the result, given the fact that the present situation is unacceptable and that we have no real alternative but to work for Black Power. The final truth is that the white society is not entitled to reassurances, even if it were possible to offer them.

We have outlined the meaning and goals of Black Power; we have also discussed one major thing which it is not. There are others of greater importance. The advocates of Black Power reject the old slogans and meaningless rhetoric of previous years in the civil rights struggle. The language of yesterday is indeed irrelevant: progress, non-violence, integration, fear of "white backlash," coalition. Let us look at the rhetoric and see why these terms must be set aside or redefined.

One of the tragedies of the struggle against racism is that up to this point there has been no national organization which could speak to the growing militancy of young black people in the urban ghettos and the black-belt South. There has been only a "civil rights" movement, whose tone of voice was adapted to an audience of middle-class whites. It served as a sort of buffer zone between that audience and angry young blacks. It claimed to speak for the needs of a community, but it did not speak in the tone of that community. None of its so-called leaders could go into a rioting community and be listened to. In a sense, the blame must be shared—along with the mass media—by those leaders for what happened in Watts, Harlem, Chicago, Cleveland and other places. Each time the black people in those cities saw Dr. Martin Luther King get slapped they became angry. When they saw little black girls bombed to death *in a church* and civil rights workers ambushed and murdered, they were angrier; and when nothing happened, they were steaming mad. We had nothing to offer that they could see, except to go out and be beaten again. We helped to build their frustration.

We had only the old language of love and suffering. And in most places— that is, from the liberals and middle class—we got back the old language of patience and progress. The civil rights leaders were saying to the country: "Look, you guys are supposed to be nice guys, and we are only going to do what we are supposed to do. Why do you beat us up? Why don't you give us what we ask? Why don't you straighten yourselves out?" For the masses of black people, this language resulted in virtually nothing. In fact, their objective day-to-day condition worsened. The unemployment rate among black people increased while that among whites declined. Housing conditions in the black communities deteriorated. Schools in the black ghettos continued to plod along on outmoded techniques, inadequate curricula, and with all too many tired and indifferent teachers. Meanwhile, the President picked up the refrain of "We Shall Overcome" while the Congress passed civil rights law after civil rights law, only to have them effectively nullified by deliberately weak enforcement. "Progress is being made," we were told.

Such language, along with admonitions to remain nonviolent and fear the white backlash, convinced some that that course was the *only* course to follow. It misled some into believing that a black minority could bow its head and get whipped into a meaningful position of power. The very notion is absurd. The white society devised the language, adopted the rules and had the black community narcotized into believing that that language and those rules were, in fact, relevant. The black community was told time and again how *other* immigrants finally won *acceptance:* that is, by following the Protestant Ethic of Work and Achievement. They worked hard; therefore, they achieved. We were not told that it was by building Irish Power, Italian Power, Polish Power or Jewish Power that these groups got themselves together and operated from positions of strength. We were not told that "the American dream" wasn't designed for black people. That while today, to whites, the dream may *seem* to include black people, it cannot do so by the very nature of this nation's political and economic system, which imposes institutional racism on the black masses if not upon every individual black. A notable comment on that "dream" was made by Dr. Percy Julian, the black scientist and director of the Julian Research Institute in Chicago, a man for whom the dream seems to have come true. While not subscribing to "black power" as he understood it, Dr. Julian clearly understood the basis for it: "The false concept of basic Negro inferiority is one of the curses that still lingers. It is a problem created by the white man. Our children just no longer are going to accept the patience we were taught by our generation. We were taught a pretty little lie—excel and the whole world lies open before you. *I obeyed the injunction and found it to be wishful thinking.*" (Authors' italics) [3]

A key phrase in our buffer-zone days was non-violence. For years it has been thought that black people would not literally fight for their lives. Why this has been so is not entirely clear; neither the larger society nor black people are noted for passivity. The notion apparently stems from the years of marches and demonstrations and sit-ins where black people did not strike back and the violence always came from white mobs. There are many who still sincerely believe in that approach. From our viewpoint, rampaging white mobs and white night-riders must be made to understand that their days of free head-whipping are over. Black people should and must fight back. Nothing more quickly repels someone bent on destroying you than the unequivocal message: "O.K., fool, make your move, and run the same risk I run—of dying."

When the concept of Black Power is set forth, many people immediately conjure up notions of violence. The country's reaction to the Deacons for Defense and Justice, which originated in Louisiana, is instructive. Here is a group which realized that the "law" and law enforcement agencies would not protect people, so they had to do it themselves. If a nation fails to protect its citizens, then that nation cannot condemn those who take up the task themselves. The Deacons and all other blacks who resort to self-defense represent a simple answer to a simple question: what man would not defend his family and home from attack?

But this frightened some white people, because they knew that black people would now fight back. They knew that this was precisely what *they* would have long since done if *they* were subjected to the injustices and oppression heaped on blacks. Those of us who advocate Black Power are quite clear in our own minds that a "non-violent" approach to civil rights is an approach black people cannot afford and a luxury white people do not deserve. It is crystal clear to us—and it must become so with the white society—*that there can be no social order without social justice.* White people must be made to understand that they must stop messing with black people, or the blacks *will* fight back!

Next, we must deal with the term "integration." According to its advocates, social justice will be accomplished by "integrating the Negro into the mainstream institutions of the society from which he has been traditionally excluded." This concept is based on the assumption that there is nothing of value in the black community and that little of value could be created among black people. The thing to do is siphon off the "acceptable" black people into the surrounding middle-class white community.

The goals of integrationists are middle-class goals, articulated primarily by a small group of Negroes with middle-class aspirations or status. Their kind of integration has meant that a few blacks "make it," leaving the black community, sapping it of leadership potential and know-how. As we noted in Chapter I, those token Negroes—absorbed into a white mass—are of no value to the remaining black masses. They become meaningless show-pieces for a conscience-soothed white society. Such people will state that they would prefer to be treated "only as individuals, not as Negroes"; that they "are not and should not be preoccupied with race." This is a totally unrealistic position. In the first place, black people have not suffered as individuals but as members of a group; therefore, their liberation lies in group action. This is why SNCC—and the concept of Black Power—affirms that helping *individual* black people to solve their problems on an *individual* basis does little to alleviate the mass of black people. Secondly, while color blindness *may* be a sound goal ultimately, we must realize that race is an overwhelming fact of life in this historical period. There is no black man in this country who can live "simply as a man." His blackness is an ever-present fact of this racist society, whether he recognizes it or not. It is unlikely that this or the next generation will witness the time when race will no longer be relevant in the conduct of public affairs and in public policy decision-making. To realize this and to attempt to deal with it does not make one a racist or overly preoccupied with race; it puts one in the fore-front of a significant *struggle*. If there is no intense struggle today, there will be no meaningful results tomorrow.

"Integration" as a goal today speaks to the problem of blackness not only in an unrealistic way but also in a despicable way. It is based on complete acceptance of the fact that in order to have a decent house or education, black people must move into a white neighborhood or send their children to a white school. This reinforces, among both black and white, the idea that "white" is automatically superior and "black" is by definition inferior. For this reason, "integration" is a subterfuge for the maintenance of white supremacy. It allows the nation to focus on a handful of Southern black children who get into white schools at a great price, and to ignore the ninety-four per cent who are left in unimproved all-black schools. Such situations will not change until black people become equal in a way that means something, and integration ceases to be a one-way street. Then integration does not mean draining skills and energies from the black ghetto into white neighborhoods. To sprinkle black children among white pupils in outlying schools is at best a stop-gap measure. The goal is not to take black children out of the black community and expose them to white middle-class values; the goal is to build and strengthen the black community.

"Integration" also means that black people must give up their identity, deny their heritage. We recall the conclusion of Killian and Grigg: "At the present time, integration as a solution to the race problem demands that the Negro foreswear his identity as a Negro." The fact is that integration, as traditionally articulated, would abolish the black community. The fact is that what must be abolished is not the black community, but the dependent colonial status that has been inflicted upon it.

The racial and cultural personality of the black community must be preserved and that community must win its freedom while preserving its cultural integrity. Integrity includes a pride—in the sense of self-acceptance, not chauvinism—in being black, in the historical attainments and contributions of black people. No person can be healthy, complete and mature if he must deny a part of himself; this is what "integration" has required thus far. This is the essential difference between integration as it is currently practiced and the concept of Black Power.

The idea of cultural integrity is so obvious that it seems almost simpleminded to spell things out at this length. Yet millions of Americans resist such truths when they are applied to black people. Again, that resistance is a comment on the fundamental racism in the society. Irish Catholics took care of their own first without a lot of apology for doing so, without any dubious language from timid leadership about guarding against "backlash." Everyone understood it to be a perfectly legitimate procedure. Of course, there would be "backlash." Organization begets counterorganization, but this was no reason to defer.

The so-called white backlash against black people is something else: the embedded traditions of institutional racism being brought into the open and calling forth overt manifestations of individual racism. In the summer of 1966, when the protest marches into Cicero, Illinois, began, the black people knew they were not allowed to live in Cicero and the white people knew it. When blacks began to demand the right to live in homes in that town, the whites simply reminded them of the status quo. Some people called this "backlash." It was, in fact, racism defending itself. In the black community, this is called "White folks showing their color." It is ludicrous to blame black people for what is simply an overt manifestation of white racism. Dr. Martin Luther King stated clearly that the protest marches were not the cause of the racism but merely exposed a long-term cancerous condition in the society.

## NOTES

[1] Lewis Carroll, *Through the Looking Glass*. New York: Doubleday Books, Inc., p. 196.
[2] Christopher Jencks, "Accommodating Whites: A New Look at Mississippi," *The New Republic* (April 16, 1966).
[3] *The New York Times* (April 30, 1967), p. 30.

*For Dr. Martin Luther King, Jr., Black Power had a
different meaning from that expressed by Carmichael and
Hamilton. He regarded Black Power as a form of
separatism. He believed that in a multiracial society,
no single group could make it alone and that the
acquisition of power required the forging of alliances
with sympathetic Whites not only in the long run
but in the short run as well.*

# Black Power

## Martin Luther King, Jr.

. . . . . . . . . . . . .

Nevertheless, in spite of the positive aspects of Black Power, which are compatible with what we have sought to do in the civil rights movement all along without the slogan, its negative values, I believe, prevent it from having the substance and program to become the basic strategy for the civil rights movement in the days ahead.

Beneath all the satisfaction of a gratifying slogan, Black Power is a nihilistic philosophy born out of the conviction that the Negro can't win. It is, at bottom, the view that American society is so hopelessly corrupt and enmeshed in evil that there is no possibility of salvation from within. Although this thinking is understandable as a response to a white power structure that never completely committed itself to true equality for the Negro, and a die-hard mentality that sought to shut all windows and doors against the winds of change, it nonetheless carries the seeds of its own doom.

Before this century, virtually all revolutions had been based on hope and hate. The hope was expressed in the rising expectation of freedom and justice. The hate was an expression of bitterness toward the perpetrators of the old order. It was the hate that made revolutions bloody and violent. What was new about Mahatma Gandhi's movement in India was that he mounted a revolution on hope and love, hope and nonviolence. This same new emphasis characterized the civil rights movement in our country dating from the Montgomery bus boycott of 1956 to the Selma movement of 1965. We maintained the hope while transforming the hate of traditional revolutions into positive nonviolent power. As long as the hope was fulfilled there was little questioning of nonviolence. But when the hopes were blasted, when people came to see that in spite of progress their conditions were still insufferable, when they looked out and saw more poverty, more school segregation and more slums, despair began to set in.

Unfortunately, when hope diminishes, the hate is often turned most bitterly toward those who originally built up the hope. In all the speaking that I have done in the United States before varied audiences, including some hostile whites, the only time that I have been booed was one night in a Chicago mass meeting by some young members of the Black Power movement. I went home that night with an ugly feeling. Selfishly I thought of my sufferings and sacrifices over the last twelve years. Why would they boo one so close to them? But as I lay awake thinking, I finally came to myself, and I could not for the life of me have less than patience and understanding for those young people. For twelve years I, and others like me, had held out radiant promises of progress. I had preached to them about my dream. I had lectured to them about the not too distant day when they would have freedom, "all, here and now." I had urged them to have faith in America and in the white society. Their hopes had soared. They were now booing because they felt that we were unable to deliver on our promises. They were booing because we had urged them to have faith in people who had too often proved to be unfaithful. They were now hostile because they were watching the dream that they had so readily accepted turn into a frustrating nightmare.

But revolution, though born of despair, cannot long be sustained by despair. This is the ultimate contradiction of the Black Power movement. It claims to be the most revolutionary wing of the social revolution taking place in the United States. Yet it rejects the one thing that keeps the fire of revolutions burning: the ever-present flame of hope. When hope dies, a revolution degenerates into an undiscriminating catch-all for evanescent and futile gestures. The Negro cannot entrust his destiny to a philosophy nourished solely on despair, to a slogan that cannot be implemented into a program.

The Negro's disappointment is real and a part of the daily menu of our lives. One of the most agonizing problems of human experience is how to deal with disappointment. In our individual lives we all too often distill our frustrations into an essence of bitterness, or drown ourselves in the deep waters of self-pity, or adopt a fatalistic philosophy that whatever happens must happen and all events are determined by necessity. These reactions poison the soul and scar the personality, always harming the person who harbors them more than anyone else. The only healthy answer lies in one's honest recognition of disappointment even as he still clings to hope, one's acceptance of finite disappointment even while clinging to infinite hope.

We Negroes, who have dreamed for so long of freedom, are still confined in a prison of segregation and discrimination. Must we respond with bitterness and cynicism? Certainly not, for this can lead to black anger so desperate that it ends in black suicide. Must we turn inward in self-pity? Of course not, for this can lead to a self-defeating black paranoia. Must we conclude that we cannot win? Certainly not, for this will lead to a black nihilism that seeks disruption for disruption's sake. Must we, by fatalistically concluding that segregation is a foreordained pattern of the universe, resign ourselves to oppression? Of course not, for passively to cooperate with an unjust system makes the oppressed as evil as the oppressors. Our most fruitful course is to stand firm, move forward nonviolently, accept disappointments and cling to hope. Our determined refusal not to be stopped will eventually open the door to fulfillment. By recognizing the necessity of suffering in a righteous cause, we may achieve our humanity's full stature. To guard ourselves from bitterness, we need the vision to see in this generation's ordeals the opportunity to transfigure both ourselves and American society.

In 1956 I flew from New York to London in the propeller-type aircraft that required nine and a half hours for a flight now made in six hours by jet. Returning from London to the United States, the stewardess announced that the flying time would be twelve and a half hours. The distance was the same. Why an additional three hours? When the pilot entered the cabin to greet the passengers, I asked him to explain.

"You must understand about the winds," he said. "When we leave New York, a strong tail wind is in our favor, but when we return, a strong head wind is against us." Then he added, "Don't worry. These four engines are capable of battling the winds."

In any social revolution there are times when the tail winds of triumph and fulfillment favor us, and other times when strong head winds of disappointment and setbacks beat against us relentlessly. We must not permit adverse winds to overwhelm us as we journey across life's mighty Atlantic; we must be sustained by our engines of courage in spite of the winds. This refusal to be stopped, this "courage to be," this determination to go on "in spite of" is the hallmark of any great movement.

The Black Power movement of today, like the Garvey "Back to Africa" movement of the 1920's, represents a dashing of hope, a conviction of the inability of the Negro to win and a belief in the infinitude of the ghetto. While there is much grounding in past experience for all these feelings, a revolution cannot succumb to any of them. Today's despair is a poor chisel to carve out tomorrow's justice.

Black Power is an implicit and often explicit belief in black separatism. Notice that I do not call it black racism. It is inaccurate to refer to Black Power as racism in reverse, as some have recently done. Racism is a doctrine of the congenital inferiority and worthlessness of a people. While a few angry proponents of Black Power have, in moments of bitterness, made wild statements that come close to this kind of racism, the major proponents of Black Power have never contended that the white man is innately worthless.

Yet behind Black Power's legitimate and necessary concern for group unity and black identity lies the belief that there can be a separate black road to power and fulfillment. Few ideals are more unrealistic. There is no salvation for the Negro through isolation.

One of the chief affirmations of Black Power is the call for the mobilization of political strength for black people. But we do not have to look far to see that effective political power for Negroes cannot come through separatism. Granted that there are cities and counties in the country where the Negro is in a majority, they are so few that concentration on them alone would still leave the vast majority of Negroes outside the mainstream of American political life.

Out of the eighty-odd counties in Alabama, the state where SNCC sought to develop an all-black party, only nine have a majority of Negroes. Even if blacks could control each of these counties, they would have little influence in over-all state politics and could do little to improve conditions in the major Negro population centers of Birmingham, Mobile and Montgomery. There are still relatively few Congressional districts in the South that have such large black majorities that Negro candidates could be elected without the aid of whites. Is it a sounder program to concentrate on the election of two or three Negro Congressmen from predominantly Negro districts or to concentrate on the election of fifteen or twenty Negro Congressmen from Southern districts where a coalition of Negro and white moderate voters is possible?

Moreover, any program that elects all black candidates simply because they are black and rejects all white candidates simply because they are white is politically unsound and morally unjustifiable. It is true that in many areas of the South Negroes still must elect Negroes in order to be effectively represented. SNCC staff members are eminently correct when they point out that in Lowndes County, Alabama, there are no white liberals or moderates and no possibility for cooperation between the races at the present time. But the Lowndes County experience cannot be made a measuring rod for the whole of America. The basic thing in determining the best candidate is not his color but his integrity.

Black Power alone is no more insurance against social injustice than white power. Negro politicians can be as opportunistic as their white counterparts if there is not an informed and determined constituency demanding social reform. What is most needed is a coalition of Negroes and liberal whites that will work to make both major parties truly responsive to the needs of the poor. Black Power does not envision or desire such a program.

Just as the Negro cannot achieve political power in isolation, neither can he gain economic power through separatism. While there must be a continued emphasis on the need for blacks to pool their economic resources and withdraw consumer support from discriminating firms, we must not be oblivious to the fact that the larger economic problems confronting the Negro community will only be solved by federal programs involving billions of dollars. One unfortunate thing about Black Power is that it gives priority to race precisely at a time when the impact of automation and other forces have made the economic question fundamental for blacks and whites alike. In this context a slogan "Power for Poor People" would be much more appropriate than the slogan "Black Power."

However much we pool our resources and "buy black," this cannot create the multiplicity of new jobs and provide the number of low-cost houses that will lift the Negro out of the economic depression caused by centuries of deprivation. Neither can our resources supply quality integrated education. All of this requires billions of dollars which only an alliance of liberal-labor-civil-rights forces can stimulate. In short, the Negroes' probem cannot be solved unless the whole of American society takes a new turn toward greater economic justice.

In a multiracial society no group can make it alone. It is a myth to believe that the Irish, the Italians and the Jews—the ethnic groups that Black Power advocates cite as justification for their views—rose to power through separatism. It is true that they stuck together. But their group unity was always enlarged by joining in alliances with other groups such as political machines and trade unions. To succeed in a pluralistic society, and an often hostile one at that, the Negro obviously needs organized strength, but that strength will only be effective when it is consolidated through constructive alliances with the majority group.

Those proponents of Black Power who have urged Negroes to shun alliances with whites argue that whites as a group cannot have a genuine concern for Negro progress. Therefore, they claim, the white man's main interest in collaborative effort is to diminish Negro militancy and deflect it from constructive goals.

Undeniably there are white elements that cannot be trusted, and no militant movement can afford to relax its vigilance against halfhearted associates or conscious betrayers. Every alliance must be considered on its own merits. Negroes may embrace some and walk out on others where their interests are imperiled. Occasional betrayals, however, do not justify the rejection of the principle of Negro-white alliance.

The oppression of Negroes by whites has left an understandable residue of suspicion. Some of this suspicion is a healthy and appropriate safeguard. An excess of skepticism, however, becomes a fetter. It denies that there can be reliable white allies, even though some whites have died heroically at the side of Negroes in our struggle and others have risked economic and political peril to support our cause.

The history of the movement reveals that Negro-white alliances have played a powerfully constructive role, especially in recent years. While Negro initiative, courage and imagination precipitated the Birmingham and Selma confrontations and revealed the harrowing injustice of segregated life, the organized strength of Negroes alone would have been insufficient to move Congress and the administration without the weight of the aroused conscience of white America. In the period ahead Negroes will continue to need this support. Ten per cent of the population cannot by tensions alone induce 90 per cent to change a way of life.

Within the white majority there exists a substantial group who cherish democratic principles above privilege and who have demonstrated a will to fight side by side with the Negro against injustice. Another and more substantial group is composed of those having common needs with the Negro and who will benefit equally with him in the achievement of social progress. There are, in fact, more poor white Americans than there are Negro. Their need for a war on poverty is no less desperate than the Negro's. In the South they have been deluded by race prejudice and largly remained aloof from common action. Ironically, with this posture they were fighting not only the Negro but themselves. Yet there are already signs of change. Without formal alliances, Negroes and whites have supported the same candidates in many *de facto* electoral coalitions in the South because each sufficiently served his own needs.

The ability of Negroes to enter alliances is a mark of our growing strength, not of our weakness. In entering an alliance, the Negro is not relying on white leadership or ideology; he is taking his place as an equal partner in a common endeavor. His organized strength and his new independence pave the way for alliances. Far from losing independence in an alliance, he is using it for constructive and multiplied gains.

Negroes must shun the very narrow-mindedness that in others has so long been the source of our own afflictions. We have reached the stage of organized strength and independence to work securely in alliances. History has demonstrated with major victories the effectiveness, wisdom and moral soundness of Negro-white alliance. The cooperation of Negro and white based on the solid ground of honest conscience and proper self-interest can continue to grow in scope and influence. It can attain the strength to alter basic institutions by democratic means. Negro isolation can never approach this goal.

In the final analysis the weakness of Black Power is its failure to see that the black man needs the white man and the white man needs the black man. However much we may try to romanticize the slogan, there is no separate black path to power and fulfillment that does not intersect white paths, and there is no separate white path to power and fulfillment, short of social disaster, that does not share that power with black aspirations for freedom and human dignity. We are bound together in a single garment of destiny. The language, the cultural patterns, the music, the material prosperity and even the food of America are an amalgam of black and white.

James Baldwin once related how he returned home from school and his mother asked him whether his teacher was colored or white. After a pause he answered: "She is a little bit colored and a little bit white." [1] This is the dilemma of being a Negro in America. In physical as well as cultural terms every Negro is a little bit colored and a little bit white. In our search for identity we must recognize this dilemma.

Every man must ultimately confront the question "Who am I?" and seek to answer it honestly. One of the first principles of personal adjustment is the principle of self-acceptance. The Negro's greatest dilemma is that in order to be healthy he must accept his ambivalence. The Negro is the child of two cultures—Africa and America. The problem is that in the search for wholeness all too many Negroes seek to embrace only one side of their natures. Some, seeking to reject their heritage, are ashamed of their color, ashamed of black art and music, and determine what is beautiful and good by the standards of white society. They end up frustrated and without cultural roots. Others seek to reject everything American and to identify totally with Africa, even to the point of wearing African clothes. But this approach leads also to frustration because the American Negro is not an African. The old Hegelian synthesis still offers the best answer to many of life's dilemmas. The American Negro is neither totally African nor totally Western. He is Afro-American, a true hybrid, a combination of two cultures.

Who are we? We are the descendants of slaves. We are the offspring of noble men and women who were kidnaped from their native land and chained in ships like beasts. We are the heirs of a great and exploited continent known as Africa. We are the heirs of a past of rope, fire and murder. I for one am not ashamed of this past. My shame is for those who became so inhuman that they could inflict this torture upon us.

But we are also Americans. Abused and scorned though we may be, our destiny is tied up with the destiny of America. In spite of the psychological appeals of identification with Africa, the Negro must face the fact that America is now his home, a home that he helped to build through "blood, sweat and tears." Since we are Americans the solution to our problem will not come through seeking to build a separate black nation within a nation, but by finding that creative minority of the concerned from the oft-times apathetic majority, and together moving torward that colorless power that we all need for security and justice.

In the first century B.C., Cicero said: "Freedom is participation in power." Negroes should never want all power because they would deprive others of their freedom. By the same token, Negroes can never be content without participation in power. America must be a nation in which its multiracial people are partners in power. This is the essence of democracy toward which all Negro struggles have been directed since the distant past when he was transplanted here in chains.

Probably the most destructive feature of Black Power is its unconscious and often conscious call for retaliatory violence. Many well-meaning persons within the movement rationalize that Black Power does not really mean black violence, that those who shout the slogan don't really mean it that way, that the violent connotations are solely the distortions of a vicious press. That the press has fueled the fire is true. But as one who has worked and talked intimately with devotees of Black Power, I must admit that the slogan is mainly used by persons who have lost faith in the method and philosophy of nonviolence. I must make it clear that no guilt by association is intended. Both Floyd McKissick and Stokely Carmichael have declared themselves opponents of aggressive violence. This clarification is welcome and useful, despite the persistence of some of their followers in examining the uses of violence.

Over cups of coffee in my home in Atlanta and my apartment in Chicago, I have often talked late at night and over into the small hours of the morning with proponents of Black Power who argued passionately about the validity of violence and riots. They don't quote Gandhi or Tolstoy. Their Bible is Frantz Fanon's *The Wretched of the Earth*.[2] This black psychiatrist from Martinique, who went to Algeria to work with the National Liberation Front in its fight against the French, argues in his book—a well-written book, incidentally, with many penetrating insights—that violence is a psychologically healthy and tactically sound method for the oppressed. And so, realizing that they are a part of that vast company of the "wretched of the earth," these young American Negroes, who are predominantly involved in the Black Power movement, often quote Fanon's belief that violence is the only thing that will bring about liberation. As they say, "Sing us no songs of nonviolence, sing us no songs of progress, for nonviolence and progress belong to middle-class Negroes and whites and we are not interested in you."

As we have seen, the first public expression of disenchantment with nonviolence arose around the question of "self-defense." In a sense this is a false issue, for the right to defend one's home and one's person when attacked has been guaranteed through the ages by common law. In a nonviolent demonstration, however, self-defense must be approached from another perspective.

The cause of a demonstration is the existence of some form of exploitation or oppression that has made it necessary for men of courage and goodwill to protest the evil. For example, a demonstration against *de facto* school segregation is based on the awareness that a child's mind is crippled by inadequate educational opportunities. The demonstrator agrees that it is better to suffer publicly for a short time to end the crippling evil of school segregation than to have generation after generation of children suffer in ignorance. In such a demonstration the point is made that the schools are inadequate. This is the evil one seeks to dramatize; anything else distracts from that point and interferes with the confrontation of the primary evil. Of course no one wants to suffer and be hurt. But it is more important to get at the cause than to be safe. It is better to shed a little blood from a blow on the head or a rock thrown by an angry mob than to have children by the thousands finishing high school who can only read at a sixth-grade level.

Furthermore, it is dangerous to organize a movement around self-defense. The line of demarcation between defensive violence and aggressive violence is very thin. The minute a program of violence is enunciated, even for self-defense, the atmosphere is filled with talk of violence, and the words falling on unsophisticated ears may be interpreted as an invitation to aggression.

One of the main questions that the Negro must confront in his pursuit of freedom is that of effectiveness. What is the most effective way to achieve the desired goal? If a method is not effective, no matter how much steam it releases, it is an expression of weakness, not of strength. Now the plain, inexorable fact is that any attempt of the American Negro to overthrow his oppressor with violence will not work. We do not need President Johnson to tell us this by reminding Negro rioters that they are outnumbered ten to one. The courageous efforts of our own insurrectionist brothers, such as Denmark Vesey and Nat Turner, should be eternal reminders to us that violent rebellion is doomed from the start. In violent warfare one must be prepared to face the fact that there will be casualties by the thousands. Anyone leading a violent rebellion must be willing to make an honest assessment regarding the possible casualties to a minority population confronting a well-armed, wealthy majority with a fanatical right wing that would delight in exterminating thousands of black men, women and children.

Arguments that the American Negro is a part of a world which is two-thirds colored and that there will come a day when the oppressed people of color will violently rise together to throw off the yoke of white oppression are beyond the realm of serious discussion. There is no colored nation, including China, that now shows even the potential of leading a violent revolution of color in any international proportions. Ghana, Zambia, Tanganyika and Nigeria are so busy fighting their own battles against poverty, illiteracy and the subversive influence of neo-colonialism that they offer little hope to Angola, Southern Rhodesia and South Africa, much less to the American Negro. The hard cold facts today indicate that the hope of the people of color in the world may well rest on the American Negro and his ability to reform the structure of racial imperialism from within and thereby turn the technology and wealth of the West to the task of liberating the world from want.

The futility of violence in the struggle for racial justice has been tragically etched in all the recent Negro riots. There is something painfully sad about a riot. One sees screaming youngsters and angry adults fighting hopelessly and aimlessly against impossible odds. Deep down within them you perceive a desire for self-destruction, a suicidal longing. Occasionally Negroes contend that the 1965 Watts riot and the other riots in various cities represented effective civil rights action. But those who express this view always end up with stumbling words when asked what concrete gains have been won as a result. At best the riots have produced a little additional antipoverty money, allotted by frightened government officials, and a few water sprinklers to cool the children of the ghettos. It is something like improving the food in a prison while the people remain securely incarcerated behind bars. Nowhere have the riots won any concrete improvement such as have the organized protest demonstrations.

It is not overlooking the limitations of nonviolence and the distance we have yet to go to point out the remarkable record of achievements that have already come through nonviolent action. The 1960 sit-ins desegregated lunch counters in more than 150 cities within a year. The 1961 Freedom Rides put an end to segregation in interstate travel. The 1956 bus boycott in Montgomery, Alabama, ended segregation on the buses not only of that city but in practically every city of the South. The 1963 Birmingham movement and the climactic March on Washington won passage of the most powerful civil rights law in a century. The 1965 Selma movement brought enactment of the Voting Rights Law. Our nonviolent marches in Chicago last summer brought about a housing agreement which, if implemented, will be the strongest step toward open housing taken in any city in the nation. Most significant is the fact that this progress occurred with minimum human sacrifice and loss of life. Fewer people have been killed in ten years of nonviolent demonstrations across the South than were killed in one night of rioting in Watts.

When one tries to pin down advocates of violence as to what acts would be effective, the answers are blatantly illogical. Sometimes they talk of overthrowing racist state and local governments. They fail to see that no internal revolution has ever succeeded in overthrowing a government by violence unless the government had already lost the allegiance and effective control of its armed forces. Anyone in his right mind knows that this will not happen in the United States. In a violent racial situation, the power structure has the local police, the state troopers, the national guard and finally the army to call on, all of which are predominantly white.

Furthermore, few if any violent revolutions have been successful unless the violent minority had the sympathy and support of the nonresisting majority. Castro may have had only a few Cubans actually fighting with him, but he would never have overthrown the Batista regime unless he had had the sympathy of the vast majority of the Cuban people. It is perfectly clear that a violent revolution on the part of American blacks would find no sympathy and support from the white population and very little from the majority of the Negroes themselves.

This is no time for romantic illusions and empty philosophical debates about freedom. This is a time for action. What is needed is a strategy for change, a tactical program that will bring the Negro into the mainstream of American life as quickly as possible. So far, this has only been offered by the nonviolent movement. Without recognizing this we will end up with solutions that don't solve, answers that don't answer and explanations that don't explain.

Beyond the pragmatic invalidity of violence is its inability to appeal to conscience. Some Black Power advocates consider an appeal to conscience irrelevant. A Black Power exponent said to me not long ago: "To hell with conscience and morality. We want power." But power and morality must go together, implementing, fulfilling and ennobling each other. In the quest for power I cannot by-pass the concern for morality. I refuse to be driven to a

Machiavellian cynicism with respect to power. Power at its best is the right use of strength. The words of Alfred the Great are still true: "Power is never good unless he who has it is good."

Nonviolence is power, but it is the right and good use of power. Constructively it can save the white man as well as the Negro. Racial segregation is buttressed by such irrational fears as loss of preferred economic privilege, altered social status, intermarriage and adjustment to new situations. Through sleepless nights and haggard days numerous white people struggle pitifully to combat these fears. By following the path of escape, some seek to ignore the questions of race relations and to close their minds to the issues involved. Others, placing their faith in legal maneuvers, counsel massive resistance. Still others hope to drown their fears by engaging in acts of meanness and violence toward their Negro brethren. But how futile are all these remedies! Instead of eliminating fear, they instill deeper and more pathological fears. The white man, through his own efforts, through education and goodwill, through searching his conscience and through confronting the fact of integration, must do a great deal to free himself of these paralyzing fears. But to master fear he must also depend on the spirit the Negro generates toward him. Only through our adherence to nonviolence—which also means love in its strong and commanding sense—will the fear in the white community be mitigated.

A guilt-ridden white minority fears that if the Negro attains power, he will without restraint or pity act to revenge the accumulated injustices and brutality of the years. The Negro must show that the white man has nothing to fear, for the Negro is willing to forgive. A mass movement exercising nonviolence and demonstrating power under discipline should convince the white community that as such a movement attained strength, its power would be used creatively and not for revenge.

In a moving letter to his nephew on the one hundredth anniversary of emancipation, James Baldwin wrote concerning white people:

The really terrible thing, old buddy, is that *you* must accept *them*. And I mean that very seriously. You must accept them and accept them with love. For these innocent people have no other hope. They are, in effect, still trapped in a history which they do not understand; and until they understand it, they cannot be released from it. They have had to believe for many years, and for innumerable reasons, that black men are inferior to white men. Many of them, indeed, know better, but, as you will discover, people find it very difficult to act on what they know. To act is to be committed, and to be committed is to be in danger. In this case, the danger, in the minds of most white Americans, is the loss of their identity. . . . But these men are your brothers—your lost, younger brothers.

And if the word *integration* means anything, this is what it means: that we, with love, shall force our brothers to see themselves as they are, to cease fleeing from reality and begin to change it. . . .[3]

The problem with hatred and violence is that they intensify the fears of the white majority, and leave them less ashamed of their prejudices toward Negroes. In the guilt and confusion confronting our society, violence only adds to the chaos. It deepens the brutality of the oppressor and increases the bitterness of the oppressed. Violence is the antithesis of creativity and wholeness. It destroys community and makes brotherhood impossible.

My friend John Killens recently wrote in the *Negro Digest:* "Integration comes after liberation. A slave cannot integrate with his master. In the whole history of revolts and revolutions, integration has never been the main slogan of the revolution. The oppressed fights to free himself from his oppressor, not to integrate with him. Integration is the step after freedom when the freedman makes up his mind as to whether he wishes to integrate with his former master." [4]

At first glance this sounds very good. But after reflection one has to face some inescapable facts about the Negro and American life. This is a multiracial nation where all groups are dependent on each other, whether they want to recognize it or not. In this vast interdependent nation no racial group can retreat to an island entire of itself. The phenomena of integration and liberation cannot be as neatly divided as Killens would have it.

There is no theoretical or sociological divorce between liberation and integration. In our kind of society liberation cannot come without integration and integration cannot come without liberation. I speak here of integration in both the ethical and the political senses. On the one hand, integration is true intergroup, interpersonal living. On the other hand, it is the mutual sharing of power. I cannot see how the Negro will be totally liberated from the crushing weight of poor education, squalid housing and economic strangulation until he is integrated, with power, into every level of American life.

Mr. Killens' assertion might have some validity in a struggle for independence against a foreign invader. But the Negro's struggle in America is quite different from and more difficult than the struggle for independence. The American Negro will be living tomorrow with the very people against whom he is struggling today. The American Negro is not in a Congo where the Belgians will go back to Belgium after the battle is over, or in an India where the British will go back to England after independence is won. In the struggle for national independence one can talk about liberation now and integration later, but in the struggle for racial justice in a multiracial society where the oppressor and the oppressed are both "at home," liberation must come through integration.

Are we seeking power for power's sake? Or are we seeking to make the world and our nation better places to live. If we seek the latter, violence can never provide the answer. The ultimate weakness of violence is that it is a descending spiral, begetting the very thing it seeks to destroy. Instead of diminishing evil, it multiplies it. Through violence you may murder the liar, but you cannot murder the lie, nor establish the truth. Through violence you may murder the hater, but you do not murder hate. In fact, violence merely increases hate. So it goes. Returning violence for violence multiplies violence, adding deeper darkness to a night already devoid of stars. Darkness cannot drive out darkness: only light can do that. Hate cannot drive out hate: only love can do that.

The beauty of nonviolence is that in its own way and in its own time it seeks to break the chain reaction of evil. With a majestic sense of spiritual power, it seeks to elevate truth, beauty and goodness to the throne. Therefore I will continue to follow this method because I think it is the most practically sound and morally excellent way for the Negro to achieve freedom.

In recent months several people have said to me: "Since violence is the new cry, isn't there a danger that you will lose touch with the people in the ghetto and be out of step with the times if you don't change your views on nonviolence?"

My answer is always the same. While I am convinced the vast majority of Negroes reject violence, even if they did not I would not be interested in being a consensus leader. I refuse to determine what is right by taking a Gallup poll of the trends of the time. I imagine that there were leaders in Germany who sincerely opposed what Hitler was doing to the Jews. But they took their poll and discovered that anti-Semitism was the prevailing trend. In order to "be in step with the times," in order to "keep in touch," they yielded to one of the most ignominious evils that history has ever known.

Ultimately a genuine leader is not a searcher for consensus but a molder of consensus. I said on one occasion, "If every Negro in the United States turns to violence, I will choose to be that one lone voice preaching that this is the wrong way." Maybe this sounded like arrogance. But it was not intended that way. It was simply my way of saying that I would rather be a man of conviction than a man of conformity. Occasionally in life one develops a conviction so precious and meaningful that he will stand on it till the end. This is what I have found in nonviolence.

## NOTES

[1] In *The Negro Protest,* Kenneth B. Clark (ed.), Beacon, 1963.
[2] Evergreen, 1966.
[3] *The Fire Next Time,* Dial, 1963, pp. 22–23.
[4] November, 1966.

*Harold Cruse's important work,* The Crisis of the Negro
Intellectual, *appeared in 1968 with a great flurry of
critical interest. Although a radical himself, Cruse is
highly critical of current Black radicalism, which he
regards as emotional and unoriginal. Cruse also assails
the African mystique among American Blacks which, he
says, will lead nowhere unless channeled into direct
action aimed at getting power for the Black community
in America. For Cruse, emigration to Africa is similarly
fruitless for it would draw off the talent and energy
required to attain the goals that are relevant in the
American context.*

# Ideology in Black: African, Afro-American, Afro-West Indian and the Nationalist Mood

## Harold Cruse

It should not be construed from what has been said thus far that this
study is so pro-nationalist it finds only the integrationist wing deserving of
criticism. For the nationalist wing is by no means so solvent, nor is it an
aggregation of groupings so well-oriented that its criticisms of the integrationists make it a viable factor in the world of reality. On the contrary, the
nationalist wing might know what it wants generally but does not know
how to achieve it specifically. In short, the nationalist wing today does not
know where it is going. On the other hand, the integrationist wing, which is
dominant, knows exactly what it wants and where it wants to go, even if
it is blocked in these aspirations by the stubborn facts of interracial realities.
And while the nationalist wing may criticize the integrationist aims in life,
the integrationists at least have a program which (the impact of a Malcolm
X notwithstanding) the nationalists do not.

In using the term nationalist wing, I am making an arbitrary distinction
between the members of the Nation of Islam (Muslims) and others who
take various anti-integrationist, pro-African, pro-black, pro-nationalist positions. This distinction must be made because the Muslims do have a working
program that is effective. But the religio-separatist nature of the Muslims is

unacceptable to many nationalist elements in the North who remain free-roving, unaffiliated groupings. Since these unaffiliated nationalist trends are composed mostly of young people, the remnants of the old Garveyites cannot be included in the same category. Yet this lone faction, gravitating around what could be called in nationalist terms, the vital center, has, at this moment, the most dynamic potential; it is, at the same time, the most disorganized, disoriented, and planless. When the passing of Malcolm X left this faction without an effective spokesman, the Muslims made certain inroads by capitalizing on that void.

Like the Negro movement as a whole, Afro-American Nationalism has inherited a raft of problems accumulated from the past. It is almost impossible today to codify nationalist thought so as to make much practical and programmatic sense in political, economic and cultural terms. Afro-American Nationalism is so fragmented into sects, factions, and cliques that it is a morass of self-inflicted immobility and frustration. But, though the decriers of black nationalism may not realize it, a very extensive bloc of the American Negro population of all classes could be influenced by this group, should it ever organize itself into a unified force with a clear "line." But the Afro-American Nationalists cannot come to terms with themselves as American products, created out of American conditions and ingredients, requiring, in the final analysis, an American solution. Having rejected Americanization out of hand as a past, present or future commitment, they function from day to day, variously isolated from American social realities. Many Afro-American Nationalists cultivate an existence that reduces any contact with whites to the barest minimum. Many others live in an intellectual world of the teachings of Islam or the history of the glories of Africa past and present, or the projection of a future return to Africa.

The old Garveyite Back-to-Africa dream still exists for many of the new Afro-American Nationalists, but not in the strict terms of the old Garvey program. Today it is merely a spiritual return, another side of the anti-American mood and its modern form of alienation. This Back-to-Africa mood is a romance of the mind and a balm for the psyche which has a bolstering effect on black self-esteem. It is the impact of the birth of free African states with presidents, premiers, protocol and international prestige—all lending vivid substance to Back-to-Africa voyages of the imagination. This is borne out by American Negroes who wear native African costumes at parties, balls, and local poetry readings. But you will not, to be sure, see any mass emigration stampede back to the homeland. Of course, even should one million blacks return to Africa, there would still remain a race problem to be solved in the United States. There are many Afro-American Nationalists who talk as if they do not realize this. And ironically, when the

African diplomats, intellectuals, bureaucrats and other spokesmen come to America, they associate not with the Afro-American Nationalists but with the prestigious integrationists of the NAACP, the American Society of African Culture, the African-American Institute, and so forth.

Today, Garveyism is a dream deferred, because the realities of African independence and the relationships of American Negroes to the African scene do not fulfill what Garveyism promised. Things have turned out differently, and both Africans and Afro-Americans have to face up to domestic and international realities not prophesied in the 1920's. The truth of the matter is that many Afro-American Nationalists do not understand the essentials of the African Revolution any better than the so-called Black Revolution in the United States. Yet they cannot escape the facts of history, a history that created that far-flung triangular relationship between Africa, the West Indies and the United States, based on the slave trade. These historical antecedents still hang heavy over the fortunes of black destiny today, and in many imponderable ways color the outlook of the Afro-American Nationalists.

The African (whether he speaks French, English or Swahili), the West Indian, and the American Negro are so similar and yet so different, that Afro-American Nationalists are all the more pressed to program a clear-cut attack on the problems they face. For no matter how much he tries, the Afro-American Nationalist cannot tear himself away as cleanly as he thinks from the ideals, values, strivings, liabilities, achievements—the sins and virtues of the entire American Negro world. He might decry the values of the integrationists and the failings of the black bourgeoisie, but he knows that in doing so, he is criticizing a recognizable reflection of himself.

But what are the dreams of the African, and that other branch of African progeny in the Western Hemisphere, the so-called Afro-West Indian? How related really are their dreams in relation to their common ancestry? How well do these people—who are as variegated as a black-hued rainbow—really understand each other? Let us examine the things some of them have been heard to say.

Back in the middle 1950's, at an interracial party, a minor African official listened to American Negroes having a discussion on the possibilities of returning to Africa; he replied most indignantly that Africa did not want any of "you Negroes" over there, and proceeded to derogate the American Negro's attitudes, habits, and general condition.

In 1962, a very well-known woman jazz singer said, "The hell with Africans! They have their own thing going over there and they have little in common with us, and care less."

Another woman, majoring in sociology and born in the United States, identifies with Africa so strongly that she is almost tribalistic in outlook. For her, the American Negro can achieve nothing in America unless his movement is predicated on a reverent identification with Africa. But her outlook is conditioned by the fact that her parents are from the West Indies; she was therefore disturbed that, when in Ghana, she was classified as an American Negro. This young woman, of course, while belonging in the Afro-American Nationalist category admits to a dual identification.

Another woman jazz singer, now retired, with a background of travel in Europe and the Far East, wants to meet Africans but feels that there is not much rapport between them and the American Negroes. She feels also that American Negroes are divided along regional lines—North, South, East and West—thus in her view seriously weakening the civil rights movement. This woman is also highly antagonistic to West Indians, who she feels do not identify with American Negroes. West Indians play a "two-faced, under-handed role with white people in undercutting American Negroes," she remarked, that having been her experience in working with West Indians professionally.

A composer-pianist of West Indian parentage has strong ambivalences on the African-American Negro identification question. He has the physical characteristics of a "mixed-blood," and constantly seeks to explain that he is not of pure African descent. Yet, his real link with his heritage is through music, and he is deeply immersed in the Afro-American musical tradition. Aware that the origins of African music are in Uganda, he derides a certain African composer who is known to favor Western forms—accusing this composer of denying his own cultural roots in music. His own roots are in the American Negro folk music tradition and he admits that his own musical development was influenced by Sissle and Blake, Ellington and others. Yet on American Negro experiences on the social, political, economic, and civil rights fronts, he often refuses to commit himself.

A West Indian couple who were friends of an American Negro couple from Virginia had to be coaxed before they would agree to visit the South. They were afraid of Southern whites. In New York, it has been noted that even the grandchildren born in the United States of West Indian immigrants are taught to make distinctions among their parents' friends. They often embarrass their parents by referring to certain visitors as either "West Indian" or "American." This is true even in the case of former Virgin Islanders: They identify with the British West Indies proper, even though all Virgin Islanders have been American citizens since 1927. The stereotype of American Negro inferiority is so strong among many West Indians that to them, an extra-intelligent American Negro either has distant West Indian antecedents, or else the ability to "think like a West Indian." This has led to another West Indian myth—that the British West Indies were peopled by a different breed of African slaves (when indeed West Indians will admit to slavery) than those who landed at American ports.

During the 1950's in the Greenwich Village interracial scene, it was noted that certain West Indian males formed themselves into a semi-exclusive social club from which camp they competed with American Negro males for the favors of white women (mostly Jewish). The West Indian women on the scene were hardly ever seen at this club's functions, for they usually consorted with white men, as did most of the American Negro women. Most of the West Indian men were ever alert to emphasize that they were "not American Negroes." The West Indian women, though fewer in number, reacted similarly, and one remarked, "You Negroes have contributed nothing to the United States but jazz music." When asked what the West Indians had contributed to the British Empire aside from calypso and labor—both slave and cheap—she replied, "Oh, that's different."

The Village interracial scene offered the best of all social laboratories for a study of race and ethnic group contacts and attitudes involving American and West Indian Negroes, Jews, Anglo-Saxons, Italians, Latins and even Indians. On the Harlem scene, the West Indian attitude has to be gauged by class, as does the American Negro attitude in reverse. One West Indian of long residence in Harlem constantly used to remark during race discussions, "What I want to know is, what is this Negro going to do?" Even after the civil rights upsurge he was unimpressed—and asked the same question. And so it goes . . . the West Indian psychology is a thing apart . . . distinguishing itself through myriad ways, but principally by not accepting the American Negro social status as it has been fashioned by the American way of life. Even when the West Indian finds a way of accommodating to this status, it is usually with certain reservations. Perceptive whites have noted this attitude and used it on all levels of black and white relations, including the Communist leftwing. Yet despite this subcultural antagonism between the two groups, one West Indian woman was heard to scoff: "What are they bickering about, they are all the same!"

Claude McKay was the perfect example of the difficulty the West Indian creative artist and intellectual, even when born in the United States, has in identifying with the American Negro. For one thing, because of the contrasts in the cultural and political developments in black America and the black West Indies, there is a clash of cultural backgrounds. Moreover, the black West Indies never experienced the kind of cultural renaissance that took place among American Negroes from the 1890's, to the 1920's, culminating in the advent of mass media. In fact, West Indians living through this renaissance understood it even less than the American Negroes—and they failed to conceptualize what they felt intuitively. McKay, for example, never grasped the cultural side of the American revolution.

The Trinidadian scholar and historian, Eric Williams, gives some answers to the background of this cultural differentiation: "The racial situation in the Caribbean is radically different from the racial situation in the United States and is thus rather incomprehensible to the native of the United States, black or white." [1]

In the United States, the West Indian complains that the American Negro lacks cohesiveness; thus to make an even more incomprehensible comparison, Williams said: "The racial consciousness which permeates the American Negro is also not found in the islands. This is a constant source of surprise and even exasperation to the American Negro visitor or student, who goes to the islands with his clichés and his prejudices, seeking for any violations of his own code of racial solidarity." [2]

Race militancy, then, is one thing in the West Indies and something else in the United States. This clash of cultural traditions creates other confusions of values. Booker T. Washington, for example, has been symbolized as the antithesis of race militancy, by the DuBois tradition in the United States. But in Williams' criticism of the backward educational systems in the Caribbean, the worst of which was the British system, he wrote: "The education provided is furthermore woefully unsuited to local conditions. Along liberal lines, little attention is paid to vocational education, and the Caribbean has produced no Booker T. Washington." [3]

For that very reason, Marcus Garvey admired Booker T. Washington, and tried to link his movement with Washington's Tuskegee institution. Yet you will never get a young nationalist militant to admit that today, especially if he is West Indian. He will invariably uphold Garvey, put down Washington, and be confused about DuBois. This, despite the fact that Mrs. A. Jacques Garvey, herself, wrote: "While in Alabama [in 1923] we went to Tuskeegee Normal and Industrial Institute. Primarily to pay homage to the late Booker T. Washington. . . ." Garvey and his wife were of the opinion that: "Since the death of Booker T. Washington there was no one with a positive and practical programme for the masses—North or South." [4]

Contrary to Eric Williams, this conflict of cultural values prompts the West Indian militant to claim more racial solidarity for his kind than for the American Negro. This ideological gambit cropped out again during the summer of 1966 when CORE and SNCC went over to the Black Power position. Prominent among the new Black Power supporters were three West Indians: Stokely Carmichael, Trinidad; Lincoln Lynch, Jamaica; and Roy Inniss, Virgin Islands. To back up their rationalizations for their new position of Black Power, all three cited the political and racial status of the black West Indies. As a result, the New York press was moved to cite "the strong Caribbean and West Indian influence in the black power philosophy." [5] Overlooked was the fact that the term Black Power was copied from Adam Clayton Powell who first gave it currency in his commencement speech at Howard University on May 29, 1966 (he had also mentioned it in Chicago at a rally during May, 1965), where he said: "To demand these God-given human rights is to seek black power." But what *is* Black Power —in either West Indian or American Negro terms?

Carmichael, Lynch, and Inniss cited their West Indian background, and Lincoln Lynch was quoted as saying: "I was shocked when I came here and found that the word 'black' was almost a cuss word with the American Negroes. . . . It must have something to do with the adjustment [we West Indians] make when we come here."

The three West Indians seekers of Black Power said that their "stance of black consciousness was alienating middle-class Negroes [Americans, that is] and white supporters in Congress and in the public in general." Further, "They were tired of unenforced laws and felt that many middle-class Negroes [Americans] were trying to escape their race." What is needed, the West Indians say, is "for Negroes to reject integration as their major aim and to band themselves together into a racially oriented mass movement. . . ." If this fails, the Black Power advocates say "armed revolt" is the answer against whites. Lynch and Carmichael emphasized the fact that in Jamaica and Trinidad there "is a lot of poverty but we felt proud in being black." [6] Moreover the West Indians have political power (*i.e.,* black policemen, civil servants, public officials, etc). Naturally these West Indians cited the Marcus Garvey nationalist precedent.

Eric Williams shows, however, that the Black Power concept, predicated on a West Indian social rationale, is deceptive, especially with regard to the actual political and class situation in the Caribbean. That the West Indian Black Power supporters are following in the footsteps of Garvey does not prove what they want it to prove. Garvey did not establish any Black Power in the West Indies because of the opposition of the West Indian black bourgeoisie: "The West Indian middleclasses were, almost without exception, viciously hostile." [7]

This West Indian middle class also has the deepest of skin-color phobias; to them, the word "black" is even more opprobrious than Lincoln Lynch found in the United States. Even though the West Indian middle classes had their social power whittled down during the West Indian working-class unrest of the 1930's, it was the labor movement that was responsible for this progress, not the Garveyites. As Williams points out, the Garveyite success was in the United States, but Garveyism left "not much to be seen in the islands in the way of concrete organization." Thus, today we have West Indian nationalists in the United States but no nationalist movement in the black West Indies. Hence, in West Indian terms, "political independence" is "integrationism"; what Stokely Carmichael calls Black Power in Trinidad is not nationalist separation from the British Crown, but gradualistic, integrated Commonwealth-partisanship within the Empire. Moreover, in Trinidad, as in former colonial days, the two major economic activities— oil and sugar—are still in foreign (white) hands. There is fourteen per cent unemployment (in 1966) and the job market is shrinking. This is typical of the entire black West Indies, where Black Power has not changed the economic situation at all; where in Trinidad the per capita income is $520 per annum. It is these conditions that force all the West Indian nationalists out of the West Indies to other places, such as New York, where the wages are infinitely higher, even *without* American Negro Black Power. But, they say, if Black Power is not achieved by the American Negro he should resort to armed revolt to get it. Why then, the question arises, *was there no armed revolt in the black West Indies where the blacks are in the majority?* For one thing, Black Power in the Caribbean has not created and brought to the fore a black Fidel Castro—which explains a lot about the black West Indies today.

The West Indian Black Power sponsors want the American Negro, as a minority, to win economic power in the United States, yet they suggest no program to achieve this. Roy Inniss of CORE, for example, reveals considerable misunderstanding of Negro leadership trends. He tells the press that *he* is in favor of lionizing certain Negro leaders over others, such as Frederick Douglass, Nat Turner, Denmark Vesey, Garvey, and Malcolm X . . . people like that, because they are historic exemplars of race militancy. (The American Negro needs the *right* sort of heroes.) As Inniss could not fit Washington and DuBois into this militant trend, he left them out— without explaining how, historically, he can separate Washington from Garvey. He also claimed that the CORE members who favored interracialism and intermarriage as a solution to the race problem were trying to bring about *his* "genetic destruction." (Presumably Inniss momentarily forgot that Frederick Douglass, the great militant Abolitionist, had married a white.)

Because of the West Indian's peculiar cultural history, the alienation of the West Indian creative intellectual in the United States has come to take on unique forms. He, or she, is often faced with the problem of relating artistically to two different cultural personalities—the West Indian or the American Negro. Some solve the problem by going completely aracial and Universal; others reach back for the West Indian novel, the West Indian play. One novelist is known to have failed to publish a first West Indian novel but succeeded with a second American Negro novel. Claude McKay achieved both. One of the most outstanding West Indian novelists is known to be aracial and an acculturated black Englishman who hardly ever speaks loudly about racial differences. But he functions in England for the most part.

The American Negro actor's fight against stereotyped Negro roles in films and theater is complicated by the fact that actors of West Indian background do not object to these roles for the same reasons of image that American Negro actors do. Since the West Indian actor has problems of identification with the American idiom, "in life," stage and film artistry presents merely another level of interpretive discord. This conflict has often been observed in drama groups, especially if it concerns characters written by a Negro playwright.

A composer of Trinidadian parentage inwardly blames the American Negro situation for *his* failures in winning recognition in America. He has threatened many times to move to England. But he always fends off the rejoinder he invites from American Negroes, by declaring, "I can't go to Trinidad because there's nothing happening there [musically]." Hence he deteriorates in New York. The peculiar nationalism of the West Indian on the identity question crops out in the case of a West Indian professor of literature. Coming out of the black majority racial status of the Caribbean, this professor identifies quite strongly with the new African literary flowering—also emerging from a black majority racial and cultural background. In his lectures it was noted that the professor attempted to link the West Indian and African literary trends in terms of the anti-colonialist imperative, although the West Indian literary output was never very extensive. However he made a slight distinction concerning the South African black (or colored) writers. In South Africa the black population is subject to the most industrially advanced white population on the African continent, and also the most numerous. This implicit psychological parallel apparently prompted the professor to link the South African writers with the American Negro writers.

The cultural, political, and class background of the Afro-West Indies makes many West Indians, in America, claim they are British or French or Spanish, or Cuban, or even Puerto Rican. This is to avoid saying, "I am an American (Negro)." If they are truly anti-colonialist (which many are not), they will claim to be Jamaican or Trinidadian, or Martiniquan, Nevisian, Barbadian, etc. All of these national groups names, such as Jamaican, were created and given to them, you will note, by white people who "discovered" these islands and called them the West Indies. Thus the name "West Indian" is acceptable to African descendants who are, racially, far removed from people who are called Indians. Yet, there are West Indians, such as Richard B. Moore, who argue about the word "Negro" on the basis that this name was given to African descendants by white men. Although the word comes from the Portuguese and Spanish, meaning "black," it has come to connote the branding of slave status in the black psychology. But the white Englishmen also call Africans in the Caribbean "Negroes"; if black West Indians refuse to use it, it means merely that they prefer another name, also given by white men and just as indicative of a strong identification with those white men. This curious semantic transference of identity values explains a lot about West Indian nationalism, which, as Eric Williams [8] points out, is incomprehensible in American terms. Williams wrote: "In the United States there were Negroes who were nationalists, in the Caribbean there were nationalists who were Negroes." [9]

This explains why nationalists who were black in the Caribbean became, not *black nationalists,* but national spokesmen for their island nations: for instance, Antonio Maceo and Juan Gualberto Gomez, who were *Cuban* nationalists, not *black* nationalists; or Jose Celso Barbosa of Puerto Rico, a leader of "color" who spoke for his people of all races, rather than for *his* race. It almost could be said that Frederick Douglass fitted this category —it was the black slave's minority status in America that made Douglass's role that of a special pro-Negro spokesman over and above that of the nationalist Martin R. Delany. On the other hand, it does explain why American Negro Crispus Attucks, reputedly the first American to die fighting against the British in the Revolutionary War, is not today a hero to the young Afro-American Nationalists as Maceo is a hero to black Cubans for his leadership in the struggle against Spain. This peculiar historical development of nationalism in the West Indies, as opposed to that among American Negroes, helps to explain why Garveyism could take root in the United States but not in the West Indies. Garvey, unlike Maceo in Cuba, did not fight for complete independence from Great Britain, but merely commonwealth status (which Britain only recently granted).

Inherited, then, is a very muddled, distorted nationalist tradition, wherein West Indian nationalists have become adept at using the Garvey tradition demagogically, inasmuch as the 1920's nationalist wave was largely West Indian.[10] Opposition to Garveyism by American Negro middle-class leaders such as DuBois and Randolph is singled out as proof of the American Negro's lack of militancy. However, the latter-day Garveyites never mention the fact that the bulk of opposition to Garveyism also came from West Indians both in New York and in Jamaica.

A good deal of the internal dissension today among the younger trend of Afro-American Nationalists stems from this undercurrent of West Indian vs. American Negro rivalry. This competition was a strong factor in the collapse of the Freedom Now Party's Organizing Committee, mentioned before. During this effort, the most vocal dissenters and no-confidence voters were all of West Indian origin. At a conference of young Afro-American nationalists held in Harlem in April, 1965, any positive clarification was negated and disrupted by Garveyites, one of whom charged that any Negro who preferred to remain in the United States and fight for equality is a "house nigger." This slash, of course, was aimed at American Negroes— not at West Indian nationals who were migrating to the British Isles and the United States (instead of Africa).

West Indian conservatism takes other overt forms, especially in connection with the identification dilemma. The majority of West Indians today do not identify with Garveyism in America but with a conservative kind of group identity of their own. The younger ones, who are not essentially middle class and who break away from the West Indian group to join the white Left or some trend of the civil rights movement, usually strive to maintain their separate identity. In these cases they generally become the staunchest allies of the whites. If they tend toward "Afro-American Nationalism" they are apt to accentuate their identification with everything African (another way of not identifying with the American Negro). Much of the West Indian's attitude toward the American Negro is based on the latter's lack of a cohesive ideology—which the West Indian can retain in America because his group is much smaller. The American Negro who dislikes the West Indian bases it on the latter's "pushiness." The West Indian, who usually refuses to abide by the American Negro's accepted status of social inferiority, blames the American for his lack of militancy concerning the very issue on the West Indians themselves never forced until the 1920's. However, after the Watts, Los Angeles, uprising of 1965, one of the loudest denouncers of this militant action was a well-known West Indian who said he felt ashamed that he was an American Negro—a classification that he had quite probably been denying since he arrived.

It is a fact that most Africans seem to agree with the West Indians in their general attitude toward the American Negro, citing his lack of racial cohesiveness. This point of view, of course, stems from the African and West Indian social backgrounds in which, colonialism aside, Africans and West Indians are the racial majority. The fact that the North American Negro has existed as a decided minority within a European-derived majority has given him his native psychology, however one cares to evaluate it. Hence, in certain specific terms, Africans, Afro-Americans and Afro-West Indians (not born in America) do not share the same psychology toward whites—yet in general terms, they do. On closer examination, differences are more of degree than of kind.

If an American Negro becomes more American than the Americans, the West Indian becomes more British than the Britisher; the same is true of British and French Africans. One of the politico-ideological factors behind this is that Africans and West Indians were never allowed to forget that they were colonial subjects. But the fact that the American Negro was also a subject, of a special kind of North American domestic colonialism, was never fully accepted either by the Negro himself nor by Africans or West Indians. Back in the 1920's, during the Haywood-Huiswoud-Briggs controversy within the Communist Party, the West Indians did not want to classify American Negroes as colonials. It was not until 1962 that even the new Afro-American Nationalists began to see the domestic colonialist nature of the Negro's position in the United States. It is only when such factors are grasped that it is possible to get to the bottom of the many misconceptions the African, Afro-American, and West Indian share about each other. One begins to see that these three do not really understand each other's black revolutions. And the least understood of all is the American variety. In the meantime, however, many facts are revealed and many myths are exploded.

The dynamics of the colonial revolution reveal that neither the African nor the West Indian possesses the kind of cohesiveness hitherto claimed— as the "Federation" and "African Unity" fiascos have revealed in the West Indies and in Africa. Despite the fact that Africans and West Indians are the overwhelming racial majorities in their respective regions, their accession to political independence has not broken the chains of economic bondage to the European powers. Economic neo-colonialism is the African reality. In the West Indies, the economic control is still in the hands of whites, Chinese, Indians, Syrians and other non-blacks. In Africa, overwhelming black majorities in several "new nations" are unable to oust white minorities from political control, not to mention economic entrenchment. Yet criticisms are heard from both Africans and West Indians that the American Negro has not achieved what he might have both before and since the Supreme Court action of 1954. The bulk of these African and West Indian critics, of course, do not participate very demonstrably in the Black Revolution. Principally, they are as sideline observers with an eagle eye open for every opportunity to lap up whatever crumbs the power structure tosses to the civil righters, or to profit from whatever barriers are breached to enhance middle-class status. We see this all over New York City in the social, political, cultural and entertainment world.

"These American Negroes," say most Africans, "have no cohesion; they have no race consciousness; they don't identify with us Africans." But do not ask these Africans to facilitate or abet cohesion with the Negro by, perhaps, living too closely with him or by socializing more intimately than State Department protocol would allow. That would be an affront to their "new nation" status within United Nations society. "We are Africans, not 'American Negroes.' They are ex-slaves, we are ex-colonial slaves (but in our own country)—that makes a big difference." Yet ironically deep down in the soul of many American Negroes, is ingrained the conviction that the African has just barely emerged out of his primitive-tribal past!

But even those American Negroes who go to Africa with a certain show of brotherhood idealism, to help "build," often fail the test. One African Hausa student who was working with some American Negroes in Ghana came to America embittered by the privileges the Americans received and gladly accepted. He described how a certain New York commercial artist was given a six-room apartment with three baths, one shower, an extra servant's room, on the fourteenth story of a hotel, which afforded the artist an expansive view of all Accra. This hotel, which was described as of "all-glass" construction, had two special guards from the Mossi Tribe of Upper Volta stationed there at all times. The African student claimed that the New York artist was paid about three hundred dollars a month for a job in Ghana's state-sponsored equivalent of a Madison Avenue advertising company. Out of this salary, the artist's rent for the spacious lodging, the student said, was about seven pounds, roughly twenty dollars at the present rate of exchange. The African student claimed that groups and individuals who allege to be helping Africa develop cannot demand such privileges and, at the same time, insist that they are "one with the people." However, he did not question the political sincerity of the governmental caste who allotted such privileges to the Americans. More than that, he did not know that these American Negroes had the background of membership in the privileged elite colored section of the political leftwing in New York. Hence, as a matter of course, they demanded and got what they had been accustomed to before.

There are naturally many living exceptions to generalized attitudes. Many Africans and West Indians have transcended group differences and collaborated with American Negroes, and vice versa. In 1960, Leopold Senghor, who later became President of Senegal, came to the United States and had much trenchant advice for American Negroes on cultural matters. Although Senghor speaks no English, he had a deeper understanding about this aspect of Afro-Americana than many of the English-speaking Nigerians and Ghanaians. Many African students work closely with American Negro students. Many West Indians work closely with American Negroes. Yet this collaboration does not proceed without complaint and friction. In the case of the

African and the American Negro, it is more often the latter who causes the African to complain. On the other hand, with the American Negro and the West Indian, it is usually the latter who becomes the source of conflict and irritation. Under all circumstances the West Indian will let it be known, one way or the other, that he considers himself "different." The Negro is more tolerant than the West Indian—perhaps too tolerant for his own good. But this is also a reason why the American Negro is less conservative. Of all three, the African has the most liberated personality, which is not to be thought synonymous with revolutionary. As far as the Caribbean area is concerned, when one compares the English-speaking West Indians with the Cubans, Santo Domingans, and Puerto Ricans—black West Indians are the most conformist and accommodative people in the Caribbean. Moreover, it is difficult to determine who is leaving home at a faster rate—white Cubans escaping Castroism or black West Indians escaping "Federated" political independence. Yet to observe all three groups in America is to see that Africans and West Indians are much more concerned about their "image" than the American Negro usually is. In expressing this concern both the African and the West Indian reveal to what extent they have accepted the American stereotype of the Negro, a stereotype from which they try mightily to except themselves. Even their attempt to escape that myth merely creates others.

The superior attitude of the West Indians has long irked many American Negroes. One method of bolstering this superiority complex is the West Indians' old saw that there was never any slavery in the British West Indies. It is also known that in certain parts of Africa, for example in Ethiopia, American Negroes have been openly ridiculed as ex-slaves. Considering Ethiopia's history and distance from the slavery of the New World, this attitude is more understandable. But the British West Indies was the main bastion of the African slave trade long before the invention of the cotton gin transformed the United States South into the most lucrative dumping ground for human commodities. If the American Negro sharecropper remained the slave of cotton well after Emancipation, our Caribbean historian could say, as late as 1942, of the black laborer in the West Indies: "The black man, emancipated from above by legislation or from below by revolution, remains today the slave of sugar." [11] The slavery trauma of the West Indian manifests itself in many ways, even today.

In the *Freedomways* issue for the winter of 1963, a West Indian-American [12] wrote a communication protesting a David Brinkley television broadcast depicting life on the West Indian island of Nevis. According to the writer (a woman), Brinkley's broadcast had racist overtones because his choice of topic and panelists tended to put Nevis conditions in a bad light. Ninety-eight per cent of the people on the island are of African descent, but a colored Nevisan told Brinkley that most of them "were lazy and didn't want to work." The writer, whose family comes from Nevis, objected to scenes on the television screen showing black servant women laying out meals while a white woman spoke of the servants in the most degrading manner. The white woman "called them lazy and stupid," saying also, "they were even too stupid to make a cup of tea." The writer said of the white woman—"Her hatred of the Nevisans in particular and of colored people in general came across the TV screen sharp and vicious." The writer protested that Brinkley could have obtained better information from Nevisans and their United States descendants (one of whom is Hope Stevens) from the Nevis Benevolent Society in New Haven, Connecticut, and in Harlem. She went on to say:

The Nevisans do not have the facilities for cultivating the land nor do they have people experienced in agricultural methods and animal husbandry. Most of the young people leave the island as soon as possible.

Today there are only two doctors on the island, one hospital and clinic.

In all the years Britain had occupied the island, there was no road built.

Federation of the West Indies islands failed, the writer pointed out, but:

Survival of the people of Nevis and other islands depend on their uniting their forces and resources to mutually aid each other economically, politically and socially.

Much of Nevis is still unexplored bush country which if cleared and cultivated could make a big difference in the economy of the country.

After explaining further that the economy of Nevis was depressed because of failure of the sugar industry, the writer added this last defense on behalf of the Nevisan image: *"Britain was never able to subjugate the people of the West Indies to accept slavery."* True to form, the writer had to use the occasion to defend the West Indian image against what is by now a dead issue—slavery. The West Indians did not "accept" slavery, implying thereby two things:

(1) *There was never any slavery in the West Indies.*

(2) There were other people who were subjugated and who did accept slavery. (Who? American Negroes.)

When the average West Indian looks askance at the American Negro's social status—his low economic level and other social disabilities—it is always the Negro's fault. "He is not militant enough. He does not stand up to *his* white folks. Unlike the black Nevisan servants depicted on David

Brinkley's program, these American Negroes *are* really lazy and also a little stupid, and don't want to work," says the West Indian. "Of course, in Nevis things are backwards because *our* white folks didn't do anything for *us*. But the trouble with these American Negroes is that they are always begging *their* white folks for things they could do for themselves (as we do after we leave Nevis to come to the U.S.A. seeking a better life)." However, if we are to accept the facts of Nevis as they are today, it is to be seen that things have not changed much since the last Nevisan slave was liberated.

Why so? Because no Nevisan leaves Nevis to train in medicine in order to return to increase the number of doctors or to plan for those missing hospitals and clinics. Because none of the young people who leave, return bearing their American or British training in agriculture and animal husbandry or road building. That "unexplored bush country" of Nevis might be quite lush and could be "cleared and cultivated" to help the economy of the island. However, Metropolitan New York, London, and other Western cities far from Nevis are much lusher and the white folks who did nothing to build up the island economy are not forcing Nevisans and others in the Caribbean to build anything with their political independence one way or the other. Black West Indians are the majority and they are free to determine their own fate. But they cannot determine their own unity even under the most favorable conditions.

People who cannot achieve political cohesion in their own countries cannot afford to be supercilious and supercritical about the political failings of others. All their claims to the contrary, there is considerable doubt as to how much West Indians really love their island homelands. For it appears that West Indians are never so much in love with Caribbean heritage, or never so vehement in defending the West Indian image, as when they are indulging these sentiments from afar in England or North America. From these vantage points, such nostalgia and identification are food to the ego, but after political independence, the time has come to show just how ready people are to enter the mainstream of world history through the mastery of political, economic and social organization *in one's own homeland*.

In the American context, and on other levels, this same tenor of criticism applies to the new Afro-American Nationalists, whose minds too are enmeshed in their own social myths. Afro-American Nationalists are faced with a whole raft of very practical political, economic and cultural problems that they must solve for themselves. No one else can or will solve these problems for them. Certainly the integrationist Negroes cannot and will not, but it is a tactical error for nationalists to waste their time, energies and propaganda fighting and criticizing integrationists. The fallacies and weaknesses of integrationist programs can be exposed only to the degree that the nationalists initiate counter programs along political, economic and cultural lines. But, at the same time, this does not mean that separatism is the perfect antidote for integrationism. An Afro-American Nationalist program that is politically, economically, and culturally effective must be a dynamic program. It cannot be a program that retreats from social realities of the white power structure under the guise of separatist nationalistic moods. It is perfectly understandable why many new Afro-American Nationalists in the cities of the North must experience a separatist mood of withdrawal from any or all contacts with the white world. The historical character of black and white social relations in America makes such a mood a prerequisite for positive reexamination and reevaluation of the black personality. For groups as well as for individuals it is often necessary to retreat into isolation in order to determine who one is. But in the world of realities such isolation cannot be maintained for too long, and there comes a time when one must emerge from it and deal with the hard facts of life. People, no matter how diverse, are interrelated and diverse peoples must, of necessity, deal with the practical facts of their inter-relationships.

So far, the Afro-American Nationalists have not distinguished the difference between having a nationalistic mood and having nationalist objectives in politics, economics, and culture that relate to how Negroes as a people exist in America. The mere fact of self-identification, of the ideology of pro-blackness, the glorification of the black skin, the idealization of everything African, the return to the natural quality of African hairstyles, the rediscovery of black female beauty, or the adoption of African tribal dress—all of these phases and moods signify a return to the root origins of self which can also be transformed into protective mystiques. If these black mystiques are suffused with a contempt for, a hatred and a rejection of, everything white, instead of being channeled into positive trends of action, such mystiques are capable of veering off into dangerous nihilistic fantasies of black supremacy that have little to do with the actualities of the real world. In this world of fantasy there will be a pecking order of blackness—"I am more black and more pure than thou"—in which case the enemy ceases to be whiteness but other less black breeds. This has already been manifested by the hate fringe of black nihilism—more threatening to blacks than to whites. Long predicted, this nihilistic black fringe was bound to develop when the Afro-American Nationalists failed to transcend their mystical and romantic phase.

It is the easiest thing in the world to shift the blame for the murder of Malcolm X to the CIA or their alleged black agents in the Negro community, but this murder signifies something more sinister than the followers of Malcolm X care to admit. It signifies that the nationalist wing of the black movement is capable of terrorism—aiming to obstruct, defeat, subvert and destroy every effort on the part of other Negro militants to develop positive programs of any kind. This nihilistic trend in Harlem, it must be remembered, accused Malcolm X of selling out simply because the man broke with the Nation of Islam and proceeded to modify his original attitude toward whites and his definition of nationalism.

The collapse of the Black Arts Repertory Theater and School is another case in point. Here was one of the most positive institutions established in Harlem during the last twenty-five years, with the support of a very broad representation from the Harlem youth. But this school was destroyed from the inside, and taken over by the terrorists who forced out everyone else who would not agree with their mystique. The Black Arts episode ended in a shooting which might easily have been fatal.

The Organization for Afro-American Unity has not been able to deal at all with the internal confusions and disabilities of the Afro-American Nationalist trends, become even more pronounced since the passing of Malcolm X. Taken as a whole, the various factions do not really know what they want. They do not know whether they want to see the United States reformed or revolutionized, destroyed or democratized, abandoned, overthrown, or obliterated. The Afro-American Nationalists cannot make up their minds whether they want to emigrate, separate, migrate, or simply sit still in the ghettoes admiring each other during the quiet lulls between uprisings. The Afro-American Nationalists are faced with so many ghetto problems of such monumental proportions, which they are neither prepared nor equipped to tackle, that it is small wonder so much frustration reigns in their ranks. The black ghettoes are in dire need of new organizations or parties of a political nature, yet it is a fact that most of the leading young nationalist spokesmen are apolitical. It might not be entirely true, but talk in Harlem had it that even Malcolm X was cool to the idea of a political party. The black ghettoes are in even more dire need of every possible kind of economic and self-help organization, and a buyers and consumers council, but the most militant young nationalists openly ridicule such efforts as reformist and a waste of time. For them politics and economics are most unrevolutionary. What they do consider revolutionary are Watts-type uprisings—which lead nowhere. Listen to this editorial:

Bourgeois Nationalism, or militant "Booker T-ism" (self-improvement) states that black people should strive to control the areas of the black ghettoes and communities, substituting black-owned businesses and establishments for the white-owned businesses. The "radical" wing of "Bourgeois Nationalism" seeks to separate the black people from White America by either acquiring separate states within this nation, or being allowed to establish a repatriation program back to Africa, to help develop it into an economic power. The more moderate wing seeks to develop black political power by forming an independent political party within the current structure; thereby electing congressmen, assemblymen, and other officials, to office—responsible to said party. . . . As time goes by, "Bourgeois Nationalism" becomes increasingly conservative—losing its militant stance and potential initiative; emphasizing "culture" and "economics" instead of politics.[13]

These are the thoughts of some of the leading exponents of the new Afro-American Nationalism. But note that in one paragraph this trend clearly reveals the depths of its own disorientation. They attempt to demonstrate how revolutionarily modernistic they are, by downgrading "Booker T-ism," the real historical meaning of which they have not yet understood. After that they dispose of Garveyism for the wrong reasons, and then the Nation of Islam's Muslims (probably because they do not like religion and the Muslims would demand too much discipline for free-wheeling young souls). They then scoff contemptuously at such efforts as the Freedom Now Party as a useless pastime for "moderates." But, interestingly enough, these young super-nationalists go even further than that—they cut the ground from under Malcolm X's OAAU because it had to be built upon the very political, economic, and cultural premises that many young nationalists reject as reflecting a childish attitude toward white America. In fact, the tentative outline of the OAAU's program, as drafted, was predicated on such political, economic and cultural ideas; and even before, these same ideas had been projected in the draft program of the Freedom Now Party published in the *Liberator* magazine of February, 1964. Recall that the Freedom Now Party platform was attacked from Detroit by James Boggs for being meaningless. Correspondingly, the young nationalists rejected the basis of the OAAU's program even before it was written. Yet in the very same issue of their publication these young nationalists refer to Malcolm X as a "real revolutionary," and take issue with those who were trying to "assert that brother Malcolm was moving closer to the mainstream of the civil rights movement."

There are serious contradictions in all of this, because although Malcolm X made revolutionary statements, his OAAU program was definitely written as a reformist document. So, also, in tone, was the draft platform of the Freedom Now Party—but merely because any political platform in America must be reformist in premise before it can be revolutionary. Otherwise such a party will never get off the ground even with strong and perceptive leadership (which the FNP did *not* have). On the other hand, even when a reformist organization such as the OAAU is established by a strongman leader like Malcolm X, it collapses if the leader is removed. This reveals an almost incurable Messiah complex, characteristic of Negro emotionalism. There must always be the great Individual Leader—the Messiah, the Grand Deliverer, the cult of the Irreproachable Personality who, even if he does not really have all the answers to the problem, can never be wrong. Negroes, including the nationalists, are led by their emotions rather than by reason or the guideposts of social analysis. This political immaturity is sustained by two factors: Negroes are not really sure what they want out of life; and, they do not understand that American society is much too complex today for the human limitations of one individual leader to encompass. What the Afro-American Nationalists need is a collective leadership, a guiding committee of political, economic and cultural experts to tackle an agreed-upon set of social goals. But who, out of the morass of nationalist confusion, can establish any goals?

In Harlem today, the American capitalist-welfare state dynamic rules supreme, with the aid of the police department. What was once truly the cultural capital of the Negro world has become a social disaster area, a dehumanized desert of mass society in black. As a community, Harlem is beyond the purview of the integrationist program, hence it falls, by default, within the purview of the nationalist wing. If the nationalist wing fails in the task of rehabilitation, then Harlem is a lost world. What stands between the nationalist wing and the capitalist-welfare state power apparatus are various groupings of Negro middle-class integrationist forces, emanating from civil rights organizations, newspaper groups, political machines, churches, social agencies and business groups. From these circles come the decision makers of Harlem, and since these rulers are now powerless to rehabilitate and improve the community, their permanent function is to control it. Manifested in this situation is Harlem's class problem. The nationalist wing calls it the problem of the black bourgeoisie or the middle-class Negro, and it is this that trips them up. The term Black Bourgeoisie was first popularized by E. Franklin Frazier, in his study of the same title. Previously, the common term was middle-class Negroes, its archetype the class of Negroes who ran the NAACP. However, it is clear that many Negroes who glibly use the term black bourgeoisie have not read Frazier's book at all, or if they have, need to reread it. They will note that Frazier's subtitle for his book is "The Rise of a *New* Middleclass." This meant that insofar as civil rights organizations like the NAACP and the Urban League are middle class, they are, in the main, pre-World War Two middle class, or older generation bourgeois. But Frazier's "new middle class" comprises a younger generation that was certainly not a part of the older middle-class entrenchment within the NAACP. The social status of this new wave middle-class

Negro was based on new developments in the American economy. Frazier wrote:

The relative size of the black bourgeoisie in the Negro population has increased during the past decade largely because the proportion of Negro workers in clerical and kindred occupations has more than doubled and the proportion of female clerical workers quadrupled since 1940. . . . During and especially since World War II, Negro men and women in the North have been entering clerical occupations, both in public and private employment, as the result of political pressure and the Fair Employment Practices Laws enacted in eleven states and twenty-five cities.[14]

Hence the greater proportion of the Negro middle class today claims a status that is based more on occupational achievements than on family background or inherited economic and social status. And it so happens that a very large number of Afro-American Nationalists are young people who fall within this occupational range. They are clerical and professional workers, teachers, students, social welfare employees, struggling writers and journalists, etc. Many who are unemployed, aspire only to these kinds of occupations, or are aspirants for a college degree, looking forward to better jobs. Despite their nationalistic ideology they are people "on the make," and they are also some of the loudest denunciators and critics of the black bourgeoisie. Everyone who is not a factory worker, service industry employee, domestic or porter is bourgeois-tainted (with the exception of themselves), but they would be scandalized if they were offered a job in a factory or service industry. In this fashion, the Afro-American Nationalists labor under the unconscious but self-engendered liability of reflecting the values of the very class they attack. Unaware that this is but the American capitalistic dynamic at work the nationalists are sufficiently muddled, confused and blinded that they mishandle and distort the question of the black bourgeoisie. The nationalist movement cannot succeed unless it establishes firm alliances with certain sections of the black bourgeoisie wherever possible. However, the Afro-American Nationalists have shown a strong tendency to reject certain of the sons and daughters of the black bourgeoisie in their early twenties on a class, skin-color, and hair-texture basis. Here, the black skin and the *au naturel* hairdo becomes the nationalist standard of ideological purity. But lurking behind the façade of many of an Afro-American Nationalist dressed like a native Nigerian, is an incipient black bourgeois, American-Negro style.

One can see such people at the African parties, consular fêtes, and the Africanized cultural events where the outward symbols of the African identification also become credentials to new social status: the personal alliance with new-nation power, the job in the African-American hierarchy, or even the sinecure in Africa, if one learns the politics of cliques. In this way, the problem of the black bourgeoisie has been internationalized, from New York to Accra, Lagos, Dakar, Conakry—"back where our history began."

Moreover, the middle-class muddle within the Afro-American Nationalists undermines a positive approach to the role of the black intelligentsia, inasmuch as the nationalists are without a skilled and well-oriented group of intellectuals. Lurking behind the anti-bourgeois sentiment is the more dangerous prejudice of anti-intellectualism. But the Afro-American Nationalists cannot afford the luxury of indulging in this typical white American prejudice against intellectualism. It is true that intellectuals are a part of what is called the educated class. But a race of people who clamor for the rights to higher education as much as Negroes do cannot contradict themselves by rejecting the class results of this higher education, without due appraisal. It so happens that there are intellectuals who seek bourgeois status and the fulfillment of the American Dream, and there are those who do not. The same applies to those nationalists who disclaim intellectualism, but who consider themselves much too knowledgeable to accept the economic and social status of the masses. America is a difficult society to live in without succumbing to the blandishments of bourgeois values. The real question is which bourgeois values are *positive* and which are *detrimental* to social progress. At any rate, the Afro-American Nationalists find they must depend on their intellectuals to arbitrate class conflict within the Negro group. To a great degree in America, the Negro intellectual is actually *declassé,* or at least he must steer clear of class association in order to play any kind of role. To the degree that the Negro intellectual fails to understand this is the measure of his deep crisis in America. But if the majority of the Afro-American Nationalists fail to understand this, they will but repeat a black sectarianism that resembles the early sectarianism of the fledging Communist Party of the 1920's. The Communists, too, went through a phase where class purity, style of dress, ideological exclusiveness, and anti-intellectualism took precedence over political maturity and awareness of American realities.

In Harlem today, among the Afro-American Nationalists, there is little awareness of practical political realities. Behind the pretext of rejecting everything white, lies the easy path to political escapism and irresponsibility. The Afro-American Nationalists have created for themselves a detached world of their own, full of confused and contradictory motivations. It is an inbred, exclusive, and often a make-believe world that exists only for itself, without specified goals. It is a world that awaits the arrival of an Armageddon, a day of racial reckoning, but that rationalizes away every possible positive action on the political, economic and cultural fronts. Lacking any program, the Afro-American Nationalists allow the capitalistic-welfare state power apparatus to move in and take over, by co-option, every issue on which a program could be based. On the one hand, the Afro-American Nationalists will say that you cannot trust the white man's Federal power to aid and abet the Negro's struggle. On the other, they leap on the band-wagon of every anti-poverty handout from the Federal power, and then complain that the Federal power is not doing enough. But the Afro-American Nationalists refuse to launch an independent political party of their own in order to deal more effectively with the Federal power. Their excuse is, that politics is moderation, yet they refuse to see the contradiction here that leads them deeper into immobility.

The Afro-American Nationalists fail to see the politically strategic nature of the Harlem community. Instead, they allow integrationist political leaders elected from the community to launch a widely advertised program aimed at breaking up, through planned integration, the present ethnic composition of Harlem. Such a plan, if carried out, would have very profound political and economic ramifications. It would critically undermine the Negro's already precarious political situation in New York, and rule out any possible future economic rehabilitation of Harlem *in the Negro's favor*. It is not understood by the Afro-American Nationalists that if Negroes lose the racial majority in Harlem, they are lost. Harlem is the Negro's main urban bastion in the entire country and he must fight to keep control of it. This fundamental truth could have been the rallying point for popular opinion in the Harlem Nationalists' confrontation of integrationist policies. If one talks of Afro-American unity, Harlem is the place where all of its theories and practice must be tested and proven. As a black principality within the leading metropolis in the western world, Harlem is a black city in economic bondage, lacking adequate political representation. It is presided over like a racial reserve by the armed police power of the state. It has no local press that speaks with the sentiments of the grass roots. It has no cultural institutions that cultivate the personalities of its people. There is not a single publication coming out of Harlem reflecting the deep imperatives of its blighted existence, playing the role of opinion-molder in the interests of social progress.

The Afro-American Nationalists are boxed in by these paradoxes and the pressures of reforms. Indulging in talk about revolution, they meanwhile gather in every possible crumb from the reformers. But they do not publish a single, inexpensive newspaper. The Organization of Afro-American Unity has not yet taken what should be the first step of any movement that aims to influence public opinion—to issue a regular periodical expressing the organization's views. The activist leadership tradition of oratory is too strongly adhered to by Negroes. They do not realize that the base of a new kind of movement with new ideas can be cemented only with the help of a publication. As long as the Afro-American Nationalists leave the information and propaganda field open, to be monopolized by the integrationist-reformers, they will be unable to mount a counter program.

The large cities, especially in the North, are where the decisive struggles of the Negro movement will be waged. It will be a difficult and complex struggle, but the Negro movement must win political and economic power within these urban communities, while seeking cultural freedom and equality there and beyond, in the broad cultural context. Even the land question can be solved only from an urban base of political power. In an advanced society such as the United States, the agrarian problem ceases to be a countryside "conquest" issue. The politics of land ownership and distribution stems from the political power invested in groups or state agencies located in capital cities. More than that, the land question—unsettled ever since post-Civil War Reconstruction failed to expropriate the land of the ex-slaveholders—is now an international issue involving Africa. Black Africa, the ancestral home of the Negro, is an underpopulated continent. There may well come a time when the race question in Africa will have to be solved by admitting specified numbers of white Rhodesians, Angolans, and South African Afrikaners into the United States, in exchange for an equal number of Afro-Americans to take their places in Africa. The political side of the international land question is certainly beyond the ken of the Afro-American Nationalists. Indeed, they are far from a definitive understanding of how Afro-American Nationalism relates to domestic and international situations in any organizational, political or theoretical fashion.

## NOTES

[1] *The Negro in the Caribbean* (Washington, D.C.: Associates in Negro Folk Education, 1942), p. 62.

[2] *Ibid.*, p. 63.

[3] *Ibid.*, p. 75.

[4] *Garvey and Garveyism*, A. J. Garvey, 1963 (Published by the author, 1963), p. 26.

[5] *The New York Times*, July 24, 1966, p. 51.

[6] *Idem.*

[7] Eric Williams, *op. cit.*, p. 93.

[8] Eric Williams is now Prime Minister of Trinidad.

[9] Eric Williams, *op. cit.*, p. 87.

10 A few years ago the Jamaican authorities in Kingston started hearings for a treason trial against Garvey's latter-day followers, the Rastafari cult, for preaching Back to Africa.

11 Eric Williams, *op. cit.*, p. 16.

12 Louise Jeffers, Nevis, West Indies, pp. 99–102.

13 "A New Philosophy for a New Age," *Black America,* Summer-Fall, 1965, p. 8.

14 E. Franklin Frazier, "Negro Middle Class and Desegregation," *Crosscurrents,* Summer, 1957, pp. 49–50.

*The following essay by Rupert Emerson and Martin
Kilson of Harvard University originally appeared in
Daedalus, the Journal of the American Academy of Arts
and Sciences. It speaks of the broadest consequences
of the rise of independent Africa and the assertion of
Black equality, value, and power in America.*

# The American Dilemma in a Changing World:
# The Rise of Africa and the Negro American

## Rupert Emerson and Martin Kilson

From great wars come unexpected consequences—certainly consequences unforeseen, and usually undesired, by those responsible for shaping
the policies which led to war. Of such consequences none is more striking
or more profound in its implications than the change in the relationship
between the races that has come in the aftermath of World War II, bearing
out the prophetic dictum of W. E. B. Du Bois at the turn of the century that
"The problem of the twentieth century is the problem of the color line—
the relation of the darker to the lighter races of man in Asia and Africa,
in America and the islands of the sea." [1] The peoples of Asia and Africa
have risen to demand their own independent and equal position in the world
society, and in their revolt against the old order of colonialism they have
been joined by the refusal of the Negro American to linger at some halfway
point between slavery and freedom. In particular, the relations of Africa
and America, of Africans and Americans, always difficult and ambivalent,
have taken on new dimensions, some calculable and others lending themselves to no more than an appreciation of general magnitude. The determination of cause and effect and of interconnections on the two sides of
the Atlantic, and of the Pacific as well, will occupy the historians far into
the future.

The immense impact of the Second World War inevitably had its effect
upon the social structure of the United States, and in no sphere more significantly than in Negro-white relations. The ramifications of the attack
upon the established patterns of segregation and discrimination are asserting
themselves today in a manner that few could have predicted twenty years
ago. Perhaps most significant of all, what had been a domestic problem of

From Talcott Parson and Kenneth B. Clark, eds., *The Negro American.* Reprinted
by permission from DAEDALUS, Journal of the American Academy of Arts and
Sciences, Boston, Mass., vol. 94, no. 4.

the United States has become part of a global problem, inextricably en-
tangled with the destiny of other peoples and continents and profoundly
affecting America's standing in the world.[2]

The Negro American has played a role in the stimulation and shaping of
African nationalism, and the mere existence of the newly sovereign African
states, now constituting a quarter of the membership of the United Nations,
has changed the nature of the American scene. The restructuring of American race relationships is taking place within a new framework deriving from
international situations generated in good part by World War II. The principal elements involved are America's status as a superpower whose interests reach to every corner of a shrinking world and whose actions affect
every people, no matter how remote; the coming of the Cold War and the
global confrontation with Communism; and the debut of problems of race
and color on the international stage consequent upon the rise of postwar
Asian and African nationalism.

The high expectations among Negro Americans that the post-World
War II era would bring change had their counterpart at the close of World
War I, but with the all-important difference that the world was not then
watching what was going on in the United States nor were Americans so
much concerned with world opinion. American race relations were essentially a matter of parochial concern, interesting relatively few outside this
country. Today Negro agitation and the way in which it is handled by the
United States, both nationally and locally, is a matter of crucial concern
not only to heads of state around the world but also to many millions of
people in many countries. What they think of American intentions and of
the way in which the civil rights struggle is handled, brought to them in
stories on the air and in the press and in appalling pictures, is a matter which
Americans can ignore only at their peril. The one world of political unity
and peace among men which many hoped would emerge from World War II
failed to materialize, but the globe has unquestionably closed in on all its
inhabitants. The United States can no longer live unto itself, nor can Asia
and Africa be seen, or see themselves, as isolated continents: we have all
become integral parts of a single field of interaction embracing all mankind.
Certainly no one can contend that the American pattern of racial discrimination was any more morally defensible after the First World War than
after the Second, but what the rest of the world was then prepared to toler-
ate indifferently has now become internationally intolerable. This revolutionary change in the world's climate has imposed upon American political
leaders the necessity of taking speedy and radical action in a sphere in which
they could formerly delay action from year to year and decade to decade.

With full recognition of this unique difference between the two eras, it is

useful to survey what happened in the United States in the aftermath of
World War I. The small group of Negro intellectuals and professionals that
had emerged before 1914, the new body of skilled Negro laborers produced
during the war, and the thousands of Negro servicemen who for the first time
saw foreign lands and ways were all hopeful that the war's impact would
favorably alter American race relations. Thus in 1918, Du Bois, the ablest
spokesman for the Negroes at this period, reflected this hope in the editorial
pages of *The Crisis,* the official organ of the NAACP:

> This war is an End and, also, a Beginning. Never again will darker people
> of the world occupy just the place they had before. Out of this war will rise,
> soon or late, an independent China, a self-governing India, an Egypt with rep-
> resentative institutions, an Africa for the Africans, and not merely for business
> exploitation. Out of this war will rise, too, an American Negro with the right
> to vote and the right to work and the right to live without insult.[3]

Du Bois saw rightly what the future was to bring, but it was to come to
realization late rather than soon. The Wilsonian call for self-determination
and a world safe for democracy was applied neither to the vast colonial
sphere nor to the Negro American. The international circumstances which
have aided the Negro to breach the ramparts of segregation and discrimination in the last years were virtually non-existent in the interwar decades.
The League of Nations was in operation but, save for the Mandates, it paid
no attention to the colonial problem, and the later concern for human rights
was essentially beyond its purview.

In the United States the expectations of Negroes were shattered by organized white violence, abetted by the inertia or indifference of our national
institutions, both governmental and private. In the so-called "red summer"
of 1919 ("red" because Negro blood was spilled at the hands of white
mobs) such anti-Negro riots as those in Chicago, East St. Louis, Omaha,
Washington, D.C., Longview, Texas, and elsewhere were unmistakable
signs that whatever the progressive impact of World War I may have been
in other parts of the world, its meaning would be denied the Negro American.

This white reaction was a particularly hard blow to the NAACP, whose
leaders' faith in American democracy was tried nearly to the breaking point.
A great effort was made to obtain federal action to end lynching. In 1922
an NAACP anti-lynching advertisement proclaimed that it was "The shame
of America—that the United States is the *Only Land on Earth* where human
beings are BURNED AT THE STAKE. In Four Years 1918–1921,
Twenty-Eight People were Publically BURNED BY AMERICAN
MOBS." [4] Basic as the purpose of the NAACP's anti-lynching program

was to the fulfillment of American democracy, no such legislation was ever enacted by Congress; nor was the United States internationally pilloried in shame then as it has been more recently.

The even greater Negro expectations for a new deal in the post-World War II period were similarly met at the outset by white violence in innumerable cities and towns. This violence, often directed against Negro ex-servicemen, also sought to cow the Negro, who had been immensely stirred by the war, into passive acceptance of his lot. While the anti-Negro violence that followed World War I largely succeeded in its purpose, the violence at the end of and after World War II was doomed to failure. Why was this so? The reasons are many, and such domestic changes as the increasing concern of our national institutions and the slow but clear assumption by the white upper classes of their proper responsibility in the racial sphere will, in the final reckoning, be given much importance. These changes did not come of themselves.

They became possible in part because the international situation after 1945 provided a new climate of *political necessity,* within which our national institutions, as they relate to the Negro, were given new opportunity (and possibly their last) to fulfill the aims, purposes, and hopes which had inspired the Founding Fathers. Necessity, we suspect, is as much the mother of institutional as it is of technological-scientific innovation. The domination of the world by the Western European white man and his descendants overseas, belatedly joined by the Japanese, was speedily drawing to a close, and the United States was forced to adapt itself to a fundamentally changed international environment. As Harold R. Isaacs has put it,

The downfall of the white-supremacy system in the rest of the world made its survival in the United States suddenly and painfully conspicuous. It became our most exposed feature and in the swift unfolding of the world's affairs, our most vulnerable weakness ... when hundreds of millions of people all around looked in our direction, it seemed to be all that they could see.[5]

Although the outburst of Asian and African nationalism after World War II was the primary element involved in the great transformation, the racial issue had been simmering internationally for a long time. Japan had already done its utmost to make use of it in the effort to discredit the United States and to subjugate Asia.[6] This undoubtedly predisposed Asians to emphasize the racial element in their postwar response to Western dominance, even though they repudiated Japan's version of Asia for the Asians. Equally influencing this response was the West's own assumption that its hegemony represented, *inter alia,* the natural subordination of "lower" to "higher" races. Shortly after the commencement of the Cold War, Nehru, speaking

at a private meeting with Negro and white American civil rights leaders
which was organized at his request by Ralph J. Bunche and Walter White,
gave the following account of the racial factor in Asian perception of the
West:

Whenever I warn against acceptance of Soviet promises of equality because
they are so frequently broken, I am answered quite often by questions about
America's attitude toward dark-skinned people. The people of Asia don't like
colonialism or race prejudices. They resent condescension. When Americans
talk to them about equality and freedom, they remember stories about lynchings. They are becoming increasingly aware that colonialism is largely based
on color—and, for the first time in the lives of many of them, they realize that
they are colored. With what is happening to the dark-skinned native population
of South Africa at the hands of Malan and what the French are doing in
Indochina our people are developing a sense of sympathy and unity with dark-
skinned victims of exploitation all over the world.[7]

African nationalism, of course, was even more engulfed with matters of
race in its postwar encounter with the West. Colonial rule in Africa was
explicitly associated with ideas regarding the inferiority of black or Negro
peoples, which were also an explicit part of American racism, and offered
the Communists a magnificent weapon with which to attack the Western,
and especially the American, response to African nationalism.

The Communist claim to be free of the racism characteristic of American
society has been belied by several incidents of discrimination and even violence against African students in Soviet bloc countries, but the Communists
have made good use for their purposes of the sins of the United States and
of colonialism, including the crises of white-dominated southern Africa and
such Congolese problems as the use of white mercenaries. To lay great stress
on the Communist role is, however, to miss the fundamental realities of the
situation. There is indeed no reason to think that events or attitudes would
have been markedly different if no Communists had existed. Both colonialism and racism spoke for themselves, and no Communists were needed to
point out the moral of the widely circulated pictures and stories concerning
the shocking inhumanity which has accompanied the desegregation drive
in the United States.

## THE EMERGENCE OF ASIAN AND AFRICAN STATES

The heart of our theme is not the Cold War nor the success or failure of
the Communists in stirring up trouble and capitalizing on the sins and errors
of the West. These are matters which are on the fringe of the great postwar
development which challenged the white control of the world and brought
into being a host of new states almost wholly inhabited by people of color.

The membership of the United Nations is only one indicator of the change, but a striking one. At the end of 1945 the U.N. had fifty-one members, of which six were located in the Middle East, four in Africa (including Egypt), and three in Asia. Twenty years later the total had soared to one hundred fifteen, among which the Africans numbered thirty-six, the Asians fifteen, and the Middle East eleven.

A new world of states has come into being, and it will be long before we fully discern its meaning and adapt ourselves to the complexities and new modes of action which are called for, but it is evident that it has already had a great effect on the American domestic scene.

A few basic facts stand in sharp relief. To state the matter in its largest and most neutral terms, the massive emergence of Asia and Africa from colonialism is juxtaposed and coincides in time with the attack upon the segregated and inferior position of the Negro in the United States. The two are separate developments and yet intimately and intricately interrelated. At another level of discourse, the American stance in world affairs has inevitably been affected by the revolutionary changes taking place in Asia and Africa, and these changes have been in varying degree influenced by American attitudes, policies, and activities. The traditional anti-colonial outlook of the United States, however much it may have been muted as an active force in recent years, played its part in creating the contemporary climate of anti-colonialism which facilitated the growth of nationalist movements. American diplomacy both within and without the United Nations has had to take into consideration the multiplicity of new states which open a wide range of new opportunities and of new uncertainties and insecurities. For the 20,000,000 Americans of African or partial African descent a new avenue of experience, perhaps of vital import, emerged when the continent of their origin burst forth in an unprecedented luxuriance of sovereign states, with more still to come.

No more than a most summary review need be attempted here of what the United States has done, and has not done, in relation to Africa. Since the record is an irregular and sometimes internally contradictory one, there is wide disagreement about where the emphasis should be placed. American policy has constantly tended toward a middle course. As a result, the swings to this side and that, could they be charted, might be reduced to a middle line which would have a large measure of consistency; but anyone who so chooses can stress the zigs or the zags and the opposing courses which they represent. Even though the United States may be said to have adhered quite closely to a moderate and responsible position, the partisans of none of the several camps which are involved, including Americans with strong views of any sort, are likely to be much pleased with it. The past and present colonial powers and South Africa tend to see the United States as meddling in their affairs, irresponsibly encouraging the anti-colonialists and nationalists, while the more militant Africans see America at best as a lukewarm supporter of their cause and at worst as an ally and supplier of the colonial powers and South Africa, and as itself a major practitioner of neo-colonialism. The widespread African good will on which America could earlier count has receded sharply in recent years. American endorsement of Tshombe's return to the Congo in 1964 and participation with Belgium in the paratroop drop on Stanleyville—which was launched from a British island-base—produced bitter hostility in many African quarters.

For nearly a century starting with the Civil War the American connection with Africa was very limited, the controlling circumstance for most of the period being European colonial domination of the continent. The assumption that Africa was inhabited by primitive peoples who had barely made a start toward civilization rendered all the more tempting the inclination to abstain from concern with the continent. This assumption was primarily responsible also for the widespread tendency of the Negro American to look down on Africa and to be wary of identifying himself with what were reputed to be the black savages across the sea. World War II brought about a new awareness of Africa, politically, economically, and strategically, but it also enhanced the strength of the American bonds to the colonial powers. The onset of the Cold War rendered any change in the status quo suspect of being of possible benefit to the enemy, and the acceptance of anti-Communism as the dominant theme in American foreign policy was, as the Africans and many Americans saw it, an undesirable and irritating substitute for the direct sponsorship of independence and development.

In the 1950's, the decisive decade for Africa, the United States was more a follower than a leader. The independence of Tunisia, Morocco, the Sudan, the Gold Coast, and Guinea between 1956 and 1958, followed by a stream of other countries, forced an almost total recasting of American relations with Africa. The sedate and measured tread which the United States envisioned for an ultimate African advance to the right of self-determination for those mature enough for independence was outpaced not only by the passionate determination of African leaders to be rid of colonialism but also by the actual rush of events accepted, and even abetted, by Britain, France, and Belgium. Washington was confronted by the necessity to make its peace with the African nationalists and with the multitude of new African states.

Without wholly discarding the caution which had characterized American policy, the United States made some drastic changes. The few consulates which had existed in some of the African colonies were now hastily replaced by an embassy in each of the new countries, equipped in the modern style with aid, information, and other services. At home a change of marked significance in the State Department was a gradual curtailing of the control over Africa of the European desks, culminating in 1958 in the appointment of an Assistant Secretary of State for African Affairs heading an autonomous African Bureau. The number of people dealing with Africa at home and abroad had to be increased dramatically, but a distressingly weak point was the failure to multiply adequately the number of Negroes above the menial and minor clerical level in the Department and the several categories of the Foreign Service.[8] With only one Negro in the corps of Foreign Service Officers before 1950, the various urgent calls for the enrollment of Negroes in the Department and abroad, whether in the newly opened African posts or elsewhere, have still not achieved satisfactory results.

The first major postwar changes in this sphere came through a few spectacular appointments of Negroes as consultants and alternate delegates to the United States delegation at the United Nations. In the immediate postwar years these included Du Bois, Walter White, and Channing Tobias, all closely associated with the NAACP; and the Eisenhower administration made similar appointments, including two Negro women as alternate delegates.

It remained for the Kennedy administration to initiate a new approach to this problem. In August 1961, at a conference on equality of opportunity in the Department of State, attended by leading Negroes, the Secretary of State, Dean Rusk, explained the context of the administration's thinking as follows:

The biggest single burden that we carry on our backs in our foreign relations in the 1960's is the problem of racial discrimination here at home. There is just no question about it.

We are dealing with forty or fifty new countries that have become independent since 1945, and we are living through a decade of readjustment of the relationships between Western Europe and the rest of the world—a decade when the white race and the nonwhite races have got to re-examine and readjust their traditional relationships.

Our attitude on a question of this sort is of fundamental importance to the success of the foreign policy of the United States.

Although this conference made strong recommendations that the number of Negroes in the upper ranks should be increased through promotion from below and through lateral transfer to the Foreign Service Officer Corps from related services, the results have been disappointing. A major reason for the relative failure of the campaign to draw in more Negroes is undoubtedly the inadequacy of education in Negro colleges and universities, which leads to a low level of success on the Foreign Service examinations; but a more aggressive and inventive attack on the problem should have been able to produce better results. In any case, in 1964, of the 10,987 persons at a professional level in the Department of State and the three categories of the Foreign Service, including the Reserve and the Staff Corps, only 205 were Negroes. Of these 21 were counted among the 3,698 Foreign Service Officers proper, including three with the rank of ambassador. In the two decades since the end of World War II, a round dozen Negroes have been assigned to ambassadorial posts, several in Africa but increasingly in other countries as well, including Norway, Finland, Luxemburg, and Syria, and also as American representative to the U.N. Economic and Social Council. The way in which the process has been speeded up is indicated by the fact that in midsummer 1965 five Negroes were simultaneously serving or had been named as ambassadors, two of them appointed in the present year by President Johnson.

A much debated and still unanswered question, given increased urgency by the emergence of the new Asian and African states, concerns the desirability of sending Negro ambassadors and other high-ranking personnel to posts abroad. It is necessary to consider whether Africans are pleased to see one of their own people, so to speak, coming to represent the United States, or whether they feel that they are securing only second-rate representation, lacking influence in Washington, since Negroes are disfavored at home. The goal here as elsewhere is surely that members of the Foreign Service and others should be appointed to diplomatic posts regardless of color and on the basis of their ability, seniority, and the kind of contribution they can be expected to make. A precondition for the realization of this goal is that the number of qualified Negroes available for such appointments be greatly expanded; otherwise special consideration must inevitably be accorded the few Negroes who can be called upon. The rise of the new countries has called attention to the shortcomings in the racial balance of America's diplomatic personnel, but it is evident that the attainment of an appropriate number of qualified Negroes cannot be expected without a fundamental improvement in the position of the mass of the Negroes in American society. Although the traditional policy of indifference has been discarded, much remains to be done.

The same moral—that no truly satisfactory answer can be found short of a basic change in the status of the Negro in America—attaches to the reverse side of the coin, the appearance in this country of a number of Asian and African diplomats and visitors of many sorts, including a greatly expanded contingent of students. To put the matter in its crudest terms a society in which segregation and discrimination continued to be, in varying degree, a standard feature was suddenly confronted by the need of dealing with a relatively large body of nonwhite emissaries from a variety of countries, who were far from ready to accept being "pushed around" or tolerated as inferiors who should know their place. In point of fact, their inherent demand that they be treated as human beings and as distinguished representatives of their countries was very likely to be coupled with an oversensitivity to anything which was felt to be a slur or insult—a reaction stemming in part from the colonial experience just left behind them. The issue, peculiarly acute in New York and Washington and the much-travelled strip of Maryland lying between the two, was unhappily precisely one of color. *The Washington Post,* editorially chiding Representative Adam Clayton Powell on May 9, 1961, for introducing a bill imposing heavy penalties on any persons who denied business facilities, services, or accommodations to ambassadors, public ministers, and their staffs because of their racial origin, pointed out the sad truth: "The bill seems to assume that foreign envoys travelling in the United States are special objects of discrimination. But the fact is that they suffer discrimination only when they are mistaken for American citizens."

Housing, meals, schools, transportation, recreation—these were all spheres in which rebuffs were likely to be experienced, and apologies after the fact, even when delivered by the President of the United States in person, could not wipe out the incident itself. Nor was it adequate to seek to explain the intricacies of the American federal system and the limited power of the government in Washington to control the attitudes and actions of states, cities, and private persons. Particularly under President Kennedy, in part because of a change in outlook but also because of the extraordinary increase in the number of African states represented in the U.N. and in Washington, very serious efforts were made by the State Department and other agencies and groups to find solutions. No solution was possible, however, unless the American Negro came to be accepted as a person of worth and dignity. The gap between the ideals of which the United States boasted and the social habits which it tolerated was so great as to cast grave doubt on the justification of the American claim to lead the free world; and indignities inflicted upon U.N. delegates and personnel brought demands for a removal of the United Nations from the United States—a United Nations, be it noted, in which the peoples of color played an increasingly decisive role. To maintain its standing in the world the United States had inescapably to deal with the way envoys and others from abroad were treated in American society. In many instances Asians and Africans were not prepared to accept special favors for themselves which were not made equally available to all others: this housing or that social gathering might be opened to Africans of appropriate standing, but were they equally open to colored Americans? Why should the Negro American accept exclusion when the Indian or African was accepted? The ability to escape the consequences of American prejudice by wearing African national dress served only to underline the shoddy nature of the compromise which sustained Jim Crow while evading some of its penalties; and some Africans have refused to avail themselves of the privilege.

Significant headway appears to have been made in dealing with parts of the problems raised by the visitors from the new countries, but no workable or acceptable solution is possible until the racial issue has been settled domestically by ridding American society of segregation and discrimination. What has become inescapably clear is that this is no longer a parochial issue for Americans to settle when they get around to it, but a matter of urgent international importance which gravely affects many aspects of American policy.

## AFRICA AND THE NEGRO AMERICAN

The issues which have just been discussed are, in good part at least, within the realm of the calculable and as such are susceptible of reasonably precise analysis. Another order of discourse is exposed when inquiry turns to the questions of the attitudes of Negro Americans toward Africa and the effect upon them of African independence. Even though exposure to Africa might frequently confirm the conviction of the Negro that he was American rather than African, Africa's liberation has beyond any shadow of doubt helped to liberate the Negro in America as well. Like emancipation from slavery, the breach with colonialism was an indispensable part of the Negro's rise to equality, and its repercussions have been strongly felt on this side of the Atlantic. Two quite different but inter-related propositions are involved. One is that the end of colonialism so changed the balance of forces in the world as to compel the United States to undertake at long last a major attack upon the racial situation at home. Thus James Baldwin, among others, gives primary credit for the civil liberties campaign to the rise of Africa in the context of the Cold War.[9] The other is that the emergence of sovereign states in Africa has changed the Negro American's image of himself and of his place in the world. Israel is not necessarily the homeland of the American Jew nor Africa of the American Negro, but both Jew and Negro have gained in stature from the existence of independent countries created by peoples to whom they have a special relationship. For the Negro in particular it has been a unique and stirring experience to see whole societies and political systems come into existence in which from top to bottom, from president through civil service to office boy, all posts are occupied by black men, not because of the sufferance of white superiors but because it is their sovereign right. In contrast to the Negro's experience of the American society, the control of the new African states and societies is in African hands, and where white expertise is needed it is employed by African governments on African terms.

Africa, in one form or another, has always been a part of the reality of Americans of African descent. The relationship has often been tortuously ambivalent and confused, but given the segregated framework of Negro acculturation to American standards and the influence of white supremacist values, this was not surprising. Nor was it unique to Negro Americans. British and French West Indian Negroes, Brazilian Negroes, and others in the New World had a not dissimilar experience. All have been shaped in their behavior and self-definition by the standards of the politically dominant white populations. Thus the trend among Negro American women at the turn of this century away from forms of African cosmetic standards for treating the hair, which persisted in the American South for centuries, to those of the white women has its counterpart throughout the Caribbean Negro communities, urban Brazil, and, interestingly enough, in urban West Africa.[10] Likewise, the sense of being ashamed of one's black skin, rooted in the Negro American's subordination to white standards and representing the ultimate of self-rejection, has its counterpart in the Caribbean communities and Brazil, and, alas, has not been unknown among acculturated Africans.[11]

The tragedy bequeathed by racist beliefs and practices has in modern times been experienced by no other people, save for the Jews who fell into Hitler's hands, so deeply as by the Negro Americans. Unlike the Portuguese system in Brazil which granted the African slave and his family-unit legal standing, with the result that whole clusters of African culture (language, family organization, religion, and so forth) persist until today, North American slavery, conceiving the slave as chattel—property pure and simple—cut his indigenous organization into shreds. Neither the law, the religion, nor the sense of decency of American slavocracy prevented the separation of husband and wife, mother and child, or tribal kinsmen, as black and white met in the slave-auction market place. Yet not everything African was destroyed among the slaves. An array of persistent Africanisms has been discovered among Negro communities in the rural South,[12] and in the urban South and the urban North, where the Negro's acculturation to American standards was greatest, the Negro subculture maintained a subterranean and private world of rituals, symbols, and motifs, where a bit of Africa persisted through time. In a real sense, however, it was no longer *African,* but *Afro-*

*American* [13]—and more American than African because the ultimate measurement was white America which held the keys to life or death. When this measurement was brought into play, the result was all too often a self-repection and a rejection of Africa, envisioned as a savage land, but in the Negro's subterranean world sufficient self-value was preserved to make group survival possible.

One aspect of the political significance of these dimensions of the Negro's world is that occasionally the poorer Negro masses and some well-educated Negroes have rallied to the banners of black nationalism.

The greatest movement toward black nationalism has invariably come at moments of high expectations among Negroes that change will occur, on the one hand, and of white America's unwillingness to permit it, on the other. This was precisely the situation after World War I when Marcus Garvey's Universal Negro Improvement Association rallied hundreds of thousands of adherents, and perhaps several million sympathizers, to its black nationalist banner whose aim was to return to Africa. The Garvey Movement never returned any Negroes to Africa, partly because of the inefficiency and corruption of its petty bourgeois, semi-literate leadership, the rock on which most black nationalist political movements in America have foundered and may continue to founder. But it displayed vividly that the Negro's subterranean world possessed enough kinship with Africa to be stirred by a black nationalist defense of her name.[14]

Since the end of the Second World War the black nationalist political response has reappeared, partly as a reflection of the international situations affecting the Negro protest or civil rights movement. The Black Muslims, led by Elijah Muhammad, represent the most articulate of the postwar groups, but a return to Africa is not a part of their program. Unlike the Garvey Movement's hundreds of thousands of adherents and sympathizers, they have little more than 15,000 souls and few keen sympathizers,[15] although they have had a striking influence.

In light of our analysis, this is not surprising. The postwar era has qualitatively altered the response of our national institutions and upper classes to the Negro's quest for equality. Though the intent to move forward is stronger than the actual movement, the Negro has reasonable grounds for expecting bona fide progress. Not only does he expect it, but, unlike any other period since slavery's end, the postwar era has brought all segments of the Negro community, rich and poor, highly educated and semi-literate, into articulate support for equality within the changing American national framework.

Yet the Black Muslims still represent, at the level of the Negro's subterranean world, a force of ultimate significance. This is found in its influence upon the new stage in the Negro's self-definition. This stage, moreover, has been reinforced by the rise of more rational black nationalist conceptions than those represented by the Black Muslims, and all of them have been affected by the debut of African nationalism on the international scene. It exaggerates the facts of the case only slightly to suggest that when Garvey was active the world at large was not listening very intently to him, whereas the murder of even a single dissident Black Muslim leader, Malcolm X, early in 1965 attracted world-wide attention and comment and was seized upon as a vehicle for political propaganda and accusations of various shades and dimensions.

Postwar African nationalism and the establishment of new African states have provided the Negro American his first examples of the black man's full entry into the modern world. Though Liberia, Ethiopia, and Haiti have long been ruled by black or colored men, they were either not effectively in control of blacks or were unhappy examples of modern black rule. No doubt some of the new African states are also not under effective black control, and some will prove sad models of modern government and development. But, unlike the period before the war, the Negro American is himself in movement toward fulfillment within his society. It is, then, this simultaneous movement of all black men (indeed all men of color, including Asians) [16] toward self-realization which renders postwar Africa an unquestioned source of inspiration and pride to the Negro American.

The Black Muslims are only one type of Negro organization that reflects the impact of postwar African developments upon Negro Americans. There are, however, many other groups of this sort, and they are likely to have a more sustained influence upon the Negro's new thrust for self-realization in American society than the Black Muslims. Unlike the Black Muslims these organizations are secular in orientation, intellectually capable of coping with the modern world; and they reject naive political goals like the establishment of a Negro state within the jurisdiction of the United States. The Afro-American Research Institution in San Francisco, which publishes a quarterly journal, *Soulbook,* represents one type of such organizations; it endeavors to apply lessons from African nationalist developments to the Negro movement for equality, emphasizing self-help programs (for example, it runs a technical school for Negro youth) and political action which excludes white participants. Another type of organization is represented by the Freedomways Associates and the Liberation Committee on Africa, both headquartered in New York. Through their journals, *Freedomways* and *Liberator,* they, among other things, orient their readers toward identification with the radical, mainly Marxian-Socialist, tendencies in Africa and in the Third World generally. The Liberation Committee, for instance, supports the Pan-

African policy of the Nkrumah regime in Ghana which seeks an immediate union of African states along Marxian-Socialist lines, and has staunchly defended the Castro government in its struggle with the United States—a defense which is greatly influenced by Cuba's governmental policy of upgrading the status of its large Negro population. There is, finally, an array of organizations whose main concern is the redefinition of the Negro's self-image in American society through artistic, literary, and other intellectual activities. The more interesting of these groups include the American Society of African Culture (New York), the Society of Umbra (New York), the Black Dialogue Associates (Los Angeles), the Harlem Writers' Guild, and the Harvard-Radcliffe Association of African and Afro-American Students. The American Society of African Culture, the largest of these organizations, is particularly concerned, in the words of its President, John Aubrey Davis,

to bring to the American Negro . . . an understanding of the continuing value of our gifts and a pride in our origins, so that we may join other Americans who feel secure in the traditions of their past and their contributions to America. Thus, we have sponsored demonstrations of African culture, such as art exhibits; we have encouraged the exchange of views between African and American Negro writers, artists, and musicians both in the United States and Africa; and we have explored the historic relationship . . . between the American Negro and Africa in lectures, panels, symposia, and publications.[17]

Ralph Ellison reports that, significantly, in Harlem the reply to the greeting "How are you?" is very often, "Oh, man, I'm nowhere."

The phrase "I'm nowhere" expresses the feeling borne in upon many Negroes that they have no stable, recognized place in society. One's identity drifts in a capricious reality in which even the most commonly held assumptions are questionable. One "is" literally, but one is nowhere; one wanders dazed in a ghetto maze, a "displaced person" of American democracy.[18]

In the swift cycle of recent events the Negro American's "nowhere" begins to give way to a more concrete and identifiable reality. It is in this context that the Black Muslims and other mainly nonpolitical black nationalist conceptions have their meaning for Negroes. All of these groups assert or seek, in one guise or another, an identification with America, but all of them also have bolstered their formulations through identification with postwar Africa as well, thereby demonstrating Africa's world significance for the Negro American. It is one thing to be the descendant of a slave born in a colonial country of an allegedly barbaric continent, and another to be linked racially to a continent suddenly peopled with independent states making a strident and impressive entry into the world's affairs. The Italian attack on Ethiopia in 1935, it has been said, had the effect of giving large numbers of Negroes a sense of involvement in world events for the first time,[19] even though the Ethiopians were then by no means sure that they wanted to be counted among the black Africans. The tidal wave of independence which swept over Africa from the middle of the 1950's brought to the Negro American a far more vivid and intimate sense of both world and African involvement. Although some Negroes no doubt still repudiate Africa and many know little or nothing about it, something of a new universe has been created for them whether they take any active share in it or not. Let there be no mistake about it: the way both whites and Negroes look at color is inevitably transformed when large numbers of men of color take over positions of great prominence and authority which had formerly been virtually a white monopoly.

Dining with Elijah Muhammad and a contingent of Black Muslims, James Baldwin was struck by Elijah's comment that no people in history had ever been respected who had not owned their own land, to which others at the table responded, "Yes, that's right." Baldwin adds that

I could not deny the truth of this statement. For everyone else has, is, a nation, with a specific location, and a flag—even, these days, the Jew. It is only "the so-called American Negro" who remains trapped, disinherited, and despised, in a nation that has kept him in bondage for nearly four hundred years and is still unable to recognize him as a human being.[20]

For the majority of Negro Americans, it is evident that the land and the flag—the nation—which they "own" will not be African, even though increasing numbers find their way to Africa. Short of some unexpected cataclysmic change, no more than a trickle of Negro Americans will decide, or have an opportunity, to cast in their lot with Africa; but for many, and probably for most, a sense of racial community with Africa and of some vicarious sharing in the sovereignty of African States will be a significant part of their social awareness. How significant such a sense will be and what kind of a cultural and political role it will play can now be estimated only on the most meagre evidence. Factors which would have a determining influence are presumably the success of the United States in achieving an open and color-blind society and the success of African peoples in achieving societies which are at once stable and progressive. But it may be that other less calculable elements of attraction or repulsion will bring about results not presently foreseeable, including, perhaps, sharp divisions within the Negro community over such matters as the proper American attitude toward the Congo or South Africa or the extent and conditions of American aid to Africa. Certainly it cannot be assumed that considerations favorable to Africa will necessarily be the dominant ones. It is equally within the realm of experience that Negro American students may resent scholarships and other favored treatment given to African students coming to this country, and that envious eyes may be cast by underprivileged Negroes, whether in Harlem or in the South's Black Belt, on American largesse to Africa. As African states, parties, and ideologies have differed among themselves, so will Negro Americans continue to differ among themselves about attitudes toward Africa and other matters.

## THE FOREIGN AND THE DOMESTIC SCENE

The interplay between domestic race relations and American foreign policy in a swiftly changing world was officially perceived immediately after the war, and the awareness of it has constantly grown. Both the Truman and the Eisenhower administrations sought, however fitfully, to give executive leadership to the protection of a wide range of civil rights long guaranteed to the Negro by the Constitution but subverted by the states. No major civil rights legislation was secured from the Congress, but a Civil Rights Commission, now under a Negro chairman, was established which has provided an invaluable body of information by means of investigations and public hearings throughout the country.

Another facet of the impact of the postwar world upon our race relations may be seen in the response of the federal courts to demands to desegregate public education. The judiciary reached its apogee in this sphere with the Supreme Court's decision on desegregation of public schools in May 1954. Long cognizant of the social and political environment within which it functions, the Court's decision in *Brown v. Board of Education* was as much influenced by America's postwar circumstances as the decision supporting segregated schools in *Plessy v. Ferguson* in 1896 was shaped by the post-Reconstruction era. The supporting brief of the Justice Department in submitting the segregation cases to the Supreme Court in December 1952 indicated full awareness of the contemporary international atmosphere and pressures. It declared that

it is in the context of the present world struggle between freedom and tyranny that the problem of racial discrimination must be viewed. . . . Racial discrimination furnishes grist for the Communist propaganda mills, and it raises doubt even among friendly nations as to the intensity of our devotion to the democratic faith.

This observation was further bolstered by a quotation in the brief from the Secretary of State:

The segregation of school children on a racial basis is one of the practices in the United States which has been singled out for hostile foreign comment in the United Nations and elsewhere. Other people cannot understand how such a practice can exist in a country which professes to be a staunch supporter of freedom, justice, and democracy.[21]

A sphere in which desegregation has moved ahead more fully than in the schools is represented by the armed services. In World War I Negro servicemen were organized into four entirely segregated regiments. The 920,000 Negroes who served in World War II had the same experience, although the Army officer-candidate schools were conducted on an integrated basis. But this latter concession to decency in the midst of the worst armed encounter democratic government had ever faced appears small when it is noted that only 2,484 of the 174,000 commissioned officers and 152 of the 6,000 warrant officers were Negro.[22]

At the end of the war the Truman administration moved slowly toward integration of the armed services, issuing an executive order in 1948 declaring equality of treatment and opportunity for all men bearing arms, regardless of race, color, religion, or national origin. The Navy, which did not even deem the Negro fit for recruitment until 1943, moved first toward full integration and was followed by the Air Force. The Army dragged its feet and did not reach a stride comparable to that of the Navy and Air Force until the Korean War, the first major encounter between the United States and the Soviet bloc in the Cold War.[23]

C. Vann Woodward records the Korean War's impact on integration in the Army thus:

With a surplus of Negro troops piling up behind the lines and a critical shortage of white troops, who were bearing the brunt of casualties, one regimental commander in Korea explained that the "force of circumstances" compelled him to integrate surplus Negroes into his decimated white platoons. It worked. Platoon leaders were delighted to have them. Men in the ranks accepted them. The Negroes fought better than they had before. Race relations took a turn for the better instead of for the worse as feared. General Matthew R. Ridgway asked and was granted permission to integrate Negroes throughout his Korean command.[24]

Following these Korean experiences integration was pushed throughout Army units overseas and in training bases at home, with the result that today the armed forces are one of the most effectively integrated of our national institutions. Thus, under the grim necessity of the Korean War, racial democracy did away with the intolerable situation which allowed men to die for their country only on a segregated basis.

It was not until the last year of the Kennedy-Johnson administration that Congress enacted the first major piece of civil rights legislation in this century—the Civil Rights Act of 1964—which was attained under the pressure of the tragic events surrounding the assassination of President Kennedy. The attention and anxiety of the world, and especially of the nonwhite peoples, were centered upon the death of an American President whose administration symbolized as no other in our history the Negro's quest for full status and who had on a number of occasions demonstrated his concern for Africa and the march toward African freedom. Fortunately for the international standing of the United States, Congress did enact the legislation on which the late President had staked a large part of his career.

Equally fortunate for our political system's future esteem in the world's eyes was the result of the 1964 election, which much of the world saw as directly related to the events surrounding President Kennedy's death and the enactment of the Civil Rights Act. In returning Lyndon B. Johnson to the White House the electorate overwhelmingly endorsed a President who stood firmly behind the civil rights program in the face of a political campaign in which a major party, the Republican party, exploited the fears and prejudices of whites regarding the Negro's militant quest for equality.

The international impact of the election was comparable to that of the adoption of the Civil Rights Act. For instance, the normally anti-American press and information media in Ghana took momentary leave of their anti-American line to express gratification at the defeat of Goldwater and the white Southerners whose support he openly sought. Any other decision on either the Civil Rights Act or the Goldwaterites' bid for power would have produced a very different reaction in Ghana and elsewhere in Africa and Asia.

## AFRICA AND AMERICA

The affairs of Africa and the United States have come in the last decade to be deeply enmeshed with each other, primarily because of the changed role of each in the world but also in part as the culmination of the forced migration of millions of Africans to America in earlier centuries. For good or ill, that relationship is more likely to intensify than to diminish in the years ahead between both governments and peoples. In the latter sphere more and more Negroes, and other Americans as well—more, perhaps, than the Africans will always welcome—will surely concern themselves with Africa and will travel there to see for themselves and, for a few, to settle in with a greater or less degree of permanence. In all probability the reverse flow will also continue to increase as more Africans come to the United States on official business, as students, and as visitors.

Governmental relationships can be expected to be increasingly diverse, complicated, and difficult. At the outset of African independence there were few states to deal with and the rough edges of forthcoming problems were obscured by an aura of optimism. Even though the United States had played no significant role in pressing for self-determination and the end of colonialism in Africa, American good will toward the African states and peoples tended to be taken for granted, and Africans in general welcomed the wider contact with America which independence brought. Aside from the suspicions of a small number of ideologically motivated Africans, the first disillusionment on the African side perhaps derived from the French-inspired delay of the United States in recognizing Guinea's independence when Sékou Touré secured an overwhelming "No" vote in the 1958 referendum on the De Gaulle constitution. Nonetheless, the belief was widespread that the United States would back African freedom and development, just as many Americans generally assumed that the abandonment of colonialism, particularly when it came about through freindly agreement with the colonial powers, would lead to democracy and orderly progress.

The easy assumptions of good will and amicable cooperation are still by no means wholly destroyed, but many events have intervened to challenge their universality and air of innocence. From the American standpoint a significant feature has been the multiplication of African states which has brought a diversity of governmental structures and political styles, including sharp clashes between African states and divergent views on foreign policy. The turn toward one-party systems, usually with one strong man dominating the scene, has undermined the hopes for the emergence of liberal constitutional democracies, and charges of corruption and other abuses are common.

Although the United States has sought to hold itself aloof from intra-African disputes whenever possible, it has on a number of occasions been forced to take sides with one or another state or grouping, as in relation to the Congo and the countries of southern Africa. Since the American position is generally middle-of-the-road, or veering to the right of the middle, difficulties have arisen most frequently with the more militant and left-inclined states, parties, and leaders, who are already the most exposed and most susceptible to Communist denunciation of the United States as the arch-imperialist, the leader of the neo-colonialists. Such attacks are, of course, certain to be amplified by the American left and in particular by the radical nationalist elements in the Negro community. As the world now operates it is virtually impossible for the United States to avoid some measure of embroilment in any major African controversy, and any such controversy is sure to have significant reverberations within this country. Thus the murder of Lumumba and the secession of Katanga became American issues, fought over with bitterness in this country.

The most sustained and vitriolic onslaught upon the United States was provided by the reactions of the African representatives at the United Nations to the airlift of white hostages from Stanleyville in November 1964, which itself followed the much-criticized American backing of Tshombe when he returned to the Congo earlier in 1964 as Premier. What the United States portrayed as a humanitarian rescue mission was denounced by African spokesmen as premeditated aggression involving the wanton and deliberate massacre of the black inhabitants. The bitter fury of some Africans was reflected in the shrill charge of the *Ghanaian Times* on November 28, 1964, that "after killing thousands to free their few spies, the Americans and Belgians stayed on to aid the already entrenched mercenaries to exterminate Congolese citizens in an effort to reintegrate Stanleyville into the Leopoldville administration.[25] Yet Nigeria and most of the former French African territories either endorsed the airlift or took it calmly. While the militants and "progressives" backed the rebel forces and demanded that the imperialists withdraw their support from Tshombe and his white mercenaries, many members of the Organization of African Unity protested the effort to force them to intervene in Congolese affairs. No matter how the United States played its cards it could not help falling afoul of one camp or the other, even, perhaps, if it had wholly abstained from action in the Congo.

African disenchantment with the United States was at least as multi-faceted as that of the United States with Africa. At the head of the list stood the American handling of the racial problem: stories and pictures of murders, beatings, burning and bombing of churches, attacks by police dogs, and the exclusion of children from schools inflamed African opinion. In good part the African denunciation of the airlift was merely one form of the expression of pent-up African feelings toward the American treatment of black men. Few Africans who have visited or lived in the United States have escaped encounters with racial discrimination, including those escorted around the country by Department of State protocol personnel in hope of special protection. As long as racial discrimination exists in this country we can expect African attacks and, in all probability, proposals to bring the issue to the floor of the U.N.

As many Africans saw it, the American attitude toward southern Africa, including the Portuguese colonies, was quite unacceptable and demonstrated a readiness to accept gross evils thrust upon Africans, while lesser injuries and indignities inflicted by Communist states were subject to stern and immediate censure. The United States was accused of subordinating the struggle against colonialism to the maintenance of good relations with the NATO allies and to the continuation of its profits from its South African trade and investments. Accusations were made that America was intervening in African affairs and American aid programs were denounced as having strings tied to them and, perhaps contradictorily, as being both subtle instruments of neo-colonialism and too limited in scope.

## IMAGE AND IDENTITY

In the contemporary idiom, problems of image and identity are crucial in the relations between Africa and America, Africans and Americans; but here it is far easier to ask questions than to answer them. What image does Africa (which, of course, means millions of Africans with divergent opinions, just as America is synonymous with millions of Americans) have of the United States, and what image will it come to have? The United States can be seen as a generous and freedom-loving country, afflicted by a racial conflict which it is desperately seeking to solve in a humane fashion, or as the stronghold of capitalist imperialism, seeking globally to hold down the revolution which threatens its white ruling class and their super-profits. What of the American image of Africa? The rise of the new African states and the unexpected claims to leadership of Ethiopia and Liberia have undoubtedly had a great effect in dispelling the image of Africa as a primitive continent hopelessly behind the rest of mankind. Not only Negro Americans but the majority of white Americans repudiated Senator Ellender when he proclaimed in the course of his 1962 African tour that no Africans were fit to govern themselves and that South Africa was on the right track, and yet he presumably spoke for many of his fellow Southerners and other conservatives. Of one thing we can be sure: he impaired the African image of America. It is implausible to go one hazardous step further and suggest that the new American image, Negro and other, of Africa still rests on fragile foundations, and that if, say, the Congo were to disintegrate into tribal strife and other countries were to follow suit, the older derogatory image of Africa might seep back in? And, if so, what effect would it have on Negro Americans, on their attitudes, and on their standing in the American society?

The identity of Africans among themselves raises serious and fascinating questions, but they need not concern us here, save perhaps to remark that the concept of pan-Africanism is a product primarily of the Negroes on this side of the Atlantic.

The identity of the Negro American is, however, central to our inquiry. Many people have sought to define it, to distinguish the elements which enter into it, and to determine the many forms and shadings which it can take. Here we can do no more than reiterate that the Negro American's sense of identity has been greatly influenced by the emergence of the new Africa and that it is likely to be more rather than less influenced by Africa as time goes by. Failure to integrate the Negro into the total American society must surely intensify his alienation from that society, and hence make more likely an identification with Africa. It is more dubious that the reverse proposition follows with an equal necessity. For example, imagine the full integration of the American Negro, accompanied by a growing conflict in the Congo and, even more dangerous, open strife and bloodshed, perhaps on an international scale, in South Africa. If the United States should stand aside or, worse, join in the support of white domination—which currently seems an improbable outcome—where would the loyalty of Negro Americans lie, in what fashion would their identity assert itself? Africa is a part of the identity of the Negro American: how large and what kind of a part has varied from man to man and generation to generation. The future destiny of that identity depends on the United States, on Africa, and on the relation between the two.

## CONCLUSION

The twentieth century has not found the answer to the problem of the color line, but it has witnessed a uniquely massive drive in search of an answer. The colonial system has almost been swept away. Aside from stray bits and pieces of empire, what is left is the large and dangerous expanse of southern Africa, white dominated and largely white settled. The resolution of the Negro American's status has been well begun but still has a long distance to travel before it achieves its goals, and, in the present close-knit world, what happens abroad and the way the United States reacts in Africa and elsewhere may have drastic repercussions on the domestic scene. Both at home and abroad major transformations in our policies and in the traditional uses of our national institutions must still be made if we are to meet the present challenge.

The inescapable issue of identity was well posed by Chief S. O. Adebo, Permanent Representative of Nigeria to the U.N., in a speech to the American Negro Leadership Conference on September 29, 1964, in which he pointed out the similarity between the problems of Nigeria and Negro Americans.

A great many of the things that happened to you here, which you thought happened to you because you were a minority people, happened to us in Nigeria. ... I no longer think simply as a Nigerian; I no longer think simply as an African. I think more as a person of color. And the objective of all of us is to restore to the man of color, wherever he may be, whether in Nigeria, or in the United States, or in Moscow, or in Brazil, the dignity of a human being. That is why we are involved in the same struggle in Africa, here, and elsewhere.[26]

This latter half of the twentieth century has presented us with a different world to live in—a world of color—and the way in which we adapt ourselves to it and make use of our opportunities, or deny them, will in great measure determine our future at home and abroad. The entire context in which we live has changed. Until the day before yesterday some Americans could delude themselves that they lived in a white country which also contained a subordinate minority of Negroes, almost wholly excluded from the serious conduct of affairs. Can we now bring ourselves to see, and to act upon the vision, that America's twenty million Negroes are not to be considered a burden and liability to be shunted off into a segregated corner, but an asset as great as any we possess in our effort to live in the new world which has sprung up about us? [27]

What lies before us is to create, as we have not succeeded in creating in the past, a nation in which all Americans without regard to "race, color, and previous condition of servitude" have equal and unquestioned access to human decency, dignity, and rights. If we can now succeed, spurred on by the rise of Asia and Africa, we will have mastered our greatest problem at home and established our claim to esteem and influence in the multicolored world which in the last years has swept white domination aside. The challenge to America is immense as the once sharp line between the domestic and the international becomes blurred and fades away.

## NOTES

[1] Harold R. Isaacs, *The New World of Negro Americans* (New York, 1963), p. 211.

[2] This turn of events was foreseen by Gunnar Myrdal who was writing his classic study of the American racial problem during the war years. Pointing out that the Negro problem had already become national in scope, after having been mainly a Southern worry, he commented that it had now "acquired tremendous international implications" in the course of a war which could be seen as ending American isolation. "Statesmen will have to take cognizance of the changed geopolitical situation of the nation and carry out important adaptations of the American way of life to new necessities. A main adaptation is bound to be a redefinition of the Negro's status in American democracy." *An American Dilemma* (9th edn.; New York & London, 1944), pp. 1015–1016.

[3] W. E. B. Du Bois, *The Crisis*, 1918.

[4] Facsimile of advertisement in James Weldon Johnson, *Along This Way—the Autobiography of James Weldon Johnson* (New York, 1933), pp. 364–365.

[5] Isaacs, *op. cit.*, pp. 6–7.

[6] Pearl Buck commented in 1942 on Japan's use of race matters in its propaganda as follows: "Japan . . . is declaring in the Philippines, in China, in India, in Malaya, and even in Russia that there is no basis for hope that colored peoples can expect any justice from the people who rule in the United States, the white people. For specific proof the Japanese point to our treatment of our own colored people, citizens of generations in the United States. Every lynching, every race riot, gives joy to Japan. The discriminations of the American army and navy and the air forces against colored

soldiers and sailors, the exclusion of colored labor in our defense industries and trade unions, all our social discriminations, are of the greatest aid today to our enemy in Asia, Japan." Pearl S. Buck, *American Unity and Asia* (New York, 1942), p. 29.

[7] Quoted in Walter White, *How Far the Promised Land?* (New York, 1953), p. 13.

[8] This and the immediately succeeding material is drawn from two unpublished papers, each entitled "The Employment of American Negroes in the Foreign Service of the United States," prepared by John A. Davis for the first and second American Negro Leadership Conferences on Africa, held in 1962 and 1964.

[9] "Most of the Negroes I know do not believe that this immense concession would ever have been made if it had not been for the competition of the Cold War, and the fact that Africa was clearly liberating herself and therefore had, for political reasons, to be wooed by the descendants of her former masters. Had it been a matter of love or justice, the 1954 decision [concerning school segregation] would surely have occurred sooner; were it not for the realities of power in this difficult era, it might very well not have occurred yet." *The Fire Next Time* (New York, 1964), pp. 117–118.

[10] One of the authors was resident in Ghana in 1964–65 where he heard conversations between urbanized African women about the respective value of "good" hair (meaning straight hair of whites) and "bad" hair (meaning curly or wooly hair of blacks). He found the conversations disturbingly reminiscent of his American childhood when such talk was legion. And there was a certain irony in encountering the urbanized African female adopting the hair-straightening styles of the Negro American female as her model, insofar as the younger generation of college-educated Negro American female, influenced by the postwar militancy of the Negro protest movement, shows a tendency toward discarding these styles.

[11] On the interesting features of this problem among Brazilian Negroes who represent nearly 40 per cent of the population, see Donald Pierson, *Negroes in Brazil* (Chicago, 1942). Brazil's most effective exponent of theories of Negro inferiority was himself of mixed blood, and the relationship of most mulatto Brazilian Negroes to the darker Negro is one of rejection. On the Negro American aspect of this phenomenon, see the excellent study by Harold R. Isaacs, *The New World of the Negro American, op. cit.* See also E. Franklin Frazier, *Black Bourgeoisie* (Glencoe, Ill., 1957).

[12] Newbell N. Puckett, *Folk Beliefs of Southern Negroes* (Chapel Hill, N. C., 1926). Cf. Melville Herskovits, *The Myth of the Negro Past* (New York, 1941).

[13] For a brilliant analysis of this transformation, see LeRoi Jones, *Blues People* (New York, 1963).

[14] The best account of the Garvey Movement is E. Cronon, *Black Moses* (Madison, Wis., 1955).

[15] See C. Eric Lincoln, *The Black Muslims in America* (Boston, 1961); E. Essien-Udom, *Black Nationalism: The Search for Identity in America* (Chicago, 1962).

[16] Asia, incidentally, has figured in a curious way in the ideology of several Negro American black nationalist propositions, and especially that of the Black Muslims. Their Allah, W. D. Fard, the progenitor of the Muslim sect, was supposed to have been born in Asia, not Africa. Asia, or more particularly the Middle East (especially Egypt), is more often referred to as the prime example of the great contribution of black men to world civilization. "Black" in this context is expanded to include all men of color, preposterous as this may seem. Among other things, this use of Asia or the Middle East as the black man's historical reference point reflects more the

impact of the American experience upon the Negro than it does of informed history and anthropological knowledge. It is a curious working out of the inferiority complex imposed by white America upon the Negro—a facet of the Negro's ambivalent relationship to Negro Africa's objective position in world history. This position, for the most part, left Negro Africa at the stage of the Neolithic (along with North American Indians, the aborigines of Australasia, and the peoples of Melanesia and Polynesia). Confronted with white supremacist beliefs and practices, the Negro American and other New World Negro communities quite naturally gave this position a negative valuation. It was not until the post-World War I era that a new evaluation could be hammered out of the existential dialectic of the Negro's subterranean world, which was done in the first instance by the Harlem Renaissance group of Negro intellectuals, and subsequently, in the late 1930's, given explicit conceptual definition by the Negro poet from French Martinique, Aimé Césaire, who invented the term "negritude." This term signifies a meaningful synthesis of the historical experience of peoples of African descent, enabling them to discard the debilitating effects of the inferiority complex. No longer, thus, must one deny history or distort it by claiming for black men what is not theirs, or partake in romantic glorification of a past that, whatever historical research ultimately allocates to it as its true historical position, was no more romantic than any other segment of the human situation. Rather one can now take hold of reality with the aid of that measure of humanity which the Negro can claim, with its own unique twist, along with all other men:

> Hurray for those who have invented nothing!
> Hurray for those who have explored nothing!
> Hurray for those who have conquered nothing!
> But who in awe give themselves up to the essence of things.
> Ignoring surfaces, but possessed by the rhythm of things.
> Heedless of taming, but playing the game of the world.
> Truly the elder sons of the world.
> Flesh of the flesh of the world,
> Throbbing with the very movement of the world.
>
> Aimé Césaire

[17] John A. Davis, "An Editorial Statement," *African Forum,* Vol. 1, No. 1 (Summer 1965), p. 3.

[18] *Shadow and Act* (New York, 1963), p. 300.

[19] Harold R. Isaacs, *op. cit.,* p. 151.

[20] *The Fire Next Time,* pp. 100–101.

[21] Quoted in C. Vann Woodward, *The Strange Career of Jim Crow* (New York, 1935), pp. 120–121.

[22] Florence Murray, *The Negro Handbook, 1949* (New York, 1949), pp. 242 ff.

[23] See *ibid.,* pp. 263–265.

[24] Woodward, *op. cit.,* pp. 137–138.

[25] The virulence of the attack upon the United States appears vividly in *The Spark* (an Accra journal which declares itself to be "A Socialist Weekly of the African Revolution") of February 26, 1965. Here, in an article headed "Who Killed Malcolm X, a Negro American," W. G. Smith accuses the "leaders of fascist imperialism who control the invisible government of the United States" of murdering not only Malcolm X, but Lumumba, President Kennedy, three officials of the Congo-Brazzaville, the Prime Minister of Burundi; of bombing Uganda and North Vietnam, of plotting

to overthrow the revolution of Tanzania, of toppling the government of the Sudan, and of being linked with the South African Nazi slaughter of the Congolese people. "The death lashes of the imperialist monster, in its long drawn out agony, are sometimes terrible." In an accompanying editorial, *The Spark* accuses the American ruling class of assassinating Malcolm X because nine African states, influenced by him, are to raise the question of American race discrimination in the U.N. "Even a member of their own class, like the millionaire Kennedy is rubbed out because he evinced the slightest desire for changing the tactics of American foreign and military strategy."

26 Photocopy of transcript of speech, pp. 5–6. Chief Adebo also spoke warmly of a speech made earlier at the Conference by Secretary of State Rusk, but objected to the Secretary's assertion that the world's greatest problem is Communism, remarking that "I think we must be pardoned for thinking that the greatest problem of this world is South Africa." pp. 14–15.

27 Seeing international leadership passing to the United States as World War II progressed, Gunnar Myrdal held that all the world would be given faith if America could succeed in integrating the Negro into modern democracy. "In this sense the Negro problem is not only America's greatest failure but also America's incomparably great opportunity for the future. . . . America would have a spiritual power many times stronger than all her financial and military resources—the power of the trust and support of all good people on earth. *America is free to choose whether the Negro shall remain her liability or become her opportunity.*

"The development of the American Negro problem during the years to come is, therefore, fateful not only for America itself but for all mankind." *An American Dilemma,* pp. 1021–1022.

*The final essay in this collection was written by the editor of this book for the* Outlook *section of the Sunday* Washington Post *on November 24, 1968. It is an attempt to trace the parallels in history and experience of the Black man in America and the Black man in Africa.*

# Two Continents' Black Pasts Run Parallel

## Ross K. Baker

In the odyssey of the American black man through deportation, slavery, paraslavery and revolution, the ancestral homeland of Africa has exerted strong but sporadic attractions. And the struggle of Africans toward national independence, economic development and self-realization has focused from time to time on the parallel effort of their black kinsmen abroad.

The angry writings of the black physician and revolutionary theorist Frantz Fanon have pointed up, in a cogent and articulate manner, the similarities between the dynamics of independence in the Third World and in the New World. In his most renowned book, "The Wretched of the Earth," Fanon described color, historical oppression and intense aspiration as the common bonds among the world's men of color.

His prescription for liberation is the same for all blacks: therapeutic and cathartic violence against the oppressor not only to achieve political freedom and economic self-sufficiency but also as a purgative to rid the black soul of dependency, self-doubt and delusions of inferiority.

Black men in Africa and America have come to regard Fanon's book as having universal applicability. His passionate words pointed for the first time to the indivisibility of black freedom and to the common aspirations of all oppressed blacks.

## THE COLONIAL RELATIONSHIPS

The analogies between the quest for African independence and the Afro-American's campaign for recognition, equity and political power are quite persuasive.

Basically, both groups of black men existed in a colonial relationship to white men, who wielded predominant political and economic power and who determined the nature of the social relationships in their respective societies.

Although, technically, Africans were never slaves of the white European

From *The Washington Post,* Sunday, November 24, 1968, p. B3. © *The Washington Post.*

colonialists, severe infringement on personal liberty were features of both French and Belgian rule. The most palpable form of quasislavery was *travail forcé* (forced labor)—a lineal descendant of the *corvee* system that prevailed in France before the French Revolution.

Under this arrangement, an African male was required to pay a tax in cash or goods toward upkeep of the colonial administration. Failing this, he was required to put in a prescribed number of days patching roads or working on European-owned plantations.

Since few Africans could afford the cash assessments, they were taken from their villages by the colonial police, often during harvest time when their own crops required attention, to serve the colonial government or a privately owned farm for what the government or planter deemed an appropriate time. Evasion of these laws was often regarded as a major felony punishable by prison, extended forced labor or even death.

Forced labor programs were most strenuously pursued by the Belgians in the Congo. The American journalist Richard Harding Davis and an Irish observer, Sir Roger Casement, both reported instances of Belgian colonial police attacking and burning villages in which there were men in arrears on their taxes or labor quota.

In the post-Civil War South, the Black Codes established a form of social control similar in many respects to colonial Africa under *travail forcé*.

The Mississippi laws of 1865–7, which rendered emancipation a fraudulent illusion, stipulated that any black man not lawfully employed by January, 1866, was to be arrested as a vagrant. If he was unable to pay his $50 fine, he would be hired out to the man who could pay it. Historian John Hope Franklin points out that under Mississippi law, any person was authorized to apprehend a black man who fled from his job.

## LEGAL AND POLITICAL STATUS

In the area of legal relationships, the position of the African and the Afro-American in the South were similar—except that they were invariably better in Africa under the colonial powers.

In both places, however, it was virtually impossible for a white man to be convicted for any crime against a black man or for a black man to escape from a judicial proceeding with anything less than the maximum punishment.

As for political position, the black man in pre-independence Africa was probably better off than his American counterpart, although this too varied from colony to colony. French and Belgian political direction was more explicit, direct and paternal. British political rule was more subtle, ingenious, hierarchical and manipulative.

The writ of French and Belgian political authority tended to run directly to the individual African through the district commissioner or *chef du cercle*. Overall French colonial police for West Africa, for example, was made at Dakar by the governor general and administered locally by French civil servants.

The British, on the other hand, employed a method known as "indirect rule." The creation of Sir Frederick D. Lugard and Sir George Goldie, two of the country's principal colonial officers in the late 19th and early 20th centuries, this arrangement allowed the British to rule through local political, tribal and religious leaders, who in turn enforced the British laws through a structure of native courts, administrators and constabularies.

This "native authority" government was an economical way to run a colony. Rather than employing hordes of tax collectors from England, the British used African personnel, thus saving huge amounts on administrative costs. The local leaders were established figures of authority and gave the coloration of self-government to what was essentially a dependency relationship.

The Afro-American, too, has experienced a form of indirect rule, although it has not been of a legal or official nature. In those areas of the United States where the black man had a vote it was subject to the manipulation of a black political leader who usually existed as part of a white-controlled machine.

The manipulation of ethnic voting blocs by local and national parties in the United States has probably benefited black people less than any other group. The value of being catered to as a bloc is directly related to the bloc members' conscious sense of identity and political efficacy. It has only been since the articulation of black power, black pride and black awareness that concrete goals for black participants in the political system have been made manifest.

One need only look at the goals that a black voter might want in order to see the utter political impotence of the black man as a bloc voter. Quality education, adequate housing, decent neighborhoods, job opportunities—the absence or inadequacy of all these indicates that the black voter, from the point of view of bettering his lot through the political process, has been emasculated.

Virtually no ethnic group has been as chronically loyal to the Democratic organizations that control most cities and received less in return. (This is no implied accolade to the Republicans, on whom the black voter has justifiably given up.)

Indirect rule in America, by the white political machine through the black leader, has failed to provide even the minimum conditions of local self-rule accorded Africans by the British, where, at the very least, an African villager could get a hearing from an African judge who understood his problems, be apprehended by a native policeman who was a fellow villager or have his property and domestic disputes adjudicated by a man fully conversant with the way of life in which such problems were rooted. In many ways, the African could obtain more responsiveness, understanding and justice than his black brother in America could under our own system of indirect rule.

## 'PARLOR' VS. 'VERANDAH'

This, of course, brings up the question of the nature of pre-independence African leadership in Africa and pre-revolutionary black leadership in America. The parallels again are compelling. The Ghanaians have the phrases for it—"parlor boys" and "verandah boys."

Under British rule in the Gold Coast (now Ghana), a small African elite was allowed to develop and to approach the inner reaches of colonial power. This handful of lawyers, professors and merchants were the "symbolic Africans" to whom the British could point.

These were the men of flawless education—a black Oxbridge set, respectable, gradualist in their assertion of African independence. They were the group designated by the British as natural leaders when the colony would be granted independence. The late Dr. J. B. Danquah and K. A. Busia are commonly looked on as archetypes of the "parlor" group.

The "verandah" group was epitomized by Kwame Nkrumah, late of the University of Pennsylvania and Lincoln University: bruised by white racism in America, demanding immediate independence, abrasive in style, flamboyant, reasonably well organized and possessed of the principal intangible asset of a successful mass leader-charisma.

Through the judicious use of his party apparatus, Nkrumah persuaded the British to appoint him head of government business under a transitional regime rather than turning to the parlor group, which, however moderate and reasonable, had been unimaginative and unexciting.

Nkrumah made it respectable and even fashionable to go to jail for opposing the British. He captured the imagination of the people and supplanted those originally groomed for leadership in much the same way that radical black leaders in America have seized power from older and more conservative individuals by dint of sheer brilliance, articulateness and uncompromising dedication to freedom.

Nkrumah, incidentally, accomplished this by having himself appointed secretary general of the moderate United Gold Coast Convention and then changing the tone and style of the group. In America, the militant leaders have turned in somewhat the same direction.

Both SNCC and CORE are far different groups from what they were in 1963 and there is now evidence of significant change within the Urban League and the NAACP. Of the older generation of black leaders in America, perhaps only Whitney Young has been astute enough to detect a changing mood among the mass of black people and has modified his own views and those of his organization to bring them into harmony with the more militant sentiments. The American "parlor" group has clearly been superseded.

## EXERCISE IN SELF-DECEPTION

The symbolic black man so beloved of propagandists has lost his claim on leadership because he approached the white man—American politician or British colonial administrator—as a supplicant. What marginal benefits he obtained were through white largesse.

He was an indispensable appendage of a white establishment, for his presence could defuse an explosive group by allowing the white man to say, "Look at your brother who made it by his deferential, diligent and respectful manner. Now why don't you all go home and do the same?"

This creation of black paragons is a favorite device of the South Africans, whose elaborate exercises of self-deception call for the Prime Minister to be photographed at the opening of Parliament with delegations from the bantustans, who, we are assured by the brochures, are anti-Communist. To the credit of the intelligence of the American people, it must be said that this sort of primitive contrivance is no longer widely believed.

The colonial holdouts in Africa and the white supremacist regimes such as Rhodesia and South Africa are manipulators of a technique which also has an analogue in American black-white relations and may be called "the swimming pool syndrome" or "how to appear to foster black equality by turning on fire hydrants."

This time-honored tactic involves quieting discontent by giving people gifts—schools, swimming pools, community centers or hospitals. In South Africa and Mozambique, the colonialists point to modern schools or hospitals and say that such facilities do not exist for black people in black-governed Nigeria or Tanzania. Like the American mayor who promises swimming pools to a crowd of angry black men, the building of clubhouses in a bantustan confuses material deprivation with the desire for significant political participation and the right to control one's own destiny.

To attempt to circumvent confrontation by offering material inducement is the supreme manifestation of condescension. Gifts are no substitute for political and spiritual independence, whether in Watts or Windhoek.

## THE MOTHER-IN-LAW

The perceptions and attitudes of black Americans and Africans are some-what different, however, in the area of relationship between black and white.

The black American is in the process of disengaging from the white com-munity. The most articulate sections of black opinion in America are in-creasingly seeking to divorce themselves even from those "white men of good will" who sympathize in large measure with the goals of the black revolution.

White sympathizers feel rebuffed and hurt by being asked to leave meet-ings of the Black United Front or being made uncomfortable in a CORE group. The fact remains, however, that the black revolution in America is necessarily and appropriately the black man's "bag." John Brown, were he alive today, would receive the same treatment.

The assertion of group identity does not admit of outside support. Black men want to achieve their own objectives and be able to say that they did it themselves.

From the abolition movement to the sit-ins in the South, the white man has figured prominently. But, like the well-meaning mother-in-law who lives with a married couple, bails them out of financial difficulty and minds the grandchildren, the white man must realize that the black people, like the couple, have to solve their own problems and deserve any credit for main-taining family harmony and achievement.

Only now is the white man gaining acceptance in Africa for what techni-cal skills and expertise he can offer. Having achieved their primary goal of political independence, the African republics can again look upon the white man as a friend and collaborator in achieving economic development, edu-cational advancement and public well-being.

The more secure an African state is in its political independence, the more the white man has received genuine acceptance as an equal and a friend. Where insecurity and national self-doubt exist, the white man is accepted grudgingly and in some cases, like the Congo until recently, regarded with hostility.

In those states where the colonial presence is still in evidence, where neocolonialism is a fact of life and where national independence is a mask for economic dependency, deep-seated resentment exists despite surface signs of acceptance.

In Africa as well as America, the relations between black and white are, in large measure, determined by the level of freedom possessed by the black man. In both cases, there is strong reason to believe that black-white rela-tions will never be totally normal until black and white are completely equal.

The determining perception of equality in both places is, pre-eminently, the black man's.

## IN THE AMERICAN CONTEXT

It is only now, with the concerted effort on the part of large numbers of American black men to re-establish links with their African heritage, that a coherent program of cultural liaison has been established. The American black man, however, is conducting his campaign for equality and recognition within the American context.

There is little inclination on the part of black Americans to forfeit the social, economic and political credit they have built up in America. Quite the contrary; they mean to collect on it.

The black man's equity in America has been earned by two centuries of slavery and a century of persecution and struggle. It drew interest in every American war, interest compounded through years of darkness.

The African, though his sympathies may be with his black kinsman in America, can never really be a part of this struggle. He has already achieved important political goals that still elude the black American. The black American, on the other hand, has attained a degree of economic security which his African brother has not yet acquired.

Although the analogies and commonalities are striking, the black American and the African are very different people. What they have in common is a history of persecution and exploitation, an unfulfilled present in which the most significant areas of their lives are beyond their control and an uncertain future both in regard to their relations with the white man and with men who share their color.

Their skin—the cachet of their brotherhood—is the most palpable common factor and their pride in it is the surest road to fulfillment.